THE OXFORD ENCYCLOPEDIA OF
ANCIENT GREECE AND ROME

THE OXFORD ENCYCLOPEDIA OF
ANCIENT GREECE AND ROME

Michael Gagarin

EDITOR IN CHIEF

Elaine Fantham

ASSOCIATE EDITOR IN CHIEF

VOLUME 2

Bilingualism and Multilingualism–Dura-Europos

OXFORD

UNIVERSITY PRESS

2010

OXFORD

UNIVERSITY PRESS

Oxford University Press, Inc., publishes works that further
Oxford University's objective of excellence in research,
scholarship, and education.

Oxford New York
Auckland Cape Town Dar es Salaam Hong Kong Karachi
Kuala Lumpur Madrid Melbourne Mexico City Nairobi
New Delhi Shanghai Taipei Toronto

With offices in
Argentina Austria Brazil Chile Czech Republic France Greece
Guatemala Hungary Italy Japan Poland Portugal Singapore
South Korea Switzerland Thailand Turkey Ukraine Vietnam

Copyright © 2010 by Oxford University Press

Published by Oxford University Press, Inc.
198 Madison Avenue, New York, NY 10016
www.oup.com

Oxford is a registered trademark of Oxford University Press

The Library of Congress Cataloging-in-Publication Data

The Oxford encyclopedia of ancient Greece and Rome / Michael
Gagarin, editor in chief ; Elaine Fantham, associate editor in chief.
p. cm.
Includes bibliographical references and index.
ISBN 978-0-19-517072-6 (hardback) – ISBN 978-0-19-538839-8 (drs)
1. Greece–Encyclopedias. 2. Rome–Encyclopedias. 3. Civilization,
Classical–Encyclopedias. I. Gagarin, Michael. II. Fantham, Elaine.
III. Title: Encyclopedia of ancient Greece and Rome.
DE5.O95 2010
938.003–dc22   2009028496

 3 5 7 9 8 6 4 2
Printed in the United States of America on acid-free paper

Common Abbreviations Used in This Work

AUC	*ab urbe condita*, from the founding of the city of Rome
b.	born
BCE	before the common era (= BC)
c.	*circa*, about, approximately
CE	common era (= AD)
cf.	*confer*, compare
d.	died
diss.	dissertation
ed.	editor (pl., eds), edition
f.	and following (pl., ff.)
fl.	*floruit*, flourished
frag.	fragment
l.	line (pl., ll.)
m	meter, meters
n.	note
n.d.	no date
no.	number
n.p.	no place
n.s.	new series
p.	page (pl., pp.)
pt.	part
r.	reigned
rev.	revised
ser.	series
supp.	supplement
s.v.	*sub verbo*, under the headword
vol.	volume (pl., vols.)
*	reconstructed or hypothetical form
[ ]	false or doubtful attributions

The Ancient Greek and Roman World

CALEDONIA

MARE GERMANICUM

N

Hadrian's Wall

HIBERNIA

Eboracum

Albis

BRITANNIA

Londinium

Gastra Vetera

GERMANIA

Rhenus

Augusta Treverorum

Mogontiacum

Durocortorum

MARE ATLANTICUM

Sequana

Argentorate

AGRI DECUMATES

Danubius

Vindobona

Carnuntum

Aquincum

RAETIA

NORICUM

Liger

GALLIA

Dravus

DACIA

Burdigala

Lugdunum

Rhodanus

ALPES MONTES

Mediolanum

Padus

Aquileia

PANNONIA

Sarmizegetusa

Sirmium

Garumna

Nemausus

Pont du Gard

Ravenna

MARE ADRIATICUM

Viminacium

Legio VII Gemina

Narbo

Arelate

APENNINI MONTES

Salona

ILLYRICUM

Durius

PYRENEES

Numantia

Iberus

Massilia

CORSICA

Aleria

Roma

ITALIA

MACEDONIA

HISPANIA

Tagus

Tarraco

SARDINIA

Brundisium

EPIRUS

Anas

Emerita Augusta

Baeares Insulae

Actium

Corduba

Baetis

Italica

Urso

Caralis

Gades

Carthago Nova

SICILIA

Siculum Fretum

Sparta

Tingi

Fretum Herculeum

Iol Caesarea

Syracusa

Cirta

Carthago

NUMIDIA

MAURETANIA

Thamugadi

MARE INTERNUM

AFRICA

Lepcis Magna

Cyrene

0   100   200   300 mi

0   100 200 300 400 500 km

THE OXFORD ENCYCLOPEDIA OF
ANCIENT GREECE AND ROME

B

CONTINUED

BILINGUALISM AND MULTILINGUALISM

In the ancient world in general bilingualism and multilingualism were more common than monolingualism.

Bilingualism in Greece. In Greece of the Classical period citizen elites may have been monolingual as a result of their feeling of cultural superiority. The Athenians in Herodotus 8.144 boast of the "kinship of all Greeks in blood and speech." Plato shows no interest in foreign languages in his etymological discussions in the *Cratylus*, simply dismissing all non-Greek languages as barbarian, and the historian Herodotus seems to have known no other languages and had to make use of interpreters on his travels around the Mediterranean world (e.g., in Egypt 2.125). Nevertheless, the majority of inhabitants in a city such as Athens, those coming in from outside, traders, slaves, and specialized workers such as the Scythian archers in Aristophanes' *Ecclesiazousae* (Women in Parliament) 1,001–1,225 would certainly have been at least bilingual in Greek and their native tongue. According to the Old Oligarch (or *Constitution of the Athenians* 2.8) the Athenian dialect took elements from all other Greek dialects and its language was "a mixed form, with loans from both Hellenes and barbarians."

At an earlier period Ionian and Carian mercenaries serving in Egypt, or specialists such as the Greek-speaking doctor Democedes of Croton who worked for the Persian king Darius (Herodotus 3.129–130, 133–134) must have been bilingual, and the same is true of the Greek colonizers and traders of the Archaic period. Later, in the time of Alexander the Great, inscriptional evidence shows that Aramaic as well as Greek was used in the administration of the Seleucid kingdoms. In Ptolemaic Egypt, Greek was the official language, and ambitious local officials must have become bilingual in Greek and the Egyptian Demotic. Some adopted double names, one Egyptian and one Greek, and there is evidence for scribes fluent in both languages. There was probably some limited use of Egyptian Demotic by Greeks, at least at the level of everyday interactions.

Bilingualism in Rome. In Rome, as in the Greek cities of the Classical period, the traders, lower-class immigrant workers, and slaves must have been bilingual from an early period. Slaves in Plautus, for example, are characterized by their use of Greek phrases, although in real life some slaves would have been bilingual in languages other than Greek— languages that would have been less appropriate for use in a Roman literary context. Inscriptions from Rome by sub-elite bilinguals include mixtures of Latin and Greek in Greek script. In epitaphs it is common for a Latin text to be preceded or followed by a conventional formula in Greek or vice-versa. In the same way Hebrew tags are found added to Jewish funerary inscriptions in Greek or Latin.

There was no official policy of enforcing Latin in the empire. Bilingual inscriptions show that ambitious provincials were keen of their own accord to learn and use Latin, at least in official contexts. A number of bilingual texts from Rome and Italy in the last two centuries BCE in Latin and Oscan, Umbrian, and Venetic attest to a sensitivity to a mixed and changing linguistic identity among these communities. Bilingual texts in Punic, Aramaic, Hebrew, Egyptian Demotic, and Coptic show recent immigrants to Rome addressing the locals in public inscriptions in their own language while retaining through the use of their native tongue their own sense of local identity, particularly in religious contexts. The Roman army took conscripts from all over the empire and was polyglot, with Latin used as the lingua franca (Tacitus *Historiae* 2.37, 3.33). Knowledge of Latin varied, with some recruits having little or no competence in the language. Orders were often given in a stereotyped form of Latin to make them more generally comprehensible.

With the growing Hellenization of Rome, especially from the first century BCE, educated Romans were expected to have at least a working knowledge of Greek. As early as 131 BCE we learn that the proconsul of Asia, Publius Licinius Crassus, could speak in any of five Greek dialects (Valerius Maximus 8.7.6). Crassus' depth of knowledge was exceptional, but those whose Greek was not adequate were disparaged (cf. Cicero's comments about Gaius Verres at *In Verrem* 4.127). The author of the *Rhetorica ad Herennium* (first century BCE) points to the importance of Greek rhetorical theory in the development of Latin oratory, and Cicero tells us that he declaimed in Greek to shape his Latin usage (*Brutus* 310; *Ad Atticum* 9.4). The practice of "code-switching" or the use of individual Greek words and runs of Greek within Cicero's private Latin letters marks an interest in Greek culture that would be shared by his elite Roman correspondents. It does not imply a thoroughgoing bilingualism (indeed Cicero and other Latin authors, such as Lucretius

and Virgil, made mistakes in their translations from Greek) or for that matter a genuine biculturalism, but is simply an expression of Roman elite culture of the time. An influx of Greek intellectuals in this period meant that Greek became the language of science, medicine, and philosophy. The early learning of Greek by the children of the Roman intelligentsia is advocated by Quintilian (*Instituto oratoria* 1.1.12–14), who advises the learning of Greek before Latin, and both Tacitus (*Dialogus de oratoribus* 29.1) and Soranus (*Gynaeceia* 2.19.5) recommend the use of Greek wet nurses for the same purpose. Interpreters for Greek were not required in the senate in Cicero's time (*De finibus* 5.89; *De divinatione* 2.131).

Tiberius disapproved of the use of Greek at senatorial meetings (Suetonius *Tiberius* 71). Augustus was fluent in written Greek but preferred not to speak it in public. Most later emperors were fluent in both written and spoken Greek. Marcus Aurelius chose to write his *Meditations* in Greek; the emperor Septimius Severus was trilingual in Latin, Greek, and Punic, and Severus Alexander (222–235 CE) was better at Greek than Latin. Greek was more widely used as the language of administration in the east; official documents and letters intended to be sent to the eastern provinces were regularly translated into Greek before being dispatched from Rome. Greek was the language of the early Christian Church. Latin, however, remained the language of law, and it was not until the time of Severus Alexander that Greek was allowed to be used in wills. Ulpian (Domitius Ulpianus), writing in the same period, informs us that even Punic, Gallic, Syriac, and other languages could be used for certain financial transactions (recorded in Justinian's *Digest* 32.11. preface). From the fourth century Greek became less widely known among the educated Roman elite, and from this time Latin was increasingly used as the main administrative language in the eastern provinces.

Evidence for the knowledge of languages other than Greek by educated Romans is patchy. Ennius was trilingual in Latin, Greek, and Oscan (according to Aulus Gellius 17.17.1) and possibly knew Messapic as well. Varro in his *De lingua latina* is able to

Bilingual Inscription. Bilingual inscription in Latin and Etruscan. Museo Oliveriano, Pesaro, Italy/Scala/Art Resource, NY

identify Latin words of Hispanic and Gaulish origin as well as Etruscan and Oscan (called Sabine by Varro, a native of Sabine Reate), but this does not prove any thoroughgoing fluency in such languages. The existence of bilingual treaties between Rome and Carthage presumes some knowledge of Punic, at least in the Republican period. Etruscan was the other language associated with an ancient literate culture that Romans were not ashamed to acquire. The emperor Claudius in his youth composed histories of Carthage and the Etruscans, making use of sources in the original languages. Ovid in exile at Tomis claims to have learned Getic and Sarmatian (*Tristia* 5.7.56), to be contemplating the composition of a poem "in Getic measures," and to have written a poem in Getic in Latin measures (*Ex Ponto* 4.13.19–20). On the whole the educated Romans were not much given to learning languages other than Greek, but their experience of empire probably made them more aware of linguistic diversity than their fifth-century Greek counterparts.

[*See also* Greek, *subentry* The Greek Language; Italy, Languages of; Language, Theories of; Latin, *subentry* The Latin Language; *and* Translation, Ancient.]

BIBLIOGRAPHY

Adams, James N. *Bilingualism and the Latin Language.* Cambridge, U.K., and New York: Cambridge University Press, 2003.

Horsfall, N. "Doctus sermones utriusque linguae?" *Échos du monde classique/Classical News and Views* 23 (1979): 79–95.

Kaimio, Jorma. *The Romans and the Greek Language.* Helsinki, Finland: Societas Scientiarum Fennica, 1979.

Momigliano, Arnaldo. *Alien Wisdom: The Limits of Hellenization.* Cambridge, U.K., and New York: Cambridge University Press, 1975.

Swain, S. "Bilingualism and Biculturalism in Antonine Rome: Apuleius, Fronto, and Gellius." In *The Worlds of Aulus Gellius*, edited by Leofranc Holford-Strevens and Amiel Vardi, pp. 3–40. Oxford and New York: Oxford University Press, 2004.

Robert Maltby

BIOGRAPHY

Biography emerges from a natural interest in persons that predates any formulation of a genre. The *Odyssey* focused on a single individual, characters inhabited histories, and encomiums praised important men before "lives," as they were called, were recognized as a literary type of their own. The boundaries of biography always remained blurred in antiquity because human beings would continue to be depicted in other genres, and biography never became as structured and subject to rules of composition as epic in poetry or declamatory rhetoric in prose. But by the end of the first century BCE, an author could state with confidence that he was writing biography, what Arnaldo Momigliano describes as "an account of the life of a man from birth to death."

Greek Beginnings. Biography began to gain definition in the fourth century BCE in response to philosophical interest in the moral choices of individuals. Isocrates' prose encomium for the Cypriot king Evagoras (c. 370 BCE) described events chronologically but recorded the accomplishments of his subject separately. Not long afterward Xenophon wrote an encomium for the Spartan king Agesilaus. It was similarly in two parts, a chronological presentation of events followed by a non-chronological listing of virtues. Aristotle and his followers contributed further. Their emphasis on research led to the collection and publication of anecdotes, especially those pertaining to writers and to schools of philosophy. Aristoxenus of Tarentum, a pupil of Aristotle, is credited with the first proper biographies, a series of lives of philosophers (late fourth century BCE). Portions of four are extant, among them Socrates and Plato.

In the Hellenistic period lives in series came to be the norm, a practice that points to an interest in types as much as to curiosity about specific individuals. Subjects might be poets or kings or generals as well as philosophers who remained of interest. The collections addressed the question of what made a man a good philosopher or poet when measured against others of his kind. These are known largely through fragments or reference in other authors. Diogenes Laertius, in the third century CE, would follow the tradition with his *Lives of Eminent Philosophers*—biographies and descriptions of philosophical schools that preserve the content of some of this material. The historical accuracy of these early lives is questionable. In the case of poets, facts were extrapolated from the contents of their work.

These Hellenistic lives developed various compositional strategies. Some were narrated chronologically while others were arranged by topic. Although the latter included the birth and death of their subjects, they described their characteristics one at a time, a structure suggested by Isocrates' *Evagoras* or Xenophon's *Agesilaus*. Another strategy was revealed by the discovery of a fragment of a life of Euripides written by Satyrus the Peripatetic in the third century BCE. One of a series of lives of poets, it was in dialogue form. For political figures, there was the option of a related format. A historical monograph centered on the public actions of a single man, although it did not trace his life from birth to death.

Biography comes into view more clearly near the end of the first century BCE, a period from which more examples have survived. Nicolaus of Damascus, a Greek contemporary of Augustus, wrote a biography of the emperor, a large portion of which is extant. The earliest examples of Latin lives also come from the end of the Roman Republic and from the reign of Augustus, and more of this survives than does the Greek biography from which it was derived. It helps reveal the nature and scope of what had gone before.

The Roman Contribution. Roman biography had native origins as well. Romans always took ancestries seriously. Funeral orations praised the achievements of the dead, and epitaphs could be elaborate, such as the *Laudatio Turiae*, addressed to a deceased wife (late first century BCE). Augustus outlined his life's accomplishments (*Res gestae*), engraved the document in bronze, and placed it on his mausoleum. Varro, at the end of the republic drew on the idea of death masks (*imagines*) of prominent ancestors that were paraded in funerals for his own *Imagines* or *Hebdomades vel de imaginibus*. This work (now lost) was a large portrait collection of some seven hundred famous Greeks and Romans of all sorts, each image accompanied by an epigram and perhaps a prose description.

Cornelius Nepos also lived and wrote at the end of the Republic. A prolific writer, his contribution to biography is *De viris illustribus* (On Famous Men), a collection of about four hundred biographies, among them lives of historians and generals. His series drew on both Varro's *Imagines* and on the well-established Hellenistic practice of grouping persons by type. Extant are the lives of two historians, Cato the Elder and Titus Pomponius Atticus, and a series devoted to "renowned generals of foreign nations." He states quite clearly that he has consciously chosen his genre: "I fear that if I begin to set forth the deeds [of the fourth-century BCE Theban leader Pelopidas], I will seem not to be narrating a biography but rather writing a history" (*Pelopidas* 1.1). And he apologizes at the beginning of his preface for his choice: "I do not doubt . . . that there will be many readers who will judge this kind of writing trivial and unworthy of the roles played by great men." A whole life included intimate details as well as the great deeds that were the property of history.

It may have been Nepos who originated the idea of comparing Romans and non-Romans, a comparison more fully developed by Plutarch (d. after 120 CE), who wrote in Greek but belonged to the broad Roman world at the end of the first century. He, like Nepos, states clearly, "I am writing not history, but lives" (Life of Alexander 1.1). His *Parallel Lives* of Roman and Greek public figures, which were intended to teach moral lessons by examples of virtue or of vice, paired Julius Caesar with Alexander, for example, and Cicero with Demosthenes. Twenty-three pairs of the lives survive, along with two of Plutarch's several biographies of Roman emperors (Galba and Otho).

The historian Tacitus wrote a biography of his father-in-law, Gnaeus Julius Agricola, imperial legate to Britain under the emperor Domitian. He describes Agricola's ancestry, his early life, and his death, but his narrative centers on the general's achievement as governor and commander. In this respect the text owes as much to the tradition of historical monograph as to that of biography. Tacitus also used the *Agricola* as a vehicle to express his distaste for Domitian's oppressive rule and the relief he felt after his death.

More important for the history of biography is the work of Suetonius, who wrote early in the second century CE. Like Nepos, he wrote a series *De viris illustribus* (On Famous Men), the biographies of poets, orators, philosophers, historians, and a more novel category, rhetoricians and grammarians. His

---

Plutarch *The Life of Alexander* 1.2

"A small thing, a word or a jest, has often illuminated character better than has a battle in which ten thousands have died or a massive gathering of troop or the siege of cities."

Lives of the Caesars were imperial biographies like those of Plutarch. Twelve in number, they begin with Julius Caesar and end with Domitian. Whereas Plutarch wrote narrative, Suetonius arranged his information by rubrics, a strategy again derived from the Hellenistic model that separated chronologically arranged information from the systematic examination of character and practices. Topics might be the emperor's presentation of games or his dispensation of justice. Or they might be his modest behavior or his cruelty.

Suetonius was influential throughout late antiquity both with his method and in the very idea of imperial biography. In the third century, Marius Maximus continued with a *Caesars* of his own, now lost. The *Historia Augusta*, outrageously fanciful biographies of second- and third-century emperors beginning with Hadrian, attributed to fictional authorship, followed in the fourth century. Even in the ninth century, Suetonius' Life of Augustus was a model for Einhard's Life of Charlemagne.

[*See also* Historia Augusta; Julius Caesar; Plutarch; Suetonius; Tacitus; *and* Xenophon.]

BIBLIOGRAPHY
Primary Works
Cornelius Nepos. Translated by John C. Rolfe. Loeb Classical Library. Cambridge, Mass.: Harvard University Press; London: Heinemann, 1984.
Cornelius Nepos: A Selection, Including the Lives of Cato and Atticus. Translated with introduction and commentary by Nicholas Horsfall. Oxford: Clarendon Press; New York: Oxford University Press, 1989.
Diogenes Laertius. *Lives of Eminent Philosophers.* Translated by R. D. Hicks. 2 vols. Loeb Classical Library. Cambridge, Mass.: Harvard University Press; London: Heinemann, 1972.

Nicolaus of Damascus. *Life of Augustus*. Edited and translated with commentary and introduction by Jane Bellemore. Bristol, U.K.: Bristol Classical Press, 1984.

Res Gestae Divi Augusti: The Achievements of the Divine Augustus. Edited and translated by P. A. Brunt and J. M. Moore. London: Oxford University Press, 1967.

Suetonius. *Works*. Translated by J. C. Rolfe. 2 vols. Rev. ed. Loeb Classical Library. Cambridge, Mass.: Harvard University Press, 1997.

Tacitus. *"Agricola" and "Germany."* Translated by Anthony R. Birley. Oxford and New York: Oxford University Press, 1999.

Secondary Works

Cartledge, Paul. "Agesilaos, Xenophon, and the Sources of Evidence." In his *Agesilaos and the Crisis in Sparta*, pp. 55–73. London: Duckworth, 1987.

Dorey, Thomas. A., ed. *Latin Biography*. London: Routledge and Kegan Paul, 1967.

Geiger, Joseph. *Cornelius Nepos and Ancient Political Biography*. Wiesbaden, Germany: Steiner, 1985.

Lefkowitz, Mary R. *The Lives of the Greek Poets*. Baltimore, Md.: Johns Hopkins University Press, 1981.

Momigliano, Arnaldo. *The Development of Greek Biography*. Expanded edition. Cambridge, Mass.; London: Harvard University Press, 1993.

Stuart, Duane R. *Epochs of Greek and Latin Biography*. Berkeley: University of California Press, 1928.

Syme, Ronald. "Biographers of the Caesars." *Museum Helveticum* 37 (1980): 104–128.

Donna W. Hurley

BIRTH AND REPRODUCTION

Childbirth was the defining moment in the life of a Greek or Roman woman, the moment when she fully acquired her status as an adult and as a wife. Marriage was undertaken to procreate children, and there was much anxiety around female sterility: medical treatises were devoted to its treatment (e.g., the Hippocratic *Sterile Women*); women consulted the god Asclepius to be relieved from it, as stories of miraculous cures preserved at the sanctuary of Epidaurus testify (stories of Agameda of Ceos and Nicasiboula of Messena: *Inscriptiones Graecae* 4.2.1.121–122); and the legend has it that the first Roman divorce occurred (c. 230 BCE) because the wife of Spurius Carvilius Ruga was barren (Aulus Gellius *Attic Nights* 4.3.2; 17.21).

Hippocratic medical writers of the fifth or fourth century BCE considered pregnancy as essential to a woman's health and recommended it as a cure for various diseases, whereas virginity could potentially be dangerous for the pubertal girl (*On the Nature of Woman* 2 = Littré 7.314; *On the Diseases of Young Girls*). Soranus, writing after 100 CE, on the other hand, considered pregnancy to be unhealthy and hazardous and saw no problem in permanent virginity (*Gynecology* 1.42). Whether these diverging medical theories had any impact on the age of women at marriage is difficult to determine. Roger S. Bagnall and Bruce W. Frier have estimated that a woman in the Greek and Roman world had to bear five or six children (a gross reproduction rate of over 2.5) to maintain the population, and this may have had an impact on how early women married and bore children.

Divinities Presiding over Childbirth. Numerous divinities presided over the various aspects of pregnancy and childbirth. In Greece, Eileithyia had been invoked by women in labor since the Bronze Age as the personification of safe delivery (*Iliad* 11.269–271). Her name was the epithet of various goddesses of women, in particular of Artemis, whose other childbirth-related epithets included Locheia, Lecho (both meaning "in childbed"), and Lusizonos (meaning "who loosens the girdle"). As shown by Helen King, Artemis had special links with the blood shed during childbirth, and personified the natural, almost savage, aspect of the process. Hera, the nymphs, the Moerae (Fates), Selene, and Hecate were also venerated as birth goddesses. At Rome, Juno Lucina presided over childbirth; on the anniversary of the foundation of her temple, the first of March, were celebrated the Matronalia (Ovid *Fasti* 2.451–452 and 3.167–258). The Romans also invoked Parca, one of the three Parcae (equivalent of the Greek Moerae), Carmentis, and numerous special goddesses who represented individual aspects of the birth process.

Pregnancy. The ancients considered a normal pregnancy to last from seven to eleven months (Censorinus *The Birthday Book* 7.2), but it was generally acknowledged that a child born at seven months had better chances of surviving than an eight-month child (Hippocratic *On the Seven and Eight Month Fetus*; Aristotle *History of Animals* 7.4, 584a). The inscriptions of gratefulness to Asclepius at Epidaurus (*Inscriptiones Graecae* 4.2.1.121–122) testify to pregnancies lasting three (pregnancy of Ithmonica of Pellene) and even five years (pregnancy of Cleo). Being pregnant with a boy was considered a better experience than expecting a girl (*Aphorisms* 5.42 = Littré 4.546; Aristotle *History of Animals* 7.4, 584a).

The Hippocratic gynecological writers enjoined their readers to trust experienced women with matters of pregnancy and childbirth, as women knew their body better than anyone else (*On the Seven Month Fetus* 4 = Littré 440). Inexperience, on the other hand, could lead to involuntary abortions (miscarriages), and both medical and lay authors encouraged women to take all precautions in order to avoid such an accident (*Diseases of Women* 1.25 = Littré 8.68; Pliny the Younger *Letters* 8.10–11). Even though the Hippocratic Oath prevents the use of pessaries to procure an abortion, the Hippocratic gynecological treatises contain many recipes for abortive pessaries and other abortifacients (e.g., *Diseases of Women* 1.78 = Littré 8.178) and one recipe to prevent conception for a full year (*atokion*: *Diseases of Women* 1.76 = Littré 8.170). Soranus had a more formal distinction between contraceptive (*atokion*) and abortive (*phthorion*) drugs and methods: the former prevented conception, while the latter destroyed what had already been conceived. He also made a distinction between abortions performed for medical reasons and those performed for a woman to preserve her looks or destroy the product of adultery (*Gynecology* 1.60). Nonmedical abortions were often condemned by Latin authors (Ovid *Amores* 2.13–14; Juvenal *Satyres* 6.591–600; Seneca *Consolation to Helvia* 16.3), but abortion was considered criminal only when practiced without the consent of the potential father.

Labor and Birth. The author of the Hippocratic *Nature of the Child* (30 = Littré 7.530–532) argued that the onset of labor was caused by the fetus, who, after depleting his reserves of food, became restless and broke the birth membrane. The Hippocratic writers, even though they had noticed birth contractions (*Diseases of Women* 1.34 = Littré 8.80), considered the child to be the active element in birth, while the mother was passive. Galen, writing in the second century CE, on the other hand, attributed the onset of labor to the uterus, whose retentive faculty was then overcome by its propulsive faculty (*On the Natural Faculties* 3.2–3 and 12 = Kühn 2.145–152 and 182–186). The ancients described labor as pains (Greek: *ponoi* or *odynai*), felt in various parts of the body (Aristotle *History of Animals* 7.10, 586b). To alleviate them and speed up the birth, drugs, incantations, and amulets were used (*Diseases of Women* 1.77 = Littré 8.170–172; Plato *Theaetetus* 149d; Pliny *Natural History* 37.180; Soranus *Gynecology* 3.12).

As described by Ann E. Hanson, the ancient birth room was a crowded place: in addition to midwives, female friends, and family members, male doctors and fathers could be present at the birth. Soranus gives us a detailed account of "normal" childbirth attended by midwives, who assisted dilation of the cervix with gentle massaging, reassured the mother, and encouraged her to breathe well, without screaming (*Gynecology* 2.2–6). He also describes a birthing chair, a cut-out seat with backrest and armrests, which corresponds to visual representations found on funeral stelae and amulets (*Gynecology* 2.3; stele of the midwife Scribonia Attica: Ostia, Antiquarium, inv., 5203; Campbell Bonner D145). In the case of an abnormal presentation (the ancients considered cephalic presentation to be normal), a version (turning) could be attempted (*Diseases of Women* 1.69 = Littré 8.146). Shaking (*Excision of the Fetus* 4 = Littré 8.514–516) and drugs could also help in difficult labors. Episiotomies, forceps births, and Caesarean sections are not mentioned in medical texts and were probably not practiced in antiquity. If all failed, doctors could perform an embryotomy, the cutting and extraction of the fetus, in order to save the mother (*Excision of the Fetus* 1 = Littré 8.512–514; Celsus, *On Medicine* 7.29). A parturient could die of exhaustion, hemorrhage, or fever. Both maternal and neonatal mortality are generally assumed to be high, but as Tim G. Parkin has argued, estimates of death rates are difficult—if not impossible—to establish. In Greece, the parturient and all those present at the birth were considered polluted (Cyrene cathartic law *Supplementum Epigraphicum Graecum* 9.72 = Sokolowski 115, lines 16–20; Euripides *Electra* 654).

After the birth, the midwife cut the umbilical cord (*Diseases of Women* 1.46 = Littré 8.106; Aristotle, *History of Animals* 7.10, 587a; Soranus, *Gynecology* 2.6), and inspected the baby for defects. It was the father, or the legal guardian, who decided whether the newborn should be raised by the family or not. Various rituals signaled that the child was formally accepted into the family: in Greece the Amphidromia (when the child was carried around the hearth); in Rome, the symbolic gesture of lifting the child from the ground (*levare* or *tollere infantem*); and in both cultures naming ceremonies. If the father chose not to raise the child, it could be exposed (that is, abandoned). Evidence relating to exposure (not to be confounded with infanticide, the killing of an infant) is difficult to interpret (Plato *Theatetus* 160e–161a; Aristotle *Politeia* 7.15, 1335b; Soranus *Gynecology* 2.10).

Representations of Childbirth in Drama. While discussing childbirth in real life may have been regarded as embarrassing (Theophrastus *Characters* 20.5–8), childbirth was a significant concern of both tragedy and comedy, as described by Edith Hall. In Euripides' tragedy, Medea draws a homology between war and childbirth, claiming that she would rather go three times to battle rather than give birth once (*Medea* 248–251). Several of Euripides' plays have a "baby" theme, in particular *Electra*, where the vengeful heroine pretends having given birth to a boy to lure her mother, Clytemnestra, to her house, and with the help of Orestes and Pylades, bring her down. In comedies, pretended pregnancies and births appear in Aristophanes' *Lysistrata* (742–757) and *Women at the Thesmophoria* (502–516). The lost comedy of Nicomachus entitled *Eileithyia* probably had a childbirth-related theme. Aulus Gellius informs us that one of Menander's plays, the *Plocium*, featured a maiden who went into labor

backstage, her cries being heard on stage (*Attic Nights* 2.23.18). In Latin, Plautus' *Truculentus* tells the story of the prostitute Phronesium who, having smuggled a baby, pretends she has borne it to the Babylonian soldier Stratophanes.

[*See also* Children and Childhood; Gynecology; Hippocratic Corpus; Marriage and Divorce; Sexuality; *and* Women.]

BIBLIOGRAPHY

Bagnall, Roger S., and Bruce W. Frier. *The Demography of Roman Egypt.* Cambridge, U.K., and New York: Cambridge University Press, 1994.

Bonner, Campbell. *Studies in Magical Amulets, Chiefly Graeco-Egyptian.* Ann Arbor: University of Michigan Press, 1950.

Dasen, Véronique. *Naissance et petite enfance dans l'antiquité: Actes du colloque de Fribourg, 28 novembre–1er décembre 2001.* Fribourg, Switzerland, and Göttingen, Germany: Vandenhoeck & Ruprecht, 2004.

Demand, Nancy. *Birth, Death, and Motherhood in Classical Greece,* Baltimore, Md., and London: Johns Hopkins University Press, 1994.

Hall, Edith. *The Theatrical Cast of Athens: Interactions between Ancient Greek Drama and Society.* Oxford and New York: Oxford University Press, 2006.

Hanson, Ann E. "A Division of Labor: Roles for Men in Greek and Roman Births." *Thamyris* 1 (1994): 157–202.

King, Helen. *Hippocrates' Woman: Reading the Female Body in Ancient Greece.* London and New York: Routledge, 1998.

Parkin, Tim G. *Demography and Roman Society.* Baltimore, Md., and London: Johns Hopkins University Press, 1992.

Riddle, John M. *Contraception and Abortion from the Ancient World to the Renaissance.* Cambridge, Mass., and London: Harvard University Press, 1992.

Sokolowski, Franciszek. *Lois sacrés des cités grecques.* Paris: École française de Athens, 1969.

Laurence M. V. Totelin

BITHYNIA

Bithynia is situated in the northwestern part of Asia Minor. Herodotus (7.75), Thucydides (4.75.2), and Xenophon (*Hellenica* 1.3.2 and 3.2.2; *Anabasis* 6.4.2) report that its population was of Thracian origin (cf. Arrian *Anabasis* 1.29.5), which is corroborated by a large number of Thraco-Bithynian personal names in the inscriptions of the Hellenistic and Roman imperial periods. In Hellenistic times Bithynia was a kingdom ruled by an indigenous dynasty and a landowning warrior elite. After the incorporation of several Greek colonies on the coast of the Propontis—Astacus, Cios, and Myrlea, which received the dynastic names Nicomedia, Prusias ad Mare, and Apamea, respectively—Bithynia constituted an area that was situated approximately east of the river Rhyndacus, north of the river Sangarius, and west of the city of Heraclea. In addition a number of cities were (re)founded, such as Prusa ad Olympum, Nicaea, Prusias ad Hypium, and Bithynium.

The last king of Bithynia, Nicomedes IV (c. 94–754 BCE), bequeathed the heavily indebted state to the Romans, so that upon his death and Rome's victory in 63 over Mithradates VI Eupator in the Third Mithradatic War, Pompey organized Bithynia as a province, thereby adding considerable parts of the former Pontic kingdom. Consequently the (double) province was from the early imperial period onward called "Pontus and Bithynia," notwithstanding some short-lived territorial changes. To facilitate the administration, Pompey divided Bithynia into twelve and Pontus into eleven territories, each with a city as its center.

Under Augustus the province was assigned to the senate and administered by a proconsul of Praetorian rank. This changed briefly under Trajan, who appointed Pliny the Younger—whose letters to the emperor are a valuable source for the history of the province—and then Gaius Julius Cornutus Tertullus as his *legati* (c. 109–115 CE); in the later part of Antoninus Pius' reign (r. 138–161), Bithynia was placed permanently under the direct authority of the emperor, represented by a *legatus Augusti pro praetore*.

Owing to Pontus and Bithynia's nature as a double province, the Greeks of each part founded a common assembly of elected city representatives, the *koinon Bithynias* and *koinon Pontou*, with a *Bithyniarchēs* and a *Pontarchēs*, respectively, as its head figure; the two functions could, nevertheless, be occupied by a single man. The assembly was responsible for the imperial cult and functioned as an intermediary with the central power in Rome. The first imperial temple was erected in the capital, Nicomedia, for Roma and Augustus in 29 BCE.

The two most important cities, Nicomedia and Nicaea, long struggled for primacy in the province, reflected in the competition for city titles (inscriptions, coins). In this context each of them sided with one of the rival emperors in 193 CE: Nicomedia chose Septimius Severus, and Nicaea chose Pescennius Niger, which resulted in a brief fall from imperial favor for Nicaea.

With the redrawing of provincial boundaries from the mid-third century onward, Pontus and Bithynia underwent several administrative and territorial changes until the creation of the provinces of Bithynia, Honorias, Paphlagonia, and Hellenopontus in the fourth century. Bithynia was the birthplace of the orator Dio Chrysostom (from Prusa; born about 40 or 50 CE) and the historian Cassius Dio (from Nicaea; born about 164 CE).

[*See also* Anatolia; Asia; Bithynia, Kingdom of; *and* Pontus, Kingdom of.]

BIBLIOGRAPHY

Corsten, Thomas. "The Rôle and Status of the Indigenous Population in Bithynia." In *Rome and the Black Sea Region: Domination, Romanisation, Resistance*, edited by Tønnes Bekker-Nielsen, pp. 85–92. Black Sea Studies 5. Århus, Denmark: Århus University Press, 2006.

Marek, Christian. *Pontus et Bithynia: Die römischen Provinzen im Norden Kleinasiens*. Mainz, Germany: Von Zabern, 2003.

Thomas Corsten

BITHYNIA, KINGDOM OF

A region in northwestern Asia Minor, Bithynia was bounded on the west by the Sea of Marmara and the Thracian Bosporus, on the north by the Black Sea, on the east by the River Billaeus (Filyos), and on the south by Phrygia Epictetus.

Well watered by several rivers, streams, and lakes, Bithynia was one of the most fertile regions of Asia

Minor, producing, in the words of Xenophon, "barley, wheat, beans of all kinds, millet and sesame, figs in abundance, plenty of grapes yielding a good sweet wine, and in fact everything except olives." Bithynia was also rich in forests, yielding excellent timber for shipbuilding, and quarries for marble. There were (and still are) famous thermal baths. The region had strategic importance as it formed the eastern shore of the Thracian Bosporus, the vital section of the maritime route between the Black Sea and the Aegean world.

Thracians, the first attested inhabitants of Bithynia, migrated to Asia Minor sometime during the first quarter of the first millennium. The urbanization of Bithynia began with the Greek colonization. In the seventh century, the Greeks colonized the coasts of Bithynia, founding Cyzicus (Belkıs), Cius (Gemlik), Chalcedon (Kadıköy), and Chrysopolis (Üsküdar), at the entrance of the Bosporus, and Heraclea Pontica (Karadeniz Ereğlisi) on the Black Sea, about 120 miles (190 kilometers) east of the Bosporus. Xenophon says that the Bithynian Thracians abused outrageously any Greeks they encountered. On the other hand, Heracleots and Byzantines reduced some of the Bithynians to serfdom.

Bithynia came under Lydian rule in the seventh century and then Persian rule in 545 BCE. The Persians controlled it through the satraps at Daskyleion. Alexander ignored Bithynia on his way to Persia, but his generals attempted to control it after his death. In 297 BCE Zipoetes, a local Thracian chieftain, freed his country from Lysimachus and assumed the royal title. The main policy of the Bithynian kings was to defend their kingdom against the Seleucids who claimed all Asia Minor as theirs. Zipoetes' son and successor Nicomedes I (c. 279–255 BCE) formed an alliance, called "the Northern League" by modern scholars, with the other kingdoms and Greek poleis in northwestern Asia Minor to ward off Seleucid encroachment. Nicomedes invited the Celtic tribes to Asia Minor and used them as mercenaries and allies against his brother, a rival claimant for the Bythinian throne, and Antiochus I. He may even have settled them in central Asia Minor to create a bulwark against the

Seleucids. Nicomedes I's successor Ziaelas (c. 255–230 BCE) established friendship with the Ptolemies most likely aimed at the Seleucids and their ally Pontus. After thus containing the Seleucid threat, the Bithynian kings began to expand eastward toward Paphlagonia and southwestward to Mysian Olympus (Uludağ). This aggressive expansionist policy inevitably brought about clashes between Bithynia and other cities and kingdoms of Asia Minor, notably Heraclea Pontica, Byzantium, and Pergamum. Prusias I attacked Heraclea Pontica and captured its dependent settlements Cierus and Tieum and renamed the former as Prusias on the Hypios. He was also involved in the great trade war between Byzantium and Rhodes (220–218 BCE), attacking and capturing some of the Byzantine possessions in Asia Minor. He also attacked Pergamum and seized its northern territories. The expansion of the Bithynian kingdom was cut short in 189 BCE when the Romans defeated Antiochus III near Magnesia. In this pivotal struggle the Attalids of Pergamum sided with the Romans and thus were richly rewarded, while Prusias I remained neutral and gave refuge to Hannibal, the great enemy of Rome. Thereafter the Bithynian kings had to take into account Roman influence in the eastern Mediterranean and act accordingly. In the first quarter of the first century, the Bithynians were caught between the struggles of the Romans and Mithradates VI of Pontus and suffered much from the activities of Roman and Italian businessmen and slave dealers, which ruined the social and economic fabric of the Bithynian kingdom and drained its population. The unfortunate king Nicomedes IV bequeathed his much ravaged kingdom to Rome in 74 BCE.

The Bithynian kings were philhellenes and encouraged the spread of Greek culture. Like other Hellenistic kings they founded a number of cities throughout their kingdom. Nicomedes I founded Nicomedia (İzmit) on the Propontis as his capital. Prusias I (c. 230–182 BCE) laid the foundations of Prusia (Bursa) at the foot of the Mysian Olympus. Although they had other motives for founding cities, this policy doubtless accelerated the Hellenization of their country.

[*See also* Attalids; Bithynia; Byzantium; Pergamum, *subentry* Historical Overview; Pontus, Kingdom of; Ptolemies; *and* Seleucids.]

BIBLIOGRAPHY

Burstein, Stanley Meyer. *Outpost of Hellenism: The Emergence of Heraclea on the Black Sea*. Berkeley: University of California Press, 1976.

Jones, A. H. M. *Cities of the Eastern Roman Provinces*. 2nd ed. Oxford: Clarendon Press, 1971.

Vitucci, Giovanni. *Il regno di Bitinia*. Rome: A. Signorelli, 1953.

Mehmet Fatih Yavuz

BLACK SEA

The Black Sea (also known as the Pontus or Euxine Sea), connected to the Mediterranean through the Bosporus, the Sea of Marmara (Propontis), and the Dardanelles (Hellespont), is bordered by the modern countries of Bulgaria and Romania on the west, Ukraine on the north, Russia and Georgia on the east, and Turkey on the south. There are regional variations in the climate, which in ancient times was most probably colder than it is now. The level of the sea has experienced six significant changes in the past six thousand years, the last being in the first centuries CE when it rose by some 10–13 feet (3–4 meters), submerging many ancient sites and eroding other ancient coastal remains.

There are no large islands; the few small offshore islands were anciently peninsulas. The modern Crimea forms a significant peninsula to the north, and separates the Black Sea from the Sea of Azov (ancient Lake Maeotis), reached through the Kerch Strait. The sea is 730 miles (1,170 kilometers) in length and 160 miles (260 kilometers) across at its shortest point with an overall area of about 163,000 square miles (423,000 square kilometers). Herodotus (4.85) was the first to estimate its extent, reckoning its length at 11,100 furlongs (roughly 1,300 miles, or 2,100 kilometers) and its (widest) breadth as 3,300 furlongs (about 400 miles, or 640 kilometers). Its original name most probably meant "dark" as, in many local languages, does the present one.

Initially, the Greeks called it "Inhospitable" (*Axeinos*), but as they became more familiar with it they renamed it "Hospitable" (*Euxeinos*). The Latin name is Pontus Euxinus. In Greek mythology, the Black Sea, the eastern edge of the known world, remained a distant area, famed for its riches, populated by Amazons and mythical creatures—the one-eyed Arimaspeans, griffins, and the like. Hercules spent some time in the land of the Scythians; Iphigenia was an exile in the land of the Taurians. Achilles lived here after death; Prometheus was chained to Mount Elbrus in the Great Caucasus range. The most popular myth was that of Jason and the Argonauts and their voyage to find the Golden Fleece in the kingdom of Aia (later identified with Colchis) on the eastern rim of the Black Sea, also known to Greeks as the border between Asia and Europe.

Although the date of the first Greek penetration of the Black Sea remains in dispute, based on available archaeological evidence the first Greek settlements around the sea were founded in the last third of the seventh century BCE. Greek colonization here was undertaken chiefly by Ionia and its main city, Miletus, initially under the pressure of Lydian and later Achaemenid expansion and conquest. According to ancient authors, between seventy-five and ninety colonies were established (Seneca, *Ad Helviam* 7.2; Pliny, *Natural History* 5.112), numbers that are probably exaggerated; in reality, there were but twenty major settlements in the early stages, the others arising through secondary colonization by or the expansion of these twenty over time.

In about 630 BCE, Histria was founded in the west and Berezan and Taganrog settlements in the north; and in the late seventh century, Sinope and Amisos were settled in the south and Apollonia Pontica in the west. The sixth century saw mass colonization, during which such cities as Panticapaeum, Nymphaeum, Theodosia, Myrmekion, and Nikonion (in the north), Phasis, Dioscurias, and Gyenos (in the east), and Odessos and Tomis (in the west) were established, most by the city-state Miletus. Heracleia Pontica (in the south) was a Megarian and Boeotian foundation (of c. 554 BCE), establishing two colonies of its own—Chersonesus in the Crimea in 422/1 BCE, and Callatis in the west in the early fourth century. In c. 542 BCE Phanagoria was founded on the Taman Peninsula, opposite the eastern Crimea, by the people of Teos in Ionia. Nearby was Hermonassa, a joint foundation of Miletus and Mytilene.

The Greek colonies soon became centers of trade and craft production. Many cities possessed good harbors, and some had several. It is very difficult to say precisely what the Black Sea exported; it changed over time. Written sources of the Classical period and later name honey, wax, fish, cattle, slaves, animal skins, and timber; in return came olive oil, wine, and luxury goods. The export of grain, especially from the area of the Bosporan kingdom, did not start until the late fifth to fourth centuries BCE. Grain was sent to Athens when there were shortages there. Often the Black Sea colonies themselves needed to import grain, particularly from the Hellenistic period.

Many parts of the Black Sea region were populated before the Greeks arrived. Most prominent were the Thracians and Getae in the west, the Scythians and Maeotians in the north, the Colchians in the east, and the Mariandyni, Chalybes, Mossynoeci, and Macrones in the south. Relations between Greeks and locals were mainly friendly, except in the south. Some tribes, especially those inhabiting the foothills of the Caucasus, made a livelihood from piracy and attacking Greek cities. From the Late Archaic to the Classical period, when local kingdoms such as the Odrysian, Colchian, and Scythian arose, the relationship was modified. Some Greek cities became their tributaries, and, within ever deepening economic links, the expertise of Greek craftsmen was used by local rulers to build, decorate, and furnish their residences, even their stone chamber-tombs, and produce precious metal objects that acted as symbols of their power, wealth, and prestige.

[See also Achaemenids; Anatolia; Asia; Bithynia; Bosporus, Kingdom of; Jason and the Argonauts; and Miletus.]

BIBLIOGRAPHY

Avram, Alexandru, John Hind, and Gocha Tsetskhladze. "The Black Sea Area." In An Inventory of Archaic and Classical Poleis, edited by Mogens Herman Hansen and Thomas Heine Nielsen, pp. 924–973. Oxford and New York: Oxford University Press, 2004. Site by site survey of major Greek colonies from their establishment down to the Hellenistic period.

King, Charles. The Black Sea: A History. Oxford and New York: Oxford University Press, 2004. A good overview of the Black Sea and its surroundings from antiquity to the recent past. Stronger on medieval and modern periods.

Tsetskhladze, Gocha R. "Greek Penetration of the Black Sea." In The Archaeology of Greek Colonisation: Essays Dedicated to Sir John Boardman, edited by Gocha R. Tsetskhladze and Franco De Angelis, pp. 111–135. Oxford: Oxford University Committee for Archaeology, 1994. A survey of the establishment of Greek colonies in the Archaic period, sources, and reasons for colonization.

Tsetskhladze, Gocha R., ed. The Greek Colonisation of the Black Sea Area: Historical Interpretation of Archaeology. Stuttgart: F. Steiner, 1998. Sixteen chapters by a diverse body of international scholars. Presents both general studies of the phenomenon and detailed accounts of particular settlements, and examines relations between Greeks and locals.

Gocha R. Tsetskhladze

BODY

See Nudity.

BOEOTIA

Boeotia is the spacious and fertile region in central Greece bounded in the north by Phocis and Opuntian Locris and in the south by Attica. Lake Copais and Mount Helicon divide Boeotia into a larger southern part dominated by Thebes and a smaller northern part dominated by Orchomenus. Nature encouraged prosperous and populous cities and villages with easy communications connecting them.

Although archaeology proves inhabitation from the Paleolithic period, Boeotia thrived only in the Late Helladic period in the second millennium BCE. Mycenaean palaces graced Thebes, Orchomenus, and Gla. Herodotus speaks of Phoenicians under Cadmus settling Boeotia (2.49; 5.57), but the "Cadmian letters" that Herodotus saw in Thebes (5.59) were probably letters akin to Ionic Greek. A Linear B tablet uncovered in the twentieth century CE bears the name "Thebes." Homer (2.494–510) and Thucydides (1.12; cf. Plutarch *Cimon* 1.1) speak of "Boiotoi" before the Trojan War. Hesiod (fl. c. 800 BCE), who lived in Boeotia, portrays the Boeotia of his own day as an agricultural society marked by smallholdings and governed by *basileis* (kings). Numismatic evidence of the late sixth century BCE indicates a nascent confederacy of small cities, doubtless under Theban hegemony.

The early years of the fifth century proved crucial for Boeotian developments in two ways. First, these years saw the earliest discernible attempts by Thebes to organize other Boeotian cities in a stable confederacy. Second, during these years Thebes and the rest of Boeotia went into open conflict with Athens, conflict that lasted for a century. In 519 the two developments coalesced in Theban efforts to force Plataea into the growing federation (Herodotus 6.108). Opposing the federation, Athens defeated the Boeotians in battle, thereafter forbidding any further Theban political coercion in the area. Athens notwithstanding, the fifth century saw the voluntary evolution of the Boeotian Confederacy, the first effective, widely based federal government in Greece. From that time also dated the enduring hostility between Boeotia—Thebes especially—and Athens. Of the Boeotian cities only Plataea remained loyal to Athens, although it, too, subsequently joined the confederacy.

Xerxes' invasion of Greece in 480–479 BCE further contributed to the antipathy between Boeotia and Athens. When Xerxes demanded submission, nearly all of Boeotia obeyed (Herodotus 6.49; 7.132). Only Plataea, which had supported Athens at Marathon (490), remained loyal to Athens. It did so from hostility toward Thebes and friendship with Athens. After their victory over the Persians at Plataea in 479, the Greeks punished Thebes but left the rest of

Boeotia in peace. Only numismatic evidence testifies that the confederacy increasingly grew to represent all the major and some minor cities.

External forces in 457 thrust Boeotia back into the mainstream of Greek affairs when a Spartan army entered Boeotia. An alliance between the two states ensued. Together they crushed a preemptive Athenian invasion at Tanagra that inflicted heavy losses. Undeterred, the Athenians returned sixty-two days later to defeat Boeotia and overrun all of it and Phocis. Although under Athenian control, Boeotia retained its political cohesion. In 447, Boeotia defeated Athens at Coronea. Boeotia thereafter rebuilt its federal organization along truly representative lines (Thucydides 5.38.2; *Hellenica Oxyrhynchia* 19). The federal government consisted of electoral units that included one or more cities that contributed a boeotarch, or elected chief magistrate, sixty members to a federal council, and units to the army. Individual cities continued to govern their own internal affairs.

Boeotia supported Sparta in the Peloponnesian War, with Thebes helping to inflame the war by besieging Plataea in 431. Boeotia thereafter thoroughly defeated Athens at the battle of Delium in 424 and fought under Sparta at Mantinea in 418. During the Decelean War (412–404) many Boeotians enriched themselves by plundering eastern Attica. At the end of the war Boeotia demanded the destruction of Athens, which Sparta firmly rejected.

Peace gave way to a period in which Boeotia lived up to its sobriquet "the dancing floor of war." In 395, Boeotia allied itself with other cities in the Corinthian War (395–386) to end Spartan domination of Greece. Boeotia and its allies won the battle of Haliartus in 395, lost at Nemea River later that year, and won again at Coronea in 394. The war devolved into stalemate that ended with Sparta joining Persia to impose the King's Peace of 386, which dissolved the Boeotian Confederacy.

In 379, Boeotia defiantly created a new confederacy with democratic citizenship and Theban leadership. With its victory at Leuctra in 371, Boeotia became ascendant. Thebes eliminated internal opposition by seizing Plataea, Thespiae, and Orchomenus. Yet rather than create an empire in Greece, Thebes encouraged federal governments there. Even victory against Sparta at Mantinea in 362 failed to bring success. Boeotia entered the Third Sacred War (356–346) to liberate Delphi from Phocian tyrants, which ultimately involved its alliance with Philip II of Macedonia. The growth of Philip's power led to an alliance between Boeotia and Athens that failed to defeat Philip at the Battle of Chaeronea in 338.

After Chaeronea, Philip reinstated the disenfranchised cities. Boeotia sided with the Macedonian general Antipater during the Lamian War (323–322) and sent forces to Thermopylae in 279 to stop Brennus' Gauls. Though it remained neutral in the Chremonidean War (267–261)—when a coalition of Greek cities again sought to end Macedonian domination—Boeotia supported Philip V of Macedon against Rome in the so-called Second Macedonian War in 200 (Philip was defeated in 197) and supported Perseus in the Third Macedonian War (170–168), only to fall to Rome in 147 BCE.

[*See also* Chaeronea, Battle of; Corinthian War; Epaminondas; Lamian War; Leuctra, Battle of; Macedonian Wars; Peloponnesian Wars; Plataea; Sacred Wars; *and* Thebes.]

BIBLIOGRAPHY
Buck, Robert J. *Boiotia and the Boiotian League, 432–371 B.C.* Edmonton: University of Alberta Press, 1994.
Buck, Robert J. *A History of Boeotia.* Edmonton: University of Alberta Press, 1979.
Fossey, John M. *Topography and Population of Ancient Boiotia.* Chicago: Ares, 1988.
Gullath, Brigitte. *Untersuchungen zur Geschichte Boiotiens in der Zeit Alexanders und der Diadochen.* Frankfurt am Main, Germany: P. Lang, 1982.

John Buckler

BOETHIUS

(Anicius Manlius Severinus Boethius; c. 474 or 480–524 or 525 CE), late Roman philosopher and politician. A Roman aristocrat, Boethius spent most of his life in the leisured study of philosophy, although in 522 he accepted the high governmental position of *magister officiorum* (master of offices). Most sympathetic to Neoplatonism, he nevertheless drew widely from various philosophical schools. Like many Neoplatonists, he found no incompatibility between Aristotelian and Platonic thought. To demonstrate this thesis, he planned to translate all of Plato and Aristotle into Latin. He succeeded only in translating Aristotle's logical works, writing two commentaries each on the *Categories* and *On Interpretation* and probably one (now lost) commentary on the *Topics*. To these he added commentaries on Cicero's *Topics* and Porphyry's *Isagoge* (an introduction to the *Categories*). Before he could finish his ambitious project, Boethius was accused and convicted of treason for reasons that remain unclear but probably stem from his orthodox Catholicism and pro-Byzantine sympathies at a time when Italy was ruled by King Theoderic, an Ostrogoth and Arian Christian whose relationship with the Eastern empire was unstable. Faced with ruin, Boethius wrote his masterwork, the *Consolation of Philosophy*. He was executed in 524 or 525. He had also written four works on mathematics (including astronomy and music, the latter important in the Middle Ages) and five short but logically rigorous theological treatises. The example of those treatises, coupled with Boethius' efforts in Aristotelian logic, inspired later medieval thinkers to ground their own theological writing in Aristotelian logic.

Theological Treatise 4, *On the Catholic Faith*, actually the earliest of Boethius' five theological works, outlines a range of theological issues, while the remaining four offer solutions to particular and often pressing theological problems of Boethius' time. Treatise 5, *Against Nestor and Eutyches*, employs Aristotelian logic to argue for the orthodox doctrine that Christ is one person with two natures, human and divine. To resolve disagreements over the nature of the Trinity, Boethius wrote Treatises 1 and 2, which develop Augustinian thought by exploring the logic of propositions about the Trinity. Treatise 3, later called by the mysterious name *On the Hebdomads*, explains how all substances are good because they have being when they are not substantial goods, thereby laying the groundwork for later medieval theories of the convertibility of being and goodness.

Although Boethius' philosophical commentaries are among his least innovative works, two modestly original discussions stand out as particularly influential on later thought. (1) In his *Second Commentary on Porphyry's "Isagoge,"* Boethius explains that if there were universals, they would be common to many (a) as a whole, (b) simultaneously, and (c) as constituents. Reporting (without explicitly endorsing) Alexander of Aphrodisias' view, Boethius holds that even though such universals do not exist, we abstract universal concepts from particulars in such a way that our thoughts still accurately represent reality. (2) In his *Second Commentary on Aristotle's "On Interpretation,"* Boethius develops an Aristotelian solution to Aristotle's own worries about logical determinism. For any pair of contradictory assertions about the future, such as (a) "There will be a sea battle tomorrow" and (b) "There will not be a sea battle tomorrow," one is true and the other false. If, for instance, (a) is true, then it appears that the sea battle, and by extension all future events, are necessary and inevitable. Against this deterministic argument, Boethius contends that propositions such as (a) are only indeterminately true. Because only determinate truths about future events rule out contingency, some future events are contingent.

While imprisoned, Boethius wrote the *Consolation of Philosophy*, an eloquent prosimetric work (i.e., alternating prose and verse) aimed at a wide audience. As the book opens, the character Boethius bewails his loss of the goods of fortune, such as political power and glory for political service. Lady Philosophy, personifying the philosophical tradition, comes to offer him consolation through philosophical therapy. Philosophy describes Fortune as a goddess whose constantly turning wheel will sweep us down as readily as it once raised us up: Fortune's only constancy is inconstancy. Boethius' loss, however, is of little importance, according to Philosophy. Implying Stoic and Aristotelian arguments, she convinces him that the downturn in his fortune is no injustice, because the goods he lost were always Fortune's to give and take. Moreover, because they never made him genuinely happy, their loss cannot make him wretched now. Turning to Plato, Philosophy argues that God orders the universe in such a way that the virtuous alone have the only power worth having: the power to attain happiness. Finally, Philosophy argues, divine foreknowledge does not leave us unfree. Because (as the Neoplatonists had argued) knowledge takes its character from the knower and not from what is known, God can have necessary knowledge even of future contingent events because of the unique character of God's knowledge. To clarify her contention, she asserts that God is eternal, having the fullness of his life all at once. Because he sees all events timelessly, his necessary knowledge of what happens imposes no more necessity on them than our knowledge of what is happening now. The *Consolation*'s influence can be found not just in later philosophy, but in medieval literary works such as Jean de Meung's *Roman de la Rose* and Geoffrey Chaucer's *Troilus and Criseyde*, *Knight's Tale*, and *Tale of Melibee*.

[*See also* Allegory; Church Fathers; Consolation Literature; Fortune; Neoplatonists; *and* Philosophy as Therapy.]

BIBLIOGRAPHY

Works of Boethius

Comentarii in librum Aristotelis Peri hermeneias. Edited by Karl Meiser. 2 vols. Leipzig, Germany: Teubner, 1877–1880.

In Isagogen Porphyrii commenta. Edited by Samuel Brandt. Corpus Scriptorum Ecclesiasticorum Latinorum, vol. 48. Vienna: Tempsky; Leipzig, Germany: Freitag, 1906.

The Theological Tractates, translated by Hugh F. Stewart, Edward K. Rand, and S. J. Tester, and *The Consolation of Philosophy*, translated by S. J. Tester. New ed. Loeb Classical Library. Cambridge, Mass: Harvard University Press, 1973. Latin text with English translation on facing pages.

Five Texts on the Mediaeval Problem of Universals: Porphyry, Boethius, Abelard, Duns Scotus, Ockham. Translated by Paul Vincent Spade. Indianapolis, Ind.: Hackett, 1994. Contains a translation of Boethius' seminal discussion of the problem of universals.

On Aristotle's "On Interpretation" 9. Translated by Norman Kretzmann. London: Duckworth; Ithaca, N.Y.: Cornell University Press, 1998. Contains a translation of Boethius' first and second commentaries, including his treatment of logical determinism.

De consolatione philosophiae and Opuscula theologica. Edited by Claudio Moreschini. Munich, Germany: K. G. Saur, 2000.

Secondary Works

Chadwick, Henry. *The Consolations of Music, Logic, Theology, and Philosophy.* Oxford: Clarendon Press; New York: Oxford University Press, 1981. A general study of Boethius.

Courcelle, Pierre. *La "Consolation de philosophie" dans la tradition littéraire.* Paris: Études Augustiniennes, 1967. Focuses on Boethius' sources and on his influence on later writers.

Marenbon, John. *Boethius.* Oxford and New York: Oxford University Press, 2003. A general study that argues for Boethius' originality as a philosopher.

Jeffrey Hause

BOOKS

Books in the form of rolls ("bookrolls") were the norm for Greek and, later, Roman literary texts from the beginning through the early Roman era. We hear of leather bookrolls as early as Herodotus (5.58), but these were relatively rare. Far the dominant material was papyrus, following an Egyptian tradition of papyrus bookrolls that stretches back at least to the third millennium. The earliest vase representation of a Greek papyrus bookroll dates to the first half of the fifth century BCE, and we can infer its use from at least a century earlier for epic and other poetic texts.

The bookroll was written in columns from left to right, and held horizontally in the hands. Bookrolls were constructed from premanufactured rolls (not sheets) of papyrus, cut away or pasted together so as to form a suitable length for a given text. Bookroll construction could therefore have been casual, but judging from extant papyri, it was not. We see many particulars, such as evenness in writing and spacing and exacting attention to layout, that imply the activity of scribes trained to the craft.

The appearance of the bookroll is remarkably stable over time and place, despite some stylistic variation. Surviving fragments of over 3,000 papyrus bookrolls allow us to give particulars. The height of the roll tends to about 7.5–13 inches (19–33 centimeters), mostly shorter (7.5–10 inches or 19–25 centimeters) in the Ptolemaic period and taller (10–13 inches or 25–33 centimeters) in the Roman era. Prose texts were written in columns that are narrow relative to their height and in a compact arrangement, roughly analogous to a modern newspaper. Verse texts are different, since the column width is simply a function of script size and verse length, but here too there was aesthetic attention to the flow of the columns. Margins on the top and bottom tend to be considerably more generous than strict functionality demands. Titles were added at the end, and, since there was no spine, also as tags that stuck out from the rolled up bookroll.

The writing itself is almost always a "book hand," an expensive script (two to two and one-half times the cost of a script used for contracts, says the Edict of Diocletian) formed with a view to clarity and without connecting strokes, the precursor of our capital letters. The letters are laid out continuously (*scriptio continua*), that is, without spaces between words or paragraphing. Punctuation is limited, in general, to major points of division, such as full sentence stops (periods), changes between speakers in drama, or divisions between poems in a poetry collection, and is done simply, by insertion of a raised dot or horizontal line. Aids to reading like accents or breathings, and minor pauses such as those marked by today's commas, seem to have been deliberately avoided by most scribes (though sometimes added by a reader). The net result is (to us) a radically unencumbered stream of letters.

The bookroll had, then, a distinct look and feel, and together with that a directed set of cultural resonances. The bookroll is designed for clarity and for beauty, but not for ease of use, much less for mass readership. The very fact that word division, which was usual in early Latin texts, was discarded by the Romans in deference to the Greek habit of *scriptio continua* tells us that functionality was less important than cultural cachet. The book-roll seems, rather, an egregiously elite product that required a great deal of education to use properly.

In general, one can assume that one literary work or one book of a work (say, a play of Sophocles or a book of Virgil's *Aeneid*) was equivalent to one roll, though there are complications and exceptions. Certain short works could be combined into a single roll; and there seems to have been a point at which a very large book might be divided into two. Normative lengths range from roughly 10 to 50 feet (3–15 meters) for bookrolls, quite a broad range: there was no standard length to which bookrolls tended. The size of the bookroll had its own cultural register. The smallest were works like books of romances or certain kinds of poetry, such as the *libelli* (notebooks) of the Roman lyric and elegiac poets, following in Callimachus' footsteps. The largest were large-scale histories and other works of explicit self-importance, whose thick diameter and heavier weight made them "monumental" in look and feel as well as in content.

The literary codex (our modern form of book) comes firmly into the historical record in the first century CE (Martial 1.2, 14.184–192). Over the course of the second to fourth centuries, the codex came to replace the bookroll as the normative idea of "book"

for literary texts. There remains lively debate as to whether the parchment or papyrus codex came first, but parchment became an important material in the record in the fourth century, predominating by the seventh. In the writing, scribes generally follow the same conventions of *scriptio continua*, sparse punctuation, and the like, as for the bookroll. But the look and feel is noticeably distinct from the roll, since individual (double) pages, typically with a single column per page, confront the reader rather than a tight, continuous stream of written columns.

A different history and set of cultural associations accompanies this difference in aesthetic. Among early codices, two prominent facts emerge from what survives. The causes remain murky, but there is a marked preference for the codex form among Christian literary texts. Almost all biblical texts are in codex form, and many apocrypha and theological writings as well. Also, early codices are more likely than bookrolls to be written in workaday hands (labeled "reformed documentary" by Roberts). Some scholars have been quick to associate the workaday character of the writing with the idea of working-class Christian communities, but that has been challenged. Others have highlighted the ability of the codex to embrace in one package

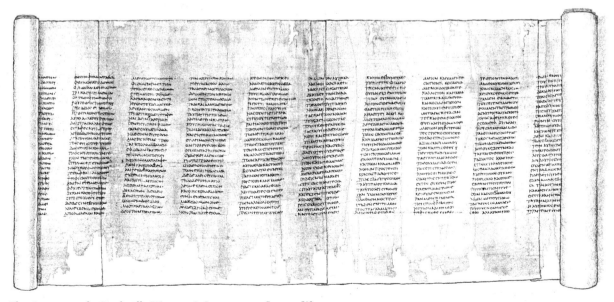

The Anatomy of a Bookroll. WILLIAM A. JOHNSON AND SHIRLEY WERNER

the whole of the developing Christian canon, but surviving early codices suggest no particular interest in that capability. It has also been supposed that a foundational text, such as a Sayings of Jesus (Roberts and Skeat) or the Pauline Epistles (Gamble), circulated in the form of a codex and thereby established the iconographical preference for the codex.

As book form, the codex had some distinct advantages. Several bookrolls could be fashioned into a single codex, and the parchment codex, especially, was far less prone to damage, facts which will have great consequence for the use and survival of classical literature. Ease of access and economy of material are also cited as advantages, probably wrongly. There was in any case one distinct disadvantage, which is that book production for the codex was considerably more complicated, involving the planning of quires and sewing of binding and covers. Without implying direct cause and effect, we can see that medieval characteristics such as the rise of scriptoria, renewed encyclopedism, and the habit of extensive marginal annotation can be located within the series of changes we associate with the shift to codex form.

[See also Libraries; Literacy, Greek; Literacy, Roman; Paleography; and Reading and Readers.]

BIBLIOGRAPHY

Gamble, Harry. *Books and Readers in the Early Church: A History of Early Christian Texts.* New Haven, Conn.: Yale University Press, 1995.

Johnson, William A. *Bookrolls and Scribes in Oxyrhynchus.* Toronto: University of Toronto Press, 2004. The foldout plates are the best available illustrations of ancient bookrolls.

Roberts, Colin H., and T. S. Skeat. *The Birth of the Codex.* London: Oxford University Press, 1983. The story of the Christian preference for the codex.

Turner, Eric S. *Greek Manuscripts of the Ancient World.* Revised by P. J. Parsons. 2nd ed. London: University of London, Institute of Classical Studies, 1987. Fine illustrative plates and annotated bibliography.

Turner, Eric S. *Greek Papyri: An Introduction.* Oxford: Clarendon Press, 1968. Rev. ed., 1980. Magisterial introduction to the Greek papyri.

William A. Johnson

BOSPORUS, KINGDOM OF

The kingdom of Bosporus, otherwise known as the Bosporan kingdom, was situated on the northern Black Sea littoral in the area known in ancient times as the Cimmerian Bosporus. It was divided into two parts, European and Asian, by the Kerch Strait, which connects the Sea of Azov (ancient Lake Maeotis) with the Black Sea. The European part comprised the eastern part of the Crimea, where Panticapaeum (modern Kerch), its capital, was situated. The Asian part, whose main city was Phanagoria, covered the entire Taman Peninsula. This area was colonized by Greeks in the sixth century BCE when the main cities, such as Panticapaeum, Nymphaeum, Theodosia, Hermonassa, Cepoi, and Phanagoria, were established. Panticapaeum was the most prominent, a colony of Miletus since the 570s BCE, and soon founded its own offshoots— Myrmekion, Tyritake, and Porthmeus—all within a radius of 6–8 miles (10–12 kilometers) of it.

The generally accepted date for the establishment of the Greek Bosporan kingdom is c. 480 BCE, the event interpreted as Greek cities coming together under Panticapaeum to withstand Scythian pressure. The only source is Diodorus (12.31.1), whose information is unclear and open to a different reading. Furthermore, there is little if any evidence of a Scythian threat. Evaluation of all existing evidence shows that the Archaeanactid dynasty, probably of Milesian origin, came to power in Panticapaeum in about 480, but that the beginnings of the kingdom are not really to be found until circa 436, when the Archaeanactids were succeeded by a new dynasty, the Spartocids, probably of Thracian origin, who called themselves archons or kings in inscriptions found in Bosporan territory. A few ancient authors described them as tyrants. They ruled for more than three hundred years.

From the outset, the Spartocids' main aim was to consolidate and expand the state, seeking to incorporate forcibly Phanagoria, Theodosia, and Nymphaeum, the cities most opposed to them. In this they succeeded, but not until the time of King Leucon I (389/8–349/8). Another policy, the incorporation of the local population living just beyond the Taman Peninsula, was pursued from the end of the fifth century. Such locals as the Sindians, Toreti, Dandarii, Maeotians, and others were included, peacefully in the main, by the middle of the fourth century. Settlements had been established in their territories to effect Bosporan penetration. The most prominent was Labrys/Labryta (Semibratnee city-site), which was refounded by Leucon I in the early fourth century after he had expelled the Sindian king and became a Bosporan administrative center. Greek Sindike (otherwise Sindik Harbor) was renamed Gorgippia after the king's brother Gorgippos, who became its governor. New cities were established on the Kerch Peninsula too (Akra, Cimmericum, Cytai, and others). In the time of Perisades I (344/3–311/10 BCE) Bosporan territory reached its greatest extent, stretching from the lands of the Taurians in the Crimea to the Caucasian Mountains. Bosporan kings called themselves in inscriptions "Archon of Bosporus" or "Archon of Bosporus and Theodosia" and, subsequently "King of the Sindi, Toreti, Dandarii, and Psessi" or of "the Sindi and Maeotae." Agriculture, crafts, and trade flourished.

Close relations between Bosporus and Athens, which had started in the late fifth century BCE, peaked in the fourth century. During the reign of Leucon I Athens enjoyed many commercial privileges in the grain trade with Bosporus. Bosporan kings were honored by Athens for sending ships loaded with grain during famine, sometimes so many that surplus grain could be sold for profit.

Expansion of the Bosporan kingdom continued in the Hellenistic period as well. Tanais was established in the Don delta. It was "a common emporium, partly of the Asiatic and the European nomads, and partly of those who navigated the lake from the Bosporus, the former bringing slaves, hides, and such things as nomads possess, and the latter giving in exchange clothing, wine, and the other things that belong to civilised life" (Strabo 11.2.3).

From the late fourth or third century BCE migrant Sarmatians settled in Bosporan territory. With the appearance of these nomadic tribes, the Bosporan kingdom began its gradual decline. After the death of the last Spartocid (109 BCE), the Bosporan kingdom became part of the Pontic empire of Mithradates VI Eupator (r. 120–63 BCE). With Roman expansion into the Black Sea, the kingdom fell into the Roman orbit, ruled by Roman client kings. It formed the most important buffer state between the Roman provinces and the threat of invasion by the Scythian and Sarmatian inhabitants of the rest of the Crimea and much of the South Russian/Ukrainian steppes, until the arrival of the Goths in the third century CE cast a severe blow to Roman dominance. The kingdom was destroyed by the Huns in the fourth and fifth centuries CE, after which life continued there on a much reduced scale.

The art of the Greek Bosporan kingdom, like the state itself (with its non-Greek Thracian dynasty) is actually Greco-barbarian. Many of the large local population included within its borders came to live in its Greek cities where Greek and local cultural and artistic features mixed and combined to create something hitherto unknown: what modern theorists might describe as hybridization or multi-culturalism.

[*See also* Black Sea; Central Asia; Colonies and Colonization, Greek; Pontus, Kingdom of; *and* Scythia.]

BIBLIOGRAPHY

Fornasier, Jochen, and Burkhard Böttger, eds. *Das Bosporanische Reich: Der Nordosten des Schwarzen Meeres in der Antike.* Mainz, Germany: von Zabern, 2002. A collection presenting the results of recent archaeological investigations of major Bosporan cities.

Gajdukevic, Viktor F. *Das Bosporanische Reich.* Berlin: Akademie-Verlag, 1971. The most comprehensive book ever written about the Bosporan kingdom. Covers from the sixth century BCE to the sixth century CE.

Hind, John. "The Bosporan Kingdom." *Cambridge Ancient History.* 2nd ed. Vol. 6, *The Fourth Century BC*, edited by D. C. Smith, pp. 476–511. Cambridge, U.K.: Cambridge University Press, 1994. Survey of the geography, sources, and political and cultural history of the Cimmerian Bosporus in the sixth to the third/second centuries BCE.

Tsetskhladze, Gocha R. "A Survey of the Major Urban Settlements in the Kimmerian Bosporos (with a Discussion of their Status as *Poleis*)." In *Yet More Studies in the Ancient Greek Polis*, edited by Thomas Heine Nielsen, pp. 39–81. Stuttgart, Germany: F. Steiner, 1997. Site by site survey (with plans) of nearly all settlements and an overview of the Bosporan kingdom and relationship between Greeks and native population down to the Hellenistic period.

Gocha R. Tsetskhladze

BOTANY

The particular richness in botanical species of the Mediterranean area results from the interaction of natural processes of evolution and diversification, together with human-induced domestication and naturalization of nonnative plants, the last of which extended well into the historical period. Although no documentation of a study, inventory, or classification of the botanical world is currently known from before the fifth and fourth centuries BCE, the archaeological evidence suggests both that human communities interacted with their botanical environment from their earliest settlement and also that they represented different plant species as having distinctive characters. An ethnobotanical analysis of preserved written documentation suggests that populations started early analyzing plants according to a binary system of similarities (which made it possible to create plant families) and differences (which made it possible to individualize single plants unambiguously). Such cognitive perception of the botanical world went along with the discovery of the therapeutic properties of plants, be it by imitation of animals, by accidental discoveries (probably sometimes lethal), or by experiments perhaps made on the basis of remarkable characteristics of plants (e.g., color, structure, or exudates).

From the fifth century BCE, physicians appear to have had an excellent knowledge of a range of plants, although that range was not as vast as sometimes claimed. Half of the formulas for medicines in the Hippocratic corpus are made out of forty-five common plants, such as hellebore, garlic, celery, and beet. This range of plants not only confirms the origin of medicine suggested by Hippocratic literature—namely, that medicines are by-products of food—but also allows a look at the natural environment of human settlements, be they urban or rural.

The first attempts to conceptualize the world of plants came from Aristotle, whose *De plantis* has not, however, been preserved in its original version. Nevertheless, it seems that one of the major questions that Aristotle's work studied was the notions of *genos* and *eidos* as levels in a classification hierarchy. Aristotle's student Theophrastus applied to botany the method of analysis developed by Aristotle in zoology. Not only did he study the process of plant generation (*De causis plantarum*), but also he distinguished the different parts of plants, described their characteristics (with their seasonal changes and local variations), and gave them names. In addition, in *Historia plantarum* he classified all plant species according to a four-type system: trees, shrubs, undershrubs, grasses. Significantly, he included in the same treatise an entire book on medicinal plants, for which he collected information from several sources including practitioners, shepherds, and plant collectors.

Alexander the Great's expedition to the East modified the Mediterranean botanical environment by introducing into the area nonnative plants species. Although no documentary evidence has been preserved, it seems reasonable to assume that both this newly introduced plant material and the native species were systematically analyzed following Alexander's expedition. In the natural history and therapeutic literature of the early Roman Empire—Pliny the Elder's *Naturalis historia* and Dioscorides' *De materia medica*, originally written in Greek—some seven hundred plant species are analyzed in an almost systematic way, according to what could be called a standardized protocol. If such an organized program existed, it would probably not be wrong to locate it in the Alexandria of the first Ptolemaic kings, where an early form of scientific research took place.

Although artists in the fifth and fourth centuries were said to be able to depict plants so realistically that birds could be deceived into thinking the depictions real, it has traditionally been considered that botanical illustration did not start before Cratevas, supposedly the physician of Mithradates VI Eupator, the king of Pontus from 120 to 63 BCE. Cratevas is said to have compiled an album of plant representations of which some items were integrated into the set of illustrations in the manuscripts of Dioscorides' *De materia medica*. Though widely accepted, this history of the origin of botanical illustration is not supported by available evidence, be it textual or iconic.

In the first century CE, botanical knowledge reached its zenith with the compilations by Dioscorides and Pliny. Particularly in Dioscorides' work, plants are described in a fairly systematic way and are grouped in botanically and pharmacologically coherent sets; these sets are classified on a scale that considers therapeutic properties, supposed origin in the cosmogony, and cultural values.

In several manuscripts Dioscorides' text is completed with representations of plants, the origin and style of which have been much debated. Although there is some agreement that the representations probably do not date back to Dioscorides, they exactly correspond to the text, of which they are a visualization. As such they might have the same origin as the information in the text—which does not necessarily mean that they were made for Dioscorides' work. As for their style, it is supposed to have been realistic at the start, and to have become more schematic over time. The truth might be the opposite, however, because illustrations were aimed to make textual data visual. Schematism was accentuated over time, probably more because of a wish to make the identification of plants unambiguous than because of an inaptitude of the artists to reproduce models faithfully, even though some degree of artistic inability should be taken into account. In some cases, however, artists represented plants in a more realistic way possibly on the basis of some direct observation of nature.

From late antiquity until the Renaissance, botanical knowledge was almost exclusively pharmaceutical—except in the Arabic world, where botany and agronomy were newly developed—and the field was dominated by Dioscorides' *De materia medica*. The treatise was condensed, excerpted, and rearranged, translated into Latin (perhaps in the sixth century), assimilated in actual practice and amalgamated with local knowledge, and used as a source for new manuals.

[*See also* Aphrodisiacs; Gardens; Pharmacology; *and* Science.]

BIBLIOGRAPHY

Primary Works

Aristotle. *De plantis*. Edited by H. J. Drossaart Lulofs and E. L. J. Poortman. Amsterdam: North-Holland Publishing Company, 1989.

Dioscorides. *De materia medica*. Edited by Max Wellmann. 3 vols. Berlin: Weidmann, 1906–1914. Translated by Lily Y. Beck. Hildesheim, Germany: Olms-Wiedmann, 2005.

Pliny. *Naturalis historia* 12–19. Edited and translated by H. Rackham. 2 vols. London: Heinemann; Cambridge, Mass.: Harvard University Press, 1945–1950.

Theophrastus. *Historia plantarum*. Edited and translated by A. Hort. 2 vols. London: Heinemann; Cambridge, Mass.: Harvard University Press, 1916–1926.

Theophrastus. *De causis plantarum*. Edited and translated by Benedict Einarson and George K. K. Link. 3 vols. London: Heinemann; Cambridge, Mass.: Harvard University Press, 1976–1990.

Secondary Works

Greene, Edward Lee. *Landmarks of Botanical History*. Edited by Frank N. Egerton. 2 vols. Stanford, Calif.: Stanford University Press, 1983. Vol. 1, pp. 120–233.

Morton, A. G. *History of Botanical Science: an Account of the Development of Botany from Ancient Times to the Present Day*. London: Academic Press, 1981. Pp. 19–81.

Repici, Luciana. *Uomini capovolti: Le piante nel pensiero dei Greci*. Biblioteca di Cultura Moderna 1152. Rome: Laterza, 2000.

Touwaide, Alain. "Bibliographie historique de la botanique: Les identifications de plantes médicinales citées dans les traités anciens après l'adoption du système de classification botanqiue de Linné (1707–1778)." *Lettre d'informations médecine antique et médiévale, Université Jean-Monnet Saint-Etienne (Centre Jean-Palerne)* 30 (December 1997–January 1998): 2–22 and 31 (July–September 1998): 2–65.

Touwaide, Alain. "La botanique entre science et culture au Ier siècle de notre ère." In *Geschichte der Mathematisch- und Naturwissenschaft in der Antike*, edited by Georg Wöhrle, vol. 1: *Biologie*, pp. 219–252. Stuttgart, Germany: Franz Steiner Verlag, 1999.

Alain Touwaide

BOUDICCA

(d. 61 CE), queen of the Iceni, a Celtic tribe inhabiting what is now Norfolk county in eastern England. (Her name is sometimes rendered incorrectly as Boadicea.) Boudicca commanded the last British rebellion to threaten Roman occupation in the first century CE. Bearing the name Victory (from the Celtic *bouda*), Boudicca led her armies to defeat a Roman legion and destroy three Roman-British settlements, Camulodunum (Colchester), Londinium (London), and Verulamium (St. Albans), slaughtering some seventy thousand allies and citizens (Tacitus *Annales* 14.33). Although all British tribes chafed after Claudius' conquest in 43 CE, under property confiscations, attacks on the Druids, and oppressive taxation under Roman administration, Boudicca's personal grievances were the immediate cause of the uprising (*Annales* 14.31). Her husband, Prasutagus, an ally of Rome, had died in 60 CE, willing his client kingdom to his daughters and the emperor Nero in hopes of preserving its independence. Instead, his home and kingdom were treated as booty; upon her complaint, his wife was whipped, his daughters raped, his nobles debased. Before her final battle, Boudicca, standing in a chariot with her daughters, addressed her soldiers and tribal families, blaming the rebellion on Roman arrogance and abusiveness (*Annales* 14.35). The Greek historian Cassius Dio describes her as more intelligent than usual for women, tall, formidable of face and voice, with long red-blond hair, dressed in a gold torque, a multicolored tunic, and a cloak fastened with a brooch (*Epistula* 62.2). He portrays her with a spear, speaking not about her wrongs but her people's loss of freedom and dignity. She praises British masculine hardiness and mocks Roman effeteness, particularly Nero's: she addresses him by the feminine form of his family name as "Lady Domitia" (*Epistula* 62.3–6). Tacitus reports her final taunt: she, a woman, decided to die, leaving it to men to live as slaves if they chose; after her army's defeat she took poison (*Annales* 14.37). It is unclear why, during this same period (c. 51–69 CE), another British queen, Cartimandua of the neighboring Brigantes, received full allied support from the Romans. This disparity in treatment calls into question whether the Romans' brutal treatment of Boudicca was the result of her gender, as has been claimed by various commentators over the centuries.

[*See also* Britain.]

BIBLIOGRAPHY

Adler, Eric. "Boudica's Speeches in Tacitus and Dio." *Classical World* 101.2 (2008): 173–195.

Braund, David. *Ruling Roman Britain: Kings, Queens, Governors, and Emperors from Julius Caesar to Agricola*. London and New York: Routledge, 1996.

Dudley, Donald R., and Graham Webster. *The Rebellion of Boudicca*. New York: Barnes and Noble, 1962.

Webster, Graham. *Boudica: The British Revolt against Rome A.D. 60*. 2nd ed. London and New York: Routledge, 2000.

Ann R. Raia

BOULE

See Council.

BOULETERION

See Agora *and* Council.

BRICK

Mud brick, made from sun-dried clay and straw, was commonly used in the Mediterranean for millennia before fired terra-cotta was systematically used for roof tiles in both Greece (Corinth) and Etruria (Murlo, Aquarossa) in the seventh century BCE. The later use of flat bricks for walls and floors developed out of this initial move toward creating a waterproof roof covering. The replacement of thatch roofs with terra-cotta tiles was originally dependent on mass production using molds, which was a technique of terra-cotta production for figurines introduced from the Near East. With the introduction of roof tiles also came design changes in the buildings, such as the elimination of apsidal ends, the adoption of gabled roofs, and the lowering of the slope to prevent the tiles from sliding down. The need to prevent leaks and a desire to provide decorative roof elements resulted in complex interlocking forms and increasingly advanced production and firing methods. Because of the precision required to fit the pieces together, the tiles for roofs were initially produced locally for individual buildings, thus resulting in the development of regional styles with little standardization until well into the sixth century BCE.

Until the Hellenistic period, fired terra-cotta for architecture was limited largely to roof tiles and decorative building elements that often protected exposed wooden parts. Early examples of fired bricks for walls and floors appear in the fourth century BCE at Olynthus in Greece and at Gela in Sicily. In mainland Italy, early examples of bricks occur at the Greek colony of Velia in the third century BCE. The examples from both Gela and Velia occur in bath buildings, the growing popularity of which no doubt influenced the production of this fireproof material. Brick remained a material particularly associated with baths during the Roman imperial period.

In Rome, the use of flat bricks for wall facing developed later than the Greek examples and was originally an outgrowth of roof-tile production. Tiles with the flanges knocked off began to appear as a facing for concrete during the first century BCE, and by the mid-first century CE flat, square bricks were produced in three standard sizes: *bessalis* (two-thirds of a Roman foot), *sesquipedalis* (one and a half feet), and *bipedalis* (two feet). Facing bricks were often created from triangles cut from the larger bricks. They did not go through the entire thickness of the wall but rather were used to provide a smooth and vertical wall surface. Occasionally a course of *bipedales* ran through the wall, usually at significant points in the construction, such as where scaffolding was attached or where arches sprang. The standardization of brick sizes led to the use of standard wall thicknesses of two feet, two and a half feet, three feet, and so on.

Stamps on bricks and roof tiles provide information about manufacture. Those from Velia displayed ΔΗ (*dēmosia*), indicating public production for or by the *dēmos*, or populace (third century BCE). Names of deities, kings, local magistrates, or private producers also appear. Occasionally stamps had the names of the Roman consuls, thus providing a date for the production of the brick, which in turn is important evidence for dating a structure. The brick stamps in Rome often name the owner (senatorial class) of the brickyard or clay beds and the person (usually slave or freedman) responsible for the workshop making the brick.

As the brick industry in Rome expanded during the late first century CE, it provided a means of social advancement for the lower classes, whose careers can be traced through the stamps. The stamps also show that female landowners made up almost 30 percent of the named landowners recorded and 6 percent of the brickmakers. By the time of Marcus Aurelius (r. 161–180 CE), most of the brickyards had passed into the hands of the emperor through legacies, and the industry eventually became a virtual imperial monopoly. The stamps disappeared during the economic turmoil of the third century but reappeared under Diocletian (r. 284–305 CE), who initiated large building projects. Imperial production of stamped bricks continued in Rome until the reign of Theodoric (r. 493–526 CE) and appeared in the new capital at Constantinople after its creation in 330 CE.

Bricks were produced in other parts of the empire but not on such an industrialized scale as in the capital. Military bricks and tiles were often stamped with the name of the legion or auxiliary unit responsible and can provide information on military movements throughout the empire. Privately produced bricks outside Italy were sometimes stamped as well, demonstrating that production was often linked to the villa economy of a region. Unlike in Rome, which could support mass production and stockpiling, production elsewhere was more likely on an ad hoc basis when bricks were needed.

[See also Building Materials and Construction.]

BIBLIOGRAPHY

Anderson, James C. *Roman Architecture and Society.* Baltimore: Johns Hopkins University Press, 1997. See pages 151–165; contains a good overview of the information on Roman brick stamps and the brick industry in Rome.

McWhirr, Alan, ed. *Roman Brick and Tile: Studies in Manufacture, Distribution, and Use in the Western Empire.* BAR International Series 68. Oxford: British Archaeological Reports, 1979. A series of articles on a variety of different aspects of Roman brick production and trade.

Spawforth, Tony. *The Complete Greek Temples.* London: Thames & Hudson, 2006.

Lynne C. Lancaster

BRIDGES

The world's oldest surviving stone bridge appears to be a viaduct leading to the Palace of Knossos in northern Crete, dated by Evans as early Middle Minoan, or circa 1900 BCE. It has nine spans, each about 7.4 to 10 feet (2.25 to 3.1 meters), with pier widths of 10.8 to 15 feet (3.3 to 4.6 meters). Although only lower portions of the piers are intact, Evans discovered in "the fallen debris . . . a series of blocks with a bevelled face, such as were employed for horizontal arches"—his term for the corbelled arch common in other early Greek bridges. Crete had at least two other stone bridges: one at Eleutherna and one farther west, across the Almyros River, "with Hellenic foundations."

North of Crete is the Argolis peninsula of mainland Greece, famous for the *tholos* tombs of Mycenae, built about 1500–1300 BCE, each with a stone dome and an access passage through the covering mound of soil. Mycenae also had the Lion Gate, built about 1330 BCE. All these structures illustrate the use of the corbelled arch. A wall opening was roofed by stones extending horizontally from the sides, each cantilevering out beyond the stone beneath. A good example is in the access passage to the Clytemnestra tomb. Difficulties arose in the vault, however, because of the lack of stability achieved by the upper stones in a wall, and this led to a change in shape.

Wace speaks of the well-organized road system around Mycenae, with bridges in the causeway, on the road to Berbate, and east of Nauplia, near the fort of Kasarmi. This third bridge shows the difficulty in using the corbelled arch for a vault, for the masonry is irregular, the stones lean in against each other, and the triangular opening is small. This bridge may be later than Mycenae, possibly from about 1100–700 BCE. Other Greek bridges had this form, such as one across the Eridanos in Athens and another on the ancient road to Marathon. At Brauron, near the coast east of Athens, is a simple stone slab bridge. Ancient timber bridges also existed—such as one built about 425 BCE at Amphipolis (or Nine Ways), east of Thessalonica—and the floating bridge was also known.

The Greeks built bridges in Asia Minor, such as one at Çesme, near Cnidus, from about 300 BCE. This bridge had substantial approaches leading to a triangular arch with a span of ten feet (three meters), now collapsed. The so-called Caravan Bridge at Smyrna has been said to be the oldest in existence, but this is difficult to justify. Another bridge, over the Selinus River at Pergamum, may be called a true arch and is curved in elevation, with individual stones or voussoirs shaped so that the joints radiate from a center. The true arch was used by the Greeks in buildings as early as the fourth century BCE, but it was uncommon in their bridges.

The Greeks built only a small number of roads and bridges, possibly because of difficult terrain, but the Romans were some of the world's great bridge builders. O'Connor lists 330 stone bridges, 34 timber bridges, and 94 aqueducts, with locations from Italy to Africa, Britain, Turkey, and Palestine, but this is only a sample of the whole. Completion dates range from 174 BCE to 560 CE, with many built between 50 BCE and 150 CE. The Romans' stone bridges and aqueducts all used the true arch, typically with a semicircular profile. The Romans' technology was remarkable: they could cut and drive timber piles, could saw stones, and had cranes capable of lifting up to almost seven U.S. tons (six metric tons)—the form is shown in a relief dated about 100 CE and held in the Vatican. The maximum span of Roman bridges increased from 80 feet (24 meters) in 142 BCE to 115 feet (35 meters) by Augustus' reign (27 BCE–14 CE) and was not exceeded until about 605 CE, by the span of 120 feet (37 meters) of the bridge at Zhao-Zhou in China. This progress in Roman bridges can best be illustrated by a few examples.

The two oldest dated Roman bridges are both from about 174 BCE, the Ponte San Lorenzo at Bulicame in ancient Etruria and the initial Ponte di Nona in Rome. Considering that work on the Via Appia began in 312, however, other bridges were probably built before these. By 142 BCE the maximum span had increased to 80 feet (24 meters) in the Pons Aemilius (or Ponte Rotto) across the Tiber in Rome; this bridge had six spans, of which only one remains. The Ponte dell'Abadia (c. 90 BCE), near Vulci in Etruria, had a span of about 82 feet (25 meters) and a height of 115 feet (35 meters). In Rome the Pons Fabricius of 62 BCE had spans of 79.4 and 80.4 feet (24.2 and 24.5 meters). Farther north, at Narni, the Via Flaminia crossed the Nera River over the Ponte d'Augusto (c. 27 BCE), with four spans from 52 to 105 feet (16 to 32.1 meters)—only one now stands. Then, probably during the reign of Augustus (27 BCE–14 CE), the remarkable Pont-Saint-Martin was built in northern Italy, east of Aosta, with a span of 117 feet (35.6 meters).

These large spans were not limited to Italy. The Alcántara Bridge in Spain, for example, was completed in 104 CE and had a remarkable symmetrical system of six arches, a fine central triumphal arch, a maximum span of 94 feet (28.8 meters), and an overall height of 203 feet (62 meters) from the stream bed. There were also many long Roman bridges, including the Puente Romano, which crosses the Guadiana at Mérida, Spain, to a stone castle on the northern bank. As originally built in 25 BCE, this bridge had twenty-one spans and a length of about a sixth of a mile (256 meters). After a flood cut through the north bank, another ten spans were built (c. 40 CE), giving a total length of about a third of a mile (500 meters). But then another flood cut through the southern bank, causing further spans to be built. The final bridge, completed during the reign of Trajan (98–117 CE), has about sixty spans and a total length of almost half a mile (721 meters).

Roman aqueducts were even longer and included major bridges, such as the Pont du Gard in southern France. The Romans also built timber bridges: in England, for example, most, if not all, of the Romans' eighty-seven bridges were of timber on stone piers. The extraordinary timber bridge of Apollodorus (c. 105 CE) crossed the Danube with twenty-one arch spans, each about 100 feet (30 meters) clear.

The Roman use of the true arch was significant. The arches were not always semicircular, and some were segmental, as in the Pont-Saint-Martin, with an included angle of 144°; at Alconétar, Spain, with an included angle of about 120°; and at Limyra, Turkey, with an included angle of about 83°. The timber bridge of Apollodorus was also segmental. Many of the Romans' stone bridges are still used.

[*See also* Aqueducts; Arch; *and* Engineering.]

BIBLIOGRAPHY

Evans, Sir Arthur. *The Palace of Minos at Knossos.* 2 vols. London: Macmillan, 1928. Describes a very old stone bridge.

Gazzola, Piero. *Ponti romani.* 2 vols. Vol. 2: *Contributo ad un indice sistematico con studio critico bibliografico.* Florence, Italy: L. S. Olschki, 1963. A classic reference.

O'Connor, Colin. *Roman Bridges.* Cambridge, U.K.: Cambridge University Press, 1993. A thorough study of Roman bridges and their technology.

Wace, Alan J. B. *Mycenae: An Archaeological History and Guide.* Princeton, N.J.: Princeton University Press, 1949. Describes three Greek bridges and illustrates the use of the corbelled arch.

Colin O'Connor

BRITAIN

The Iron Age communities of Britain were essentially agrarian societies in loosely defined tribal territories, with those of the southeast characterized by long-established links with northern Gaul. Julius Caesar's expeditions of 55 and 54 BCE left no permanent trace, but he imposed tribute payments on some native leaders, and the area maintained contacts with the Roman world. This is reflected in rich graves containing imports and possibly diplomatic gifts, and it is possible that some tribal leaders were educated at Rome.

The Claudian Conquest. The annexation of Britain, one of the last provinces to be added to the Roman Empire, came in 43 CE under the emperor Claudius. Britain's separation from the continent by the much-feared Atlantic Ocean added prestige to Claudius' triumph in Rome, but also contributed to the island's marginal position with respect to the empire. The invading four legions landed in southeast England either at Rutupiae (Richborough) or near Fishbourne and Chichester, and following a battle at the Thames conquered Camulodunum (Colchester), the center of the important Catuvellauni tribe. Archaeological evidence for Roman assaults on hill forts is known from Hod Hill and Maiden Castle in Dorset. The south was quickly subdued, and troops moved into Wales and the north. However, a revolt of native tribes led by Boudicca in 60–61 CE led to the destruction of emerging urban centers at Londinium (London), Verulamium (St. Albans), and Camulodunum. The difficult terrain and determined native opposition meant that the conquest of Wales was not completed until the Flavian period, and the area remained heavily garrisoned throughout Roman rule. In the north, the governor Gnaeus Julius Agricola (c. 77/8–83/4) penetrated into northeastern Scotland, winning a crucial battle at the not-yet-located site of Mons Graupius. However, Roman control of these northernmost areas was brief, resulting in gradual withdrawal to the Tyne-Solway line. Here construction of Hadrian's Wall, consisting of a masonry wall and ditch and controlled by forts and mile castles, commenced circa 122 CE. The border was moved north when a new wall was constructed under Antoninus Pius between the Firth of Forth and Firth of Clyde in central Scotland. This was abandoned by 165 CE, and, despite campaigns in Scotland under Septimius Severus from 208 to 211 CE, Hadrian's Wall remained the border for the remainder of Roman rule. It is in northern Britain and in Wales that the majority of auxiliary units were stationed, with legionary fortresses located at Isca Silurum (Caerleon), Deva (Chester), and Eboracum (York). While these military installations brought wealth to some of the local inhabitants, it has been argued that they impeded the development of urban centers and villas in these areas of the province.

The Archaeological Evidence. Archaeologically, Britain is one of the most thoroughly investigated provinces in the empire, with especially detailed data on settlements and material culture. Other than agriculture, the Romano-British economy revolved around the exploitation of precious metals, notably gold from Dolaucothi in Wales and silver and lead from the Mendips, and the supply of the army. Much of the trade is archaeologically invisible (e.g., slaves, wool, grain), with pottery often acting as a marker of trade networks. While pottery was largely imported in the early Roman period, large workshops developed later in the south of Britain, often in rural locations.

Much recent work on Romanization has begun to explore the potential of nonelite material culture, exploring emerging Romano-British art styles and religious practices as well as changing dietary patterns to measure acceptance of, and resistance to, Romanized ways. The picture is complicated by an increasing awareness of the diversity of the "Roman" garrison, which was composed of German, Gaulish, Danubian, and North African troops, although in the later empire military units recruited locally. Incomers have been identified among the later Roman inhumation cemeteries at Eboracum and at Lankhills near Venta Belgarum (Winchester). Epigraphy remains one of the main sources for the

Hadrian's Wall. Near Sewing Shields Crag, Northumberland. © EDIFICE/THE BRIDGEMAN ART LIBRARY

identification of individuals and their origin, and for the names of Romano-British deities, but the epigraphic habit is largely limited to military sites, with other evidence such as small bronze figurines or Romano-Celtic temples painting a very different picture of religious worship in the province. Christianity is attested throughout the province by the fourth century CE, mainly in the form of lead tanks and portable objects decorated with Christian symbols.

The Roman conquest had brought major changes to land proprietorship. The majority of the population of the province lived and worked in the countryside, as demonstrated by an increasing amount of evidence from aerial photography and field surveys, which have begun to show the density of small rural sites such as villages, hamlets, and farms. Their archaeological exploration still lags behind that of villas, with their often substantial masonry remains, mosaics, and rich material culture, although it should be noted that villas display considerable variability, ranging from cottages to palatial complexes. In Britain, villas are largely concentrated in the southeast, and their distribution appears closely linked not just to the underlying soil and its agricultural potential but also their proximity to urban centers.

Some Roman towns in Britain developed on the site of military installations while others grew out of existing Iron Age central sites. *Coloniae*, the highest status urban sites, are known at Camulodunum, Glevum (Gloucester), Lindum (Lincoln), and Eboracum. More common were *civitas capitals*, the administrative centers of the tribal areas, and so-called small towns. The latter often lack the public buildings and planned layout of the larger sites, but appear to have developed as market or religious centers, such as the major religious site at Aquae Calidae, or Aquae Solis (Bath).

The nature of late Romano-British urbanism is much contested, with evidence for dark earth often interpreted as indicating decline and the creation of allotments within towns. There is also evidence for a lack of maintenance of major facilities such as public baths, and for the use of administrative buildings such as the forum basilica at Calleva Atrebatum (Silchester) for metal working. Most towns were equipped with walls during the third century CE, although it is debatable whether their primary function was defensive.

As in other parts of the empire, the province was divided into two in the early third century CE (with Londinium and Eboracum as their respective capitals), and into four provinces in about 300 CE (with capitals at Londinium, Lindum, Corinium [Cirencester], and Eboracum). A further subdivision, Valentia, is known in the fourth century in northern Britain, but its exact location is unknown.

The End of Roman Britain. Britain was a relatively peaceful province during the later Empire, but it did see a number of usurpers, notably Carausius (r. 286–293) and Allectus (r. 293–296), who created a separate empire centered on Britain. The piecemeal construction of the so-called Saxon Shore forts along the southeast coast may have been related to this breakaway empire, or it may have begun in response to problems caused by raiders from across the North Sea. Another interpretation of these forts (e.g., at Burgh Castle, Rutupiae, and Portchester) is that they acted as transshipment centers for military supplies and taxes collected in kind.

In 367 CE there appears to have been a combined attack by Saxons, Picts, and Scots, although its severity may have been embellished in the account celebrating the military campaign by Theodosius I. The removal of troops from Britain in 383 and 407 CE to support the campaigns of the usurpers Maximus and Constantius III left a depleted garrison unable to defend the province, which gradually fell to the Saxons, with only the Christian church in the west providing ties to the Roman Empire.

[*See also* Boudicca; Hadrian's Wall; *and* London.]

BIBLIOGRAPHY

Frere, Sheppard. *Britannia: A History of Roman Britain.* 3rd ed. London: Routledge and Kegan Paul, 1987.

Jones, Barri, and David Mattingly. *An Atlas of Roman Britain.* Oxford: Oxbow, 2002.

Mattingly, David. *An Imperial Possession: Britain in the Roman Empire, 54 BC–AD 409.* London: Allen Lane, 2006.

Millett, Martin. *The Romanization of Britain: An Essay in Archaeological Interpretation.* Cambridge, U.K.: Cambridge University Press, 1990.

Hella Eckardt

BRONZE AGE

See Greece, *subentry* Prehistory to the End of the Bronze Age.

BRUTUS, LUCIUS JUNIUS

(d. 509 BCE) Roman consul. Lucius Junius Brutus is credited with being the founder of the Roman Republic, the man who "liberated" Rome from monarchy. His story is most fully and famously told by the historian Livy (1.57–2.7), with additional details in Dionysius of Halicarnassus (4.67–5.18). The son of Tarquinia, sister of the Etruscan king of Rome Lucius Tarquinius Superbus, Brutus accompanied two of Tarquin's sons to Delphi to inquire about the significance of a snake that had slithered out of a pillar in the temple of Jupiter Optimus Maximus, Tarquin's great legacy to Rome. To avoid the fate of his father, who had been murdered by the king, Brutus had feigned "stupidity" ("brutus"= stupid). A transparent etiology, the story nonetheless accounts for how Brutus was sufficiently trusted to travel to Delphi and, more importantly, managed to survive Tarquin. When Lucretia was raped by the king's youngest son, Brutus arrived on the scene with Lucretia's husband Lucius Tarquinius Collatinus. Horrified, he vowed vengeance on the king and all his relatives, swearing that Rome would endure kings no more. Brutus forthwith convened a meeting in the Forum and delivered a heated speech detailing the atrocities of the Etruscan kings, thereby prompting the exile of Tarquin and his family. This paved the way for the creation of the Republic; Brutus was one of its first consuls. Tarquin, however, presently assembled a force to recover his position, against which Brutus led an army with his fellow consul Publius Valerius Publicola. Brutus was killed shortly thereafter. The historicity of Brutus and the stories associated with him have often been questioned, but regardless of how much Livy's version owes to fiction and folklore, it captures the great importance later Romans attached to Brutus.

[See also Lucretia; Rome, subentry Early Rome and the Republic; and Tarquin the Proud.]

BIBLIOGRAPHY

Cornell, Timothy J. The Beginnings of Rome: Italy and Rome from the Bronze Age to the Punic Wars (c. 1000–264 BC). London and New York: Routledge, 1995.

Alain M. Gowing

BRUTUS, MARCUS JUNIUS

(c. 85–42 BCE), best known as one of the assassins of the dictator Julius Caesar, the man perceived to be a threat to the political traditions and even structure of the Roman Republic. While this may be his chief claim to fame, prior to the Ides of March Brutus had begun to acquire a reputation as an effective advocate or lawyer, attracting the attention of the famous orator Cicero (who addressed to him the admonitory Brutus of 46 BCE, a treatise that is in essence a history of Roman oratory, as well as three other works). Brutus himself penned several works, all indicative of a deep interest in ethics and moral philosophy, among them On Virtue (dedicated to Cicero) as well as On Duties (Cicero also composed a celebrated work on the same subject). While none of his writings survive, they were probably all composed in the late 50s and early 40s, when not coincidentally Cicero himself was busy writing many of his own philosophical works. Brutus' penchant for philosophy figures prominently in accounts of his role in the assassination of Caesar.

In the civil war between Pompey and Caesar, Brutus supported the former, even participating in the battle of Pharsalus in 48 BCE. Pardoned by Caesar, Brutus eventually returned to Rome, presumably to resume his political career. He was clearly back in Caesar's good graces, for he received the proconsulship of Cisalpine Gaul for 46 BCE, quite a prize for someone whose previous political office had been that of quaestor in 53 BCE. He held this post through the spring of 45. Later that year he divorced his wife Claudia, soon remarrying, however, this time to Porcia, the daughter of Cato the Younger, the bitter opponent of Caesar who had famously taken his own life in April of 46 BCE in order to avoid capture by Caesar. Cato also happened to be Brutus' uncle. In short, in terms of his family connections if not of his own political leanings, Brutus was consistently allied with the anti-Caesarian cause.

Caesar appointed Brutus praetor urbanus for 44 BCE, the same year in which Cassius (Gaius Cassius Longinus) would serve as praetor peregrinus. Like Brutus, Cassius had also fought on the side of Pompey and, like Brutus, had been pardoned by Caesar. Caesar's clemency proved ill placed, however, for in 44 BCE the pair conspired with some sixty individuals to murder him. Following the Ides, the tyrannicides were for a time granted amnesty and even assigned important commands in the East, but with the formation of the triumvirate in the autumn of 43 a military confrontation became inevitable. Thus in October of 42 BCE the armies of Mark Antony and Octavian (later Augustus) met and defeated the forces of the tyrannicides at Philippi. Brutus, like his colleague Cassius, took his own life rather than face capture.

The "afterlife" of Brutus is almost as interesting as his actual career. Revered by many as a "liberator," heir to the legacy of his ancestor Lucius Junius Brutus, legendary founder of the Roman Republic, Brutus (along with Cassius) was often appropriated by the imperial opposition, a symbol of liberty lost as well as of the possibility of liberty regained.

[See also Cassius; Julius Caesar; Philippi, Battle of; and Rome, subentry Early Rome and the Republic.]

BIBLIOGRAPHY

Clarke, M. L. The Noblest Roman: Marcus Brutus and His Reputation. London: Thames and Hudson, 1981.

MacMullen, Ramsay. Enemies of the Roman Order: Treason, Unrest, and Alienation in the Empire. Cambridge, Mass.: Harvard University Press, 1966.

Rawson, Elizabeth. "Cassius and Brutus: The Memory of the Liberators." In Past Perspectives: Studies in Greek and Roman Historical Writing; Papers Presented at a Conference in Leeds, 6–8 April 1983, edited by I. S. Moxon, J. D. Smart, and A. J. Woodman, pp. 101–119. Cambridge, U.K.: Cambridge University Press, 1986.

Alain M. Gowing

BUILDING MATERIALS AND CONSTRUCTION

Construction projects represent considerable economic investments, so the study of the materials and technology used provides insight into the priorities of the individuals and societies that sponsor the projects. The development of building practices in the Greco-Roman world can be generally characterized as moving from available natural materials, such as timber and stone, to manufactured ones, such as fired brick and concrete. With the change in materials also came a development from a simple post-and-lintel structural system to one employing complex vaulting.

Greek Materials and Construction. The most basic building materials were wood for columns and beams, mud brick often covered by a coating of lime plaster for walls, and thatch for roofing. The beginnings of monumental architecture are signaled by the introduction at Corinth of fired terra-cotta roof tiles in the first half of the seventh century BCE. By the beginning of the sixth century BCE monumental stone structures appear, as in the temple of Artemis on Corfu. The move toward monumental architecture in Greece reflects increasing wealth and enough confidence in the future to embark on long-term projects. The degree of Egyptian influence is debated, but developments in Greece may well have been stimulated by contact with the monumental stone architecture of Egypt, where the Greek trading colony of Naucratis existed from the mid-seventh century BCE.

The structural system used for both stone and wood structures was the simple post and lintel in which columns support a horizontal beam. Once stone lintels replaced wooden ones, the construction process relied on the ability to lift heavy blocks and place them accurately. Originally this was accomplished by ramps as used in pharaonic Egypt. Direct evidence occurs for compound pulleys only in the third century BCE and for cranes only in the first century BCE (Vitruvius *De architectura* 10.1.1–2), but the existence of cranes rigged with compound pulleys is implied by the forceps and lewis hole cuttings in blocks of some late sixth century BCE temples at Delphi, Olympia, and Athens. Building monumental temples was a statement of pride and piety by the people of the cities that erected them, and technological innovation played an important role in the message conveyed.

The earliest temples were built of local stone and covered in lime plaster, but the most impressive temples were built of marble, which often had to be transported long distances by both land and sea. Land transport for any type of large stone was an expensive and challenging endeavor. Often it was moved by sledges and rollers, though wheeled carts were also used. In either case unpaved roads were used, so the dry summer months were best for heavy loads.

The development of carved stone architecture was dependent on metal technology. Iron was used in Greece by 1000 BCE, and tempering, which allowed for iron chisels that were tough without being brittle, was known by the eighth century BCE. Once the Greeks began to add optical refinements, such as entasis (a slight outward bulge in columns), to their buildings in the sixth century BCE, good-quality iron chisels were necessary to create precise joints. To aid in joining the blocks and reducing work time, a technique called "anathyrosis" was developed in which the center of the block was carved down, leaving only a smooth band around the edge to form the contact surface. Iron wedges, levers, and mallets were also used to quarry the blocks, and dowels and clamps of various shapes set in lead were used to connect the blocks, though wood was also used. The most common example of wooden connectors was the system of empolia used for aligning column drums, which would then be carved with vertical fluting. The Greek interest in precision and the quest for optical perfection is also reflected in contemporary figural sculpture, from which—as demonstrated by the guiding role of Phidias in both the architecture and sculpture programs of the Parthenon—architecture cannot be entirely separated.

As buildings became larger, another constructional issue was the roofing method. Typically the

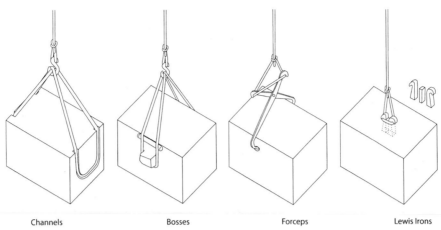

Channels   Bosses   Forceps   Lewis Irons

Lifting Methods. COURTESY OF LYNNE LANCASTER

cella was spanned by large beams, and the sloping rafters of the roof were supported on props above the walls and columns. One of the largest examples of this system was the Parthenon, with a cella span of thirty-six feet (eleven meters). The development of the truss, which is a triangular frame with a tie beam in tension running along the bottom, greatly increased the distances that could be spanned, but the date of its introduction is unclear; some scholars argue that the truss could have been used as early as the sixth century BCE in Sicily, and others argue for much later dates. In any case the ability to acquire large timbers of lightweight but stiff wood would have been critical for large spans, and inscriptions from Athens and Epidaurus testify to the long-distance importation of large beams of fir and cypress.

Even as stone architecture developed, well into the Hellenistic period fortification walls continued to be constructed of mud brick, perhaps because of the belief that mud brick provided a shock-absorbing quality to walls that had to resist the newly developed siege machines. However, the Greek focus on aesthetics resulted also in very elegant examples of stonework in both polygonal and ashlar masonry, as seen in fortification walls at Heracleia Latmus in Asia Minor and elsewhere. They were typically built in a style called *emplecton* in which two outer skins of finely fitted stone blocks were filled with rubble bound with mud mortar and reinforced with cross blocks to bind the two wall faces (Vitruvius *De architectura* 2.8.7).

Greek building accounts (Erechtheum in Athens, Sanctuary of Asclepius at Epidaurus) and even working drawings inscribed on the buildings themselves provide some idea of the building process. The building accounts typically list the contracts for supplying materials or labor for a project, naming the person and his pay for a specified task, thus demonstrating the reliance on individual workmen and the fairly simple organizational model used. These inscriptions were set up by the city council to make transparent the process of public building and are reflections of the democratic beliefs of Greek society. Drawings found on some monuments also demonstrate that the builders often used both full and scaled drawings to work out details. One example on the inner sanctuary wall of the temple of Apollo at Didyma (c. 300 BCE) even demonstrates the way in which the entasis in columns was laid out.

Roman Materials and Construction. Subsequent to their first use in Greece, the earliest terra-cotta roof tiles in Etruria and Latium appeared in the second half of the seventh century BCE (Murlo, Acquarossa) and led to increasingly larger and more elaborate structures. However, in central Italy wood played a greater role than in Greece, with the earliest monumental architecture having

Optical Refinements

In the sixth century BCE, Greek builders began to add optical refinements to their designs, such as leaning columns inward, making the corner columns slightly larger than the inner ones, and adding curvature to horizontal and vertical lines. The culmination of such refinements is represented in the Parthenon, where the platform on which the outer colonnade stands is curved upward such that the center is a few inches higher than the ends. The same curvature is found in the entablature blocks that form the roof. Evidence for how the curvature was laid out has been found at Cnidus where holes were first drilled to different depths to establish points along the curve in the floor. Moreover, columns themselves also have a slight outward bulge, called *entasis*. Vitruvius (*De architectura* 3.5.3–4, 12) explains that such refinements were meant to correct optical distortions. A flat platform or straight column would appear to be concave if the lines are not bowed outward to counter this optical illusion. As a result there are no right-angled blocks, and each block had to be carved for its individual place within the structure, thus requiring a high level of carving skill.

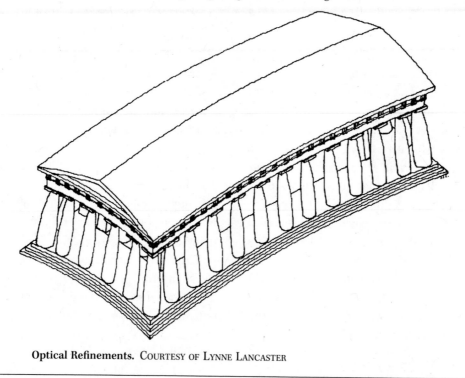

Optical Refinements. COURTESY OF LYNNE LANCASTER

foundations of local volcanic tuff surmounted by wooden and mud-brick superstructures and terra-cotta tiles and decorative elements for roofs. Nevertheless the width (about 177 feet, or 54 meters) of the enormous volcanic-stone foundations of the temple of Jupiter on the Capitoline in Rome (509 BCE) rivals that of the temple of Artemis at Ephesus (mid-sixth century BCE) and demonstrates the level of monumentality attained at this time also in Rome, though the exact size of the temple itself has recently been disputed, and evidence for the materials used for the earliest superstructure is lacking.

Roman builders are best known for the use of the arch, which was a means of spanning a distance by using wedge-shaped stones (voussoirs) that transferred the weight of the structure to either side, thus maintaining compression between the stones.

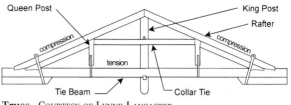

Truss. Courtesy of Lynne Lancaster

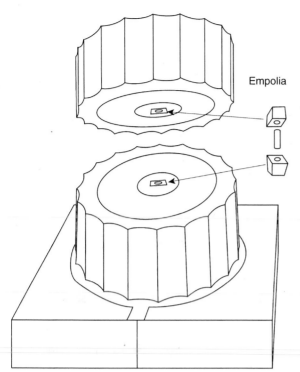

Empolia

Empolia. Drawing after Francis Cranmer Penrose, *An Investigation of the Principles of Athenian Architecture* (London, 1888), fig. 2. Courtesy of Lynne Lancaster

In Rome the earliest stone barrel vault has been discovered in a cistern dating to the sixth century BCE and located on the slopes of the Palatine. The most notable Roman exploitation of the stone arch was its use in aqueducts bringing fresh water into Rome, the earliest of which was the aqua Appia (312 BCE). The water channel of an aqueduct had to retain a constant incline from source to destination, so builders tunneled through hills and built aqueduct bridges across valleys by raising them on arches.

In the third century BCE, builders in central Italy began experimenting with *opus caementicium*, or concrete, in which small stones were held together with a lime mortar. By the mid-second century BCE they had combined the new material with the arched form to create concrete vaulting, as in the Sanctuary of Fortuna at Palestrina and the so-called Porticus Aemilia in Rome, recently identified as a mid-second century BCE ship shed (*navalia*). The combination of concrete and arched stone construction was critical in the development of two of the most representative of Roman buildings, the bath and the freestanding theater/amphitheater. The water- and fireproof nature of concrete was much better suited to the bath environment than were wooden roof structures. The combining of an arched stone skeleton with concrete vaulted stairs resulted in structures, such as the Theater of Pompey (55 BCE), that allowed multitudes to enter or exit quickly and efficiently.

The idea of combining materials of different strengths led the Romans to develop a hierarchy of materials whereby denser and more resistant stones were used in places where loads were concentrated, such as under columns, thus producing a somewhat modified form of the continuous foundations that had been used by the Greeks. The same concept was applied to the superstructure, so once concrete vaults became larger and were combined in complex ways, they were often reinforced with stone or brick ribs to help control the loads within the structure. With the peace brought by Augustus in 27 BCE, the seaborne trade throughout the Mediterranean was made safe and the exchange of both materials and ideas increased, which influenced building methods. Two building materials that became important at this time were bricks and window glass, both of which affected bath design: bricks because they were resistant to fire and retained heat and glass because it served both to keep the heat within a room while also allowing for natural light. The result of the introduction of window glass can best be seen at Pompeii by comparing the dark and windowless Stabian Baths of the second century BCE to the new Central Baths of 62–79 CE, with large windows within brick-faced walls facing onto the palaestra.

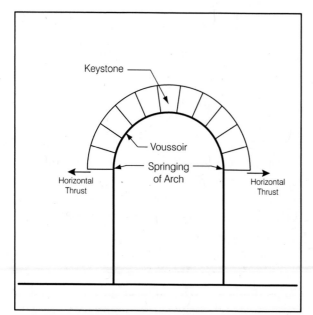

Arch. COURTESY OF LYNNE LANCASTER

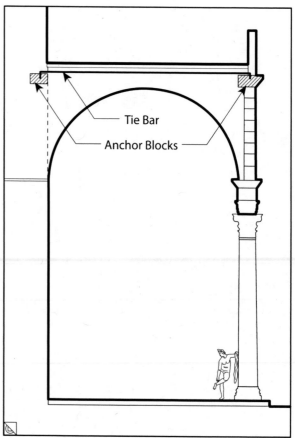

Tie Bar. COURTESY OF LYNNE LANCASTER

A prime example of the effect of the new empire-wide trading network and organizational infrastructure is demonstrated by the difference between multiple-drummed Greek columns and monolithic Roman columns of colored marble. As revealed by Greek building accounts, building parts for Greek projects were contracted with individuals, whereas those for Roman projects were often mass-produced in imperially controlled quarries and shipped on long-distance trade routes, as shown by quarry inscriptions and finds from shipwrecks. Such trading networks created greater availability and standardization of building elements, which in turn resulted in less emphasis on labor-intensive optical refinements and more on the elaborate display of exotic materials.

A further result of the interest in new materials and forms can be seen in the development of iron tie bars, which allowed the Roman builders to combine the post-and-lintel system borrowed from the Greeks with their own concrete vaulted system. The builders used iron tie bars to connect a colonnade to an adjacent wall so that it could resist the outward thrust of the vault. This system was typical of the colonnades in the palaestrae of the imperial baths of Trajan, Caracalla, and Diocletian and was eventually used in later church architecture.

Two other aspects of the imperial system that ultimately affected Roman construction were the movements of the legions and the necessity of providing food for Rome and the armies. For example, in Britain hollow terra-cotta voussoirs that were used to create heated ceilings in bath buildings were probably introduced by Roman military terra-cotta production units there. In Rome, empty amphorae that had brought olive oil—as tax—from Spain were sometimes built into concrete vaults to conserve on materials and in some cases to lighten the structure. Moreover, the increase in long-distance trade for both military and civilian purposes required more advanced harbors, which were made possible by the development of hydraulic pozzolana mortar for concrete construction. Ultimately many of the technological advances in Roman construction resulted from the exchange of ideas that resulted from trade infrastructure that developed in the imperial period.

[*See also* Architecture, *subentry* Forms and Terms; Brick; Concrete; Domestic Architecture; Marble; Parthenon; Technology; Temples; *and* Vaults and Vaulting.]

BIBLIOGRAPHY

Adam, Jean-Pierre. *Roman Building: Materials and Techniques.* Translated by Anthony Mathews. London: Batsford, 1994.

Camp, John McK., II, and William B. Dinsmoor Jr. *Ancient Athenian Building Methods.* Athens, Greece: American School of Classical Studies at Athens, 1984. A small pamphlet giving a good overview of Greek building methods.

Coulton, J. J. *Ancient Greek Architects at Work: Problems of Structure and Design.* Ithaca, N.Y.: Cornell University Press, 1977. Deals with specific design and structural issues encountered by Greek designers.

Lancaster, Lynne C. *Concrete Vaulted Construction in Imperial Rome: Innovations in Context.* New York: Cambridge University Press, 2005. An examination of the materials and building techniques employed in concrete structures in imperial Rome.

Oleson, John Peter, ed. *The Oxford Handbook of Engineering and Technology in the Classical World.* New York: Oxford University Press, 2008. A collection of essays on every aspect of materials and technology in the Greek and Roman world, all with thorough bibliographies.

Rowland, Ingrid, trans. *Vitruvius: The Ten Books on Architecture.* Commentary and illustrations by Thomas Noble Howe, additional commentary by Ingrid Rowland and Michael J. Dewar. New York: Cambridge University Press, 1999. An annotated and illustrated translation of Vitruvius.

Spawforth, Tony. *The Complete Greek Temples.* London: Thames & Hudson, 2006. Has a section on building materials and techniques and a good bibliography.

Ulrich, Roger B. *Roman Woodworking.* New Haven, Conn.: Yale University Press, 2007.

Wilson Jones, Mark. *Principles of Roman Architecture.* New Haven, Conn.: Yale University Press, 2000. Focuses on design and the process of building; extensive bibliography.

Lynne C. Lancaster

BUILDING TYPES

See Basilica; Temple; *and* Theater Buildings.

BUREAUCRACY

See Political Structure *and* Ideology, Roman.

BURIAL

See Death, *subentry* Death and Burial in the Ancient World; Funeral Oration, Greek; *and* Funerals, Roman.

BUSTS

See Portraiture.

BYZANTIUM

Located at the apex of a triangular peninsula at the southern end of the Bosporus, Byzantium was surrounded by sea on three sides that formed, as the sixth-century CE Byzantine historian Procopius put it, "a garland around the city." The city was bounded on the south and west by the Propontis and on the north by the Golden Horn, a seven-mile-long (11.3-kilometer-long) natural bay that served the city as a port. The city prospered since it held a key position on the maritime trade route between the Black Sea and the Aegean and controlled the mainland routes between Europe and Asia. Besides its excellent strategic location, Byzantium possessed a large and fertile territory. The city controlled its Thracian hinterland as far as the Çekmece lakes in the west, and as far as the Black Sea shore in the north. It even controlled territories on the Asian eastern shores of the Propontis, extended at times as far west as Lake Dascylitis. Byzantium produced enormous amounts of grain from its territories. Part of their agricultural wealth was produced by the Bithynians who were reduced to the status of serfs by the Byzantines. The water around Byzantium was teeming with fish, which contributed much to the economy of the city.

Byzantium was founded c. 660 BCE in a joint enterprise led by Megarians and some other Greek poleis. Later in the Archaic period another party of Megarian colonists came to Byzantium. There is no information about early Byzantium but sources suggest that its inhabitants were continuously in conflict with the Thracians in their hinterland. The Byzantines submitted to Persian suzerainty in 514 BCE when Darius I crossed the Bosporus on his way to Scythia. The Byzantines suffered under Persian rule, revolting twice and witnessing the destruction of their city in 493 BCE. Persian rule lasted until 478 BCE when Greek forces led by Pausanias liberated the city. The Spartan commander Pausanias, however, ruled the city tyrannically until he was expelled by the Athenians in 471 BCE. From then until 405 BCE the city was an important member of the Athenian League, contributing money, ships, and manpower. In 440–439 and 411 BCE, however, the Byzantines revolted against the Athenians and the city remained under Spartan control from 405 until 394 BCE. Byzantium was one of the first states to join the second Athenian League, founded in 378 BCE. When Athenian aggression in the northern Aegean and the Hellespont alienated the Byzantines, they revolted against Athens and joined the Theban League (364 BCE) and shortly thereafter supported the revolt of Rhodes, Chios, and Cos against Athens in the Social War of 357–355. In 340 BCE Philip II of Macedon besieged Byzantium but failed to capture it thanks to Athenian and Persian help. In the Hellenistic period, although the Byzantines suffered Thracian attacks, Celtic pressure, and Seleucid threats, they remained important international actors in the Greek world. They were embroiled with the Rhodians in a war that involved the kingdoms of Bithynia and Pergamum between 220 and 218 BCE.

When the Romans appeared in the east in the second and first century BCE, the Byzantines shrewdly sided with them. However, during the last century of the Roman Republic and early Empire the city was overburdened by the passage of Roman armies. Nevertheless, Byzantium shared the prosperity prevalent in the Roman world. Authors of the early Principate period stress the wealth it derived from fishing, agriculture, and trade.

During the civil wars following the death of Publius Helvius Pertinax, the Byzantines supported Pescennius Niger against Septimius Severus (193 CE). Though Niger was defeated and killed, the Byzantines refused to surrender and were besieged for more than two years (193–196 CE). When the town surrendered, Septimius burned it to the ground and reduced it to village status dependent on the neighboring Perinthus. Shortly after its destruction, Septimius Severus refounded Byzantium as Antoninia Augusta and built several important buildings. However, the city was so weakened that in the following century it could not stop the invasion of the Goths, who, after sailing through the Bosporus, wreaked havoc in the Aegean world, sacking Ilium, Athens, Sparta, and Delphi.

In 324 CE Constantine defeated his rival Licinius around Chrysopolis near Chalcedon and decided to refound Byzantium as his own city, perhaps as a Christian capital of the empire. He began its reconstruction on 8 November 324. He enlarged the city, built magnificent buildings, and beautified it with ancient works of art brought from all over the empire. Constantine dedicated his new city on 11 May 330. From then on the city was called Constantinopolis, and sometimes Nova Roma (New Rome) or Altera Roma (Second Rome).

[*See also* Constantinople; Megara; Persian Wars; *and* Thrace.]

BIBLIOGRAPHY

Isaac, Benjamin H. *The Greek Settlements in Thrace until the Macedonian Conquest.* pp. 215–237. Leiden: E.J. Brill, 1986.

Krautheimer, R. *Three Christian Capitals: Topography and Politics.* Berkeley: University of California Press, 1983.

Müller-Wiener, Wolfgang. *Bildlexikon zur Topographie Istanbuls: Byzantion, Konstantinupolis, Istanbul bis zum Beginn des 17. Jahrhunderts.* Tübingen: Wasmuth, 1977.

Mehmet Fatih Yavuz

C

CADMUS

See Thebes, *subentry* Theban Myths.

CAESAR

See Julius Caesar.

CALENDAR, GREEK

Greek calendars variously made use of the cycles of the sun, the moon, and the stars. The moon formed the basis of all city-state festival calendars, while the star-almanacs—which traced the rising and setting of stars—helped time agricultural activities, and perhaps regulated some civil calendars, and the sun, after initially loosely helping mark out seasonal periods in the agricultural cycle, eventually formed the basis of some civil calendars. A year measured by the sun and the stars is practically of the same length, at least over an individual's lifetime. From early in the Hellenistic period solar months were generated from the time taken by the sun to pass through the twelve signs of the zodiac. A lunar "year," however, is always incommensurate with a seasonal or solar year, as twelve lunar months fall eleven days short of a solar year. Various intercalary cycles were devised to realign the lunar calendars with the sun, and hence with the seasons, a matter of great importance in a society whose religious life was agriculturally based.

The Linear B tablets from Knossos (c. 1370 BCE) and Pylos (c. 1200 BCE) provide the earliest evidence for calendar systems in ancient Greece. The relevant tablets (e.g., Knossos Fp1) are fragments of ritual calendars, in which the offerings for the gods are listed on a monthly basis. That the calendar was lunar is implied etymologically by the use of the word *me-no* for "month," but there is no way now to understand how this might have been correlated with the seasonal, solar year. The names of eight months survive from Knossos, and three from Pylos, but the two sites seem to have held none in common. Only four names are suggestive of later historical months: *di-wi-jo-jo* (Dios), *ra-pa-to* (Lapato), *di-pi-si-jo* (Dipsios), and *ka-ra-e-ri-jo* (Klareon). All names appear either to be theophoric or toponymic.

In literature, the *Iliad* and *Odyssey* (c. 750–700 BCE) display awareness of the use of both the sun and the moon as means of reckoning time, the sun for the seasonal year, and the moon for other measures, such as the length of a pregnancy, a form of time reckoning which has continued to the present day. No calendar as such is mentioned, nor are months named, but instead the risings and settings of a few significant stars are used to signal certain periods in the seasonal year. Hesiod's *Works and Days* (c. 700 BCE) utilizes this approach more thoroughly in his account of the agricultural year. Ten observations are provided of the rising, setting, or (in one instance) culmination of five stars or constellations, which help to mark out four seasons. Hesiod's farmer is also expected to note other coincident signs from the natural world, notably the arrival of migrating birds. Only occasionally is the moon used to indicate the appropriate time—or otherwise—for activities; lucky and unlucky lunar days would have a greater future under the Romans.

Star-based almanacs remained in use throughout the Greek and Roman periods, providing historians with better temporal fixes for their narratives than the relatively discordant local state calendars. Thucydides (c. 420 BCE), for instance, famously recommends the use of summers and winters to mark the passage of time from one year to the next in the Peloponnesian War (5.20.1–2); elsewhere (2.78.2; 7.16.2) he uses the first visible dawn rising of the star Arcturus and the winter solstice as temporal markers.

All the Greek city-states used lunar calendars, but New Year's Day could differ from city to city because each city began its year with the first new moon after or near one of the four tropical points of the solar year—the summer or winter solstice, or the spring or autumn equinox. This combination of lunar and solar phenomena made the beginning of the year similar to Christian Easter, in that it was mobile within a prescribable period of time, but dissimilar to the Islamic religious calendar, which is purely lunar and wanders through the whole of the seasonal year over time. A mixture of observation and schematic calculation seems to have been used in deciding when a month started and when it ended, with the start being marked by the evening sighting of the new moon's crescent. It may be that star-almanacs (*parapēgmata*), helped to regulate some cities' calendars.

The Athenian year is the best known, but we can reconstruct several others. In Athens the year began after the summer solstice, about halfway through a Julian year. The names of the months—Hekatombaiōn, Metageitniōn, Boēdromiōn, Pyanepsiōn, Maimakteriōn, Poseideōn, Gamēliōn, Anthestēriōn, Elaphēboliōn, Mounichiōn, Thargēliōn, Skirophoriōn—reflect religious festivals in the respective months. The reconstruction of other cities' calendars is enabled by epigraphical and literary evidence, often in the form of records preserved by the local religious bureaucracy, such as the series of slave manumission inscriptions from Delphi, or the financial records of the Temple of Zeus Olympios at Locri in South Italy.

Difficulties arose in antiquity in correlating dates across the various states from different timings of the observation of the same new moon's crescent, and more particularly from ad hoc insertions of intercalary months, which were designed to bring the lunar and solar years back into synchrony. Various systems of intercalation were devised, notably the eight-year and the nineteen-year, or Metonic, cycles (the latter named after the Athenian astronomer Meton, who invented it in the 430s BCE). In the eight-year cycle three of the lunar years were given an extra month, while in the Metonic cycle seven years gained an extra month. The quadrennial games at Delphi and Olympia were governed by eight-year cycles. It appears increasingly likely that Athens utilized the Metonic cycle to regulate its calendar through the Hellenistic period, and perhaps into the Imperial Roman period as well.

The Macedonian calendar became the most utilized Greek calendar throughout the Hellenized world in the wake of the conquests of Alexander the Great (356–323 BCE). Its months were: Dios, Apellaios, Audnaios, Peritios, Dystros, Xanthikos, Artemisios, Daisios, Panēmos, Lōios, Gorpiaios, Hyperberetaios. The new year began after the autumn equinox. It was absorbed into the calendrical systems of Egypt and the former Persian Empire. In the Persian Empire there already existed a lunisolar calendar of great antiquity, regulated since the fifth century BCE by its own nineteen-year cycle. The Macedonian calendar was absorbed into this much older, but very similar, system without any loss. In Egypt, however, a near-solar calendar of 365 days was used. Each of its twelve months was of thirty days, and five extra ("epagomenal") days made up the balance. The Macedonian calendar was drawn into this system, with the final result being that the Macedonian months were directly equated to the regular Egyptian ones. The lack of an extra ("leap") day every four years caused the Egyptian year to wander slowly but regularly ahead of the true solar year. A proposal in 238 BCE under the Ptolemies to introduce a leap-day failed to take hold, but ironically it was an Egyptian Greek, Sosigenes, who formulated for Julius Caesar the solar calendar with which we still, in effect, live.

[*See also* Calendar, Roman.]

BIBLIOGRAPHY

Bickerman, E. J. *Chronology of the Ancient World.* London. 2nd ed. Ithaca, N.Y.: Cornell University Press, 1980. An accessible study of Greek and Roman calendars and chronology, with useful tables and lists.

Hannah, Robert. *Greek and Roman Calendars: Constructions of Time in the Classical World.* London: Duckworth, 2005. A study of the development of Greek and Roman calenders, set in their cultural contexts.

Lehoux, Daryn. *Astronomy, Weather, and Calendars in the Ancient World: Parapegmata and Related Texts in Classical and Near Eastern Societies.* Cambridge, U.K.: Cambridge University Press, 2007. A specialized study of star-almanacs in the Near Eastern, Greek, and Roman worlds.

Samuel, Alan E. *Greek and Roman Chronology: Calendars and Years in Classical Antiquity.* Munich: Beck, 1972. An excellent standard reference work on all aspects of Greek and Roman calendars.

Trümpy, Catherine. *Untersuchungen zu den altgriechischen Monatsnamen und Monatsfolgen.* Heidelberg, Germany: Universitätsverlag C. Winter, 1997. A specialized study of Greek months.

Robert Hannah

CALENDAR, ROMAN

The original form of the Roman calendar was attributed to Romulus and supposedly comprised 304 days divided into ten lunar months: Martius, Aprilis, Maius, Junius, Quintilis, Sextilis, September, October, November, December. The two moons of midwinter agricultural inactivity were not counted.

Numa Pompilius, the legendary second king of Rome (r. 715–673 BCE), was credited by Livy, Ovid, and Macrobius with being the calendar's first reformer and the city's religious founder. He added Ianuarius and Februarius to complete a twelve-month lunar year of 355 days; he divided each month into days, each day having a particular character to regulate religious and civic activities; he introduced a system of intercalation to synchronize the lunar year with the seasons when discrepancies became too obvious; and he founded the college of pontiffs to control the calendar so that sacrifices and rituals could be performed on the correct days and with proper procedure for the preservation of the *pax deorum* (goodwill of the gods).

The earliest contemporary representation of the Roman Republican calendar is from the colony of Antium in the mid-first century BCE. It organizes in tabular and abbreviated form the names of the months, and it includes coded information such as letters (A–H) signifying the eight days of the market cycle and the character of individual days; the calends, nones, and ides denoting the lunar phases; and notices of festivals and foundation dates of temples. The calendar comprises twelve months—four months of thirty-one days, seven of twenty-nine days, and one of twenty-eight days—totaling 355 days for a year. A thirteenth column shows an intercalary month, inserted every other year, at which time February was reduced to twenty-three days; twenty-two or twenty-three days were added after the Terminalia (23 February). The five remaining days of February were added at the end of the intercalary month, so that the Intercalaris, or Mercedonius, consisted of twenty-seven or twenty-eight days.

The peculiar features of the Republican calendar, as seen by Censorinus (238 CE), were the length of the months and the intercalation system. He saw them as an (unsuccessful) attempt to synchronize the civil and solar years. The Roman quadrennial system comprised 355 + 378 + 355 + 377 days, a cycle that added up to 1,465 days, four days longer than four solar years. Thus the calendar lagged behind four days every quadrennium in relation to the four seasons. Greater discrepancy could be caused by the pontiffs, who were sometimes suspected of abusing their powers by intercalating for political rather than religious reasons. During the civil wars of the mid-first century, intercalation was neglected. By 46 BCE there was a ninety-day discrepancy between the civil year and the solar year. The harvest thanksgiving was being celebrated before the crops had ripened.

Julius Caesar, *pontifex maximus* (chief pontiff) and now dictator, employed the Alexandrian mathematician Sosigenes to align the solar and civil year. The lunar calendar was abandoned and replaced with a solar calendar of 365.25 days, with a single day intercalated every fourth year. In 46 BCE, ninety days were added to the lunar year to give it a total of 445 days, the longest year in Roman history. It was described by Macrobius as *annus confusionis ultimus* (final year of confusion).

Caesar's reform was as much a political maneuver as it was a mathematical adjustment. From 1 January 45 BCE the Julian calendar began to provide the populace with unprecedented stability in every aspect of daily life. In wresting the calendar from manipulative pontiffs, the Julian calendar transferred control of time from the senate to the people of Rome. It also preserved continuity with the traditional calendar in form and emphasis: it retained the names of the months, their division by calends, nones, and ides, the character of the days, and the dates of all the major festivals. This was achieved by adding the extra days at the end of the shorter months. Roman collective identity remained intact.

The personal cult of Caesar and his successor, Augustus, was gradually inscribed in the new calendar alongside the ancient traditional festivals. The months of Quintilis and Sextilis were renamed July and August, respectively, and anniversaries of the imperial family were incorporated. The decentralized religion of the Republic and the centralizing religion of the Empire coexist in extant remnants of many inscribed calendars of the early Empire, especially the *Fasti Praenestini* (c. 6–10 CE). Ovid's Roman calendar (*Fasti*, 4–16 CE) creates an ideological connection between the two religions. The Roman people were able to embrace the ruler-cult while still clinging to their old idols and myths of identity. The Codex-Calendar of 354 indicates that they adopted Christianity in the same way.

[*See also* Calendar, Greek; Festivals, Roman; Ovid; *and* Religion, *subentry* Roman Religion.]

BIBLIOGRAPHY

Bickerman, E. J.. *Chronology of the Ancient World.* 2nd ed. Ithaca, N.Y.: Cornell University Press, 1980.

Degrassi, Attilio. *Inscriptiones Italiae.* Vol. 13, fasc. 2: Fasti e Elogia. Rome: La Libreria dello Stato, 1963.

Feeney, Denis. *Caesar's Calendar: Ancient Time and the Beginnings of History.* Berkeley: University of California Press, 2007.

Herbert-Brown, Geraldine. "Ovid's *Fasti*: The Poet, the Prince, and the Plebs." In *The Blackwell Companion to Ovid*, edited by Peter Knox. Forthcoming.

Michels, Agnes Kirsopp. *The Calendar of the Roman Republic.* Princeton, N.J.: Princeton University Press, 1967.

Salzman, Michele Renee. *On Roman Time: The Codex-Calendar of 354 and the Rhythms of Urban Life in Late Antiquity.* Berkeley: University of California Press, 1990.

Scullard, Howard H. *The Festivals and Ceremonies of the Roman Republic.* Ithaca, N.Y.: Cornell University Press, 1981.

Geraldine Herbert-Brown

CALIGULA

(Gaius Julius Caesar, 12–41 CE), emperor (r. 37–41 CE). Although often referred to by modern historians as Caligula, Gaius Julius Caesar was known as Gaius in the Roman world and that is the name used in this article. The youngest son of Germanicus Julius Caesar and Agrippina the Elder (Vipsania), he was taken as a toddler to his father's military post on the Rhine frontier and there dressed as a little soldier. He received the nickname "Caligula," or "Little Boots," from the word for legionary footwear. He accompanied his parents to his father's Eastern command as well. After Germanicus' death, he returned to Rome with his mother.

When Gaius was growing up, his older brothers, possible successors to Tiberius, were exiled and imprisoned along with their mother. All were dead by 33 CE. Tiberius controlled Gaius by bringing him to his retreat on Capri in 31. He was given priesthoods and then became quaestor. When the emperor died in 37, the praetorian prefect Macro had the guard salute Gaius as emperor and prepared the senate to give him by a single vote all the powers that Augustus had acquired in a lifetime. Hailed as the son of the still-popular Germanicus, Gaius entered the city to a hopeful populace.

Gaius began well, setting himself apart from his unpopular predecessor. He granted amnesty to exiles, abolished treason trials, burned papers that attacked his family, and paid the benefactions of Tiberius' will, even though it had been officially set aside. He reinstated his mother and brothers as members of the imperial family pantheon and honored his three living sisters extravagantly. Since he had as yet no children of his own, he named as regent Aemilius Lepidus, the husband of one of them, Drusilla. His piety was not without calculation, however, for without military credentials or much experience, he needed his family, who were his only asset, to validate his position. Later in 37 Gaius fell ill, and shortly after he recovered the following year, there began the first of many executions that would take place in his reign. A coup may have been under way. Soon Drusilla died. Gaius mourned her to excess and the next year had her declared a goddess, the first woman to receive this honor.

By 39 CE Gaius' relations with the senate had deteriorated to the point that he berated it openly. In defiance he engineered the most ambitious of his many extravagant displays, a causeway of boats across the Bay of Naples, and traversed it in mock triumph. In September of that year, he removed the consuls from office, left Rome, and journeyed north. In northern Italy he executed Drusilla's former husband, Lepidus, and sent his remaining sisters, Livilla and Agrippina the Younger, into exile. Continuing on, he relieved Gaetulicus (Gnaeus Cornelius Lentulus Gaetulicus), general for the army of Upper Germany, of his command and executed him, evidently because he believed that a plot against him had been formed.

This journey north was preliminary to a serious plan to invade Britain. Gaius engaged in minor incursions across the Rhine before moving a large force to the Channel coast. Although the invasion was aborted, he declared victory and returned to Rome in the spring of 40 CE. Intent on celebrating a triumph, he had to settle for an ovation. His relations with the senate now reached their nadir, but the final attempt on his life came from another quarter, from officers of the Praetorian Guard. In January of 41, he was ambushed on the Palatine and died on the spot from multiple stab wounds. Along with the praetorian tribunes, conspirators may have included the praetorian prefects, imperial freedmen, senators, and even his successor, his uncle Claudius.

Although Gaius' reign had promised well, he soon met with distrust fueled by his own arrogance, extravagance, and unpredictable behavior. Hostility arose when he refused to maintain the pretense that the senate and the emperor were equal partners. Gaius insulted others easily but was thin-skinned himself. He held extravagant banquets and adorned his favorite horse with gold and jewels. His attention to his sisters was suggestive of incest with all three, especially Drusilla. He executed many cruelly. Despite tales of conversing with gods and the establishment of a priesthood for himself, he probably did not claim outright divinity.

Gaius' mental health has always been the subject of curiosity and conjecture. He may have been bipolar, for his excesses seem manic, but it is impossible to know, since ancient prejudice obscures evidence. Those who evaluated his reign could not accept this singularly unsuccessful representative of the emerging principate as a model. He could be disposed of by calling him mad.

[*See also* Agrippina the Elder; Claudius; Germanicus; Julio-Claudian Emperors; *and* Rome, *subentry* The Empire.]

BIBLIOGRAPHY

Balsdon, John P. V. D. *The Emperor Gaius (Caligula).* Oxford: Clarendon Press, 1934 and various reprints.

Barrett, Anthony A. *Caligula: The Corruption of Power.* London: Batsford, 1989, and New Haven, Conn.: Yale University Press, 1990.

Wiedemann, T. E. J. "Gaius Caligula." In *Cambridge Ancient History*. 2nd ed., *The Augustan Empire, 43 B.C.–A.D. 69*, edited by Alan K. Bowman, Edward Champlin, and Andrew Lintott, vol. 10, pp. 221–229. Cambridge, U.K.: Cambridge University Press, 1996.

Donna W. Hurley

CALLIMACHUS OF CYRENE

(fl. c. 280–245 BCE), Hellenistic poet and scholar. Callimachus represents himself as "Battiades," that is, "son or descendant of Battus," a reference either to the name of a real ancestor (as in the biographical tradition, which makes him the son of Battus and Mesatma) or to his homeland (of which Battus was the founder). Callimachus flourished during the reign of Ptolemy II Philadelphus (r. 282–246 BCE), but some poems date from the reign of Ptolemy III Euergetes (r. 246–222 BCE), including several in honor of that king's wife Berenice II. Although Callimachus was an active participant in the scholarly life of the Alexandrian Museum, he never served as its director.

According to the catalog of his works in the tenth-century encyclopedia known as the *Suda*, Callimachus was the author of eight hundred books, and even if one allows for some exaggeration, he must be counted as one of the most prolific and important figures of the Hellenistic period. He compiled a bibliography of Greek literature in 120 books called the *Pinakes* (Tables), in which he cited the first line of each of the works held at the Alexandrian Library. The titles of his numerous prose works on a wide range of topics—including an attack on the philosopher Praxiphanes of Mytilene and treatises on rivers, winds, nymphs, barbarian customs, birds, the names of fishes and of months, athletic contests, and wonders and paradoxes—reveal his astonishing erudition, but except for citations in the secondary tradition, these works have been almost entirely lost.

Callimachus composed poems in a wide range of meters and genres, including epic (*Hecale*), hymn (a series of six hymns playing with the conventions of the *Homeric Hymns*), elegy (*Aetia*), iambic (a collection of thirteen *Iambi*), lyric, and epigram. In all of his compositions he plays with the traditional conventions of—and blurs the formal and thematic boundaries between—literary forms. Meter and dialect, two important markers of genre in Archaic and Classical poetry, are a frequent vehicle for experimentation, such as in his book of *Iambi*, which include a range of meters and dialect forms.

By any standard, Callimachus was a talented poet, and his work is of enormous literary influence and importance. Often witty and wry, he is capable of great pathos as well, and the corpus as a whole is marked by great tonal variety. Erudition, however, is the most obvious characteristic of Callimachus' poetry. In practically every passage he engages in a learned way with earlier literature (including prose as well as poetry), simultaneously displaying his intimate knowledge of it while also making clear his independence. Thus, for example, in a passage of the *Aetia*—a fragmentarily preserved four-book elegiac poem in which he recounts a series of stories explaining the origins of various, often obscure, local rites and rituals from throughout the Greek world—Callimachus cites a prose history of Ceos as the inspiration for "his Muse" in telling the story of Acontius and Cydippe. The Homeric poems are a particularly important model for Callimachus. At the level of diction, for instance, Callimachus frequently uses words in ways that implicitly stake out positions in contemporary critical debate about their proper Homeric meaning or form, and on the frequent occasions that he draws on Homeric words or phrases—rarities being a particular subject of his interest—he regularly alters them in subtle ways.

The tension between tradition and innovation is evident in other aspects of the poet's work. In the prologue to his *Aetia*, a text that exerted tremendous influence on later poetry, Callimachus defends himself from unnamed critics for not having composed a poem of many thousands of lines on kings and heroes by imagining Apollo expressing a preference for finely honed "thin" poetry over "big" or "fat" poetry, and urging the poet to traverse the literary road less traveled. Though the precise point of the passage has been widely debated, the opposition between "thin" and "fat" poetry here and elsewhere in the corpus—Callimachus playfully declares, for example, that "a big book is a big bad"—probably amounts not to general rejection of long epic poems as a viable poetic mode, as was once often claimed, but instead to a preference for highly refined compositions in which every word is chosen with care over those written in uncreative imitation of Homer. Such refinement plays out not only in his diction, but also in his metrical practice—his hexameter, for instance, noticeably regularizes some of the tendencies of the form from Homer on—and narrative technique. The *Hecale* provides a good example of the poet's novel approach to traditional subject matter. The poem, once probably more than one thousand verses long but now surviving only in fragments, contains a miniature account of a heroic legend, Theseus' capture of the Marathonian bull. The focus of the narrative, however, is not on Theseus' encounter with the beast, but on his visit along the way to the home of an aged woman.

Callimachus worked under the patronage of the early Ptolemies, and a number of passages contribute to the image and reflect the interests of the Alexandrian court: for example, his *Hymn to Zeus* subtly allows for slippage between Zeus and Ptolemy, and the opening of the third book of his *Aetia* honors Berenice II in the manner of Pindar's odes in honor of athletic contests. Callimachus often adopts a polemical stance in his poetry, but the precise nature of his relationship to his contemporaries is generally hard to pin down. The story of a dispute between Callimachus and Apollonius Rhodius (Apollonius of Rhodes) about the status of epic in general and Apollonius' *Argonautica* in particular is probably a biographical fiction, but there can be no doubt that Callimachus disagreed with the early third-century epigrammatist Asclepiades of Samos about the quality of the *Lyde*, an elegiac poem by Antimachus of Colophon.

It is hard to underestimate Callimachus' importance for subsequent Greek and Roman literary history, even if his influence was long obscured by the loss of so much of his scholarly and poetic output. Other than the hymns and epigrams, Callimachus' work survives only in quotations in other texts and in numerous papyrus fragments. His *Hecale* and *Aetia* seem to have survived intact at least until the Fourth Crusade, because they were known to Michael Choniates around 1200. Although his learned approach was sometimes the subject of criticism, Callimachus' poetry was important to Roman literature as early as Quintus Ennius, and no account of the work of the Latin poets of the first centuries BCE and CE can ignore its influence on their style, narrative technique, and representation of Rome's burgeoning empire. His influence on Greek poetry continued well into the Byzantine period.

[*See also* Apollonius of Rhodes; Encyclopedias and Dictionaries; Literary Criticism, Ancient; Pindar; *and* Poetry, Greek, *subentries* Didactic Poetry, Epic, Post-Classical Greek Epic, Lyric, Epinician Poetry, Elegiac Poetry, Epigrams, *and* The Iambic Tradition.]

BIBLIOGRAPHY

Acosta-Hughes, Benjamin. *Polyeidea: The Iambi of Callimachus and the Archaic Iambic Tradition.* Berkeley: University of California Press, 2002.

Cameron, Alan. *Callimachus and His Critics.* Princeton, N.J.: Princeton University Press, 1995.

Fantuzzi, Marco, and Richard Hunter. *Tradition and Innovation in Hellenistic Poetry.* Cambridge, U.K.: Cambridge University Press, 2004.

Harder, M. A., R. F. Regtuit, and G. C. Wakker, eds. *Callimachus.* Groningen, The Netherlands: Egbert Forsten, 1993.

Harder, M. A., R. F. Regtuit, and G. C. Wakker, eds. *Callimachus II.* Dudley, Mass.: Peeters, 2004.

Hunter, Richard. *The Shadow of Callimachus: Studies in the Reception of Hellenistic Poetry at Rome.* Cambridge, U.K.: Cambridge University Press, 2006.

Kerkhecker, Arnd. *Callimachus' Book of Iambi.* Oxford: Clarendon Press; New York: Oxford University Press, 1999.

Pfeiffer, Rudolf, ed. *Callimachus.* 2 vols. Oxford: Oxford University Press, 1949.

ALEX SENS

CAMBRIDGE RITUALISTS

"Cambridge Ritualists" is a name given to a group of three classicists, Jane Harrison (1850–1928), Gilbert Murray (1866–1957), and Francis Cornford (1874–1943), who worked together at the beginning of the twentieth century, applying the methods and findings of anthropology to the field of ancient Greek religion. Like many of their contemporaries in the social sciences, they sought origins, which for religion meant primitive ritual. They believed that ritual lay behind many later practices and that myth was an attempt to explain ritual long after its original meaning was lost. (James George Frazer and Arthur Bernard Cook, their contemporaries at Cambridge, also worked in the same area, but independently.) Harrison drew Murray and Cornford into her own research and inspired them with her contagious fervor. In Murray's words, "we were out to see what things really meant, looking for a new light our elders had not seen" (letter to Jessie Stewart, 26 October 1953). The books and articles they published ranged in subject matter from ancient Greek religion to Greek literature, archaeology, and art. However, their collaboration consisted as much in hammering out their ideas together as in individual publications.

Harrison scoured Greek art and literature for evidence of primitive practices, producing a mass of detail that had lain neglected while other classical scholars, more concerned with the rational and aesthetic influence of Greece, had regarded Greek religion as beginning with Homer (9th–8th century BCE) and centering on the Olympian gods. Traveling in Greece, Harrison encountered firsthand survivals of primitive rituals among the peasant folk and learned from archaeologists, notably Wilhelm Dörpfeld and Arthur Evans. She read widely in the social sciences and was particularly influenced by Émile Durkheim. Her work culminated in the assertion that behind all the different manifestations of spirits lay one concept, that of a dying and rising god, ritually celebrated each spring. She called this the *eniautos daimōn*, or "Year Spirit." A barely enunciated corollary was that Jesus Christ was no more than yet another manifestation of this universally worshipped god.

While scholars raised academic eyebrows, the work of the ritualists resonated with the public, whose interest in the "primitive" had been piqued by recent anthropological discoveries of explorers and missionaries and by the exciting archaeological finds of Heinrich Schliemann and Arthur Evans. The ritualists themselves wrote with this wider readership in mind and even went so far as to suggest that the timeless values of Greek religion offered a religion for their own day.

Although Harrison, Murray, and Cornford are often referred to collectively as the "Cambridge Ritualists," there were deep intellectual differences between them. Harrison, despite protestations to the contrary, was fascinated by the irrational and the "primitive" for its own sake, whereas Murray's interest lay in his vision of Hellenism as a struggle from murky origins toward perfection, and Cornford likewise was primarily interested in how Greek thought developed. After World War I, Murray's association with the League of Nations drew him away from scholarly work, while Cornford applied himself to ancient philosophy. Harrison abandoned Classics for Russian language and literature.

[*See also* Classical Scholarship, *subentry* Modern Classical Scholarship.]

BIBLIOGRAPHY
Primary Works
Cornford, Francis M. *From Religion to Philosophy: A Study in the Origins of Western Speculation.* London: E. Arnold; New York: Longmans, Green, 1912. Reprint, New York: Harper and Row, 1957. Explores the social significance of Greek philosophy.
Harrison, Jane Ellen. *Prolegomena to the Study of Greek Religion.* Princeton, N.J.: Princeton University Press, 1991. First published 1903 by Cambridge University Press. A detailed study of rituals and festivals of ancient Greece, Harrison sets out her theory of the evolution of gods and goddesses. The last section, almost half the book, is devoted to Dionysus and the Orphics. This book is not an easy read, but chapter 5, "The Demonology of Ghosts and Sprites and Bogeys," is a good introduction to Harrison's method.

This Mythos edition includes a valuable introduction by Robert Ackerman.

Harrison, Jane Ellen. *Themis: A Study of the Social Origins of Greek Religion.* Cambridge, U.K.: Cambridge University Press, 1912. Reprint, London: Merlin Press, 1963. Includes contributions from Cornford and Murray.

Murray, Gilbert. *Five Stages of Greek Religion: Studies Based on a Course of Lectures Delivered in April 1912 at Columbia University.* London: Watts, 1935. An early version of this work was published as *Four Stages of Greek Religion Based on a Course of Lectures Delivered in April 1912 at Columbia University* (New York: Columbia University Press, 1912). A much shorter and more accessible book than Harrison's *Prolegomena*.

Secondary Works

Csapo, Eric. *Theories of Mythology.* Oxford: Blackwell, 2005. A superb and lucid introduction, with a chapter on ritual theories that situates them in their intellectual and historical context. Good bibliographies at the end of each chapter.

Calder, William M., III, ed. *The Cambridge Ritualists Reconsidered: Proceedings of the First Oldfather Conference, Held on the Campus of the University of Illinois at Urbana-Champaign, April 27–30, 1989. Illinois Classical Studies,* Supplement 2. Atlanta: Scholars Press, 1991. Two articles in this book are particularly helpful: "The Cambridge Group: Origins and Composition," by Robert Ackerman, and "Prolegomena to Jane Harrison's Interpretation of Ancient Greek Religion," by Renate Schlesier.

Robinson, Annabel. *The Life and Work of Jane Ellen Harrison.* Oxford: Oxford University Press, 2002.

Annabel Robinson

CAMEOS

Cameos were produced from about the time of Alexander the Great (r. 336–323 BCE) and right through the Roman period. In this context the word "cameos" refers to gemstones—often layered chalcedonies (onyx, sardonyx), but also single-colored stones, among them cornelians, emeralds, garnets, sapphires, and other hard stones—carved in relief. They served as settings for rings, brooches, or pendants, or in some instances served as miniature relief sculptures that were set in frames or as carvings in the round. The production of such works was painstaking, and the resultant cameos were very highly valued.

Some cameos depicting images of rulers—notably Ptolemaic kings and queens—and, later, members of the Roman imperial family, often known as Staatskameen (state cameos), were carved in official workshops and given as presents to supporters of the regime. Famous examples of such specially commissioned gems include the Tazza Farnese (in Florence), a carved agate bowl depicting the goddess Isis—here standing in for Cleopatra VII—and various personifications representing the prosperity of Egypt; the Gemma Augustea (in Vienna) honoring Augustus and his conquests; and the Grand Camée de France (in Paris), which is similar but glorifies Tiberius. This visual language was used into late antiquity, and the great cameo in the Dutch royal collection celebrates, in all probability, Constantine's triumph over Maxentius at the Milvian Bridge (28 October 312).

Many cameos are simply portraits of the ruler and other members of his family, especially frequent when the dynasty was unsure of itself. In Ptolemaic Egypt the portraits of Isis, frequently perhaps to be equated with Cleopatra VII, may reflect the uncertain hold on power of this famous woman. From the Roman period, cameos of Divus Augustus produced early in Tiberius' reign and contemporary portraits of Tiberius himself highlight the succession. Later, Claudius and his successor, the young Nero, both essentially usurpers, were glamorized in cameo art. In the late second and early third century Septimius Severus, his wife Julia Domna, and later their elder son Caracalla are especially in evidence in cameo art. Clearly some of the most skilled artists of the time, including Augustus' own gem cutter Dioskourides, carved cameos.

Because the audience for such works was restricted to an inner circle of family members and courtiers, the propaganda messages they contain are often rather sycophantic. The emperor or empress may sometimes appear as a god; thus Augustus on the Gemma Augustea appears in conversation with Dea Roma as an earthly Jupiter accompanied by his eagle; Claudius, too, is a thunderbolt-bearing

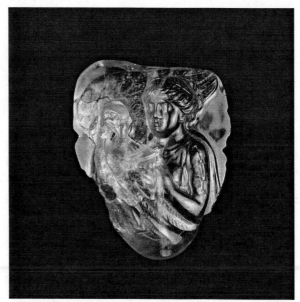

Aphrodite Cameo. Cameo of Aphrodite feeding an eagle, Roman. THE BRIDGEMAN ART LIBRARY

cameos were especially common in the third and fourth centuries CE. A large number of such cameos are portraits of women, sometimes clearly equated with Venus by emphasizing the sexuality of the subject. These seem to have been given by male lovers to their girlfriends. Other cameos, notably ones showing mourning cupids and also probably those depicting lions, were probably memento mori reminding the wearer to make the most of life while it lasts.

[*See also* Augustus, *subentry* Portraits of Augustus; Gems; Jewelry; Portraits and Portraiture; *and* Propaganda, Roman.]

BIBLIOGRAPHY

Henig, Martin. *The Content Family Collection of Ancient Cameos.* Oxford: Ashmolean Museum; Houlton, Maine: D. J. Content, 1990.

Henig, Martin, and M. Vickers. *Cameos in Context: The Benjamin Zucker Lectures, 1990.* Oxford: Ashmolean Museum; Houlton, Maine: D. J. Content, 1993.

Megow, Wolf-Rüdiger. *Kameen von Augustus bis Alexander Severus.* Berlin: Walter de Gruyter, 1987.

Richter, Gisela M. A. *The Engraved Gems of the Greeks, Etruscans, and Romans.* 2 vols. London: Phaidon, 1968–1971.

Martin Henig

Jupiter triumphant over the hapless Britons on a cameo in Vienna; Julia Domna on a cameo in the British Museum drives the chariot of the goddess Juno-Caelestis, drawn by bulls; and Constantine's chariot on the cameo in the Dutch royal collection, with its centaur mounts, likewise places the emperor in a mythological realm. A sapphire cameo, the largest ancient sapphire known (now in Cambridge, U.K.), is cut with a depiction of Venus, Augustus' supposed divine ancestor, feeding the eagle of imperial power. The purple color of the stone, imported from as far away as Sri Lanka, emphasizes the manner in which the propaganda of these Roman gems was directly derived from that of Hellenistic monarchy.

Most cameos, however, were much more personal in nature and include exquisite representations of Bacchic scenes evoking prosperity; Medusa masks, heads of mime actors, and busts of Minerva, which were all regarded as effective against the baleful influences of the Evil Eye; and love charms, including images of cupid, hands tweaking ears (for remembrance), clasped hands of concord (for betrothal), and mottos, often bantering remarks between lovers with an erotic significance. Such essentially private

CAMP, ROMAN

See Fortifications and Forts; Warfare, *subentry* Roman Warfare.

CANNAE, BATTLE OF

Hannibal's most celebrated victory and Rome's most notorious defeat took place near the Apulian town of Cannae—now Canne della Battaglia—in the summer of 216 BCE. The battle was almost certainly fought on the right bank of the Aufidus River—the modern Ofanto—on a broad and virtually level plain downstream from the hill of Cannae.

In the spring of 216, Hannibal, who had previously won major victories in northern Italy, captured the Roman grain depot at Cannae and gained a dominant position over the Apulian coastal plain. Rome reacted by abandoning the previous year's attrition strategy and sent the consuls, Lucius Aemilius Paullus and Gaius Terentius Varro, with fresh troops to join the army in Apulia. According to Polybius, the combined army of 80,000 infantry and 6,000 cavalry was the largest Rome had ever fielded. This tradition is broadly supported by Appian, Plutarch, and Livy, though Livy also notes an alternative tradition that only 10,000 new troops were raised.

Allowing for the absence of camp guards, perhaps 65,000 Roman infantry and 6,000 cavalry took the field under Varro at Cannae, facing about 40,000 Carthaginian infantry and 10,000 cavalry. Both armies deployed with regular infantry in their centers, cavalry on their wings, and skirmishers in front. The Roman infantry were deployed more deeply and densely than usual, while the Carthaginian infantry were drawn forward at the center in a crescent of alternating units of Spaniards and Celts, with the most experienced Libyans at the crescent's convex horns.

After the initial skirmishing, the Roman infantry pushed forward, slowly driving the convex crescent concave, but falling into confusion and disarray as they advanced into the Carthaginian trap. Meanwhile, the Spanish and Celtic cavalry forced back the Roman cavalry along the river. On routing them, they rode to aid the Numidian cavalry who had been skirmishing with Rome's allied cavalry in the open plain. The allied cavalry fled, pursued by the Numidians. With the Roman cavalry vanquished, the infantry's flanks were exposed, and the Libyans moved forward to attack them, while the Spanish and Celtic cavalry turned to attack the Roman rear. The Romans were surrounded.

The most conservative ancient estimate for the subsequent slaughter has 48,200 Romans being slain and 19,300 being captured, which, if anyway accurate, would represent the highest casualty rate for a single day's fighting in the history of western warfare.

Hannibal has often been criticized for failing to press his victory, but such criticism is surely misplaced, given that it would have taken three weeks for his depleted and exhausted army to march the 250 miles (over 400 kilometers) to Rome, which was heavily fortified and had no shortage of defenders. In any case, his strategy relied on winning decisive victories that would tempt Rome's allies to join him, and although many did so, the core of Rome's Italian confederacy remained loyal. The scale of Hannibal's victory at Cannae may have been paradoxically counterproductive, as it discouraged the Romans from directly confronting him in the field again, depriving him of the propagandist victories and subsequent defections he so desperately needed.

[*See also* Hannibal; Punic Wars; *and* Warfare, *subentry* Roman Warfare.]

BIBLIOGRAPHY

Daly, Gregory. *Cannae: The Experience of Battle in the Second Punic War*. London and New York: Routledge, 2002.

Lazenby, John Francis. *Hannibal's War: A Military History of the Second Punic War*. Warminster, U.K., and New York: Aris and Phillips, 1978.

Gregory Daly

CAPITAL PUNISHMENT

See Punishment.

CAPITALS

Used as the crowning element on a cylindrical or square column, a capital—from Latin *capitulum*, diminutive of *caput*, "head" (Vitruvius *De architectura* 4.1.6)—constitutes one of the most important decorative elements of ancient architectural designs. Most commonly capitals occur in buildings, primarily in temples, but occasionally they also occur as part of pedestals or bases for dedicatory statues or other objects. The history of column capitals is connected with the much-disputed origin of the architectural styles of buildings, a topic referred to by the Roman architect Vitruvius in his work *De architectura*, written in the first century BCE. In his discussion of *genera* (4.2.3), commonly translated as "orders" but more correctly as "types," Vitruvius attributes the origin of the superstructure of temples, including columns and capitals, to the use of wood, which was gradually replaced by stone in the earliest Doric temples, dated circa 600 BCE. Other theories propose a gradual development of forms, originating with Bronze Age Mycenaean architecture—for example, the Lion Gate and the Treasury of Atreus—or a more sudden influence from Egyptian architecture in the late seventh century BCE.

Greek Types of Capitals. Based on Vitruvius' account, there are three main types of capitals: Doric (*De architectura* 4.3), consisting of a square abacus or "slab" and a round echinus or "cushion"; Ionic (3.5), characterized by a pair of curved volutes; and Corinthian (4.1), bell-shaped with rows of acanthus leaves. Variations include the Aeolic capital, sometimes called "proto-Ionic," which combines a pair of vertical volutes with a palmette; the Tuscan capital, similar to the Doric, with a square abacus and a round echinus, which includes both the original Etruscan capital and its Roman adaptation; and the Composite capital, which combines the Ionic and the Corinthian.

Whereas the capitals formed an integral part of the structure of a building, providing the transition from the vertical columns to the entablature and the roof, the decorative elements of the capital's different forms are used to identify the style and chronology of the building, as well as its geographical context. Thus the Doric temple of Hera at Olympia, built around 600 BCE, was described by the Greek traveler Pausanias in the second century CE as still containing one wooden column—and presumably capital? (*Tour of Greece* 5.16.1)—whereas the Doric temple of Apollo at Bassae (430–400 BCE) added both Ionic and Corinthian capitals. Examples of the Aeolic capitals come from Larissa and Neandria in Asia Minor, where the style flourished in the sixth century BCE and spread over to the Greek mainland, where it

continued to be used primarily on columns supporting statuary.

Characteristic for the capitals used in buildings on the Greek mainland is that the primary styles (Doric, Ionic, Corinthian) display a gradual change of proportions and execution of details such as the rounded and curved moldings, and these changes serve to establish a fairly secure dating. On the other hand, the Greek temples in Magna Graecia, including both southern Italy and Sicily, express different traditions, perhaps influenced by Etruscan and Italic architecture. Most conspicuous is the overall difference in scale between contemporary mainland temples, such as the temple of Zeus at Olympia and the Parthenon in Athens compared to the temples at Paestum, Agrigento, and Selinus.

Etruscan and Roman Types of Capitals. Similarly, in the Etruscan area of Italy the form and decoration of column capitals reflect a variety of traditions, some perhaps Greek, others local. Thus Etruscan rock-cut tombs such as the Tomb of the Doric Columns at Cerveteri (Caere), dated to the sixth century BCE, preserve columns crowned by capitals that resemble the Greek Doric, but with proportions that are decidedly non-Greek. Likewise, forms such as the Aeolic capitals occur in tombs, also at Cerveteri, ranging in date from the sixth to the third century BCE (Tomb of the Capitals, Tomb of the Reliefs). Here as in other areas of Etruscan art, styles seem to be local and regional rather than chronological.

In Etruscan architecture, column capitals with a characteristic Etruscan round molding and of non-Greek proportions represent one aspect of what Vitruvius refers to as the "Tuscan" style (4.7.1–5; a more correct translation of his term *Tuscanicus* would be "Tuscan-like," or "derived from Tuscan," as in Etruscan). Although his description probably refers to buildings contemporary with his lifetime (first century BCE) rather than to Etruscan monuments of the Archaic period (sixth century BCE) or later, characteristic of both styles is the rounded echinus on which rests the square abacus. The best-preserved capitals come from rock-cut tombs, whereas the evidence from Etruscan monumental buildings, including temples, is scarce. In some cases it is also not clear whether a fragment with an Etruscan round should be interpreted as a column base or a capital (as seen in examples from Rome, Pompeii, and Minturnae).

Because of its location in Italy between the Greek colonies in the south and the Etruscan cities to the north, the ancient city of Rome found itself at the crossroads of architectural traditions. It is therefore not surprising that the column capitals preserved on Roman buildings reflect a continued use of the Greek Doric, Ionic, and Corinthian types of capitals, but with the addition of the Tuscan and Composite capitals. Of these, the Roman architects seem to have combined the Doric and the Tuscan into a distinctive unit that, unlike Greek Doric, included a column base, used by itself or in the lowest tier of tall buildings such as amphitheaters (for example, the Colosseum). Placed over the Tuscan, the Ionic type gained a fixed position in Roman buildings such as the Theater of Marcellus and the Colosseum, but it is also found in temples in Rome and Tivoli and in the basilica at Pompeii.

It was, however, the Corinthian capital and its more elaborate form, the Composite, that came to dominate all of Roman architecture; according to Wilson, "Corinthian is the Roman order." Whether its invention should be credited to a nurse in Corinth who placed a basket on top of an acanthus plant in memory of a young girl, as told by Vitruvius (*De architectura* 4.1.9), is questionable, but this capital's possibilities, both architectural and symbolic, were endless. By the time of Augustus the use of the Corinthian capital was well established in Rome itself, and from there spread throughout the empire, to Baalbek in the east, to Sabratha and Leptis Magna in Libya, and to Bath in England.

[*See also* Sculpture, Architectural.]

BIBLIOGRAPHY

Coulton, J. J. *Ancient Greek Architects at Work: Problems of Structure and Design.* Ithaca, N.Y.: Cornell University Press, 1977. A discussion of building technique and architectural tradition.

Meritt, Lucy T. Shoe, and Ingrid E. M. Edlund-Berry. *Etruscan and Republican Roman Mouldings.* Philadelphia: University Museum, University of Pennsylvania, for the American Academy in Rome, 2000. First published in 1965 as vol. 28 of the Memoirs of the American Academy in Rome. A study of architectural details used to determine location and geographical distribution within ancient Italy.

Vitruvius. *Ten Books on Architecture.* Translated by Ingrid D. Rowland; commentary and illustrations by Thomas N. Howe. Cambridge, U.K., and New York: Cambridge University Press, 1999. A recent translation of *De architectura*, with important analysis and commentary.

Wilson Jones, Mark. *Principles of Roman Architecture.* New Haven, Conn.: Yale University Press, 2000. An analysis of Roman architectural design and its influence on the Renaissance.

Ingrid E. M. Edlund-Berry

CAPPADOCIA

Cappadocia is a region in central Asia Minor bounded on the west by the Halys River, on the south by Mount Taurus, on the east by the Euphrates River, and on the north by Galatia and Pontus. Cappadocia was of cardinal strategic importance as it was crossed by major highways connecting western Asia Minor with Persia, Syria, and Mesopotamia.

During the period of Persian domination, Cappadocia was ruled through two satrapies, governed by a line of hereditary satraps, who claimed descent from one of the seven companions of Darius I. After the fall of the Persian Empire, Ariarathes I, the satrap of Cappadocia, resisted Alexander and his generals. Perdiccas defeated and executed him. Thereafter Cappadocia came into possession of various generals and successors of Alexander.

Sometime in the 270s Ariaramnes, a grandson of Ariarathes I, regained control of Cappadocia and minted coins. In about 255 BCE his son and successor Ariarathes III declared his independence and assumed the title of king, founding the Ariarathid dynasty, which lasted until 96 BCE. The Ariarathids came to terms with the Seleucids and pursued a pro-Seleucid policy, marrying the daughters of the Seleucid kings. Ariarathes IV supported Antiochus III against the Romans at Magnesia in 190 BCE, but he and his successors wisely adopted pro-Roman policies thereafter. The next Cappadocian king, Ariarathes V (r. 163–130 BCE), was a notorious philhellene. He was educated at Athens, received Athenian citizenship, and corresponded with his tutor, the philosopher Carneades. He also sponsored Greek games both in Cappadocia and in Athens. Most important, he founded cities that had quintessential features of Greek civic life: city councils, civic cults, festivals, and gymnasiums. The philhellene Cappadocian ruler died fighting on the side of Romans against Aristonicus. His successors Ariarathes VI and VII were assassinated by the intrigues of the king of Pontus, Mithradates the Great (r. 120–63 BCE), who installed his own son on the Cappadocian throne and killed the last Ariarathid, ending the old royal family. Finally the Romans expelled Mithradates' son and declared Cappadocia free in 96 BCE. When the Cappadocians asked for a ruler ("for they were unable to bear freedom," according to Strabo), the Romans put Ariobarzanes, a native Cappadocian noble, on the throne. The Ariobarzanids ruled until 36 BCE, mostly trying to defend themselves against Mithradates and his son-in-law Tigranes of Armenia. Antony finally ended Ariobarzanid rule when it proved ineffective in his Parthian campaign and appointed Archelaus as king of Cappadocia (36 BCE). Archelaus appears to have been an energetic and effective ruler who controlled his realm for more than a half century. When he died in Rome, where he was being tried, Tiberius annexed Cappadocia and appointed an equestrian prefect to govern it in 17 CE.

Of the three native royal families, it was the Ariarathids who tried to spread Greek culture in their realm. Since, however, Cappadocia proper had no access to the sea, which meant the curtailment of the presence of Greeks and Greek culture, urbanization and Hellenization did not really penetrate the whole country. Cappadocia remained a world of villages and tribes.

[See also Anatolia.]

BIBLIOGRAPHY

Cohen, Getzel M. *The Hellenistic Settlements in Europe, the Islands, and Asia Minor.* Berkeley: University of California Press, 1995.

Jones, A. H. M. *Cities of the Eastern Roman Provinces.* 2nd ed. Oxford: Clarendon Press, 1971.

Mehmet Fatih Yavuz

CAPRI

Capri (Greek, Kapríe or Kapriai; Latin, Capreae), the southern of the two major islands that help form the Bay of Naples (Ischia is the other island), is a craggy calcareous island about four miles (six kilometers) long, two miles (three kilometers) wide, and ten miles (sixteen kilometers) in circumference (Pliny *Natural History* 3.83), with one large harbor facing north. Capri is only about three miles (five kilometers) from Sorrento, to which it was joined during the Paleolithic period. The island is best known for its famous resident the emperor Tiberius, who lived there from 27 CE until his death in 37.

In contrast to the island of Ischia, Capri has not revealed significant archaeological material illuminating early Greek colonization in the West. But ceramic, epigraphic, and literary evidence suggests that Capri played a role in the important maritime trade of Greeks, Phoenicians, and Italic peoples along the Italian coast from the seventh century at the latest, when the Greek colony of Cumae claimed the island. Two centuries later Capri was part of the territory of Naples, in which status it remained until the early Augustan period. Then, purportedly because Augustus had received a propitious omen on the island, the emperor acquired Capri as imperial property from Naples in exchange for Ischia. He frequented Capri and its adjacencies (Suetonius *Divus Augustus* 92, 98; Cassius Dio 52.43; Strabo 5.4.9), and it remained in imperial hands, with its curious fossils (Suetonius *Divus Augustus* 72.3), picturesque grottoes, and various summits including the sites of the modern cities of Capri and Anacapri (at, respectively, 466 feet or 142 meters and 932 feet or 284 meters above sea level).

The island was damaged by the eruption of Vesuvius in 79 CE. More than a century later Commodus' wife, Crispina, and his sister, Lucilla, were exiled here (Cassius Dio 72.4). The scarce inscriptions indicate that Greek was the predominant language and that most inhabitants were imperial dependents. A suspect document holds that Capri was donated to the Abbey of Montecassino in the sixth century.

The archaeology of Capri is problematic. Intense antiquarian and tourist interest since the eighteenth century has caused many ancient structures and objects to be reused or exported without sufficient archaeological scrutiny: the Villa San Michele, for example, rises on a late Republican structure in Anacapri, and the early imperial Villa Damecuta and Palazzo a Mare are damaged because of Bourbon and British fortifications on Capri's northwest corner and at Marina Grande. When Tiberius withdrew to Capri in 27—drawn by its balmy climate, spectacular views, Greek background, and seclusion—his isolation generated rumors including that he constructed twelve dwellings to accommodate his vices (Suetonius *Tiberius* 39–41; Tacitus *Annales* 4.57–58, 67). In the 1930s Amadeo Maiuri excavated some seventy-five thousand square feet (seven thousand square meters) of an extensive villa on Capri's northeastern promontory. Now called Tiberius' Villa Jovis, this early imperial structure comprises cisterns, baths, reception areas, private rooms with panoramic views, service quarters, and a lighthouse. Popular identification of Tiberius with other remains is less archaeologically justifiable.

Geology and natural beauty encouraged the construction of various Roman nymphaea, including in the Grotta Azzura (Blue Grotto) and on the south side of the island (the so-called Matromania). Most of these and other archaeological sites are not protected, and no public museum has yet been built.

[*See also* Tiberius.]

BIBLIOGRAPHY

De Caro, Stefano, and Angelo Greco. *Campania*. Guide Archeologiche Laterza, 10. 2nd ed. Rome and Bari, Italy: Laterza, 1993.

Federico, Edouardo, and Elena Miranda. *Capri antica dalla preistoria alla fine dell'età romana*. Capri, Italy: Edizioni La Conchiglia, 1998.

Mary T. Boatwright

CARACALLA

(Marcus Aurelius Antoninus; Septimius Bassianus, 188–217 CE), Roman emperor (4 February 211–8 April 217). Caracalla was born (Lucius?) Septimius Bassianus in Lugdunum (Lyon, France) on 4 April 188. At age seven—as Caracalla's father, the emperor Septimius Severus (r. 193–211), consolidated his authority—Caracalla was renamed Marcus Aurelius Antoninus after the emperors Antoninus Pius (r. 138–161) and Marcus Aurelius (r. 161–180). The nickname "Caracalla," which refers to a hooded cloak popular in Gaul, was used by writers to distinguish this emperor from his namesake, though in official documents his name is always given as Marcus Aurelius Antoninus.

Caracalla was designated as Severus' heir from the time of his name change and shortly thereafter was officially promoted to the rank of Augustus. In 202 the young teenager was married to Plautilla, the daughter of the Praetorian prefect Plautianus. Caracalla disliked his wife, and they had no children. Caracalla divorced Plautilla in 205 after he had her father executed.

Caracalla and his younger brother Publius Septimius Geta accompanied their father on campaign in Britain, where Geta was himself promoted to Augustus. The rivalry between the brothers was bitter and did not improve after Severus' death in York on 4 February 211. Both brothers theoretically had equal authority, but the twenty-two-year-old Caracalla—who was eleven months older than Geta—expected deference from his brother. The brothers returned to Rome, but their quarrels brought government to a standstill. Caracalla had Geta killed in late December 211, and a violent purge of Geta's supporters was carried out. With his sole authority firmly established, Caracalla authorized important changes in government operations, including increased pay and privileges to soldiers and bestowal of Roman citizenship on all free residents of the empire.

Caracalla spent most of the rest of his reign outside Rome, visiting Gaul in 213 and leading a military campaign in southern Germany. The following year he embarked on a journey to the East for a war against the Parthians. Along the way the emperor displayed an increasing fascination with Alexander III of Macedon (Alexander the Great).

Roman armies faced little opposition as they marched through the tottering Parthian Empire. Edessa and its hinterland were annexed as the Roman province of Osroene, and Caracalla used the rebuff of his offer to marry the Parthian emperor's daughter as an excuse to sack the cities of Mesopotamia. Caracalla also used his time in the East to cultivate a growing interest in religion, including participation in the rites of the temple of Asclepius in Pergamum and the temple of Serapis in Alexandria. Caracalla may also be the Antoninus mentioned in the Talmud engaging in discussions with the Jewish rabbinic leader Judah haNasi. A visit to the temple of the moon god near Carrhae occasioned the emperor's assassination on 8 April 217. A rogue bodyguard was officially blamed, though Caracalla's successor as emperor, the Praetorian prefect Macrinus, was suspected of arranging the murder.

Contemporaries were critical of Caracalla's reign, particularly the killing of his brother Geta. Moralizing about fratricide has obscured the influence of the emperor's policies. Universal citizenship and the increased importance of soldiers became characteristic features of the Roman Empire in the third century and beyond.

[*See also* Antonine Family and Dynasty; Citizenship, Roman; Elagabalus; Praetorian Guard; *and* Septimius Severus.]

BIBLIOGRAPHY

Birley, Anthony Richard. *Septimius Severus: The African Emperor.* Rev. ed. New Haven, Conn.: Yale University Press, 1988.

Meckler, Michael. "Caracalla and His Late-Antique Biographer: A Historical Commentary on the 'Vita Caracalli' in the *Historia Augusta*." PhD diss., University of Michigan, 1994.

Michael Meckler

CARIA

The region known as Caria was a mountainous land in southwest Asia Minor, bounded on the north by Lydia and Ionia, on the northeast by Phrygia, on the east by Lycia, and on the south and the west by the Mediterranean and the Aegean Sea, respectively. Caria was of strategic importance: first, it controlled a key maritime route between the Aegean and the Mediterranean, and second, the Maeander valley, which divided Caria from Ionia, was an important corridor connecting the Aegean coast and inland Anatolia.

Caria was inhabited by two major ethnic groups, the Carians and the Greeks. The Carians' origin is unknown. Like Greek, Carian is an Indo-European language, but its relationship to other Anatolian languages is not clear. The Carians claimed that they were indigenous, though the Greek historians, including Herodotus and Thucydides, insist that they migrated from the Aegean islands in the second millennium BCE. The Greeks colonized coastal Caria toward the end of the second millennium BCE. The Carians lived mostly in hilltop settlements in the interior, centered around religious sanctuaries, and were ruled by native dynasts until the fourth century BCE. They also intermingled with the Greeks living on the coast of Caria. Extensive use of Carian personal names attested in classical Halicarnassus suggest peaceful, intimate relations between the Greeks and the native Carians. In fact Herodotus, the "father of history," was half Carian and half Greek.

The Carians who lived on the coast were experienced seamen. Herodotus mentions a famous Carian explorer, Scylax of Caryanda, who explored the Indus for Darius. The Carians were also proverbial fighters and soldiers. Since their land was not rich in agricultural resources, the Carians turned to mercenary service, hiring themselves out to the Near Eastern powers such as the Lydians and Egyptians. Above all, the Carian mercenaries served the pharaohs of the Twenty-sixth Dynasty in Egypt where they were settled in garrison towns. The ancient Greeks believed that the Carians invented the crest and shield handles, and that they were the first recorded mercenaries. A Greek proverb reveals how the Carians were perceived by others: "We shall let the Carian [mercenaries] take our risks," that is, let someone else face danger in our place.

Since the Carians lacked political unity, they were first conquered by the Lydians and then by the Persians in 545 BCE. After the Persian Wars, some of the Carian communities joined the Delian League in 478 BCE, though the inland Carian communities were still under Persian rule. The Athenian general Cimon's victory at the battle of the river Eurymedon in 469 BCE persuaded many other Carian communities to join the Delian League. However, the Athenian Tribute Lists suggest that by 440 the Athenians were losing the loyalties of inland Carian communities, perhaps as a result of Persian machinations. In 428 BCE the Athenian general Lysicles made an expedition to inland Caria to collect tribute, but he was attacked and killed by the Carians. Thereafter, inland Caria once again came under Persian control. The famous Persian satrap Tissaphernes had estates in northern Caria, and he appears to have controlled Caria as a satrap dependent on the satrapy of Sardis.

About 492 BCE, after the execution of Tissaphernes, the Persians made Caria an independent satrapy and entrusted it to Hecatomnus, the local dynast of Mylasa, whose ancestors appear in the pages of Herodotus. Under the rule of Hecatomnus and his children, Caria reached its zenith in the fourth century BCE. The most important member of the family was Hecatomnus' son Mausolus (r. 377–353 BCE). He gained control of Rhodes, Cos, and Chios, and became a prominent international figure joining the Great Satraps' Revolt and instigating the Social War of 357 BCE. He founded several cities, moved the capital of his dynasty from inland Mylasa to Halicarnassus on the coast, and accelerated the Hellenization of his country. His monumental tomb at Halicarnassus, the Mausoleum, was considered one of the Seven Wonders of the ancient world.

The Hecatomnid rule continued even after the conquest of Caria by Alexander the Great in 334 BCE. Alexander appointed Ada, one of the children of Hecatomnus, as satrap of Caria. After the death of Alexander, Caria became a bone of contention among the Seleucids, the Ptolemies, and the Rhodians. Epigraphic evidence shows that these powers founded a number settlements in Caria to bolster and secure their claim over the region. After the battle of Magnesia, Romans gave Caria to Rhodes. After the battle of Pydna (168 BCE), however, the Romans declared Caria free to punish Rhodians who displayed lukewarm support during the Third Macedonian War. When the Romans created their first province in Asia Minor in 129 BCE, Caria became part of the Roman province of Asia.

[*See also* Anatolia; Aphrodisias; *and* Cnidus.]

BIBLIOGRAPHY

Fraser, P. M., and G. E. Bean. *The Rhodian Peraea and Islands.* London: Oxford University Press, 1954.

Hornblower, Simon. *Mausolus.* Oxford: Clarendon Press; New York: Oxford University Press, 1982.

Ruzicka, Stephen. *Politics of a Persian Dynasty: The Hecatomnids in the Fourth Century B.C.* Norman: University of Oklahoma Press, 1992.

Mehmet Fatih Yavuz

CARTHAGE

Located on the Gulf of Tunis in what is now Tunisia, Carthage—Phoenician *Qart Hadasht* (New City), Greek *Karchēdōn*, Latin *C/Karthago*—was founded, according to legend, by Queen Elissa-Dido of the Phoenician city of Tyre (in present-day Lebanon) in 814 BCE. To date, however, archaeological evidence places the layout of formal sectors of the city, such as funerary, domestic, and religious zones, to the second half of the eighth century BCE. Three known necropoleis point to a sizable population already in the seventh century BCE; this growth is attributable to Carthage's ideal situation for controlling trade networks to the west, particularly for the acquisition of gold, silver, and tin.

Economy. Carthage established a strong naval fleet in order to protect its trading interests; circa 535 BCE it formed an alliance with the Etruscans to block the Phocaeans' trading settlement on Corsica. Naval power was also instrumental in territorial expansion; by the end of the fifth century BCE, neighboring coastal towns as well as Sardinia and the western part of Sicily were in Carthaginian hands, although control of Sicily was contested by the Greeks and Carthaginians down to the third century BCE. Carthage maintained ties with its mother city, Tyre, particularly by sending annual tribute to its patron god, Melqart, but when the Assyrians overtook Tyre in the early sixth century BCE, Carthage became the key Punic (from Latin *Poenus*, "Phoenician") center of the Mediterranean. Outside of formal Carthaginian territory, Carthaginian politics and culture influenced the inhabitants of the coast of North Africa from Libya to Morocco and into southern Spain.

The Phoenician colonists had originally agreed to pay the local Africans an annual tribute in exchange for the land where they established Carthage. This obligation ended in the sixth or fifth century BCE when the Carthaginians gained control of the interior, including the fertile Bagradas (Medjerda) River Valley. Carthaginian skill in agriculture was renowned; the works of the agronomist Mago were even translated into Greek and Latin. The main crops—grains, olives, and fruits, including grapes and figs—were produced in part on estates owned by wealthy citizens of Carthage and grown for both local consumption and sale abroad. Other exports included textiles, worked ivory, pottery, and jewelry.

Economic status was a key component of the Punic city's political system, which seems to have been based on a hereditary oligarchy. At its head were two leaders, in Latin called *suf(f)etes* (singular *suf(f)es*), who were elected annually based on wealth and merit. They were assisted by the Council of Elders, a deliberative assembly of some antiquity,

and as of the early fourth century they were held in check by a tribunal known as the One Hundred and Four. The People's Assembly was additionally responsible for electing war leaders. Aristocratic status also seems to have been the basis of human sacrifice to the Carthaginian god, Baʿal Hammon, and his consort Tanit. Modern scholars have long debated whether reports of child sacrifice by immolation were the propaganda of hostile Greek and Roman writers, but written evidence from the Near East and archaeological evidence from Punic settlements including Carthage strongly suggest that leading citizens were obliged to offer a child or an animal substitute in order to appease their gods.

Carthage and Rome. The city's political and economic growth rivaled that of Rome, with which Carthage signed treaties governing zones of influence and trade in 509 and 348 BCE; the two cities were allies against Pyrrhus in his invasions of Italy and Sicily in the early 270s BCE. However, the dominance of these two central Mediterranean powers was drawing them inexorably toward conflict. Carthage unsuccessfully fought three so-called Punic Wars against Rome and faced harsh war reparations after each defeat, beginning with the loss of Sicily, Sardinia, and Corsica after the First Punic War (264–241 BCE). Carthage's problems in dealing with unpaid mercenaries after that conflict were dramatized by Gustave Flaubert in his novel *Salammbô* (1862). After Hannibal's defeat in the Second Punic War (218–201 BCE), the Numidian king Masinissa took advantage of his alliance with Rome to infringe on Carthaginian territory. Carthage's need to defend against this threat, combined with the contention of a conservative faction at Rome that Carthage must be destroyed, precipitated the outbreak of the Third Punic War in 149 BCE. In 146, Scipio Aemilianus captured Carthage, which was then plundered, destroyed, and placed under a curse that it never again be inhabited. The further story that the Romans sowed Carthage under with salt to render its soil infertile is a modern fabrication, although a ceremonial plowing ritual may have taken place.

Despite the curse, Carthage's location and the agricultural productivity of its hinterland were too significant for the Romans to ignore. Only a quarter of a century after the Punic city's destruction, Gaius Sempronius Gracchus proposed the creation of the *colonia* Junonia near the ancient site, but political intrigue at home prevented the execution of more than preparatory surveying. Julius Caesar revived the idea, which was then carried to fruition under Augustus in 29 BCE. The Colonia Iulia Concordia Karthago became the capital of the Roman province of Africa Proconsularis and, thanks to Rome's dependence on its grain, also became one of the most important and most populous imperial cities. At its height in the second century CE, Carthage's imperial-style baths were being supplied with water via the longest-known aqueduct, from Zaghouan (ancient Ziqua), some 82 miles (132 kilometers) away. It was at Carthage that Gordian I first asserted and then lost his claim as Roman emperor in 238 CE.

A strong Christian community was well established in Carthage by the third century; its members included Tertullian, Cyprian, and Augustine. The schismatic Donatist church arose out of controversy over the powerful Carthaginian bishopric in the early fourth century. Despite the construction of heavy fortification walls, the city was captured by the Vandals in 439, then fell a century later to Byzantine forces. After the Arab conquest of 698, the adjacent site of Tunis displaced Carthage as the focal point of the region.

[*See also* Archaeology, *subentry* Sites in North Africa; Hannibal; Phoenicia; Punic Wars; Rome, *subentry* Early Rome and the Republic; *and* Vandals.]

BIBLIOGRAPHY

Aubet, María Eugenia. *The Phoenicians and the West: Politics, Colonies, and Trade.* Translated by Mary Turton. Cambridge, U.K.: Cambridge University Press, 1993. An English translation of *Tiro y las colonias fenicias de Occidente*, first published in 1987.

Lancel, Serge. *Carthage: A History.* Translated by Antonia Nevill. Oxford: Blackwell, 1995. An English translation of *Carthage*, first published in 1992.

Ridley, R. T. "To Be Taken with a Pinch of Salt: The Destruction of Carthage." *Classical Philology* 81 (1986): 140–146.

Rives, J. B. *Religion and Authority in Roman Carthage from Augustus to Constantine.* Oxford: Clarendon Press; New York: Oxford University Press, 1995.

Jennifer P. Moore

CASSANDRA

Although early accounts of the Cassandra story vary in their details, the myth eventually coalesces around a standard narrative: daughter of Priam and Hecuba, she was a prophetess who could never be fully understood or heeded. As the common story goes, she received the gift of prophecy from Apollo in return for promises of sexual favors; when she reneged on her promises, he caused that her prophesies would never be believed. After the war, she was dragged from the altar of Athena by Ajax, son of Oileus, and chosen to be the war-prize of Agamemnon; finally, she met her death at the hands of Clytemnestra and Aegisthus when she arrived at the palace in Argos as Agamemnon's concubine.

It is clear that her prophetic powers were a feature of the epic tradition, since the *Cypria* mentions this aspect of her myth. However, the *Iliad* overlooks her prophetic aspect, stressing instead that she was the most beautiful of Priam's daughters (*Iliad* 13.365). The *Iliu Persis* mentions the story of Ajax dragging her from the altar. Scholia to the *Iliad* preserve hints of another story: that, as children, she and her brother Helenus received their prophetic powers when they were licked by Apollo's sacred serpents. However, this account does not appear elsewhere; instead, it is the story of Cassandra pursued and punished by Apollo that predominates, and she comes to embody the prophet of doom whom no one will credit. So in Aeschylus' *Agamemnon* (1072–1330), Cassandra stands before the palace in Argos, foretelling her imminent death and that of Agamemnon, but the chorus of elders claim they cannot or must not believe her. In Euripides' *Trojan Women*, her prophesies regarding her death and

Odysseus' homecoming are dismissed as the ravings of a mad woman, and the chorus in Euripides' *Andromache* allude to the story that she warned to no avail that the infant Paris was destined to be a destructive force. The *Alexandra*, a long poem by the Hellenistic writer Lycophron, is largely constructed as a prophetic recitation by Cassandra of Troy's history and the fates of the heroes in the aftermath of the war, the tragic tone underscored by Cassandra's awareness that she will not be believed. Finally, Virgil exploits her image in *Aeneid* 2, as Cassandra warns the Trojans about the danger even as they bring the Trojan horse inside the gates of the city, again to no avail (246–247); later, she is dragged from the temple of Athena, "turning her eyes to the heavens in vain" since the Greeks have bound her hands (403–407). Scenes of Cassandra being dragged by Ajax from the altar of Athena were especially popular in the visual arts of both Greece and Rome.

The figure of Cassandra has inspired numerous artists using classical motifs; in the twentieth century, the German author Christa Wolf wrote *Cassandra*, a feminist meditation on war that reworked the story of the Trojan War from the perspective of Cassandra, suggesting that Cassandra symbolized the suppression of women's voices and rejection of women's perceptiveness.

[See also Priam and Hecuba; Trojan War; and Women, *subentry* Women in Greek Literature.]

BIBLIOGRAPHY

P.G. Mason, "Kassandra," *Journal of Hellenic Studies* 79 (1959): 80–93; Joan Breton Connelly, "Narrative and Image in Attic Vase Painting: Ajax and Kassandra at the Trojan Palladion," in *Narrative and Event in Ancient Art*, edited by Peter J. Holliday (Cambridge, U.K., and New York: Cambridge University Press, 1993): 88–129; Orazio Paoletti, "Kassandra," *Lexicon Iconographicum Mythologiae Classicae* 7.1 956–970.

Jennifer Clarke Kosak

CASSIUS DIO

See Historiography, Latin.

CASSIUS

(Gaius Cassius Longinus, ?80 BCE–42 BCE), leader, with Marcus Junius Brutus, of the senatorial conspiracy that assassinated Julius Caesar. As quaestor in 54 he went on Marcus Licinius Crassus' disastrous expedition into Mesopotamia, but salvaged his troops from the defeat at Carrhae and stayed on in Syria as proquaestor. In 51, deputizing for the incoming governor, Cassius successfully repelled a Parthian raid. As tribune of the Plebs in 49 (with his kinsman Quintus Cassius Longinus, also tribune in 49, who took refuge with Caesar in Gaul, alleging violation of his sacrosanctity), Cassius fought for Pompey and the republicans, serving as a naval commander against Caesar. After the defeat of Pharsalus in 48, he sought and received pardon from Caesar and on Caesar's nomination was *praetor peregrinus* in 44. In the nominal amnesty and uneasy standoff after Caesar's assassination, Cassius was afraid to preside over the funeral games at Rome and withdrew to Antium. Through his mother-in-law, Servilia's, machinations he and Brutus were transferred from nominal provinces, Cassius receiving the unarmed province of Cyrene and Brutus Crete. Instead Cassius went to Syria and Brutus to Macedonia, where they levied ruthless taxation and raised armies. Despite Cicero's attempts to reconcile the parties, Cassius and Brutus faced the armies of Octavius Caesar and Mark Antony at Philippi in August 42. Cassius was the first to be defeated and committed suicide.

Our main sources besides Appian's *Civil War*, book 2, are Plutarch's Life of Brutus and Cassius' correspondence with Cicero: five letters between 51 and 46 from Cicero to Cassius (15.14–18), with one reply from Cassius joking about his interest in Epicurean physics and optics (*Epistulae ad Familiares* 15.19), then after the assassination ten letters of political information and advice from Cicero up to July 43, with three lively and diplomatic replies (*Epistulae ad familiares* 12.11–13) from Cassius himself.

[See also Brutus, Marcus Junius; Crassus; Julius Caesar; and Philippi, Battle of.]

BIBLIOGRAPHY

Osgood, Josiah. *Caesar's Legacy: Civil War and the Emergence of the Roman Empire.* Cambridge, U.K., and New York: Cambridge University Press, 2004.

Syme, Ronald. *The Roman Revolution.* Oxford: Oxford University Press, 1939, often reprinted.

Elaine Fantham

CASTOR AND POLLUX

Castor and Pollux are twin heroes of Greek and Roman myth who are known in Greek as the Tyndaridae, in post-Homeric sources as the Dioscuri (from *Dios kouroi,* "sons of Zeus"), and in Latin as the Gemini ("twins").

The parentage of Castor and Pollux (Polydeuces in Greek) varies with the source. Their mother was Leda, the wife of King Tyndareus of Sparta; she bore several other children, among whom were Helen, the wife of Menelaus, and Clytemnestra, the wife of Agamemnon. In the *Iliad,* Castor and Pollux are referred to as the sons of Tyndareus, and both have died by the time of the Trojan War, but in later sources (for example, Pindar *Nemean Odes* 10; Apollodorus 3.10.7; *Homeric Hymn to the Dioscuri* [33]) Pollux, like Helen, is the child of Zeus, who coupled with Leda while in the form of a swan. Some accounts say that both Castor and Pollux were the sons of Zeus and were hatched from an egg. One brother, Castor, was mortal, while Pollux was immortal—a fact that becomes significant later in their story.

As the sons of Tyndareus, the brothers were especially venerated in Sparta, where they had numerous shrines, including one known as the Menelaion where Castor and Pollux, as well as Helen and Menelaus, were said to be buried. Although they did not fight at Troy to retrieve their sister Helen (see *Iliad* 3.237–242), the brothers did invade Attica to recover her when Theseus abducted her as a child. They also took part in the hunt for the Calydonian Boar and in the voyage of the Argonauts. During the voyage, just as a storm was ceasing, stars appeared on the heads of the twins—thus the twin lights of the phenomenon of Saint Elmo's fire became associated with them, and they became known as patrons of sailors.

Castor and Pollux wanted to marry Phoebe and Hilaeira, the daughters of King Leucippus of Sicyon. Because the young women were already betrothed to Lynceus and Idas, the brothers abducted them (the subject of Peter Paul Rubens's *The Rape of the Daughters of Leucippus*) and carried them off to Sparta, where each of the women bore a son. A fight occurred—either because of the women or over a cattle raid—between Castor and Pollux and Lynceus and Idas, and all except the immortal Pollux were killed. Zeus brought Pollux to Olympus, but Pollux's grief for Castor was so great that he begged Zeus to allow him to share his immortality with his brother. Zeus consented, and each twin lived half of each year on Olympus and half in the underworld; or, as in both Pindar's *Pythian Odes* (11.61–64) and Homer's *Odyssey* (11.300–304), they lived one day on Olympus and the next in the underworld. Zeus finally placed them in the sky as the Gemini, the "heavenly twins."

In addition to the shrines at Sparta, there were temples to the Dioscuri in Athens and in Rome, where they were greatly revered and where a temple of Castor was erected in the Forum in the fifth century BCE. Both of the brothers were associated with horses and have often been portrayed in art as being on horseback. The Roman *equites* regarded Castor and Pollux as their special patrons.

[*See also* Atreus, House of; Gods, Greek, *subentry* Lesser Greek Gods; *and* Jason and the Argonauts.]

BIBLIOGRAPHY

Burkert, Walter. *Greek Religion.* Translated by John Raffan. Cambridge, Mass.: Harvard University Press, 1985.

Grimal, Pierre. *The Dictionary of Classical Mythology.* Translated by A. R. Maxwell-Hyslop. Oxford and New York: Blackwell, 1996.

Kerényi, Karl. *The Heroes of the Greeks.* Translated by H. J. Rose. London: Thames & Hudson, 1959.

Georgia S. Maas

CATACOMBS

The word "catacomb" refers to a subterranean cemetery constructed during the Roman Empire or late antiquity (second to seventh century CE). The word itself originally indicated a specific location for a Christian burial ground *ad catacumbus* ("near the hollows"), probably a pozzolana quarry off the Via Appia near Rome, but the true meaning of the word is impossible to determine.

Although catacombs are also found elsewhere, including Naples, Malta, and Alexandria, most known examples surround the city of Rome, with the largest concentration along the Via Appia to the south. It remains unclear why Roman Christians began using catacombs for interment; they probably borrowed the practice from the city's Jewish communities, whose catacombs replicated earlier Palestinian rock-cut tombs.

Modest catacomb complexes contain only a few hundred burials, while the largest extend for miles, with galleries accommodating thousands of burials on as many as five separate levels. Dug to order, without a centralized plan, adjacent catacombs often were merged to form larger complexes. Those seeking burial space initially exploited abandoned quarries or cisterns; only from the fourth century were catacombs dug systematically following a gridlike "fishbone" plan of long, straight galleries at 90-degree angles. Some catacombs feature our earliest examples of Christian fresco painting, and are thus of particular value to historians of art and of the Christian church.

Burials in catacombs follow a number of architectural types:

- *Loculus* or "slot" burials were used for the poor. Burials are in vertical rows along passageway walls; these *loculi* were closed with slabs—sometimes unmarked, sometimes identified with a painted or (occasionally) incised text—affixed into place with wet clay.
- *Arcosolium* burials are horizontal tombs recessed lengthwise into walls with arch-shaped plastered areas above them for decoration.

- A *cubiculum* (chamber) contains several burials generally of the *arcosolium* type; *cubicula* contained the bodies of an extended family, *collegium*, or a group of clergy (as in the "Crypt of the Popes" in the Catacomb of Callixtus).

A burial might be single or double (*bisomus*); *trisomus* and *quadrisomus* graves are rare. We also find secondary burials (*formae*), sometimes from a later period, sunk directly into the floor. Only a small proportion of catacomb graves were labeled. Occasionally we find other identification markers, including coins, beads, dolls, or animal teeth, set into the grave's seals. Although care was taken to provide respectful and safe disposal of the dead, catacombs do sometimes contain mass graves, presumably from epidemics when gravediggers were overwhelmed. A few cremation burials in urns are also known.

Catacombs contain few areas for public assembly. Airshafts provided minimal ventilation; terra-cotta oil lamps furnished meager light. Remains of perfume ampules suggest that the catacombs smelled foul and were unsuitable gathering places. Although families celebrated funerary meals on cemeterial grounds, it is unlikely that food preparation or consumption would have happened underground. Some catacombs—notably on Malta—have carved dining benches outside *cubicula*, but their use was probably only symbolic, given subterranean conditions. We also find carved *mensae* (dining tables), sometimes with plates affixed. Food offerings were likely placed on these tables, probably as a variation on the ancient Roman practice of pouring oil or wine down libation tubes to the deceased. Graves with such libation tubes still exist in the catacombs.

According to ecclesiastical sources, one major Roman catacomb, Saint Callixtus, came to be administered by the city's clergy in the third century, becoming a burial site for many church leaders. A guild of gravediggers (*fossores*) dug and sold burial plots to individuals. Under Pope Fabian (236–250) other catacombs were associated with the seven administrative districts of Rome and their *tituli*; thus each *titulus* church ("inscribed" with a signal honor) had a corresponding suburban burial ground. However, Christians presumably could choose to be buried at the site of their choice, and it is likely that despite the claims of our Christian sources, bureaucratic organization and administration of Rome's catacombs really happened only in the early fifth century or later.

Until the early fifth century, catacombs were purely cemeterial, with family members visiting graves on the death anniversary of the deceased and on various other Roman festivals for the dead, such as the Rosalia or the Parentalia. This private cemeterial function was eclipsed in late antiquity by the new interest in martyrs, leading to the renovation of catacombs in decline. The private cemeterial use of catacombs continued, but with a renewed emphasis on the construction of subterranean chapels, *martyria*, and burials of the faithful *ad sanctum* (next to the martyrs' tombs). By the ninth century, the practice of transferring the relics of martyrs into churches led to the gradual abandonment of the catacombs. Christians, free to bury their dead beneath or beside saints' bones in churches, no longer favored catacomb burial.

[*See also* Cemeteries; Christian Art, *subentries* Overview and Egypt; Christianity; Church Fathers; Death, *subentry* Death and Burial in the Ancient World; Funerary Art; *and* Tombs.]

BIBLIOGRAPHY

Bodel, John. "From *Columbaria* to Catacombs: Communities of the Dead in Pagan and Christian Rome." In *Roman Burial and Commemorative Practices and Earliest Christianity*, edited by L. Brink and D. Greene, pp. 177–242. Berlin and New York: Walter de Gruyter, 2008.

Fiocchi Nicolai, Vincenzo, Fabrizio Bisconti, and Danilo Mazzoleni, eds. *The Christian Catacombs of Rome: History, Decoration, Inscriptions*. Leipzig, Germany: Schnell & Steiner, 1999.

Rutgers, Leonard V. *Subterranean Rome: In Search of the Roots of Christianity in the Catacombs of the Eternal City*. Leuven, Belgium: Peeters, 2000.

Nicola Denzey Lewis

CATILINE

(Lucius Sergius Catilina, c. 108–62 BCE), Roman demagogue. A patrician, Lucius Sergius Catilina served under Gnaeus Pompeius Strabo during the Social War of 91–87. Our main sources, the biased evidence of both Cicero and Sallust, reveal an enigmatic first-century BCE aristocrat unscrupulously in pursuit of a successful political career. As Sulla's legate during the civil war of the 80s and the ensuing proscriptions, Catiline acquired a reputation for his involvement with political assassination, proscribing even his brothers-in-law, Marcus Marius Gratidianus and Quintus Caecilius. In 73 Catiline was accused of adultery with the Vestal Fabia, but acquitted.

Catiline was elected praetor in 68 and governed Africa for the following two years. Imminent prosecution for provincial extortion prevented the well-connected Catiline from standing for the consulate during 66 and 65. Cicero initially contemplated speaking for his defense, but withdrew to obtain the *optimates*' support as candidate for the consulship. Despite rumors about a conspiracy to assassinate both incoming consuls for 65, Catiline was acquitted, allegedly assisted by his prosecutor, Publius Clodius Pulcher.

During 64 Catiline and Cicero were rivals for the consulate of the following year. Cicero, supported by wealthy equestrians who opposed Catiline's policy of debt cancellation, defeated him. Catiline also failed to win the support of the poor and politically disgruntled in the next campaign. In October, amid rumors that a frustrated Catiline was plotting violent sedition, Cicero charged him with treason, persuading the senate to pass an ultimate decree (*senates consultum ultimum*) outlawing Catiline. Early in November Cicero delivered his first Catilinarian oration, whereupon Catiline fled Rome to take command of an uprising in Etruria. The senate declared Catiline a public enemy, and on the evidence of Allobrogan envoys, the remaining leaders of the conspiracy were arrested and executed. Republican forces defeated Catiline in battle at

Pistoria, where he perished bravely at the hands of Marcus Petreius.

[*See also* Cicero, *subentry* Life of Cicero; Cato the Younger; Clodius; Crassus; Rome, *subentry* Early Rome and the Republic; *and* Sulla.]

BIBLIOGRAPHY

Sallust. *Catiline's War, The Jugurthine War, Histories.* Translated by A. J. Woodman. London and New York: Penguin, 2007.

Wilkins, Ann T. *Villain or Hero: Sallust's Portrayal of Catiline.* New York: Peter Lang, 1994.

Maridien Schneider

CATO THE ELDER

(Marcus Porcius Cato, 234–149 BCE), Roman public and literary figure. Called "the Elder" or "the Censor" to distinguish him from his great-grandson Cato of Utica, Caesar's unbending opponent, Cato ranks among the most significant (and problematic) figures of the middle Republic. Facts and fictions concerning him can be difficult to distinguish. His public career is fairly well documented. What Romans called a "new man" (*novus homo*), that is, the first of his family to enter the senate, Cato served with distinction in the war against Hannibal before launching a political career under the patronage of Lucius Valerius Flaccus. He governed Sardinia as praetor in 198, reached the consulship (with Flaccus) in 195, and the Censorship (again with Flaccus as colleague) in 184. His extraordinary rise was clearly the result of extraordinary ability. A highly competent soldier—he celebrated a triumph for his success in Spain as consul and proconsul— Cato contributed to important military victories from the Metaurus in 207, where Livius Salinator prevented a Carthaginian army from reinforcing Hannibal, to the defeat of Antiochus III at Thermopylae in 191, which ended Seleucid adventurism in the west. Cato's censorship was famously contentious. He and Flaccus together exercised their responsibilities with rigorous honesty, punishing even prominent figures for their peccadilloes and advancing an aggressively moral social agenda. Always scrupulous in the letting of contracts for public works, they consistently championed the public good over aristocratic privilege.

No hypocrisy is evident in Cato's moral rigor, but there was certainly ostentation. A strict disciplinarian, he shared his soldiers' hardships on campaign. A firm supporter of sumptuary laws, he lived a conspicuously austere life. In the course of a long and litigious career, he attacked the corruption of provincial governors, the vanity of generals, and the conspicuous consumption of the elite. He held strong views on every significant issue of the time. Though a firm supporter of traditional Roman values and often cast by later tradition as the enemy of Hellenism, his attitude toward Greek culture was in fact complex. He called the Greeks "a vile and unruly race" and advised his son to examine their literature without studying it deeply: too much Greek literature would corrupt everything. In 155, he urged that an embassy of Athens' leading philosophers be sent home before they corrupted the Roman youth. He consistently argued against involvement in Greek affairs, and he ridiculed Scipio Africanus for philhellenic affectations. Yet Cato was himself fluent in Greek, knew Greek literature well, and kept a Greek tutor in his household. In his dialogue *On Old Age*, Cicero makes Cato the spokesman and apologist of old age, casting him as a philosophizing sage, citing Xenophon as readily as the Roman magistrate-lists. That characterization is probably exaggerated, but not false. Cato's own writings reveal both deep familiarity with Greek traditions and a desire to have them serve Roman interests.

Greek connections are not immediately apparent. Cato's main historical work, *The Origins* (*Origines*), seems on first glance to repudiate the Greek historiographic conventions that informed the writing of Rome's earliest historians, Fabius Pictor and Cincius Alimentus. Cato's was the first history written in Latin, and it avoided such Greek conventions as dating by Olympiads. Its first book covered the period from the founding of Rome to the expulsion of the kings; books 2 and 3 traced the origins and customs of the towns of Italy. The historical narrative resumed in book 4 with the First Punic War (the early Republic received scant attention) and continued through book 7 into Cato's own time. He was still adding to it at his death. The work giving Romans their own history in their own language nevertheless owed much to Greek tradition. Cato's preface echoed Xenophon's *Symposium*, and his attention to origins reflected the Hellenistic interest in foundation legends (*ktiseis*). He clearly knew the work of Timaeus of Tauromenium, the great historian of the Greek West, though when dating Rome's foundation from the fall of Troy he followed the chronology of the Alexandrian polymath Eratosthenes of Cyrene. Famous Greek deeds like the Spartan Leonidas' stand at Thermopylae provided a measure for the greatness of Roman achievements. The history was also remarkable for avoiding the names of Roman magistrates, though it recorded individual soldiers of note and the name of at least one Carthaginian elephant. Such priorities suggest a deliberate counter to the aristocratic focus of his predecessors and recall Ennius' decision in the final books of his *Annals* to emphasize the heroism of ordinary soldiers.

The only senator known to figure prominently in the *Origins* was Cato himself: he included at least two of his own speeches at appropriate places. The one delivered in 167 on behalf of the Rhodians and included in book 5 became a literary benchmark: Cicero's literary executor Tiro eventually subjected it to an extended stylistic critique (Gellius 6.3). Cicero himself knew as many as 150 speeches. Fragments of about eighty survive. We might expect them to be fairly crude, and not just because Roman oratory was still a developing art. Two of Cato's sayings, "Stick to the subject; the words will follow" and "an orator is a good man skilled at speaking" (a favorite of Quintilian) imply distaste for the niceties of Hellenistic rhetoric. Cicero, who gives Cato a prominent place in the *Brutus*, his history of Roman oratory, acknowledges that Cato's stylistic effects were unpolished by the standards of his own day. The fragments nevertheless reveal considerable skill in the manipulation of language: much assonance, alliteration, repetition, and word play, a sensitivity to rhythm (though not Cicero's sophisticated rhythmic effects), effective use of rhetorical figures. Whether Cato's practice reflects direct knowledge of Greek rhetorical theory or simply a natural flair for Latin expression is ultimately less significant than its result: the first great achievement in the history of Latin prose.

Other works by Cato known in antiquity include collections of moral instruction addressed to his son and treatises on civil law and military affairs. Only a few fragments and testimonia remain. One work, a compilation of advice on estate management (*De agricultura*) survives intact.

[*See also* Agricultural Treatises; Latin Literature, Beginnings of; *and* Military Treatises.]

BIBLIOGRAPHY
Works of Cato the Elder
Historicorum romanorum reliquiae. Edited by Hermann Peter. 2nd ed. Vol. 1, pp. 55–97. Leipzig, Germany: Teubner, 1914. Fragments of his *Origines.*
Oratorum romanorum fragmenta liberae rei publicae. Edited by Enrica Malcovati. 3rd ed. Vol. 1, pp. 12–97. Turin, Italy: Paravia, 1953. Fragments of his oratory.
Les origines (fragments) de Caton. Edited by Martine Chassignet. Paris: Belles Lettres, 1986. Text with French translation and limited annotation.
Opere di Marco Porcio Catone Censore. Edited by Paolo Cugusi and Maria Teresa Sblendorio Cugusi. 2 vols. Turin, Italy: UTET, 2001. Now the edition of choice, complete with Italian translation, notes, and excellent bibliography.

Secondary Works
Astin, Alan E. *Cato the Censor.* Oxford: Clarendon Press, 1978.
Gruen, Erich S. "Cato and Hellenism." In *Culture and National Identity in Republican Rome*, pp. 52–83. Ithaca, N.Y.: Cornell University Press, 1992.
Plutarch. "Cato the Elder." In *Roman Lives.* Translated by Robin Waterfield, pp. 3–35. New York and Oxford: Oxford University Press, 1999. Oxford World's Classics. The major ancient source for Cato and highly instrumental in shaping his image for later centuries.

Sander M. Goldberg

CATO THE YOUNGER

(Marcus Porcius Cato; Cato Uticensis, 95–46 BCE), Roman politician. The younger Cato, great-grandson of Cato the Elder (Cato the Censor), was more important as a symbol after his death than in life: the most memorable times of his career came at its beginning and end. Orphaned in his childhood, Cato grew up a defiant and obstinate figure. After military service, he made his name as quaestor for rooting out the corruption of the public accounts in the treasury. Hostile to popular issues, such as restoring the full powers of the tribunate, he reversed his stance to be elected tribune for 63 so that he could oppose the bill proposed by Quintus Metellus Celer to recall Pompey to Rome with an armed force to suppress the Catilinarian conspiracy. It was when the senate deliberated over the punishment of the confessed conspirators in December 63 that Cato made his name. The consul-elect, his brother-in-law Silanus, had proposed executing the prisoners: but when the praetors-elect spoke, Julius Caesar argued for a milder penalty and warned against the precedent this would set of usurping the rights of a popular trial. It was Cato as tribune-elect who rallied the original decision on the grounds of national security: the situation was too urgent to indulge in mercy to acknowledged terrorists. The speech attributed to him in Sallust's *Bellum Catilinae* is the historian's reconstruction, but Sallust also singles out Cato and his enemy Caesar as the two men great beyond the level of their peers, Cato in severity, Caesar in generosity.

Opposed to the domination of political life by military power, Cato must take some blame for the alliance of Pompey and Caesar in 60 after Cato had refused a marriage alliance with Pompey and opposed the settlements Pompey needed for his veterans and the newly conquered Middle Eastern provinces. According to Plutarch's *Cato Minor*, Pompey admired him in his presence but felt relief whenever Cato left him. Throughout the 50s Cato obstructed the "triumvirs." Removed from Rome for two years by an honorific and lucrative mission to take over the province of Cyprus, he resumed his filibustering with demands that Caesar be recalled and impeached for massacring the German Usipetes during a truce. Elected praetor in 54, he was a severe presiding magistrate in the courts, but alienated pragmatic politicians like Cicero and many wealthy voters by his refusal to compromise: he failed to be elected consul in 51.

It was Cato who proposed offering a sole consulship to Pompey in 52, and again urged that Pompey be authorized to defend the state and take charge of its forces against Caesar in January 49. (We have one sample of his personality in his disingenuous reply to Cicero's request for support in seeking a triumph in *Epistulae ad familiares* 15.5.)

Cato took a noncombat role in the civil war and refused the command offered to him after Pompey's death. Plutarch devotes a fifth of the *Cato Minor* (based on the memoirs of Cato's friend Munatius Rufus and their rewriting by Thrasea Paetus) to Cato's final defense of Utica after the defeat of Thapsus and his negotiations on behalf of the city and Roman residents. But what gave his life meaning for posterity was his suicide: after a convivial dinner reading Socrates's final discussion of the soul in Plato's *Phaedo*, Cato withdrew to his chamber and demanded his sword. But he failed to kill himself outright: when his friends heard his cries, their doctor bound him up, but as soon as he was alone he ripped the wound open and disemboweled himself.

The cult of Cato began with eulogies by his nephew Marcus Junius Brutus and Cicero (countered by Caesar himself with the *Anticato*) and continued with Sallust's encomium. Horace (*Carmina* [*Odes*] 1.12.35) celebrates his noble death, and Virgil's *ekphrasis* of the shield of Aeneas includes Cato sitting in judgment in Hades over sinners like Catiline (*Aeneid* 8.668–70). To Seneca, Cato was the sole honorable supporter of the Republic against the massed forces of Pompey and Caesar, and Lucan takes him as arbiter of right and wrong ("the gods approved the victorious cause but Cato the defeated," 1.126). Both Lucan and Plutarch report two more quixotic actions. To oblige his old friend

Quintus Hortensius Hortalus he divorced his loyal wife Marcia, who married Hortensius and gave him a child: when Hortensius died in 50, Cato took back Marcia, made wealthy by her inheritance from Hortensius. In Africa after Pompey's death, Cato led his army in a week's march through the hardships of a snake-infested desert in a display of endurance that killed no enemies and tested his mettle against Nature at her most severe.

[*See also* Cato the Elder; Civil War; Pompey; and Rome, *subentry* Early Rome and the Republic; *and* Scipio Africanus.]

BIBLIOGRAPHY

MacMullen, Ramsay. *Enemies of the Roman Order: Treason, Unrest, and Alienation in the Empire.* Cambridge, Mass.: Harvard University Press, 1966.

Syme, Ronald. *The Roman Revolution.* Oxford: Clarendon Press, 1939.

Elaine Fantham

CATULLUS

(Gaius Valerius Catullus, mid-first century BCE), Roman poet. Gaius Valerius Catullus was born in Verona, and died in Rome in his thirtieth year. The source that tells us this (Jerome's fourth-century CE additions to Eusebius' *Chronici canones*, probably derived from Suetonius' lost *De poetis*) also dates his birth to 87/86 and his death to 58/57 BCE; but since all the dateable poems in the collection belong to 56–54, that must be an error.

The few ancient authors who quote Catullus by title refer to his *Hendecasyllabi* (which included poems 42 and 53), *Epithalamium* (poem 62), *Priapus* (?), *Phasma* (a play), *Laureolus* (a play), and *Peri mimologion* (?), which was evidently a prose work; there is also a reference to a lover's magic incantation, as in Theocritus' second idyll. The two plays are generally attributed to "Catullus the Mimographer," a supposedly different author also writing in the 50s BCE; but since our Catullus demonstrably wrote works other than those in the surviving corpus, there seems to be no good reason to imagine two authors of the same name who lived at the same time.

Our Catullan collection is ultimately dependent on three fourteenth-century manuscripts derived from a lost copy (or copy of a copy) of a single text, which was supposedly found somewhere "under a bushel" and brought back to the poet's native city from far away by an anonymous citizen of Verona; so at least we are told in a teasingly inexplicit poem by Benvenuto Campesani of Vicenza that is reproduced in two of the surviving manuscripts.

The collection contains 116 poems, clearly divided into three main sections: 1–60, short poems in various meters; 61–64, long poems in various meters (two wedding songs, a narrative hymn, and a mythological epic); 65–116, poems in elegiac couplets. Since poem 1 is a dedication poem, and each of the "sections" opens with a reference to one or more of the Muses, the order of poems is clearly not random. It used to be attributed to an imagined "posthumous editor," on the arbitrary assumption that Catullus died in 54 BCE. More probably the order of poems represents the poet's own arrangement, either as his own single three-volume collection or as the later combination of separate collections and longer poems.

We know from the poems themselves that Catullus was a Transpadane (from the once-Gallic lands north of the river Padus [Po]); that his home was at Sirmio on Lake Garda, which was in the territory of Verona; that he served in Bithynia in northern Asia Minor on the staff of a proconsul called Memmius; that he was on familiar terms, friendly or otherwise, with men and women of high rank in Rome, such as the drunken lady Postumia and the patrician Torquatus, for whom he wrote a wedding song; that he knew Cicero and Caesar, and attacked the latter in slanderous invectives; that he pursued a coquettish boy of good family called Juventius; and that he had a stormy relationship, ranging from infatuated love to furious jealousy and hatred, with a married lady, evidently aristocratic, whom he called "Lesbia." The Bithynia trip can be dated by other sources to 57–56 BCE; Apuleius, writing in the second century CE but probably using well-informed earlier authors, identifies "Lesbia" as Clodia (which might refer to any of three known Clodia sisters); Suetonius tells us that Caesar stayed with Catullus' father when in Transpadana during the winters of his Gallic campaign, and that he won the poet over by reacting to his attacks with a dinner invitation.

Everything else in the poet's "biography" is modern speculation. One of his friends, also from Verona, was called Caelius; one of his enemies was called Rufus. However, there is no reason to suppose that either was Caelius Rufus, lover of the wealthy patrician widow Clodia Metelli in the years 59–57 BCE, and the common belief that this Clodia was "Lesbia" requires the poems about her to be dated before early 59 BCE (when her husband died), even though all the securely dateable poems in the collection are three or four years later than that. The identification was first made by Ludwig Schwabe in 1862; astonishingly, many scholars still take it seriously.

Among the poet's close friends were Veranius and Fabullus, who had been on provincial service in Spain under a proconsul called Piso; Licinius Calvus, descended from plebeian heroes of the fourth century BCE, who was not only a distinguished poet but also one of Rome's foremost orators (Catullus refers to his famous prosecution of Caesar's ally Vatinius); and another poet, Helvius Cinna, who himself had been in Bithynia, and later met a tragic death on the Ides of March 44 BCE, when the Roman mob mistook him for one of the assassins of Julius Caesar.

As writers, Catullus, Calvus, and Cinna all followed the learned example of Callimachus and the other poets of Hellenistic Alexandria; Catullus' poem 66 is a translation (with additions) of part of Callimachus' *Aitia*. Their favorite genre was the mini-epic, allusive and highly wrought mythological narrative on erotic and/or melodramatic themes. Calvus wrote an *Io*, on the girl turned into a heifer by jealous Juno; Cinna's *Zmyrna*, on the incestuous mother of Adonis, is praised by Catullus in contrast with the lamentable efforts of less gifted contemporaries. We hear also of Valerius Cato's *Dictynna* and Cornificius' *Glaucus* (both Callimachean subjects), and Catullus refers to a poem on the Great

Mother by his friend Caecilius. By the time Cicero referred to "the younger men" (*neoteroi*) in 50 BCE, and "the new poets" in 46, they probably formed an influential literary school.

Catullus' own epic, poem 64 on the wedding of Peleus and Thetis, subtly undermines the unparalleled happiness of the hero who marries a goddess with two long and brilliantly dramatic insertions: the description of the coverlet of the bridal bed, with its narrative of Ariadne's betrayal by Theseus and of the revenge Jupiter grants her, and the song of the Fates at Peleus' wedding, with its prophecy of the murderous career of the son (Achilles) who is about to be conceived. The poem ends with the reflection that the vices of the contemporary world have made it impossible for the immortals even to visit men, much less marry them.

A different view of divine attitudes to mortals is offered in poem 63, a variant on the story of the goddess Cybele's human lover Attis. (The Phrygian goddess had been worshipped in Rome since 204 BCE as the Great Idaean Mother of the Gods.) Catullus' Attis is a Greek youth, star of the racetrack and the wrestling ring, who comes to Mount Ida to devote himself to Cybele's service. She requires self-castration; in his madness Attis mutilates himself, runs to the wild mountain, and falls asleep in exhaustion. At dawn he wakes, sane again and knowing what he has done. He goes back down to the shore, where his long lament of loss has much in common with that of Ariadne in poem 64, except that for him there is no way out of the despair. The goddess sends her lion to drive him back to the wild mountain and lifelong slavery. It is all narrated in the frantic Galliambics that were used for hymns to the Great Mother by her real-life eunuchs, the Galli, and like a hymn it ends with a prayer: "Goddess, great goddess Cybele, goddess lady of Dindymus, / Far from my house may all your fury be, mistress: / Drive other men frenzied, drive other men insane."

However, it was not for these masterpieces that Catullus was best known in the ancient world. The Romans prized him for his invectives ("iambics"), but above all, as we moderns do, for his love poetry.

By the time we have read the first eleven poems of the collection we know all we need to know about the course of the love affair that for most readers defines Catullus' poetic achievement: the tentative approach via the "sparrow poems" (2 and 3), the triumphant but precarious defiance of convention in the "kiss poems" (5 and 7), the attempt to come to terms with rejection in poem 8, the bitter message of farewell in poem 11. That is as much narrative as the reader needs to have, just enough to understand the other poems about "Lesbia" as they come up in the collection—for instance poem 51, a translation of Sappho (with additions) that only at this point explains the name he gave his mistress. The poems are arranged not for chronology but for artistic variety; what matters is not what happened but how that range of emotions can be turned into art.

In the elegiac poems in the third part of the collection, Catullus uses a different technique to explore what "Lesbia" meant to him. In the long and carefully wrought poem 68b ("poem 68" is probably two quite separate poems wrongly run together in the manuscripts), the Muses are invited to reward Catullus' friend Allius for providing the lovers with a safe house. The scene of her arrival, like a bride to her husband or the epiphany of a goddess, is suddenly interrupted with a mythological simile (Laodamia to Protesilaus) that develops into an elaborate narrative constructed concentrically around the notion of Troy as a scene of death. The key word, emphatically repeated, is *coniugium*, marriage, but when the scene at Allius' house resumes, the poet admits that his love is adulterous and that he must share his mistress with other lovers too. But she is still his light, the source of his life's happiness, and the gods must bless the man who made their liaison possible.

In the center of the Laodamia simile Catullus laments the death of his own brother at the site of Troy. Only three other poems refer to this event (65, 68a, 101), which must have happened shortly before the assembling of the collection, and may have been the reason for it. Catullus is explicit that his brother's death has made impossible the whole business of love poetry (*totum hoc studium*, 68a.19). We need not suppose he gave up literature altogether. The references to other works (see above) show that at one time there was more Catullus to be read than there is now. But his writing career was not a long one. Ovid, who should have known, implies

Catullus Reading. Painting (1885) by Stepan Vladislavovich Bakalovich (1857–1947). TRETYAKOV GALLERY, MOSCOW/THE BRIDGEMAN ART LIBRARY

that Catullus and Calvus both died young, and Jerome's report that Catullus died in his thirtieth year may be accurate, even though his dates are not.

The great villa at Sirmio, dated to the Augustan period, was probably built by the poet's descendants; they were well known in Roman public life in the first century CE, intermarrying with old patrician families and even intimate with emperors. Catullus himself is named as an honored predecessor by the Augustan poets Tibullus, Propertius, and Ovid, and by Martial a century later; the Transpadane Pliny the Younger liked to imitate his style, and he was still "the most elegant of poets" for Aulus Gellius in the late second century. But after that he seems to have gone out of favor, and since he was never an author taught in school, texts of his poems may have become rare by late antiquity. Eventually, his survival through the Middle Ages depended on just that single copy that was brought to Verona sometime about 1300.

The first printed edition was published in Venice in 1472—a still very corrupt text, accompanied by a brief and not wholly inaccurate biography—and in 1492 the city of Verona adorned its new Loggia del Consiglio with a statue of Catullus. In England, the poets of the sixteenth and seventeenth centuries knew him as a love poet, but there was no complete English translation until 1795. For the past two centuries he has been admired and deplored for many reasons: "tenderest of Roman poets" (Tennyson), "the most hard-edged and intense of the Latin poets" (Ezra Pound), "vindictive, venomous, and full of obscene malice" (Harold Nicholson).

[See also Clodia; and Poetry, Latin, subentry Lyric.

BIBLIOGRAPHY
Works of Catullus
Carmina. Edited by R. A. B. Mynors. Oxford: Clarendon Press, 1958.
The Poems: Edited with Introduction, Revised Text, and Commentary. Edited by Kenneth Quinn. London: Macmillan, 1970.
Catullus, Tibullus, and "Pervigilium Veneris." Edited and translated by Francis W. Cornish et al. Loeb Classical Library, 1913. 2nd ed. revised by G. P. Goold. Cambridge, Mass.: Harvard University Press, 1988.
The Poems of Catullus. Edited and translated by Guy Lee. The World's Classics. Oxford and New York: Oxford University Press, 1990.
Catullus: Edited with a Textual and Interpretive Commentary. Edited by Douglas F. S. Thomson. Toronto: University of Toronto Press, 1997.
The Complete Poetry of Catullus. Translated with commentary by David Mulroy. Madison: University of Wisconsin Press, 2002.
The Poems of Catullus. Translated with commentary by Peter Green. Berkeley: University of California Press, 2005.

Secondary Works
Fordyce, Christian J. *Catullus: A Commentary.* Oxford: Clarendon Press, 1961. Latin text with English commentary.
Gaisser, Julia Haig. *Catullus and His Renaissance Readers.* Oxford: Clarendon Press; New York: Oxford University Press, 1993.
Gaisser, Julia Haig, ed. *Catullus.* Oxford Readings in Classical Studies. New York: Oxford University Press, 2007.
Skinner, Marilyn B., ed. *A Companion to Catullus.* Malden, Mass.: Blackwell Publishing, 2007.
Wiseman, T. P. *Catullus and His World: A Reappraisal.* Cambridge, U.K., and New York: Cambridge University Press, 1985.
Wray, David. *Catullus and the Poetics of Roman Manhood.* Cambridge, U.K., and New York: Cambridge University Press, 2001.

T. P. Wiseman

CAUSATION, THEORIES OF

The Greek word *aition* (or *aitia*) is sometimes translated as "cause" (an ontological category) and sometimes as "explanation" (an epistemological category). Understood in a narrow sense, causation is the activity of something that exists prior to, and is productive of, its effect. In that sense it is misleading to talk about ancient theories of "causation," since (for example) Aristotelian formal and final causes are neither prior to nor productive of their effects. However, to call *A* the "cause" of *B* in a broader sense is simply to identify *A* as being somehow causally relevant to, or explanatory of, *B*. (For this reason some prefer "reason" or "explanatory factor" to "cause.") The ancients can be said to have been interested in causation in this broader sense, covering a wide range of relations.

The ancients differed widely on the nature of causation; nevertheless, there are at least three things on which almost all agreed. First, to be a cause is to be that "because of which" something comes about. Second, causes are *things* rather than events or states of affairs. Finally, they all agreed on the principle (derived from the Eleatic school of Zeno and Parmenides) that something cannot come into being out of nothing. To some (though by no means all) this meant that nothing is uncaused. Apart from this, there was no clear consensus on how to understand the concept of *aitia*.

Platonic and Aristotelian Theories. In the *Cratylus*, Socrates tells Hermogenes that "cause" refers to "that through which (*di' ho*) a thing comes to be" (413a). It is impossible to pin down a single Platonic theory of causation that is consistent across all dialogues (assuming Plato even had any fully worked-out account of *aitia* at all). Instead one must take care to consider what Plato says about causes on each separate occasion. The two most sustained discussions of causation come in the *Phaedo* and *Timaeus*. In the *Phaedo*, Plato introduces a causal theory that treats forms as causes (though in what sense remains controversial). The *Phaedo* develops two models of form causation. On the "safe but naive" model (100b–102a), forms are responsible for particular things having specific properties by virtue of standing in a certain relation to them, often referred to as "participation" (though the *Phaedo* remains uncommitted to any precise characterization of that relation). For example, all beautiful things are made beautiful by participating in the form of beauty, which is said to exist "itself by itself." The more "sophisticated" model (105b–c) introduces a third element into the picture, immanent characters, which are said to "bring the forms along with them." To use Plato's example, soul makes a body living because it carries vitality (the immanent character), which brings along with it the form of life itself. While the *Phaedo* downgrades the physical causes of natural science to

things without which the real causes could not operate (98b–99c; cf. *Laws* 10), the *Timaeus* affords them the status of *co*-causes (*sunaitia*). The real cause (*aitia*) of order and goodness in the cosmos is Intelligence, which uses natural necessity as a tool for achieving that end (46c–e). According to the *Timaeus*, a complete explanation is one that "weaves together" these two causes, Intelligence and Necessity, into a single account (68e–69a). Forms figure into this picture as the paradigms that Intelligence looks to in constructing the visible world (29a).

The concern for causes penetrates deep into the foundations of Aristotelian epistemology. Scientific knowledge not only involves knowing *that* something is the case but also *why* it is the case, and that requires grasping its cause. Definitions of key scientific terms, which are among the first principles of a science, must also state the cause so that knowing *what* something is and knowing *why* it is come to the same thing (*Analytica posteriora* 1.2, 2.1–2). Finally, genuine proofs in science take the form of demonstrations whose middle terms identify the causal connections between attributes and their subjects. Aristotle's whole scientific enterprise is thus dominated by the search for causes.

Even outside the *Analytics*, Aristotle insists that we do not know a thing until we have grasped the "Why?" of it and that to grasp this is to grasp its primary causes (*Physics* B3, *Metaphysics* A3). He argues that there are four primary causes and that it is the job of the natural scientist to know about all four. The "material" cause refers to "that out of which" a thing is made. Thus, for example, the bricks and timber are material causes of the house. The "formal" cause corresponds to the essence that makes something what it is: what makes something an eye is the function of seeing. The "efficient" cause is the productive source of a change: the builder is the efficient cause of the house. And the "final" cause is the end for the sake of which the change comes about: the builder builds the house for the sake of shelter.

The Neoplatonists (200–600 CE) offered a hybrid model that distinguished six causes (Proclus *In Timaeus* 1.263,19–30; Olympiodorus *In Gorgias*

5.1–6.1). In addition to the standard four Aristotelian causes, they added the "instrumental" cause (e.g., the hammer is an instrumental cause of the house) and the "paradigmatic" cause (the role played by separately existing forms in Plato's *Timaeus*). Of the six, three (efficient, final, paradigmatic) are identified as true causes, while the others (including the Aristotelian enmattered form) are merely co-causes (Simplicius *In Physics* 3.16–19). Drawing on Plato's treatment of the soul in the *Phaedrus* and *Laws*, the Neoplatonists also argued that only incorporeal things (e.g., Platonic forms) can act as causal agents; body as such lacks all form of agency (Proclus *Elements* 80).

Hellenistic Theories. The Hellenistic philosophers took causes to be corporeal things. The Epicureans revived the theory of mechanical causation developed by the early atomists, Democritus and Leucippus. In this system, impacts at the atomic level become the ultimate source for all change. Everything we see happening at the macroscopic level is the effect of collisions taking place at the microscopic level. The Epicureans acknowledged three basic kinds of atomic motion: downward motion, due to an atom's own weight; rebounding motion, resulting from the impact between atoms (Lucretius *De rerum natura* 2.80–141); and the "swerve," which was introduced in part to explain how atoms falling straight down collided to produce impacts (2.196–264). This swerve is the only uncaused motion in an Epicurean world that is otherwise completely deterministic.

While the Platonists and Aristotelians allowed for a broad conception of *aitia*, the Stoics took a fresh approach by narrowing the notion of cause to active causes; causes have to *do* something in order to bring about their effects (Sextus Empiricus *Outlines of Pyrrhonism* 3.14, Seneca *Epistulae* 65.4; for the general shift in the meaning of cause see Frede 1980). Like the Epicureans, the Stoics held that every cause is a body and what it acts on are other bodies. But what causes are cause of are not bodies but incorporeal predicates. For example, the teacher, by acting on the student, brings it about that the predicate "is learned" is truly said of the student (hence effects are "sayables," *lekta*: Clement of Alexandria *Miscellanies* 8.9.26.3–4). The Stoics cataloged a "swarm of causes" as a way of allocating responsibility among those factors that actively contribute to the effect (Alexander of Aphrodisias *On Fate* 191.30–192.28; Clement 8.9.33.1–9; Cicero *On Fate* 39–43). According to Clement, the Stoics distinguished four kinds of cause. Preliminary (*prokatarktikon*) causes are triggers whose activity is prior to the effect, while sustaining (*sunektika*) or complete (*autoteles*) causes are responsible for a thing's continued existence and are thus simultaneous with their effect. For example, the preliminary cause of a cylinder's rolling down a hill is the agent that pushed it, while the sustaining cause is its shape. Auxiliary (*sunerga*) causes are those that work in conjunction with the sustaining cause to amplify its effect (e.g., the smoothness of the path along which the cylinder rolls), while co-causes (*sunaitia*) work in conjunction with other co-causes in order to bring about the effect (e.g., each string of a lyre is a co-cause of the harmony).

The interest of the Hellenistic philosophers in causation was bound up with their concern for human freedom and responsibility. The Epicureans worried that if everything is necessitated by antecedent causes, then nothing would be up to us and everything would be fated; thus, we could not be held morally responsible for our actions (Epicurus *Letter to Menoeceus* 133–134; Lucretius *De rerum natura* 2.251–293). Epicurus used the atomic swerve, which is an uncaused event, as a way of releasing humans from the bonds of fate (though exactly how remains controversial). By contrast, the Stoics embraced determinism where everything happens as part of a fixed and inescapable sequence of causes, which they identified with fate. Nothing is outside the causal nexus; for if anything did arise without a cause, that would be tantamount to something coming to be out of nothing (Alexander *On Fate* 191.30–192.28). The Stoic distinction between types of causes is supposed to have arisen in part as a response to the problem of how to reconcile their determinism with the prospect of human freedom (see, especially, Cicero *On Fate* 39–43).

[*See also* Fortune; Freedom; Philosophy, *subentry* Overview; *and* Science.]

BIBLIOGRAPHY

Fine, Gail. "Forms as Causes: Plato and Aristotle." In *Mathematik und Metaphysik bei Aristoteles*, edited by A. Graeser, pp. 69–112. Berner Reihe philosophischer Studien 6. Bern, Switzerland: Haupt, 1987.

Frede, M. "The Original Notion of Cause." In *Doubt and Dogmatism: Studies in Hellenistic Epistemology*, edited by Malcolm Schofield, Myles Burnyeat, and Jonathan Barnes, pp. 217–249. Oxford: Clarendon Press; New York: Oxford University Press, 1980.

Hankinson, R. J. *Cause and Explanation in Ancient Greek Thought*. Oxford: Clarendon Press; New York: Oxford University Press, 1998.

Long, A. A., and David Sedley, eds. *The Hellenistic Philosophers*. 2 vols. Cambridge, U.K., and New York: Cambridge University Press, 1987.

Sorabji, Richard. *Necessity, Cause, and Blame: Perspectives on Aristotle's Theory*. Ithaca, N.Y.: Cornell University Press; London: Duckworth, 1980.

Devin M. Henry

CAVES

A cave is any rock shelter that can be used as a dwelling or for other activities; in the Mediterranean caves were used throughout antiquity beginning in the Paleolithic period. One of the most fully documented caves is the Franchthi Cave in the southern Argolis, which was occupied from the Upper Paleolithic to the Early Neolithic periods. It served as either a seasonal or a permanent settlement, and its remains reveal the remarkable development over several millennia from mainland hunting and gathering to fishing and then to agriculture.

Caves played an important role in ritual worship. The finds from numerous caves on the island of Crete attest to their importance for the Minoan people of the Bronze Age and as late as the Roman period. Cult practice at the Dictaean Cave, the legendary birthplace of Zeus, continued uninterrupted from Middle Minoan II (c. 1925/00–1750/20 BCE) until the Geometric period (eighth century BCE). Its construction included an upper chamber for worship, a *temenos* with altar, and an underground pool.

Objects found there include bronze statuettes of male and female devotees, animal figurines, jewelry, weapons, miniature double-axes, and pottery. Another cave important for our understanding of Iron Age cave activity on the island is the Idaean Cave, also sacred to Zeus, which has yielded an abundance of Geometric tripod cauldrons similar to those found at Olympia and Delphi.

The natural setting of caves made them good locations for oracular activity. The oracle of Trophonius was established in a cave at Lebadeia in Boeotia. The Corycian Cave on the slopes of Mount Parnassus above Delphi was sacred to Pan and the nymphs. Cult activity here began in the Neolithic period, was abandoned in the Bronze Age, and began again at the end of the eighth century. The most spectacular find at this cave was an estimated twenty-five thousand bored, flattened, lead-weighted, and inscribed *astragaloi* (knucklebones) that had been deposited as votives. These may have been game pieces that belonged to youths from Delphi, who dedicated them as a rite of passage prior to marriage. Alternatively their inscriptions suggest that they were instruments of divination related to the oracle of Apollo at Delphi. Finally, the remote location of the Corycian Cave made it a good refugee shelter. The citizens of Delphi hid there from invaders during the Persian Wars (490 and 480/479 BCE), the Greek war of independence in the early nineteenth century, and World War II.

In the Archaic and Classical periods, caves were frequently dedicated to Pan and the nymphs. In the late fifth century BCE a Theran named Archedemus dedicated the Vari Cave on the south slope of Mount Hymettus, although the cave was in use before his time. The original focus of the cave may have been a spring at its lowest point. Archedemus carved a portrait of himself as a craftsman, and a rupestral inscription described him as endowed with nympholepsy, a heightened state of fluency and verbal ability. Many rock-cut niches, statuary, a carved flight of steps, and other inscriptions to Pan, Apollo, and the nymphs were found in the cave. Seven marble reliefs depicting Hermes, Pan, the nymphs, and Achelous were located there, along with several terra-cotta statuettes, lamps, libation saucers, drinking cups, lecythi, loutrophoroi, and goat horns.

In Greek literature caves often served a symbolic purpose. Mythology associated caves with birth, dwellings for monsters, and illicit affairs. Hesiod's *Theogony* states that Zeus was born in a cave on Mount Aegeon. In Homer's *Odyssey*, Polyphemus and his flock inhabit a cave, while the enchantress Calypso detains Odysseus in her cave on Ogygia. In the *Republic*, Plato contrasts the inner darkness of the cave with the exterior light to represent the enlightenment of the philosopher.

Caves also played a significant role in Roman mythology. The cave of the Lupercal was said to be the site where the she-wolf suckled Rome's legendary founders Romulus and Remus after their abandonment. The Lupercalia, a fertility festival connected with the worship of Lycaean Pan, was celebrated there annually on 15 February. The emperor Augustus rebuilt the cave, and excavators rediscovered it in 2007 on the Palatine Hill. In Virgil's *Aeneid* (6.45ff.), Aeneas learns the early history of Rome from the Sibyl in a cave at Cumae. Just as other caves had oracular activity, so the Sibyl's prophesies were written on oak leaves and scattered by the wind. A cave is also the location where Aeneas weds the Carthaginian queen Dido.

Caves embellished with sculpture served as retreats for Roman emperors. On the island of Capri, several seaside caves have been discovered with carved niches, seats, pools, and sculptural decoration. Most notably, the cave at Sperlonga, belonging to the emperor Tiberius, had a dining facility and a sculptural program from the Trojan cycle. According to Porphyry's *De antro nympharum* (third century CE), caves were central to the practice of Mythraism because their structure represented the cosmos into which the soul could descend and return during initiation into the mysteries.

BIBLIOGRAPHY

L'Antre Corycien. Bulletin de Correspondance Hellénique, Supplements 7 and 9. Athens, Greece: Ecole Française d'Athènes; Paris: Boccard, 1981–1984. A complete report and analysis of the excavation history and finds from the Corycian Cave.

Weller, Charles Heald, et al. "The Cave at Vari: I. Description, Account of Excavations, and History." *American Journal of Archaeology* 7, no. 3 (1903): 263–288. Although the interpretation of the finds is art historical rather than archaeological, this excavation report of the cave at Vari is followed by reports for each category of finds from the cave.

Wickens, Jere Mark. "The Archaeology and History of Cave Use in Attica, Greece from Prehistoric thru Late Roman Times." PhD diss., Indiana University, 1986. A thorough explanation of the variety of uses of caves, focusing on those from the Attic countryside.

Eric Andrew Cox

CELTS

Geographically the Celts were the most extensive population group identified by classical authors to the north of the Mediterranean domain in Europe. They were at least a component of the cultural pattern from present-day Anatolian Turkey west to Iberia, south into Italy, and north to the British Isles, albeit at different times and for different durations, during the pre-Roman Iron Age (from the eighth century BCE to—for the northern areas—the first century CE). Literacy being little developed in protohistoric Celtic societies, they are identifiable from contemporary historical documentation composed by their literate neighbors, by surviving place- and personal names, by linguistic patterning within the Celtic language group—traits that help identify speakers of Celtic languages—and, although more contentious, by genetic evidence.

As proxy evidence, the widespread material culture record furnished by archaeology is important. This comprises traces primarily and successively of the Hallstatt (First Iron Age; eighth to mid-fifth centuries BCE) and La Tène (Second Iron Age; thereafter until the early years of the Christian era) cultures, focused on the zone north of the Alps from central France east to Hungary and the middle Danube Valley. Material culture peripheral to this zone, notably from south of the Pyrenees in Iberia and along the Atlantic coastlands to the British

Isles, is more or less closely—and sometimes only remotely, as in, for example, southwest Ireland—related to the west-central European sequence. At the subcontinental scale, there is no absolute spatial or chronological fit between material culture and linguistic and toponymic evidence.

For most of the chronological span, the settlement record of Celtic temperate Europe is dominated numerically by small-scale agricultural holdings of rectangular—on the northwestern periphery, round—timber-built buildings, sometimes enclosed by stockades or ramparts, and accompanied by ancillary structures. Both cereal cultivation and livestock rearing manifest increasing sophistication and success, particularly from about the third century BCE when iron technology became increasingly widespread. A strengthening subsistence economy undoubtedly contributed to rising population numbers. Of rising importance, too, during this period in both quality and quantity are horses: initially small draft ponies for wagons and carts, but later cavalry steeds. Superimposed on this agricultural stratum at least intermittently are settlement sites of considerably greater political and economic complexity, suggesting enhanced hierarchical differentiation.

Funerary Record. Funerary sites, whether cremations or inhumations under barrow mounds or flat inhumation graves in cemeteries, numerically dominate the archaeological record in certain sectors and for certain periods (e.g., in northeast France in Early La Tène times). The frequent occurrence of grave goods, both locally produced and, relatively rarely, imported from Mediterranean cultures—a particular status indicator—provides intimations of significant wealth and social differences. Famous cemeteries like the eponymous Hallstatt (Salzkammergut, Austria) have been studied since the nineteenth century. Underpinned by long-distance exchanges inspired by the export of locally mined rock salt, some burials here from the eighth to sixth century BCE demonstrate high-quality imports from Slovenia, northern Italy, and nearby areas, as well as, for example, amber from Baltic shores. Both male and female graves can be wealthy;

rich children's graves indicate inherited, rather than ascribed, status.

In succeeding generations across temperate Europe, the best-furnished individual graves under barrows continue to indicate that females as well as males could enjoy elevated status, whether secular or religious. A key example found at Vix in Burgundy and dating from circa 500 BCE, that of a middle-aged, physically deformed woman with, among other things, gold jewelry, a dismantled elaborate wagon, and a massive wine krater imported from a western Greek colony, has attracted divergent opinions—secular ruler, shaman, priestess? Both rich female and male graves continue into the succeeding La Tène Iron Age; in these examples local high-quality craft products, now decorated in the first style within Early Celtic art, are found alongside southern imports, as at Reinheim in western Germany.

Thereafter cemeteries, primarily of inhumations accompanied by warrior panoplies—typically sword, swordbelt, shield fitments, and spear—tools, and other status markers such as jewelry, correspond more or less neatly with historical accounts of Celtic migrations, notably toward the Middle Danube in Hungary, on to the Balkans, and ultimately to Asia Minor and the Black Sea coastlands. In many areas toward the end of the period, unaccompanied or poorly accompanied cremation cemeteries predominate; these are less readily identifiable by archaeological fieldwork. In a few areas, however, elite burials continue into the early Roman period and include indications of individual wealth, of feasting and drinking (they contain plentiful Italian wine amphorae), and sometimes, to judge from the weaponry, of military service as Roman auxiliaries. Such graves are found in southeast England, the Duchy of Luxembourg, and central France.

Social and Economic Developments. At certain periods the settlement record and its patterning suggest the evolution of rather more complex sociopolitical and economic arrangements. This is especially clear in the second and first centuries BCE with the development of major proto-urban settlements, such as Manching (Bavaria), Stradoniče (Bohemia), and Mont Beuvray (Burgundy), surrounded by elaborate, resource-consumptive defenses enclosing up to a few hundred hectares, the interior marked on excavation by indications of dense settlement, industry, and commerce (notably, in western examples, imports of wine amphora from Italy). Such *oppida*—archaeological usage follows Caesar's descriptions in *Bellum Gallicum*, but examples also occurred earlier in Gallia Cisalpina, northern Italy—were in some instances the centers of emergent secondary states. By the time of the Roman advance starting in the later second century BCE, examples in Gaul included Bibracte of the Aeduan tribe (= Mont Beuvray) and Avaricum of the Bituriges Cubi (= modern Bourges [Berry]), both also described by Caesar. Though some *oppida* failed rapidly as towns, others flourished through Roman times, such as Lutetia of the Parisi, now Paris.

An earlier, albeit short-lived, episode of greater social and economic complexity is apparent in the sixth and fifth centuries BCE, across the Hallstatt–La Tène transition. Marked by the emergence of elite fortified hilltops termed "princely seats," with aristocratic housing, plentiful evidence for high-quality craftsmanship, and nearby sumptuous burials, these are epitomized by Heuneburg on the Upper Danube in Baden-Württemberg and by Mont Lassois in Burgundy. These, too, were nodes through which exchange with the South—Etruscan Italy, the western Greek colonies, notably Massalia —passed. Compared to the subsequent episode, Mediterranean imports were fewer but of higher quality. The last of these ephemeral principalities were in marked decline by the later fifth century BCE, close in time to the historically and archaeologically attested invasions of northern Italy—where Celtic cemetery evidence is much more readily distinguished than that of their settlements.

Recent academic study of the temperate European Iron Age shows divergent trends. In Britain and Ireland many archaeologists have become increasingly skeptical about the characteristics of Celtic pre-Roman insular communities. Here, as on the Continent, a massive upswing in the quantity of rescue archaeological fieldwork has produced a wealth of new detailed evidence, not only for agricultural settlement but also for religious and ritual

Celtic Metalwork. Bronze fittings from a chariot, from the tomb of a princess of Vix, Burgundy, France. MUSÉE ARCHÉOLOGIQUE, CHÂTILLON-SUR-SEINE, FRANCE/GIRAUDON/ THE BRIDGEMAN ART LIBRARY

practices, most remarkably in the sanctuary sites of Picardy, France, and for the disposal of the dead— from human sacrifices in the peatlands of eastern Ireland to a cart burial (with similarities to a series from the Belgian Ardennes) from lowland Scotland. It is becoming increasingly plain that the Celtic societies of later prehistory, though essentially agrarian and rural in character, varied substantially over time and by region. Some were heavily indebted culturally to their southern neighbors; others, much less so. Although shared characteristics, notably the styles that constitute Early Celtic art (i.e., the art, dominantly on metalwork, of the La Tène culture), remain discernable, no single social, economic, or political model can readily accommodate all the evidence: internal diversity is a keynote of the Celtic Iron Age of Europe.

[See also Barbarians; Druids; Gaul; and Trier.]

BIBLIOGRAPHY

Buchsenschutz, Olivier. Les celtes de l'âge du fer. Paris: Armand Colin, 2007.

Cunliffe, Barry W. The Ancient Celts. Oxford: Oxford University Press, 1997.

Green, Miranda J., ed. The Celtic World. London: Routledge, 1995.

Koch, John T., in collaboration with Raimund Karl, Antone Minard, and Simon Ó. Faoláin. An Atlas for Celtic Studies: Archaeology and Names in Ancient Europe and Early Medieval Ireland, Britain, and Brittany. Oxford: Oxbow, 2007.

Moscati, Sabatino, ed. The Celts. Milan: Bompiani, 1991. Includes the catalog of an exhibition held at the Palazzo Grassi, Venice, 1991.

Rieckhoff, Sabine, and Jörg Biel. Die Kelten in Deutschland. Stuttgart, Germany: Konrad Theiss, 2001.

Ian Ralston

CEMETERIES

Disposal of the dead is a concern for any society and takes an organized form through the use of cemeteries, or areas reserved for burial. The cemeteries of ancient Greece and Rome assume a wide range of types, from small, inconspicuous graveyards without architectural elaboration to long segments of major roads lined by tombs built to catch the gaze of the passerby. Most cemeteries share a common location type. Factors including religious pollution, hygiene, accessibility, and efficient land use resulted in the typical placement of cemeteries close to, but outside, the settlement of the living. A second role of cemeteries as sites for commemoration is documented for most periods. Long after the funeral, regular visits would be made for tombside feasts, libations, and other rituals that cemented the bond between the worlds of the living and the dead.

Greece. The cemeteries of Athens, particularly the Kerameikos cemetery, are the best studied post–Bronze Age burial grounds in Greece. The locations of sub-Mycenaean through Geometric cemeteries, presumably associated with adjacent settlements, are scattered and suggest both continuity and rupture with their Bronze Age predecessors. Burials occupied the area of the Classical Agora from the late Bronze Age to the Geometric period, and numerous Geometric wells close to small groups of contemporary graves document habitation in the immediate vicinity. In contrast, the Kerameikos cemetery, located immediately outside the Classical Dipylon gate, has a sub-Mycenaean foundation. Here, and by other later gates, cemeteries line major roads by the eighth century BCE. These cemeteries were the ones to survive as a major shift took place: the almost complete cessation of adult burial within central Athens in the seventh century. The erection of the fifth-century fortification circuit made explicit the exclusion of the Kerameikos and other peripheral cemeteries from the community of the living, and these cemeteries expanded outward, growing to tremendous sizes as additional graves were added through the Roman period. New cemeteries sometimes sprang up, but they consistently respected the boundary of the city wall. Classical texts offer no evidence for legislation restricting intramural burial, so this shift may represent a redefinition of settlement space as perceived by an expanding urban community without need of legal codification.

The Kerameikos was unquestionably the foremost cemetery in ancient Athens. Located on land that was cut by the course of the Sacred Way, it was the setting for aristocratic burial mounds of the seventh and sixth centuries BCE. In the fifth century the road linking the adjacent Dipylon Gate to the recently renovated Academy became lined by the tombs of the Demosion Sema, or state burial ground, where soldiers and important individuals who died in the service of Athens were laid at government expense and honored annually with speeches and races. Beginning in the late fourth century, extravagant family tomb monuments with ashlar facades lined the Kerameikos' streets, presenting the passerby with an ensemble of architecture and sculpture that commemorated the leading members of society. Like other major Athenian cemeteries, the Kerameikos continued in use through the Hellenistic and Roman periods, when spatial demands caused an unneeded street at the site to be filled with earth so that additional graves could be laid. Patterns of development for other Greek cities seem to present a generally similar picture to that of Athens, although city walls were not strictly observed as a cemetery boundary, as demonstrated by the famous roadside cemetery that entered Corinth at the city's Kenchrean gate.

Etruria. In central Italy the cemeteries of the Etruscan civilization are best represented by Cerveteri's Banditaccia cemetery, Tarquinia's Monterozzi cemetery, and Orvieto's Crocifisso del Tufo cemetery. The hills and ridges around these cities were first established as highly visible burial grounds by the proto-Villanovan and Villanovan civilizations of the ninth to eighth centuries BCE, and the same cemetery sites were frequently used when the Etruscans emerged in the seventh century. In the most common early cemetery format, chamber tombs covered by tumuli were irregularly scattered across the landscape. Regional variation, due in large part to the natural environment, produced some cemeteries of strikingly different types. At inland sites in southern Etruria like San Giuliano, chamber tombs were carved into high cliff faces; tombs for the most important individuals were installed on the hills topping the cliffs.

In the late sixth century increased regularization came to the Banditaccia cemetery, as well as some other burial grounds, through the advent of single-chamber cube tombs that were arranged in rows along cemetery roads and plazas. This kind of organization reached its pinnacle at Orvieto's Crocifisso del Tufo Cemetery in the late sixth to early fifth centuries. While formally planned Etruscan cemeteries are thought to reflect the urban plan of the Etruscan city, this development may further represent a more egalitarian social climate expressed through both a common tomb type and a broadened burial group. Traditional cemeteries declined as the Etruscans became Romanized in the late Republican period. At Tarquinia's massive Monterozzi cemetery, the last chamber tomb wall paintings belong to the late second century BCE, and tombs were reused without significant elaboration into the first century CE.

Rome. Rome's Iron Age burials, which should relate to nearby settlements, are found primarily in the later Roman Forum, on the Palatine and Esquiline hills, and in the later Augustan Forum. As Rome became urbanized, the Roman Forum was first limited to infant burials and then went out of use completely circa 600 BCE. Scattered burials from the sixth to third centuries have been recovered from the land extending outward from Rome's gates and may have been sited on the estates of the deceased. Though intramural burial was restricted in the fifth century by the Twelve Tables law code, elite Republican Romans, and later some emperors, were granted the right to bury within the city. In the Republican period the Esquiline Hill remained a major cemetery and was described by Cicero (*Philippics* 9.17), along with the Campus Martius, as a site favored by Romans granted an honorary burial by the senate. The Esquiline was not exclusively the domain of the elite, however. Literary sources (Horace *Satires* 1.8; Varro *De lingua Latina* 5.25) describe burial pits provided for the poor that are traditionally associated with an excavated group of at least seventy-five large stone-lined burial chambers of the third to second centuries.

Cemetery use in the city of Rome was transformed, beginning in the second century BCE, through the development of grave-lined streets, a practice that spread to Italian cities like Pompeii and Ostia in the following century. The highly visible land fronting major thoroughfares leading into Rome gradually became filled with monumental tombs built to honor leading individuals and their families. This cemetery format was clearly indebted to Greek models like the Athenian Kerameikos cemetery, but it was through Rome that tomb streets reached new heights of architectural elaboration and spread throughout the empire. Beginning in the Julio-Claudian period the social composition of these cemeteries was dramatically altered as they became dominated by the freedman class, often as members of *collegiati* (professional associations) who shared the costs of burial in columbarium tombs that could accommodate hundreds of cremation burials within urns.

The diminution of the mortuary sphere's role as a venue for the expression of personal power along with cemetery expansion redefined the character of tomb streets over the course of the first two centuries CE. Attention was redirected from the increasingly plain tomb facade to the building's interior, where the celebration of cult, invisible to the passerby, took on a role of heightened importance. In terms of layout the cemetery became a network of tomb rows linked by secondary pathways and interior plazas that shifted tomb orientation from the main avenue toward these internal spaces. The same movement away from burial as a monumental social statement to an emphasis on cult, coinciding with land-use pressures, culminated in the extension of large sections of Roman cemeteries underground in the second and third centuries in the form of catacombs.

Late Antique Greece and Rome. The key development of late antique cemeteries is traditionally identified as the large-scale introduction of burial within the city walls in the sixth century CE. In Rome, the last dated catacomb burial was made in 535, and in the same century graves, sometimes in small groups, sprang up throughout the urban interior. The densest burial area seems to have been the Campus Martius, placing the dead in close proximity to the living within this heavily populated district. The transfer of saints' relics from the catacombs to urban churches and the Gothic siege of Rome in 537–538 have each been advanced as the impetus for this phenomenon. While the latter factor must have been particularly influential for the city of Rome, a broader view suggests a gradual shift that included both a more fluidly defined urban space and changing attitudes toward the bodies of the dead. Cemeteries had already occupied positions close to the walls of Italian towns like Brescia in the third to fourth century, and in the fourth century these towns received small groups of intramural burials. Christianity played a major role within this process by reshaping the classical urban fabric with new ecclesiastical focal points that provided a desirable setting, in close proximity to saints' relics, for the church burial of clergy and elite members of society. Such church interments were exceptional, however, and the general movement of burial into the city should not be regarded as a strictly Christian phenomenon.

The picture for late antique Greece is somewhat different and reveals change within the midst of considerable continuity. Although regional practices varied throughout the East, the sixth century witnessed no widespread intramural burial adoption of the sort experienced by Rome. In Athens and other cities many of the old extramural cemeteries continued to function until at least the early seventh century. Newly installed cemeteries of the fifth to sixth centuries sometimes occur in the immediate vicinity of decayed buildings, including the Theater of Dionysus at Athens and the Sanctuary of Asclepius at Corinth. While these sites lay within the boundaries of the most extensive phases of city fortifications, they usually remained outside the contracted late antique administrative and economic centers. The topographic qualities of such cemeteries, including proximity to settlement, ease of access via major roads, and readily known and remembered locations are the most important factors contributing to their mortuary reuse. Churches are sometimes associated with fifth- to sixth-century Greek cemeteries, and usually seem to be constructed in the vicinity of preexisting burial grounds.

[*See also* Archaeology, *subentries* Overview, Sites in Greece, *and* Sites Elsewhere in Europe; Architecture, *subentry* Historical Overview; Catacombs; Death, *subentry* Death and Burial in the Ancient World; Etruscans, *subentry* Art and Archaeology; Funerals, Roman; Funerary Art; Sarcophagus; *and* Tombs.]

BIBLIOGRAPHY

Cantino Wataghin, G. "The Ideology of Urban Burials." In *The Idea and Ideal of the Town between Late Antiquity and the Early Middle Ages*, edited by G. P. Brogiolo and B. Ward-Perkins, pp. 147–180. Leiden, The Netherlands, and Boston: Brill, 1999. A useful overview of scholarship on late antique intramural burial in Italy that stresses the need for a diachronic analysis of mortuary practices.

Hesberg, Henner von, and Paul Zanker. *Römische Gräberstrassen, Selbstdarstellung, Status, Standard: Kolloquium in München vom 28. bis 30. Oktober 1985.* Munich, Germany: Verlag der Bayerischen Akademie der Wissenschaften, 1987. A superb, multilingual collection of papers on tomb-lined streets in Italy and the provinces that presents much new evidence.

Kurtz, Donna, and John Boardman. *Greek Burial Customs.* London: Thames and Hudson, 1971. A classic and still valuable treatment of burial practices in Greece for the Iron Age to the Classical period.

Morris, Ian. *Burial and Ancient Society: The Rise of the Greek City-State.* Cambridge, U.K.: Cambridge University Press, 1989. A provocative study of Iron Age burial practices that identifies a widening of the group receiving formal burial as a sign of an early rise of the polis circa 750 BCE.

Steingräber, Stephan. *Etrurien: Städte, Heiligtümer, Nekropolen.* Munich, Germany: Hirmer, 1981. A well-illustrated gazetteer of Etruscan sites accompanied by a substantial bibliography.

Tzavella, E. "Burial and Urbanism in Athens (4th–9th C. AD)." *Journal of Roman Archaeology* 21 (2008): 352–376. The first comprehensive investigation of Athenian cemeteries for late antiquity through the Dark Age of the seventh to ninth centuries. Includes much unpublished data.

Jeremy Ott

CENSOR

See Magistrates and Officials, Roman

CENTAURS

The mythical Centaurs, wild, mountain-dwelling creatures who were part man and part horse, appear frequently in Greek and Roman art. Unlike the satyrs, who shared the Centaurs' taste for wine and women, Centaurs were brave and aggressive, leading to violent encounters with Greek heroes. On the other hand, two Centaurs, Chiron and Pholos, were renowned for their wisdom, and it is this duality of both form and character that make Centaurs a potent symbol of man's divided nature.

A handful of Bronze Age figurines may represent Centaurs, but the earliest certain occurance in Greek art is a large terra-cotta statuette from Lefkandi, in Euboea, that dates to the late tenth century BCE. Nearly two centuries pass before their next appearance, in the third quarter of the eighth century, when small Centaurs in the Geometric style were cast in bronze as votive dedications. Among these is a group in the Metropolitan Museum of Art, said to be from Olympia, with a Centaur battling a human warrior. The suggestion of narrative invites identification with mythical fights known from later works and literary accounts, but in this early period it is difficult to identify specific combats.

It was not until the seventh century that recognizable battles between heroes and Centaurs began to occur on bronze plaques and painted Corinthian and Athenian vases, such as the great Protoattic amphora in New York that shows Heracles (Hercules) killing the Centaur Nessus for insulting his wife Deianeira. Other Protoattic vases show Peleus presenting his son Achilles to his teacher Chiron, and a bronze plaque from Olympia portrays an episode at the wedding in Thessaly of Pirithous, at which the drunken Centaurs fell upon the Lapith women: two Centaurs are pounding into the ground the otherwise invulnerable Greek warrior Caineus. These subjects continued to be represented by artists throughout the Archaic and Classical periods, alongside such related episodes as Chiron urging Peleus to assault Thetis and the old Centaur's subsequent attendance at their wedding. The latter was painted by the Athenian black-figure artist

Kleitias on the François Vase (c. 570 BCE); in another frieze on the vase the death of Caineus is set amid the fight at the wedding of Pirithous.

The Thessalian combat became the model for future "Centauromachies," with Centaurs brandishing boulders and branches in frenzied battle with Greek opponents. It was continued in numerous Athenian red-figure vase paintings of the fifth century, when the role of Pirithous' friend Theseus is emphasized. In the first half of the century the Centauromachy was the subject of a mural by the painter Polygnotus in the Theseion at Athens and appeared in monumental form in the west pediment of the temple of Zeus at Olympia. Most famous of all are the south metopes of the Parthenon (c. 438 BCE), where the struggle with the Centaurs may symbolize the Greek defeat of the barbarian Persians. In the sixth century, another mythical Centauromachy, between Hercules and the Peloponnesian Centaurs who interrupted his visit to the Centaur Pholos, was portrayed in carved reliefs on the temple of Athena at Assos (Turkey). An earlier episode from the same story, with Pholos watching Hercules open a jar of wine, was a favorite of Athenian vase painters.

Centaurs loom larger in art than in literature. Homer does not mention them by name, but Hesiod and Pindar know Chiron and Nessus, and several authors mention the conflict with the Lapiths. The revenge of Nessus was the subject of Sophocles' *Trachiniae*, and Pholos was featured in a comedy by Epicharmus. Later writers, such as Apollodorus and Diodorus Siculus, flesh out details of the old myths.

Most early Centaurs were represented with the body and hind legs of a horse attached to the rear of a fully formed man. From the beginning, however, some Centaurs were depicted with the upper body of a man and the body and four legs of a horse. The more human type persisted until the end of the sixth century, after which it was reserved for depictions of Chiron, a mark of his civilized nature and his status as an immortal son of Cronus. Both types commonly are depicted with long hair and beards. Chiron often wears human clothing, but most Centaurs are nude except for an occasional animal skin.

Narrative scenes involving Centaurs became less common in the fourth century, but the Thessalian Centauromachy again was splendidly portrayed in sculpted reliefs on the temple of Apollo at Bassae. As part of the established Greek repertory, Centaurs continued to be depicted throughout antiquity in every scale and medium, from seals and jewelry to mosaics and statuary. Impressive Roman sculptures in colored marble of a young and an old Centaur, the latter bound and ridden by Eros, probably were based on Greek originals of the late third or second century BCE. Although Centaurs now mostly occurred in decorative roles, in marble sarcophagus reliefs Roman sculptors continued to represent their battles with Hercules and the Lapiths, perhaps symbolizing man's struggle to overcome his divided nature and attain spirtual unity.

[*See also* Monsters *and* Mythic Wars and Battles.]

BIBLIOGRAPHY

Baur, Paul Victor Christopher. *Centaurs in Ancient Art, the Archaic Period.* Berlin: K. Curtius, 1912.

Padgett, J. Michael. *The Centaur's Smile: The Human Animal in Early Greek Art.* Princeton, N.J.: Princeton University Art Museum, 2003.

Schiffler, Birgitt. *Die Typologie des Kentauren in der antiken Kunst vom 10. bis zum Ende des 4. Jhs. v. Chr.* Frankfurt am Main, Germany: Lang, 1976.

J. Michael Padgett

CENTRAL ASIA

Central Asia, in spite of the name, has often been marginalized in modern studies of the ancient world. From the broader perspective of world rather than Western civilization, however, the region is indeed central to the interwoven histories of China, India, Persia, Parthia, Egypt, Greece, and Rome. No greater symbol of that centrality exists than the fabled Silk Road of Central Asia, one of the world's first truly international trade networks. If all roads led to Rome, then some of the longest had as their nexus such Central Asian cities as Samarqand and Bactra.

As a cultural or geopolitical construct, Central Asia has no fixed boundaries. The term generally refers to the expansive landlocked regions that stretch from the Caspian Sea to western China, and from the southern Urals to the Hindu Kush Mountains. Six of the modern so-called 'stans fall wholly or in part within this territory: Afghanistan, Tajikistan, Uzbekistan, Turkmenistan, Kyrgyzstan, and Kazakhstan. "Inner Asia," often used as a synonym, more precisely adds the regions of Tibet and Mongolia, so that one might think of Central Asia as essentially the westward (Islamic) arm of Inner Asia. Vast, varied, and complex (Curtius 7.4.26), Central Asia embraces broad open steppes, towering mountain ranges, arid deserts, powerful rivers, and lush oases. These diverse features produce extremes of climate and habitation, imposing natural limits on settlement patterns, military and trade routes, agricultural production, and population densities. The steppes naturally fostered a horse-based culture, and from ancient Central Asia came important innovations in the use of rigid saddles and armored cavalry. For the most part, the region is dominated by pastoral nomadism; farming along river valleys and around oases relies heavily on irrigation. The economy, therefore, revolves around sheep, goats, cattle, and horses, plus scattered harvests of fruits and the staple crops of barley and wheat. Major rivers such as the Oxus (modern Amu) and Jaxartes (modern Syr) tended to bring together, sometimes violently but usually symbiotically, the nomadic and sedentary cultures of Central Asia. This dynamic relationship can be traced as far back as the Bronze Age, when the nomadic Andronovo culture of the northern steppes interacted with a major indigenous civilization (the so-called Bactria-Margiana Archaeological Complex, or Oxus civilization) that rivaled its contemporaries in Egypt, Crete, Anatolia, and elsewhere (c. 2200–1700 BCE). Urban centers benefited from Eurasian commerce and exhibited a high degree of cross-cultural influence. In Islamic tradition, Bactra (modern Balkh in Afghanistan) ranks as the oldest city in the world.

Under Achaemenid rule (539–330), Bactra served as the satrapal capital of Bactria-Sogdiana, a province that extended from the Hindu Kush northward across the Oxus to the Jaxartes. Revered among the Persians as the birthplace of Zoroaster and associated with the legendary exploits of Ninus, Semiramis, and (among the Greeks) Prometheus, Hercules, and Dionysus, Bactria and its environs sometimes sound like a Neverland in our sources. Griffins and other beasts allegedly lived there among such tangible exotica as lapis lazuli, gold, silphium (a rare medicinal plant), camels, prized ("heavenly") horses, and even petroleum. The long and brutal military campaign of Alexander the Great (late fourth century BCE) ended Persian sovereignty in this part of Central Asia, and introduced a strong Greek presence by way of thousands of settlers whose purpose, in part, was to isolate and defend the satrapy from nomadic Saka (Scythian) tribes beyond the Jaxartes. The construction of Alexandria-Eschate ("the Furthermost") on the Jaxartes was one aspect of this grand enterprise. Other Greek foundations, including the excavated site at Ai Khanoum, attest to the resources and manpower required to hold this area in check. Seleucus, one of Alexander's generals and the founder of the Seleucid Empire, renewed these efforts early in the Hellenistic era.

In the middle of the third century BCE, Bactria and Sogdiana broke free of Seleucid control and sustained itself as an independent Hellenistic state, ruled at first by the Diodotid dynasty. When King Antiochus III attempted to reassert Seleucid power in Central Asia at the end of the century, Euthydemus I of Bactria prevailed by enduring a long siege at Bactra (208–206 BCE) and warning Antiochus of a pending nomadic invasion by the Sakas (Polybius 10.49 and 11.34). Antiochus conceded the royal title to Euthydemus and marched away. Some fifty years later, during the reign of Eucratides I the Great, the Sakas did invade Sogdiana while the once-nomadic Parthians encroached upon western Bactria. Greek rule in Central Asia ended once and for all when migrating Yuezhi tribes, displaced from the north by the powerful Xiongnu, overran Sogdiana (Kangju) and Bactria (Daxia) by circa 130 BCE. Chinese sources offer us a valuable snapshot

Central Asian Crown. Crown from the excavations of the necropolis at Tillya Tepe, Afghanistan, first century BCE–first century CE. KABUL MUSEUM, AFGHANISTAN/THE BRIDGEMAN ART LIBRARY

of this process, derived from the mission of Zhang Qian (d. 114 BCE) to secure for his emperor access to the celebrated "heavenly" horses of the Fergana Valley. By the middle of the first century CE, one branch of the Yuezhi led by Kujula Kadphises settled into a powerful state that absorbed the lingering vestiges of Central Asian Hellenism. The Greek alphabet was used, and Hellenistic-style coins were minted. The Greek pantheon fused with a variety of religious influences from Iran and India, including Buddhism. The gigantic Buddhas of Bamian, destroyed by the Taliban in 2001, were once a remarkable reminder of this development. This eclectic state became the wealthy and powerful Kushan Empire, a vital link in the long Silk Road connecting the empires of China, Parthia, India, and Rome. Kushan expansion into India linked the lucrative land and sea routes between East and West. The dazzling golden hoard of Bactria, excavated from the graves of Kushan aristocrats interred at Tillya-Tepe in northern Afghanistan, exemplifies the riches and far-flung contacts of this Central Asian Empire.

In the third and fourth centuries CE, the Kushans lost territories to the ascendant Sassanid Persians, who had succeeded the Parthians as an Iranian superpower. Finally, the Kushans succumbed to the Hephthalites (the so-called White Huns) in the fifth century, playing out a scenario in Central Asia not so unlike the one overwhelming the Romans in the West.

[*See also* Alexander the Great, *subentry* Life and Career; Bosporus, Kingdom of; Nomads; Persia, *subentries* Arsacid and Sassanian Persia *and* Achaemenid Persia; Scythia; *and* Seleucids.]

BIBLIOGRAPHY
Benjamin, Craig. *The Yuezhi: Origin, Migration, and the Conquest of Northern Bactria*. Turnhout, Belgium: Brepols, 2007.
Briant, Pierre. *Histoire de l'empire perse: De Cyrus à Alexandre*. 2 vols. Paris: Fayard, 1996. Translated by Peter T. Daniels as *From Cyrus to Alexander: A History of the Persian Empire*. Winona Lake, Ind.: Eisenbraun, 2002.
Holt, Frank L. *Alexander the Great and Bactria: The Formation of a Greek Frontier in Central Asia*. Leiden, The Netherlands, and New York: E. J. Brill, 1988.
Holt, Frank L. *Thundering Zeus: The Making of Hellenistic Bactria*. Berkeley: University of California Press, 1999.

Frank L. Holt

CERES

The Roman goddess Ceres boasts a Latin name that suggestively connects her to generation (*creare*) and growth (*crescere*). Ancient antiquarians suggested such associations (Servius' commentary on Virgil *Georgics* 1.7), and modern linguists affirm them. May we conclude, then, that Roman farmers first conceived of Ceres as an impersonal force akin to the agrarian goddess of mildew, Robigo? In almost all other respects, Ceres appears thoroughly Hellenized. According to our historical sources, she was formally identified with Demeter of Enna in Sicily (Cicero *In Verrem* 2.4.108) when, after consultation of the Sibylline Books, her temple was vowed in response to famine in 496 BCE (Dionysius of Halicarnassus *Antiquitates Romanae* 6.17). In this Greek guise, Ceres retained her customary consorts in a triad that was Latin only in name: Ceres, Liber, and Libera (i.e., Demeter, Dionysus, and Kore).

At Rome, Ceres was worshiped in the Greek language by priestesses imported from Greek cities in southern Italy (Cicero *Pro Balbo* 55; Valerius

Maximus 1.1.1). Her sacrifices, sows, were made according to the "Greek rite," that is, with head uncovered. Cassius dedicated the temple, formally called Aedes Cereris Liberi Liberaeque, on the Aventine near the Circus Maximus in 493, and Greek artisans inscribed their names (Pliny the Elder *Naturalis historia* 35.154). Historical context reveals more distinctively Roman outlines: Ceres was the plebs' patron, and her Aventine temple served as the headquarters for Plebeian aediles who were responsible for the grain supply. It also served as their treasury and archive. All fines levied for violations against the sacred persons of the people's tribunes were forfeited to Ceres (Livy 3.55.7; Dionysius of Halicarnassus *Antiquitates Romanae* 6.89). Tribunes received and stored senatorial decrees here (Livy 3.55.13).

Plebeian aediles were originally in charge of games held in honor of Ceres from the 12th through the 19th of April, the last day of which constituted the Cerialia proper. Festivities included feasting, gladiators, and tying burning torches to foxes' tails (Ovid *Fasti* 4.681–2). A second feast, enjoined by the Sibylline Books in 191 BCE for every four years—eventually observed annually on 4 October—was celebrated solely by women and required preparatory fasting and sexual abstinence (Ovid *Amores* 3.10.1–2; cf. the Greek Thesmophoria).

Ceres appears also in our most ancient fragments of Roman law (Twelve Tables 8.5 = Pliny *Naturalis historia* 18.12): those who stole crops by night were executed "for Ceres" and suspended from trees (on Ceres and trees, cf. Ovid *Metamorphoses* 8.741–742). Ovid tells that Ceres, a goddess of peace, could avert war (*Fasti* 4.407–408), Cicero tells that Ceres taught justice, morality, and humanity (*In Verrem* 2.5.187–188), and Festus tells that she served as a foundation for marriage (*De verborum significatione*, in the excerpts of Paul under the word *facem*). On the other hand, she is sometimes portrayed as the patron of divorce (in the augmented edition of Servius' commentary on Virgil *Aeneid* 3.139; cf. Plutarch *Romulus* 22).

Because the father (Jupiter = Zeus) of her daughter Proserpina (Persephone) had conspired to wed the maiden to his brother Pluto (Hades) in "infernal marriage" (*Orci nuptiae*), Ceres was associated also with the dead. Those who had failed to fulfill funeral duties could, for example, try to make amends by sacrificing a sow to Ceres (Aulus Gellius 4.6.8). Her association with Earth (Tellus) also contributed to such conceptions. During the Empire, Ceres continued to appeal. Her worship was widespread. Curse tablets testify to her popularity as well as power to punish. Augustus and Tiberius rebuilt her temple after it burned in 31 BCE (Tacitus *Annales* 2.49). She was associated first with the empress Livia Drusilla and was more generally, especially on coins, linked to *annona* (the grain supply). Claudius attempted (Suetonius *Divus Claudius* 25), and Hadrian was able (Aurelius Victor 14.4), to introduce the Eleusinian mysteries to Rome. Latin literature is full of elaborations and allusions to the myth of Ceres, but see especially Ovid's *Fasti* (4.393–620), Ovid's *Metamorphoses* (5.341–571), and Claudian's *De raptu Proserpinae*.

[*See also* Demeter; Eleusis and the Eleusinian Mysteries; *and* Mythology, Roman.]

BIBLIOGRAPHY

Hinds, Stephen. *The Metamorphosis of Persephone: Ovid and the Self-Conscious Muse.* Cambridge, U.K.: Cambridge University Press, 1987.

Le Bonniec, Henri. *Le culte de Cérès à Rome, des origines à la fin de la République.* Paris: Klincksieck, 1958.

Simon, Erika. *Die Götter der Römer.* Munich: Hirmer, 1990. See pages 43–50.

Spaeth, Barbette S. *The Roman Goddess Ceres.* Austin: University of Texas Press, 1996.

Hans-Friedrich Mueller

CHAERONEA, BATTLE OF

Philip II, after bringing to an end the Sacred War and negotiating the Peace of Philocrates (346 BCE), had been anxious to bring Athenians into alliance with Macedon. But the Athenians' fears of Macedonian expansion in the Thraceward and Hellespontine regions, which was an area of vital economic interest, led eventually to a coalition of Thebes and Athens, whose forces confronted Philip at Chaeronea in Boeotia. The battle occurred on 2 August 338 BCE (for the date, 7 Metageitnion, see Plutarch *Camillus* 19.7), pitting thirty thousand Macedonian infantry and two thousand cavalry against an army of roughly equal size (Diodorus 16.85.5). Philip's forces stretched from the hilly ground at the foot of the Chaeronean acropolis to the Cephisus River; the king commanded the forces on the right, while his eighteen-year-old son Alexander led the cavalry on the left. This placed Alexander directly opposite the Sacred Band, the vaunted three-hundred-man infantry unit of the Thebans. But Philip, by allowing the Athenians to push back the Macedonian infantry on the right, created a gap in the Greek line, for the Thebans were prevented from moving directly forward by the marshy area near the Cephisus. This gap was exploited by Alexander's cavalrymen, who isolated the Sacred Band and took them in the flank. Philip, meanwhile, had backed up, drawing the Greek infantry forward until he recoiled with devastating effect.

The combined efforts of father and son dealt a crippling blow to the coalition and utterly destroyed the Sacred Band. The Athenians lost one thousand killed and two thousand wounded (Diodorus 16.86.5–6). The grave of the Sacred Band—the remains of 254 dead have been discovered—was marked by the Lion of Chaeronea (Pausanias 9.40.10), one of the most impressive war monuments of the Greek world.

Chaeronea has come down in history as the battle that destroyed Greek liberty, but Philip's treatment of the two enemies was significantly different: Thebes was garrisoned and forced to ransom her prisoners of war; Athenian prisoners were released without ransom, and their city, along with the other Greek states (with the exception of the Spartans, who stubbornly refused), signed a Common Peace and constituted the League of Corinth (337 BCE) with Philip as its *hēgemōn*. It was with the aid of league forces that Philip planned to launch his Persian War. In the event, Philip was assassinated and the role of *hēgemōn* and leader of the expedition was inherited by Alexander, who achieved spectacular results.

[*See also* Alexander the Great, *subentry* Life and Career; Philip II; *and* Sacred Wars.]

BIBLIOGRAPHY

Davis, Paul K. *100 Decisive Battles from Ancient Times to the Present*. Oxford: Oxford University Press, 1999. See pages 29–31.

Fuller, J. F. C. *The Generalship of Alexander the Great*. New Brunswick, N.J.: Rutgers University Press, 1960.

Hammond, N. G. L. "The Two Battles of Chaeronea (338 B.C. and 86 B.C.)." *Klio* 31 (1938): 186–218.

Hammond, N. G. L., and G. T. Griffith. *A History of Macedonia*. Vol. 2. Oxford: Clarendon Press, 1979. See pages 596–599.

Waldemar Heckel

CHALCIS

Chalcis is a major town in the middle of the west coast of Euboea located strategically on a small peninsula. The location commands the narrowest part of the Euripus strait and controls sea traffic. Domination over the fertile plains in the surrounding regions was equally important to the development of the town and was accomplished by the success in a dispute with Eretria for the possession of the fertile Lelantine plain to the south (Thucydides 1.15.3). In the eighth century BCE, Chalcidians participated with other Euboeans in the foundation of the colonies in South Italy and Sicily, while in the Chalcidice peninsula, many colonies claimed Chalcis as their mother city. After an alliance with the Boeotian League against Athens (Herodotus 5.74.2), the city was defeated, and in 506 BCE Athenian *clerourchoi* (settlers) were installed in the fertile lands of the local aristocracy, the *hippobotai*, who were expelled. A fort on the site of Vrachos—overlooking the Lelantine plain—might be associated with the Athenian cleruchy (settlement). During the Persian wars, Chalcidians fought both at Artemision (Herodotus 8.1.2) and Salamis (Herodotus 8.46.2). Chalcis was a member of the Delian League, an Athenian-controlled alliance against the Persians. Chalcis appears in the tribute lists from 448/7 BCE (*Inscriptiones Graecae* vol. 1 [3rd ed.] 269.V31). But in 446 BCE, the town led a revolt of Euboean cities against Athens. Defeated by Pericles (Thucydides 1.114.1–3; Plutarch *Pericles* 23.4), it became a tributary ally and lost its independence. In 331 BCE, Philip II imposed a Macedonian garrison after the battle at Chaeronia. Aristotle died there in 322 BCE. In the Hellenistic period, Chalcis was involved in the wars of the Diadochi. In 196 BCE, Titus Quinctius Flamininus revived the Euboean League and proclaimed Chalcis an autonomous city. He was honored with races and a gymnasium. After a brief occupation under Antiochus of Syria (192/1 BCE), it was partly destroyed in 146 BCE by the Romans for allying against them with the Achaean League. The city declined until the Byzantine period, when it became an administrative and cultural center. In 1210 CE it was captured by the Venetians and declared the capital of the kingdom of Negroponte.

The modern town, which is built on the top of the ancient one, allows only random archaeological investigation. More information, however, is offered by the surrounding areas. To the north, the Early Bronze Age site at Manika, with rich cemeteries and a well-organized settlement, testifies to the early significance of the area. Equally rich tombs are dated to the Mycenaean period. Patchy traces of Early Iron Age cemeteries and domestic deposits denote the settlement's importance during this period. It must have been comparable to others on the island such as Eretria and Lefkandi. This might be when Amphidamas was king; Hesiod attended his funerary games and won a tripod for a song (*Opera et Dies* 654–655). The Archaic and Classical city extended around the foothills of Mount Vathrovounia, which was occupied from the Neolithic period. The acropolis might have been on Arethousa hill, one of the town's highest. Remains of fortifications with towers have been located and are dated to the fourth century BCE. The Arethousa springs were the main source for supplying water to the city. Below Arethousa is located the natural harbor of Agios Stephanos, which is not affected by

the currents of Euripus. To the west of the modern city might have been the location of the Kanethos hill known from the sources (Strabo 10.1.8). Doric capitals were found in the wall of the medieval castle (*Kastro*) and might belong to the Temple of Olympian Zeus (*Inscriptiones Graecae* vol. 1 [3rd ed.] 40.35.61–62). In 410 BCE, Chalcis was connected with Boeotia by a bridge (Diodorus Siculus 13.47.3–6; Strabo 9.2.8). Inscriptions dated to the late Classical and Hellenistic periods refer to the existence of a gymnasium, a stadium, a theater, and various sanctuaries.

From the ancient sources we learn that Chalcis was renowned for its rich agricultural resources (especially its olive trees), for its excellent metalworking, for the production of purple dye, and, above all, for its fine lifestyle. Athenaeus (4.132) speaks admirably of its symposia and high-quality seafood.

[*See also* Chaeronea, Battle of; Euboea; *and* Lelantine War.]

BIBLIOGRAPHY

Bakhuizen, S. C. *Studies in the Topography of Chalcis on Euboea.* Leiden: Brill, 1985.

Reber, Karl, Mogens Herman Hansen, and Pierre Ducrey. "Euboia." In *An Inventory of Archaic and Classical Poleis*, edited by Mogens Herman Hansen and Thomas Heine Nielsen, pp. 643–663. Oxford: Oxford University Press, 2004.

Sapouna-Sakellaraki, Efi. *Chalkis.* Translated by W. Phelps. Athens: Greek Ministry of Culture, 1995.

Irene S. Lemos

CHAOS AND COSMOS

See Causation, Theories of *and* Creation.

CHARIOT RACING

Detailed accounts of organized chariot races can be found in the earliest Greek literature. Homer's lengthy description of the funeral games for Patroclus in book 23 of the *Iliad* gives pride of place to the *tethrippon*, the four-horse chariot event, a prominence paralleled at the Panhellenic games. According to tradition, chariot racing was introduced in the twenty-fifth Olympiad (680 BCE), a late addition that may reflect the growing regional importance of the Great Games and their ability to attract competitors and audience from a broader catchment zone.

Greece. Elites competing for status in the Hellenic world deployed athletic contests for the display of leadership and virtue. Sponsorship of racing teams carried a higher cost than did other events, a factor elevating the prestige of the commitment even though sponsors did not, with few exceptions, personally participate in the event. From the late sixth century BCE the richest and most ambitious victors used a range of media to publicize their success to a broader, even diachronic, audience. These included epinician odes (victory odes) like those of Pindar and Bacchylides, statues of themselves with their winning teams in a Panhellenic sanctuary or their home city (the famous charioteer at Delphi is a portion of such a monument), or coin images, which achieved yet another kind of circulation for the celebration of victory. In their repeated references to the victor's public-mindedness, his selflessness with money, and the honor brought by his victory to his home city, the odes reflect a certain tension between the acclaim that a champion received for individual achievement and the corporate interests of the civic community. Status gained from a *tethrippon* victory could disrupt the balance of power within the ruling class. Herodotus specifically connects success in chariot racing to a number of would-be tyrants in Athens, including Cylon and Miltiades. The same combination of ambition and threat lurks in Alcibiades' sponsorship of no fewer than seven chariot teams at Olympia. Indeed, many of Pindar's victory odes celebrated the Sicilian tyrants of Syracuse and Acragas (Agrigento).

Hellenistic dynasts and their courts also appropriated equestrian victories within the panoply of royal image building. Among these champions a striking number of elite women and queens were actively engaged in equestrian competition. The poetry of Posidippus and Callimachus honors Berenice II, who brought much glory to the Ptolemies for her chariot successes at Nemea, Isthmia, and Olympia. Statues and inscriptions applaud Zeuxo of Cyrene and her three daughters, who took home crowns from multiple equestrian victories at the Panathenaea of 202 and 198 BCE. The epitaph for Damodika of Cyme explicitly compares her racing victory to her motherhood, both honorable achievements that she leaves to posterity. Such examples point to the greater public presence of women as civic benefactors and wielders of economic power in the Hellenistic world.

Rome. In Rome, the *ludi circenses* were cherished as the oldest of spectacle events, dating back to the city's legendary founder. The organization of *ludi* as annual public festivals started in the fourth century BCE with the Ludi Magni, which featured chariot races in honor of Jupiter. The magistrates who organized the *ludi* seized the opportunity to demonstrate their generosity and capacity for cultural as well as political leadership. Triumphant Roman generals likewise competed to produce dazzling victory games. Contemporary Hellenistic dynasts and their pageants of royal power were models for the development of Roman *ludi*, more than the Great Games of the Classical period were. Members of the Roman elite did not, however, compete either as owners of stables or as charioteers themselves. Instead of relying on individuals' racing stables, the Roman Republic developed a corporate system of training and support of horses and drivers by a limited number of color-coded collectives: the Red, White, Blue, and Green *factiones*. Individual elite *editores* produced spectacles as a whole, arranging contracts with providers for different performances in the program. The relationship constructed between the producer of Roman spectacle and the audience, grateful and supportive recipients of this gift, was crucial to the magnates of the late Republic and to the emperors, their successors to power.

Normally spectacle was an occasion for positive interaction between the emperor and his people. It was important that the emperor be seen to share popular pleasures, as a demonstration of his engagement with the lives and needs of the Roman people. He was expected to cheer vigorously; choosing a circus faction to root for conferred an important social identity on the *princeps*. Even so, a certain restraint was also expected: examples of imperial misbehavior include Caracalla's setting his soldiers on rival fans who had dared to boo his favorite driver. The exchange between emperor and audience went beyond spontaneous reaction to the races. Spectators could and did request further gifts, favors, and even reform of unpopular policies. The emotional resonance of the setting and the high visibility of the exchange explain the significance attributed by ancient authors to incidents of failed communication. On the whole, however, races made Romans happy.

The great popularity of the races was a result of the intensity of the experience: the speed, the pounding of the hooves, the dust, the sweat, the brilliant colors, and, always, the combined fear and hope of an accident, a *naufragium* (literally "shipwreck"). Educated viewers recognized different strategies of winning, distinguishing between the driver who held the lead throughout the race, the strong competitor who finally managed to pass the leader, and the charioteer who burst from behind to win in the last moments. Teams from the same faction might cooperate to break rivals' focus, pressure them out of coveted inside lanes, even foul targeted opponents. The limited number of teams in the faction system channeled fan enthusiasm into more intense rivalries, more intense feelings of group identity, expressed vividly by the habit of wearing faction colors on game days. Action in the stands seems also to have been a real draw for many: some hoped to hook up romantically in this heady environment, others were lured by the range of door prizes given a lucky few spectators. Risk was personalized by the thrill of betting on the outcome. Ancient gamblers weighed career records of horses and drivers or bet on favorite colors to show their fan-club solidarity.

Outstanding drivers were embedded in a cult of celebrity, their portraits captured in a broad range of media, their images built on their strength, skill, and cool attitude. Entourages followed them in public, eager for reflected glory. The acclaim was

Chariot Racing. *Pompa circensis*, the ceremony that opened chariot races. Panel in opus sectile from the Basilica of Junius Bassus, Rome, fourth century CE. Museo Nazionale Romano (Palazzo Massimo alle Terme), Rome. PHOTOGRAPH BY ROBERT B. KEBRIC

perhaps heightened by the fact that many died young, like Crescens, dead at twenty-two with career winnings of more than 1.5 million sesterces. Legally, however, chariot drivers, like other performers, suffered *infamia*, a loss of status and privilege imposed on all occupations in which one's body was used to please the public. Those in elite classes who trained and even raced in public were pushing the limits of socially acceptable behavior; additional legislation, aimed at the upper classes, tried to restrict these crimes of status, or at least make them less visible. Inappropriate racing enthusiasm was a source of criticism for some emperors: Caligula's "treats" bestowed on the racehorse Incitatus, including a senatorial toga as a stable blanket, became symbols of his habitual abuse of political privilege.

Loyalty to a circus color was extreme among many fans and became a core social identity in late antiquity, a time when such identity was compressed by dwindling opportunities for public involvement. Fan clubs had high visibility as civic groups: members in their colors sat in reserved sections, to cheer and chant petitions, their fervor escalating because of proximity and perceived connection. Such partisanship could slip into violent action, a phenomenon seemingly more frequent and severe in the later Eastern empire. The most notorious example of politicized circus rioting is the Nika riot of 532 CE, in which growing tensions over tax reforms and government corruption were exacerbated by the emperor Justinian's botched response to the demands of circus fans. Widespread mayhem destroyed public buildings, and the rioters elevated a new candidate to the purple as army loyalties wavered in the face of such uncertainty. The empress Theodora's grim resolution, encapsulated by her famous epigram "The purple makes a good shroud," bolstered Justinian's stance enough to launch a counterassault on the circus crowds. Order was restored, but suppression of the revolt entailed the massacre of thousands of civilians drawn in by the network of circus fans.

[*See also* Athletics, Greek; Circus; Games, *subentry* Roman Games; *and* Stadium.]

BIBLIOGRAPHY

Bergmann, Bettina A., and Christine Kondoleon, eds. *The Art of Ancient Spectacle.* Washington, D.C.: National Gallery of Art, 1999.

Cameron, Alan. *Bread and Circuses: The Roman Emperor and His People.* London: King's College London, 1974.

Cameron, Alan. *Circus Factions: Blues and Greens at Rome and Byzantium.* Oxford: Clarendon Press, 1976.

Hornblower, Simon, and Catherine Morgan, eds. *Pindar's Poetry, Patrons, and Festivals: From Archaic Greece to the Roman Empire.* Oxford: Oxford University Press, 2007.

Rouché, Charlotte. *Performers and Partisans at Aphrodisias in the Roman and Late Roman Periods: A Study Based on Inscriptions from the Current Excavations at Aphrodisias in Caria.* London: Society for the Promotion of Roman Studies, 1993.

Alison Futrell

CHARYBDIS

See Scylla and Charybdis.

CHERSONESUS, PONTIC

See Asia.

CHERSONESUS, THRACIAN

See Thrace.

CHILDBIRTH

See Birth and Reproduction.

CHILDREN AND CHILDHOOD

In the summer of 413 BCE, the Athenians sent a force of Thracian mercenaries back to their homeland in the north, with instructions to do what harm they could to the enemy on the way. Finding the small Boeotian city of Mycalessus unguarded, they attacked it. The Athenian historian Thucydides describes what happened next:

> The Thracians rushed into Mycalessus and set to wrecking the houses and shrines and killing the people. They spared neither old nor young, but killed whomever they came upon, one after the other, children and women too, and farm animals besides—every living thing they saw. For the people of Thrace are like most barbarians, most murderous when they think things are going their way.... They also attacked a boys' school, the largest one there, just when the boys had gone inside it, and cut them all down. This terrible disaster was the worst for the whole city as it fell upon it unexpectedly (author's translation; Thucydides *History of the Peloponnesian War* 7.29.4).

It is the deaths of the schoolchildren on which Thucydides chooses to focus: they are the climax of the catastrophe. A general himself, he was well aware of how war can affect children—and of how their deaths can affect everyone else. He blames the Thracians for the tragedy. They are barbarians, non-Greek—indeed, the brutal and indiscriminate killing, in a school of all places, characterizes them as uncivilized. The implication is that Greeks cared for their children—and that this was both desirable and distinctive. We need not accept what he says at face value. It is easy to point to Greek atrocities against children in war: the Trojan prince Astyanax, hurled down from the towers of Troy in a war Thucydides himself thought historical, and princess Polyxena, sacrificed over the tomb of Achilles. Closer to Thucydides' own day, Xenophon praises the Spartan king Agesilaus for looking after young children abandoned when he moved his camp on campaign; slave dealers did not want to carry and feed those left unsold (Xenophon *Agesilaus* 1.21). Such consideration was obviously rare. And the Thracians did not commit their crimes on their own. They had, as it happens, an Athenian commander—though Thucydides is silent on his role. Greek (and Roman) attitudes and actions toward children were complicated: diverse from place to place, over time, across social classes, and according to gender, they also (as in this case) enter our sources for many rhetorical reasons. A short article can hardly provide more than a glimpse of such complexity, evident from the beginning of a child's life.

Greeks and Romans did not raise all the children born into their households and regarded those who did (Jews, Egyptians) as unusual. At Athens, the decision was the prerogative of the *kyrios*, the adult male who headed it. At Sparta, on the other hand, children were brought before the elders of the tribesmen, who had rejected newborns hurled into a chasm at the base of Mount Taygetus (Plutarch *Lycurgus* 16.1). Their role may have improved a child's odds—the elders would place considerable weight on Sparta's need for military manpower—or impaired them. (The elders would lack a father's emotional interest in his child.) At Rome, the life-or-death power of the *paterfamilias* was theoretically extended to older children under his control, even after they had become adults, though in practice it too was exerted only over newborns. Here, as at Athens, those rejected—"exposed"—were set out in places well known for this purpose, and might be rescued. Most were likely raised as slaves but freeborn foundlings might be able to reclaim their original status later in life. In general, Roman law required that those who took them in be repaid for the costs of rearing them; Greek law did not. Slave children, the illegitimate, and the visibly handicapped were most likely to be rejected. (Agesilaus, lame in one leg, may have been an exception.) There is some evidence that girls too made up a group at risk. For example, a law ascribed to Romulus allegedly required Romans to raise all their sons but only their firstborn daughters (Dionysius of Halicarnassus *Roman Antiquities* 2.15.1). However, this law (if it ever existed) was no longer in force during Dionysius' lifetime. (Spartan girls may not have undergone the scrutiny by the elders; in any case, it is unclear how this would have affected their chances of survival.) Though some intellectuals (such as the Stoic Gaius Musonius Rufus) disapproved of exposure, legal restrictions were rare. A Theban law once forbade the practice but allowed the very poor to turn a newborn over to the authorities, who in turn gave it to another citizen to raise as a slave. It was only under the Christian empire of the fourth century CE that exposure was treated as a form of murder before the law.

Though the extent of exposure is unknown, its very existence may be thought to undermine Thucydides' implicit contrast between Greeks and barbarians. Indeed, some scholars have argued that adults in high mortality populations (including the Greeks and Romans) felt relatively little for individual children: their all-too-frequent deaths made emotional ties a poor investment. But our evidence suggests, to the contrary, that Greek and Roman parents responded to the prospect of the deaths of the children they had decided to raise by taking every precaution they could, from folk remedies—plants, charms, magical stones, apotropaic names, the amulets which hang around boys' necks on many Roman reliefs and protect against the evil eye—to the best advice of specialists. (Doctors thought the fortieth day and seventh month after birth especially dangerous and handbooks interpreted dreams that might reveal less predictable perils.) When these means failed, they mourned their dead, supported by familiar ritual practices and a community in which many had suffered the same sorrow. And the killing of children who had been accepted into the household was always regarded as murder. Medea was a maternal monster for Greeks and Romans alike.

Athenians welcomed wanted children with the *amphidromia*, a ritual celebrated on the fifth or seventh day after birth, and named them then or on the tenth day. At Rome, the *paterfamilias* signaled a child's acceptance by lifting it from the ground. Naming took place at a ceremony of purification, the *lustratio*, which (like the *amphidromia*) involved moving in a circle. This was held on a girl's eighth day, a boy's ninth. An Athenian boy was presented to his father's *genos* as a baby, to his phratry (another kin-based group) as a toddler and again (perhaps) at sixteen. His civic debut may have occurred at the spring festival of the Anthesteria during his third year, when gifts of small vases depicting children's activities were customary. Athenian girls followed a different ritual curriculum,

likely confined to a select group: *arrhephoroi* (serving Athena and Artemis) at seven, *aletrides* (grinding meal for sacred cakes) at ten, and *arctoi* (literally, "bears") in honor of Artemis before marriage. A boy reached adulthood on admission to his father's deme at seventeen or eighteen, a girl at marriage (in her mid- to late teens).

Unlike other Greeks (and Romans), Spartan boys took part in a compulsory, community-run course of education from the age of seven; from the Roman period at least, the last seven years were each designated by a distinctive name. They left childhood when voted into one of the city's common messes at twenty; similarly, their sisters married a little later than other Greek girls. Among the Romans, boys exchanged the *toga praetexta*, with its purple stripe, for the plain white *toga virilis* at the age thought fit by the *paterfamilias*. About sixteen or seventeen during the later Republic, this might be reduced to allow the sons of the elite to marry (their puberty was legally set at fourteen) or hold office. Girls could be married as young as twelve, but most in fact wed in their mid- to late teens (with the earlier marriages more common for the elite).

These stages coincide only roughly with the ideas of ancient theoreticians and the deductions of modern scholars. So Plato and Aristotle seem to operate with a five-step scheme of child development, each stage exhibiting physical and psychological characteristics of its own: babyhood (until two, when a child is weaned and can talk); early preschool (from three to five, a period of increased bodily activity and independent play); preschool (at six or seven, a time for children to form their own social networks); school (until puberty at fourteen); and adolescence. The play of Roman children has also been periodized. "Practice play" (with rattles and bright stones) was a feature of the first eighteen months, followed by playing house or building sand castles until age four. Children then acted out adult roles, girls playing with bride dolls and boys establishing status. (In one ball game, a "king" triumphed over "sheep.") After, at seven, they embarked on games with set rules, usually involving strength, risk, and strategy.

Throughout these stages, whether ritual, social, or developmental, children were regarded as vulnerable, weak, foolish, fearful, driven by desire, and much in need of molding. (It was Hannibal's childhood which was responsible for his love of slaughter; Seneca *On Anger* 2.5.4.) They shared many of these attributes with other groups who did not have the roles and responsibilities of adult male citizens: women, animals (Spartan boys were organized into "herds"), the very old, and slaves. (In both Greek and Latin, common words for "child"—*pais, puer*—regularly meant "slave" as well.) But some imperfections (impetuosity, lisping speech) could be cute. And there were significant distinctions between children and other subordinate statuses too. Boys participated in the competitive festivals that were a defining characteristic of the Greek way of life; Roman writers caution that the corporal punishment suitable for a slave was unseemly and ineffective for a son. And children's otherness might bring them into contact with higher forces as well, as priests and priestesses, acolytes (for good luck, both parents had to be alive), or mediums.

Still, children did spend much of their early years with women, a custom accentuated by the traffic flow of the Athenian home (in which areas were off limits to adult male outsiders) and the fact that Spartan men did not live with their families for the first few years after marriage. Roman women had a more direct role in the acculturation of their children: Cornelia, the mother of the Gracchi, was given credit for the brothers' oratorical skills (though not for the use they made of them). Furthermore, slave wet nurses and nannies were common, and *paidagogoi* accompanied even adolescent boys as they traveled through the city, often to schools operated by slave and former slave entrepreneurs.

Such associations were a source of concern: children might drink in immorality with a slave's milk, mimic the imperfections in a slave's speech. Yet slaves must also have supplied stability in families regularly disrupted by divorce and death, and their children (or others they nursed) were among a child's first playmates. Seneca writes of visiting his suburban villa and meeting with the pet slave of his

Child with Goose. Marble figure found at Ephesus. Roman copy (second century CE) of a Greek bronze of the early third century BCE. KUNSTHISTORISCHES MUSEUM, VIENNA/ERICH LESSING/ART RESOURCE, NY

youth, the son of his old steward (Seneca *Moral Letters* 12.3). Links of this sort might involve more than friendship alone. Sexual ties between grown men and adolescent boys were accepted by the Greeks, and slaves replaced citizen boys as the passive partners at Rome. What did Seneca's slave think of their relationship and the wretched state to which (Seneca says, not very sympathetically) the years had brought him? How much choice would he have in a culture where slave children were thought ready for work at five and even poorer citizen children might be expected to tend animals, gather fruit, or care for still younger children before they were in their teens and could be apprenticed to a skilled craftsman at twelve? As always, we are left to speculate on the experiences and emotions of Greek and Roman children themselves.

[*See also* Birth and Reproduction; Education; *and* Toys and Games.]

BIBLIOGRAPHY

Bradley, Keith R. *Discovering the Roman Family: Studies in Roman Social History*. New York and Oxford: Oxford University Press, 1993. Especially good on child labor, the roles of slave nannies, and the importance of slaves in providing continuity when families were disrupted by death and divorce.

Golden, Mark. *Children and Childhood in Classical Athens*. Baltimore and London: Johns Hopkins University Press, 1990. Standard survey with special focus on social history.

Kennell, Nigel M. *The Gymnasium of Virtue: Education and Culture in Ancient Sparta*. Chapel Hill and London: University of North Carolina Press, 1995. Groundbreaking and myth-busting examination of the upbringing of Spartan boys in particular.

Neils, Jenifer, and John H. Oakley, eds. *Coming of Age in Ancient Greece: Images of Childhood from the Classical Past*. New Haven, Conn., and London: Yale University Press, 2003. Richly illustrated catalog and collection of chapters, some on topics omitted here (such as Bronze Age childhood).

Pache, Corinne Ondine. *Baby and Child Heroes in Ancient Greece*. Urbana and Chicago: University of Illinois Press, 2004. Extended investigation of the myths and cults of Opheltes, the children of Medea, and other children worshiped in Greece, often in the context of athletic festivals.

Rawson, Beryl. *Children and Childhood in Roman Italy*. New York and Oxford: Oxford University Press, 2003. Thorough account by a pioneer in the field who makes good use of images, inscriptions, and legal sources.

Uzzi, Jeannine Diddle. *Children in the Visual Arts of Imperial Rome*. New York and Cambridge, U.K.: Cambridge University Press, 2005. Outlines the role of representations of children in expressing Rome's national and imperial identity.

Wiedemann, Thomas. *Adults and Children in the Roman Empire*. New Haven, Conn., and London: Yale University Press, 1989. Lively and wide ranging, with an emphasis on change over time.

Mark Golden

CHIOS

Chios is the name of one of the larger Aegean Islands (328 square miles [850 square kilometers]), located 4.3 miles (7 kilometers) from Asia Minor, and of the single polis of the island (on its eastern coast). The island's northern part is mountainous. The largest plain is around the city; the southern hills are also cultivable. Little is known about its prehistoric population. It was colonized by Ionians from Euboea circa 900 BCE, with possible Aeolian admixture. Its fifth century BCE tragedian Ion recounted its foundation (Pausanias *Tour of Greece* 7.4). It seems that Oenopion of Crete (a son of Dionysus and Ariadne) was recognized as the chief founder.

Chios had a strong claim to be the homeland of Homer (9th–8th century BCE). In the Archaic and Classical periods the guild of the Homeridae (performers of Homer's poetry) flourished there. Chios controlled the Oenussae Islands, at least since the fifth century BCE, and Psará (intermittently). In the early seventh century, it colonized Maroneia (Thrace) and in the sixth it participated in the foundation of the Hellenion at Naucratis (Egypt). Aspects of its political regime (especially the administration of justice) are codified in the *rhētra* (a boustrophedon inscription), among the oldest Greek constitutional documents (c. 575–550 BCE), though only half preserved (*Annual of the British School at Athens* 51 [1956]:157–167). It refers to a council (*boulē*) of the people with fifty members per tribe (though the number of tribes is unknown) and an assembly. Effective kingship seems to have been abolished: the office is referred to in the plural.

Chios fought against Erythrae over its mainland possessions (*peraia*) and against Samos. It had one of the most powerful Greek navies and traded in Asia Minor, the Black Sea, and Egypt. Exports included its famous wine and mastic (a resinous material from the mastic tree). In Classical times, it was regarded as the greatest of the Ionian cities and the richest among the Greeks. Its easy lifestyle gave rise to many proverbs and expressions. Based on the size of its fleet at Lade, the free population may have been as high as eighty thousand; this could have been sustained only through the importation of food. Thucydides claims Chios had more slaves than any other city except Sparta (8.40.2). Theopompus (b. c. 380 BCE) claimed that the Chians were the first to buy slaves from abroad (rather than conquer them), and thus they faced many slave revolts.

Chios remained independent of Lydia, but by the time of Darius I's Scythian expedition (513 BCE), Persia had imposed a tyrant (Strattis). Chios played a prominent role in the Ionian revolt (500–493 BCE), fighting ferociously at the naval battle of Lade, for which it was punished with destruction and enslavement. Strattis returned. It was around this time that Chios dedicated the altar of Apollo at Delphi. After the Persian Wars it joined the Delian League, contributing ships rather than tribute, and remained loyal to Athens until 412 BCE, when it rebelled along with most of the Aegean allies seeking Spartan help (and briefly inducing Lesbos to rebel). It was possibly then that it freed many slaves, probably for recruitment. We know little about its constitution at that time.

Chios' history in the fourth century was complex, as it passed from the Spartan hegemony to the Second Athenian Alliance, the Theban Alliance, and finally fell under the Carian Hecatomnid rule of Mausolus. Two letters of Alexander III (Alexander the Great) to the Chians survive epigraphically: the first (*Sylloge Inscriptionum Graecarum*, 3rd ed. 283; of 332 BCE) commands them to restore democratic exiles, provide twenty triremes, and accept (and pay for) a garrison; the second letter is obscure. One of the exiles, though not a democrat, was Theopompus, an important historian with wide-ranging interests who was involved in most political and intellectual developments of his time, especially rhetoric, philosophy, and the rise of Macedonia. He was very polemical and was exiled again after the death of Alexander. In the Hellenistic era, Chios passed from the hegemony of Antigonus to Lysimachus and then the Ptolemies. After the mid-third century it was independent and allied with Aetolia, the victor of the Gauls, who gave Chios a vote in the Amphictyonic Council, which administered the Panhellenic sanctuary of Apollo at Delphi. The alliance provided for mutual rights between Chios and Aetolia. Chios sided with Rome in the second-century wars, being among the first Greek cities to establish a cult of Roma, but little is known of its history until it sided with Mithradates VI Eupator of Pontus in the early first century and was captured by Sulla.

The polis of Chios was probably always the most important settlement on the island, but continuous occupation precludes excavation. The most important excavated site is Emporio, a natural harbor on the southeast coast. Inhabited intermittently since the Neolithic, the Bronze Age phase was destroyed circa 1100 BCE. The Archaic village was abandoned circa 600 BCE, but a temple of Athena was built on the hillside in the sixth century BCE (and restored at the end of the fourth); a second temple was built by the harbor.

Chios was a naval power that sought wealth and independence. It made allies throughout its history to prevent domination by a single power. Except for its reliance on slavery, it had a remarkably stable society.

[*See also* Aegean Sea.]

BIBLIOGRAPHY

Boardman, John, and C. E. Vaphopoulou-Richardson, eds. *Chios: A Conference at the Homereion in Chios, 1984.* Oxford: Clarendon Press; New York: Oxford University Press, 1986.

Graf, Fritz. *Nordionische Kulte: Religionsgeschichtliche und epigraphische Untersuchungen zu den Kulten von Chios, Erythrai, Klazomenai und Phokaia.* Rome: Schweizerisches Institut in Rom, 1985.

Sarikakes, Theodōros. *Hē Chios stēn archaiotēta.* Athens: Eriphylē, 1998.

Anthony Kaldellis

CHOREGIA

See Liturgy.

CHOREGIC MONUMENTS

Although they are found elsewhere, choregic monuments are most closely associated with Athens and the Athenian institution of the *chorēgia*. One of several liturgies, or sponsorships, that wealthy citizens provided for the benefit of the polis or city-state, the *chorēgia* supplied the choruses for tragedies and comedies as well as for dithyrambic (lyric) contests for men and boys that were performed in festivals held throughout the year. Once chosen, the sponsor, the *chorēgos*, became responsible for all costs associated with the choral performance: stipends and daily expenses of the *choreutai* (chorus members) as well as that of their trainer and the flute player who accompanied them; the *chorēgos* also paid for costumes and masks needed in the production and provided space for training. Choral performances were highly competitive, and *chorēgoi* commemorated their victories with various dedications. For theatrical performances, these included *pinakes* or painted panels, sculptural reliefs, *phalloi*, and statues. In dithyrambic contests a triumphant *chorēgos* was awarded a bronze tripod and received permission from the state to erect, at his own expense, a base on which to place the tripod.

The simplest and most modest type of base was a stepped pedestal, several examples of which are known. More monumental were single freestanding columns whose capital supported the tripod. Most famous, however, are those choregic dedications that so outstripped in scale their function as tripod bases that they are usually considered in studies of monumental Greek architecture alongside temples, stoas, and other public structures. Three in particular are well known: the monument of Lysikrates, dated 335/34 BCE, and the monuments of Thrasyllos and Nikias, both firmly dated to 320/19 BCE. Of these, the Lysikrates Monument is the best preserved, standing to a height of 32.8 feet (10 meters). A square pedestal made of limestone acts as the base for an elaborate marble *tholos* (round building): Six monolithic Corinthian columns stand on a ring of three steps and support an entablature that includes both a sculpted frieze and dentils. The marble roof, decorated in a pattern of overlapping scales, is crowned with a finial on which rested the tripod. The Lysikrates Monument thus represents the first use of the Corinthian order on the exterior of a building; it is also one of the earliest examples of the combination of frieze and dentils. It was located along the Street of the Tripods leading to the

sanctuary of Dionysus, so called because of the many large and elaborate choregic monuments that bordered it. The Thrasyllos Monument was set high above the orchestra of the Theater of Dionysus itself. An example of pure facade architecture, two pilasters flanked a central pier in the Doric order, decoratively covering a natural cavity in the rock face of the Acropolis and acting as the base for the tripod perched atop the entablature. The Nikias Monument is the largest of the three, although today it is the least well-preserved, most of its superstructure having been transported and rebuilt in another location. Placed just west of the theater, it was built in the form of a small Doric *naos* or temple. Both the Thrasyllos Monument and the Nikias Monument imitated elements of design found in the famous *propylaia* (double gateway) to the Athenian Acropolis built by the architect Mnesicles as part of the Periclean building program a century earlier. As such they represent a classicizing trend in fourth-century Athenian architecture that contrasts with the extravagant look of the Lysikrates Monument.

The date of origin of the *choregia* (and thus choregic monuments) is uncertain but is known from the introduction of democracy at the end of the sixth century BCE. Henceforward it was inextricably linked with this institution, embodying as it did values central to Athenian culture of the fifth and fourth centuries BCE: competition, public acclaim, and reciprocal obligations. The choregic monument was the visible and lasting symbol of the choregos' victory, the approbation that accompanied it, and the expectation of public favor in return for his service. Evidence for the appearance of choregic dedications in the fifth century is slim, but there is general recognition that the monuments became grander over the course of the fourth century. If, or how, this may have related to a transformation in democratic ideology itself is debated. What is certain is that soon after the collapse of democracy in 322/21 BCE the philosopher and statesman Demetrius of Phaleron passed sumptuary legislation that outlawed choregic monuments and curtailed the practice of the *chorēgia* as it had existed for the previous two hundred years.

[*See also* Architecture, *subentry* Forms and Terms.]

BIBLIOGRAPHY

Goette, Hans R. "Choregic Monuments and the Athenian Democracy." In *The Greek Theatre and Festivals: Documentary Studies,* edited by Peter Wilson, pp. 122–149. Oxford: Oxford University Press, 2007. Description of the basic types and examples of choregic monuments in Athens.

Townsend, Rhys F. "The Philippeion and Fourth-Century Athenian Architecture." In *The Macedonians in Athens, 322–229 BC: Proceedings of an International Conference Held at the University of Athens, May 24–26, 2001,* edited by Olga Palagia and Stephen V. Tracy, pp. 93–101. Oxford: Oxbow, 2003. Semiotic analysis of Athenian choregic monuments in the cultural context of later fourth-century Greece.

Wilson, Peter. *The Athenian Institution of the "Khoregia": The Chorus, the City, and the Stage.* Cambridge, U.K.: Cambridge University Press, 2000. Authoritative study of the institution of the choregia.

Rhys F. Townsend

CHORUS

See Dance.

CHRISTIAN ART

[*This entry includes two subentries, an overview and a discussion of Christian art in Egypt.*]

Overview

Early Christian art usually is identified as such by its subject matter—that is, by the fact that it depicts recognizably Christian symbols or biblical motifs. Christian iconography, however, often bears obvious similarities in themes and style with non-Christian art of the same place and period, which renders clear distinctions difficult to sustain. To add to the complexity of definition, prior to the Constantinian era, Christian artworks were not found in exclusively Christian contexts, nor were they associated with specific, known Christian patrons. Despite these cautions, examples of generally accepted Christian artworks arguably reveal an evolution in content, composition, and context that allows broad categorization of their pictorial elements as well as their placement. In general, Christian art proceeds from being primarily symbolic, to representing biblical narratives, to reflecting dogmatic developments, and finally to embracing iconic, or portrait, types; it also proceeds from domestic and funereal settings to monumental, ecclesial spaces.

Surviving examples of distinctively Christian art cannot be securely dated prior to the early third century. Some scholars have argued that this relatively late emergence demonstrates early Christian repudiation of figurative art, either in continuity with Jewish observance of biblical prohibitions or reflecting specifically Christian theological objections to images of the gods. Other scholars argue that the lack of identifiable Christian art in the first two centuries was more likely the result of the social or economic status of the faithful: most early Christians were financially unable to purchase specially made Christian artworks to decorate their homes, assembly halls, or tombs. A third argument is that pre-third-century Christians produced works of art that are now difficult to distinguish from other Greco-Roman artifacts. Proponents of this argument view Christian art as a subcategory of Roman art, adapting Roman art's motifs, styles, and techniques.

This last viewpoint may be coordinated with the approach taken by early Christian apologists, whose arguments elucidated the faith for their Greco-Roman audiences by referring to well-regarded philosophical ideals or by contrasting familiar stories of the gods. In a similar manner artisans adapted popular mythological or decorative motifs to convey Christian messages in the visual language of the predominant culture. These artisans likewise followed prevailing artistic styles and techniques. Early Christian wall paintings were executed in a sketchy, impressionistic style and were framed with colored borders similar to—although not usually as carefully executed as—those produced for contemporary Roman tombs and domestic interiors. Only once the content of the works became unambiguously Christian could they be identified as such.

This line of reasoning discounts the existence of exclusively Christian workshops, deeming it more likely that artisans accepted commissions from both pagan and Christian clients. The probable priestly supervision of Christian cemeteries may have meant a certain degree of official oversight or approval of their decoration, but it seems as likely that content and quality were entirely personal choices based on financial means and personal preferences. In any case the only possible support in the material evidence for an anti-image attitude on the part of early Christians is the absence of surviving pre-third-century examples.

Textual evidence, however, suggests that early Christians disapproved of pagan idols in particular. Further, certain New Testament passages indicate that Christians resisted making visual representations of their God (cf. Acts 17:29), and second- and third-century writers criticized their pagan neighbors for making or owning cult statues and paintings (cf. Justin Martyr, 1 *Apology* 9.1–9; Clement of Alexandria *Exhortation to the Heathen* 4; Tertullian *On Idolatry* 3–4). At the same time, some of these writers testify to Christians' owning objects decorated with Christian imagery. For example, Tertullian refers to drinking glasses or sacramental chalices etched with the figure of a shepherd carrying a sheep over his shoulders (*On Modesty* 7.1, 10.12), and Clement of Alexandria provides a list of appropriate symbols that Christians could engrave on their signet rings (*Instructor* 3.11.59). Clement's list of approved motifs includes a dove, fish, ship, lyre, and anchor, while he specifically rejects images of pagan gods or of weapons, and references to drinking or licentious behavior. This evidence suggests disapproval of cult images that depicted or displayed divine beings or immoral activities, and acceptance of discreet but identifiable Christian figures or signs on modest, everyday objects. In any case no extant documents support the supposition that early Christian authorities were hostile to art per se. Instead it appears that they denounced only the practice of offering prayers, sacrifice, or other honors to images of the pagan gods and resisted making cult images of their own.

Early Christian Symbols. The oldest surviving material evidence corroborates this conclusion and to a large extent reflects Clement's instructions. Images of doves, fish, boats, and anchors were popular for early Christian epitaphs, as well as for inscribed gems. As Tertullian noted, representations of a shepherd carrying a sheep appeared on drinking glasses, as well as on lamps, dishware, paintings, and sculpture. The shepherd images were not representations of the deity, but rather were symbolic references to the character of the savior. The other symbols alluded to key Christian beliefs, values, and aspirations.

The largest part of the surviving evidence comes from a Roman funerary context: the wall paintings in the Christian catacombs and carved sarcophagi. Influenced by popular Roman decorative motifs, the most common themes for Christian funerary art were maritime, floral, and pastoral subjects. In addition to fish, boats, and anchors, walls and vaults of burial chambers were painted with flowers (especially roses), grape vines, bowls of fruit, fountains, animals, and birds of all kinds (doves, quail, and peacocks). Specific Christian meanings are difficult to discern, but these paintings almost certainly alluded to safe passage to a blissful afterlife in a paradisiacal garden. The fish, however, signified a number of possible ideas, including the acrostic based on the letters of the Greek word *ichthys* (fish) that represents the first letter of each word in the title *Iēsous Christos Theou Huios Sotēr* (Jesus Christ, Son of God, Savior; cf. Tertullian *On Baptism* 1; Sibylline Oracles 8.217–250; Optatus of Milevis *Against Parmenian* 3.2.1). Because fish also appear frequently in New Testament stories—as in the multiplication of loaves and fish or in the miraculous catch of fish—the fish may have alluded to one or more biblical narratives.

Added to these simple symbols were three regularly recurring human figures, also prevalent in non-Christian funerary art. One of these was the orant, or praying figure. Normally a standing female with raised arms and veiled head, this figure also represented the virtue of *pietas* (piety). In funerary contexts she may have been intended to symbolize the soul of the deceased, especially because she frequently has a portraitlike visage or is joined by individual family members. The identification of the orant with the departed soul is strengthened by the regular addition of the prayerful phrase *in pace* (in peace).

The second figure, a shepherd, typically wears a short tunic and boots and carries a sheep over his shoulders. Although somewhat more distinctively Christian than the orant, this figure, too, has pagan roots. Appearing on pottery lamps, bowls, glasses, gems, and wall paintings from the early third century onward, this pastoral figure almost certainly alluded to the biblical "Good Shepherd" (cf. John 10.1–9). Yet this image had a pagan precedent in a depiction of Hermes, the gods' messenger and care-taking guide to the underworld, sometimes shown as a young shepherd carrying a ram.

The shepherd and the orant frequently appear with a third figure: a seated reader garbed as a philosopher. Together this trio personified piety, philanthropy, and love of wisdom—virtues that suit-ed the religious sensibilities of pagan and Christian clients alike. Christian teachers, however, claimed that theirs was a "true" philosophy. The three per-sonifications might also have referred to the theo-logical virtues of faith, hope, and charity (cf. 1 Corinthians 13).

Like Hermes the shepherd, Christianized versions of images of the Sun God (Sol Invictus), Apollo, Hercules, and Orpheus were ways of depicting Christ as bringer of light, doer of miraculous deeds, or tamer of souls. Rather than evidence of syncretism, such iconographic adaptation demonstrates how specific attributes of a well-known hero or deity could be transferred to Christ, showing him as the superior god who possesses every divine quality. A similar favorable comparison was drawn by apologists like Justin Martyr (cf. 1 *Apology* 21ff.). Jesus is shown not only as god but as better than all the gods, particu-larly because his is true, not false divinity.

A scene of five or seven diners sitting at a horseshoe-shaped table is another common motif in Christian art, occurring dozens of times in cata-comb frescoes or on sarcophagus reliefs. The almost identical image was equally popular in pagan funer-ary art. Both pagans and Christians may have wanted to depict an aspect of a blessed afterlife—a merry banquet. The image also alluded to actual funeral meals shared by the deceased's family and friends at the tomb. The diners' sharing of wine, bread, and a platter of fish has led some interpreters to see a sacramental significance in the scene. Agape meals could be indicated, because they were understood to be prefigurations of the heavenly banquet. The fish could indicate Christ, lending a eucharistic significance to the eschatological one (cf. Paulinus of Nola *Epistle* 13.11). In some instances the diners are served by female figures named Irene (peace) and Agape (love/charity).

The particular suitability of pastoral motifs or banquet scenes for funerary contexts is obvious. They express hope that the deceased will be safely led to a bliss-filled heavenly abode. Yet many of these same symbols and motifs appear on extant small nonfunerary objects such as lamps, glasses, gems, and bowls. Still, because of its underground venue, and because it was not as likely to be replaced by rebuilding and renovation, the pre-ponderance of early Christian art has a funerary provenance. A significant exception (in addition to the small, personal items) allows a cautious com-parison to nonfunerary iconography. This is the unique house church discovered at Dura-Europos in Syria (c. 256). Probably not the only decorated church assembly space, Dura's Christian building nonetheless is the sole surviving example of pre-fourth-century Christian ecclesiastical decoration.

Biblical Narrative Art. Excavated in the mid-twentieth century by French and American ar-chaeological teams, the Dura church is a converted domestic building that enclosed both a small assem-bly hall and a room designed for administering baptisms. This baptismal room had a rectangular font at one end, covered by an arched vault. It also had wall paintings that were mostly intact when the building was discovered. The ceiling was painted blue with white stars, as was the vault of the font. The arch was decorated with grapes, pomegranates, and wheat, and behind the font a lunette painting included images of a shepherd with his flock, along with a (much smaller) Adam and Eve. The rest of the wall paintings showed the Samaritan woman at the well, David slaying Goliath, and Jesus walking on the water, stilling the storm, and healing the paralytic. The interpretation of a partially destroyed image of women processing toward a rectangular structure with a pitched roof and pediment is disputed. It may be the three women arriving at Christ's empty tomb, or three of the five wise brides coming to the bridegroom's tent.

Throughout the third century, as in the Dura-Europos baptistery, single symbols (e.g., fish, anchor) and single figures (e.g., orant, shepherd) were joined or elaborated by innovative illustrations of stories taken from the Old and New Testaments. Among the first narratives to be pictorially depicted were Adam and Eve eating the forbidden fruit, Noah in the ark, Abraham offering his son Isaac for sacrifice,

Moses striking the rock in the wilderness, Susanna and the Elders, Daniel in the lions' den, the Three Youths in the Fiery Furnace, and Jonah being swallowed and then spit up by the sea creature. Each of these images appears frequently and with a fairly standardized composition. Noah is ordinarily shown in a small boxlike ark with his hands lifted in the prayer posture, while Daniel, also an orant, is represented as a heroic nude. He faces forward with a lion on each side.

The popularity of these characters from Hebrew scripture is not easily explained, although some scholars have posited a lost illuminated Septuagint as a model. Nevertheless, even if such a model existed (and there is no certain evidence that one did), the earlier and more frequent appearance of Moses striking the rock instead of Moses leading the Israelites through the Red Sea suggests that either iconographic models or hermeneutic practice influenced the choice of stories. For example, Jonah's unusual sequential representation includes his being thrown overboard, his being spit back up on dry land, and his safe rest under the gourd vine,

Jonah and the Whale. Mosaic pavement from the basilica at Aquileia, Italy, early fourth century. THE BRIDGEMAN ART LIBRARY

but not his call to Nineveh or that city's salvation from destruction. The story of Jonah thus may reflect the way the story was interpreted as a figure of Christ's death and resurrection (cf. Matthew 12.40). Art historians also have noted Jonah's similarity in appearance to the hero Endymion on pagan sarcophagi. Jonah's nude repose thus could also allude to a blissful afterlife. Other scholars have suggested that prayers offered for the souls of the dead or alluding to the promise of salvation through baptism are the source of the iconography.

Gospel scenes were depicted as well, especially in the late third and early fourth centuries, although representations of John baptizing Jesus appeared somewhat earlier, at least by the mid-third century. More scenes from Jesus' ministry gradually appeared on tomb walls and sarcophagus reliefs, especially scenes of Jesus healing the paralytic, the woman with the issue of blood, and the man born blind. Other popular compositions included the adoration of the magi, and Jesus raising Lazarus, meeting the Samaritan woman at the well, multiplying the loaves and fish, and changing water to wine. Depictions of Jesus performing miracles such as raising Lazarus generally show him wielding a staff, a possible reference to the supernatural powers of Moses or Aaron. This staff's similarity to a thaumaturge's baton, along with the iconographic emphasis on Jesus as healer, has led some commentators to argue that the images alluded to the healing or magical arts of other contemporary wonderworkers.

Other Old Testament scenes appeared in the fourth century, including some still unique depictions of stories from the Joseph cycle found in the Via Latina catacomb. Besides these stories, this catacomb, which also had wall paintings depicting pagan gods, contained representations of Abraham entertaining his three angelic guests and of Moses and the Israelites crossing the Red Sea—a scene that also began to be carved on sarcophagus reliefs. Other new images designed for these marble coffins included the Trinity creating Adam and Eve, Cain and Abel presenting their sacrifices to God, Elijah's ascent to heaven, Jesus entering Jerusalem seated on a donkey, and Jesus taking the role of Ezekiel by raising the dry bones.

The book of Acts inspired an image of Peter's arrest, which was frequently juxtaposed with an image of the saint striking a rock to baptize his Roman jailers, an image that has a surviving textual parallel in a later apocryphal source, the Acts of Peter. Clearly based on an earlier representation of Moses striking the rock, this iconographic transformation indicates the important role of Peter as a "new Moses" or the rock on which Jesus would found his church (cf. Matthew 16.18). During this period of innovation in iconography, compositions became more complex, and the quality of technique, workmanship, and materials improved. One famous example, the Junius Bassus sarcophagus, shows extraordinary skill and sophistication.

Dogmatically and Imperially Inspired Art. By the mid-fourth century, biblical narrative scenes of Jesus' miracles and Peter's adventures were joined by more dogmatically inspired images. These compositions, which appeared at the time that Christianity was in transition from an unpopular and persecuted sect into a religion patronized by the first Christian emperor, emphasized Jesus as lawgiver and heavenly sovereign. Scholars often have described this change of emphasis—from Jesus as healer or miracle worker to Jesus as enthroned king—as the adaption of imperial iconography. As the newly secure faith ultimately became the official state religion, imperial themes and styles undeniably affected Christian art, much of it financed by the imperial fisc. However, the enthroned Christ was not only the emperor's personal patron: he was Jupiter's replacement. Christ had conquered the pagan gods as much as he had overthrown death. The triumphant image of an empty cross surmounted by a victor's wreath or of a regnant Lord of Lords prepared to judge the living and the dead were dogmatic and ecclesiastical messages as much as political ones.

Constantine's patronage of Christianity included his building of churches in Rome and the Holy Land, and his example inspired a building boom in general as a new group of upper-class Roman Christians redirected their wealth from sponsoring civic projects to generously endowing ecclesial

Christ the Lawgiver. Roman marble, fourth century. © CZARTORYSKI MUSEUM, KRAKÓW, POLAND/THE BRIDGEMAN ART LIBRARY

foundations. Basilicas now built exclusively for Christian worship were lavishly decorated with artworks, furnishings, and liturgical vessels made from precious metals. According to later records, among the many gifts that Constantine donated to his first Roman basilica—now known as Saint John Lateran but originally dedicated to Christ the Savior—was a hammered silver *fastigium* (a pediment supported by bronze columns) with two life-size images of Christ, sitting on a throne and on a chair, facing toward both the front and the back of the building. The enthroned Christ was joined by four spear-carrying angels, and the frontally facing Christ was flanked by his twelve apostles. In addition to these impressive (and heavy) silver figures, the pediment supported gold and silver lamps and wreaths (*Liber Pontificalis*, Sylvester 34.9).

Even more splendid were the monumental mosaics that adorned apses and walls. In addition to its rich silver and gold *fastigium*, Constantine endowed the Lateran basilica with gold foil and glass mosaic to decorate its apse vault. This application of colored small tesserae to walls and vaults was a technical innovation, replacing the painted walls of the previous era. The image placed in this large curved space also replaced the cult statue in earlier Roman basilicas. Rather than the idol-like dominance of a three-dimensional figure, the Christian church developed the two-dimensional yet curved and glittering glass mosaic, making the apse both an architectural and a liturgical focal point, as well as a place for artistic experimentation. The light refracted by the small pieces of glass and gilding would have allowed the composition to shimmer—creating an awe-inspiring effect.

Although the vicissitudes of conquest, fire, earthquake, or renovation have destroyed much of the original material evidence, written records and contemporary parallels allow hypothetical reconstruction of the actual iconography that adorned those first Christian apses. The current mosaic in the Lateran is presumed to have been based on the original design. The upper portion shows a bust of Christ surrounded by angels. Below, a gemmed cross rises from a rocky mound from which spring the four Edenic rivers. Deer and sheep drink from these living waters (a reference to Psalms 23 and 41). Saints stand to the right and left looking toward the cross. A river populated with sea life, boats, and fishing cherubs flows across the bottom, a possible allusion to the Jordan as a passage to Paradise.

Saint Peter's apse, probably completed by Constantine's son Constans I, was destroyed in the sixteenth century, but ancient drawings show Christ handing a scroll of the law to Peter and Paul—a composition often referred to as the *traditio legis*. Usually depicting the ascended Jesus regally enthroned or standing on an outcropping of rock from which the four rivers spring, this image had special significance in Rome, the site of both apostles' martyrdom and burial. This image became widespread elsewhere and was a popular subject for sarcophagus reliefs, perhaps because of its eschatological significance. Two apses in the mausoleum of Constantine's daughter, Constantina (c. 345–350), depict contrasting (and much restored) compositions of this sort: one shows a fair-haired and youthful Jesus standing handing the scroll inscribed *dominus legem dat* to Paul while Peter looks on, and the other shows a majestic, dark, and bearded Jesus handing over keys to Peter—the city's first bishop and the basis for the claimed primacy of his successors.

A surviving fourth-century apse mosaic in a chapel attached to Milan's basilica of San Lorenzo depicts a slightly different scene of Christ seated, surrounded by his apostles and with a box of scrolls at his feet. His wears the white tunic and pallium of the philosopher, and his face is youthful and beardless. A very different Christ appears on another surviving (but heavily restored) late fourth-century apse, in Rome's church of Santa Pudenziana. Here a full-bearded Christ sits on a high-backed throne before a cityscape reprsenting the Heavenly Jerusalem (Revelation 21.2). He holds an open book that reads *Dominus conservator Ecclesiae Pudentianae* (the Lord is the preserver of the church of Pudentiana). His apostles sit on either side; to his immediate left and right are Peter and Paul, respectively. These two apostles are being offered wreaths by women who represent the churches of the Jews and the Gentiles. Christ's throne, like his robe and the cross rising behind him, is golden and studded with gems; the four beasts of John's apocalypse loom above, against a streaky sunset sky.

Throughout the fifth and sixth centuries the decorative programs of churches became more and more elaborate and iconographically innovative. The mosaics that decorated the triumphal arch of the church of Santa Maria Maggiore (built by Sixtus III, c. 435) depicted the scenes from the Virgin Mary's youth (based on the *Protevangelium of James*) and from Christ's nativity, including the adoration of the magi and the massacre of the innocents. By contrast, the original arch program for San Paolo Fuori le Mura, created about the same time, had an image that clearly adapted pagan and imperial iconography to portray a biblically inspired scene. On the uppermost register a bust of Christ adorned with the radiate nimbus of the sun god hovered among the four beasts of Paradise and above the twenty-four elders of Revelation bearing crowns to cast before him (cf. Revelation 4.1–11).

Paulinus, an aristocratic early fifth-century bishop who built several churches on his ancestral lands between Rome and Naples, described two different apse themes he commissioned. One, at Fundi, depicted the final judgment. Christ appeared as a lamb beneath a bloody cross. Above him hovered the Holy Spirit in the form of a dove, and the hand of God descended to offer a crown. The Christ-lamb was busy separating sheep from goats, with the assistance of the Good Shepherd, who herded off the goats and welcomed the lambs into a bucolic paradise. For his church at Nola, Paulinus commissioned a representation of the Holy Trinity, which was symbolically depicted as Christ in the form of a lamb standing on a rock from which four rivers flowed, the Father's voice (almost certainly depicted as a hand from heaven), and a dove for the Holy Spirit. The central image was a cross within a wreath (Paulinus of Nola *Epistle* 32.10–17).

Images of Christ's Passion. The wreathed cross appears on many Christian sarcophagi, especially those discovered in Rome and dated from the mid- to late fourth century. Frequently designated "passion sarcophagi" because their iconographic motifs include scenes from Christ's arrest and trial, their common central motif is a cross whose horizontal bar supports a christogram—a symbol made up of the Greek letter chi bisected by a rho, the first two letters of the title *Christos*—encircled by a wreath. Doves usually perch on the cross's horizontal bar, and in certain instances two Roman soldiers are shown at its base, resting on their shields.

This particular motif was undoubtedly influenced by imperial imagery, most notably the Constantinian labarum—a military standard adopted by the emperor after his conversion to Christianity and based on his recorded dream vision of the Chi-Rho monogram and divine instructions to place it on the shields and helmets of his soldiers to assure a military victory (cf. Lactantius *Death of the Persecutors* 44.5). The placement and posture of the two Roman soldiers correspond to those of the figures of kneeling captives often seen on reverse coin types minted during the fourth century. Scholars have frequently noted these parallels and cite them as evidence of the turn toward imperial motifs in fourth-century Christian art. However, the existence of the two doves, as well as the passion scenes, also suggests that the key message may have been Christ's triumph over death rather than the emperor's earthly conquests—especially on a funerary monument such as this. Furthermore, crowns or wreaths were presented to martyrs as well as to soldiers and

emperors. And although pagan sarcophagi often depicted battle scenes with heroes conquering barbarian enemies, Christians arguably aspired to a different kind of glory and honor.

Whatever their intended message, these sarcophagus reliefs are the earliest monumental references in pictorial art to Christ's passion. In fact, pre-sixth-century depictions of Christ on the cross (and not merely an empty cross) are extremely rare. A small group of early gems engraved with crucifixion images has been hypothetically dated as early as the late third or early fourth century, and certain Egyptian papyri include a symbol constructed of a tau and rho into a pictogram that may have been meant to represent the crucifixion. A well-known third-century graffito of a figure saluting a crucified donkey-headed figure bears the inscription "Alexamenos worships his god." Discovered on a plaster wall on Rome's Palatine Hill, this unique grafitto is generally regarded as a mocking reference to Christianity and not made for or by one of the faithful.

Two early and certainly Christian crucifixion images date to roughly the same time period, about 430. One, a small panel of the carved wooden doors of Rome's basilica of Santa Sabina, depicts Christ naked except for a loincloth and standing between two smaller-stature nude men, probably meant to be the two thieves crucified with Christ. All three figures appear to be standing (rather than hanging) with their arms outstretched as if either crucified or in prayer. Actual crosses seem missing, except by allusion in the architectural structures behind the three men. The second early crucifixion image is one of four ivory plaques that were originally the sides of a small box or reliquary casket. Here Christ is shown nailed by his hands to a cross. The cross includes the legend "REX IUD." Christ is presented frontally with eyes wide open. He is nude except for a simple loincloth, and his body appears upright and robust. Mary and John stand to the left. At the right the Roman centurion acknowledges Christ as the son of God. The plaque also includes an image of Judas hanging from a tree—a stark contrast to the living, vigorous Christ.

The image of the crucifix became more widespread from the sixth century onward, although the earliest originate in the eastern parts of the Empire—for instance, a leaf from the Syrian Gospel of Rabbula (c. 586) and a large group of pilgrimage tokens known as *ampullae*. The images on these pilgrimage tokens may have been based on the lost apse mosaic in the Constantinian basilica (the Martyrium) adjoining Jerusalem's Holy Sepulcher.

Given their contexts, the early images of Christ crucified were not designed to be venerated, or even the focus of prayer. They continued the tradition of narrative iconography and were not holy images as such. Thus they could not be confused with pagan idols (statues in particular). By the end of the fourth century, however, the practice had changed. According to documents, Constantine presented life-size sculptures of Christ and John the Baptist to the Lateran baptistery along with the silver *fastigium* placed in the main basilica (*Liber Pontificalis*, Sylvester, 34.13). A portrait of Christ's face and shoulders appeared on the tomb ceiling in the Catacomb of Commodilla around the end of the century. Soon more of these images appeared also in precious metals, mosaic, gold glass, and ivory —and eventually icons painted on wood panels. These images presented the face or figure of a holy person, usually frontally, with little obvious narrative content or context. In Rome portraits of Peter and Paul, often shown together, were especially popular. Other saints were favorites, preeminently the Virgin Mary, who frequently appeared with the child Jesus on her lap, flanked by angels and apostles and, sometimes, a deceased petitioner.

Thus beginning around 400, Christian art gradually became dominated by iconic portraits of Christ and the saints, while narrative compositions became less typical for wall painting or apse programs. Sarcophagus reliefs, meanwhile, tended to use stock symbolic images, such as floral and bucolic motifs. Around this time, however, illustrated Bibles appeared, providing a different venue for scripture-based images. The oldest surviving example of these, the Quedlinburg Itala, dates to the early fifth century and consists of five leaves from the books of Samuel and Kings. The style of these manuscript illuminations starkly contrasts with that of the catacomb paintings. Richly detailed and finely painted, a complete manuscript may have had dozens of illustrations, presented in sequenced cycles. These books, or the models on which they were based, may have influenced the development of narrative art in other media, including ivory and glass mosaic. A good example is the central nave mosaics of the basilica of Santa Maria Maggiore (c. 430) that depict more than twenty scenes from the Old Testament stories of Abraham, Jacob, Moses, and David. Smaller liturgical or personal objects—such as textiles, ivory diptychs and book covers, reliquaries, communion plates, chalices, or pyxides—similarly portrayed biblical narratives, including scenes from the life of Christ or his mother.

In summary, from the early third to the end of the fifth century, Christian art developed from simple symbolic figures through narrative and dogmatic representations, and finally to iconic images. The function and place of art had become increasingly varied and complex, as had the materials and venues for its creation and display. Art served many purposes, including edification, adornment, and inspiration. By the end of the Early Christian period, visual art also provided a means by which the viewer could directly encounter the holy and a focus for offering prayer and praise.

[*See also* Basilica; Catacombs; Cemeteries; Christianity; Church Buildings; Church Fathers; Dura-Europos; *and* Funerary Art.]

BIBLIOGRAPHY

Blaauw, Sible de. "Imperial Connotations in Roman Church Interiors: The Significance and Effect of the Lateran Fastigium." In *Imperial Art as Christian Art, Christian Art as Imperial Art: Expression and Meaning in Art and Architecture from Constantine to Justinian*, pp. 137–156. Rome: Bardi Editore, 2001.

Brandenburg, Hugo. *Ancient Churches of Rome from the Fourth to the Seventh Century: The Dawn of Christian Architecture in the West.* Translated by Andreas Kropp. Turnhout, Belgium: Brepols, 2005.

Cartlidge, David, and J. Keith Elliott. *Art and the Christian Apocrypha.* London and New York: Routledge, 2001.

Elsner, Jaś. *Imperial Rome and Christian Triumph: The Art of the Roman Empire AD 100–450*. Oxford and New York: Oxford University Press, 1998.

Finney, Paul Corby. *The Invisible God: The Earliest Christians on Art*. New York and Oxford: Oxford University Press, 1994.

Holloway, R. Ross. *Constantine and Rome*. New Haven, Conn.: Yale University Press, 2004.

Jensen, Robin M. *Face to Face: Portraits of the Divine in Early Christianity*. Minneapolis, Minn.: Fortress Press, 2005.

Jensen, Robin M. "The Passion in Early Christian Art." In *Perspectives on the Passion: Encountering the Bible through the Arts*, edited by Christine Joynes and Nancy Macky, pp. 53–84. New York: T&T Clark, 2008.

Jensen, Robin M. *Understanding Early Christian Art*. London and New York: Routledge, 2000.

Lowden, John. *Early Christian and Byzantine Art*. London: Phaidon, 1997.

Malbon, Elizabeth Struthers. *The Iconography of the Sarcophagus of Junius Bassus*. Princeton, N.J.: Princeton University Press, 1990.

Mathews, Thomas F. *The Clash of Gods: A Reinterpretation of Early Christian Art*. Rev. ed. Princeton, N.J.: Princeton University Press, 1993.

Milburn, Robert. *Early Christian Art and Architecture*. Berkeley: University of California Press, 1988.

Murray, Mary Charles. *Rebirth and Afterlife: A Study of the Transmutation of Some Pagan Imagery in Early Christian Funerary Art*. Oxford: B.A.R., 1981.

Noga-Banai, Galit. *The Trophies of the Martyrs: An Art Historical Study of Early Christian Silver Reliquaries*. Oxford: Oxford University Press, 2008.

Snyder, Graydon F. *Ante Pacem: Archaeological Evidence of Church Life before Constantine*. Rev. ed. Macon, Ga.: Mercer University Press, 2003.

Spier, Jeffrey. *Late Antique and Early Christian Gems*. Wiesbaden, Germany: Reichert Verlag, 2007.

Spier, Jeffrey, ed. *Picturing the Bible: The Earliest Christian Art*. New Haven, Conn.: Yale University Press, 2007. See in particular Johannes G. Deckers, "Constantine the Great and Early Christian Art" (pp. 87–110), Robin M. Jensen, "Early Christian Images and Exegesis" (pp. 65–85), Herbert L. Kessler, "Bright Gardens of Paradise" (pp. 111–139), Herbert L. Kessler, "The Word Made Flesh in Early Decorated Bibles" (pp. 141–168), Mary Charles Murray, "The Emergence of Christian Art" (pp. 51–63), and Jeffrey Spier, "The Earliest Christian Art: From Personal Salvation to Imperial Power" (pp. 1–23).

Weitzmann, Kurt. *Late Antique and Early Christian Book Illumination*. New York: G. Braziller, 1977.

Weitzmann, Kurt, ed. *Age of Spirituality: A Symposium*. New York: Metropolitan Museum of Art, 1980. See in particular Beat Brenk, "The Imperial Heritage of Early Christian Art" (pp. 39–52), George M. A. Hanfmann, "The Continuity of Classical Art: Culture, Myth, and Faith" (pp. 75–99), and Ernst Kitzinger, "Christian Imagery: Growth and Impact" (pp. 141–163).

Weitzmann, Kurt, ed. *Age of Spirituality: Late Antique and Early Christian Art, Third to Seventh Century*. New York: Metropolitan Museum of Art, 1979. The catalog of an exhibition held at the Metropolitan Museum in 1977–1978.

Weitzmann, Kurt, and Herbert L. Kessler. *The Frescoes of the Dura Synagogue and Christian Art*. Washington, D.C.: Dumbarton Oaks, 1990.

Robin M. Jensen

Egypt

Excluding a few large cities—cosmopolitan Alexandria was a world apart—late-antique Egypt was a rural country with small villages and towns. Daily life was rooted in a Hellenistic tradition, mixed with local beliefs and practices. Christianity, attested already in the first century, and paganism coexisted well into the sixth century. Egyptian art was always often hybrid, blending pharaonic and Greco-Roman style and iconography, and gradually markers of Christian faith emerged. Pagan and mythological motifs continued to exist, adapted to new settings and meanings. Derived from pharaonic Egypt are the ankh cross—or ansate cross or crux ansata, a cross with a loop for the upper vertical arm, from the hieroglyph "life" or "to live"—and the representation of the Virgin nursing her son modeled after representations of Isis nursing Horus; Nilotic scenes, celebrating nature and rural life, came to evoke Paradise.

The dry climate of Egypt has preserved an extraordinary number of objects and architectural remains, mainly in regions that became deserts early on. The permanent habitation of the limited area of cultivated land led to continuous rebuilding. This has resulted in an uneven distribution of material remains. Dating Egyptian art and architecture on the basis of style is problematic. New research, modern excavation technology, and dating methods will provide a more secure chronology. Older literature should be treated with caution: recent research and discoveries have often changed established views.

Architecture. Although written sources testify to third-century churches, the oldest architectural remains date to the fourth century. The majority of church buildings belong to the traditional Roman basilica type: an oblong structure consisting of a nave and side aisles, with, at the eastern end, an apse or square altar room with side chambers. Trilobate sanctuaries can be found in Upper Egypt, such as the White and Red monasteries near Sohag, dating to 455 and the early sixth century. Low or high screens closed off the sanctuary (designed for the clergy) from nave and aisles, where the congregation assembled. Typical Egyptian elements are the western return aisle and the decorative use of wall niches. A baptistery could be housed in one of the side chambers or in a cluster of additional rooms; freestanding baptisteries have not been found. Building material was usually mud brick, seldom stone (often taken from pharaonic monuments) or burned brick.

Early monastic churches were small and simple (e.g., Kellia, fourth or fifth century). Monumental exceptions are the churches of the White and Red monasteries. Urban churches followed the trend of cosmopolitan cities such as, and above all, Alexandria (the churches in the pilgrimage center of Abu Mina, or Saint Menas, near Alexandria, fifth–sixth century) or Hermopolis Magna (al-Ashmuneyn; two episcopal churches dating to the fifth century). The main media of church decoration were sculpture and painting.

Sculpture, Painting, and Textiles. Sculpture, of stone and of wood, was chiefly architectural. *Spolia*—"spoils," that is, columns, capitals, and friezes taken from Hellenistic buildings—were blended with elements made to order. These elements show decorative and plant designs, crosses, animals, and sometimes figurative reliefs, and originally they were painted. Examples are found at Cairo's Coptic Museum, such as the doors of Saint Barbara Church

(Old Cairo) from the fourth to fifth century. Furniture in wood or stone is rarely preserved; an exception is a fifth-century wooden altar in the Coptic Museum.

Stelae—tombstones, wood or stone, the oldest dating to the fourth century—mainly show an architectural structure with the deceased in orant (praying) position, mother and child, crosses, and eagles. Texts, including names, dates, and invocations in Greek or Coptic, were engraved or painted. Decoration and formulas bear regional characteristics. Mythological subjects dating to the fourth to fifth century from Heracleopolis Magna (Ahnas) or Oxyrhynchus (Bahnasa; now at Cairo, Coptic Museum) were long thought to be Christianized sculptures. They probably come from pagan mausoleums.

The oldest-known wall paintings with Christian subjects are now destroyed: the Karmuz catacomb (Alexandria), with standing saints, and a frieze of Miracles of Christ, from the third century. Tomb chapel domes in the necropolis of al-Bagawat, near al-Kharga Oasis, show biblical scenes, saints, and personifications of virtues (Exodus Chapel, fourth century; Chapel of Peace, fifth century). In a tomb chapel in Antinoë, Middle Egypt (fifth century), the saints Colluthos and Mary accompany the deceased lady Theodosia. The upper part of the nave of the funerary church of the Monastery of Apa Bane in Middle Egypt (fifth century) preserved gemmed crosses with animals.

Figurative friezes present scenes in a continuous background. A large fourth-century painted piece with Old Testament scenes (now at Riggisberg, Switzerland, Abegg-Stiftung) also shows this principle. A classical approach with depth, movement, and expression is predominant. The heritage of Greco-Roman art is evident in the profusion of decorative borders and patterns. Nearly all murals were executed in *al-secco* (paint applied to a dry layer of plaster).

In the fourth to fifth century came a frontal and formal approach to the people depicted, an approach characterized by a lack of depth, clear outlines, sharp folds, and large eyes. However, a subtle play of colors and thin lines to model faces can often be observed, and secondary characters, animals, and background frequently represent a classical style. This frontality demonstrates that the intention of images had changed: the persons depicted are no longer part of a real world but, instead, are part of a world to come.

The system of wall decoration of tombs and churches belongs to the Hellenistic tradition: a dado with panels imitating *opus sectile* (a geometric pattern of inlaid stones), a painted curtain, or a space-filling floral or geometrical design, as well as an upper register with figurative paintings. Altar-room decoration has rarely been preserved. The principles of decorative programs reflect the function and symbolic meaning of the space: the church as House of God and the Gate of Heaven, the tomb chapel in the expectation of Resurrection and Paradise.

Early textual sources mention the veneration of icons, but at present the oldest saint portraits on wood date to the fifth or sixth century from Antinoë, Middle Egypt (now at Cairo, Egyptian Museum, and at Florence, Museo Egizio). It is generally acknowledged that technique—encaustic (wax as binding agent) or tempera (a water-soluble medium)—and meaning (object of veneration) originate from pagan cult portraits and Egyptian mummy portraits of the first to fourth centuries. The Christian images show the frontality, clear outlines, and large eyes of contemporaneous wall painting, which find predecessors in part of the pagan portraits.

Among the thousands of objects of daily use from late-antique Egypt (table and kitchen ware, lamps, household furniture and furnishings, toilette implements, clothing, jewelry, musical instruments, and so on) in various media, it is only decoration (crosses, saints, biblical scenes) that identifies artifacts made for Christians or a Christian context (e.g., the ivory comb with Miracles of Christ, sixth century, at Cairo, Coptic Museum). Textiles of linen, wool, and silk are especially well known. Woven in various techniques, clothing and furnishings have mainly been found in burials, the oldest fabrics dating to the second to fourth centuries. Papyri testify to a large textile production and extensive international trade. Until the sixth century, silk was most probably imported.

[*See also* Christianity *and* Egypt.]

BIBLIOGRAPHY

Gabra, Gawdat, and Marianne Eaton-Krauss. *The Treasures of Coptic Art in the Coptic Museum and Churches of Old Cairo*. Cairo, Egypt: American University in Cairo Press, 2006.

Grossmann, Peter. *Christliche Architektur in Ägypten*. Leiden: The Netherlands, Brill, 2002.

Schrenk, Sabine, and Regina Knaller. *Textilien des Mittelmeerraumes aus spätantiker bis frühislamischer Zeit*. Riggisberg, Switzerland: Abegg-Stiftung, 2004.

Török, László. *Transfigurations of Hellenism: Aspects of Late Antique Art in Egypt, A.D. 250–700*. Probleme der Ägyptologie 23. Leiden, The Netherlands: Brill, 2005.

Gertrud J. M. van Loon

CHRISTIANITY

Christianity traces its origins to Jesus, a Jew from the village of Nazareth in Galilee. Born around 4 BCE, he had a public career as an itinerant preacher and healer that lasted perhaps less than one year. He gathered twelve disciples, later called "apostles," who traveled with him and shared in his ministry. At the core of his message was the imminent arrival of the "kingdom of God," which he probably conceived as God's definitive intervention in human history that would bring about the transformation of the world according to the divine will. Around 30 CE (between 29 and 33), he and his twelve disciples went to Jerusalem to celebrate Passover, where he shared a final meal with them, was arrested and tried by religious and civil authorities, and executed by the Roman government.

Three days after his death, his tomb was discovered empty. His disciples and others claimed that Jesus had appeared to them, neither as a resuscitated corpse nor as a ghost, but "resurrected"—still corporeal, but radically transformed and not subject to ordinary physical limitations. The disciples' experience of the resurrected Jesus is the decisive event for the origins of Christianity. He was now viewed as the means of salvation, that is, for entering the kingdom of God. Convinced that Jesus was vindicated and transformed by his resurrection, the disciples began to preach this good news, or "gospel" (Greek, *euangelion*), and to proclaim his victory over death.

The so-called "Jesus movement" took shape initially in Jerusalem. Initially, its adherents were known as "Nazarenes" (Acts 24:5) or followers of "the Way" (Acts 9:2). Hostility from some local leaders as well as normal travel led to a dispersal of believers from Jerusalem to other parts of Judaea, Samaria, Syria, Phoenicia, Cyprus, and beyond. At Antioch, the followers of Jesus were called "Christians" for the first time (Acts 11:26). Apostles and missionaries such as Paul of Tarsus established communities of followers throughout Syria, Asia Minor, and Greece, so that Christianity reached Rome by the mid-first century and was established in most of the major cities of the Mediterranean basin by the end of the first century. It continued to grow at a moderate pace through the early fourth century, when its legalization by Constantine sparked an upsurge in membership.

The Organization of Christianity. The structure of leadership in early Christian communities developed over time. Initially, multiple "presbyters," or "bishops" (*episkopoi*), oversaw a community as pastors and leaders of worship, and "deacons" (*diakonoi*) were responsible for practical service, like almsgiving. Apostles were considered a source of authoritative teaching about Jesus (thus, "the apostolic tradition"). There were also "prophets" who offered inspired utterances and "teachers" who gave instruction; these offices waned, or were assumed by others during the second century. The monepiscopacy (one bishop at the head of each local church) became standard in the middle of the second century. The single bishop presided at church assemblies, preached, taught, administered and governed the local church, oversaw charitable works, and represented the local church in correspondence and councils. Bishops came to be thought of as the successors to the twelve apostles and guardians of the apostolic tradition. Though bishops were equal to each other, those who

presided over churches in metropolitan cities like Rome, Alexandria, Antioch, and Jerusalem had preeminence. In the fourth and fifth centuries, Constantinople competed with these older cities for prominence in the ecclesiastical realm, at times with considerable discord and acrimony. Constantine also granted bishops judicial power, thereby incorporating them into the governing structure of the empire. He conferred on them other privileges as well, enabling bishops to acquire political power unimaginable a century earlier. The offices of presbyter and deacon developed into separate, lower clerical grades whose members assisted bishops in their responsibilities.

Each local Christian community was called a "church" (*ekklēsia*). Churches were initially in communion with each other through a shared belief in Jesus, exchange of letters, and mutual support. Later, the local bishop played a crucial role in maintaining communion with other churches. Initially, the local community gathered in the house of one of the members, a practice that continued until the fourth century. Dedicated church buildings also began to be constructed in the third century. In the fourth century and later, magnificent churches were built through imperial patronage, particularly in Rome, Constantinople, and Palestine.

Christian Rituals and Festivals. Baptism was the ritual of initiation into the Christian community. Having its origin in ritual washings of Judaism, baptism was a sign of repentance, an inner purification, a new birth in Christ, and the forgiveness of one's sins. Postbaptismal sins were forgiven by performing an appropriate penance, although some argued through the third century that such sins could not be forgiven. While lighter sins required public confession, more serious sins like murder and adultery necessitated a period of excommunication before a ceremony of reconciliation.

Three kinds Christian meetings predominated in the early centuries. The *synaxis*, or service of the word, continued a Jewish synagogue practice that consisted of reading Scripture, interpreting it, singing psalms, and reciting prayers. The Lord's Supper, or Eucharist, was a reenactment of Jesus' last supper with his disciples before his crucifixion. The Agape, or love-feast, was a fellowship meal shared among believers that had both Jewish and pagan precedents.

Originally, the Eucharist and Agape were apparently conjoined, but in the early second century they began to be celebrated separately, and the Eucharist became joined to the synaxis. The central ritual of the Eucharist involved the body and blood of Jesus in the form of bread and wine. All those who were baptized consumed the bread and wine, thereby renewing their communion with Jesus and each other. In the beginning, these rituals were marked by spontaneity and diverse practices, but they soon became formalized and gradually institutionalized. The synaxis-plus-Eucharist (eventually known as the "Divine Liturgy" or the "Mass") was celebrated weekly in commemoration of the resurrection of Jesus on Sunday, "the Lord's day." Daily celebration of the Eucharist was infrequent, but not unheard of, in the early Christian centuries.

The Eucharist was also celebrated upon festival days. The most important of these was Pascha, or Easter, which by the early second century was celebrated in conjunction with the Jewish Passover as an annual commemoration of Jesus' resurrection. Baptisms would take place at this time. By the beginning of the third century, the celebration had expanded into a commemoration of Jesus' passion, death, and resurrection—the essentials of what would become Holy Week. By the end of the fourth century, Lent, a forty-day period of catechetical and ritual preparation for Easter, had developed. The feast of Pentecost, celebrated fifty days after Easter, commemorated the ascension of Jesus and the descent of the Spirit (Acts 2:1f.). Epiphany, celebrated on 6 January, initially commemorated both the birth of Jesus and his baptism. A separate festival marking the birth of Jesus on 25 December—Christmas—was not generally celebrated until the end of the fourth century, although the Jerusalem church did not celebrate it until the sixth century. Related to these celebrations was pilgrimage to the Holy Land (Palestine) in order to visit and pray at the sites associated with Jesus. Though this practice was known in the second century, it became a popular

Eucharistic Image. Multiplication of the loaves. Fresco, Catacomb of San Callisto, Rome, third century. ALINARI/THE BRIDGEMAN ART LIBRARY

phenomenon in the fourth century and was promoted by the imperial family.

Christian festivals were not limited to commemorations of events in the life of Jesus. In the third century the cultic veneration of martyrs (see below) spread throughout the church. These annual celebrations on the date of the martyr's death included the Eucharist, the reading of an edifying account of the martyrdom, preaching, the veneration of the martyr's relics, and a kind of funerary meal. The latter was often subject to abuse, and some church leaders tried to suppress it. In the fourth century, memorial buildings (*martyria*) were sometimes built to house relics and became pilgrimage destinations. The relics of the martyrs and other saints were believed to be conduits of divine power, able to effect healing and other miracles, and were thus highly prized and jealously guarded.

Christian Identity. Christianity's self-understanding evolved over time in response to various challenges. Roman authorities generally tolerated Christians in the pre-Constantinian period, even though some Christian practices were considered unusual and rumors of cannibalism and incest were persistent. From time to time tensions arose between Christians and their non-Christian neighbors for a variety of reasons, though rarely because of divergent religious beliefs. Hostilities toward Christians during the first two centuries were sporadic and isolated, carried out by local governments or mobs in response to accusations. In this period, a number of Christian "apologists" composed works that defended Christianity, arguing for the reasonableness and uprightness of their religion, and for their concern for the welfare of the empire. Nonetheless, Decius inaugurated an empire-wide, systematic persecution of Christians in 249–251, blaming their failure to supplicate the Roman gods for the woes of the empire. This practice was revived by Diocletian, who launched the so-called "Great Persecution," which lasted from 303 to 305 in the western part of the empire, but as late as 313 in the East. These persecutions left an indelible mark upon the church, which came to conceive of martyrdom as the highest expression of Christian discipleship.

In 313, Constantine and Licinius issued the so-called "Edict of Milan," which proclaimed religious tolerance and ordered the restoration of confiscated Christian property or compensation. This legalization of Christianity was a watershed event, ushering in new relationships with political authorities. Various models of church-state relations emerged. Some held that the church had nothing in common with the state. Others saw the emperor as enjoying a special relationship with God that enabled him to guide the church as well as the empire. Most adopted a middle position wherein it was held that the church and state had distinct spheres of responsibility, but must nonetheless cooperate in the common pursuit of justice and peace. The legislation of Theodosius I in the late fourth century made Christianity the official religion of the Roman Empire.

Separation from Judaism was another defining feature of the first Christian centuries. Initially,

Christian Emperor. Fourth-century bronze statue, possibly of the emperor Valentinian I (321–375; r. 364–375), called the Colossus of Barletta (Italy). ALINARI/THE BRIDGEMAN ART LIBRARY

those who believed in the resurrected Jesus constituted but one of several subgroups within Judaism, and Jewish observance persisted in several groups that venerated Jesus. But growing numbers of Gentile believers and the Jewish war with Rome (66–70 CE) encouraged the separation of churches from standard Jewish practice and belief. By the early second century, Christianity had moved from being fundamentally Jewish to seeing itself as superseding the religion from which it had sprouted. In the ensuing centuries, this view developed at times into full-blown anti-Judaism, in which Jews were blamed for the death of Jesus and the destruction of the Jerusalem temple was seen as divine punishment for their murderous actions. Through the fifth century and beyond, preachers consistently inveighed against "Judaizing," the voluntary adoption of Jewish practices. While this indicates abiding Christian concern to define itself over against Judaism, it also reveals the continued appeal that Judaism had for many ancient Christians.

Christianity also defined itself over against other movements, the most significant of which was Gnosticism. "Gnostic" is a term used by modern scholars to describe a wide variety of texts that espouse two common doctrines: that the Creator God and the God who sent Jesus are different, and that the material cosmos is to be escaped if at all possible. Little is known about Gnostic groups: some intermingled with mainstream Christians; some met separately. Such interaction led to disputes about correct doctrine and authoritative texts, and eventually to arguments about which writings would be included in the emerging Christian canon of Scripture.

Related canonical questions were also raised by the late second-century Marcion, who denied that the Old Testament and certain "Jewish" parts of the New Testament were authoritative for Christians. Most Christians rejected his claims, thereby affirming the continuity between Judaism and Christianity. Nonetheless, consensus on the canon was attained only in the fifth century as the result of a gradual recognition of which books most Christians used as authoritative and scriptural; it was not a determination of the canon "from above" by the bishops or the emperor.

The limitation of inspiration to ancient texts associated with the apostles was one way of marginalizing later prophetic movements within Christianity. The most important of these movements was late-second and third-century "New Prophecy," also known as Montanism. Montanism can be understood as a protest against the laxity of the ecclesiastical organization. Montanists ascribed authority to the Spirit rather than to ecclesial structures and officials, and combined this with a revived apocalyptic expectation. For them, the Spirit reinforced church discipline and was thought to be the guarantee of correct scriptural interpretation before the return of Christ. The New Prophecy was rejected by mainstream Christians primarily because of its rigorism in ecclesial practice, not its doctrinal aberrations.

Other movements, such as asceticism, were channeled and incorporated into Christianity. The voluntary exercise of self-denial was part of Christianity from its earliest days, but extreme ascetic practices were still mostly condemned in the second and third centuries. By the early third century, however, perpetual sexual abstinence (celibacy or virginity) came to be extolled as a higher state of Christian living than marriage, an attitude that remained constant through the fifth century and beyond. In the fourth and fifth centuries, asceticism became institutionalized as monasticism, a distinct lifestyle that was marked by withdrawal from local communities and other social structures in order to foster full devotion to prayer and ascetical practice. Monks and ascetics came to represent a new ideal of Christian holiness since martyrdom was no longer possible in an increasingly Christianized empire.

The prominence of asceticism in Christianity led to competing theological anthropologies. The older tradition, associated mainly with the Greek East but also having adherents in the Latin West, was highly optimistic about the human capacity for the performance of good works, the freedom of the will, the possibility of gaining merit through them, and thus the reward of salvation. Augustine of Hippo formulated an alternative view in the course of his early fifth-century controversy with Pelagius, who subscribed to this older tradition. Augustine maintained that the sin of Adam—the progenitor of the human race—had so vitiated human beings' natural capacities, and in particular their free will, that they could not even choose, and still less perform, good works without divine "grace." Hence salvation is not achieved, but is a gift freely given without prior merit according to God's predestination. Augustine's views on the fallen human condition and the necessity of grace became deeply ingrained in the Latin West, whereas his doctrine of predestination found limited acceptance. His thought as a whole had little effect on eastern theologians.

Christian Doctrine. The two most fundamental, distinctive, and contested tenets of Christianity were its doctrines of Christ and the Trinity. These doctrines attained their classic expressions only in the fourth and fifth centuries, yet even beyond this period there was disagreement, particularly regarding Christological doctrine. The earliest Christians affirmed that Jesus was "Lord" (Hebrew *Adonai*; Greek *Kurios*; Rom. 10:9; 1 Cor. 12:3)—a startling statement that identified him with the one true God—and also acknowledged the activity of God's Spirit in the world. Hence, the earliest Christians recognized three divine agents—God the Father; Jesus Christ, the Son of God; and the Holy Spirit—but struggled to provide a satisfactory account of how these three entities did not undermine their insistence upon monotheism.

Second-century attempts at resolution focused upon the relation between God and Christ, who was identified with the pre-existent Word (*Logos*) of God (John 1:1). The divine Word was thought to have been "uttered" by God for the purposes of creation. He was thus seen as a mediating principle between God and the created world, divine but subordinate to and numerically distinct from God. The Spirit was considered along similar lines.

In the early third century a reaction to this theology emerged that stressed the divine unity and "monarchy" (the single divine principle). Seeking to avoid the implied polytheism of their opponents, Monarchians viewed "Father," "Son," and "Spirit" as names for the single God's changing roles or modes—hence, their theology was called "modalism." A subtle form of Monarchianism developed by the early third-century Sabellius aroused refutation well into the fifth century.

In response to Monarchianism, theologians like Tertullian of Carthage and Origen of Alexandria reformulated Trinitarian theology. They stressed that there were eternal relations between the Father, Son, and Spirit, who shared in a single divinity in varying degrees. The Son was subordinate to the Father, and the Spirit to the Son. Hence monotheism was maintained by allowing for grades of the single divine nature in a hierarchical Trinity.

In the early fourth century, the legacy of Origen was interpreted diversely. Some, like Arius of Alexandria and Eusebius of Caesarea, emphasized the unique status of God the Father as alone possessing the fullness of divinity. Others, like Alexander of Alexandria and his successor Athanasius, argued that the Son's co-eternity with the Father implied that his divinity was equal to the Father's. To put an end to such debates, Constantine convened the Council of Nicaea in 325—the first council whose episcopal participants came from all corners of the empire. The council promulgated a creed that was meant to exclude the theology of Arius, and did so by asserting that the Son was "of the same substance" (*homoousios*) as the Father and "from his substance." Such language sounded hopelessly materialistic to many contemporaries, was believed to be susceptible to a Sabellian interpretation, and was largely rejected in the years immediately following the council. At this stage, Christians had no concept that conciliar decisions and creeds were normative for all churches; the Nicene Council and its Creed only acquired this status later in the fourth century.

From 325 to around 360, eastern theologians sought—without lasting success—to formulate a consensus Trinitarian theology that excluded the extreme views of Arius, Athanasius, and Marcellus of Ancyra (an ally of Athanasius whose views were widely interpreted as Sabellian). The late 350s saw the rise of Heteroousian theology (from *heteroousios*,

Christian Symbols. Sarcophagus of Livia Primitiva, Rome, early third century CE. At bottom are images of a fish, the Good Shepherd, and an anchor. Musée du Louvre, Paris. PHOTOGRAPH BY ROBERT B. KEBRIC

"different in substance"), which distinguished God from the Son in terms of substance. In other words, they held that the Father, as the only true God, possessed divinity in the fullest sense, and that the Son's divinity was essentially different from his. The Homoiousians argued against Heteroousians that the Father and Son were "like in substance" (*homoiousios*), a position that sought to avoid the extremes of *heteroousios* and the Nicene *homoousios*. This controversy sparked a reaction from Basil of Caesarea, who on a broadly Homoiousian basis affirmed that the Father and Son shared a single divinity, but were distinguished by certain properties that accounted for their distinct identities. Basil's insights were developed by his fellow Cappadocians, Gregory of Nazianzus and Gregory of Nyssa.

From the 360s onward, due to groundwork laid by Athanasius and Basil, a pro-Nicene alliance began to form that viewed the Nicene Creed as the best possible statement for achieving consensus in Trinitarian matters. The Nicene Creed came to be viewed as a cipher for a Trinitarian theology in which the three, the Father, Son, and Holy Spirit,

are irreducible and one nature, power, and will. In the 370s, pro-Nicene theology attracted more and more support, and received imperial approval at the Council of Constantinople in 381. In the last years of the fourth century, when Theodosius made Christianity the official religion of the Roman Empire, its prescribed form was the Nicene orthodoxy ratified at the 381 council.

The history of Christological doctrine was a gradual articulation of the sense in which Jesus could be considered both human and divine. Already by the early second century, two extremes were largely rejected: "adoptionism," which maintained that Jesus was a human being who was uniquely allocated divine power and adopted as the Son of God, and "doceticism" (including most Gnostic Christologies), which held that he was a divine being who only appeared (*dokeō*) to be human. By the fourth century, the debate had shifted to determining the extent to which Jesus was divine, with the Council of Constantinople affirming that he possessed the same divinity as God the Father and was thus equal to him (i.e., the Nicene formulation *homoousios*).

This conclusion prompted questions regarding the unity of Christ's personhood. An early solution, associated with Apollinaris of Laodicea, was to argue that Christ lacked a human mind or soul, which was replaced by the divine Word; in other words, Christ's humanity was limited to corporeality. This position was soon considered untenable because of its denigration of Christ's full humanity. By the late fourth century, Christian theologians routinely affirmed Christ's full divinity (*homoousios*, the same as the Father's) and full humanity (consisting of mind, soul, and body).

But Christological controversy was renewed in the late 420s when Nestorius, the bishop of Constantinople, was accused of separating the divinity and humanity of Christ to such an extent that the unity of Christ's personhood was impugned. In other words, while a staunch advocate of the full humanity and divinity of Christ, Nestorius was interpreted as teaching that Christ was internally divided into distinct human and divine "persons," or two subjects of consciousness and activity. Against him, Cyril of Alexandria strongly affirmed the single personhood of Christ, affirming that Christ was "one incarnate nature of God the Word." At the Council of Ephesus in 431, he orchestrated the condemnation of Nestorius, leading to a breach with Syrian bishops sympathetic to Nestorius. The dispute was resolved only in 433 when Cyril recognized in the "Formula of Reunion" the legitimacy of speaking of Christ as one person who was an unconfused union *out of* two natures, the human and divine. The Formula was interpreted by some as a tacit endorsement of Nestorianism because it allowed for two natures in Christ, but Cyril defended himself against the charge. Debate continued in no small part because of the ongoing ambiguity of key terms, like "nature" (*physis*) and "person" (*prosōpon* or *hypostasis*).

Cyril died in 444, and his legacy was fiercely contested. The Council of Ephesus in 449 accepted a parody of Cyril's Christology as interpreted by Eutyches, affirming that Christ was one nature dominated by divinity to such an extent that his full humanity was compromised. This position was quickly reversed at the Council of Chalcedon in 451. The Christology of the *Tome* of Leo of Rome, which had been rejected at Ephesus in 499, was acclaimed as the orthodox Christology, affirming the full divinity and full humanity of Christ in one whole person. The Chalcedonian Definition stated that Christ was "in two natures without confusion, without change, without division, without separation." Though Chalcedonian Christology became the standard in the Latin West and the Greek East, the council was largely rejected by Syriac- and Coptic-speaking Christians. They considered it unfaithful to Cyril's Christology because it allowed for a union *in* two natures rather than *out of* two natures, the former being interpreted as fundamentally Nestorian. Those churches that rejected Chalcedon remain juridically separated from their Latin and Greek counterparts to the present day.

[*See also* Acts of the Apostles; Bible, *subentry* Christian Scripture and Other Writings; Christian Art; Church Buildings; Church Fathers; Constantine; Jews and Judaism; Marriage and Divorce, *subentry* Christian Marriage; Martyrs, Martyrdom, and Martyr Literature; Monasticism; Philosophy, *subentry* Christian Polemical Writing against the Greek Philosophers; *and* Religion, *subentry* Christian Views of Greek and Roman Religion; *and the following biographies*: Augustine; Constantine; Helena; Jesus; Paul; Perpetua.]

BIBLIOGRAPHY

Ayres, Lewis. *Nicaea and Its Legacy: An Approach to Fourth-Century Trinitarian Theology.* Oxford and New York: Oxford University Press, 2004.

Chadwick, Henry. *The Church in Ancient Society: From Galilee to Gregory the Great.* Oxford History of the Christian Church. Oxford and New York: Oxford University Press, 2001.

Davidson, Ivor J. *The Birth of the Church: From Jesus to Constantine, A.D. 30–312.* The Baker History of the Church. Grand Rapids, Mich.: Baker Books, 2004.

Davidson, Ivor J. *A Public Faith: From Constantine to the Medieval World, A.D. 312–600.* The Baker History of the Church. Grand Rapids, Mich.: Baker Books, 2005.

Drobner, Hubertus R. *The Fathers of the Church: A Comprehensive Introduction.* Translated by Siegfried S.

Schatzmann. Peabody, Mass.: Hendrickson Publishers, 2007.

Esler, Philip Francis, ed. *The Early Christian World.* 2 vols. London and New York: Routledge, 2000.

Frend, W. H. C. *The Rise of Christianity.* Philadelphia: Fortress Press, 1984.

Grillmeier, Aloys. *Christ in the Christian Tradition.* Vol. 1, *From the Apostolic Age to Chalcedon (451).* Translated by John Bowden. Rev. ed. Atlanta: John Knox Press, 1975.

Hall, Stuart G. *Doctrine and Practice in the Early Church.* London: SPCK, 1991.

Kelly, John N. D. *Early Christian Doctrines.* 5th ed. London: A. C. Black, 1977.

Pelikan, Jaroslav. *The Christian Tradition: A History of the Development of Doctrine.* Vol. 1, *The Emergence of the Catholic Tradition (100–600).* Chicago and London: University of Chicago Press, 1971.

Wilken, Robert. *The Spirit of Early Christian Thought: Seeking the Face of God.* New Haven, Conn., and London: Yale University Press, 2003.

Young, Frances, Lewis Ayres, and Andrew Louth, eds. *The Cambridge History of Early Christian Literature.* Cambridge, U.K., and New York: Cambridge University Press, 2004.

Mark DelCogliano

CHRISTIAN WRITERS

See Church Fathers.

CHRONOLOGY

There were two basic types of yearly time reckoning used by Greek and Roman historians and states: dating by eponymous magistrates and dating by era. And there were a bewildering number of each type. During the Archaic period (750–500 BCE), as Greek communities organized themselves into city-states with well-defined institutions, including annually elected magistrates, law codes, and archives of written records, it became important to keep track of the passage of time. The most common solution was for a community to keep an official list of the names of one of its annually elected chief magistrates as the year's eponym (the one whose name was given to the year). In Sparta, for example, one of the five annually elected ephors was the eponymous magistrate, and a list of their names began to be recorded from the year 754 BCE onward; in Athens one of the nine annually elected archons was the eponymous archon, and a list of their names began to be recorded from the year 683 BCE. Moreover, we possess an inscription from Miletus that lists the local eponymous priest (*stephanēphoros*, or "crown wearer") that begins in the year 525 and ends in 314 BCE.

Greece. With the rise of historical writing during the fifth century BCE, Greek historians realized the need to have a uniform system of annual time reckoning for recording events involving the various city-states. Because Athens had emerged as a dominant cultural center, the Athenian list of eponymous archons became one of the more commonly used systems for constructing a historical chronology. An alternative system that emerged was a form of era dating. Era dating dates events in reference to a fixed date in the past. Because the Olympic games, celebrated every four years, were one of the most important, commonly shared cultural events of the numerous city-states, dating by Olympiads became increasingly popular as a means of dating all events among the Greeks. Hippias of Elis, who flourished during the second half of the fifth century BCE, drew up the first complete chronology based on Olympiads, beginning with the first Olympic games in 776 BCE. An event could be dated by specifying the Olympiad number and the year of that Olympiad (first, second, third, or fourth). Thus, for example, the Battle of Salamis, which occurred in 480 BCE, could be dated as having been fought in the first year of the seventy-fifth Olympiad. Olympiad dating became well established among Greek historians from the fourth century BCE onward and was used, for example, by Polybius during the later second century BCE and by Diodorus Siculus (together with Athenian archons) during the later first century BCE.

Another form of era dating emerged in the aftermath of Alexander the Great's death in 323 BCE. The Asiatic portion of his vast conquests soon developed into the Seleucid Empire, taking its name from its first ruler, Seleucus I Nicator. Dating from the Seleucid era (year one equals 312 BCE) was widely adopted by communities in western Asia for the next several centuries.

Rome. As Rome emerged as the dominant power of the Mediterranean from the second century BCE onward, Rome's own system of yearly time reckoning was increasingly used by Greek and Roman historians, as well as being recognized by communities that came under Roman rule. Like Athens and Sparta, Rome since the inception of the Republic in 509 BCE had used a system of eponymous magistrates to record officially the passage of the years. These magistrates were the two annually elected consuls, who served as heads of state and as Rome's paramount military commanders. Thus according to this system the plebeian tribune Tiberius Sempronius Gracchus (d. 133 BCE) was slain in the consulship of Publius Mucius Scaevola and Lucius Calpurnius Piso Frugi.

As the Romans from the second century BCE developed their own tradition of historical writing to narrate the events of the Roman state, they also eventually created their own form of era dating. Before 509 BCE the Roman state had been ruled by kings, and Roman historians, writing centuries later, established a standard list of seven kings, but they differed somewhat as to exactly when Romulus, the first king, had founded Rome. Nevertheless, during the closing years of the Roman Republic (40s and 30s BCE) two scholars, Titus Pomponius Atticus and Varro, worked out a systematic chronology of Rome's past that fixed the city's foundation to the year 753 BCE. This date henceforth became widely accepted and was used along with the eponymous consuls to form what is termed the A.U.C. dating system (*ab urbe condita*, or "from the founding of the city"). Thus Tiberius Gracchus was slain in the year 621 A.U.C.

With the advent of the Principate established by Augustus in 27 BCE, Rome's republican institutions were overshadowed by the position of the emperor, and dating by the eponymous consuls was supplemented by a new method of time reckoning: the year of the emperor's tribunician power.

Thus the emperor Augustus died in the year 14 CE in the consulship of Sextus Pompeius and Sextus Appuleius and in the thirty-seventh year of his tribunician power.

These different chronological systems were used throughout the western half of the Roman Empire until its disintegration during the fifth century CE and were in use much longer in the eastern half of the Roman Empire, which evolved into the Byzantine Empire. In 525, Pope John I commissioned the mathematician-astronomer Dionysius Exiguus to draw up an "Easter table," showing on what day of the year Easter (the first Sunday following the first full moon after the vernal equinox) had occurred in the past and would fall in the future. Dionysius devised a new form of era dating by taking as his starting point his estimation of the year in which Jesus was born. This system, *anno Domini*, abbreviated A.D. and meaning "in the year of the Lord," was adopted in the early eighth century by the Venerable Bede in his *Historia ecclesiastica gentis Anglorum* (Ecclesiastical History of the English Nation), after which the system gradually became the standard in western medieval Europe and thence into modern times.

[*See also* Calendar, Greek; Calendar, Roman; Encyclopedias and Dictionaries; Periodization; Time and Timekeeping, Greek; *and* Time and Timekeeping, Roman.]

BIBLIOGRAPHY

Bickerman, E. J. *Chronology of the Ancient World.* 2nd ed. Ithaca, N.Y.: Cornell University Press, 1980.

Samuel, Alan E. *Greek and Roman Chronology: Calendars and Years in Classical Antiquity.* Munich: Beck, 1972.

Gary Forsythe

CHRYSIPPUS

(c. 280–208/4 BCE), Stoic philosopher. Born in Soli in what is now Turkey, Chrysippus came to Athens, presumably as a young man, and studied philosophy both with Cleanthes, the second head of the Stoic school, and in the skeptical Academy before embarking on a teaching career in part outside the Stoa. Anecdotes suggest an uneasy relationship with Cleanthes, but these may simply be fictional re-creations, at the personal level, of Chrysippus' thoroughgoing renovation of the teachings of the school of which he himself became head in 232 BCE. His death is conventionally located between 208 and 204 at age seventy-three, but we are also told that in his eightieth year he began the thirty-ninth book of his opus *Logical Questions*—a highly specific report that deserves more weight than it is usually given.

By a strange coincidence, a book of this same work is one of only three, out of a reported total of 705 books (i.e., papyrus rolls), known for certain to have survived in something like its original form, albeit only in part. The two other books belong to a more famous work, *On Providence*. All were preserved in the Villa dei Papiri in ancient Herculaneum, buried by the eruption of Vesuvius in 79 CE. For the contents of the rest of Chrysippus' production—311 books, we are told, on logic alone, the area of Stoic philosophy that he more or less created—we are entirely reliant on quotations, citations, and reports in other ancient writers, many of them hostile, ignorant, or negligent.

The most extensive set of quotations was extracted in the second century CE by the medical writer and philosopher Galen from the first book of Chrysippus' *On the Soul* and from his *On the Passions*. These permit a more balanced assessment of ancient reports that Chrysippus himself padded out his works with quotations. Neither sensory evidence nor syllogistic proof is available, Chrysippus argues, for determining the location in the body of the mind, which Stoics called the "ruling part" of the soul; so instead Chrysippus proposes to extract information implicit in ordinary linguistic behavior and in poetry and myth. These represent largely unreflective expressions of *logos* (reason), the immanent cosmic structuring principle—identical with perfect rationality, god, fate, and providence—that is also present in the imperfectly rational human soul. Similarly, Chrysippus' reported tendency toward repetition and irrelevance may in fact manifest a commitment to exhibit the thoroughgoing interconnectedness of the Stoic system's three parts, logic, ethics, and natural philosophy.

Despite the dearth of firsthand evidence, Chrysippus' contributions were manifestly so extensive, and so remarkable for both philosophical creativity and dialectical ingenuity, that it was said that without him there would have been no Stoa; and certainly no mere summary can do justice to them. A small selection of his achievements will highlight his contributions to the school's doctrinal orthodoxy and to his sophisticated (re)interpretation of doctrines that he inherited from Zeno of Citium, founder of the school, in an unacceptably vulnerable, underconceptualized form.

Chrysippus was almost certainly responsible for the Stoic doctrine of "kinds" or *genera* (the Aristotelianizing term "categories" is misleading), the four ontological levels that a body may occupy. This metaphysical theory was not merely a bulwark against Academic deployment of the so-called growing argument, which challenges the ordinary notion of objects persisting and changing over time. It was also developed to defend both an ethical doctrine and an epistemological one. The ethical doctrine defended was that the virtues constitute internally differentiated cognitive states, not (as the early Stoic Aristo of Chios claimed) a single such state differentiated purely externally, by the objects on which it operates. The epistemological doctrine defended was that the possibility of our enjoying exact and reliable ("apprehensive") sensory appearances of individuals is not thwarted by the existence of exactly similar objects: each genuine unity is uniquely characterized by a "peculiar quality," a unique combination of "common qualities." Chrysippus thus defends both his own interpretation of Zeno's somewhat ambiguous pronouncements about the virtues and also Zeno's doctrine (under threat from the Academy) of the apprehensive appearance as the "criterion of truth" and the foundation for knowledge.

"Qualities" for Chrysippus are "breaths" (*pneumata*), currents of fire and air conjoined. Whereas Zeno and Cleanthes seem to have thought of (a form of) fire as the divine, intelligent substance permeating and shaping the world, Chrysippus instead postulated *pneuma*—the peculiar constitution of which allows simultaneous contraction and expansion—to explain the stable differentiation of elements, natural substances, and (especially) organisms, with their potential for autonomous change and movement. He shared the Hellenistic schools' wide acceptance of the principle that only bodies are capable of this or any causal interaction, in which incorporeal universals (as distinct from common qualities) can play no part. Indeed, although talk about universals is permitted as useful shorthand in definitions—central to Chrysippus' exposition of key concepts and their interrelations—it is devoid of ontological implications, and may even be misleading, universals themselves being metaphysical chimeras (as Chrysippus' deployment of the well-known "no man" argument was meant to establish).

Chrysippus also decisively influenced Stoic etiology and the school's mature teaching about fate. For Zeno and Cleanthes, fate had been the traditional, quasi-personal force of Greek myth, but in Chrysippus' hands it became an ineluctable chain of causes that is one manifestation of the divine rational principle. A crucial distinction is drawn between an individual's causal potential (inherent in its *pneuma* as its "sustaining cause") and other, occurrent, causal factors, such as our impressions of the world. In the case of human agents, fate works, not coercively *on* us, but cooperatively *through* us: it is the character of one's own soul, a concentration of *pneuma*, that fixes one's choice of actions. This version of compatibilism, aiming to secure our responsibility for our actions even as they form an integral part of the cosmic causal nexus, proved as influential, and as controversial, as the theory of "total mixture" that Chrysippus used to account for *pneuma*'s unique structure and its capacity for retaining its nature while diffused throughout an object of any kind or size.

In the field of logic Chrysippus' best-known achievement, as one of antiquity's greatest logicians, is probably the identification of the five inference-schemata known as the "indemonstrables," together with rules for reduction of other arguments to these; but other innovations complemented his etiological theory. The modal concepts are defined so as to embody a distinction between a proposition's intrinsic truth-receptiveness and extrinsic factors that may prevent that receptiveness from being exercised. Conditional propositions—which can express the dependence of future events on past or present ones—were assigned truth-conditions different from the truth-functional ones favored by early Stoics. Instead, what must hold between the "if . . ." and the "then . . ." components of a true conditional is, it seems, necessary and conceptual in nature (its precise nature is much debated). Hence there can be true predictions of future events—and Chrysippus strenuously defended both the possibility of true prophecies and the principle of bivalence, which he deemed essential for avoiding causal lacunae. But prophecies cannot be linked to the past or present by the kind of necessary connection that would ground a true conditional.

In one area of philosophy, moral psychology, Chrysippus' authority was challenged within the school by Posidonius of Apamea (first century BCE); besides criticizing Chrysippus' definition of the ethical end, Posidonius also, we are told, argued in favor of a Platonizing division among the rational, appetitive, and anger-related functions of the soul. In contrast, the Chrysippean soul is rational through and through, so that passions (*pathē*) such as anger and fear are to be understood, not only as physical states of the soul, but also as beliefs—erroneous value judgments—that are "irrational" only in that they represent impulses exceeding the natural limits imposed by rationality. The wise man, the model of human behavior, instead consistently matches his impulses to the true value of their objects. Here again Chrysippus is probably interpreting, expanding, and justifying Zeno's underdeveloped, underconceptualized views on the topic. As he is reported to have said to Cleanthes: "Give me the doctrines, and I will discover the arguments for myself."

[*See also* Grammarians; Posidonius of Apamea; Stoicism; *and* Zeno of Citium.]

BIBLIOGRAPHY
Primary Works

As noted, none of Chrysippus' works survives intact.
The classic collection of quotations, citations, and testimonies (including Galen's lengthy excerpts from *On the Soul* I and *On the Passions*) remains Hans von Arnim, ed., *Stoicorum Veterum Fragmenta*, vol. 2: *Chrysippi fragmenta logica et physica*, and vol. 3: *Chrysippi fragmenta moralia, Fragmenta successorum Chrysippi* (Leipzig, Germany: Teubner, 1903). A more extensive collection of Stoic dialectic teaching is Karlheinz Hülser, ed., *Die Fragmente zur Dialektik der Stoiker*, 4 vols. (Stuttgart, Germany: Frommann-Holzboog, 1987–1988). For *On Providence* (Herculaneum Papyri 1421, 1038) and *On Fate*, see Alfred Gercke, "*Chrysippea*," in *Jahrbücher für klassische Philologie*, Supplement vol. 14 (Leipzig, Germany: Teubner, 1885), pp. 689–781. For the remains of the book of the *Logical Questions*, see Livia Marrone, "Le *Questioni logiche* di Crisippo (*PHerc.* 307)," *Cronache Ercolanesi* 27 (1997): 83–100.

Secondary Works

Atherton, Catherine. *The Stoics on Ambiguity.* Cambridge, U.K.: Cambridge University Press, 1993.

Bobzien, Susanne. *Determinism and Freedom in Stoic Philosophy.* Oxford: Clarendon Press, 1998.

Bréhier, Emile. *Chrysippe et l'ancien Stoïcisme.* Rev. ed. Paris: Presses Universitaires de France, 1951.

Frede, Michael. *Die stoische Logik.* Göttingen, Germany: Vandenhoeck & Ruprecht, 1974.

Inwood, Brad. *Ethics and Human Action in Early Stoicism.* Oxford: Clarendon Press, 1985.

Tieleman, Teun. *Galen and Chrysippus on the Soul: Argument and Refutation in the "De Placitis," Books II–III.* Leiden, The Netherlands: Brill, 1996.

Catherine Atherton

CHTHONIC GODS

The term "chthonic" comes from the Greek *chthonios*, meaning of, in, or under the earth. The term can be most simplistically applied to gods associated directly with the earth and also by extension to those with any interest in corporeal or mundane matters of creation and destruction. This seems intrinsically to contrast chthonic gods with the sky and the "heavenly" Olympians, but in fact the term "chthonic" is typically is used to distinguish an attribute or aspect of a particular god, including the Olympians. Though the association with earth most readily calls to mind an agricultural aspect, gods involved with what is lower than, or under, the earth—namely, the grave and the underworld—are the ones more commonly called "chthonic." The sense of gloom and fear associated with death and the underworld, as opposed to the openness and light of the sky, can also imply more sinister and dark powers for chthonic gods.

Chthonic gods thus run the gamut from the benevolent energy of fertility and harvest deities to the demonic spirits associated with the darkest corners of the underworld. In both its agricultural and its death-related sense, the epithet is fairly loosely applied. Gaia (Earth herself), Demeter, and, particularly in Homer, Hades and Persephone naturally belong to this group—Hades doubly so, both as the lord of the dead and as the Roman Pluto, the bringer of crops. The term is also applied to others whose jurisdiction falls anywhere within man's earthly-into-afterlife existence, such as the Moerae (Fates), Charon the ferryman into the underworld, and Hypnos (Sleep). At the more mysterious, and sometimes darker, end are the Erinyes (Furies) and destructive spirits such as Thanatos (Death) and the Ceres (female death spirits), as well as those whose dwelling place is Tartarus (literally, "deep place").

"Chthonic" is widely applied—for instance, in Homer and Hesiod—to the earthy and sometimes darker aspects of the Olympians, such as to Artemis in her "magical" and nocturnal aspect Hecate, to the chthonic Hermes in his role as the psychopomp, and to the chthonic Zeus, that is, Zeus active in the underworld. In Egypt, Osiris and Anubis, as gods of the underworld and the dead, as well as the (atypically) masculine earth god Geb and the Babylonian keeper of the dead Ereshkigal, can also be called "chthonic." In essence, any activity related to the cycle of earthly life, from fertility to death and the subsequent return of the body to the earth, is chthonic, and virtually every god has some role that could qualify as such.

The cult and worship of chthonic gods has not been shown to be distinctly different from the purposes or manner of worship of the Olympians. Certainly the chthonic gods would be appealed to for the requisite blessings related to successful farming and from a desire to gain blessings for deceased loved ones, but they were also beings to be appeased in an effort to ward off dread events, such as death, and evil in general. Certain material differences in ritual are sometimes highlighted, such as possible human sacrifice or the offering of libations, particularly of blood, which flows down into the earth, as opposed to the burning of meat, the smoke of which is carried up into the sky. However, though certainly true, these differences are not ubiquitous, nor are they exclusive to these two classes of deity.

The chthonic cult in practice differed from the civic cult in that the civic cult, as the citizens' public and group worship of the deity or deities associated with a particular city-state, served a collective, and often political, set of purposes. Though involving some element of public good, at least in the agricultural benefits, chthonic cults included a somewhat more personal benefit, particularly when related to dead kin or the personal fear of evil spirits. In these ways the chthonic cult more closely resembles the ancestral. Both related to death and the dead, with the ancestral cult often about the living appealing to deceased kin in the expectation that the deceased might exert some influence over the fortune of the living. The ancestral cult also served to honor the solidarity of the bloodline and the idea of a collective existence. For similar purposes, the heroic cult held the worship of the immortalized dead, frequently near the believed grave of the deceased. Though because of their mortuary element either of these could technically be described as chthonic, the usual chthonic cult did not appeal to the deceased themselves. Rather appeals were made to those who rule over the underworld and to those who have the power or possible inclination to destroy—to gain some favor for a deceased loved one (or perhaps gain some disfavor for a deceased

enemy), to solicit protection from possible evil influences on behalf of the living, or to circumvent the wrath of those deities with possible sinister designs.

[See also Autochthony and Underworld and Afterlife.]

BIBLIOGRAPHY

Burkert, Walter. "The Dead, Heroes, and Chthonic Gods." In his Greek Religion, pp. 190–215. Translated by John Raffan. Cambridge, Mass.: Harvard University Press, 1985.

Fairbanks, Arthur. "The Chthonic Gods of Greek Religion." American Journal of Philology 21, no. 3 (1900): 241–259.

Hägg, Robin, and Brita Alroth, eds. Greek Sacrificial Ritual, Olympian and Chthonian: Proceedings of the Sixth International Seminar on Ancient Greek Cult, Göteborg University, 25–27 April 1997. Sävedalen, Sweden: Svenska Institutet i Athen, 2005.

Paley, F. A. "On Chthonian Worship." Journal of Philology 1 (1868): 1–14.

Amber Fischer

CHURCH, CHRISTIAN

See Christianity.

CHURCH BUILDINGS

The earliest sources for the meeting habits of the Jesus movement are textual, and no identifiable church building predates the third century. Scant material remains, however, should not frustrate our inquiry into the development of worship space after the death of Jesus. Textual evidence from late-second-century Alexandria tells us that at least some Christian communities there already talked of "going to church" (Clement of Alexandria Paedagogus 3.11). No physical traces of these churches have been identified, however, and it may be that the buildings themselves were not distinguishable. During this period Christianity was evolving from an offshoot of Judaism into an independent religious orientation. Indeed, there is no evidence that early followers of Jesus ever conceived of themselves as

"Christians" until later in the first century (Acts 11:26), and even then, the term probably began in Antioch as a local slur. Thus, the origins of a distinctly Christian architecture took place within the same centuries which also witnessed the transformation of the nascent "Jesus movement" into a distinct religion.

Early Meeting Places. The early textual sources for church meetings include letters of Paul and the narrative account known as the Acts of the Apostles. The latter tells us that worshippers initially met in houses, gathering "at home" in the context of a communal dinner (Acts 2:46; see also 5:42). This evidence dovetails nicely with information gleaned from Paul and others, who refer to these assemblies as meetings of "the church (Greek: *ekklēsia*; Latin: *ecclesia*) in the house" of various individuals (Romans 16:4–5; see also Colossians 4:15). In addition, Paul specifically names several heads of households whom he knew throughout the Mediterranean. Examples include a patron named Philemon (Philemon 2) and a community led by the couple Aquila and Prisca (1 Corinthians 16:19). By taking into account the social dynamics that lay behind these meetings, scholars have shown that patronage, hospitality, and friendship played a key role in the emergence of assembly spaces for the Jesus movement. Consistent with the Greco-Roman ethos of civic and religious patronage, which cut across gender lines, both men and women played the roles of host and patron. Early "church" buildings themselves, however, remain wholly invisible to us from an archaeological point of view, owing to the fact that their constituents often met in these sorts of adopted settings.

Christian Structures. Why and how did this situation change? Earlier scholars offered a theological answer, drawing upon ideas popularized by John Calvin during the Protestant Reformation. Calvin was the first to suggest, by scriptural exegesis, that the purity of these early church assemblies had been gradually corrupted by "pagan," or Greco-Roman, concepts of sacred space. This type of theological explanation, however, assumes that scripture is the normative lens through which all historical questions should be investigated. In fact, by drawing attention to the many local factors that influenced the early Jesus movement, historians and scholars of religion have long demonstrated that such a normative, or fixed, perception of either the early churches or of first-century Judaism is not historically defensible. This paradigm shift itself was the product of a growing interest in textual criticism during the nineteenth and early twentieth century, the period when literary-historical tools began to be applied to the interpretation of scripture. By challenging many of the theological assumptions that had informed the reading of Christian scripture up to that time, these scholars laid the foundation for how later social and cultural historians would approach the study of Christian architecture.

Since the 1980s and 1990s, for example, research on early Christian architecture has focused on comparisons with the architectural habits of other Greco-Roman social and religious organizations. The followers of Mithras in Rome, the worshippers of Serapis on Delos, and the local Jewish community in the Syrian city of Dura-Europos offer three case studies. Despite their geographic and religious differences, none of these associations in their early stages of local formation ever gathered in a building that had been purposely or primarily designed for their specific needs. Instead, each met in an adapted environment, such as a house, apartment, or small bath complex owned by a local individual. These spaces were only secondarily transformed to meet the needs of the larger group, an act that depended heavily upon the wealth and benefaction of local individuals who could marshal the money and space to facilitate architectural change.

The construction of a banqueting hall for the Shipbuilders Guild (the Fabri Navales) at Ostia is an excellent illustration of this process. At some point during the first century CE, a Late Republican residence in this area was demolished and replaced with a peristyle house. In the middle of the second century, this newer house was adapted to provide a communal dining space for the Shipbuilders Guild, who assembled there and also maintained a sanctuary space across the street. This building sequence suggests that, by the middle of the second century, the logistical needs of the guild at Ostia had far outstripped the social and religious meeting space originally available to them. It is possible that the wealthy owner of the house even played an important role in raising the urban profile of the guild. This interplay between patronage and architectural adaptation offers a useful lens through which we can glimpse how similar groups might have developed their own visible presence in cities throughout the empire.

Architectural developments that accompanied the rise of "Christianity," as it came to be known in the early decades of the second century, are best seen within this context. Like other associations, Christian communities, too, gradually developed a need for more formalized spaces, such as larger assembly halls and places for baptism. The first identifiable church building, located in Dura-Europos, is an example of adaptation. The building, originally a domestic structure, was constructed as a series of rooms facing a central court. Between

241 and 256, the house was transformed into a Christian meeting space, whose identity was confirmed by the presence of Christian graffiti. During this renovation, two rooms in the southern part of the house were combined into one large hall, and a raised platform was added at one end, mostly likely for the reading of scripture. Across the courtyard, a baptismal font, identifiable by its form and by the surrounding Christian wall paintings, was installed in a room that had once served a utilitarian purpose.

The developments at Dura-Europos were not unique, nor did examples of local adaptation automatically cease with the legalization of Christianity in 313. On the contrary, Christian transformation of preexisting space is attested in textual and material sources throughout the third, fourth, and fifth centuries. The fact that buildings constructed specifically as churches also emerged in the late third and fourth century should, therefore, be seen as a simultaneous, organic development, not an architectural innovation attributed solely to Christianity's legalization. In fact, some of the first

Santa Sabina. Central nave, c. 400. SCALA/ART RESOURCE, NY

known instances of original church construction were based not on a formal articulation of space, like the Roman basilica with its aisles and central nave. Rather, they were often conceived as a simple, open assembly hall that frequently lacked any interior divisions. The early church of Saint Chrysogonus (San Crisogono) in Rome, built around 310, possessed this kind of open floor plan.

At the same time, other buildings, like that of Saint John Lateran (San Giovanni in Laterano) in Rome (c. 314–319), did begin to evince more formal, interior divisions, characterized by side aisles and a central, longitudinal nave. These features, with the addition of a cross aisle, or transept, eventually became standard for the Christian basilica. Nevertheless, fourth-century church buildings defy easy categorization or chronological typology. With the emperor's patronage, for example, other more visible church forms also flourished, such as the rotunda erected at the so-called Holy Sepulcher in Jerusalem (c. 326–335). These developments took place alongside the continued construction of open "hall churches," as at Philippi in Macedonia (343–344). Thus, it was imperial support, explicit or otherwise, that frequently determined the appearance of a fourth-century church. Only after the fourth century did the basilica as we recognize it today assume a more prominent place in church construction.

Finally, it is important to note that archaeological evidence for the conversion of temples into churches during the fourth century is extremely rare, even after the legislation establishing Nicene Christianity as the official religion of the empire (380 CE). Some Christians did, however, begin to forcibly appropriate synagogues during this time (Ambrose *Letters* 40.6–7). Architecturally, it is these instances of synagogue appropriation, not the systematic conversion of the temples, that have often propagated a view of the fourth century as the period of Christian "triumph."

[*See also* Archaeology, *subentry* Sites Elsewhere in the Middle East; Architecture; Basilica; Christian Art; Christianity; Constantine; Dura-Europos; *and* Synagogues.]

BIBLIOGRAPHY

Finney, P. Corbey. "Early Christian Architecture: The Beginnings (A Review Article)." *Harvard Theological Review* 81 (1988): 319–339.

Krautheimer, Richard. "The Beginnings of Early Christian Architecture." *Review of Religion* 3 (1939): 144–159. Reprinted in his *Studies in Early Christian, Medieval, and Renaissance Art.* New York: New York University Press, 1969.

Schüssler Fiorenza, Elisabeth. *In Memory of Her: A Feminist Theological Reconstruction of Christian Origins.* New York: Crossroad, 1983.

Synder, Graydon. *Ante Pacem: Archaeological Evidence of Church Life before Constantine.* Macon, Ga.: Mercer University Press, 1985.

Wharton, Annabel. *Refiguring the Post-Classical City: Dura Europos, Jerash, Jerusalem, and Ravenna.* Cambridge, U.K.,: Cambridge University Press, 1995.

White, L. Michael. *The Social Origins of Christian Architecture.* 2 vols. Valley Forge, Penn.: Trinity Press, 1996–1997.

Douglas Ryan Boin

CHURCH FATHERS

The development of the Eastern and Western patristic traditions from the church's origins in the first century up until the mid-fifth century owed as much to the contributions of outstanding individuals as it did to the historical events that shaped their responses to the challenges of Christianity. These outstanding individuals are known as the church fathers, by virtue of both their gender and their influence on the later church through the survival of their writings. From this period of four centuries a remarkable amount of patristic literature has survived in Greek, Latin, Coptic, Armenian, and Syriac manuscripts. In this article some of the major themes of the most important of these writings are surveyed. Of necessity, many important themes and figures are omitted, and there is a greater representation from the fourth century than from any other. This was truly the golden age for the church fathers.

The figures under discussion have been selected for the broadness of their contribution in a range of areas. They are presented in chronological order: Tertullian, Irenaeus, Cyprian, Athanasius, Ambrose, Augustine, the Cappadocians, Cyril of Alexandria, Nestorius, and Leo the Great. One major theme has been selected from the writings of each figure or group. This will enable us to cover, however briefly, the most significant historical developments within the delimited chronological period. These themes include criteria for salvation; Christian identity; developing sacraments, particularly baptism; establishing and maintaining authority as Christian leaders; defining and dealing with schism and heresy; Christology and the church councils; and the church's relationship with temporal power.

Tertullian of Carthage. One of the most controversial figures of the early church, both in his own time and today, was Tertullian of Carthage (c. 155 or 160–after 220), a highly educated layman who wrote in North Africa toward the end of the second century. His didactic and uncompromising style earned him a not undeserved reputation as a firebrand, a puritan, a misogynist, and a rigorist. Tertullian did more to define the Christian identity against the prevailing Greco-Roman culture than perhaps did any other individual up to his day. He spoke out strongly against Christians joining the military, against Christians marrying outside the faith, and against pagan religious practices.

Tertullian's best-known work remains his *Apology*, an extended treatise in defense of the Christian faith addressed to the Roman governors of his province. Tertullian sought in this treatise to expose traditional Greco-Roman religion as a sham. He even took the irenic imperial attitude to Christianity to task, attacking Trajan's policy of toleration as inconsistent and unjust. Trajan had earlier advised Pliny the Younger, governor of Bithynia, that he was to leave Christians in peace unless they drew attention to themselves. As Pliny the Younger records, if an accusation was brought against Christians, they were to be tried, and only if they were found guilty of atheism or of disbelief in the Roman gods should they be punished (*Epistulae* 10, 97). Tertullian complains in *Apology* 2: Trajan "says that they should not be sought [out]—as though they were innocent; then prescribes that they should be punished—as though they were guilty!"

In his later years Tertullian adhered to the teachings of the Montanist sect, with its emphasis on the gifts of the Holy Spirit, especially that of prophecy. This sect granted a greater leadership role to women than did the mainstream churches, and it seems that these charismatic leaders posed quite a challenge to episcopal authority. In the opinion of some scholars, Tertullian put himself outside the limits of orthodoxy in this final stage of his life. The continuing debate over this bears witness to the fluidity of sectarian boundaries in the church in this very early period.

Irenaeus of Lyons. Another outstanding apologist of the second century was Irenaeus of Lyons (c. 120–200). Irenaeus' main opponents were the adherents of Gnosticism, a raft of esoteric beliefs promoted by various teachers such as Basilides of Alexandria and Valentinus of Rome. Gnosticism incorporated a range of Jewish, pagan, and oriental ideas about the *plērōma*, a hierarchy of divinities and demigods, and the role of secret knowledge in attaining salvation. In his tract *Against the Heresies* and his second major work, *Proof of the Apostolic Preaching*, Irenaeus sought to counter this exclusivist approach by proposing his own model of salvation for all. Ironically, Irenaeus did more than any other writer to preserve the teachings of the Gnostics for posterity, albeit from a critical perspective.

Irenaeus sought to establish twin authorities for the church: the continuous tradition handed down from the time of Christ, and the canon of Christian scriptures. Irenaeus recognized the importance of defending the Hebrew scriptures against those who wished to reject them as portraying a very different God from that embraced by Christianity. The heretic Marcion was the first to make a canon of scripture consisting only of selected New Testament books, excluding all of the Old Testament. That this teaching was rejected as heretical was largely thanks to Irenaeus' efforts.

Cyprian of Carthage. The greatest contributor to the continued attempt to define the limits of schism and heresy was Cyprian, bishop of Carthage

(248–258) and head of the North African church. The stakes were quite high at this time of large-scale persecution of the Christian church under Emperor Decius in 249–251. During this persecution Cyprian went into hiding for a year. Many Christians, even some bishops, complied with imperial demands to burn incense in front of an image of the emperor, thus showing their allegiance to both the emperor and state religion. When some of those who had lapsed in this way, and who had handed over scriptures to be burned, wished to return to the church, an angry reaction ensued from those who had remained faithful. This resulted in the formation of sects of rigorists, such as the Novatianists, who wished to reject those who had betrayed their beliefs, and an opposing sect of laxists who advocated a more moderate treatment of the lapsed. When those who had been baptized in either sect wished to rejoin Cyprian's community, a second, "true" baptism was the condition of their reentry.

Cyprian's stance on baptism of the lapsed led to conflict with Stephen, bishop of Rome (254–257), who insisted that the laying on of hands by church elders was sufficient for heretics or schismatics who wished to rejoin the church. Cyprian's model of ecclesiology, which precluded salvation outside the church, did much to strengthen the North African church's claim to authority, even against the bishop of Rome. Cyprian himself died as a martyr during the persecution of Valerian in 258. The third and final universal persecution took place in the later reign of Diocletian (303–305).

Athanasius of Alexandria. Another victim of imperial persecution was Athanasius, bishop of Alexandria (328–373). By now, however, Byzantine emperors were—nominally at least—Christian, with the brief but luminous exception of Julian the Apostate (r. 361–363). With the conversion of Constantine in 312 and the establishment of a new capital on the Bosporus in 331, doctrinal dilemmas had become a feature of imperial life. Constantine's son and successor Constantius II (r. 337–361) was a self-professed adherent of Arianism, despite its condemnation as a heresy at the Council of Nicaea (325), over which his father had presided. Athanasius had attended this council as a young deacon and three years later became bishop of Alexandria, one of the five most powerful churches in the Roman Empire (along with those in Rome, Jerusalem, Constantinople, and Antioch). Arius, a priest of Alexandria, had found a great deal of support for his doctrine of Christ the Son as the creation, and therefore the subordinate, of God the Father. The Arian controversy continued in the East until its renewed condemnation at the Council of Constantinople (381) and in the West until the fifth century when it was brought back to Italy with the Gothic invaders.

Athanasius spent seventeen years of his bishopric in exile, first in Trier, then in Rome, and finally in the desert outside Alexandria. Two of his most influential works are his *Paschal Letter* of 367, outlining the definitive canonical list of twenty-seven books of the New Testament, and his Christological treatise *On the Incarnation.* Perhaps his most enduring work, however, is his *Life of Saint Anthony*, one of the earliest essays in hagiography, which presented the monk's struggles in the Egyptian desert and became the proof text for the burgeoning monastic movement in Egypt, Palestine, and Syria. Athanasius was able to return to his see only after the death of Constantius in 361, ironically at the time of the pagan reformer Julian's accession to the imperial throne. Julian's two-year reign saw an attempt to wrest back education of the young by banning Christian teachers in schools, but the attempt was short-lived.

Ambrose of Milan. Another advocate of spiritual authority against temporal power was Ambrose, bishop of Milan (374–397) and a former governor of Aemilia and Liguria in northern Italy. Milan by this time had replaced Rome as the administrative hub of the Western empire. Ambrose was willing and able to confront those holding secular power with the authority of the church. He convinced the young emperor Valentinian II to forbid the restoration of a statue of the goddess of Victory in the senate house at Rome. The pagan senator Symmachus' defense of the Altar of Victory is one of the most powerful orations in defense of traditional Roman values that survives. In the face of opposition from the bishop of Milan, however, no degree of eloquence proved persuasive to Valentinian II. After imperial soldiers slaughtered thousands of citizens in a stadium in Thessalonica (390) in retaliation for the murder of a Roman governor by a rioting mob, Ambrose confronted the emperor Theodosius I (r. 379–395) and forced him to do public penance. Theodosius had declared through an edict that Christianity was now the only legal religion of the empire. He banned games and the theater and forbade worship in pagan temples.

The issue of the Theodosian Code (Codex Theodosianus) by Theodosius II in 438 codified many legal reforms in line with the new religion of the empire. It addressed sixty-six laws against heretics (e.g., Codex Theodosianus 16.1.2), forbidding them the right of assembly and the right to appoint priests, as well as confiscating their meetinghouses and ordering that their books be burned. Manichaeans alone warranted the death penalty (Codex Theodosianus 16.5.9). Ambrose was also a formidable opponent of Arianism in northern Italy, and he managed to resist the empress Justina's attempts to make him hand over church buildings to the Arian faction.

Augustine of Hippo. Ambrose and his protégé Augustine, later bishop of Hippo (396–430), represent the Western church at the apogee of its powers. After initial membership in the Manichaean cult, Augustine made a formal conversion to Christianity in 386, and in 396 he became bishop of the important North African urban center of Hippo Regius, in the Roman province of Numidia. With the sack of Rome by Alaric in 410 and the loss of North Africa to the Vandals in 429, Roman power was on the decline. In the *City of God*, a history of Roman civilization, Augustine felt compelled to explain the catastrophic events of 410 as part of God's plan for Rome. In this work he sought to avert the blame leveled at the Christian contingent for abandoning their traditional protectors, the Roman gods.

Augustine's writings were largely shaped by controversies, first against the Manichaeans, the cult to which he adhered in his youth. The second major controversy that consumed him as bishop of Hippo concerned the Donatists, a rival Christian sect that posed a real threat to stability in North Africa. Augustine left a lasting legacy in his doctrines of original sin and predestination, developed at least in part as a reaction to the third major challenge to his beliefs, Pelagianism. Pelagius, a monk who taught that salvation was within the grasp of all who turned their efforts toward virtuous living, had gathered a strong following in the late fourth century among the aristocratic ascetics of Rome. At the end of a long career as bishop of Hippo, Augustine on his deathbed faced the imminent destruction of his home city by Geiseric, the Vandal leader who conquered North Africa from the north, crossing over from Spain.

The Cappadocians. The third canon of the Council of Constantinople (381) made the first reference to Constantinople as the "new Rome" and granted its bishop a primacy of honor second only to that of the bishop Rome. This was reaffirmed in 451 at the Council of Chalcedon in canon 28, a source of great annoyance to Leo, bishop of Rome. As well as condemning Arianism, the Council of Constantinople placed an anathema on Apollinaris of Laodicea and his "two sons" theory, labeled thus by Gregory of Nazianzus in a letter to Cledonius against Apolinaris (*Epistle* 101). The council affirmed the presence of a human soul in Jesus Christ, which Apollinaris denied. It also affirmed the divinity of the Holy Spirit, a triumph over the Macedonian heresy for the Cappadocian fathers—Gregory of Nazianzus, Gregory of Nyssa, and his brother Basil of Caesarea, who had consistently promoted this doctrine.

The Niceno-Constantinopolitan Creed, with its emphasis on the Holy Spirit's divinity, was an expansion of the creed ratified at the first ecumenical Council of Nicaea in 325. As patriarch of Constantinople, Gregory of Nazianzus presided over the opening of the council but was soon forced by rival factions and ill health to resign his position. His successor Nectarius, who at the time of his election was unbaptized, was the choice of Emperor Theodosius.

Cyril of Alexandria and Nestorius. The Council of Ephesus (431) saw the triumph of Cyril of Alexandria over his enemy Nestorius, bishop of Constantinople (428–431); the Nestorian party had not even arrived before the council began. The council published its confession of Jesus as one person according to Cyril's phrase "one incarnate nature of God the Word," and it acknowledged Mary as the "God-bearer" (Greek *theotokos*), a term that Nestorius had rejected. The council affirmed the presence of two natures—one human and one divine—in Jesus, which increased tensions with the advocates of one-nature Christology or "monophysitism."

Callixtus and Cyprian. Saint Callixtus of Rome (d. 222) and Saint Cyprian of Carthage (d. 258). Mural, Catacomb of San Callisto, Rome, sixth century. THE BRIDGEMAN ART LIBRARY

Although the Cyrillians seemed to have had the victory, an extreme faction led by the monk Eutyches believed that Cyril had been betrayed at that council. So the Eutychians convened another council at Ephesus (449), with the support of Theodosius II and with Dioscurus, patriarch of Alexandria, presiding. This council deposed the patriarch of Constantinople, Flavian, who died shortly afterward as a result of violence inflicted upon him by the supporters of Dioscurus and Eutyches. Their violence earned the council the title of the "Robber Synod" (Latin *latrocinium*), a term coined by Leo the Great.

Leo the Great. At the follow-up council held in Chalcedon in 451, the assembled bishops condemned Eutyches and his "monophysite" doctrine—namely, the doctrine that after the incarnation the one-person Jesus Christ is marked by a single nature. Leo the Great, bishop of Rome (440–461), was instrumental in the final resolution of the issue expressed in the council's *Definition of Faith*. Although not present, he made his contribution via his *Tome* (Dogmatic Letter), addressed to Bishop Flavian of Constantinople, which included the famous formula of two natures in one person, Christ truly God and truly man (*Epistle* 28.3). The Chalcedonian *Definition of Faith* spoke of the two natures joined in Christ without confusion, without change, without division, and without separation. As Grillmeier remarks, "All future discussion on the will, knowledge and consciousness of Christ belong in the end in that area of christological problems that was marked out by Chalcedon" (p. 553). Supporters of Cyril at Chalcedon proclaimed that Cyril had spoken through Leo, and so they were satisfied. The monophysite churches of Antioch and Alexandria were permanently alienated by this council, however, along with the rest of the Greek-speaking East. Latins and Greeks from this point on began to drift apart on matters of ecclesiology, clerical discipline, and pneumatology (theology of the Holy Spirit), finally resulting in the Great Schism of 1054.

Chalcedon is thus a fitting point at which to end this brief survey of the major developments, both theological and historical, of the first four centuries of the Christian church. The nucleus of activity shifted as the various churches of Rome, Jerusalem, Antioch, Alexandria, and Carthage waxed and waned in importance. Only Constantinople, which had no claim to apostolic origins, can be said to have been on an upward trajectory from its foundation in 331. The authority of bishops of these ecclesiastical centers was often contested by schismatics, ascetics, heretics, and even other orthodox bishops. However, with the conversion of the imperial court to Christianity, the future of the religion was assured. With the influx of funds toward church building programs designed to reflect and enhance the glory of the emperor, the conversion of pagan temples into basilicas for Christian worship, and imperial subsidizing of the priesthood, the appeal of the religion was bound to increase. The emergence of those bishops, monks, and laymen who may properly be called the "fathers of the church" was a key element in promulgating the doctrines and disciplines associated with the new religion, but imperial backing was essential if a faction was to maintain its claim to represent the orthodox position.

[*See also* Augustine; Bible, *subentry* Christian Scripture and Other Writings; Boethius; Christianity; Cicero, *subentry* Philosophy of Cicero; Gnosticism; Jerome; Jesus; Martyrs, Martyrdom, and Martyr Literature; Monasticism; Monotheism; Oratory, Greco-Roman; *and* Origen.]

BIBLIOGRAPHY
Primary Works
Tertullian. *Apologetical Works*. Translated by Rudolph Arbesmann, Sister Emily Joseph Daly, and Edwin A. Quain. Washington D.C.: Fathers of the Church, 1950.
Stevenson, J., trans. *Creeds, Councils, and Controversies: Documents Illustrating the History of the Church AD 337–461*. Rev. ed. with additional documents by W. H. C. Frend. London: SPCK, 1989.
Tanner, Norman P., trans. *Decrees of the Ecumenical Councils*. Vol. 1: *Nicaea I to Lateran V*. London: Sheed and Ward, 1990.

Secondary Works
Casiday, Augustine, and Frederick W. Norris, eds. *The Cambridge History of Christianity*. Vol. 2: *From*

Constantine to c. 600. Cambridge History of Christian Thought 2. Cambridge, U.K., and New York: Cambridge University Press, 2007.

Dunn, Geoffrey D. *Tertullian.* Early Christian Fathers. London and New York: Routledge, 2004.

Esler, Philip F., ed. *The Early Christian World.* 2 vols. London and New York: Routledge, 2000.

Ferguson, Everett, ed. *Encyclopedia of Early Christianity.* 2nd ed. New York and London: Garland, 1998.

Frend, W. H. C. *The Early Church: From the Beginnings to 461.* Rev. ed. London: SCM, 1982.

Grillmeier, Aloys. *Christ in Christian Tradition.* Vol. 1: *From the Apostolic Age to Chalcedon (451).* Translated by John Bowden. Atlanta: John Knox Press, 1975.

Ramsey, Boniface. *Beginning to Read the Fathers.* Rev. ed. London: SCM, 1993.

Rousseau, Philip. *The Early Christian Centuries.* London: Longman, 2002.

Tanner, N. P. *The Councils of the Church: A Short History.* New York: Crossroad, 2001.

Young, Francis, Louis Ayres, and Andrew Louth, eds. *Cambridge History of Early Christian Literature.* Cambridge, U.K., and New York: Cambridge University Press, 2004.

Bronwen Neil

CICERO

(Marcus Tullius Cicero; 106–43 BCE), Roman politician, writer, philosopher, orator, and advocate. [*This entry includes two subentries, on the life and career of Cicero and on Cicero's philosophy.*]

The Life of Cicero

Marcus Tullius Cicero (106–43 BCE) was a Roman politician, writer, and advocate. Cicero's plausible self-description was that he was Rome's greatest orator and a voice for moderation in politics and morals, and this is largely how he has been received by later ages. In his own time, however, his life might just as well be described in terms of his complicated relationship to lethal political violence: successively he was witness to, advocate for, advocate against, and finally himself a victim of such violence. Cicero was also an associate of and is now an important source of information on Julius Caesar, Pompey, and all the other major political figures of the final period of the Roman Republic.

Sources. Cicero's life is better known to us than anyone else's from classical antiquity. In large part this is because of information that he himself left behind. Cicero's public career was principally as an orator, so his nearly sixty surviving published speeches are important primary documents of that career. (Almost as many published speeches are known to be lost, and others were never published in the first place.) There is some modern controversy over how far these texts reflect what was actually said on the original occasions, though clear instances of major rewriting are nearly unknown. It is clearer that Cicero was selective in deciding which speeches were published at all—there seems, for instance, to be a preference for court cases that he won—but his rationale in any particular instance is usually unknown.

The speeches are also an important secondary source for other parts of his life—and of the late Republic as a whole—both because Cicero was a major actor in important events under discussion and because his personality and the oratorical conventions of the day put the orator himself front and center. His philosophical and rhetorical writings play a similar dual role. Especially when Cicero is a character in his own works, they record much incidental information about his life. At the same time, these more scholarly works, which Cicero himself hoped would provide Romans with a basic corpus of ethical and political theory, seem to have substituted for more overt forms of political activity during the periods when such activity became too dangerous.

Finally, more than nine hundred letters from Cicero are extant, dating from 68 to 43; coverage is uneven, especially through the 60s. These were written to a number of correspondents, most notably Cicero's friend Titus Pomponius Atticus (nearly seven hundred pages in one standard edition) and Cicero's brother Quintus (ninety pages), but about eighty other people were the recipient of at least one letter. Most of these letters seem to have been saved archivally and published well after Cicero's death, preserving if not a purely authentic account of his thoughts, at least a version not otherwise preserved for Cicero or for anyone else of the time. Other letters preserve a record not of these intense relationships, but of the mechanics of elite social activity. For instance, a large collection exists of mostly standardized letters of recommendation written by Cicero to connections—mostly in the provinces—on behalf of a variety of lesser figures. Meanwhile at least a few letters seem to have been written with a view to publication—such as his "advice" to his more experienced brother on governing a province—and it is known that Cicero once contemplated publishing a selection (on some unknown basis) of about seventy "genuine" letters. Moreover, the collection of Cicero's letters contains a few letters by third parties providing additional insight into contemporary politics, epistolary practices, and even prose style—for instance, the dispatches of Marcus Caelius Rufus from Rome while Cicero was governor of Cilicia, and copies of letters from Caesar trying to win Cicero to his side in the civil war. Numerous as they are, letters on any given topic may be lacking both because of the collection's haphazard formation and because of the simple fact that Cicero may not have been away from his regular correspondents at the time of any particular event.

Outside Cicero's own writings, a number of other views of the man survive. Plutarch wrote a biography of him, and there is substantial relevant narrative in the histories of Cassius Dio and Appian (note, however, that all three of these sources are substantially later than Cicero's lifetime). Miscellaneous information about Cicero is scattered in many places, but a list of the most notable sources might include Aulus Gellius, Quintilian, Asconius Pedianus (a commentator on some of Cicero's speeches), and Plutarch's other late Republican biographies. All of these sources are themselves at least somewhat dependent on Cicero's writings, and they often tend to accept his interpretation of events.

Early Life and Career. Cicero was born at Arpinum, in southeastern Latium, on 3 January 106 BCE, making him a Roman citizen—as was not yet the case for all Italians. Little specific detail exists about his father and essentially none about his mother. In general, however, his immediate family seems to have been prominent in the life of the municipality and was moreover connected socially to the great Roman general and Arpinum native Gaius Marius and with other and even better-connected members of the metropolitan aristocracy.

Cicero was educated at Rome and later in Greece, and he is known to have had contact with many leading intellectual figures of the day: the politicians and orators Marcus Antonius and Lucius Licinius Crassus, the two cousins of the name Quintus Mucius Scaevola (Quintus Mucius Scaevola Augur and Quintus Mucius Scaevola Pontifex) who were both priests and jurists, the grammarian Lucius Aelius Stilo, and the Greek philosopher Philo. Cicero's education seems to have comprised both formal instruction (reading, writing, and declamation, especially from the Greeks) and the traditional apprenticeship in law, oratory, and politics with the aristocratic figures just named. His military experience seems to have been quite limited for an ambitious young man in his position, consisting of perhaps a year as a junior staff officer in 89 during the Social War.

Politics in the years from just before the war to the end of Sulla's dictatorship in 79 was alternately turbulent and stagnant. The normal mechanisms of the legislative and justice systems seem to have come nearly to a halt. The situation was aggravated for Cicero by the death (including two murders) of several of his patrons during this period. As a result he seems largely to have lain low for most of the period. At the very end of the 80s he is seen pleading for the first time in court—mostly civil-law matters, but also a homicide case (*Pro Roscio Amerino*, 81 or 80). Several of the important figures in the homicide case were loosely connected with Sulla's regime, and Cicero plays up the political implications—and so his courage in facing them—but the reality of the situation is unclear. The published texts of his speeches in the civil-law cases show a mastery of and engagement with technicalities of law that are generally absent from the later criminal cases. This probably reflects the different functions of the respective courts, but it is worth noting that Cicero felt that these drier speeches were still good advertising at the time; he seems to have given them up after the very early 60s. After a few years of this, Cicero took an extended trip to Greece and Asia Minor for advanced studies, including contact with the great polymath Posidonius. He may also have produced his first rhetorical handbook, the work-manlike *De inventione* (*On Invention*), at around this time.

Cicero was not the first Roman orator to publish texts of his speeches—that practice went back at least a century—but the scale of Cicero's publication seems to have been unprecedented. Its purpose may have changed over time. Originally the publication seems to have focused on advertising Cicero's skills to would-be clients or others in need of them. Although this function probably never disappeared entirely, a pedagogical usage eventually developed. Cicero speaks with great pride of the popularity of his speeches among youths. What these youths were supposed to learn is not entirely clear, but it probably included both the technicalities of rhetoric and also more general questions of how a Roman states-man should conduct himself. Finally, late in life Cicero seems to have become more interested in the permanence of written texts; publication as a means of immortality becomes a conscious pur-pose. Written oratory fulfilled all three of these purposes, but other kinds of writing could achieve the second and third, so it is not surprising that Cicero describes his "literary" work as part of a program continuous with his more "political" career.

Cicero also married his first wife, Terentia, in 79, and they had a daughter Tullia in 77. A son, also named Marcus, was subsequently born in 65. Terentia brought both wealth and connections to the Roman nobility to the marriage. Both Cicero and Terentia had strong personalities, but the marriage survived almost to the end of Cicero's life.

Cicero's first political office was the quaestorship that he held in 75. He was elected at the youngest possible age and with the greatest number of votes among the successful candidates, both marks of particular political success and something repeated in each of his successive campaigns. He served as an administrative officer to the governor of Sicily, working particularly with taxation and the Roman grain supply. He later noted that it was politically disadvantageous to serve his term out of the view of the voting public in Rome, and in fact he did not leave Rome on public business again until 51. His aedileship in 69 seems to have been undistin-guished; even on his own account the games he gave as part of his official duties were relatively modest. He could have run for the tribunate for 73 (or later) but chose not to do so. This decision was perhaps motivated by reservations about the popu-list connotations of the office.

Throughout the late 70s and early 60s, Cicero continued to build his reputation as an orator, pri-marily as a defense advocate in the criminal courts. Not incidentally, his defenses of leading *equites* and Italian notables helped develop a base of indebted political supporters. That his defense work was also financially profitable is suggested by his purchase of significant new estates by the early 60s. Later in life he boasted of the large sums that he inherited from his clients, who were technically forbidden from paying fees to an advocate.

Cicero's one more dramatic bid for public atten-tion was the prosecution of Gaius Verres in 70, when Cicero was campaigning to become aedile. Cicero's connection to Sicily, where Verres was extorting money from his provincial subjects, seems to have given him the opportunity to try this celebrity case. He succeeded despite Verres' high position and a powerful defense team that included the orator Quintus Hortensius Hortalus and the consul-to-be Quintus Caecilius Metellus (later Creticus). To ensure maximum publicity, Cicero published not only his application to prosecute— he had to exclude another, potentially collusive prosecutor—and his opening speech, but also five expanded versions of speeches that he could have delivered at later hearings, had Verres not given up in the middle of the trial and gone into exile.

To some extent a prosecution was a conventional move for an ambitious but not wellborn young pol-itician. At the same time a trial for public corruption resonated well with a continuing theme of Cicero's political career: that the ruling elites needed to demonstrate in practice their self-proclaimed moral superiority to justify their ongoing rule. That Cicero is known primarily through these and similar texts tends to draw attention to the more literary aspects of his advocacy, so it is worth noting that the actual trial was a triumph of research and organization at least as much as it was a triumph of eloquence.

High Politics. Cicero's time at the center of Roman politics arguably began during his praetorship in 66. His formal portfolio was charge of the court that tried extortion by provincial governors, but more important was his move into a new oratorical venue. While praetor, Cicero gave his first speech to the whole people, urging passage of the Manilian law giving Pompey great powers to cleanse the eastern Mediterranean of pirates. This was also perhaps the beginning of Cicero's intermittent attempts to attach himself to Pompey's career—and, he seems to have hoped, to make Pompey feel a need for his support. The law seems to have been highly popular, and Cicero presents himself as a moderate populist in having supported it. This has been interpreted as evidence of an early, relatively popular phase of Cicero's career, but is perhaps better understood in generic terms. That is, any Roman politician speaking before the people claimed to be their special friend. Moreover, Cicero seems to have opposed a similar law (for a different command) during the previous year; he was then won over by Pompey's personal popularity and/or his proven merits as a commander.

Cicero had some luck in the undistinguished field of competitors that he faced for the consulship of 63. The most important competitor turned out to be the several-time loser Lucius Sergius Catilina (Catiline), who attempted a coup d'état by the end of the year. Cicero's term in office saw several political incidents that may have involved—and in one case almost certainly did involve—ambitious men testing the waters for major political power grabs. As he entered office Cicero encountered a proposed law for land distribution that, he successfully argued in a series of speeches, involved too much long-term cost and too much centralization of power in the hands of the commissioners in charge. These speeches are important for the insight they give into the practice of popular legislation and the rhetorical differences involved in arguing the same issue before different audiences (senate and people). Later, the trial of one Gaius Rabirius for his part in a political killing back in 100 seems to have been designed (by Julius Caesar among others) to test the limits of vigilante activity led by officeholders in "emergency" situations; Cicero himself argued the pro-lynching position, but the trial ended without a clear resolution.

The greatest conflict arose near the end of Cicero's term as consul. Catiline, having once more been denied office (and even the opportunity to stand), decided that revolution was a better path to power. After some tense political maneuvering, Cicero got Catiline to show his hand and convinced some would-be conspirators to inform on their fellows. Those at Rome were rounded up and, after a debate somewhat foreshadowed by the trial of Rabirius, executed; Caesar was among those arguing against execution. Those in the field were subsequently defeated in battle. As part of the counterplotting, Cicero ensured the assistance of his colleague in office Gaius Antonius Hybrida by ceding to him any claim to the military governorship of Macedonia following their consulship. The lost opportunities for both profit and military glory may have cost Cicero more than he realized. Cicero depicts the suppression of Catiline's conspiracy as an unqualified success, but already at the end of his term, political enemies were making much of the "illegality" of his actions and denouncing his "kingship." Most notably, one of the tribunes prevented him from making the usual end-of-year speech summarizing his accomplishments.

In addition to the major actions just described, Cicero was also involved in some more ordinary business during his consulship. He carried one bill strengthening the law against electoral bribery and another tightening the rules on public junkets. He opposed the passage of a law restoring the civic status of the children of men proscribed under

Sulla's regime. As private counsel he defended present and potential political allies in court. In doing so he did not hesitate to play on his public position: Rabirius' defense has already been mentioned, and near the end of the year he very nearly conceded the guilt of the incoming consul Lucius Licinius Murena on a charge of electoral bribery but argued that continuity of leadership was necessary because of the then ongoing Catilinarian crisis. He had also engaged in courtroom work during his praetorship, albeit with less clear political overtones, and the Roman system apparently saw no general conflict of interest. Indeed, in 62, Cicero's defense of Publius Cornelius Sulla against charges of complicity in Catiline's conspiracy turned largely on his insider knowledge of the conspiracy as its chief opponent. A few years later he went on to publish as a unit the bulk of his known speeches from his consulship year. He also promulgated a poem on his consulship, sent a lengthy dispatch (now lost) to Pompey in the East, and made notes available to selected poets and historians in hopes that they would immortalize his deeds in independent literary form—in both Greek and Latin.

As a former consul, Cicero was henceforth one of the most senior members of the senate, and he hoped to wield political authority from that position for the rest of his life. He seems not to have contemplated a second consulship, which would have been quite unusual, or the censorship, which typically went to someone more senior and better-born and which had been vacant for some time. Still, even his power in the senate required negotiation with other figures, most notably his continuing efforts to join forces with the great (and popular) general Pompey, whom Cicero seems to have regarded as a naturally complementary figure. He continued to praise Pompey publicly and support his legislative interests while the general campaigned in the East. More broadly, Cicero argued for greater harmony between sections of the ruling class, the office-holding senators and the merely wealthy *equites.*

Despite these efforts Cicero was overtaken by other political forces. On the one hand, opposition to Cicero personally—and especially to his execution of the conspirators—coalesced around the figure of Publius Clodius Pulcher, with whom Cicero began a feud by testifying against him in a trial for impiety in 61. On the other hand, Pompey found it more useful to join forces with two other, more radical political figures: the idiosyncratic genius Julius Caesar and Pompey's earlier colleague as consul, Marcus Licinius Crassus—making the so-called First Triumvirate of 60. Cicero was asked to join this combination, perhaps in a junior capacity, but he refused. When Caesar was elected consul for 59 and began to push through a substantial legislative program (by aggressive means), the principal opposition came from figures, such as Cato the Younger, to whom Cicero was more personally sympathetic. Still, Cicero's ties to Pompey, his personal caution, and his genuine belief in the dangers of excessive political strife caused him to try to lie low at this time.

This strategy of avoidance failed when, under complex circumstances, Clodius was elected one of the tribunes for 58. Among many other legislative actions, Clodius engineered both the exile of his enemy Cicero, mainly on the grounds of having executed citizens (Catiline's conspirators) without trial, and also the confiscation of his property. Cicero had been offered but refused opportunities to go abroad on public business, which would have made him immune to prosecution, at least for the duration. He spent most his exile in Macedonia, and his mental anguish is evident in many surviving letters to friends and family back home. Fortunately, normal political flux soon broke up the configuration of forces that had driven him out: Clodius' term ended, and more sympathetic people gained other major offices; Pompey and Clodius quarreled, driving Pompey to more active support of Cicero; and Cicero's allies had time to use a different and more favorable legislative mechanism than that which had brought about his exile.

Cicero's return in 57 was marked by triumphant displays of his supporters, and his property was largely restored, though the details of this were tied up in a series of juridical-religious proceedings for a couple of years. In particular Cicero had to fight against Clodius' claim to have consecrated the site of Cicero's house on the Palatine to the goddess Liberty, and thus to have put it beyond human recovery. Though the house itself was important, Cicero also took the opportunity to attack the legality of the exile itself.

From this point on, Cicero often pointed to the honorific circumstances of his recall as proof of his standing, while ignoring the continuing disgrace of the underlying exile, which clearly did lasting damage to that standing. He reiterated versions of the narrative in speeches of thanksgiving for his return, in speeches on the matter of the house, in a series of criminal defenses in which his own biography was of disputed relevance, and even in his personal letters. Moreover, Cicero was compelled to be more cooperative with his newfound patrons in the Triumvirate. Not only did he continue to support Pompey's legislative agenda, but he pressed for power and honors for Caesar and defended the triumvirs' allies, including personal enemies of his own, in court.

Occasionally Cicero could indulge his own political hatreds, as in 55 in the long invective against Lucius Calpurnius Piso—who, as consul in 58, had colluded in his exile—but this seems to have had little practical effect. (Other than Verres', only one other actual prosecution undertaken by Cicero is known.) He also mounted relatively normal defenses of friends and allies—for instance, defense of Marcus Caelius Rufus in 56 and of Gnaeus Plancius in 54—of a type not very different from defenses of a decade earlier. At least partially in return for his cooperation with the triumvirs, he was chosen to one of Rome's coveted lifetime priesthoods, the augurate, in 53.

As the 50s went on, Cicero tended to withdraw from an increasingly chaotic and violent political scene. One notable exception was his defense in 52 of the conservative politician and gangster Titus Annius Milo on trial for the murder of his populist opposite number Clodius. Cicero's speech denying Milo's involvement failed to secure an acquittal, though the case may have been lost before it even began; the version published later put more emphasis on justification of the act.

The middle and end of the decade mark Cicero's first major period of productivity as a rhetorical and philosophical writer. The works of this period are mostly expansive, if not systematic, treatments of broad topics: *De oratore* (*On the Orator*), *De re publica* (*On the Republic*), *De legibus* (*On the Laws*; apparently not published at the time). *De re publica* includes a history of Rome's early political evolution to support Cicero's argument that the actual Roman Republic was a more plausible ideal state than were more theoretical candidates like Plato's. *De legibus* takes a similar approach, though it privileges a distinctly archaizing version of the Roman state. *De re publica* also includes a section, much excerpted in later ages, in which Scipio Aemilianus is made to recount a dream in which his ancestors show him the natural order of the universe as a guarantee of the heavenly reward awaiting committed and unselfish statesmen.

The very end of the decade also brought Cicero's brief turn in the kind of military and foreign policy position normally much sought after by Roman politicians. For largely technical legal reasons he was made governor of Cilicia in southeastern Asia Minor from mid-51 to mid-50. In this position he faced the normal variety of problems: balancing the interests of provincial subjects, individual Roman businessmen (especially government contractors), and the state itself; military threats both real (the neighboring Parthian Empire) and largely imaginary (local mountain tribes); and the politics of a Roman world on the verge of civil war.

The Last Years. Cicero took his time returning to Rome, not arriving until early January 49, days before the final break between Caesar and senatorial forces that precipitated the civil war. Cicero had hoped to be awarded a triumph for his exploits in Cilicia, but this failed because of a combination of their triviality and the growing crisis back home. He also hoped to broker a compromise between Caesar and his principal opponents, such as Cato, Lentulus Spinther, and Metellus Scipio. His sympathies were more with the opponents, but he objected both to their excessive rigor and to the practical consequences of an all-out struggle, however good the cause in theory. In fact, even when Pompey first came out fully against Caesar and withdrew, along with much of the senate, first from Rome and then in March from Italy itself to gather his forces, Cicero initially hesitated to go, and he never took up a military command on the senatorial side. His letters suggest that his heart was never really in the struggle, and after the decisive defeat of Pompey in mid-48, he sued for Caesar's clemency.

The years of Caesar's dictatorship marked the second period of semiretirement in Cicero's career. He did argue a few cases—and publish the resulting speeches—notably before Caesar acting as sole judge. These speeches contain much praise of the dictator, but it is hard to tell how much of this is necessary pretense, how much motivational, and how much simply sarcastic. But most of his literary efforts returned to rhetorical and philosophical writing. These were mostly shorter and more focused monographs than the works of the earlier period and include *Brutus* (on the history of oratory), *Topica* (as a subset of rhetorical "invention"), *De amicitia* (*On Friendship*), and *De divinatione* (*On Divination*), though there was still room for some more ambitious projects, such as *De natura deorum* (*On the Nature of the Gods*) and *De officiis* (*On Duties*). The *Tusculanae quaestiones* (*Tusculan Disputations*) weave declamatory practice with Stoic teachings to reinforce men against the fear of death and pain. Similarly, *De officiis* brings Stoic thought together with more traditional fatherly instruction to ground social roles and obligations in universal ethical principles.

Cicero was not party to the plot to assassinate Caesar, though several of the ringleaders were friends and allies of his, and he was quick to celebrate the deed after the fact. As with the breach between Caesar and the senate, Cicero initially tried to patch things up between Caesar's surviving lieutenant Mark Antony, who remained the legal head of state, and the faction around the assassins or "liberators." This soon proved impossible after harsh personal attacks between Cicero and Antony.

Cicero's fourteen speeches against Antony and on other, related topics of the day were published collectively as the *Philippicae* and make up his final oratorical output. Cicero's faction quickly lost ground, not least because Caesar's nephew and heir Gaius Octavius, later the emperor Augustus, became a powerful but unaccounted-for force, eventually in alliance with Antony. Antony and Octavian, along with one Marcus Aemilius Lepidus, were able to seize power and formally outlaw their enemies, including Cicero. He tried to escape Italy but failed and was tracked down and killed by Antony's troops near Caieta on 7 December 43. According to legend, his enemies removed his head and hand—representing his spoken and written attacks on Antony—and displayed them on the speaker's platform at Rome.

Cicero's last years had been marked by considerable turmoil in his personal life. After a long and often turbulent marriage, he divorced Terentia in 46. Then in quick succession he married and divorced a teenager named Publilia. His daughter Tullia died in childbirth in 45, and Cicero's letters show him to have been overwhelmed by grief. Though he went on to success during the early years of the Empire, the younger Marcus never showed much promise during Cicero's lifetime. Cicero had somewhat more luck with other young political figures—Caelius, Marcus Junius Brutus, his son-in-law Dolabella—but none was ever a special protégé of his, nor did any of them have unproblematic careers themselves.

Political Means. Cicero was a "new man," the first in his family to reach office at Rome. Well-connected municipal aristocrats like Cicero took such a step up every year but rarely went further, and it was extremely rare for one to reach the highest office—Cicero is the first new man known to have won the consulship at the minimum legal age. His background meant that he lacked several of the advantages that often made for success in Roman politics. He neither had striking wealth nor exercised hereditary patronage over large groups, nor was his name familiar to voters from generations of experience. Nor did he ever acquire the kind of military reputation that might in principle have been available to a man with more talent than connections (like his kinsman and fellow Arpinate, Marius). In fact, the extent to which Cicero's career almost entirely avoided the military in favor of more political activity shows a kind of specialization that was at least unconventional and would probably have been impossible a generation or two earlier. And even his small-town origins were a problem: political opponents could half-jokingly refer to him as a "foreigner" at Rome.

The most obvious counterweight to these disadvantages was Cicero's oratorical ability. In a society in which public speaking was the only real mass medium, as well as the medium of most state business, Cicero was regarded as the leading orator of the day, if not of all time, both in his lifetime and afterward. A few ancient comments, including his own, suggest that if Cicero's oratorical style had a weakness, it was that he often worked near the edge of excess. Still, he seems to have cultivated flexibility and suitability to whatever each context demanded. Both the corpus as a whole and individual speeches show considerable variety. Additionally, both in formal speaking and in conversation Cicero was noted for an exceptionally quick and sharp wit—and again, if he had a weakness here, it was perhaps in self-indulgence rather than in lack of talent.

Somewhat less obvious than these talents were the connections that from an early age Cicero had with more socially prominent figures. The men he apprenticed under in the late 90s and early 80s included some of the most distinguished political figures, and he must have benefited both from their expert instruction and from mere association with them. Cicero's Greek instructors lacked this value as patrons, but they were at least equally distinguished as technical experts. The importance of such contacts is perhaps illustrated by the rise of Cicero's rather less talented younger brother Quintus to the second-highest magistracy, though both Quintus and Marcus' eponymous son, who eventually reached the consulship himself, must have benefited from their connection to the self-ennobled Cicero. The rather limited basis of Cicero's political success may have made him particularly vulnerable—both practically and psychologically—to attacks on what he regarded as his great accomplishment: the suppression of the Catilinarian conspiracy.

Oratory was a conventional tool of Roman politics. Even the intellectual apparatus that surrounded it—"rhetoric" in the narrow sense, and typically conceived of as a Greek product—was an established, if more controversial, instrument of social contest. Cicero, however, seems to have increased the stakes in the game of deploying Greek cultural capital for social gain at Rome. It is easy to oversimplify the politics of philhellenism (and antihellenism), but clearly Cicero was more willing than most to display an interest in and mastery of Greek culture in a relatively wide variety of contexts. Moreover, he made theoretical arguments to convince his fellow citizens of the value of this learning (in relatively traditional, Roman terms), and his philosophical and rhetorical writings made Greek thought all the more readily accessible to them.

These arguments were largely confined to Cicero's more literary works themselves, but his defense of the poet Aulus Licinius Archias—on, in modern terms, immigration charges—centered on an extended discussion of the value of the literary even for the practically minded. Of course this argument was hardly disinterested; Cicero was encouraging his fellow aristocrats to be more committed to a game that he was extremely good at. His treatment of Roman law was similar to that of Greek cultural products. He had and boasted of a knowledge of the civil law deeper than that of many of his fellows who also operated as public speakers. At the same time, he argued against a contemporary trend that was making the law an area of specialist knowledge. Instead he kept it in the realm of ordinary aristocratic competence, where it could be controlled and be an instrument of social and political struggle—and again an instrument that tended to operate to his own advantage.

Even a better-connected Roman politician of the period would have depended heavily on the construction of political alliances, even if, as is now generally agreed, politics was not merely a matter of such alliances, much less their perpetuation over generations. Thus Cicero spent considerable effort trying to convince Pompey that their interests were generally shared or, conversely, trying to isolate Pompey and Caesar from each other, or demonize certain opponents (Clodius, Gabinius) before any audience that would listen. Cicero was also very solicitous of the support of figures who are less well known today, such as Appius Claudius Pulcher, the noble whom Cicero succeeded as governor of Cilicia and who was, as Cicero's letters show, always in danger of being offended. The existence of the letters also gives us an unusual window into Cicero's less (overtly) political friendships. These might be with the older orator Hortensius on the one hand, or with the younger Brutus (the eventual assassin of Caesar), whom Cicero would have liked to think of as a protégé. There were also Cicero's boyhood friend and eventually in-law Titus Pomponius Atticus, the studiously apolitical knight, and Tiro, Cicero's slave (later freedman) secretary and literary assistant.

Political Ends. Although it may or may not be psychologically accurate, one can organize much of Cicero's political program as a set of responses to his own biographical trajectory. Having moved from the periphery to the center of the ruling class, he showed something of a convert's zeal for the traditional order, and particularly for the role of a narrow oligarchy in ruling the society as a whole. On the other hand, also like a convert, he was perhaps more deeply committed to making real the public justifications of elite privilege, which might have been embraced more cynically by others. The rulers were responsible, however paternalistically, for the best interests of the community as a whole. The compromise resulting between these potentially competing pulls tended to take a form suggested by the notion of "proportional equality" in the structure of the Roman government, in which the votes of the wealthy counted for more than the votes of the poor did.

For Cicero, inequality was the natural order of things, but few people—at least, few male citizens—had no value at all. At least in principle Cicero thought that the government should take into account the needs of the poor, and he even

Cicero versus Catiline. Cicero accusing Catiline in the senate. Painting by Cesare Maccari (1840–1919), Palazzo Madama, Rome, the seat of the Italian Senate. ALINARI/ART RESOURCE, NY

granted that noncitizen subjects had legitimate claims on their Roman masters. In particular court cases Cicero showed no compunction about exploiting ethnic stereotypes against people on the other side, but such prejudices seem not to have been central to his own thinking. Similarly, he would casually exploit Roman misogyny, but he did not make much effort to incite or expand it.

Moderns reading Cicero defending values such as "liberty" or the "republic" need to keep this context in mind. As deep and even principled as his opposition to rule by autocrats may have been—even, perhaps especially, in the case of popular figures that he might call "demagogues"—his ideal was to replace them with a few hundred oligarchs. If this government might be constrained by the substantive rights of its citizens, it would be by security of private property rather than, say, by freedom of conscience.

This philosophy presupposed the existence of a common, public interest, which was undercut by too much public disagreement, especially among members of the elite. Moreover Cicero had grown up with the Social War in his late teens and the subsequent civil wars, including the bloody Sullan proscriptions. These factors led to an avoidance of conflict—and especially armed conflict—that some contemporaries saw as cowardice but that could also be described as pragmatism. So, for instance, Cicero saw it as a virtue of his suppression of the Catilinarian conspiracy that he had won without recourse to troops (at least within the city); others thought this either a sign that the danger had not been so severe in the first place or that Cicero had let his colleague do the heavy lifting.

Even short of the potentially violent clashes like this or the eventual civil wars involving Caesar and Antony, Cicero often took compromise as a value in itself, even in matters where his sympathies were clearly with one side or the other. This might be a promotion of the "concord of the orders," that recognition of shared interests among the political and nonpolitical fractions of what modern analysis would describe as a single socioeconomic ruling class. It might more specifically mean suppressing conflict within the political fraction itself. The chief underlying problem seems to have been the highly competitive nature of Roman public life. The most obvious motivations for aristocratic behavior— glory, *dignitas*, wealth—were broadly individualistic and centrifugal. Much of Cicero's theoretical political writing is designed to emphasize the collective and centripetal elements already inherent in traditional value systems. That is, superficial political success was not genuine unless it contributed to— or was at least compatible with—the common good. Much of Cicero's political effort can be seen as attempting to put the same ideas into practice.

[*See also* Catiline; Cilicia; Clodia; Clodius; Letters, Roman; Literary Criticism, Ancient; Oratory, Roman; Rhetoric, Greek; Rhetoric, Roman; *and* Rome, *subentry* Early Rome and the Republic.]

BIBLIOGRAPHY

Works of Cicero

Cicero's Letters to Atticus. 7 vols. Edited by D. R. Shackleton Bailey. Cambridge, U.K.: Cambridge University Press, 1965–1970.

Epistulae ad familiares. Edited by D. R. Shackleton Bailey. Cambridge, U.K.: Cambridge University Press, 1977. Includes a Latin text and a commentary in English.

Epistulae ad Quintum fratrem et M. Brutum. Edited by D. R. Shackleton Bailey. Cambridge, U.K.: Cambridge University Press, 1980. Includes a Latin text and a commentary in English.

Cato Maior de senectute. Edited by J. G. F. Powell. Cambridge, U.K.: Cambridge University Press, 1988. Includes a Latin text and a commentary in English.

De re publica: Selections. Edited by James E. G. Zetzel. Cambridge U.K.: Cambridge University Press, 1995. Includes a Latin text and a commentary in English.

Pro P. Sulla oratio. Edited by D. H. Berry. Cambridge, U.K.: Cambridge University Press, 1996. Includes a Latin text and a commentary in English.

Cicero on the Ideal Orator (De oratore). Translated by James M. May and Jakob Wisse. New York: Oxford University Press, 2001.

Pro Rabirio Postumo. Translated with an introduction and commentary by Mary Siani-Davies. Oxford: Clarendon Press; New York: Oxford University Press, 2001.

De natura deorum, Liber 1. Edited by Andrew R. Dyck. Cambridge, U.K.: Cambridge University Press, 2003. Includes a Latin text and a commentary in English.

Philippics I–II. Edited by John T. Ramsey. Cambridge, U.K.: Cambridge University Press, 2003. Includes a Latin text and a commentary in English.

On Divination, Book 1. Translated with an introduction and commentary by David Wardle. Oxford: Clarendon Press; New York: Oxford University Press, 2006.

Speech on behalf of Publius Sestius. Translated with an introduction and commentary by Robert A. Kaster. Oxford: Clarendon Press; New York: Oxford University Press, 2006.

Secondary Works

Alexander, Michael C. *The Case for the Prosecution in the Ciceronian Era.* Ann Arbor: University of Michigan Press, 2002.

Barnes, Jonathan, and Miriam Griffin, eds. *Philosophia togata. II: Plato and Aristotle at Rome.* Oxford: Clarendon Press, 1997.

Butler, Shane. *The Hand of Cicero.* London: Routledge, 2002.

Classen, Carl Joachim. *Recht, Rhetorik, Politik: Untersuchungen zu Ciceros rhetorischer Strategie.* Darmstadt, Germany: Wissenschaftliche Buchgesellschaft, 1985.

Connolly, Joy. *The State of Speech: Rhetoric and Political Thought in Ancient Rome.* Princeton, N.J.: Princeton University Press, 2007.

Craig, Christopher P. *Form as Argument in Cicero's Speeches: A Study of Dilemma.* Atlanta: Scholars Press, 1988.

Crawford, Jane W. *M. Tullius Cicero: The Lost and Unpublished Orations.* Göttingen, Germany: Vandenhoeck & Ruprecht, 1984.

Dyck, Andrew R. *A Commentary on Cicero, "De legibus."* Ann Arbor: University of Michigan Press, 2004.

Dyck, Andrew R. *A Commentary on Cicero, "De officiis."* Ann Arbor: University of Michigan Press, 1996.

Everitt, Anthony. *Cicero: The Life and Times of Rome's Greatest Politician.* New York: Random House, 2001.

Fantham, Elaine. *The Roman World of Cicero's "De oratore."* Oxford: Oxford University Press, 2004.

Griffin, Miriam, and Jonathan Barnes, eds. *Philosophia togata: Essays on Philosophy and Roman Society.* Oxford: Clarendon Press, 1989.

Grimal, Pierre. *Cicéron.* Paris: Fayard, 1986.

Habicht, Christian. *Cicero the Politician.* Baltimore: Johns Hopkins University Press, 1990.

Hutchinson, G. O. *Cicero's Correspondence: A Literary Study.* Oxford: Clarendon Press, 1998.

Laurand, Louis. *Études sur le style des discours de Cicéron.* 2 vols. Paris: Société d'Édition "Les Belles Lettres," 1926–1927.

Leeman, Anton D., Harm Pinkster, et al. *M. Tullius Cicero, "De oratore libri III."* 5 vols. Heidelberg, Germany: Winter, 1981–2008. A commentary; volume 5 is in English, the rest are in German.

Lintott, Andrew. *Cicero as Evidence: A Historian's Companion.* Oxford: Oxford University Press, 2008.

May, James M., ed. *Brill's Companion to Cicero: Oratory and Rhetoric.* Leiden, The Netherlands: Brill, 2002. Includes an excellent and extensive review of Cicero the orator and rhetorician by Christopher Craig.

Mitchell, Thomas N. *Cicero, the Ascending Years.* New Haven, Conn.: Yale University Press, 1979.

Mitchell, Thomas N. *Cicero, the Senior Statesman.* New Haven, Conn.: Yale University Press, 1991.

Narducci, Emanuele. *Cicerone e l'eloquenza romana: Retorica e progetto culturale.* Rome: Laterza, 1997.

Narducci, Emanuele. *Modelli etici e società: Un'idea di Cicerone.* Pisa, Italy: Giardini, 1989.

Powell, Jonathan, ed. *Cicero the Philosopher: Twelve Papers.* Oxford: Clarendon Press, 1995.

Powell, Jonathan, and Jeremy Paterson, eds. *Cicero the Advocate.* Oxford: Oxford University Press, 2004.

Rawson, Elizabeth. *Cicero: A Portrait.* London: Allen Lane, 1975.

Riggsby, Andrew. *Crime and Community in Ciceronian Rome.* Austin: University of Texas Press, 1999.

Shackleton Bailey, David R. *Cicero.* London: Duckworth, 1971.

Steel, Catherine. *Cicero, Rhetoric, and Empire.* Oxford: Oxford University Press, 2001.

Steel, Catherine. *Reading Cicero.* London: Duckworth, 2005.

Stockton, David L. *Cicero: A Political Biography.* Oxford: Oxford University Press, 1971.

Stroh, Wilfried. *Taxis und Taktik: Die advokat. Dispositionskunst in Ciceros Gerichtsreden.* Stuttgart, Germany: Teubner, 1975.

Vasaly, Ann. *Representations: Images of the World in Ciceronian Oratory.* Berkeley: University of California Press, 1993.

Wood, Neal. *Cicero's Social and Political Thought.* Berkeley: University of California Press, 1988.

Andrew M. Riggsby

Philosophy of Cicero

Cicero, born into a world in which philosophy was an almost exclusively Greek activity, did more than any other Roman writer to create a distinctly Roman philosophical tradition.

Early Philosophical Training and Writing. When they were still young, Cicero's father brought him and his younger brother Quintus to Rome to be educated. At Rome, Cicero received training in law, oratory, and philosophy. He studied oratory with the statesmen Lucius Licinius Crassus and Marcus Antonius. From the beginning Cicero combined training in oratory and philosophy. He studied with the Stoics Lucius Aelius Stilo and Diodotus, the Epicurean Phaedrus, and Philo of Larissa, the head of the Academy who came to Rome from Athens in 88. Cicero thus had early exposure to the three major Hellenistic schools of philosophy: Stoic, Epicurean, and Academic.

Epicureanism held an initial attraction for Cicero. He later wrote (*Epistulae ad familiares* 13.1.2) that in his youth he greatly respected Phaedrus the Epicurean, and that his exposure to Philo of Larissa attracted him to the New Academy. Although Cicero often argued against Epicureanism in his later philosophical works, it is clear that his knowledge of Epicureanism was deep. He also had read (*Epistulae ad Quintum fratrem* 2.10) Lucretius' Epicurean poem *De rerum natura* (*On the Nature of Things*), and according to a later tradition he edited the poem for publication. Cicero's main objections to Epicureanism were its choice of pleasure as the highest or even sole good and its recommendation that one not take part in politics.

Cicero's early training in Stoicism was even more thorough. He studied dialectic with Diodotus, a Stoic philosopher who lived in his household for more than twenty-five years. Cicero found dialectic important for his rhetorical training, and he used it to supplement his rhetorical exercises in Greek and Latin. Cicero was critical of aspects of Stoicism, but some Stoic positions remained attractive to him throughout his life, especially the views that virtue is the highest or even sole good and that to take part in politics is a duty.

During this early period the greatest influence on Cicero's philosophical development was Philo of Larissa. Philo was head of the Academy from 110, and he introduced Cicero to the particular brand of Academic skepticism that Cicero followed throughout his life. Adapting the views of earlier Academic skeptics including Arcesilaus and Carneades, Philo taught that although knowledge is unattainable, one should, after studying the views of the various dogmatic schools on particular issues, accept the view that seems most plausible or persuasive. Cicero expresses his adherence to Philo and the New Academy repeatedly in his works. Some scholars have argued that Cicero abandoned Philo's doctrines after his encounter with Antiochus of Ascalon in 79, but most scholars think that Cicero remained a follower of Philo and the New Academy throughout his life.

Cicero's allegiance to Philo had a number of important effects. First, it helped determine Cicero's relationship to the other philosophical schools of his day. As an adherent of the New Academy, Cicero was encouraged to investigate the doctrines of the other schools in order to determine which positions seemed the most probable. Second, Philo's approach to philosophy helped shape the form of Cicero's philosophical works, especially those published after 46. In many of his philosophical works Cicero presents the various positions of the dogmatic schools on a particular topic, followed by the arguments against these positions, thus allowing the reader, in good Academic fashion, to determine which one seems the most persuasive. Third, the Academic approach was quite compatible with Cicero's experience as an orator. As a student of rhetoric and advocate in the courts, Cicero had to be able to critique and speak on either side of an issue. Philo's philosophical method was ideally adapted to Cicero's temperament and calling.

It was during these years from 91 to 83 that Cicero wrote his earliest rhetorical treatise, *De inventione* (*On Invention*). The work focuses on invention, or "the discovery of things that are true or similar to the truth which make a case plausible" (1.9), and is a straightforward treatment of the topic. The work shows that at an early age Cicero was advocating that rhetoric and philosophy be combined for the good of society (1.1–5). *On Invention* also enunciates two positions that Cicero maintained throughout his life: the importance of drawing critically from many writers rather than relying on a single source (2.1–9) and the need to avoid giving rash assent to any particular doctrine (2.10).

After a successful but intense debut as an orator in 81–80, Cicero traveled to the East for further studies from 79 to 77. He spent the first six months in Athens, where he studied Epicurean philosophy with Phaedrus and Zeno of Sidon. The most important teacher that Cicero had in Athens, though, was the Academic philosopher Antiochus of Ascalon. Antiochus had broken with his teacher Philo, claiming that the skeptical turn the Academy had taken had been an aberration. Antiochus moved the Academy back to dogmatism, claiming that there was close affinity among the Platonic, Peripatetic, and Stoic schools. He adopted Stoic epistemology and taught that the discrepancies among the Academics, Peripatetics, and Stoics were differences more in terminology than in substance. Cicero was impressed by Antiochus' teaching and included arguments drawn from Antiochus in a number of his later philosophical works. During the rest of his travels in 79–77, Cicero studied with the leading Greek rhetoricians of the day. While at Rhodes he also studied with the Stoic philosopher and polymath Posidonius.

When Cicero returned to Rome in 77, he reentered the world of Roman politics, serving as quaestor in 75, praetor in 66, and consul in 63. His rise to power was followed by rapid reversal. He was forced into exile in Greece in March 58, returning to Rome in September 57. He never returned to the political prominence he had achieved as consul. During the period from 77 to 55, Cicero published no rhetorical or philosophical works, but he later noted that "when I least appeared to be doing so, I was engaged in philosophy, as my speeches show, which are full of the maxims of the philosophers" (*On the Nature of the Gods* 1.6). Several of Cicero's speeches contain passages that mention philosophical schools and doctrines, including *Pro Murena* (60–66) in 63, *Pro Caelio* (40–42) in 56, and *In Pisonem* in 55. Also during this period Cicero acquired a number of villas in the Italian countryside: in their libraries, gardens, and shaded porticoes, temporarily freed from the pressures of politics in the capital, Cicero read and discussed philosophy with his friends.

Philosophical and Rhetorical Writings, 50s BCE. During a period of enforced political inactivity in the mid-50s BCE, Cicero tried to remain in the public eye and be of service to the state by writing rhetorical and philosophical works. The three major works that resulted were the dialogues *De oratore* (*On the Orator*), *De re publica* (*On the Republic*), and *De legibus* (*On the Laws*).

Cicero finished *On the Orator* by the end of 55. One of Cicero's greatest literary and philosophical accomplishments, *On the Orator* uses Greek philosophical models and rhetorical theory to present a new cultural ideal of the Roman statesman and orator thoroughly conversant with philosophy. The work, addressed to his brother Quintus and cast as a historical-fictional dialogue between Lucius Licinius Crassus and Marcus Antonius in 91, treats the nature of oratory and the ideal orator. The earliest surviving dialogue in Latin literature, the work includes elements drawn from the dialogues of Plato and Aristotle. In book 1, Crassus argues for an expanded notion of oratory, saying that the ideal orator needs to receive both rhetorical training and an extensive philosophical education. Marcus Antonius challenges this view, maintaining that oratory rests on natural aptitude and oratorical practice. In book 2, Antonius lays out three of the five parts of oratory: invention, arrangement, and memory. Crassus is the main speaker in book 3, addressing the last two parts of oratory, style and delivery. In the course of book 3 Crassus reiterates the need for orators to acquire philosophical knowledge.

Cicero followed *On the Orator* with another of his major works, the *Republic*, which he wrote in 54–51. As with *On the Orator*, Cicero addressed the *Republic* to his brother Quintus and cast it in the form of a historical dialogue among leading Romans, this time set in 129. In his *Republic*, modeled partially on Plato's *Republic*, Cicero discusses the best form of government, the Roman state, justice, and the ideal ruler. The work, which only partially survives, consisted of six books. In book 1, Scipio Aemilianus

(Scipio the Younger) discusses the nature of the state (*res publica*) and different forms of government, and he argues that the best government is a mixed constitution like Rome's. In book 2, Scipio traces the development of the Roman state from monarchy to republic. Book 3, poorly preserved, treats the nature of justice, with Lucius Furius Philus speaking against justice as a principle that governments should pursue, and Gaius Laelius Sapiens defending it. Book 4, only a few fragments of which survive, discusses social classes and education, and book 5, also fragmentary, treats the qualities of the ideal ruler (*rector*) of the state. Book 6 discusses the actions of the ideal ruler in periods of crisis and ends with the famous *Somnium Scipionis* (*Dream of Scipio*). This passage was preserved as a separate work thanks to Macrobius' fifth-century commentary on it. One of the most famous passages in Cicero and modeled on the so-called Myth of Er that ends Plato's *Republic*, the *Dream of Scipio* is Scipio's account of a dream that he had about the nature of the universe, the insignificance of the earth and the human fame, and the nature of the soul and the afterlife.

The last philosophical work of this period is the *Laws*, which Cicero began shortly after the *Republic* but never published. It is not mentioned in the passage in *On Divination* 2.3 where Cicero lists his philosophical works. Books 1–3 of the *Laws* survive, and there are references in later authors to some additional books. Cicero set the dialogue in the late 50s BCE near Arpinum, his hometown. The influence of Plato's dialogues, especially the *Phaedrus* and the *Laws*, is apparent. The interlocutors are Cicero himself, his brother Quintus, and Cicero's friend Atticus. Book 1 discusses the concepts of justice and law. Cicero sets out the Stoic view that the universe is rational, that human beings participate in this rationality, and that natural law exists. Book 2 discusses laws governing religious practices, and book 3 treats laws governing magistrates, the senate, and assemblies.

Rhetorical Interlude, 46 BCE. After Cicero returned to Rome in 50 BCE following his successful governorship of Cilicia, political events prevented him from devoting time to philosophical writing. Civil war erupted in 49, and Cicero joined Pompey's side against Caesar. After Pompey's defeat, Cicero withdrew from the conflict and waited for Caesar's pardon. By 46, Cicero was again giving speeches, but Roman politics were completely dominated by Caesar. That year Cicero published three rhetorical works: the *Brutus*, *Paradoxa Stoicorum* (*Stoic Paradoxes*), and the *Orator ad M. Brutum*.

Cicero dedicated the *Brutus* to Marcus Junius Brutus, soon to be one of the assassins of Julius Caesar. A dialogue with Cicero, Atticus, and Brutus as participants, *Brutus* presents a history of Greek and Roman orators and is an important source for our knowledge of ancient oratory. Its final section (304–324) is autobiographical, describing Cicero's early education, rhetorical and philosophic training, and development as an orator. In *Brutus* (283–291) Cicero discusses a recent controversy between adherents of two styles of oratory, the simple "Attic" style that looked back to the Athenian orator Lysias and the more ornate "Asianic" style identified with orators of the Greek East. Cicero objects to this distinction, arguing that Demosthenes, the best Attic orator, controlled a full range of styles. Cicero concludes the work with the picture of the ideal orator and a lament that given the current condition of the state, Brutus will not have the opportunity to exercise effectively the oratory that he so carefully cultivated.

The *Stoic Paradoxes*, written in the same year, is an experiment in presenting philosophy in a more popular form. Dedicated to Brutus and written in honor of Brutus' uncle Cato the Younger, the work has a simple structure. After the dedication, six brief sections follow in which Cicero imagines that he is arguing in the Forum for six of the Stoic paradoxes: (1) moral worth is the only good; (2) virtue is sufficient for happiness; (3) all bad actions are equal, and all right actions are equal; (4) every fool is mad, only the wise man is a citizen, all fools are exiles; (5) only the wise man is free, every fool is a slave; and (6) only the wise man is rich. The work shows Cicero experimenting with how best to present technical Stoic arguments in his writings.

The *Orator* was also addressed to Brutus and discusses the best type of oratory and the ideal orator. In the introduction Cicero discusses Plato's theory of the forms, and he credits the study of Academic philosophy for his own oratorical abilities. The *Orator* is more technical than *On the Orator* is, and it includes a long section on prose rhythm and meter in speeches. It also revisits the theme, present in the *Brutus*, of the best oratorical style. Cicero argues that the best orator is one who takes Demosthenes as a Greek model and who has command of all three styles: the plain, middle, and grand.

One other work on oratory that may belong to 46—although some date it to the years 54–52—is the *Partitiones oratoriae* (*Divisions of Oratory*). Cast in the form of a dialogue between Cicero and his young son Marcus, it covers three main topics: the speaker, the speech, and the question that the speaker is addressing.

Philosophical Works, 45–44 BCE. The years 46–45 were difficult for Cicero: besides his political troubles he suffered a number of personal setbacks. He and his wife Terentia divorced in late 47 or early 46. He married a younger woman, Publilia, but the marriage soon failed. In mid-February 45, a month after giving birth, his beloved daughter Tullia died at his villa at Tusculum. The death of Tullia left Cicero completely distraught. He wrote later that the only thing that brought him relief was reading and writing, and during this period he wrote his final string of philosophical works.

Cicero finished his *Consolatio* (*Consolation*) in the months after Tullia's death. In his attempt to find solace after her death, he writes, he read every work of consolation that he could find, but to no avail. To lessen his sorrow, he took the unusual step of writing a consolation to himself. The few fragments that remain show that it was an unusual work. Normally a consolation involves two individuals: the consoler and the consoled. In the *Consolation*, Cicero takes both parts, speaking to himself in the first person. In it he gives the views of the various philosophical schools on diminishing grief, and he consoles himself on his loss of Tullia.

Cicero produced his *Hortensius* during the same period. Although it exists now only in fragments, it was one of Cicero's most famous works in antiquity. Saint Augustine remarks in the *Confessions* (3.4) that it was reading the *Hortensius*, Cicero's "exhortation to philosophy," that turned him to philosophy and God. Modeled in part on Aristotle's lost *Protrepticus*, the *Hortensius* is set as dialogue, with some of the interlocutors (including the orator Hortensius) arguing against philosophy and with Cicero, refuting their objections, arguing on philosophy's behalf.

The *Academica* (*Academics*), written soon afterward, treats the topic of epistemology (or theory of knowledge) and is often viewed as Cicero's most philosophically proficient work. Cicero originally composed the *Academics* as a dialogue in two books, named the *Catulus* and the *Lucullus* after the chief interlocutors of each book. He grew dissatisfied with his assignment of technical philosophical arguments to Roman politicians, so he recast the work as a dialogue in four books, this time with himself, his brother Quintus, and Marcus Terentius Varro, the leading Roman intellectual of the day, as the interlocutors. The *Academics* has only partially survived. From the first edition only the second half, the *Lucullus*, has survived, and from the second edition only part of the first book (out of four) has survived. In both editions Cicero represents himself and his interlocutors discussing the views of Carneades, Philo of Larissa, and Antiochus of Ascalon on whether knowledge is possible. Cicero defends Philo's skeptical position against the Stoic position, adopted by Antiochus, that the attainment of knowledge is possible.

De finibus (*On Moral Ends*), written at the same time as the *Academics*, is dedicated to Brutus and treats the views of the three major philosophical schools on the *summum bonum*, or highest good, for human beings. *On Moral Ends* consists of five books and is cast in the form of three separate dialogues: books 1 and 2 are set in the year 50 and treat the ethical views of Epicureans, books 3 and 4 are set in 52 and discuss Stoic ethics, and book 5 is set in Cicero's student days in Athens in 79 and examines the views of Antiochus. Cicero sets up each of the three sections of *On Moral Ends* as debates, with the views of the dogmatic school given first and those of the Academic refutation second.

Cicero's next composition, the *Tusculanae quaestiones* (*Tusculan Disputations*), also treats ethical topics but is a more popular, accessible work than *On Moral Ends* is. The *Tusculan Disputations* is designed to help Cicero and his readers work through important moral and psychological issues. Composed in summer 45, the work is set at Cicero's villa at Tusculum and represents a conversation between Cicero and an unnamed interlocutor on ethical topics. At the beginning of each book the interlocutor sets out an ethical thesis, and Cicero, drawing on the doctrines of the major philosophical schools, refutes it. In *On Divination* 2.2 Cicero concisely summarizes the five books of the *Tusculan Disputations*: "The first book discusses how to disregard death, the second discusses how to endure pain, the third discusses how to lessen distress, the fourth discusses other mental disturbances, and the fifth covers the topic that throws the greatest light on all of philosophy: it demonstrates that virtue by itself is sufficient for attaining happiness in life."

Cicero published *De natura deorum* (*On the Nature of the Gods*) late in 45. Dedicated to Brutus, it consists of three books and is written as a dialogue set some thirty years earlier. The work is one of our best ancient sources on Epicurean and Stoic views of the gods. In book 1, Velleius sets out Epicurean theology, and Cotta attacks it from the Academic perspective. Balbus presents the Stoic views on the divine in book 2, and Cotta gives the Academic refutation of the Stoic position in book 3. The works ends with Cicero's statement that on the whole he thinks Balbus' Stoic position nearer to the truth.

Following closely in topic is Cicero's next work, *De divinatione* (*On Divination*). The work discusses the question of whether divination exists, and Cicero presents it as a dialogue between himself and his brother Quintus. In book 1, Quintus argues for the Stoic view that divination exists, whereas in book 2 Cicero takes the Academic position and argues against divination. The work is an excellent source for Stoic views on divination.

Two shorter philosophical works were written around the same time as *On Divination*. *De senectute* (*On Old Age*), or *Cato Maior* (*Cato the Elder*), is dedicated to Atticus and is cast as a dialogue set in 150 BCE. As its title suggests, it treats the topic of aging and how best to deal with it. Closely connected to *On Old Age*, the work *De amicitia* (*On Friendship*), or *Laelius*, is also dedicated to Atticus and is set in 129 BCE.

Also written shortly after *On Divination* is the clearly argued but only partially preserved *De fato* (*On Fate*). Cicero sets up the work as a dialogue between himself and Aulus Hirtius on freedom, fate, and determinism. *On Fate* is particularly important for preserving some of the arguments of the Stoic Chrysippus, Epicurus, and the Academic Carneades on this difficult topic.

Cicero wrote the *Topica* (*Topics*), a short treatise on rhetoric, under unusual conditions: sailing on a boat between Velia and Rhegium on the southern Italian coast in July 44. Cicero addressed the work to his friend Gaius Trebatius Testa, and he claims that he based it on the *Topics* of Aristotle. The work is somewhat puzzling because it is not closely related to Aristotle's *Topics* as we know it. Rather, in his *Topics* Cicero discusses discovering arguments and other rhetorical issues in ways that are related to his earlier treatment of the topics in *On Invention* and *On the Orator*.

Cicero wrote *De officiis* (*On Duties*), his last and one of his most famous and influential writings, toward the end of 44 in the form of a letter to his son Marcus, who was studying philosophy in Athens. *On Duties* consists of three books and treats the topic of moral conduct. In the first two books Cicero follows the Stoic Panaetius' work (also called *On Duties*), discussing "the honorable" (*honestum*) in book 1 and "the useful" (*utile*) in book 2. In book 3, Cicero treats the apparent conflict of the honorable and the useful. Cicero presents the Stoic account of moral conduct as the one that seems the most persuasive to him.

Although his life was cut short not long after he finished *On Duties*, Cicero had shown in his writings how Greek philosophy could be integrated into

Roman life and letters. Combining a love of Roman political institutions and cultural values with a deep knowledge and respect for the traditions of Greek philosophy, he argued in his philosophical and rhetorical works for a fusion of Greek and Roman thought that would enable his fellow citizens to lead more successful and meaningful lives.

Legacy. Cicero's rhetorical and philosophical works had profound influence on later writers. In antiquity he was widely read. Classical authors including the elder Seneca, the younger Seneca, Tacitus (*Dialogus de oratoribus*, or *Dialogue on Orators*), and Quintilian discuss his style and views on rhetoric and philosophy, and Macrobius wrote a commentary on the *Dream of Scipio*. Cicero also had great influence on early Christian writers. Tertullian, Minucius Felix, Lactantius, Victorinus, and Rufinus wrote works heavily influenced by Cicero, and Saint Ambrose modeled his *De officiis ministrorum* (*On the Duties of the Clergy*) on Cicero's *On Duties*. Saints Jerome and Augustine each studied Cicero extensively. Jerome tells in a letter (22.30) that he studied Cicero so enthusiastically that he dreamed that a heavenly judge accused him of being, not a Christian, but a "Ciceronian." Augustine credited Cicero's *Hortensius* with turning him toward philosophy as a young man, and his style and many of his works, especially *Contra academicos* (*Against the Academics*) and the *De civitate Dei* (*City of God*), show deep Ciceronian influence.

During the Middle Ages the works of Cicero that were the most popular included *On Invention*, the *Dream of Scipio*, the *Topics*, *On Friendship*, *On Old Age*, and, to a lesser extent, the *Tusculan Disputations*, *On Duties*, and *Paradoxes of the Stoics*. In the Renaissance these works, along with *On the Orator*, influenced thinkers including Petrarch, Poggio Bracciolini, Coluccio Salutati, Lorenzo Valla, Machiavelli, Castiglione, and Montaigne. From the seventeenth to the nineteenth centuries, most educated readers in Europe read some of Cicero's rhetorical and philosophic writings. Cicero's reputation suffered a setback in the nineteenth century when in an influential history of Rome (*Römische Geschichte*, 1856) the German historian Theodor Mommsen attacked

Cicero. Portrait bust. Palazzo Nuovo, Musei Capitolini, Rome. PHOTOGRAPH BY ROBERT B. KEBRIC

Cicero's quality as a politician and thinker. Mommsen did great damage to the modern assessment of Cicero, but since the beginning of the twentieth century there has been a resurgence of interest in Cicero's rhetorical and philosophical works.

[*See also* Church Fathers; Consolation Literature; Divination and Diviners; Epicurus; Knowledge, Theories of; Mommsen, Theodor; Oratory, Greco-Roman; Platonism; Political Structure and Ideology, Roman, *subentry* The Republic; Rome, *subentry* Early Rome and the Republic; Religion, *subentry* Philosophical Criticism; Skepticism; Stoicism; *and* Values and Virtues, Roman.]

BIBLIOGRAPHY

Works of Cicero

Academica. Edited by J. S. Reid. London: Macmillan, 1885. Includes a Latin text and commentary in English.

Rhetorica. 2 vols. Edited by A. S. Wilkins. Oxford Classical Texts. Oxford: Clarendon Press, 1902–1903. Includes a Latin text.

Tusculanae disputationes. Edited by Max Pohlenz. Bibliotheca Teubneriana. Stuttgart and Leipzig, Germany: Teubner, 1918. Includes a Latin text.

Academicorum reliquiae cum Lucullo. Edited by Otto Plasberg. Bibliotheca Teubneriana. Stuttgart, Germany: Teubner, 1922. Includes a Latin text.

"De divinatione," "De fato," "Timaeus." Edited by Otto Plasberg and Wilhelm Ax. Bibliotheca Teubneriana. Stuttgart, Germany: Teubner, 1938. Includes a Latin text.

"Brutus," "Orator." Translated by G. L. Hendrickson and H. M. Hubbell. Loeb Classical Library. Cambridge, Mass.: Harvard University Press, 1939. Includes a Latin text and English translation.

"De inventione," "De optimo genere oratorum," "Topica." Translated by H. M. Hubbell. Loeb Classical Library. Cambridge, Mass.: Harvard University Press, 1949. Includes a Latin text and English translation.

Brutus. Edited by A. E. Douglas. Oxford: Clarendon Press, 1966. Includes a Latin text.

De oratore. Edited by Kazimierz F. Kumaniecki. Bibliotheca Teubneriana. Leipzig, Germany: Teubner, 1969. Includes a Latin text.

On the Good Life. Translated by Michael Grant. Penguin Classics. Harmondsworth, U.K.: Penguin, 1971. A translated selection of Cicero's writings on ethics.

Orator. Edited by Rolf Westman. Bibliotheca Teubneriana. Leipzig, Germany: Teubner, 1980. Includes a Latin text.

Tusculan Disputations I. Edited and translated by A. E. Douglas. Warminster, U.K.: Aris & Phillips, 1985. Includes a Latin text, an English translation, and commentary in English.

Cato Maior de senectute. Edited by J. G. F. Powell. Cambridge, U.K.: Cambridge University Press, 1988. Includes a Latin text and commentary in English.

"Laelius, On Friendship" and "The Dream of Scipio." Edited and translated by J. G. F. Powell. Warminster, U.K.: Aris & Phillips, 1990. Includes a Latin text, an English translation, and commentary in English.

Tusculan Disputations II and V, with a Summary of III and IV. Edited and translated by A. E. Douglas. Warminster, U.K.: Aris & Phillips, 1990. Includes a Latin text, an English translation, and commentary in English.

Cicero, "On Fate," and Boethius, "The Consolation of Philosophy" IV.57, V. Edited and translated by R. W. Sharples. Warminster, U.K.: Aris & Phillips, 1991. Includes Latin texts, English translations, and commentary in English.

De officiis. Edited by Michael Winterbottom. Oxford Classical Texts. Oxford: Clarendon Press, 1994. Includes a Latin text.

De re publica: Selections. Edited by James E. G. Zetzel. Cambridge, U.K.: Cambridge University Press, 1995. Includes a Latin text and commentary in English.

The Nature of the Gods. Translated by P. G. Walsh. Oxford: Clarendon Press, 1997. Includes an English translation.

De finibus bonorum et malorum. Edited by L. D. Reynolds. Oxford Classical Texts. Oxford: Clarendon Press, 1998. Includes a Latin text.

"The Republic" and "The Laws." Translated by Niall Rudd. With an introduction and notes by Jonathan Powell and Niall Rudd. Oxford World's Classics. Oxford: Oxford University Press, 1998. Includes an English translation.

On Obligations. Translated by P. G. Walsh. Oxford: Oxford University Press, 2000. Includes an English translation.

On the Ideal Orator (De oratore). Translated by James M. May and Jakob Wisse. Oxford: Oxford University Press, 2001. Includes an English translation.

Cicero on the Emotions: "Tusculan Disputations" 3 and 4. Translated by Margaret Graver. Chicago: University of Chicago Press, 2002. Includes an English translation and commentary.

Topica. Edited and translated by Tobias Reinhardt. Oxford: Oxford University Press, 2003. Includes a Latin text, an English translation, and commentary in English.

"De re publica," "De legibus," "Cato maior de senectute," "Laelius de amicitia." Edited by J. G. F. Powell. Oxford Classical Texts. Oxford: Clarendon Press, 2006. Includes Latin texts.

On Academic Scepticism. Translated by Charles Brittain. Indianapolis, Ind.: Hackett, 2006. Includes an English translation.

Secondary Works

Brittain, Charles. *Philo of Larissa: The Last of the Academic Sceptics.* Oxford: Oxford University Press, 2001. A detailed account of the life and philosophy of Cicero's philosophical teacher.

Douglas, A. E. *Cicero.* Greece & Rome, New Surveys in the Classics, no. 2. Oxford: Clarendon Press, 1968. Contains excellent chapters on Cicero's philosophical and rhetorical works.

Douglas, A. E. "Cicero the Philosopher." In *Cicero*, edited by T. A. Dorey, pp. 135–170. London: Routledge & Kegan Paul, 1965. An important essay for understanding Cicero's philosophical works.

Dugan, John. *Making a New Man: Ciceronian Self-Fashioning in the Rhetorical Works.* Oxford: Oxford University Press, 2005. Contains chapters on *On the Orator, Brutus*, and the *Orator*.

Dyck, Andrew R. *A Commentary on Cicero, "De legibus."* Ann Arbor: University of Michigan Press, 2004.

Dyck, Andrew R. *A Commentary on Cicero, "De officiis."* Ann Arbor: University of Michigan Press, 1996.

Fantham, Elaine. *The Roman World of Cicero's "De oratore."* Oxford: Oxford University Press, 2004. An excellent treatment of *On the Orator* in the context of Cicero's life and times.

Fox, Matthew. *Cicero's Philosophy of History.* Oxford: Oxford University Press, 2007. Includes discussions of sections of the *Republic, On the Orator, Laws*, and *Brutus*.

Gildenhard, Ingo. *Paideia Romana: Cicero's "Tusculan Disputations."* Cambridge Classical Journal, Proceedings of the Cambridge Philological Society, Supplementary vol. 30. Cambridge, U.K.: Cambridge Philological Society, 2007. Argues that the *Tusculan Disputations* should be read politically as a literary response to the tyranny of Caesar.

Griffin, Miriam, and Jonathan Barnes, eds. *Philosophia Togata: Essays on Philosophy and Roman Society.* Oxford: Clarendon Press, 1989. An excellent collection of essays on Roman philosophy, including a chapter on *On Duties*.

Inwood, Brad, and Jaap Mansfeld, eds. *Assent and Argument: Studies in Cicero's Academic Books: Proceedings of the 7th Symposium Hellenisticum (Utrecht, August 21–25, 1995).* Philosophia Antiqua, vol. 76. Leiden, The Netherlands: Brill, 1997. An excellent collection of essays on the Academics.

Long, A. A. "Roman Philosophy." In *The Cambridge Companion to Greek and Roman Philosophy*, edited by David Sedley, pp. 184–210. Cambridge, U.K.: Cambridge University Press, 2003. Includes a balanced account of Cicero's philosophical works.

MacKendrick, Paul. *The Philosophical Books of Cicero.* London: Duckworth, 1989. An overview with an introduction and chapters outlining and summarizing each of Cicero's philosophical and rhetorical writings.

May, James M., ed. *Brill's Companion to Cicero: Oratory and Rhetoric.* Leiden, The Netherlands, 2002. Includes essays on Cicero's rhetorical works.

Morford, Mark. *The Roman Philosophers: From the Time of Cato the Censor to the Death of Marcus Aurelius.* London and New York: Routledge, 2002. Contains a chapter on Cicero and his contemporaries.

Powell, J. G. F., ed. *Cicero the Philosopher: Twelve Papers.* Oxford: Clarendon Press, 1995. An important collection of essays on aspects of Cicero's philosophical works.

Walter Englert

CILICIA

"Cilicia" refers to a diverse geographical area along the southern coast of Anatolia. Rough Cilicia, or Tracheia, the rugged mountainous section in the west, is sharply distinguished from Plain Cilicia, or Pedias, the eastern fertile plain. The borders ran approximately from ancient Coracesium (modern Alanya) in the west to the Amanus (Nur) Mountains in the east, with the great Taurus Mountains to the north.

The eastern plain was settled early; Tarsus was already a regional center in the third millennium BCE. In the Bronze Age the entire area was inhabited by Luwian peoples related to the Hittites; the earliest-known Hittite treaty links the two states. Following the collapse of the Hittite Empire, smaller Iron Age kingdoms known as the "Neo-Hittites" developed in the region (extending into Syria) until their demise at the hands of the Assyrians in the ninth–eighth centuries BCE. During this period the documents of Tiglathpileser III first present the term *Hilakku* (or *Khilakku* or *Khilikku*), from which the name Cilicia (Kilikia) is presumably drawn, although the Greeks attributed the name to a putative founder, Cilix of Phoenicia. Greek and Phoenician influence is attested by Greek colonies on the coast and by Phoenician inscriptions.

During the Persian period (sixth–fourth centuries BCE), most of Cilicia maintained a semi-independent status. The annual tribute of five hundred talents (Herodotus 3.90) and the contribution of one hundred ships to the expedition of Xerxes I (Herodotus 91) bespeak a fair level of prosperity. At this time Cilicia was ruled not by satraps but by native kings with the title "Syennesis."

In the Hellenistic period (third–first centuries BCE) most of Cilicia was controlled by the Seleucids, although the coast of Tracheia was frequently contested by the Ptolemies, interested primarily in the rich and relatively accessible cedar forests for ship-building timber. The gradual decline of both those powers, along with the destruction of Carthage in the mid-second century BCE, created a vacuum filled by default by the rise of piracy throughout the Mediterranean, but especially along the coast of Tracheia. The Cilician pirates were sufficiently organized to cooperate with Mithradates VI and maintained a brisk trade in slaves, but ultimately they posed such a menace to shipping that Rome felt compelled to intervene. Already in 102 BCE, Cilicia was designated as a *provincia*, although the geographical boundaries are quite unclear and in fact may not have included much of the territory under discussion. Initial attempts at control were ineffective—Pedias was acquired by the Armenian king Tigranes the Great in 83 BCE—until Pompey the Great was granted extraordinary power (*maius imperium*) and assigned the task of clearing the seas in 67 BCE. This he did in a swift campaign that culminated in a decisive battle off Coracesium. He followed this military victory by a generous policy of resettlement.

In 51/0 BCE Cicero reluctantly assumed the rule of the province, at which time the greatest danger was posed by the Parthians farther east. That threat never materialized, and Cicero contented himself with minor campaigns against the so-called Free Cilicians in the Amanus Mountains, for which he was hailed imperator and granted a *supplicatio*.

In the late Republic the province of Cilicia seems to have been merged with Syria; it was abolished as a separate entity in 43 BCE. For about a century thereafter, Pedias remained part of Syria, while Tracheia was ruled by client kings, a policy described by Strabo (14.5.6) as more appropriate for such a remote area renowned for banditry. Indeed the tribes of Isauria (northern Tracheia) resisted settlement into cities until well into the Roman period, and they were bold enough to raid

the coast by Anemurium in 52 CE. They were pacified by the most successful of the client kings, Antiochus IV of Commagene, who also founded several towns. Following Antiochus' deposition in 72 CE on a charge of conspiring with the Parthians, Cilicia, including Pedias, was once again reconstituted as a Roman province under Vespasian, with its capital at Tarsus. That city flourished as a center of Stoic philosophy and was home to the apostle Paul. Pedias remained strategically important for the eastern policy of the empire, while Tracheia was incorporated into the Byzantine records as Isauria.

Recent archaeological survey of western Tracheia has revealed little trace of the elusive pirates, but indicates that settlements and population densities increased during the early centuries of the *pax Romana*. Like much of the Eastern Empire, the region was more obviously Hellenized than Romanized—for instance, only a handful of the thousands of extant inscriptions are in Latin—and most towns of any size are organized on the polis model, with *boulē* and *dēmos*. The nomenclature indicates, however, that the indigenous Luwian population maintained a significant presence well into the Roman period.

[*See also* Anatolia; Cicero, *subentry* The Life of Cicero; Hittites; *and* Piracy.]

BIBLIOGRAPHY

Houwink ten Cate, Philo Hendrik Jan. *The Luwian Population Groups of Lycia and Cilicia Aspera during the Hellenistic Period.* Leiden, The Netherlands: Brill, 1961.

Rauh, Nicholas. *Merchants, Sailors, and Pirates in the Roman World.* Stroud, U.K.: Tempus, 2003.

Syme, Ronald. "Observations on the Province of Cilicia." In *Anatolian Studies Presented to William Hepburn Buckler*, edited by W. M. Calder and Josef Keil, pp. 299–332. Manchester, U.K.: Manchester University Press, 1939.

Matthew Dillon

CINCINNATUS

See Rome, *subentry* Early Rome and the Republic.

CINNA

(Lucius Cornelius Cinna; d. 84 BCE), Roman general and politician, praetor by 90 BCE, and general in the Social War. Though Cinna was not a partisan of Sulla, Sulla allowed him to be confirmed consul for 87 on the condition that he swear not to encroach upon Sulla's laws. When Sulla departed, Cinna was courted by Sulla's opponents and began to propose legislation to restore the banished Marians and distribute the newly enfranchised freedmen and Italians fairly throughout the tribes. Opposed by his colleague Gnaeus Octavius and driven from Rome, he was deposed and replaced by Lucius Cornelius Merula. Then with bribes Cinna won over the troops besieging Nola and rallied the banished Marians, including Marius himself, and took Rome by force (87), killing Octavius (Merula committed suicide) and ruthlessly purging enemies. Sulla was outlawed, and Cinna and Marius were declared consuls for 86. On Marius' death, Lucius Valerius Flaccus became Cinna's consular colleague and consul for 85; when he was murdered, he was replaced by Gnaeus Papirius Carbo (consul 85–84). Following the precedent of Marius, Cinna continuously held the consulship from 87. Julius Caesar married his daughter in 85.

The sources do not allow a clear picture of Cinna's policies. He reinstated Publius Sulpicius Rufus' distribution of citizens across the thirty-five tribes and made attempts (such as debt relief and the fixing of exchange rates) to mitigate the extensive devastation of Italy. With his colleagues, he also prepared extensively for Sulla's inevitable return. Planning operations against Sulla, Cinna was killed in 84 in a mutiny at Ancona by troops reluctant to fight in a new civil war. His portrayal as a tyrant stems from Sullan sources and cannot be trusted.

[See also Julius Caesar; Marius; Rome, subentry Early Rome and the Republic; and Sulla.]

BIBLIOGRAPHY

Seager, Robin. "Sulla." In *The Last Age of the Roman Republic, 146–43 B.C.*, edited by J. A. Crook, Andrew Lintott, and Elizabeth Rawson, chap. 6. The Cambridge Ancient History, 2nd ed., vol. 9. Cambridge, U.K.: Cambridge University Press, 1994.

John Alexander Lobur

CIRCUS

The monumental circuses of imperial Rome were the largest structures in the Roman world, showcases for innovation in spectacle and display, representing the tremendous commitment of energy and resources to venues designed, first and foremost, to accommodate chariot racing. The greatest of these racing facilities was the Circus Maximus in the capital city, seating as many as 250,000 people and providing a model for similar buildings throughout the empire.

The origins of the circus venue were associated with the origins of the city. Rome's legendary founder, Romulus, is credited with the first circus games, held to honor the rustic god Consus (and to lull the Sabines) in what was the future site of the Circus Maximus, the Murcian Valley between the Palatine and Aventine hills. Romulus' games were improvised, taking advantage of the natural features of the valley setting to accommodate races and their spectators; informal arrangements like these needed only a rudimentary turning post set up on level ground to meet the basic needs of equestrian events. The Tarquin kings, linked in the Roman memory with urbanization of the city as well as with intolerable abuse of power, turned their architectural talents to constructing the archaic Circus Maximus, with track and seating.

The real development of the circus as a venue for imperial spectacle came in the late Republic, with improvements to the course and the starting gates sponsored by Julius Caesar as part of his lavish triumphal celebrations of 46 BCE. Augustus more fully realized the circus's potential as a medium for politically charged display. He built the imperial box, providing a visible focus for spectators' gratitude and enthusiasm for imperial generosity. Augustus' Palatine residence, located just above the seating on the northern side of the Circus Maximus, further linked the emperor to this greatest of spectacle venues, a connection maintained until well into the Byzantine era. Later emperors—notably Claudius, Nero, Titus, and Trajan—laid claim to the praise of posterity with further enhancement of the seating and performance area, marked by monuments within and without. In the circus

Rome's monarch hosted the glory and power of the Roman world; the color and excitement of any given race might be transitory, but the games were embedded in a divinely sanctioned order enacted by the emperor.

The Roman circus was constructed like an enormous stadium, the track following a long horseshoe shape, with spectators, ranked by status, seated in rows on banks rising from the wall around the track. The opening procession or *pompa* entered through an archway set into the curved end of the structure. The starting gates or *carceres*, twelve of them in the Circus Maximus, were staggered along the short straight end of the circus and closed off before the race by sets of double doors. One of the eagerly anticipated signals of a starting race was the whip-like crack made by the release of the latches held in place by a torsion mechanism, slamming open the gates of the *carceres*. White lines designated lanes for the first part of the race, to keep chariots separated until they reached the "break" line beside the nearest turning post, at which point the drivers could begin their struggle to reach the coveted inside position. The wide barrier or *spina* running lengthwise down the center of the track served primarily as a safety feature—to maintain control over the movement and focus of the horses, to minimize the horses' tendency to panic at the sight of oncoming teams circling an unmodified turning post. The *spina* also was a major location for monumentality in the circus, accumulating features that enhanced the spectacle and reminded the audience of past ludic and imperial victories, guaranteed by divine favor.

On either end of the *spina* were the *metae* or turning posts, each in the form of three rounded cones set high on a platform. Lap counters were also mounted on either end of the barrier, to heighten audience tension with regular marking of the race's progress. Sculpted eggs were raised on a bronze spike and lowered, one by one, after the lead team completed each of the seven laps. Bronze dolphins, mounted upright on a rod and flipped onto their tails after each lap, were added by Agrippa in 33 BCE, an allusion to victory over the naval power of Sextus Pompeius. Augustus' obelisk was also located here, imported to commemorate the emperor's victory over Egypt at Actium and to serve as a reminder of the cosmic authority of the *princeps*, friend to the god of the sun.

Display and perception were important functions of the circus. As in all spectacle structures, the political message of the circus relied on the visible presence of the emperor, his positioning within the monumental framework of the structure, and his demonstrative interactions with the audience. But the success of the racing spectacle also relied on the shared emotions directed and channeled by the circus panoply, the visual cues that helped to shape Roman identity.

[*See also* Chariot Racing.]

BIBLIOGRAPHY

Humphrey, John. *Roman Circuses: Arenas for Chariot Racing.* London: B. T. Batsford, 1986.

Köhne, Eckart, and Cornelia Ewigleben, eds. *Gladiators and Caesars: The Power of Spectacle in Ancient Rome.* Berkeley: University of California Press, 2000.

Potter, David S., and David J. Mattingly, eds. *Life, Death, and Entertainment in the Roman Empire.* Ann Arbor: University of Michigan Press, 1998.

Alison Futrell

CITIZENSHIP, GREEK

The Greek concept of citizenship emerged along with the polis, that distinctive, "face-to-face" form of community tied together by religion, law, and public participation first glimpsed in Homer's poems from the eighth century BCE. By the end of the fourth century BCE, it seemed to Aristotle that the polis was the natural "end" of human social organization and further that the important question "who is a citizen or member of the polis (*polites*)?" could be answered clearly and simply with the definition: a citizen is he who holds the offices of juryman and assemblyman (*Politics* 1275a). Aristotle's definition has long been taken as authoritative, reinforcing the common view that Greek society privileged or in fact created citizenship as the right of participation in public or group decision-making, and further that only free adult males were citizens. The insight and legacy of Aristotle's discussion, however, should not preclude the appreciation of a larger understanding of polis membership or citizenship expressed by the language of the Athenians' own "citizenship law" of 451–450 BCE proposed by Pericles: "whoever is not born from two citizens [astoi] should not have a share in [metechein] the polis" (Aristotle *Athenaion Politeia* 26.4). Using the analogy of family membership and inheritance, in which both men and women share, if in different ways, Pericles' law reveals "citizenship" not simply as having privileges or holding office but as participating in the life and goods of the polis, including religious rites, judicial protection, and economic advantage. Citizenship as "shareholding" implies the inclusion of women as citizens (here *astoi* rather than Aristotle's *politai*) and the recognition of important nonpolitical aspects of citizenship. Both Aristotle's officeholding and Pericles' shareholding are important expressions of the Greek conception of citizenship or community membership that endured long after the polis lost its autonomy and that still have relevance in the modern world.

[*See also* Cosmopolitanism; Freedom; Oaths, Greek; Perioikoi; Polis; Virtue, Popular Conceptions of; *and articles on individual Greek city-states.*]

BIBLIOGRAPHY

Patterson, Cynthia. "Athenian Citizenship Law." In *The Cambridge Companion to Ancient Greek Law*, edited David Cohen and Michael Gagarin. New York: Cambridge University Press, 2005. Discusses the development and character of Athenian citizenship law, an important basis for Aristotle's analysis and also a challenge to the sufficiency of that analysis.

Patterson, Cynthia. "Gender and Citizenship in the Ancient World." In *Migrations and Mobilities: Gender, Citizenship, and Borders*, edited by Judith Resnick and Seyla Benhabib. New York: New York University Press, 2009. Discusses the character and importance of female citizenship in Athens and Rome.

Cynthia Patterson

CITIZENSHIP, ROMAN

The conceptualization of communal membership at Rome and Roman practice in extending it have served since the second century BCE as important indices both of the difference between Rome and its peers in the ancient Mediterranean and also of the evolution of the Roman state, first from archaic to classical society with respect to individual rights, and second from city-state to imperial state, as citizenship was extended widely to the population of the empire. The history of Roman citizenship in the classical period—namely, from the end of the fourth century BCE to the early third century CE—can be usefully analyzed along two axes. One axis would study citizenship as a topic within a developing law of persons at Rome and so chart the development of particular rights and obligations as constituents or entailments of membership in the Roman state. The other axis would understand citizenship as embedded within a network of economic, legal, and political structures by which persons, property, communities, and territories were tied together and rendered both knowable and governable by the state. Of course, processes separated for the purposes of analysis are rarely distinct in history, and revolutions in the political, institutional, and geographic contexts of Roman government ultimately affected the practice of citizenship at the individual level in fundamental ways.

The Emergence of Classical Citizenship. In the archaic period—from, say, the eighth to the mid-fifth century BCE—the Roman community lacked fixed and formal criteria for membership. Rather, like the city-states of Archaic Greece, the communities of central Italy practiced considerable horizontal mobility. But whereas in the sixth and fifth centuries BCE the states of Greece almost universally developed rules that restricted citizen status to the legitimate males of citizen parentage and so came to adhere to strictly genealogical conceptions of membership, Rome developed a conception of its community as a system of porous and institutionalized mechanisms allowing new members to join.

The difference is visible at the level of language in the Roman use of Latin *civitas* to mean both citizenship and, by metonymy, community of citizens: shared citizenship is what defines the community. Greek *politeia* can mean communal membership as well as the rules by which a community governs itself, but by no standard implicature can Classical Greek denominate a community by the quality or rules of membership. Put bluntly, the Romans came to view political communities as products of human institution building; the Greeks retreated to a view of them as organic and outside the bounds of intellectual inquiry.

This development, the work of centuries, had long-standing consequences for Roman thought on the nature and ontology of cultures. Though their conception of the state was occasionally controversial, Romans of the classical period displayed an ongoing commitment to this vision in a number of ways, not least by rehearsing legends of the city's foundation through an act of asylum and through the celebration in politics, literature, and historiography of the specific, extra-Roman origins of particular families. What these stories conveyed was a sense that the boundaries of the Roman community were porous and that the community itself had grown through the regular reception of immigrants. This required among other things a shared understanding that there should be a process, however ill-defined, by which persons not Roman could become Roman.

Much of the fundamental legal and political work establishing the structures of Roman citizenship was performed early in the classical period. This is true of both the internalist perspective, focusing on the law of persons, and the constitutionalist-institutional view.

So far as the constitutionalist-institutional view is concerned, the long struggle between Rome and its neighbors in Latium, and particularly the legal structures negotiated first in the *foedus Cassianum* of 493 BCE—which allied Rome with the Latin League—and revised under Roman hegemony in 338 after the dissolution of the league, were clearly crucial to all subsequent developments. (For the former, see Dionysius of Halicarnassus *Antiquitates Romanae* 6.95.1; for the latter, Livy 8.14.) Starting

from the assumption of a basic likeness in the civil law structures of member communities—structures that may well have been underspecified or largely customary early in this period—the communities of Latium appear to have established two basic rights belonging to citizens of member communities in relation to other communities in the league. These were, first, *conubium*, the right to marry legitimately across communal boundaries, the citizenship status of children following that of the father, and second, *migratio*, the right to shed citizenship in one member community and acquire citizenship in another, through formal change of residence.

Equally crucial, and visible both before and during this same period—again, in relations with other cities of Latium—was the Roman practice of incorporating wholesale into the Roman citizen body the populations of cities conquered in war (early examples include Politorium, Medullia, Tellenae, and Ficana: Livy 1.33; c. 625 BCE). Although the Romans came to practice enslavement in war, it was very rarely practiced on wholesale populations in the early period, not least because Rome's early enemies were neighbors, sharing significant culture and language with the Romans themselves. We should not, however, be under any illusions that the grant of citizenship at the closure of war was received as a boon. In the aftermath of the war with the Latins in 338 BCE, a number of Rome's allies were offered citizenship and declined, preferring formal autonomy; citizenship without full voting rights was, however, simply imposed on the conquered. Nevertheless this history, too, contributed to a self-understanding at Rome that the passage from alien to citizen could be traversed, and traversed in multiple ways. This, coupled with the Roman practice of extending citizenship to the freed slaves of Romans, radically distinguished Rome from all Greek states. (For the Greek practice compare *Sylloge Inscriptionum Graecarum* 543.)

Thus already in the fourth century BCE the Romans had conceived of citizenship as a form of political identity that individuals acquired (or shed) by permission of the community, through their consensual commitment to its normative order. It no doubt helped that this understanding came into existence when the individuals and communities moving across the citizen-alien boundary shared the same cultural background, but the understanding persisted when that was no longer true. What is more, the ongoing porousness of the Roman community must have driven the development of that most Roman institution, the census, from a mere reckoning of potential men-at-arms to a mechanism for adjudicating questions of membership.

Turning to the law of persons, in the historical record the crucial developments of the early Republic appear in large measure to derive from the so-called Conflict of the Orders, the struggle by plebeians to place checks on the magisterial and judicial power of patricians and later to acquire access to office themselves. In stages stretching from about 450 when the content of the civil law was codified, down to the *lex Valeria* of 300 BCE—and continuing in some important respects to the *leges Porciae* of the second century BCE—a series of enactments circumscribed in several ways the power of magistrates over citizens. In later Roman legal thought—documents contemporaneous with the original enactments are lacking—some of these were conceived of as constitutional in nature, as checks upon magistrates' *imperium*. But others were conceived of as rights inhering in the citizen: most important, the right of *provocatio*—very loosely, appeal to trial by assembly over against a perceived exercise of mere coercion.

Another privilege of the full citizen was *suffragium*, the power to vote in elections; a third, connected in ancient texts to *suffragium*, was the right to stand for office. That one might be a citizen but not have *suffragium* seems to have been an innovation devised in the settlement of Latium in 338 BCE. What emerges in later, extant sources are mere terms—*civitas optimo iure*, "full citizenship"; *civitas sine suffragio*, "citizenship without the vote"—deployed as though legal structures uniform and homogeneous across time and community obtained wherever and whenever the terms are used. This is unlikely to have been the case. Two things do seem clear: such citizens bore all the duties of citizenship—they paid taxes and served in the legions even though their communities lacked full autonomy—and citizens without the right to vote were nevertheless citizens of Rome and thus governed in the final calculation by Roman magistrates and Roman courts.

Although *civitas sine suffragio* appears to have emerged as a solution to a contingent problem—namely, that although citizenship was the traditional mechanism for incorporating new members of whatever origin into the Roman community, the Romans felt misgivings about extending full citizenship to such a large body of conquered peoples all at one go—it harmonizes with other developments of the late fourth century BCE in displaying a willingness and ability on the part of Roman legal thinkers to conceptualize citizenship as conferring certain discrete rights and powers and as entailing specific obligations, rights, and obligations that might be disaggregated or bundled in different groupings as desired.

Citizenship in Italy to the Late Republic. The de novo creation of communities through treaty negotiation or unilateral legal enactment on the part of Rome points to the place of citizenship in broader problems of governance (and government) in the Italian peninsula. In the fullness of time, the inability of Roman politicians to craft enduring solutions to these problems helped bring about the end of republican government, with consequent alteration to the meaning of citizenship itself.

Communities of citizens without the franchise were but one type of community established by Rome in the late fourth century. Others were colonies of citizen or Latin status. These last consisted of individuals granted the package of rights and obligations conceded by Rome to its defeated Latin rivals in 338, which package was rapidly abstracted from the context for which it was created and was distributed first to participants in joint Roman-Latin colonial foundations outside Latium and later to ethnically non-Latin populations. Such colonies might be founded ex nihilo and implanted in or alongside preexisting urban centers. A still further type was the *municipium*, the self-governing municipality of Roman citizens. Others were created by ad hoc enactment down to the end of Hannibalic war in 201 BCE. After that date many communities underwent changes of status for all manner of reasons, but little noteworthy legal innovation took place.

What these actions brought to the fore were tensions of two kinds, which found expression in quite different ways. First, they rendered visible numerous limitations in the ability and willingness of Rome to extend the institutions of religion and government out to its constituent communities; they correspondingly threatened to expose the shallowness of republicanism as ideal and republican citizenship as lived reality. For although the granting of limited forms of autonomy to local communities solved various practical problems, permitting as it did access to law, the regulation of public properties, and the continuance of religious life, it did nothing to allow full citizens far from Rome to participate meaningfully in the political and religious life of Rome itself. Conceptual solutions to these

difficulties began to emerge only after the Social War (91–87 BCE), but the practical difficulties persisted until they were in part resolved, and in part transformed, by the emergence of the Principate.

The second tension brought to the fore by the extension of Roman power throughout Italy and the subdivision of the peninsula into communities and individuals constituted as political beings in relation to the state and to each other by the status assigned to them by Rome was as follows. The years that followed its victory over Carthage in 201 BCE brought untold wealth to Rome. Roman politicians and voters responded to the consequent social disruption by restricting the benefits of empire ever more to themselves at the expense of their allies. The close imbrication of individuals of different status within communities, and likewise of communities of different status, exacerbated the tensions this provoked. It seems that one response was the creation of the so-called *ius civitatis per magistratuum adipiscendae*, the right to obtain Roman citizenship by

Roman Citizen. Bronze diploma granting citizenship to Marcus Papirius, an Egyptian, 79 CE. © THE TRUSTEES OF THE BRITISH MUSEUM/ART RESOURCE, NY

holding a local magistracy. By it the Romans sought to co-opt the allegiance of the governing elite within local communities. The effort was not enough: Rome went to war with its allies in 91/90 nonetheless. But this right thereafter became a regular feature of grants of Latin status to provincial towns.

The outcome of the Social War was the enfranchisement of all Italy: this was accomplished at the level of persons by the extension of citizenship and at the communal level by the "municipalization" of all towns not yet incorporated along Roman lines. This process provoked a final stage in the conceptualization of citizenship in its geographic and political components, for Roman citizenship was effectively sundered from the franchise at Rome. What emerges, rather, is an apparatus for distinguishing place of origin, residence, and citizenship: *origo, domicilium,* and *civitas.* A connection earlier deemed natural, between membership in Rome and membership in a geographically determined voting tribe, long under strain, was now effectively replaced.

Imperial Aftermath. The story of citizenship during the Empire is one of gradual extension—to communities and to individuals, sometimes systematically, sometimes ad hoc. Two problems become systematically visible in the second century but were rapidly resolved by Caracalla's grant of citizenship to all freeborn residents of the empire in 212 CE. These are (1) problems of legitimacy and the devolution of property in marriages between citizens and aliens, and (2) the legal upheaval created by the grant of citizen status to select members of families when one of their number held local office or was so rewarded for service by the emperor.

Although citizenship had even prior to Augustus effectively lost its connection to genuine political agency, it continued to arouse emotion as a token of membership. As such the willingness on the part of Rome to extend citizenship to its former enemies continued to earn praise from Greeks in particular into the fourth century (see the *Orationes* of Aelius Aristides 26.59–64; Themistius 16; and Libanius 30.5).

[*See also* Colonies and Colonization, Roman; Cosmopolitanism; Democracy; Interstate Relations; Law, Roman; Oaths, Roman; Political Structure and Ideology, Roman; Rome, *subentry* Early Rome and the Republic; *and* Toga.]

BIBLIOGRAPHY

Bispham, Edward. *From Asculum to Actium: The Municipalization of Italy from the Social War to Augustus.* Oxford and New York: Oxford University Press, 2007.

Cherry, David. "The Minician Law: Marriage and Roman Citizenship." *Phoenix* 44 (1990): 244–266.

Davies, J. K. "Athenian Citizenship: The Descent Group and the Alternatives." *Classical Journal* 73 (1977): 105–121. Reprinted in P. J. Rhodes, *Athenian Democracy* (Edinburgh: Edinburgh University Press, 2004).

Gardner, Jane. *Being a Roman Citizen.* London: Routledge, 1993.

Kremer, David. *Ius Latinum: Le concept de droit latin sous la République et l'Empire.* Paris: Boccard, 2006.

Momigliano, Arnaldo. Review of Adrian N. Sherwin-White, *The Roman Citizenship* (Oxford: Clarendon Press, 1939). *Journal of Roman Studies* 31 (1941): 158–165. Contains a concise history of the scholarship.

Sherwin-White, Adrian N. *The Roman Citizenship.* 2nd ed. Oxford: Clarendon Press, 1973.

Taylor, Lily Ross. *The Voting Districts of the Roman Republic: The Thirty-five Urban and Rural Tribes.* Rome: American Academy, 1960.

Thomas, Yan. *"Origine" et "commune patrie": Étude de droit public romain (89 av. J.-C.–212 ap. J.-C.).* CÉFR 221. Rome: École Française de Rome, 1996.

Clifford Ando

CITY

[*This entry includes two subentries, a historical overview and a discussion of Roman urbanism.*]

Historical Overview and Theoretical Issues

Evidence for cities in Greek and Roman antiquity comes from both archaeological and textual sources. Although this article will stress the archaeological evidence, textual information is an inextricable part of identifying and interpreting the city and its components. Evidence for the beginnings of the classical city comes especially from archaeology; textual evidence becomes stronger for later periods.

Early Greek City-States. With the collapse of the Bronze Age states of the Aegean and Anatolia in the late thirteenth and twelfth centuries BCE, patterns of urban settlements shifted from palace-based centers with complex redistributive economies and extensive trade links to locally oriented villages. By the eighth century BCE the political organization that emerged in Greece was based on the city-state, or *polis* as the Greeks called it, an urban center with a greater or lesser amount of nonurban territory, and the *ethnos*, or "tribal state," a loose association of villages. The polis was standard in much of the Peloponnesus and the eastern half of central Greece and in the Aegean basin, the areas of Mycenaean control in the Late Bronze Age, whereas the *ethnos* characterized western and northern areas of the Greek peninsula. Each city-state and *ethnos* was independent. If this fragmentation recalls Mycenaean and, by coincidence, much older Sumerian political organization, it contrasts with the large centralized states typical of the Near East in the second and first millennia BCE and of Egypt.

The reasons for the rise of the city-state are unclear. The mountainous topography of Greece has been cited as favoring small polities. But such geography need not lead to this outcome. Sumerian city-states arose on a flat landscape, and the Greek peninsula itself from post-Classical to modern times was part of larger states. Factors particular to the Iron Age must hold the key. One such element may have been the parallel development of town and local cult, the cult center (or sanctuary) sometimes located in a rural setting, thereby establishing a distinct political, social, and ritual cluster that, by the eighth century BCE, coalesced into an independent city-state. Other elements important in the development of cities in the Iron Age were migrations—first, within the Greek peninsula itself; second, eastward across the Aegean to the Anatolian coast and islands offshore; and third and latest, to more distant coasts, notably the Black Sea to the northeast and South Italy and Sicily to the west—renewed contacts with the Near East and Egypt, and the return of literacy with the invention of the Greek alphabet.

Locations of towns varied. In some cases, such as Athens, settlements continued Late Bronze Age predecessors. In contrast the cities founded by colonizers could well be the first habitation at that place. Fortifiable sites were preferred. Athens, Corinth, and others had their "high city," or acropolis. A promontory with a harbor on each side was a favored situation on seacoasts, especially characteristic of East Aegean towns such as Smyrna and Iasos, for such a site could be easily defended. Of shorter duration were towns in remote locations; Karphi, in the mountains of Crete, was occupied for only a century, circa 1050–950 BCE.

City versus Countryside. The opposition of urban and rural is important in any consideration of ancient cities. The Greek polis normally included both. Scholars have traditionally focused on the city as the core element in the identity of a polis and its inhabitants. However, the land outside the city boundaries is fruitfully seen as complementary to that inside the city, both economically and socially. Immediately outside the city walls lay the cemeteries, areas ritually polluted for the living. This distinction, which began early in the Iron Age, was preserved throughout Greek and Roman antiquity, with only selected individuals of prominence awarded the privilege of intramural burial. Farther out, in addition to farmhouses and natural resources—such as quarries, mines, and forests—that a city-state might exploit, might be religious centers, or sanctuaries. In contrast to, say, the Sumerians, for whom temples were always inside cities, Greek sanctuaries could be situated both inside a city and in the countryside. Famous examples include the Athenian Acropolis (urban) and Olympia (rural). Even rural sanctuaries would be carefully delimited so that the area of sacred ground was clear. The influence of these major rural sanctuaries on cities could be great. Would-be colonizers consulted the oracle at Delphi for a blessing of their enterprise. A victory at the games during the famous festivals at Olympia, Nemea, Delphi, and Isthmia would make a man celebrated in his hometown.

Archaic Cities of Ionia. The cities of the eastern Aegean became prominent in the Archaic period. Coastal locations favored international trade. Miletus, one such coastal seaport, assured its prosperity by founding some ninety colonies, especially in the Hellespont, Sea of Marmara, and Black Sea regions. With the development of monumental stone architecture, thanks in part to the inspiration of Egyptian practice, several cities sponsored the building of huge temples, such as the Heraeum on Samos and the Artemisium at Ephesus. These architectural marvels and the complexes in which they stood, major religious centers, drew pilgrims from near and far. Homer, reputed to be from Chios or Smyrna, had already brought literary fame to the region. Lyric poets continued the tradition in the Archaic period. Miletus was particularly known for its philosophers Thales, Anaximenes, and Anaximander, pioneers in the quest to understand the nature of matter. Coveted by the powerful neighboring kingdom of Lydia, then captured in the mid-sixth century BCE by Cyrus the Great, founder of Achaemenid Persia, the cities of Archaic eastern Greece saw their first period of greatness come to an end in 494 BCE when an unsuccessful uprising against the Persians led to the capture and sack of Miletus. The Persian invasion of the Greek peninsula was the direct result.

Athens and Sparta. During the Archaic period the Ionian cities were not alone in their prosperity, but they were rivaled by city-states elsewhere in the Greek world. By the end of the Persian Wars (490 and 480/79 BCE), two city-states, Athens and Sparta, had obtained particular power and prestige. Their rivalry eventually led to the Peloponnesian War (431–404 BCE), a protracted conflict that engulfed the two cities and their allies and eventually resulted in a Spartan victory. But neither city ever regained the military strength that it had enjoyed in the fifth century. Although military equals, Athens and Sparta consisted of strikingly different societies and built environments, a difference that has fascinated observers of ancient Greece from antiquity to the present. Sparta, a small urban nucleus, controlled an extremely large territory, Laconia and Messenia; farm production by tenant farmers and serfs (helots) in the conquered lands allowed the citizens to devote themselves to military training. Daily life was austere; the city itself was simple (as Thucydides noted: 1.10.2). The history of Athens followed a different trajectory. In political organization, conflicts between social classes and between regions in Athenian territory were resolved by an equal distribution of power, privileges, and responsibilities—democracy for all male citizens. As for the city proper, in contrast with Sparta, Athens prided itself in the development of its urban structures, in its art and architecture, and in its other cultural achievements.

Archaeological explorations in Athens since the independence of modern Greece in the nineteenth century have supported this picture noted already in antiquity. The Acropolis—which by the late Archaic period had become a religious center focused on the cult of Athena, the patron goddess of the city—was the site of a grand rebuilding project in the second half of the fifth century BCE. In their sack of Athens in 480, the Persians had destroyed the sacred buildings on the Acropolis. After victory, the Athenians and other Greek city-states vowed never to rebuild the ruins, but to leave them as reminders of Persian aggression and Greek sacrifice. By the mid-fifth century BCE, however, the power and prosperity of Athens had increased to the point where Athenians felt the need to express this power and prosperity in publicly tangible form. Pericles, the Athenian leader, put into action a remarkable program of rebuilding on the Acropolis. Notable buildings included the Parthenon (temple of Athena Parthenos) with rich sculptural decoration, the Propylaia (the monumental entrance), the tiny temple of Athena Nike, and the Erechtheum, a multipurpose religious structure housing in particular the venerable cult of Athena Polias, patroness of the city. Exposed in the nineteenth century by the stripping away of later construction—antique, medieval, and early modern—these fifth-century buildings stand today as icons of modern Athens.

Much more informative about daily life in ancient and medieval Athens have been excavations elsewhere in the city. Excavations in the Agora, the city center, begun in 1931, have revealed civic, commercial, religious, and domestic buildings, and monuments, shrines, and objects of innumerable sorts. Other major excavation projects have included the Kerameikos cemetery outside the ancient Dipylon Gate, first explored in 1870, yielding graves, offerings, and funerary monuments of many periods, and, more recently, discoveries made during the construction of the city's subway network. All such archaeological excavations have provided an invaluable complement to the picture that can be gleaned from ancient writers.

Classical Cities: City Planning. City planning implies a conscious control of the building activities in a city, either as a whole or in part. For Greeks and Romans, such control is associated particularly with newly founded cities, or newly created districts within established cities. On rare occasions, established cities were completely renewed. The use of planning must be contrasted with the lack of planning, a feature better attested in the archaeological record than in the textual—where silence on practices in an individual city may or may not be significant. "Organic" is the adjective often used to describe a city that developed without systematic planning. Such a city might have originated as a village, growing over a long period of time, with buildings and streets added as particular needs arose. Athens is such a city. However, even in such a city, events may occur that require an interventionist response. The result might be that a section of the town was organized as an ensemble. The destruction of Athens by the Persians in 480 BCE led to the construction of the Themistoclean city wall—a marking out of the city's boundary—and eventually to the Periclean building program on the Acropolis and the planned harbor of Piraeus.

The seeming random placement of buildings in Athens and other Greek cities has been challenged by some. Constantinos A. Doxiadis proposed that for the ancient Greeks, visual relationships were carefully calculated when new buildings were erected. Vincent Scully, focusing on religious buildings, demonstrated that orientation to prominent landscape features, such as mountain peaks, was often a guiding principle in the placement of temples. Such observations have seemed self-evident to some but have been resisted by others, who find such theories to be grounded in the mind of the modern beholder.

Grid Plan. The grid or orthogonal plan (streets at right angles) is the city plan par excellence, simple but systematic. In the Greek world this layout was associated in particular with Hippodamus of Miletus, a planner of the fifth century BCE said to have worked at Piraeus (the port of Athens), and more tentatively said to have worked at Thurii (an Athenian colony in southern Italy) and Rhodes (although this last was not founded until 408/7 BCE). Hippodamus should not be considered the inventor of the grid plan, however, for this basic principle already had a long history in the eastern Mediterranean, Egypt, and the Near East. Knowledge about Hippodamus comes from various ancient writers, most notably Aristotle in *Politics* (2.5). Aristotle was interested in Hippodamus not for any practical lessons on city planning, but rather for his theoretical approach to the overall organization of a city, social and physical. Hippodamus is introduced as the one who "invented the division of cities" and who "cut up Piraeus." Division of cities, as Aristotle soon makes clear, refers not only to physical divisions, as we might first think, but also to social divisions. Hippodamus proposed that a city of ten thousand should be divided into three classes (artisans, farmers, and warriors), its land into three parts (sacred, public—to provide food for the warriors—and private). As for cutting up Piraeus, this phrase does seem to refer to physical divisions. Inscribed boundary stones from the fifth century BCE attest to different planned districts (in Greek, *neméseis*), but it seems that only the flat central section of Piraeus was laid out on a grid plan, whereas its hilly sections were not.

The grid plan works well on flat land, and so it suited new Greek cities in certain sections of South Italy (e.g., Metapontum) and along the western and northern Black Sea coast. Any topographical irregularities might necessitate adaptations. In any case, even if an overall unified grid might not be possible, sections could be laid out in grid plan, with separate orientations. Olynthus in northern Greece is one such example. Founded in 432 BCE as a regional center for Chalcidians, the city flourished until its destruction by Philip II in 348 BCE and was never rebuilt. Located on two adjacent hilltops about 100 to 130 feet (30 to 40 meters) above the plain, the city was laid out on a north-south grid with main streets of equal dimensions. Whereas the east slope outside the city wall was incorporated into the overall grid plan, the southwest hill, although inside the fortified area, could not, for the ground there was too steep. Excavations in 1928–1938 revealed some one hundred houses, a unique sample of ancient Greek domestic architecture. In contrast, no religious buildings and few public buildings were discovered. Arranged on straight, parallel streets, houses typically were grouped in double rows of five each, separated by an alley. From the street, all that one could see of a house would have been a modest entrance in a plain wall. Inside, rooms were arranged around a courtyard. Olynthus has several examples of houses with an *andrōn*, the men's dining room, usually with its own entrance, where the man of the house received his (male) guests.

Priene. A city such as Olynthus with a short history of occupation and not built upon by later settlers offers the archaeologist a more comprehensive look than does, for instance, Athens with its long, tangled building history and modern overlay. Excavations at such cities as Olynthus help us understand more easily how the parts fit together: city center, domestic quarters, temples, fortification walls, and so forth. Even more informative than Olynthus is Priene, because it has yielded a greater variety of buildings than Olynthus has, and so gives an unparalleled look at the ancient Greek city.

Priene, in southwest Turkey, was a modest city of little historical importance. Priene occupied two different locations in the valley of the Meander River. The first, attested by coins and in literary sources, has never been discovered; the continual silting caused by the river must have left the town either in marshy ground or high and dry, far from the seacoast. During the fourth century BCE the Prienians resettled downstream in order to have access to the Aegean. Although small in population—four thousand is one estimate—late Classical and early Hellenistic Priene equipped itself with the buildings characteristic of a Greek city, with its distinct political, social, and religious institutions.

Fading away in the later Hellenistic, Roman, and early Byzantine periods, the city did not redo its buildings, nor was it resettled in medieval or modern times. Excavations conducted in 1895–1898 revealed the overall town plan, providing a comprehensive look at an ancient Greek city not possible for a larger, richer, long-lived city such as Athens. The main section of Priene lies at the foot of an impressive mountain on a bluff overlooking the Meander. For the most part the layout follows a grid plan, even though the bluff is not flat. At the heart of the city is the *agora*, here a rectangular space bordered by stoas (porticoes), with, on the east end, a small temple; to the northeast behind the north stoa (also called the Sacred Stoa) are two standard civic buildings, a *bouleutērion* (council chamber) and a *prytaneion* (home of the city's sacred hearth, and used by those running the daily affairs of the city); and a food market is beyond the west stoa. A theater was built into the hillside above the agora. To its west, on its own platform, was the main temple of the city, dedicated to Athena Polias. Below the temple a large neighborhood of houses extends westward to the city gate. Below the bluff on which the agora is located, a stadium (for races) and a gymnasium (for exercising and for schooling) are found. Although the gymnasium is oriented within the overall grid, the stadium is instead wedged in diagonally to take advantage of the available terrain.

Hellenistic Cities. The conquests of Alexander the Great brought the Greeks into contact with other ethnicities, with effects on the nature of cities. In addition, the kingdoms established by his successors ended the political autonomy of the city-states, even if their institutions were perpetuated, and accentuated social differences among ruling elites, ordinary citizens, and the poor. Although established cities continued—with Athens, for example, now a cultural rather than a political center—a new range of urban formulas came into being. Alexander himself founded many new cities, the most famous of which was Alexandria on the Mediterranean coast of Egypt. Even if Alexandria was laid out by the architect Dinocrates in a grid plan, typical for new foundations, its Ptolemaic rulers nonetheless emphasized the palace district, with palaces, gardens, and the Mouseion, a research center that included a famed library. Elsewhere, prestigious monuments included the tomb of Alexander the Great and the Pharus, an imposing lighthouse on the small island of the same name that protected the city's harbors. Although little remains of Hellenistic Alexandria, the character of this city was clearly Greek. Elsewhere in Ptolemaic Egypt, traditional Egyptian buildings and imagery continued with little impact from Greek design.

Kingship is also reflected in the city layout of Pergamum, seat of the Attalid kingdom in western Asia Minor. Focused on an acropolis, a hilltop already occupied in the Archaic and Classical periods, this upper city featured the royal palaces, barracks, and armories, the great library, an astoundingly steep theater, the city's principal temple (to Athena), a monumental altar with lavish sculptural decoration, and the upper agora. Domestic quarters gradually spread down the south and east slopes of this hill in Hellenistic times, with the new fortifications of Eumenes II (r. 197–?160 BCE) reflecting the expansion. Recent research at Pergamum has included a close look at how the street system was organized on these slopes; an unusual radial grid was employed on the steeper southeast side. During the Roman Empire the city spread onto the flat plain below, following a regular grid plan. Thanks to peace, fortification walls were not necessary.

A quite different sort of city was established on the tiny Aegean island of Delos. Sacred from its association as the birthplace of Apollo and Artemis, Delos became a free port in 166 BCE. Until sacked by Mithradates VI Eupator in 88 BCE and again by pirates in 69 BCE, the city prospered from businesses that could buy, sell, and export free from taxation. Excavations since 1873 have revealed, in addition to the older sanctuaries, commercial districts and extensive residential quarters that included elegant houses. Because the island has no water sources, rainwater had to be collected in cisterns underneath courtyards.

Roman Cities: Origins. The history of the Roman city is twofold: on the one hand, the capital city itself, and on the other hand, provincial cities. Rome is well known, thanks to both textual and archaeological evidence. Its early history, bound in legend, was recorded at length by the historian Livy (59 BCE–17 CE). Founded in 753 BCE (traditional date), the town was ruled first by Latin kings (c. 753–600 BCE), then by the Etruscans (c. 600–509 BCE). Settlement began on the Palatine Hill, not far from the Tiber River and above the streams and swampy areas that the Etruscans channeled, drained, and developed as the civic center (the forum Romanum). The Etruscans built a citadel and their principal temple on the nearby Capitoline Hill, the temple of Jupiter Optimus Maximus, with three cellas, in Etruscan fashion, the homes of Jupiter, his wife Juno, and their daughter Minerva.

The expansion of Roman rule during the Republic (509–27 BCE) had a dramatic impact on the development of cities. Conquest of Etruscan and Greek regions in the Italian peninsula and Sicily by the late third century BCE in particular brought rich cultural traditions that had a striking influence on the built forms of the urban environment. Etruscan practices adopted by the Romans may have included foundation rituals and, like the Greeks, a certain fondness for the grid plan.

Foundation Rituals. Even if the theory of Greek city planning incorporated practical purposes, such as prudent exposure to the sun and various winds in order to ensure good health (e.g., Hippocrates *De aera, aquis, locis* 1–6), a cosmic element—that is, orienting streets and buildings to compass points and heavenly bodies—seems absent. The Romans, although also not cosmically minded (but this is contested), did incorporate significant rituals into the laying out of a new city, a legacy from the

Etruscans (Plutarch *Romulus* 11; Varro *De lingua Latina* 5.143). First, a trench, called the *mundus* (world), was dug in a central place; into this were thrown first fruits and earth from the founders' place of origin. The boundary line (*pomerium*) for the city would then be traced using a plow pulled by a bull and a cow. This line had a sacred quality, offering protection to the city walls normally erected nearby. At spaces reserved for city gates, however—that is, passages through which unclean items would pass—the plow was lifted up and over.

Roman City Plans. As with Greek cities, Roman cities could develop in an organic manner or, if newly founded, be laid out in a systematic fashion. Rome itself developed organically, as noted above, beginning on a few hilltops by the Tiber River. Eventually more hills were included, and the low-lying lands, crossed by streams and tending to be marshy, were drained or channeled and so made usable for building. Planning in Rome—indeed, into the twentieth century—has been marked by periodic urban renewals, with specific ensembles of buildings and streets planned together. In the ancient city the imperial forums mark such a cluster. Each of the five units just north of the forum Romanum (forums of Julius, Augustus, Vespasian, Nerva, and Trajan) are planned spaces, portico-lined courts with a prominently placed temple, and in the case of Trajan's forum, the most complex of these, various additional buildings: a basilica, twin libraries, a column decorated with commemorative relief sculptures, and an adjacent multistory commercial complex ("Trajan's Market").

These forums were designed to be experienced from the inside: squeezed together in limited downtown space, they were not arranged along grand vistas. Elsewhere, however, a broad visual impact could dictate placement. The Arch of Constantine (dedicated in 315), for example, was strategically situated along a triumphal road leading from the Circus Maximus northward between the Palatine and Caelian hills to the Flavian Amphitheater (Colosseum), the temple of Venus and Roma, and the colossal statue of the sun god Sol, with whom Constantine identified. For the late-antique Roman walking along the route, the visual relationships and the associations of Constantine with Roman glories gradually unfolded and multiplied.

Grid Plan. The planned Roman city was, like the Greek, characterized by the grid plan. Different from the Greek, however, is a variation that emphasized two main streets crossing at right angles, one north-south (the *cardo*), the other east-west (the *decumanus*). The crossing point typically marked the city center. This feature was thought by the ancients to come from the Etruscans. As revealed by excavations, the layout of Etruscan cities rarely displays such regularity; plans were determined instead by the irregular topographic conditions of each site. When sited on level ground, however, the grid plan was used. The best-known example is Marzabotto, an Etruscan colony founded in the Po River Valley near modern Bologna in the late sixth century BCE. Among the parallel streets, some are wider than the others, one running north-south, three east-west. Thanks to a surveyor's mark discovered at the intersection of the *cardo* with one of the east-west streets, the *decumanus* can be identified. No agora or other civic building marks this intersection, however. Temples stood on a terrace to the northwest of the town proper, although on the same orientation as the street grid.

Army Camps. Increased territory saw the development of a vast network of interconnected settlements. A well-maintained system of roads, newly founded towns, and army camps (*castra*, singular *castrum*) played distinct roles in this network. Army camps were also a determining influence in Roman city plans. Established throughout the empire, such camps were organized on a standard plan, a square or rectangle with straight streets crossing at right angles from an entry in the middle of each side. The commander's tent was located at the center. Barracks, storage, and other facilities were neatly arranged on subsidiary streets or paths, themselves placed at right angles and parallel. These main streets are also a form of *cardo* and *decumanus*. Many founded cities used this basic layout. Ostia, an urban sentinel at the mouth of the Tiber, was one example, originally established in the mid-fourth century BCE. In the later Republic and during the Empire, towns could be founded to settle veterans; this basic camp plan was typically the core, with the main forum at the intersection of the main streets. The cities could then expand beyond the regular core, perhaps in an organic way, as indeed happened at Ostia. Many such cities have continued to be inhabited into modern times.

Cities of the Roman Republic: Cosa and Pompeii. Although, because of alterations and overbuilding during the imperial period and beyond, Republican Rome survives poorly, thanks to archaeological work and literary sources it seems clear that during the later Republic the character of the city, with its building types and layout, was established.

Cosa. To understand the appearance of a Roman town during the Republic, however, one can look first at Cosa, 87 miles (140 kilometers) north of Rome. Cosa is to the Republican Roman city what Priene is to the Greek city: a representative example, even if small, of the ancient city, revealed through archaeological excavations. Cosa played a modest role in Roman history. Founded in 273 BCE as a colony strategically placed in land captured from the Etruscans, Cosa flourished until 70–60 BCE when it was sacked, perhaps by pirates. Subsequent occupation was minor. Archaeological excavations (1948–1954 and 1965–1972) have exposed much of the overall town; textual evidence, in contrast, is negligible.

Situated on hilly ground with a harbor nearby, Cosa was laid out on a grid plan and enclosed by a fortification wall. The highest site was occupied by a separately walled citadel, site of the temple of Jupiter—here, as at Rome, the principal shrine of the town. A large street led downhill to the forum, the city center. This rectangular open-air space was lined with civic buildings such as the *comitium* (meeting place of the assembly of the people) and the *curia* (for the senate, or council of elders). Other buildings included archive and office buildings, a shrine, a prison, and a cistern with, eventually, a basilica above it. The basilica ultimately became a standard Roman civic building, used for legal matters. Typically rectangular with interior rows of columns, its central portion rose higher than the outer sides, allowing for windows (the clerestory). In the fourth century CE the basilica design was adapted as the model for Christian churches: nave with clerestory, flanked by side aisles.

Marking the main entrance into the forum was a triple archway, an early example of the "true arch" in Roman architecture. Although invented earlier, perhaps in the Near East, the true arch became a hallmark of Roman architecture. In addition, this arch at Cosa, made in part of mortared rubble, shows an early use of concrete, a material that came to characterize the Roman city, permitting a range of building forms unimaginable in Greek architecture. Concrete is a mix of lime, sand, and water that hardens well when it dries. After Cosa and by the time of Augustus, the Romans included in the mix a volcanic dust called "pozzolana," named after the town of Pozzuoli (ancient Puteoli) on the Bay of Naples. The resulting concrete was particularly hard and had the additional virtue of setting underwater—so it could be used for harbor installations, cisterns, and aqueducts. Concrete wall cores were normally faced with more attractive materials such as expensive marble or stones, bricks, or tiles arranged in different patterns.

Pompeii. A more complex view of a provincial Roman city during the Republic and into the Empire is given by Pompeii. Founded in the late sixth century BCE, Pompeii was destroyed in 79 CE, buried in volcanic pumice and ash when nearby Vesuvius erupted. Thanks to the concrete, stone, and brick in its constructions and to the lack of later settlement, Pompeii's buildings have survived remarkably well. Excavations conducted from 1748 to the present have exposed most of this medium-sized city of about ten to twenty thousand (determining ancient populations is extremely difficult), with its unequaled view of Roman daily life: the city center (forum), streets lined with shops, extensive domestic quarters with houses ranging from rich to modest, and buildings for entertainment (theaters, an amphitheater). The rectangular portico-lined forum featured the temple of Jupiter at one of the short sides; behind the porticoes were civic offices, commercial buildings, and additional religious buildings. These last include a shrine to the deified emperor Vespasian. In imperial times, emperors were routinely deified and venerated. Established in every city, this cult served to connect people throughout this immense state.

Roman Cities: The Empire. Just as the Roman state was transformed when Republic gave way to Empire, so the capital city was given new direction during the reign of Augustus, the first emperor (r. 27 BCE–14 CE). According to his biographer Suetonius, Augustus found the city made of brick and left it made of marble. In order to make of Rome a city worthy of its great destiny, Augustus favored the integration of culturally prestigious Greek forms and materials into the Italic tradition of art and architecture. Marble, much used in Greece thanks to abundant sources in the Aegean basin, now became a material of choice to cover imperial buildings, with the opening of an Italian source, the Carrara quarries in northwest Italy.

Augustus himself lived modestly, but he promoted major building projects for the city. His forum of Augustus, enclosing a temple of Mars that successfully combines traditional Roman with Greek features, adjoined the earlier forum of Julius (Caesar). The Ara Pacis, the Altar of Augustan Peace, was the first of a series of public monuments decorated with relief sculptures that publicized imperial achievements. Although Augustus celebrated the bringing of peace after decades of civil war, later emperors glorified their military victories, as attested by the reliefs on, for example, the Arch of Titus, the Column of Trajan, and the Arch of Constantine.

Rome's population eventually swelled to perhaps a million, far larger than that of any other city in the empire. The social spread was huge as well, from the grandiose palaces of the emperors to the squalid dwellings of the poor in multistory apartment buildings. Literary evidence (e.g., Juvenal) gives us the texture of daily life in the capital. Archaeology has offered a more piecemeal vision, depending on surviving monuments (such as the Pantheon, a temple converted into a church), sectors made available for long-standing excavations (such as the forum Romanum), and the chance offered by randomly located new construction sites to peer down into the past. Discovered in dispersed contexts have been such marvels as the Forma Urbis Romae, a large—originally about 59 by 43 feet (18 by 13 meters)—marble plan of the city at a scale of 1:240, made in 203–211 and placed on the wall of the Templum Pacis (Temple of Peace) in the forum of Vespasian; only 10 to 15 percent of the original survives, however, in more than a thousand fragments.

Monumental buildings attracted attention, in antiquity as today. In addition to palaces, temples, and the forums, Roman cities were typically furnished with baths and, for entertainments, with theaters, amphitheaters, and a circus or hippodrome. The scale of building in the capital was of course grander: the late imperial Baths of Caracalla and Baths of Diocletian were staggeringly huge. Public baths had become an essential part of Roman social life and could be found in all cities. To supply water for the baths and for requirements of daily life, water was brought to the cities from sources near and far by means of carefully graded channels or aqueducts. When these channels had to cross a valley, the level of the channel was maintained by a bridgelike construction, or arcade.

Cities rivaled each other for honors, titles awarded by Rome. Benefactions might come from the emperor himself—Hadrian, the great traveler, had monuments and buildings erected in the wake of his visits—or from wealthy locals. One such benefactress was Plancia Magna at Perge (Mediterranean Turkey), the moving force in her distinguished family of the second century CE. She had the city gate renovated, complete with a court with two levels of statues of famous Pergians, and then had inscriptions carved to record her largesse.

Late Antiquity. With the fourth century the history of the city enters a new era. The first appearance of Christianity as a publicly accepted religion and the shift of the capital eastward, to Constantinople, the New Rome, garnished with prestige items from throughout the empire, symbolize both change and continuity. As social habits slowly changed, so, too, did the nature of the built environment. Although commercial activities continued, certain cultural habits fell away, such as the use of theaters, baths, and gymnasiums, as did the practice of civic institutions. The buildings that went out of use collapsed, were recycled into new construction, or were converted for new functions. From the fifth through the seventh century, with political and social fracture in the West and the Arab conquests in the eastern Mediterranean (Egypt, Syria), the transformation away from ancient patterns became greater still.

[*See also* Acropolis, Athenian; Agora; Aqueducts; Archaeology; Cemeteries; Concrete; Cosa; Delos; Marble; Pompeii; Roads; *and* Rome, *subentry* The City of Rome.]

BIBLIOGRAPHY

Brown, Frank E. *Cosa: The Making of a Roman Town.* Ann Arbor: University of Michigan Press, 1980. An excellent, well-illustrated introduction.

Cahill, Nicholas. *Household and City Organization at Olynthus.* New Haven, Conn.: Yale University Press, 2002. A detailed analysis of Classical Olynthus based on evidence revealed by Robinson's excavations of 1928–1938, with a focus on the houses.

Camp, John M. *The Archaeology of Athens.* New Haven, Conn.: Yale University Press, 2001. An authoritative introduction.

Castagnoli, Ferdinando. *Orthogonal Town Planning in Antiquity.* Translated by Victor Caliandro. Cambridge, Mass.: MIT Press, 1971. A concise survey of the grid plan as used in Greek, Etruscan, and Roman cities.

Doxiadis, Constantinos A. *Architectural Space in Ancient Greece.* Translated by Jaqueline Tyrwhitt. Cambridge, Mass.: MIT Press, 1972. On sight lines in Greek cities by a noted architect-planner; originally published in German in 1937.

Gates, Charles. *Ancient Cities: The Archaeology of Urban Life in the Ancient Near East and Egypt, Greece, and Rome.* London and New York: Routledge, 2003. A comprehensive survey of the material culture of city life from the Neolithic Near East to Constantine the Great.

Grimal, Pierre. *Roman Cities.* Translated and edited by G. Michael Woloch. Madison: University of Wisconsin Press, 1983. Grimal's concise introduction combined with Woloch's descriptive catalog of Roman cities; focuses on cities in western Europe, Italy, and North Africa.

Hammond, Mason. *The City in the Ancient World.* Cambridge, Mass.: Harvard University Press, 1972. A historical survey of Old World cities from origins into early medieval times; has no illustrations, but does have an extensive and still valuable annotated bibliography.

Hoepfner, Wolfram, and Ernst-Ludwig Schwandner. *Haus und Stadt im klassischen Griechenland.* 2nd ed. Munich: Deutscher Kunstverlag, 1994. Explores the nature of domestic architecture in selected Greek cities of the Classical and Hellenistic periods; excellent plans and reconstructions.

Marlowe, Elizabeth. "Framing the Sun: The Arch of Constantine and the Roman Cityscape." *Art Bulletin* 88 (2006): 223–242. How the fourth-century person walking along the triumphal way experienced this arch and its connections with adjacent monuments.

Martin, Roland. *L'urbanisme dans la Grèce antique.* 2nd ed. Paris: Picard, 1974. A classic study.

Osborne, Robin. *Classical Landscape with Figures: The Ancient Greek City and Its Countryside.* Dobbs Ferry, N.Y.: Sheridan House, 1987. Investigates the countryside of city-states using textual and archaeological evidence, including results from surface surveys.

Osborne, Robin, and Barry Cunliffe, eds. *Mediterranean Urbanization 800–600 BC.* Oxford: Oxford University Press for the British Academy, 2005. These papers explore early Greek and Italian urbanism in its larger Mediterranean context, from Spain to Cyprus.

Owens, E. J. *The City in the Greek and Roman World.* London and New York: Routledge, 1991. A survey of Greek and Roman city planning.

Parish, David, ed. *Urbanism in Western Asia Minor: New Studies on Aphrodisias, Ephesus, Hierapolis, Pergamon, Perge, and Xanthos.* Journal of Roman Archaeology Supplementary Series 45. Portsmouth, R.I.: Journal of Roman Archaeology, 2001. Up-to-date views from important excavations in western Turkey.

Polignac, François de. *Cults, Territory, and the Origins of the Greek City-State.* Translated by Janet Lloyd. Chicago: University of Chicago Press, 1995. On the role of early rural religious centers in the development of Greek city-states.

Rich, John, ed. *The City in Late Antiquity.* London and New York: Routledge, 1992. A companion volume to Rich and Wallace-Hadrill's; both books present papers resulting from seminars and conferences organized by the classics departments of the universities of Leicester and Nottingham, 1986–1988.

Rich, John, and Andrew Wallace-Hadrill, eds. *City and Country in the Ancient World.* London and New York: Routledge, 1991. An important collection of essays on

Greek and Roman urbanism by both archaeologists and historians.

Rumscheid, Frank. *Priene: A Guide to the "Pompeii of Asia Minor."* Translated by R. Blümel. Istanbul, Turkey: Ege Yayınları, 1998. A detailed, well-illustrated guidebook; replaces the previous standard, Martin Schede, *Die Ruinen von Priene* (1964).

Rykwert, Joseph. *The Idea of a Town: The Anthropology of Urban Form in Rome, Italy, and the Ancient World.* Princeton, N.J.: Princeton University Press, 1976. On the religious and ritual underpinnings of Roman cities.

Scully, Vincent. *The Earth, the Temple, and the Gods: Greek Sacred Architecture.* Rev. ed. New Haven, Conn.: Yale University Press, 1979. Greek temples in their natural settings; an inspired work.

Stambaugh, John E. *The Ancient Roman City.* Baltimore: Johns Hopkins University Press, 1988. An excellent, lucidly written survey.

Wycherley, R. E. *How the Greeks Built Cities.* 2nd ed. London: Macmillan, 1967. By now something of a period piece (the first edition was published in 1948), but still a good place to start.

Charles Gates

Roman Urbanism

The remains of the cities of the Roman Empire are one of its most visible legacies, and indeed "Rome" can refer either to the city or the empire. Urbanism is essentially a social practice, the engagement between people in a particular environment, usually defined in terms of population size, density, and the presence of monumental architecture. The size of the settlement itself and its hinterland are also important factors, as is the presence of particular architectural forms, some of which were related to the administration of the city. In fact, there is no single comprehensive definition of what constitutes a Roman city. Rather, there is a list of criteria to consider in relation to context, including the place of communities within the ancient urban network, and their recognition as cities on Roman terms (the recognition of the civic status of a community)—irrespective of any one necessary feature of the physical site.

By far the greater part of the population of the Roman world lived in rural areas, but it was cities that, in some ways, formed the framework for empire. This was because the network that was made up of cities throughout a large geographical area was the basis for and unit of administration. Cities were essentially nodes in this network, which also included the countryside and extended throughout the Roman world. This network was the product of different local circumstances, some of which did not previously include dense urban settlement. Naturally, then, the physical form and relationship of Roman cities with Rome herself varied widely, as did life within and around them. Given these factors, it is unsurprising that there are some things that many Roman cities have in common but also a huge amount of variability between them, due to the geographical, chronological, and cultural scope of the empire. Our sources for understanding Roman cities are numerous, from ancient authors and inscriptions, to archaeological material, or even such rare materials as depictions of cities in paintings, or the *Forma urbis romae*, the Severan marble plan of the city of Rome of which fragments are preserved. In some places where modern cities cover ancient ones, traces of the ancient city layout survive in the modern town plan.

In some geographical areas of the empire the Roman period saw the first cities to appear, as in Britain—elsewhere, such as in the eastern provinces, cities had existed before the coming of Rome for centuries, even millennia, but proliferated in the Roman period. While some scholars have taken this to indicate a deliberate policy of urbanization, this is difficult to prove. The Roman Empire started as a single settlement, and as such, the city formed one of the basic units of government. It is likely the Romans preferred this familiar organizational unit for the provinces, so cities flourished. There was a hierarchy of cities inasmuch as different cities had different and unequal relationships with Rome at the core, and while there was competition between cities, the hierarchy has to do with differing relations with Rome rather than between cities. In the west, the hierarchy moved from "native" communities, *civitates*, to those of municipal status, *municipia* and, at the top, *colonia*. In the east these titles were also used but often the central organization was around communities with *polis* status.

Elements of Roman Cities and City Planning. Another important aspect of Roman urbanism was the built environment of the cities. What constituted a Roman urban landscape varied greatly throughout the empire, but generally there are a range of features and structures that could be expected. This included religious structures—from large sanctuaries to small street shrines, the sacred topography of a city was an important characteristic, and many features of cities, such as crossroads, could take on a religious significance. Conveniences such as baths, circuses, theaters, and amphitheaters are known throughout the empire, as are administrative buildings including *basilica* (long buildings used as public meeting places), and multipurpose areas such as *fora* (open spaces often flanked by public buildings).

Open space and temporary structures would have also featured in cities. Commercial buildings found in cities included *horrea* (warehouses) for storage, markets, shops, inns, and food and drink establishments. Brothels are also known in cities, and the existence of a "moral" topography of Roman cities has been the topic of some debate. Another important aspect of the Roman city was infrastructure, not only in terms of roads but also the water supply, harbors, and sewers.

Fortifications formed a part of many cities, including city walls and associated earthworks. Other city boundaries could be demarcated with boundary stones or by other means, and could have symbolic and even religious significance. Rome herself, for instance, had the *pomerium*, the "Servian" wall, and eventually the Aurelianic wall, and the *pomerium* retained legal and religious functions even after the others were built. While many cities had all of these elements, none was absolutely necessary or definitive; indeed, the only type of building which occurred in absolutely every city, and that which formed the greatest part of all cities, was housing, which could include a range of buildings from large palaces to houses or apartments.

It is difficult to define the edges of cities—while some cities had walls, those walls need not have necessarily marked either the extent of densely inhabited area nor that the area inside them was entirely occupied. Indeed, cities always had a territory around them, but defining this territoriality is difficult. Outside of the city boundaries, but associated with cities, were cemeteries and extra-urban territories that were part of the city, including occupation which was neither completely urban nor rural. Beyond this, agricultural landscapes were also tied with cities. Cities and their surrounding countryside in fact had a close relationship, and in some ways the dichotomy between them is false. Likewise, the countryside and city alike were affected by the organization of space as a means of control by Rome.

The form cities took, or their "town plan," depended on a number of factors, including, for instance, whether or not there was an existing settlement on the site, and the local topography. While cities such as Rome had grown somewhat organically, some aspects of new cities, in particular their road systems, appear to have been planned. Where there were preexisting settlements or roads, city plans were sometimes adapted to incorporate those. On a new site, Roman cities could have roads laid out according to a grid plan, as for example is preserved in some veteran colonies such as at Timgad (Thamugadi) in North Africa. In the east, an orthogonal town plan was sometimes inherited from earlier settlements, as at Dura-Europos in Syria. Elsewhere, the Roman period saw a change in the focus of the city, as at Athens with its new Augustan forum and Hadrianic expansion. Particularly in the east, Roman control over the existing network of cities did not necessarily mean any immediate change in their physical form, and there has been a long debate on the nature of urbanization in the west as an ideological phenomenon linked with the spread of "Roman" culture.

All of the different structures and spaces that made up Roman cities, and the form cities took, were the physical manifestation of cultural, social, economic, and political practices. Monumental architecture, and the permanence and power implied by it, was used by both the wealthy and the imperial house to reify and display their power, on scales ranging from fountain-houses erected by local elites in provincial cities to the transformation in Rome of the *forum Romanum* into a monument to the Julio-Claudians, or the more systematic program of the imperial *fora*. To take the archetypal example of the Flavian Amphitheater (or Colosseum as it is popularly known), it can be understood not just in terms of a place for the masses to witness spectacle (which itself has an important social history), and as Rome's first permanent amphitheater (important architecturally), but also in terms of the source of the revenue for its construction (spoils from the sack of Jerusalem) and implications of its physical locale (taking back as public space that which had been private under Nero), all of which have wider implications.

Because of the variability of Roman cities, and because cities were constantly changing, their study is complex: the built environment of a city did not reflect that place at any one moment, but rather reflected the social, cultural, economic, political, and historical changes that formed those urban landscapes over the course of time. In past studies of Roman cities, scholars have tended to study "town planning" in terms of the layout of streets and the placement of fortifications and monumental architecture, but more recently archaeologists and historians alike have taken a more nuanced approach to understanding Roman cities, studying such aspects as domestic space, movement through cities, cities within the landscape, or their literary topography: populating Roman cities, long studied primarily for their monumental architecture, with objects and people.

Cities and the Economy. The place of the city in the Roman economy has been the topic of huge dispute. Much of this debate centers on Weber's model of the "consumer city," which involves the economic relationship between cities and the country, with the city extracting what it needs from its countryside in rents and taxes. This model might be a useful way of conceptualizing a few cities, such as Rome and Alexandria, but these are not typical.

Roman Street. Stepping-stones in a street in Pompeii, placed so that pedestrians could cross without getting their feet wet or dirty in the mud and wastes that accumulated. The stepping-stones were spaced so that carts could pass over them with their wheels in the gaps on either side. (Roman carts and chariots had a standard wheel spacing that resulted in the modern railroad gauge.) PHOTOGRAPH BY J. DONALD HUGHES

Such models do not fully explain the variety of economic interaction within and outside urban environments, and recent research suggests a series of nested economies operating within cities, ranging from small-scale local markets to interaction (and often dependence) in wider regional networks. Cities are now generally studied within their broader economic context, playing roles both as consumers and producers, as well as having ideological and administrative roles in the organization of the Roman economy. Indeed, the place of cities in the administration and collection of taxes was one of their key roles.

Roman Conception of Cities. Rome herself and Roman cities generally existed not only as physical cities but also conceptually, both symbolically within Roman worldview and as they existed in, and were constructed by, texts. The city of Rome was of course that which was most written about, and in some ways it became a world city, a microcosm for the empire of the same name. This was true not only of its public spaces and monuments, for instance with arches commemorating foreign triumphs, but also in the idea of Rome as it is presented in contemporary literature, and the importation of provincial architectural forms into the city.

In Roman writing, cities were often held up as beacons of civilization; hence Tacitus is able to give evidence of the Germans' barbarism by pointing out that they do not live in cities (*Germania* 16). So in one sense, cities were at the center of Roman social, political, and cultural life. Simultaneously though, cities were thought to be the locale of corruption, and of immoral behavior. A similar tension is felt in the attitudes toward the concepts of town and country, and while the city was the locale of civilization there was also nostalgia among the elite for the pastoral life (for instance, Varro *De re rustica* 3), which led, among a certain part of the population at Rome, to attempts at bringing the country into the city with urban villas and *horti* (palatial gardens).

Roman City. Aerial view of Pompeii, showing the forum with the basilica and the temple of Apollo. ALINARI/ART RESOURCE, NY

The sacking (and later refounding) of cities such as Carthage and Corinth, and the rhetoric surrounding these, also show the symbolic potency of cities both as inhabited places and as ideological concepts.

Roman urbanism was the product of many processes, and each city was a palimpsest. The standing remains of cities, ruins that became romanticized, were among the seeds for the burgeoning study of the ancient world in the early modern period. It is a testament to the wealth of material and textual evidence that the study of Roman cities continues to access and assess these places, where human activity in the Roman world was the densest.

[*See also* Fortifications and Forts, Roman; Forum in Rome; Police and Fire Services; Pomerium; Sanitation and Sewers; *and* Trade and Commerce, Roman.]

BIBLIOGRAPHY

Coulston, John, and Hazel Dodge, eds. *Ancient Rome: The Archaeology of the Eternal City*. Oxford: Oxford University School of Archaeology, 2000. A useful collection of thematic essays covering important aspects of the archaeology of the city of Rome.

Edwards, Catharine. *Writing Rome: Textual Approaches to the City*. Cambridge, U.K., and New York: Cambridge University Press, 1996. Important work on the significance of Rome in literature and literature in Rome, including postclassical responses to the city.

Edwards, Catharine, and Greg Woolf, eds. *Rome the Cosmopolis*. Cambridge, U.K.: Cambridge University Press, 2003. An important collection of papers employing various approaches to the city of Rome, and examining the relationship between city and empire.

Fentress, Elizabeth, ed. *Romanization and the City: Creations, Transformations, and Failures; Proceedings of a Conference Held at the American Academy in Rome to Celebrate the 50th Anniversary of the Excavations at Cosa, 14–16 May, 1998*. Portsmouth, R.I. : Journal of Roman Archaeology, 2000. An accessible collection of essays that deals primarily with the urbanization and its forms throughout the empire, with a broad range of case studies.

Goodman, Penelope J. *The Roman City and Its Periphery: From Rome to Gaul*. London and New York: Routledge, 2007. Using Gaul as a primary example, this volume examines in detail the nature of city boundaries and the periphery of cities in both archaeology and text.

Parkins, Helen M., ed. *Roman Urbanism: Beyond the Consumer City*. London and New York: Routledge, 1997. A collection of essays that addresses some of the central issues in Roman urbanism, in particular the place of the city in the Roman economy.

Stambaugh, John E. *The Ancient Roman City*. Baltimore: Johns Hopkins University Press, 1988. A useful introduction to Roman cities and their constituent parts.

Ward-Perkins, John Bryan. *Cities of Ancient Greece and Italy: Planning in Classical Antiquity*. New York: G. Braziller, 1974. A problematic but seminal short study on ancient town planning.

J. A. Baird

CITY-STATE

See Polis.

CIVIL SERVICE

See Political Structure and Ideology, Roman.

CIVIL WAR

The word *stasis* refers to civil war within a Greek city-state. The word means "standing," so *stasis* was used first to refer to a faction that took a particular political position, then to refer to conflict between two or more such factions.

Civil wars are usually represented as one of two types: (1) either the champions of the poor or democracy against the champions of the rich or oligarchy, (2) or the champions on behalf of an outside power (such as Persia, Athens, or Sparta) and its role in the life of the city-state in question against the champions of either autonomy or another outside power entirely. These motives for civil war could and did overlap. In very early Greece, too, there may have been conflict between those perceived as "natives" (i.e., pre-Dorians) and those perceived as newcomers

(Dorians). *Stasis* should not, however, be regarded as class warfare in the Marxist sense of the term, because class in ancient Greece was determined by property ownership, not by labor, and slaves filled the role of the Marxist laborer.

Although (according to Thucydides) *stasis* existed in the earliest settlements in Greece, Herodotus is the first author to record a major civil war, the conflict among the parties of the coast, the hills, and the plain in sixth-century Attica that led to the rise to power of the tyrant Pisistratus. The Athenians later interpreted the party of the hills (Pisistratus' party) as pro-democracy, the party of the plain as pro-oligarchic, and the party of the coast as pursuing a middle constitution between democracy and oligarchy. From then on, *stasis* was associated with political affiliation, and many other tyrants in Archaic Greece owed their rise to victory in a civil conflict (e.g., Theagenes of Megara, tyrant c. 640–620).

In fifth-century Greece, *stasis* generally occurred between oligarchic and democratic parties, the oligarchic parties usually supported by Sparta and the democratic parties by Athens. Both city-states used *stasis* and the victory of their own supporters in such conflicts as a means of ensuring the stability of their alliance with the city-state in question. The classic example of fifth-century *stasis* is the civil war between democrats and oligarchs in Corcyra, which led Thucydides to record the complete destruction of the normal laws and mores of Greek life: brothers betrayed brothers, oaths of loyalty no longer mattered, and "words lost their meaning" and came to mean their opposite (e.g., friendship became enmity) in such an unnatural climate.

Stasis continued to play a role in fourth-century Greece. Sparta, Athens, and Thebes continued to take one side or the other in civil conflict in order to stabilize their own foreign policies and interests abroad. Argos suffered an especially severe stasis in 370, in which the democratic mob not only murdered the leaders of the oligarchic faction, but their own leaders as well. Foreign states also did not hesitate to use this weapon against the Greeks: the Persians had done so since the Ionian Revolt around 500 BCE, and they continued to support medizing parties in the Greek city-states through the fifth and fourth centuries. Philip II of Macedon owed some of his ascendancy over Greece to his support of oligarchic parties in Greek city-states.

Between the fifth and fourth centuries the incidence of *stasis* increased, probably because democracy and insistence on popular or class rights were becoming more widespread. A corresponding concern about *stasis* arose among Greek statesmen, and some fourth-century treaties, especially those establishing federal leagues, have provisions for assistance not only against external invaders but also against revolution from within, for example, the charter of the League of Corinth guaranteed the constitutions of member states in effect at the time of their joining the League, and so attempted to protect members against *stasis*.

In many city-states, *stasis* provided an important transitional stage between oligarchy and democracy, and despite the pain and suffering that it inflicted, *stasis* was ultimately to the good of the city-state; at Athens, for instance, stasis led to strong leaders like Solon and Pisistratus, and thus ultimately to the rise of Athenian democracy. The ideal society of Plato's *Republic* is free from *stasis* because each citizen knows his place, and his ultimate goal is the good of the city-state. For Aristotle in the *Politics*, *stasis* is an undesirable condition and perhaps even impossible. His ideal city-state is politically and economically autarkic, thus removing one major motive for *stasis*; it is also static, that is, it does not promote the other conditions that lead to *stasis*. He regards the motives for *stasis* as individual ones, not valid as causes of war and disruptive to the general peace, much as Thucydides portrays civil war in his account of *stasis* at Corcyra.

In the Hellenistic world *stasis* continued, intensified by the new multicultural nature of the Greek city-state and the wars between various areas of the Greek world. Roman domination of Greece effectively put an end to *stasis*.

[*See also* Polis.]

BIBLIOGRAPHY

De Ste. Croix, G. E. M. *The Class Struggle in the Ancient Greek World: From the Archaic Age to the Arab Conquests.* London: Duckworth, 1981.

Gehrke, Hans-Joachim. *Stasis: Untersuchungen zu den inneren Kriegen in den griechischen Staaten des 5. und 4. Jahrhunderts v. Chr.* Munich: Beck, 1985.

Lintott, Andrew W. *Violence, Civil Strife, and Revolution in the Classical City, 750–330 B.C..* London: Croom Helm, 1982.

Sarah Bolmarcich

CIVIL WARS, ROMAN

See Rome, *subentry* Early Rome and the Republic.

CLASS, SOCIAL

See Social Organization, Greek, *and* Social Organization, Roman.

CLASSICAL SCHOLARSHIP

[*This entry includes five subentries:*

Antiquity
Byzantium
Western Europe in the Middle Ages and the Renaissance
Modern Classical Scholarship
History of the Study of Ancient Art and Architecture

See also Interpretations and Interpreters.]

Antiquity

Countless readers over the last several millennia have found that ancient literature is difficult to understand but rewarding enough to make the attempt worthwhile. This situation creates a demand for aids that allow the reward to be reached with less difficulty; today encyclopedias such as this one are created to meet that demand, as are dictionaries, grammars, commentaries, critically edited texts, and a host of other scholarly genres. Things were little different in antiquity: many works of ancient literature were difficult to understand even when first produced, and others became difficult after a century or two, when textual corruption and the natural processes of linguistic and social change rendered their language obscure and their allusions opaque. Because the period from the composition of the Homeric poems to the fall of the Roman Empire was well over a thousand years (hundreds of years greater than the time that separates us from Chaucer), even the plainest and simplest examples of ancient literature had ample time to become difficult. But their appeal remained strong, and therefore a large body of ancient scholarship grew up that was dedicated to elucidating this material.

Nature and Survival of Ancient Scholarship. Ancient scholars, like modern ones, produced a variety of different kinds of work. They established definitive editions of texts, wrote commentaries explaining a wide variety of points, compiled dictionaries, and produced treatises on grammar, meter, accentuation, mythology, proverbs, and other relevant topics. As with modern scholarship, this work varied widely in quality: some ancient scholars were highly intelligent, careful, accurate, and conscientious about citing sources, and others were unintelligent, lazy, sloppy, or prone to make up references rather than checking a source. Moreover, some ancient scholars had advantages that their modern counterparts can only dream of: native-speaker fluency in ancient Greek or Latin or both, access to vast numbers of papyrus texts hundreds of years older and often far less corrupt than our medieval manuscripts, firsthand knowledge of much of the ancient literature that is now lost, and contact with an explanatory oral tradition going back to the time of the classical writers themselves. Others, however, had no information not available to us and based their pronouncements on guesswork or extrapolation from information found in the texts on which they were commenting.

Ancient scholarship is useful to us today in two ways. First, it gives us crucial information about ancient literature itself: what the different ancient readings of a particular line were, what various Greek and Latin words meant, what works of literature have been lost and what was in them, and so on. Second, it tells us about the culture that produced and used the scholarship: which works they read, how they interpreted them, and what they found important about the literature of prior ages. Such insight into ancient interpretation is particularly important for understanding Latin and postclassical Greek literature, much of which was heavily influenced by scholarly work on earlier literature. Educated Greeks and Romans did not read Homer or other poets in a vacuum; they studied the Homeric poems at schools in which obscure words and complex passages were authoritatively explained, and they discussed criticism and interpretation. It was thus inevitable that authors like Theocritus, Apollonius Rhodius (Apollonius of Rhodes), Virgil, and Propertius, in composing their own poetry, relied not only on the transmitted text of Homer and other poetry, but on the traditional scholarly explanations and interpretations of such poetry.

For understanding the culture that produced and used the scholarship, surviving ancient scholarship is useful to us regardless of its quality; indeed ancient scholarly misunderstandings are often more enlightening to us than interpretations we share. But for the purpose of understanding the original work under discussion, the accurate ancient scholarship is considerably more useful than the inaccurate, and therefore it is unfortunate that the two types, which were originally largely distinct, have been mixed up in transmission to a considerable extent. Use of ancient scholarship is thus fraught with arguments about which scholar is ultimately responsible for each morsel of information, as only by means of successful attribution can we have any confidence in the information's reliability.

The vast majority of ancient scholarship is no longer extant; we know about it only from references in other works. Nearly all the rest survives only in severely mutilated form: fragments quoted by later writers, epitomes, and later works drawing heavily on sources that can be partly reconstructed from those works. Only a very few scholarly works still exist in anything resembling their original form, and most of these are relatively late in date. Although some scholarly material has been found on papyrus, the majority of what we have survived through the manuscript tradition, and in many cases its textual tradition is very poor. It is a surprising but undeniable fact that the ancient scholarship preserved on papyrus is on the whole of lower quality than that which survives in manuscripts; it seems that the initial selection of material to include in manuscripts was excellent, though its fate in transmission has often been unfortunate.

Extant material—besides the literary texts that have come down to us, which in a certain sense are all products of the ancient scholars who weeded out errors from their own copies—includes a fairly large number of glossaries and dictionaries of obscure words, most from the Roman period or later; several treatises on linguistic subjects such as grammar, syntax, and accentuation, the earliest perhaps Hellenistic; a variety of works on literary criticism, mythography, proverbs, and so on; a few intact commentaries, all either late (but using earlier material) or nonliterary (e.g., commentaries on scientific works); and a large mass of medieval marginalia, known as scholia, preserving substantial extracts from ancient commentaries that are otherwise lost. For Greek it is the scholia that are most directly relevant for understanding ancient literature, because they provide most of the information we have on what ancient scholars said about it; for Latin the surviving commentaries and other intact works are more useful.

Greek literary criticism started early, but other forms of scholarship (e.g., grammar, lexicography, textual criticism) are generally postclassical. Their roots can be found in the fifth century BCE when philosophers and teachers of rhetoric began thinking and writing about language in a way that led toward systematic linguistic scholarship and when attempts to explain Homer to schoolchildren resulted in the earliest ancestors of some of our scholia (the so-called D scholia to Homer). In the fourth century, Plato and Aristotle continued to think systematically about language and literature, while the establishment of an official text of the Athenian tragedies showed a new concern for textual authenticity and the creation of texts like that preserved on the Derveni papyrus showed the development of systematic exegesis. The Stoic philosophers also made important observations about the Greek language that laid much of the foundation for the later grammatical tradition—exactly how much is disputed, because the works in question are lost.

Alexandrian Scholarship. The Greek scholarship most famous today is Alexandrian, that is, work associated with the Museum at Alexandria in Egypt. This institute of higher learning, the first of its kind, had at its core the best library in the ancient world—the one famously, though perhaps not completely, burned by Caesar's soldiers—and was run by a succession of Librarians, most of whom made important contributions to the preservation and interpretation of Archaic, Classical, and Hellenistic literature. The Museum was founded circa 285 BCE, and the most notable of its scholars include Zenodotus of Ephesus (c. 325–c. 270), who worked on establishing the texts of Homer and the lyric poets; Aristophanes of Byzantium (c. 257–c. 180), who edited many poetic texts, divided lyric poetry into separate lines of verse, produced important lexicographical works, and wrote introductions to many plays; and Aristarchus of Samothrace (c. 216–c. 145), who produced texts and commentaries on a wide range of poetic and prose works and who was considered the greatest of all ancient scholars, particularly in regard to his work on Homer. Apollonius Rhodius, Callimachus, and Eratosthenes of Cyrene also worked there as scholars but are now more famous for poetry (Apollonius and Callimachus) and science (Eratosthenes).

The Alexandrians established definitive texts of Archaic and Classical literature, comparing the variants found in different papyrus copies and arguing in commentaries for and against different possibilities; the commentaries also contained extensive explanations of a wide variety of other interpretive problems. The guiding principle behind these explanations was "to elucidate Homer from Homer," or to support arguments about meaning or usage in a particular text by citing parallels from the same text or other works of the same author. Because Greek had many different literary dialects, and the language spoken in Hellenistic Egypt was substantially different from that of Archaic Greece, this principle was important in allowing the Alexandrians to produce accurate and nuanced explanations of Archaic poetry without allowing their own instincts to mislead them. It also provided a generally accepted basis for scholarly argumentation.

Other achievements of the Alexandrians include the invention of the accent marks still in use today (the accents themselves, as features of pronunciation, go back at least to Indo-European times, as we can tell from the fact that many words have the same accented syllable in Sanskrit as the one marked by the Greek grammarians) and the compilation of introductions to plays containing historical information about the circumstances of the original production; some such introductions are the ancestors of extant dramatic hypotheses (the short paragraphs prefaced to plays in many manuscripts and editions), though not all hypotheses have Alexandrian roots.

Shortly before the death of Aristarchus the scholars had to flee from Alexandria as a result of unsuccessful political activity; this move ultimately resulted in the dispersal of Alexandrian learning throughout the ancient world. Aristarchus' pupils established themselves in a variety of cities; one, Dionysius Thrax (c. 170–c. 90 BCE), founded a school in Rhodes and produced grammatical treatises, one of which may still be extant. That is, a treatise bearing his name survives, but since antiquity at least parts of it have been suspected of having a considerably later date. Dionysius' pupil Tyrannio (c. 100–c. 25 BCE) was at least partly responsible for establishing Alexandrian scholarship in Rome. Another disciple of Aristarchus, Apollodorus of Athens (c. 180–c. 110 BCE), moved to Pergamum, where a school rivaling that at Alexandria had grown up under the leadership of the Stoic scholar Crates of Mallus (second century BCE).

After a brief hiatus, scholarship resumed at Alexandria, where the Library still offered exceptional possibilities, but the age of glory was over. Notable during this later period was Didymus Chalcenterus (Brazen Gut), probably the most prolific of all ancient scholars but not credited with originality; he is said to have written as many as four thousand books and was nicknamed *bibliolathas* (book forgetter) because he could not remember what he had written. As well as producing lexica and monographs, he put together the writings of Aristarchus and other scholars to compile hundreds of composite commentaries on Homer, Demosthenes, and other literary works; the remains of his commentaries, preserved in the scholia, are our primary source of knowledge of the Alexandrians' critical work.

Greek Scholarship in the Roman Empire. In the Roman world, scholarship was a flourishing and widely respected profession carried out in major cities all over the empire. We have much more understanding of work from this period (particularly its apex in the second century CE) than of earlier scholarship because a significant amount survives intact. Some of this is original work of the highest quality, such as Apollonius Dyscolus' treatise on syntax; other notable scholarly contributions include treatises on accentuation by Herodian and on meter by Hephaestion, as well as a host of lexica: Erotian's and Galen's glossaries of medical terminology, Apollonius Sophista's lexicon of Homeric words, Pollux's *Onomasticon*, Harpocration's lexicon of terms used by the Attic orators, Herennius Philo's collection of synonyms and homonyms, and Diogenianus' lexicon of rare words (not independently extant, but forming the basis for Hesychius' lexicon). Many commentaries were written in the second century, a number of which are still extant. Galen (129–c. 199) is responsible for thirteen surviving commentaries on Hippocrates that are crucial for our understanding of the nature of ancient scholarship, as well as for some surviving work on Plato. The earliest surviving commentaries on Aristotle likewise date to the second century, and the most important of the Aristotle commentators, Alexander

of Aphrodisias, comes from the second and third centuries. Writers of the third century, too, produced numerous commentaries and exegetical works on ancient literature, a substantial amount of which survives: from Porphyry alone we have works on Homer, Plato, Aristotle, and Ptolemy, a mathematician and astronomer of the second century CE.

These works were intended for serious scholars and advanced students, but the Roman period also saw the proliferation of literary aids designed for the general reader: less technical commentaries and summaries of literary works, usually with an emphasis on mythology. Some of these works were prose summaries of famous poetry, often focusing on mythological details; these included a set of summaries of individual books of the *Iliad* and *Odyssey* and a collection of summaries of the plays of Euripides known today as the "Tales from Euripides." Such works may have been intended to be read instead of rather than along with the original poems or plays.

In the late antique and Byzantine periods the rise of Christianity and the breakup of the Roman Empire reduced the reading of Greek pagan literature and the demand for work on it. Nevertheless scholarship was still produced, and a considerable amount survives; it is generally considered to be inferior in quality to earlier work but is nevertheless important because it contains a substantial amount of Alexandrian and Roman scholarship that is lost in its original form. There are a number of important surviving lexica from the fifth and sixth centuries, by Hesychius, Orus, Orion, Cyrillus, and Stephanus of Byzantium. Surviving commentaries are common but focus neither on questions of interest to the literary scholar nor on matters appealing to the general reader, but rather on technical philosophical and mathematical issues. Most plentiful are commentaries on Aristotle, Plato, Hippocrates, Galen, Ptolemy, Euclid, and other technical writers. It is clear that commentaries to literary works were also composed during this period, in some cases by the same scholars as the surviving commentaries, but succeeding generations preserved only the philosophical and mathematical ones intact, while the literary ones are lost as self-standing entities—though they sometimes survive in the scholia.

Latin Scholarship. The Romans saw the Greeks as their superiors in literary culture, and much Roman scholarship is derivative from Greek; for example, Latin grammatical terminology is largely translated from the Greek. Suetonius, who left us a set of biographies of grammarians and rhetoricians as well as his more famous biographies of emperors, tells us that there were two channels of transmission by which the Greek scholarly tradition reached Rome: bilingual Greeks from southern Italy, such as Lucius Livius Andronicus and Quintus Ennius, and visits to Rome by established Greek scholars. For Suetonius the crucial visit was that of Crates of Mallus in the second century BCE; he came for a brief embassy but broke his leg falling into a sewer and so was forced to stay long enough to teach a group of disciples. Despite the neatness of this story, it is clear that other visiting Greeks were also influential: in 56 BCE, for example, Aristarchus' scholarly heir Tyrannio gave classes in Cicero's house.

This initial dependence on Greek models does not mean that early Latin scholarship was necessarily unoriginal; the extent of such originality is hotly debated. The reason for this uncertainty is that Latin scholarship is in some respects much better preserved than the Greek material. The earliest substantial piece of surviving Latin scholarship is the *De lingua latina* (On the Latin Language) of Varro, who lived from 116 to 27 BCE and thus predates almost all preserved Greek scholarship by a substantial margin. Varro had Latin predecessors, including Lucius Aelius Stilo (credited with being the first true Latin scholar) and the poets Lucius Accius and Gaius Lucilius. One significant scholar who followed Varro was Marcus Verrius Flaccus, who taught the children of Augustus' family and is credited with being the first to hold competitions among his students and give prizes; mutilated versions of two of his antiquarian works survive, though his strictly philological treatises are lost. Gaius Julius Hyginus, Augustus' librarian, composed a number of lost scholarly, historical, geographical, and antiquarian works. Quintus Remmius Palaemon was famous

both for vice and arrogance and for producing an influential, but now lost, grammatical treatise.

Several surviving works are attributed to Latin scholars of the early Imperial period. A historical commentary on some of Cicero's speeches was composed by Quintus Asconius Pedanius, and a treatise on abbreviations bears the name of Marcus Valerius Probus, as do a number of manifestly later works, including commentaries and grammatical treatises; both these men are known to have also written numerous lost works. An abbreviated grammatical treatise is attributed to Quintus Terentius Scaurus, and if the attribution is correct this would be the earliest surviving Latin grammar; more securely attributed to Scaurus is a work on orthography, and another orthographical work by Velius Longus also survives. From the later second century we have nearly intact the *Noctes Atticae* of Aulus Gellius, an eclectic collection of learned anecdotes containing much valuable scholarly information.

More survives from the late Empire. Significant extant work includes Pomponius Porfyrio's commentary on Horace, Terentius Maurus' treatises on pronunciation and meter, Gaius Marius Victorinus' treatise on meter and several commentaries (most notably one on Cicero's *De inventione*), Nonius Marcellus' dictionary, and grammars by Flavius Sosopater Charisius, Diomedes, Marius Plotius Sacerdos, and others. Aelius Donatus, living in the fourth century, has left us an immensely influential grammar (his name gives the medieval English word for a Latin grammar, *donet*), as well as the mutilated remains of fascinating commentaries on Terence and Virgil. There are also later commentaries on Donatus' *Artes* that may contain fragments of his lost work.

Perhaps the most famous piece of Latin scholarship is the commentary on the *Aeneid* attributed to Servius, who lived in the fourth and fifth centuries. This exists in two forms, so different that it is sometimes doubted whether they go back to a common source at all, but despite its difficulties it is a valuable and intriguing work; much of the material in it (especially that in the longer version, the *Servius auctus*) comes from the lost portions of Donatus' commentary. Servius also produced other scholarly works, including metrical treatises and a study of Donatus' grammar. Other commentaries on Virgil include those of Tiberius Claudius Donatus (distinct from the more famous Aelius Donatus), Pseudo-Probus, and Junius Philargyrius. There are also medieval scholia on Virgil and other Roman authors; some of these are important, but none has the status of the most famous Greek scholia.

Macrobius, writing around 400 CE, has left us a commentary on Cicero's *Somnium Scipionis*, extracts from a grammatical treatise, and an intriguing compilation entitled *Saturnalia*, which describes the dinner conversation of a group of learned men and thus preserves much scholarly information in a manner similar to that of Gellius. Martianus Capella produced a learned allegory and encyclopedia of the liberal arts—one of which was grammar—entitled *On the Wedding of Philology and Mercury*.

Late in date but of great importance are the grammatical works of Priscian, who taught Latin to Greek speakers in Constantinople in the fifth and sixth centuries. His magnificent *Institutiones grammaticae*, far more detailed and complex than the grammars of Donatus, was eclipsed by Donatus' in the early Middle Ages but reemerged by the twelfth century; it contains a summary of Greco-Roman grammatical theory—including the syntax of Apollonius Dyscolus, which is often easier to understand in Priscian than in the original—and is an invaluable source of information on Latin and the linguistic views of its speakers.

[*See also* Antiquarianism; Derveni Papyrus; Encyclopedias and Dictionaries; Grammarians; Greek, *subentry* The Pronunciation of Ancient Greek; Indo-European Languages; Literary Criticism, Ancient; Mythography; *and* Papyrology.]

BIBLIOGRAPHY
Primary Works
Erbse, Hartmut, ed. *Scholia graeca in Homeri Iliadem (scholia vetera).* 7 vols. Berlin: de Gruyter, 1969–1988. A superb edition, but not complete: see also Thiel's edition of the D scholia.

Keil, Heinrich, ed. *Grammatici Latini.* Leipzig, Germany: Teubner, 1855–1880. An important collection of texts, some now superseded.

Lallot, Jean, ed. *Apollonius Dyscole: De la construction.* Paris: J. Vrin, 1997. A superb edition of the *Syntax*, with Greek text, facing French translation, introduction, and detailed commentary.

McNamee, Kathleen, ed. *Annotations in Greek and Latin Texts from Egypt.* American Studies in Papyrology 45. New Haven, Conn: American Society of Papyrologists, 2007. A complete corpus of annotated papyri, with key discussion of ancient annotation and the development of medieval scholia.

Rossum-Steenbeek, Monique van, ed. *Greek Readers' Digests? Studies on a Selection of Subliterary Papyri.* Leiden, The Netherlands: Brill, 1998. Texts and discussion of hypotheses, Mythographicus Homericus, and so on.

Schironi, Francesca, ed. *I frammenti di Aristarco di Samotracia negli etimologici bizantini: Introduzione, edizione critica, e commento.* Hypomnemata 152. Göttingen, Germany: Vandenhoeck & Ruprecht, 2004. A complete edition of fragments of Aristarchus from the *Etymologica*, with extensive discussion.

Thiel, Helmut van, ed. *Scholia D in Iliadem* (2000). Available only on the Internet, at http://www.uni-koeln.de/phil-fak/ifa/klassphil/vanthiel/index.html. The best edition of a group of scholia omitted from Erbse; the Web site also offers a study of them and an edition of the D scholia to the *Odyssey*.

Trojahn, Silke, ed. *Die auf Papyri erhaltenen Kommentare zur Alten Komödie: Ein Beitrag zur Geschichte der antiken Philologie.* Beiträge zur Altertumskunde 175. Munich: Saur, 2002. Contains texts, translations, and excellent detailed study of papyrus commentaries to Aristophanes and Eupolis.

Uhlig, Gustav, Richard Schneider, et al., eds. *Grammatici Graeci.* Leipzig, Germany: Teubner, 1867–1910. The standard edition of the main grammatical treatises.

Wouters, Alfons. *The Grammatical Papyri from Graeco-Roman Egypt: Contributions to the Study of the "Ars Grammatica" in Antiquity.* Brussels: Paleis der Academiën, 1979. A good edition of the grammatical papyri, with thorough discussion of each one, some translations, extensive indices, and a detailed introduction.

Secondary Sources
Dickey, Eleanor. *Ancient Greek Scholarship: A Guide to Finding, Reading, and Understanding Scholia, Commentaries, Lexica, and Grammatical Treatises, from Their Beginnings to the Byzantine Period.* New York: Oxford University Press, 2007. A comprehensive

guide to ancient Greek scholarship, with extensive bibliography, glossary, and reader.

Gibson, Craig A. *Interpreting a Classic: Demosthenes and His Ancient Commentators.* Berkeley: University of California Press, 2002. A good, detailed discussion; includes texts, translations, and commentary on Demosthenes papyri.

Holford-Strevens, Leofranc. *Aulus Gellius: An Antonine Scholar and His Achievement.* Rev. ed. Oxford: Oxford University Press, 2003. A learned account of the ultimate learned Roman.

Kaster, Robert A. *Guardians of Language: The Grammarian and Society in Late Antiquity.* Berkeley and Los Angeles: University of California Press, 1988. An excellent study of Latin and Greek grammarians in the fourth and fifth centuries CE, including a prosopography of known grammarians from 250 to 565 CE.

Matthews, Peter. "Greek and Latin Linguistics." In *History of Linguistics, II: Classical and Medieval Linguistics*, edited by Giulio Lepschy, pp. 1–133. London: Longman, 1994. An accurate, balanced, and thoughtful overview of ancient grammatical thought.

Montanari, Franco, ed. *La philologie grecque à l'époque hellénistique et romaine.* Geneva, Switzerland: Fondation Hardt, 1994. A useful collection of articles on ancient scholarship.

Pfeiffer, Rudolf. *History of Classical Scholarship: From the Beginnings to the End of the Hellenistic Age.* Oxford: Clarendon Press, 1968. The standard history of Greek scholarship; superbly learned, detailed, and accurate, though now superseded on a few points.

Rawson, Elizabeth. *Intellectual Life in the Late Roman Republic.* Baltimore: Johns Hopkins University Press, 1985.

Rengakos, Antonios. *Der Homertext und die hellenistischen Dichter.* Stuttgart, Germany: F. Steiner, 1993. Considers how the scholarship of Zenodotus, Aristophanes, and Aristarchus influenced Apollonius Rhodius, Callimachus, and other Hellenistic poets.

Reynolds, L. D., and N. G. Wilson. *Scribes and Scholars: A Guide to the Transmission of Greek and Latin Literature.* 3rd. ed. Oxford: Clarendon Press, 1991. A lively and accessible introduction.

Schad, Samantha. *A Lexicon of Latin Grammatical Terminology.* Pisa, Italy, and Rome: Fabrizio Serra, 2007. Essential for reading Latin grammarians.

Schlunk, Robin R. *The Homeric Scholia and the "Aeneid": A Study of the Influence of Ancient Homeric Literary Criticism on Vergil.* Ann Arbor: University of Michigan Press, 1974.

Sluiter, Ineke. *Ancient Grammar in Context: Contributions to the Study of Ancient Linguistic Thought.* Amsterdam: VU University Press, 1990. Discusses the Stoics and Apollonius Dyscolus, with a useful summary and discussion of much earlier work on Apollonius.

Swiggers, Pierre, and Alfons Wouters, eds. *Ancient Grammar: Content and Context.* Louvain, Belgium: Peeters, 1996. A good collection of articles on ancient grammar.

Eleanor Dickey

Byzantium

Except for a few discovered on inscriptions, papyri, and magical tablets, all extant Greek texts survive because they were preserved and copied by the Byzantines. This transmission decisively shaped the corpus of ancient literature. The composition of the corpus reflects Byzantine needs and tastes: poets and orators for the school curriculum, historians for imitation, philosophers for style or to aid theology, and scientific works for practical purposes. Specialized interests account for the survival of more esoteric works, while losses of territory and the ravages of fire and war claimed much that has been lost. By 500 CE the codex had replaced the papyrus scroll, and the invention of minuscule script circa 800 necessitated the transliteration of all works that were to survive—a process that could introduce errors into the text. By then the ancient scholia on major authors, especially the poets, had begun to be copied into manuscript margins, breaking up the original self-standing Alexandrian commentaries. The two earliest minuscule texts of the *Iliad*, called D and A and dating to the tenth century, are sufficiently different to prove that Homer, at least, was transliterated more than once; the texts' respective scholia stem from different ancient traditions, too.

Education in Byzantium generally adhered to the Hellenistic curriculum, though biblically based alternatives existed. Unlike in the medieval West, interest in the classics was largely a secular activity and prepared one for a secular career at the court or administration—from which the church was but a step away. The prestige of elevated registers of

Greek and the continued performance of Attic at the court imposed high philological demands on the literate classes. Starting in the ninth century, dictionaries illustrating classical usage were compiled based on ancient lexicography (e.g., the *Etymologicum Magnum*), as were manuals of rhetoric and commentaries on ancient theorists, mainly Hermogenes. One product of the encyclopedist movement of the tenth century was the *Suda*, a kind of dictionary of classical studies with thirty thousand entries on words, terms, sayings, and people from antiquity, still a major source of otherwise lost information.

In the mid-ninth century the future patriarch of Constantinople Photius wrote 280 reviews of about 386 ancient books that he had read (the *Bibliotheca*), which included some early Byzantine texts but not standard school authors such as the poets. He offered summaries and sometimes critiques of their style. Because many of these texts have been lost, Photius' testimony is irreplaceable. In the tenth century, a circle of scholars at the court of the emperor Constantine VII Porphyrogenitus excerpted ancient and Byzantine authors, mainly historians, into a vast encyclopedia with fifty-three headings, only one of which, *On Embassies*, survives whole, though others (e.g., *On Virtues and Vices*) survive in part. This work is our main or sole source for many texts (e.g., Nicolaus of Damascus' history); the excerptors also preserved much of the history of Polybius that survives.

Classical scholarship flourished in twelfth-century Byzantium. Gregory Pardos, bishop of Corinth, wrote the only surviving treatise on the ancient Greek dialects, relying on lost ancient authorities; he also wrote a long commentary on Hermogenes. A prince of the Comnenus dynasty, Isaac, wrote a commentary on the *Iliad* prefaced by an accessible introduction to the events and heroes of the Trojan War. A series of classics for beginners was produced by professional classicists for imperial patrons. For example, John Tzetzes composed a series of book-by-book verse allegorical summaries of the *Iliad* and the *Odyssey* and three poems narrating the events before, during, and after the Trojan War.

Byzantine scholars also began again to write original and professional commentaries on ancient authors, mostly poets. Tzetzes commented on Hesiod, Aristophanes, Lycophron, Oppianus, and others, while Eustathius, later the bishop of Thessalonica, wrote long commentaries on Homer, Pindar (only the preface survives), and Dionysius Periegetes. Eustathius' verse-by verse commentary on the *Iliad*—more than 3,500 pages in the modern edition—synthesizes discussions of grammar, etymology, rhetoric, mythology (allegorically interpreted), the plot, and the cultural background. It is a major source for otherwise lost ancient scholarship, though Eustathius blends his authorities well together with his own views.

In philosophy, Michael Psellus in the eleventh century had already produced paraphrases of Aristotle and tried to reconcile Christian doctrine with Neoplatonic metaphysics, especially Proclus. His twelfth-century heirs were more cautious after his successor John Italus was tried for philosophical heresy. A circle of scholars around the princess Anna Comnena, including Michael of Ephesus and Eustratius of Nicaea, produced book-by-book commentaries on the works of Aristotle that had not been covered by the commentators of late antiquity, such as the *Ethics* and the *Generation of Animals*.

This movement ceased in the chaos following the Crusaders' overthrow of the empire in 1204. After the restoration of Byzantine power, scholars of the late thirteenth and early fourteenth centuries began again to write commentaries (for example, Thomas Magister on Pindar and the tragedians) and made advances in the editing of poetry. An understanding of ancient meter enabled Demetrius Triclinius to produce new editions of the tragedians and Aristophanes, including plays that were not in the standard curriculum. Maximus Planudes translated Christian and secular Latin authors into Greek (Augustine, Ovid). The statesman Theodore Metochites wrote a series of 120 essays touching on topics in ancient history, political theory, and literary criticism. Independent in spirit, they are alternately respectful and critical of antiquity and its authors.

Byzantine scholarly activity in any period was densely interconnected. Although the history of personal relations often eludes us, scholars—especially commentators and lexicographers—relied on each other's works. Much scholarship was geared toward classroom use, but a knowledge of ancient literature and a facility in Attic Greek could advance one's career at the court and in the church. The Byzantines divided all learning into that which was "inside" (or "ours," i.e., Christian) and that which was "outside" ("Greek"). By adapting the study of Greek culture to the needs of a post-Classical and Christian society, ameliorating its troubling aspects (especially the gods) and preserving and defining the corpus of Greek literature, the Byzantines effectively laid the groundwork for the development of classical studies as the pursuit and loving recovery of what was by then already a largely alien ancient culture.

[*See also* Byzantium; Encyclopedias and Dictionaries; *and* Philosophy, *subentry* Greek Philosophy in the Middle Ages and the Renaissance.]

BIBLIOGRAPHY

Dickey, Eleanor. *Ancient Greek Scholarship: A Guide to Finding, Reading, and Understanding Scholia, Commentaries, Lexica, and Grammatical Treatises, from Their Beginnings to the Byzantine Period.* Oxford: Oxford University Press, 2007.

Kaldellis, Anthony. *Hellenism in Byzantium: The Transformations of Greek Identity and the Reception of the Classical Tradition.* Cambridge, U.K.: Cambridge University Press, 2007.

Lemerle, Paul. *Le premier humanisme byzantin: Notes et remarques sur enseignement et culture à Byzance des origines au Xe siècle.* Paris: Presses Universitaires de France, 1971. Also available in English: *Byzantine Humanism, the First Phase: Notes and Remarks on Education and Culture in Byzantium from Its Origins to the 10th Century*, translated by Helen Lindsay and Ann Moffatt (Canberra: Australian Association for Byzantine Studies, 1986).

Wilson, Nigel G. *Scholars of Byzantium.* London: Duckworth, 1983.

Anthony Kaldellis

Western Europe in the Middle Ages and the Renaissance

Classical Latin literature continued to be copied and widely read during the late-antique period. The lavishly produced manuscripts of such authors as Virgil and Terence, as well as the subscriptions attached to many of the codices produced in this period, attest to the scholarly interest in Republican and Augustan authors. Though Christian writers often displayed an ambivalent, if not hostile, attitude toward pagan literature, they nevertheless recognized its importance for training in the disciplines of grammar and rhetoric. In *De doctrina christiana*, Augustine (354–430) advocated the use of pagan authors as an aid to the study of the Bible. By the close of the fifth century the classical texts that had been transferred from cumbersome and fragile papyrus rolls to more durable and easy-to-use parchment codices found a home in the newly established monastic foundations. In particular, the Rule of Saint Benedict (c. 480–c. 547), with its instructions for the daily monastic reading (Rule 48), played a central role in ensuring the survival of pagan literature during late antiquity.

The centuries following the collapse of Rome were a dark and bleak period for classical learning on the Continent, where the copying of classical texts virtually ceased and the tenuous link that bound this period to classical Rome was nearly severed. But in the monasteries of Anglo-Saxon England (such as Lindisfarne and Wearmouth-Jarrow), Irish and Anglo-Saxon scribes copied, studied, and transmitted the vestiges of classical learning to later generations. Manuscripts produced in England were frequently transported by missionaries to daughter houses on the Continent. Many grammatical texts, essential to the preservation of learning and scholarship, reached the Continent through Anglo-Saxon intermediaries. In Spain, Isidore of Seville (c. 560–636) wrote his massive *Etymologiae* to serve as a comprehensive encyclopedia of learning. Spain was also the conduit through which much of the Latin literature of North Africa passed to northern Europe.

Carolingian Renaissance to the Twelfth Century. The Carolingian renaissance, the revival of learning fostered by the emperor Charlemagne (742–814) in the late eighth century, reestablished the primacy of classical Latin literature within the intellectual framework of western Europe. Scribes working at monasteries closely associated with the Carolingian court, such as those at Tours, Fleury, and Lorsch, copied many of the manuscripts that serve as the oldest, or the most important, extant witnesses to a manuscript tradition. The script used, the graceful and clear Caroline minuscule, was itself an important agent of cultural transmission, because texts copied in this script were easily read. The imperial court established at Aachen gave added impetus to this intellectual movement. Poets connected with the court adopted nicknames recalling the literary figures of classical Greece and Rome. Alcuin of York (c. 735–804) took the name "Flaccus" (for Horace, Quintus Horatius Flaccus), while Angilbert (d. 814), a pupil and friend of Alcuin, took the name "Homer." Moduin (c. 770–840/43), a Carolingian court poet known as "Naso" for (Ovid, Publius Ovidius Naso), boasted that "Golden Rome renewed is once more reborn to the world."

The period of the Carolingian renaissance was the first great age of classical scholarship. Monastic libraries under Charlemagne's dominion contained important collections of classical literature, and individuals labored on specific authors or assembled new collections. About the year 800, the Irishman Dungal (d. after 827) corrected the text of Lucretius; Lupus of Ferrières (or Lupus Servatus, c. 805–c. 862) annotated manuscripts of classical authors, notably a text of Cicero's *De oratore*; and Sedulius Scottus (fl. 840–860) assembled his *Collectaneum*, a collection of excerpts from a wide range of classical and patristic authors. In the second half of the ninth century, Heiric of Auxerre (841–876) and Remigius of Auxerre (c. 841–908) lectured on such classical poets as Juvenal, Persius, Horace, Terence, and Virgil. Hrotsvitha (c. 935–c. 975), canoness of the Benedictine Abbey of Gandersheim, wrote popular comedies in Latin in imitation of Terence.

The later eleventh and early twelfth centuries witnessed a further resurgence of interest in the Latin classics. The abbey of Monte Cassino under the stewardship of Abbot Desiderius (abbot 1058–1087) recovered and preserved manuscripts of important authors that otherwise would have been lost (the *Annals* of Tacitus, the *Golden Ass* of Apuleius, Varro's *De lingua Latina*). The libraries of the monastic foundations of southern Germany, particularly those at Tegernsee, Benediktbeuren, and Saint Emmeram, contained important texts and commentaries on the Latin poets. In the Loire Valley region of France, masters at such cathedral schools as Orléans and Chartres lectured and commented on Lucan, Ovid, and Juvenal, as well as on writers less familiar today such as Martianus Capella. The exposition (allegories and grammatical glosses) by Arnulf of Orléans (fl. 1175–1180) on Ovid's *Metamorphoses* influenced interpretation down to the Renaissance. Books 1–6 of Virgil's *Aeneid* received the elaborate allegorical commentary attributed to Bernard Silvester (c. 1085–1178). The study of Platonic philosophy also flourished at Chartres, where the master Bernard (d. after 1124) elucidated the Latin translation of Plato's *Timaeus*, one of the few works of Greek philosophy known to the West before the reintroduction of Aristotle in the late twelfth century. Chartres was also renowned as a center for the study of classical Latin literature. There William of Conches (c. 1090–after 1154) composed commentaries on Boethius' *Consolatio philosophiae*, Priscian's *Institutiones grammaticae*, and Macrobius' *Commentary on the "Dream of Scipio."* (The *Dream of Scipio*, extracted from Cicero's *De re publica*, became an influential text in the Middle Ages.) The early twelfth century also witnessed the rise of the *florilegium* (literally a gathering of flowers), or select excerpts. Two of the most important florilegia circulating during the High Middle Ages, the *Florilegium Gallicum* and the *Florilegium Angelicum*, have their origin at Orléans.

The writings of two English scholars, William of Malmesbury (d. c. 1143) and John of Salisbury (d. 1180), reveal an exceptional knowledge of classical Latin literature. In his *Gesta regum anglorum*

(Deeds of the English Kings), produced around 1120, William shows an extensive knowledge of classical Latin historians. As librarian of Malmesbury, he had access to a first-rate collection of manuscripts. John of Salisbury studied under the best minds of the early twelfth century, including Peter Abelard (1079–1142) and William of Conches. His *Policraticus*, written in a style reminiscent of Cicero, one of John's favorite authors, treats of the relationship of kings to their subjects.

Though extensive knowledge of Greek virtually vanished in western Europe from the Merovingian period to the Renaissance, several writers appear to have had a limited, or even at times a strong, command of the language. The Venerable Bede (c. 672–735) shows an acquaintance with Greek and Hebrew. John Scottus Eriugena (c. 815–877), appointed librarian of the palace library by Charles the Bald (823–877), translated at royal command the works of the fifth- or sixth-century Pseudo-Dionysius into Latin. Robert Grosseteste (c. 1175–1253), bishop of Lincoln, demonstrates in his theological writings a unique ability to read Greek sources.

Increased copying and study of the classics strongly influenced literary production in Latin and the vernacular throughout the twelfth-century renaissance. Walter of Châtillon (1134?–1200?) emulated classical Latin epic in his widely circulated poem the *Alexandreis*. Alan of Lille (c. 1128–1202), in the *De planctu naturae* (The Complaint of Nature) and the *Anticlaudianus* (modeled on a work of the late fourth-century poet Claudian), drew upon the poetry of Ovid for inspiration. Ovid's love poetry, particularly the *Ars amatoria*, served as a model for poetic anthologies and courtly literature. The *Carmina Burana*, an important collection of Latin and vernacular poetry from the early twelfth century, shows close links to Ovid's love poetry, as does the poetry of Baudri de Bourgueil (c. 1046–1130). In his *De amore* (c. 1185), Andreas Capellanus (Andrew the Chaplain) conveyed the ethos of the *Ars amatoria* to a wider audience. The French vernacular poets of the late twelfth century, notably Chrétien de Troyes in such works as *Cligès* and *Erec and Enide* and Marie de France in her short poetic *Lais*, drew upon and extended the scope of Ovidian eroticism.

Nor was the study and influence of classical literature confined to the schools of the north. In the late twelfth century, Spanish vernacular literature drew upon classical sources. The anonymous *Libro de Alexandre* borrowed heavily from the poetry of Ovid. In the next century the historical works of Alfonso X (1221–1284), *Estoria de España* and *General estoria*, incorporate mythic material from the *Metamorphoses* and *Heroides*. Toledo, with a large population of Arabic-speaking Christians, became an influential center for translation. Gerard of Cremona (c. 1114–1187) translated eighty-seven books, including many works of Aristotle (*Analytics*, *Physics*, *On Generation and Corruption*, and *Meteorology*).

The Late Middle Ages. In the early thirteenth century the disciplines of theology, law, and medicine gradually eclipsed the study of classical literature as centers of learning shifted from cathedral schools to the newly established universities. Bologna was noted for its law faculty, Salerno gained renown in medicine, and Paris was distinguished for its faculty of theology. Texts of Aristotle were reintroduced to western Europe in Latin translations made from Arabic versions of the Greek originals. Nevertheless certain classical authors continued to influence the cultural landscape. Ovid's *Metamorphoses* was imaginatively reinvented in Latin and vernacular reworkings. Allegorical interpretations, such as Giovanni del Virgilio's *Allegorie* (1323), the anonymous vernacular *Ovide moralisé* (early fourteenth century), and Pierre Bersuire's *Ovidius moralizatus* (1348), a Latinized moralization that drew upon the earlier vernacular *Ovide*, became important resources for scholars and poets alike. The Loire Valley area continued to be a fruitful source for commentaries on classical authors. Guillaume de Lorris (fl. 1230) and Jean de Meung (c. 1250–c. 1305) drew upon the *Metamorphoses* in their allegorical poem the *Roman de la Rose*.

The Late Middle Ages (thirteenth and fourteenth centuries) also saw the rediscovery of many Latin authors. Works of Seneca (both the *Tragedies* and the *Dialogues*) began to circulate widely in northern

Europe. Richard de Fournival (1201–1259), an important bibliophile, owned manuscripts of Propertius and the *Tragedies* of Seneca (now Paris, Bibliothèque Nationale de France, lat. 8260). Nicholas Trevet (c. 1257–c. 1334), a Dominican master associated with the universities of Oxford and Paris, wrote a highly influential commentary on the *Tragedies*, and in the early fourteenth century the Paduan Albertino Mussato (1261–1329) modeled his Latin tragedy the *Ecerinis* on Seneca. In England a group of classicizing friars—Thomas Waleys (fl. 1318–1349), John Ridevall (d. in or after 1340), and Robert Holcot (c. 1290–1349)—incorporated classical allusions into their biblical commentaries and sermons. The monastic communities in fifteenth-century England devoted much energy to the elucidation of the classics. At Saint Albans the monk Thomas of Walsingham (d. 1422), better known as a chronicler, wrote an allegorical exposition of the *Metamorphoses*, as well as extensive biographies of classical Latin authors.

Vernacular writers in England were strongly influenced by classical models. The *Legend of Good Women* by Geoffrey Chaucer (c. 1343–1400) shows affinities with Ovid's *Heroides*; his *House of Fame* derives many of its stories from Ovid's *Metamorphoses*. John Gower (c. 1330–1408) in his *Confessio amantis* incorporates large segments from Ovid's *Metamorphoses*, *Tristia*, and *Epistulae ex Ponto*. In Italy, Dante (1265–1321) in his *Commedia* adopted Virgil as his guide through the realm of Hell, and he viewed Ovid as one of the virtuous Latin poets (*Inferno* 4.90). His earlier work, the *Convivio* (The Banquet), reveals a striking indebtedness to Boethius' *Consolatio philosophiae* and Cicero's *De amicitia*.

The medical treatises of the Roman physician Galen (129–c. 204/216) were introduced to western Europe in Latin translations made either from the original Greek text or from Arabic translations. In the early ninth century, Hunayn ibn Ishaq, known to the Latin West as Johannitius (d. 873), the Christian director of the caliph's House of Wisdom (library) in Baghdad, translated into Arabic the majority of the works of Galen and produced an introduction to the art of medicine, called the *Questions on Medicine for Scholars*, that was based on Galen's *Ars medicina*. This introduction came to the Latin West in a Latin translation under the title *Isagoge Johannitii ad Tegni Galieni* (Johannitius' Introduction to the Art of Galen). During the twelfth and thirteenth centuries the treatise became highly influential at the medical school of Salerno, and it subsequently formed part of the *Articella* (Small Art), the most popular medieval selection of basic medical texts. The rediscovery of the *De medicina* of Aulus Cornelius Celsus (c. 25 BCE–c. 50 CE) at Siena in 1426 provided a model for humanist medicine, while the books of the elder Pliny's *Natural History* devoted to medicine also influenced Renaissance teachers. By the late 1490s, humanist scholars had access to manuscripts of Galen in the original Greek. The central figure in this Galenic revival was Niccolò Leoniceno (1428–1524), who taught medicine at the University of Ferarra.

During the late eleventh century, jurists at Bologna rediscovered the key text of Roman law, the *Digest*, a codification of late imperial law compiled during the reign of the emperor Justinian (r. 527–565). This discovery fostered the new jurisprudence that established the University of Bologna as the major center for the study of civil and canon law in the later Middle Ages. By the thirteenth century, many layers of glosses had been built up surrounding the text of the *Digest*, and these glosses were synthesized by the legal scholar Accursius (Francisco Accorso di Bagnolo, c. 1182–c. 1260) between 1220 and 1240 into what became the standard exposition or *glossa ordinaria* on the *Digest*.

The Renaissance. Renaissance humanism, the rebirth of classical learning that took place in Italy during the fourteenth and fifteenth centuries, increased exponentially the educated public's acquaintance with classical literature. The pre-humanist Lovato Lovati (1241–1309), a Paduan jurist, shared his enthusiasm for classical antiquity with a tightly knit circle of scholars. These individuals were acquainted with a wide range of classical authors, including Lucretius, Horace, Tibullus, Martial, and Ovid's *Ibis*. The rediscovery (c. 1300) of Catullus through a Veronese manuscript (now lost) of his poetry reawakened the interest of scholars in this hitherto unknown Republican poet.

Verona also benefited from an important group of antiquarian scholars. Giovanni de Matociis (d. 1337), custodian of the cathedral, was the first to show that the composite Pliny of the Middle Ages actually consisted of two writers, the Younger and the Elder (*Brevis adnotatio de duobus Pliniis*). An anonymous Veronese author put together the *Flores moralium auctoritatum*, a florilegium of moralistic writings that was put together in part from earlier collections of excerpts but that also drew from manuscripts at Verona of little-known authors or works, including Catullus, the younger Pliny, the *Historia Augusta*, Varro's *Res rustica*, and Cicero's *Letters to Atticus* and *Letters to Quintus*.

The Tuscan Petrarch (1304–1374), the leading humanist of the next generation, consolidated and expanded the gains of his Paduan and Veronese predecessors. Steeped in the literature of Rome and himself a commanding poet in the vernacular, Petrarch reinvigorated the cultural and intellectual landscape of Europe. His work on the scholarly traditions of classical authors (most notably Livy), conducted during his stay at the papal court at Avignon, had lasting significance. His personal library was extensive, containing manuscripts of Virgil, Horace, Statius, Ovid, and Juvenal, as well as lesser-known authors such as Aulus Gellius. In 1345 he discovered at Verona a manuscript of Cicero's *Letters to Atticus*, on which he modeled his own extensive correspondence. His biographical compilation of famous men from antiquity, *De viris illustribus*, served as a model for later biographical compilations.

Giovanni Boccaccio (1313–1375), a younger contemporary of Petrarch, began his career as a writer of fiction in the vernacular. His *Decameron*, a collection of short tales, clearly shows his familiarity with Apuleius' *Golden Ass*. In his more mature years, perhaps influenced by his acquaintance with Petrarch, he turned to composing more scholarly works in Latin. His biographical work devoted to famous women (*De mulieribus claris*), extant in nearly one hundred manuscript witnesses, was quite popular. His *Genealogia deorum gentilium* (Genealogy of the Gods of the Gentiles), on which he labored from 1360 to 1374, represents one of the most important Renaissance handbooks of mythology. These "Renaissance" works of Boccaccio and Petrarch strongly influenced the "medieval" writings of Chaucer and Gower (see above), evidence of the rapid, though uneven, spread of classical learning in the fourteenth century.

Florence became the focal point for humanism during the later fourteenth and fifteenth centuries. Coluccio Salutati (1331–1406), chancellor of Florence for nearly thirty years, drew heavily upon the classical tradition (particularly Ovid) in his *De laboribus Herculis* (On the Labors of Hercules). Poggio Bracciolini (1380–1459), the leading Florentine humanist of the early fifteenth century, rediscovered many lost works of classical antiquity. While attending the Council of Constance in 1415, he unearthed at the Burgundian monastery of Cluny a manuscript containing Cicero's speeches. In 1416 a foray to the monastery of Saint Gall in Switzerland yielded manuscripts of a complete text of Quintilian, Asconius' commentary on the speeches of Cicero, and a copy of Valerius Flaccus' *Argonautica*. Poggio is also responsible for uncovering manuscripts of Silius Italicus, Statius' *Silvae*, and Manilius in 1417. He played a leading role in the development and dissemination of the new script called humanist minuscule, modeled on Caroline minuscule. The cursive version of the script, invented by Niccolò Niccoli around 1420, was used by humanist scholars to expedite the circulation of newly discovered classical texts.

Lorenzo Valla (1407–1457), a pupil of Leonardo Bruni (c. 1369–1444), held a chair of rhetoric at Rome from 1450. His most enduring work, the *Elegantiae*, first printed in 1471, dealt with problems in Latin style, word usage, and grammar in various authors. It strongly influenced the movement of later humanists to reform Latin prose style in imitation of Cicero. Politian (Angelo Poliziano, 1454–1494) in his *Miscellanea* set new standards for textual criticism. Distancing himself from the line-by-line commentary so favored by the early humanists, Politian used the essay form to emend corrupt passages, and he often used Greek sources to correct and illustrate Latin texts. He collated large numbers of Latin manuscripts, many of which are now lost. Filippo Beroaldo the Elder (1453–1505) produced important commentaries on a wide range of classical authors and works, including Juvenal, Pliny the Elder, Suetonius, and Apuleius' *Golden Ass.*

During the Italian Renaissance, Greek studies were reintroduced to western Europe. During the medieval period Constantinople had remained an important intellectual center. Scholars such as Eustathius (c. 1115–c. 1195) and John Tzetzes (c. 1110–1180) wrote commentaries on classical Greek texts, while Maximus Planudes (c. 1260–1310) translated into Byzantine Greek such Latin authors as Ovid (*Metamorphoses* and *Heroides*), Augustine, Boethius, and Macrobius. The visit of Manuel Chrysoloras (c. 1355–1415) to Florence in 1397–1400 invigorated the humanists' interest in the language, and the study of Greek became an increasing part of the *studia humanistica.* Many ancient Greek authors were circulated in Latin translations. Cardinal Bessarion (1403–1472), a native of Constantinople, settled in Rome and became the leading exponent of Greek studies in Italy. His extensive collection of Greek manuscripts was presented to the Republic of Venice in 1468. Scholars who left Constantinople in the decades prior to the fall of Constantinople in 1453 brought with them many manuscripts of the Greek classics.

Johannes Gutenberg's introduction of the printing press to Europe in the 1450s meant that classical literature could be disseminated to an ever-wider educated public. Multiple editions of Greek and Latin classics were printed during the next two decades. For several Latin authors the *editio princeps* was rapidly produced in Rome: Virgil (1469), Lucan (1469), Ovid (1471). Printed editions were frequently equipped with voluminous scholarly aids such as commentaries, biographical sketches, and introductions. Venice became a major center of the printing trade. The Aldine Press, founded there by Aldus Manutius (1449/50–1515), favored attractive and portable editions of the classics printed in italic type. Between 1494 and 1515, thirty-three first editions of the greatest Greek authors were issued from the Aldine Press.

By the end of the fifteenth century, Italian humanism had crossed the Alps to northern Europe and England. The study of Latin and Greek became firmly embedded at the Sorbonne in Paris. Guillaume Budé (1468–1540), the first great classical scholar of the French renaissance, was instrumental in the establishment of the Collège de France under the patronage of Francis I (r. 1515–1547). Desiderius Erasmus of Rotterdam (1466–1536) created a truly pan-European humanism. He edited anew the Greek New Testament (published at Basel by Johannes Froben, 1516), and he was drawn into the polemical debate regarding the virtues of Cicero as a Latin stylist (*Ciceronianus*, 1528).

In France during the sixteenth century, scholars further developed classical studies in several areas. Greek studies continued to flourish, and Greek texts began to appear as early as 1507. Henri Estienne (Henricus Stephanus, 1528/31–1598) published in four volumes his monumental *Thesaurus graecae linguae* (1572), an important tool for the study of Greek. In his edition of the works of Plato published in 1578, he introduced a division of the text into numbers, with each number subdivided into equal sections labeled a, b, c, d, and e. This system, known as Stephanus pagination, is still in use today. Adrianus Turnebus (1512–1565), royal reader (professor) in Greek from 1547, brought out editions of Aeschylus and Sophocles. Collectors such as Pierre Pithou (1539–1596), Pierre Daniel (c. 1530–1603), and Jacques Bongars (1554–1612) made important contributions to classical scholarship through the manuscripts they acquired. In particular, Daniel received manuscripts from the monastery at Fleury, which had been sacked by the Huguenots in 1562. To Pierre Pithou we owe important manuscripts of Juvenal and Persius (the famous Codex Pithoeanus from the monastery at Lorsch). Pierre Daniel discovered the longer version of Servius' commentary on Virgil (*Servius Danielis*). In the second half of the sixteenth century, French scholarship was dominated by the figure of Joseph Scaliger

(1540–1609), whose name is forever linked with his edition of Manilius (1579) and his studies on the chronological systems of the ancient world.

Vernacular literature in sixteenth-century France and England became increasingly indebted to the classics. The poets of the Pléiade school—Pierre de Ronsard (1524–1585), Joachim du Bellay (1525–1560), and Jean-Antoine de Baïf (1532–1589)—modeled their verse on the authors of the *Greek Anthology* and on Virgil, Ovid, and Horace. Tudor England witnessed important new translations into English: the translation by Arthur Golding (c. 1536–c. 1605) of Ovid's *Metamorphoses*, the translation by Henry Howard, Earl of Surrey (1517–1547), of Virgil, and the translations by Christopher Marlowe (1564–1593) of book 1 of Lucan's *Pharsalia* and parts of Ovid's *Amores*. The *Spanish Tragedy* (c. 1590), by Thomas Kyd (1558–1594), is strongly influenced by Seneca.

[*See also* Allegory; Antiquarianism; Books; Christianity; Classical Tradition; Collectors and Collections; Dante; Libraries; Monasticism; Paleography; *and* Philosophy, *subentry* Greek Philosophy in the Middle Ages and the Renaissance.]

BIBLIOGRAPHY

Berschin, Walter. *Greek Letters and the Latin Middle Ages from Jerome to Nicholas of Cusa*. Translated by J. C. Frakes. Washington, D.C.: Catholic University of America Press, 1988.

Bolgar, R. R. *The Classical Heritage and Its Beneficiaries*. Cambridge, U.K.: Cambridge University Press, 1954.

Clark, James G. *A Monastic Renaissance at St. Albans: Thomas Walsingham and His Circle, c. 1350–1440*. Oxford: Clarendon Press; New York: Oxford University Press, 2004.

Gaisser, Julia Haig. *Catullus and His Renaissance Readers*. Oxford: Clarendon Press; New York: Oxford University Press, 1993.

Gaisser, Julia Haig. *The Fortunes of Apuleius and the "Golden Ass": A Study in Transmission and Reception*. Princeton, N.J.: Princeton University Press, 2008.

Grafton, Anthony. *Joseph Scaliger: A Study in the History of Classical Scholarship*. 2 vols. Oxford: Clarendon Press; New York: Oxford University Press, 1983.

L'Engle, Susan, and Robert Gibbs. *Illuminating the Law: Legal Manuscripts in Cambridge Collections*. London: Harvey Miller, 2001.

Newton, Francis. *The Scriptorium and Library of Monte Cassino (1058–1105)*. Cambridge, U.K.: Cambridge University Press, 1999.

Pfeiffer, Rudolf. *History of Classical Scholarship from 1300 to 1850*. Oxford: Clarendon Press, 1976.

Rand, Edward Kennard. *Ovid and His Influence*. Boston: Marshall Jones, 1925.

Reynolds, L. D., ed. *Texts and Transmission: A Survey of the Latin Classics*. Oxford: Clarendon Press, 1983.

Reynolds, L. D., and N. G. Wilson. *Scribes and Scholars: A Guide to the Transmission of Greek and Latin Literature*. 3rd ed. Oxford: Clarendon Press, 1991.

Sabbadini, Remigio. *Le scoperte dei codici latini e greci ne' secoli XIV e XV*. Florence, Italy: G. C. Sansoni, 1967.

Sandys, John Edwin. *A History of Classical Scholarship*. 3 vols. Cambridge, U.K.: University Press, 1903–1908.

Smalley, Beryl. *English Friars and Antiquity in the Early Fourteenth Century*. Oxford: Blackwell, 1960.

Weiss, Roberto. *The Renaissance Discovery of Classical Antiquity*. Oxford and New York: Blackwell, 1969.

Wilson, N. G. *From Byzantium to Italy: Greek Studies in the Italian Renaissance*. Baltimore: London: Duckworth, 1992.

Witt, Ronald G. *In the Footsteps of the Ancients: The Origins of Humanism from Lovato to Bruni*. Leiden, The Netherlands, and Boston: Brill, 2000.

Ziolkowski, Jan M., and Michael C. Putnam. *The Virgilian Tradition: The First Fifteen Hundred Years*. New Haven, Conn.: Yale University Press, 2008.

Frank T. Coulson

Modern Classical Scholarship

Modern classical scholarship is generally considered to have begun in the Renaissance. Since that time the subject has been pursued in a variety of different ways in different times and places, so that its history in one country may be notably different from that in another. For centuries classical scholarship was an almost exclusively European preoccupation, but since the nineteenth century American scholarship has also been significant, and since the twentieth century the same can be said for that of Australia, New Zealand, South Africa, Israel, and Japan. The histories of classical scholarship in various countries are manifest today in the different interests, orientations, and knowledge of classical scholars in different places. But there has also been close interaction between the different groups, and at different periods the field has been dominated by different elements. Each such period has left its traces on the ways classical scholars think and write in the twenty-first century.

The history of modern classical scholarship is traditionally divided into four periods. The first ran from the early fourteenth to the early sixteenth century and was dominated by Italian humanist scholarship, the second lasted until the late seventeenth century and witnessed the flowering of the French *polyhistors*, the third ran to the end of the eighteenth century and was chiefly characterized by English and Dutch critical scholarship, and the fourth was the great age of German *Altertumswissenschaft* in the nineteenth and early twentieth centuries. To these one could now add a fifth period, starting from World War II, dominated by Anglo-American work, and characterized by division of the discipline into smaller specialized fields.

Italian Humanist Scholarship. At the start of the fourteenth century competence in Latin was widespread in western Europe, but the Greek language was almost completely unknown; of the body of classical literature we possess today, much of the Roman and nearly all the Greek literature appeared to have been lost. To the scholars of the Italian Renaissance we owe the rediscovery of almost all the classical literature that has been recovered since the Middle Ages, as well as the reintroduction of Greek to the Western scholarly world. This process is usually considered to have begun with Petrarch (Francesco Petrarca, 1304–1374), who as a boy read classical Latin literature in secret when he was supposed to be studying law; his father caught him and burned most of his books, but Petrarch was undeterred and went on to amass one of the greatest collections of classical literature of his day. In an age before printing, he sought eagerly for surviving copies of literary works unknown in his day, and when he found them he copied the manuscripts out by hand. He was responsible for the discovery of most of Cicero's letters and several of his speeches, as well as for firing the enthusiasm of other scholars, who made many more discoveries.

Like the other scholars of his day, Petrarch was also an author in his own right, producing significant works of both prose and poetry; indeed, one of the main reasons that the Renaissance scholars wanted to read the great works of classical Latin literature was to imitate them, both in language and in content. For this reason they are often compared to the Alexandrian scholar-poets who dominated the first great period of classical scholarship in antiquity. Petrarch's Latin prose was a conscious imitation of Cicero's, and this choice of Cicero as the model of Latin style has largely endured to the present day.

Petrarch longed to know Greek and to read Homer and Plato, of which there were not even complete Latin translations. He acquired Greek texts of both authors but never managed to learn to read them, despite repeated attempts. In the absence of textbooks, dictionaries, and grammars, the only way to learn Greek was to be taught by someone who knew the language, and at that period only Greeks, who were rare in the West, had such knowledge.

But the scholarly landscape changed rapidly during the Italian Renaissance. Increased contact with Greece resulted in the reestablishment in the West of knowledge of Greek, as well as in the rediscovery (at least from a Western perspective) of many key works of Greek literature. Greek works were rapidly translated into Latin for those unable to read them in the original, and systematic searches of monastery libraries resulted in the discovery of many previously unknown Latin texts, greatly increasing the amount of classical literature available. The foundation of academies in several Italian cities and of major libraries made lectures and texts widely available, and in the later fifteenth century the introduction of printing made possible the rapid dissemination of classical literature, translations, and scholarly works.

Among the important names that follow Petrarch's in the history of Renaissance classical scholarship are Giovanni Boccaccio (1313–1375), the first of the humanists to learn Greek, who discovered a number of important works of Latin poetry but is more famous today as the author of the *Decameron*; Leonardo Bruni (1370?–1444), the first translator of many works of Greek literature; Poggio Bracciolini (1380–1459), who rediscovered many important works, including a number of Cicero's speeches; and Lorenzo Valla (1407–1457), a bitter enemy of Poggio's who made great strides in the linguistic study of Classical Latin and its use for textual criticism, not least when he proved that the "Donation of Constantine," on which the papacy's claim to secular power was based, was an eighth-century forgery. The last of the great Italian humanist scholars was Politian (Angelo Ambrogini Poliziano, 1454–1494), a great scholar of Greek who learned the language as a child and could compose Greek verses by the age of sixteen. Aldus Manutius (1449–1515) published the first printed editions of countless Greek works and founded a publishing and printing dynasty that continued to render valuable service to scholarship until the end of the sixteenth century.

The greatest scholar of this period, however, was not Italian: Desiderius Erasmus (1466–1536) came from the Netherlands, though he also lived in France, England, Italy, Germany, and Switzerland. Erasmus' name is linked today with the Erasmian pronunciation of Latin and Greek, because he was a powerful advocate for a pronunciation approximating the ancient one. In Erasmus' day most scholars pronounced Greek like modern Greek, because contemporary Greeks had passed their pronunciation on to Western Renaissance scholars along with their language; that we now use an approximation of the ancient pronunciation is thanks in large part to Erasmus' arguments. Latin posed different problems because Renaissance scholars pronounced Latin as they pronounced their own languages, with the result that Latin speakers from different countries might be mutually unintelligible. Erasmus' proofs that these national pronunciations had no ancient authority did not bring about immediate change, but eventually scholars in many countries switched to a pronunciation closer to the ancient one. This change met with stiff opposition in many places, including England, and in some countries

was never implemented: in Italy, for example—and therefore in Roman Catholic circles throughout much of the world—Latin is still pronounced according to a pre-Erasmian system (known in English-speaking countries as the "ecclesiastical pronunciation"). In Britain, Latin pronunciation had to be readjusted for a second time in the late nineteenth century, owing to changes in the pronunciation of English since Erasmus' day, but occasionally one can still hear traces of the older English pronunciation of Latin, which is as different from the ecclesiastical pronunciation as it is from the ancient one.

Erasmus' most important work, however, was not the dialogue on pronunciation but his edition of the Greek New Testament, which was both praised and attacked by Catholics and Protestants alike and which ultimately served as the basis for Martin Luther's German translation. Erasmus also edited numerous classical and early Christian texts and produced important discussions of them and their use; for example, his dialogue *Ciceronianus* ridicules the convention of using only strictly Ciceronian Latin and sparked a violent controversy on that subject.

The French Polyhistors. Erasmus and his contemporaries went to Paris when they wanted to learn Greek properly, for the center of expertise in Greek scholarship was shifting from Italy to France at the end of the fifteenth century, and for the next two centuries it remained there. Important figures in this period include Guillaume Budé (1468–1540)—after whom the Budé editions of classical literature are named—who did key work on Roman law, numismatics, and Greek, and who was instrumental in the foundation of the Collège de France, and Jean Dorat (Auratus, 1508–1588), a prolific poet who translated and interpreted most of the known Greek poetic corpus. The scholar-printers Robertus Stephanus (Robert Estienne or Étienne, 1503–1559) and his son Henricus (Henri Estienne or Étienne, 1531–1598) produced editions of classical texts that remained definitive for centuries; the status of some of them was such that when better editions finally appeared in the nineteenth century, the page numbers of the Stephanus edition were reproduced in the margins, and even today we refer to passages in Plato by their Stephanus numbers. The elder Stephanus is also responsible for the modern numeration of the verses in the New Testament and for the great Latin dictionary entitled *Latinae Linguae Thesaurus*, which remained the standard dictionary for more than two centuries; the younger Stephanus produced an enormous Greek dictionary entitled *Thesaurus Graecae Linguae*, which in some respects has still not been superseded.

Perhaps the greatest figure of this period was Joseph Justus Scaliger (1540–1609), whose achievements include being the first scholar of modern times to understand archaic (that is, pre-Classical) Latin. Scaliger also had the necessary knowledge of ancient Oriental languages to enable him to sort out the various ancient chronological systems and indicate how they related to one another, work that is fundamental to any understanding of ancient history. Isaac Casaubon (1559–1614) produced many important commentaries, including ones on difficult authors like the late Greek rhetorician Athenaeus. Charles Du Cange (1610–1688) compiled huge dictionaries of medieval Latin and Greek that are still unsurpassed and in regular use today. The overall trend of seventeenth-century classical scholarship, however, was toward uncritical collections of descriptions of antiquities or the notes of earlier scholars on literary works.

One memorable legacy from the seventeenth century was produced by the Dutch scholar Heinrich Christian von Hennin, who in 1684 propounded an erroneous theory that ancient Greek had been pronounced, not with accents on the syllables marked in manuscripts with accent marks (the antiquity of these marks was unknown until the discovery of accented papyri long after his day), but following the same system of accentuation as Latin. Hennin's theory was at first widely accepted, and pupils began to learn Greek with his accentuation. But then his theory was discredited, and Greek pronunciation in most of Europe reverted to the Byzantine system of accentuation—that is, placing a stress on the syllable that in antiquity would have received a pitch accent. Only in England, the Netherlands, and their colonies did the Henninian pronunciation persist through the force of tradition, leading to different pronunciations of Greek in different countries. In the nineteenth century, American usage was corrected under German influence, but English and Dutch classicists still pronounce Greek with Latin stresses and in consequence have much more difficulty learning the placement of the accent marks than French, German, or American classicists do.

English and Dutch Critical Scholarship. At the end of the seventeenth century, scholarship received a new impetus from the work of Richard Bentley (1662–1742), who is often considered the greatest English classicist. Bentley won his fame by proving that the Epistles of Phalaris had not been written by the sixth century BCE tyrant of that name but came from the early Christian period; this achievement may not seem spectacular nowadays, when few people have ever heard of the Epistles of Phalaris, but in Bentley's time, when they were celebrated as some of the best productions of ancient literature, the effect of his argument was shattering. His argument sparked a furious debate that continued for decades; the extent to which Bentley was ahead of his time can be seen from the fact that discussion about the letters' authenticity could continue after Bentley had pointed out both that they contained gross historical anachronisms (such as mentioning Callimachus and other authors who lived centuries after Phalaris) and that they were composed in late Atticizing Greek rather than in either Classical Attic or the Doric that Phalaris would have used. Among Bentley's many other contributions the discovery of the letter digamma stands out: Bentley was the first to realize that certain anomalies in Homeric meter were due to the presence of a consonant *w* that had been pronounced earlier in the history of Greek but had disappeared by the time the *Iliad* was written down. Bentley made great advances in the study of Horace, Latin and Greek meters, and textual criticism, though in this last area he relied more on his own genius and thorough knowledge of the ancient languages than on a scientific study of the manuscript tradition, with the result that some of his work represents an improvement on, rather than a restoration of, the original writings of the ancients.

Other notable English scholars followed Bentley. Edward Gibbon (1737–1794) produced the monumental *Decline and Fall of the Roman Empire*, which remains an important work of ancient history; its status today as a readily available cheap paperback makes it unique among works of eighteenth-century classical scholarship. Richard Porson (1759–1808) is known for his work on Greek meter (including "Porson's Law") and for proving the spuriousness of a notoriously contested verse in the First Epistle of John 5:7. In his age and that of his immediate followers Peter Elmsley (1773–1825), Peter Paul Dobree (1782–1825), and Charles James Blomfield (1786–1857), British scholarship stood out particularly for the exact study of Attic grammar and the texts of the tragedians. Thomas Gaisford (1779–1855) produced many useful editions of Greek texts, including one of the *Etymologicum Magnum* that is still the standard text; he also persuaded Oxford's Clarendon Press to publish many important new editions of classical texts.

German *Altertumswissenschaft* and Its Influence. By Gaisford's day, however, scholarship had moved into a period dominated by German speakers, and most of the texts that his publishing program produced were edited by Germans. Classical scholarship in Germany had gotten off to a slow start, but there are some notable names before the nineteenth century. Johann Joachim Winckelmann (1717–1768), an influential and inspiring teacher, produced the all-encompassing *Geschichte der Kunst des Alterthums* (History of Ancient Art) that broke new ground by treating ancient "art" (in the broadest sense, including poetry) in the context of the historical development of a range of Mediterranean cultures. The great Homer and Virgil editions of Christian Gottlob Heyne (1729–1812) were landmarks. Heyne's pupil Friedrich August Wolf (1759–1824) was the first to describe his work as *Altertumswissenschaft*, literally the "science of antiquity." This type of classical scholarship became the glory of nineteenth-century Germany; it focused on ancient history and brought an extensive and fully integrated knowledge of languages, literatures, art, numismatics, and other disciplines to bear on the understanding and explanation of ancient culture.

Legend has it that Wolf inaugurated a new era of study at the age of eighteen, when on his arrival at university he insisted on registering to study philology rather than theology or one of the other subjects normally offered; the story appears to have been exaggerated, in that Wolf was not absolutely the first person to register for this course of study, but it shows the way he was regarded by succeeding generations of German classicists. Outside Germany, Wolf is today best remembered for his *Prolegomena ad Homerum*, the work that sparked the modern controversy on the Homeric Question that has raged ever since; the *Prolegomena* was inspired in part by the rediscovery of the A scholia to the *Iliad* and by the Alexandrian scholarship that these scholia contained. Wolf was also instrumental in developing the seminar system of advanced teaching that was used to great effect in German universities and, later, in many other parts of the world, where it became the core of modern graduate study.

Wolf's pupils were numerous and influential, and from his time onward German-speaking classical scholars led the field. Important figures of the early nineteenth century include Gottfried Hermann (1772–1848) and August Boeckh or Böckh (1785–1867), the first of whom concentrated on linguistic and the second on historical scholarship; there was considerable rivalry between these two views of the field, ultimately resolved in the position that a good classicist needs to know everything. Immanuel Bekker (1785–1871) collated more than four hundred manuscripts and produced more than sixty volumes of good editions of Greek texts, including some not yet superseded. Karl Lachmann (1793–1851) is credited with developing the modern science of textual criticism, in which the relationship of extant and lost manuscripts to one another is worked out as part of reconstructing the history of the text. A little later came the brothers Wilhelm and Ludwig Dindorf (1802–1883 and 1805–1871), who produced innumerable editions of ancient texts; Wilhelm's output was far larger than Ludwig's, but Ludwig was perhaps the sharper scholar. The standard of Dindorf editions is variable, but because they were the first proper editions of many texts, they were widely disseminated and in many cases remain the most easily available texts even where they have been superseded by better work; in some cases the Dindorf editions have still not been superseded. Theodor Bergk (1812–1881) produced major editions of the lyric poets and Pindar and a monumental four-volume history of Greek literature, full of independent thinking and valuable insights. Eduard Zeller (1814–1908) did important work on ancient philosophy. August Nauck (1822–1892), among whose works was an excellent edition of the Greek tragic fragments, moved to Saint Petersburg and was highly influential in the development of classical scholarship in eastern Europe. Hermann Diels (1848–1922) produced important work on Greek philosophy, especially the Presocratics; Eduard Meyer (1855–1930) did key work in ancient history; and Jacob Wackernagel (1853–1938) made important contributions to the understanding of the ancient languages and their literatures.

The giants of German scholarship were Theodor Mommsen and Ulrich von Wilamowitz-Moellendorff. Mommsen (1817–1903) is today considered a Roman historian, but in keeping with the spirit of his times his interests were much wider than would now be encompassed in that designation. He edited a number of Latin texts, did important linguistic work on Oscan and Italic dialects, and produced seminal works on epigraphy, numismatics, and Roman law, as well as a *Römische Geschichte* (History of Rome) that has endured like that of Gibbon; he also directed the creation of the *Corpus Inscriptionum Latinarum*, a gigantic work that consolidates the body of Latin stone and metal inscriptions and that is vital to our understanding of every aspect of Roman life and history, and he made a large contribution to the *Monumenta Germaniae Historica* series. Mommsen received the Nobel Prize in Literature in 1902. His pupil and son-in-law Wilamowitz (1848–1931) is often considered the greatest classical scholar ever,

owing to his phenomenal output, his ability to break down the barriers between disciplines and combine literary and historical perspectives, his constant awareness of the processes of transmission and of what allowances to make for them in assessing evidence, and his understanding of what questions to ask. Wilamowitz produced important editions and commentaries on Greek tragedies and comedies, as well as major works on Homer, Hellenistic poetry, Plato, Aristotle, early lyric poetry, Greek religion, and Greek meter. He was also instrumental in the editorial work for *Inscriptiones Graecae*, the Greek equivalent of Mommsen's Latin epigraphic corpus, and had exceptional influence as a teacher.

Although Germany was the acknowledged leader during this period, important work was also done in other countries. English classical scholarship, which suffered a period of decline after 1825, revived under German influence in the latter part of the nineteenth century. George Grote (1794–1871) produced a massive and fundamentally important history of Greece, as well as works on Plato and Aristotle. Henry George Liddell (1811–1898) and Robert Scott (1811–1887) compiled the great Greek lexicon that (in repeatedly updated versions) remains the main Greek dictionary of the English-speaking world; like much other English-language scholarship of this period, the lexicon was originally based on a German work by Franz Passow (1786–1833). Benjamin Jowett (1817–1893) worked on Plato, Thucydides, and Aristotle, and though the quality of his contributions is disputed, their impact was undoubtedly significant. Richard Claverhouse Jebb (1841–1905) produced magnificent editions and commentaries on Sophocles and other authors that are still widely used.

A. E. Housman (1859–1936) was exceptional among English scholars of this period in overtly rejecting German *Altertumswissenschaft*—though much of his work nevertheless presupposes acceptance of German ideas—and following in the tradition of purely textual scholarship established by Bentley; Housman did much important work, including editions of Manilius, Juvenal, and Lucan, but is better known for his own poetry. Gilbert

Murray (1866–1957) was born in Australia but worked in Britain, where he produced immensely popular translations and interpretations of Greek tragedies and played a key role in bringing understanding and enjoyment of the classical world to people outside the university setting. Poles apart from Murray in approach, John Dewar Denniston (1887–1949) did vital work, not least his enduring book on Greek particles.

An excellent school tradition of training in classics developed in nineteenth-century England, with the result that large numbers of children learned Latin and Greek at an early age and arrived at university with an excellent command of both languages; many entering undergraduates could not only read Latin and Greek easily but could write both prose and verse fluently. In the nineteenth century the division between schoolteachers and university lecturers was not as fixed as it is today, and some notable classicists worked at both levels. Some of the didactic works produced as part of this flowering of early training are still in use today: these include the *Latin Prose Composition* of Thomas Kerchever Arnold (1800–1853, not to be confused with his contemporary Thomas Arnold the headmaster of Rugby), now known as "Bradley's Arnold" owing to later revisions.

Benjamin Hall Kennedy (1804–1889), who taught at Harrow and Shrewsbury schools before becoming Regius Professor of Greek at Cambridge, is best known today for his *Latin Primer*. This work, originally entitled the *Public School Latin Primer*, was specifically designed to be a standard Latin grammar for use in select schools across England and to replace the institution-specific Latin grammars that establishments like Eton had previously produced. It therefore had tremendous influence; for example, the oft-observed fact that the order of the Latin and Greek noun cases used in Britain is different from that used in other European countries and in America can be traced to Kennedy. The order of the cases given by the ancient grammarians has been passed down through the grammatical tradition and is still used in most countries, but with the discovery of Sanskrit, whose cases had traditionally been presented in an order that groups similar endings together, it occurred to a number of scholars that the principles of the Sanskrit order would have pedagogical advantages if applied to Latin and Greek. In most countries this idea was not acted on with any long-term effect, but the authority invested in Kennedy's primer meant that when he adopted the innovation of a changed case order students all over England immediately learned the new order. To this day new Latin and Greek textbooks intended for use in Britain adhere to it.

The American education system lagged behind European ones for centuries after the foundation of the first universities there in the seventeenth and eighteenth centuries, and Wilamowitz was only moderately unjust when he turned down a proposed transatlantic exchange program on the grounds that Harvard had nothing to offer Berlin. Nevertheless there were some precursors to the remarkable flowering of American classical studies in the twentieth century. These include the Greek-born Evangelinus Apostolides Sophocles (1807–1883), whose *Greek Lexicon of the Roman and Byzantine Periods* is still the standard reference work in this area. Charlton Thomas Lewis (1834–1904) and Charles Lancaster Short (1821–1886) produced in New York the great Latin dictionary that bears their name; it was based on an earlier dictionary by another American, E. A. Andrews (1787–1858), though Andrews in turn had based his work on a German abridgment of the *Totius Latinitatis Lexicon* of Egidio Forcellini (1688–1768). Basil Lanneau Gildersleeve (1831–1924), an eloquent exponent of the Southern cause who fought for the South in the Civil War, did important work on Pindar as well as writing the Latin grammar that bears his name; many consider him the greatest American classicist. His northern counterpart William Watson Goodwin (1831–1912), who like Gildersleeve had a doctorate from Göttingen, has left us a Greek grammar, an unsurpassed work on the moods and tenses of the Greek verb, and a host of texts and commentaries on Greek authors. Herbert Weir Smyth (1857–1937) was the author of another important grammar, as well as works on Greek dialects, Aeschylus, and other authors, while Milman Parry (1902–1935) turned the study of Homer in a new direction by drawing attention to the relevance of modern orally composed epics for understanding the ancient ones.

Among the notable trends of this time, on both sides of the Atlantic, was the foundation of professional societies, such as the American Philological Association (1869), the Society for the Promotion of Hellenic Studies (1879), and the Classical Association (1903). Another was the creation of specialist scholarly journals such as the *Journal of Hellenic Studies* (1880), the *American Journal of Philology* (1880), the *Classical Review* (1887), the *Classical Journal* (1905), *Classical Philology* (1906), *Classical Quarterly* (1907), and *Classical Weekly* (1907); the last of these rather significantly changed its name to *Classical World* in 1957. The series of Oxford Classical Texts began in 1898, and the Loeb Classical Library began in 1912. The *Thesaurus Linguae Latinae* project started in 1900, became a fully international enterprise in 1949, and will clearly require a substantial portion of the twenty-first century to complete. The *Realencyclopädie der classischen Altertumswissenschaft*, a revision of a six-volume work produced by August Pauly in 1839–1852, was started by Georg Wissowa and is commonly known as the *RE* or Pauly-Wissowa; the first volume appeared in 1894 and the last in 1980.

Another feature of this period was the exponential development of technical subdisciplines of classics, most notably archaeology, papyrology, and Indo-European linguistics. (Epigraphy, the study of inscriptions, remained more a part of mainstream classics, as signaled by the work done by Mommsen and Wilamowitz on the epigraphic corpora.) All these fields had earlier antecedents: the excavations of Pompeii and Herculaneum in the eighteenth century had revealed a library of charred papyrus rolls, some of which were legible, and Sir William Jones (1746–1794), an Englishman working in India, had realized the historical relationship of Sanskrit, Greek, and Latin and so laid the groundwork for the study of Indo-European linguistics.

But it was in the late nineteenth and early twentieth centuries that all three of these disciplines really developed into professional specialties. Heinrich Schliemann (1822–1890) may not have been a very good archaeologist even by the standards of his own time, but he attracted tremendous international attention to the subject, and his excavations of Troy and Mycenae were of great importance both directly, for the advancement of knowledge of antiquity, and indirectly, for the development of scientific archaeology. His work and that of Arthur Evans uncovered the existence of the Mycenaean and Minoan civilizations and so opened a new perspective on Aegean prehistory. Excavations in Egypt led to the discovery of large numbers of papyri, both literary texts—which provided new readings, new insight into the history of texts, and in some cases entire works of literature that had been lost for centuries—and documents. Though the discoveries of literary texts caused more excitement initially, the documentary texts have over time had a greater effect because they now amount to a corpus of many thousands of letters, petitions, tax forms, census returns, receipts, and similar texts; this corpus has proven invaluable in broadening our understanding of many aspects of ancient life, as well as in revolutionizing understanding of the evolution of the post-Classical Greek language. Perhaps the best known of the pioneer papyrologists are Bernard Pyne Grenfell (1869–1926) and Arthur Surridge Hunt (1871–1934), who dug up thousands of papyri in Egypt and in 1898 produced the first in the long series of Oxyrhynchus Papyri volumes that continue to appear regularly today.

Franz Bopp (1791–1867) founded the science of Indo-European linguistics and thus profoundly altered the study of Latin and Greek grammar and etymology, which until his day had largely continued in the tradition of the ancient grammarians. The realization that the extant Indo-European languages—including not only Latin, Greek, and Sanskrit but also English, German, Russian, Lithuanian, Irish, Persian, Armenian, and many other languages ancient and modern—are descended from a common ancestor that was spoken before the invention of writing and consequently is now lost made it possible to understand the irregularities of Latin and Greek in a historical context. In the second half of the nineteenth century the subject became more scientific and exact thanks to the work of Karl Brugmann (1849–1919) and others, and in the twentieth it was given new dimensions by the discovery that Hittite and Tocharian were also Indo-European. In the early twentieth century the study of modern linguistics developed out of these Indo-European studies; since then modern linguistics has in turn provided many insights that further understanding of the ancient languages and the way they were used in speech and in writing.

Since World War II. World War II marked a significant turning point in the history of classical scholarship. With the rise of the Nazis, scholarship outside Germany received a valuable stimulus from an exodus of German scholars, driven out of their homeland because of their Jewish background or political beliefs. Many of these refugees found academic positions abroad and so spread German scholarship to other countries, but the loss of them and other effects of the war sent scholarship in Germany itself into a decline. Eduard Fraenkel (1888–1970), a pupil of Wilamowitz, came to Oxford and introduced there the German seminar system as well as his immense learning; Fraenkel's work on Plautus, Aeschylus, and Horace was of key importance, but the role that he played in training a generation of English classical scholars in the German tradition was perhaps of even greater value. Other pupils of Wilamowitz who came to Britain include Felix Jacoby (1876–1959), editor of the definitive collection of fragments of Greek historians; Paul Maas (1880–1964), author of important works on meter, textual criticism, and Byzantine studies; and Rudolf Pfeiffer (1889–1979), who did vital work on Callimachus and on Alexandrian (and later) scholarship. Werner Jaeger (1888–1961), also a pupil of Wilamowitz and the successor to his chair, fled instead to the United States, where he worked primarily on ancient philosophy.

After the war America achieved new importance in classical scholarship, as in most other areas, and British work also flourished, resulting in the current period of Anglo-American domination: since World War II a majority of important work in the field has been published in English. The nature of the subject also shifted as it became increasingly divided into specialist subfields such as history, art, literature, and philosophy. Such specialization is the antithesis of the holistic view of *Altertumswissenschaft*, which is no longer viewed as an attainable goal—though it has left us the valuable legacy of a reminder that a broader understanding is desirable.

The second half of the twentieth century is often seen as a period of decline, for the prestige of the subject has diminished along with the number of students studying it, and the number of scholars employed to teach it, in both schools and universities around the world. The decline in the quantity and quality of classical training available in schools, in particular, has had an effect on scholarship at all levels, for it means that today's classical scholars usually began their study at a later age than did those who lived a century earlier, and in consequence we often know less, particularly less Latin and Greek.

At the same time this period has seen a number of exciting developments that have allowed considerable advances despite these handicaps. In 1952 the decipherment of Linear B by Michael Ventris (1922–1956) and John Chadwick (1920–1998) gave access to written documents in Greek from as early as the fourteenth century BCE, revolutionizing the study of both Aegean prehistory and the Greek language. Classics has also profited considerably from developments in other fields, such as the improved knowledge of ancient Near Eastern languages, literatures, and cultures that has led to greater awareness of Near Eastern influences on the Greeks. New technologies, such as carbon-14 dating and imaging techniques, have greatly increased the knowledge that it is possible to gain from ancient artifacts and documents. Huge corpora of ancient texts are now available online, easily searchable from anywhere in the world. Thus classical scholarship continues to advance, to become more sophisticated, to fill in areas where knowledge was previously sketchy, and generally to edge closer to the ideal of complete and correct understanding of the ancient world.

[*See also* Afrocentrism; Antiquarianism; Cambridge Ritualists; Dilettanti, Society of; Greek, *subentry* The Pronunciation of Ancient Greek; Interstate Relations; Latin, *subentry* The Pronunciation of Latin; Linguistic Theory; Paleography; Papyrology; Textual Criticism; *and entries on the following figures*: Droysen, J. G.; Finley, M. I.; Fustel de Coulanges, Numa-Denys; Gibbon, Edward; Grote, George; Housman, A. E.; Momigliano, A. D.; Mommsen, Theodor; Murray, Gilbert; Rostovtzeff, M. I.; Schliemann, Heinrich; Syme, Ronald; Wilamowitz-Moellendorff, Ulrich von; *and* Winckelmann, Johann Joachim.]

BIBLIOGRAPHY

Allen, W. Sidney. "The Pronuncation of Greek in England" and "The Oral Accentuation of Greek." In his *Vox Graeca*, 3rd ed., pp. 140–149 and 149–161. Cambridge, U.K.: Cambridge University Press, 1987.

Allen, W. Sidney. "The Pronunciation of Latin in England." In his *Vox Latina*, 2nd ed., pp. 102–110. Cambridge, U.K.: Cambridge University Press, 1978.

Allen, W. Sidney, and C. O. Brink. "The Old Order and the New: A Case History." *Lingua* 50 (1980): 61–100.

Arrighetti, Graziano, ed. *La Filologia greca e latina nel secolo XX: Atti del congresso internazionale.* 3 vols. Pisa, Italy: Giardini, 1989.

Benario, Herbert W. "German-Speaking Scholars in the United States and Canada from the 1930s." *Klio* 83 (2001): 451–472.

Briggs, Ward W., ed. *Biographical Dictionary of North American Classicists.* Westport, Conn.: Greenwood Press, 1994.

Briggs, Ward W., and William M. Calder, eds. *Classical Scholarship: A Biographical Encyclopedia.* New York and London: Garland, 1990.

Brink, C. O. *English Classical Scholarship: Historical Reflections on Bentley, Porson, and Housman.* 2nd ed. Cambridge, U.K.: J. Clarke; New York: Oxford University Press, 1985.

Calder, William M., and Daniel J. Kramer. *An Introductory Bibliography to the History of Classical Scholarship: Chiefly in the XIXth and XXth Centuries.* Hildesheim, Germany: Olms, 1992.

Calder, William M., and R. Scott Smith. *A Supplementary Bibliography to the History of Classical Scholarship: Chiefly in the XIXth and XXth Centuries.* Bari, Italy: Dedalo, 2000.

Clarke, Martin L. *Classical Education in Britain, 1500–1900.* Cambridge, U.K.: Cambridge University Press, 1959.

Clarke, Martin L. *Greek Studies in England, 1700–1830.* Cambridge, U.K.: Cambridge University Press, 1945.

Jocelyn, H. D., ed. *Aspects of Nineteenth-Century British Classical Scholarship.* Liverpool Classical Papers 5. Liverpool, U.K.: Liverpool Classical Monthly, 1996.

Pfeiffer, Rudolf. *History of Classical Scholarship from 1300 to 1850.* Oxford: Clarendon Press, 1976.

Platnauer, Maurice, ed. *Fifty Years (and Twelve) of Classical Scholarship.* Oxford: Blackwell 1968.

Reynolds, L. D., and N. G. Wilson. *Scribes and Scholars: A Guide to the Transmission of Greek and Latin Literature.* 3rd ed. Oxford: Clarendon Press, 1991.

Sandys, John E. *A History of Classical Scholarship.* Vols. 2 and 3. 3rd ed. Cambridge, U.K.: Cambridge University Press, 1921.

Scott, Izora. *Controversies over the Imitation of Cicero as a Model for Style, and Some Phases of Their Influence on the Schools of the Renaissance.* New York: Teachers College, Columbia University, 1910. Reprint, Davis, Calif.: Hermagoras Press, 1991.

Stray, Christopher. *Classics Transformed: Schools, Universities, and Society in England, 1830–1960.* Oxford: Clarendon Press, 1998.

Stray, Christopher, ed. *Classics in 19th- and 20th-Century Cambridge: Curriculum, Culture, and Community.* Cambridge, U.K.: Cambridge Philological Society, 1999.

Stray, Christopher, ed. *Oxford Classics: Teaching and Learning, 1800–2000.* London: Duckworth, 2007.

Todd, Robert B., ed. *The Dictionary of British Classicists.* Bristol: Thoemmes Continuum, 2004.

Wilamowitz-Moellendorff, Ulrich von. *History of Classical Scholarship.* Translated by Alan Harris; edited by Hugh Lloyd-Jones. London: Duckworth, 1982.

Winterer, Caroline. *The Culture of Classicism: Ancient Greece and Rome in American Intellectual Life, 1780–1910.* Baltimore: Johns Hopkins University Press, 2002.

Eleanor Dickey

History of the Study of Ancient Art and Architecture

The disciplines of art history, architectural history, and classical archaeology all contribute to the study of classical art and architecture. The field covers prehistory through late antiquity and includes the interaction of the core cultures of Greece and Rome with civilizations in Europe, Africa, and the Near and Far East. It analyzes and interprets not only architecture, sculpture, and painting—the media granted "major" status in Western culture—but also categories of decorative and applied arts such as ceramics, coins, gems, textiles, mosaics, and furniture. Its key concepts, practices, and institutions derive from ancient models. Of particular importance is the diverse body of ancient texts, loosely called the literary tradition, that offers information about individual works and their makers, as well as theory, criticism, and historical development.

Although antiquity had no concept matching the modern notion of "art," fine arts and architecture were considered part of the inventory of *technai*, the arts of civilization, and were understood through two interpretive paradigms: one paradigm stressed patterns of origins, rise, and decline, and the other paradigm stressed progress accomplished through successive individual achievements. These ostensibly historical accounts displayed a critical bias in favor of the attainments of the fifth and fourth centuries BCE that has only recently been questioned by historians. Ancient technical, critical, and scholarly literature now survives mostly in the form of cited titles, quotations, and attributed information in texts such as the ten books on architecture by the practicing architect Vitruvius (late first century BCE), the encyclopedic *Natural History* of Pliny the Elder (23/4–79 CE), and Pausanias' guidebook to Greece (later second century CE). The nearly exclusive focus on Greece in this material, which reflects Rome's uneasy stewardship of the monuments and intellectual traditions of Greek culture, has decisively shaped post-antique scholarship.

During late antiquity and the Middle Ages, ancient buildings and works of art in both the Latin West and the Byzantine East were variously destroyed, ignored, collected, imitated, or adapted for use in new cultural circumstances; contemporary texts shed light on the processes of engagement with the remains of the classical past. In the twelfth and thirteenth centuries in the West, an emerging humanist interest in antique culture extended to art and architecture, as shown by guidebooks like the *Mirabilia urbis Romae* (Marvels of the City of Rome,

c. 1140) that offered unevenly accurate commentary. These works were gradually superseded in the years of Renaissance humanism, when travel, collecting, and antiquarian research, much of it undertaken through learned academies inspired by ancient models, began to extend the corpus of extant material and to organize it on the basis of the ancient literary tradition, which had survived unevenly but was now increasingly available in manuscript and, ultimately, printed editions. This learning, linked to civic ideology, was centered largely in Italy and was based on the conviction that the present, through imitating antiquity, could surpass antiquity's cultural achievements. This conviction is clear in works like those of the Italian artist Leon Battista Alberti (1404?–1472): *De pictura* (*On Painting*, 1435), *De statua* (*On Sculpture*, 1464), and *De re aedificatoria* (*On Architecture*; written earlier but fully published in 1485). Their mixture of description and prescription likewise characterizes the historical and critical account of ancient art and architecture that introduces *Le vite de' più eccellenti pittori, scultori, ed architettori* (*Lives of the Most Excellent Painters, Sculptors, and Architects*, 1550; 2nd ed., 1568), by Giorgio Vasari (1511–1574), a work that follows the ancient schema of rise and decline.

Seventeenth and Eighteenth Centuries. The cultural prestige of ancient art and architecture promoted by humanism assured their position as models for current practice and influenced the forms of their study throughout Western Europe. The near institutionalization of educational travel in the form of the grand tour; the collection of sculpture, gems, coins, and decorative arts; the practices of restoration and cast making; the proliferation of illustrated accounts of travel, iconographic studies, and corpora of monuments; and the continuing foundation of academies for both artistic education and the pursuit of scientific and humanistic studies all served to extend knowledge of the monuments and promote a body of historical and antiquarian scholarship in vigorous dialogue with contemporary theory and practice. The ancient literary tradition retained its scholarly and critical authority, as demonstrated by works like *De pictura* *veterum* (1637; English trans., *The Painting of the Ancients*, 1638) and the *Catalogus architectorum, mechanicorum . . .* (1694; English trans., *A Lexicon of Artists and Their Works*, 1987), by the Huguenot scholar Franciscus Junius the Younger (c. 1598–1677; active in Holland and England), which drew primarily from the ancient texts to provide historical and encyclopedic treatments of classical art and architecture.

During the eighteenth century the patronage of European royalty and nobility, increasing access to private collections of antiquities, and the emergence of public museums (e.g., the British Museum, opened 1759) fostered the study of ancient art and architecture. Some of the most influential research was undertaken in ecclesiastical circles; for example, the Benedictine monk Bernard de Montfaucon (1655–1741) published an authoritative survey of antiquities relating to the religion and daily life of the ancient world (*L'antiquité expliquée et représentée en figures*, 1719, 1724; English trans., *Antiquity Explained, and Represented in Sculptures*, 1721–1722; Supplement, 1725). Whereas papal collections and patronage had established Rome as the center of antiquarian research, the Bourbons' sponsorship of systematic excavations at Herculaneum and Pompeii beginning in the 1740s initiated a new era in the recovery of antiquities and their contexts. The work significantly expanded the corpus not only of extant sculpture but also of painting, heretofore poorly represented. Similarly, collections like those of the British diplomat William Hamilton (1730–1803) helped establish Greek painted vases as a corpus available for study and imitation.

The supremacy of classical art and architecture as cultural models, expressed in the emergence of neoclassicism, intensified the symbiosis of antiquarian scholarship and contemporary criticism. The most influential eighteenth-century scholar of classical antiquities, the German Johann Joachim Winckelmann (1717–1768), indeed called for cultural renewal through the imitation of ancient Greece. Like the work of contemporary antiquarians whose studies reflected the consciously broad scope of Enlightenment scholarship, Winckelmann's *Geschichte der Kunst des Alterthums* (1764; English trans., *History of Ancient Art*, 1849) included the art of Egypt, Phoenicia, and Etruria; his highly judgmental and prescriptive history of artistic style followed the ancient schema of rise and decline and the critical standards established by the textual tradition.

The supremacy of Greek art was disputed, however, by champions of Roman superiority like the Italian artist and architect Giovanni Battista Piranesi (1720–1778). The acknowledged problem of limited knowledge of actual Greek monuments began to be remedied by expeditions to Greece and Asia Minor that yielded influential works like *The Antiquities of Athens* (1762–1816), by the painters and architects James Stuart (1713–1788) and Nicholas Revett (1720–1804), published with support from the Society of Dilettanti, a group founded in London in 1734. Often intended to provide models for contemporary architecture, such works also furnished important material for scholarship.

Nineteenth and Twentieth Centuries. In the years following the French Revolution of 1789, changes in the structure of the European, especially German, universities and in the conception of academic disciplines fostered professionalism among scholars of antiquity. The rise of Romanticism and a succession of historicizing styles challenged the supremacy of classical models and began to distance research from criticism and practice in the arts. The strength of the academic tradition of architectural training was maintained through the century, however, and acquisitions like the sculptures from the temple of Aphaea on Aegina (1812; now Munich, Glyptothek) and the Parthenon (1816; British Museum) continued to excite enthusiasm.

After Greece became an independent state in 1832, excavations were undertaken by both Greek and foreign archaeologists; elsewhere, too, large-scale projects were managed by national antiquities authorities and foreign research institutes established under private and governmental sponsorship. Such work, extensively reported in journals and monographs, greatly expanded the corpus of buildings and works of art and fostered a tendency toward specialization. Emphasis was placed on organizing this material by establishing typologies and chronologies, debating questions like the use of color in sculpture and architecture, and tracing origins and development. Research on classical architecture continued to attempt both to recover ancient theory, principles of design, and techniques through detailed measurements of individual buildings and also to trace and explain the evolution of forms and types. *The Architecture of Ancient Greece: An Account of Its Historic Development* (1927; 3rd ed., 1950), by the American architectural historian William Bell Dinsmoor (1886–1973), which functioned as an authoritative handbook, still adhered to the ancient schema of rise and decline.

The study of Roman architecture followed different lines, recognizing the originality and power of Roman technical achievements and the dynamism of regional developments throughout Rome's empire. In the study of art, texts retained a dominant position; iconographic analysis, for instance, proceeded from the assumption that images reflected texts, and efforts to match extant painting and statuary with works named in the literary tradition continued. The attempt to recover the appearance of Greek "originals" through the analysis of Roman "copies" is associated particularly with Adolf Furtwängler (1853–1907), whose *Meisterwerke der griechischen Plastik* (1893; English trans., *Masterpieces of Greek Sculpture*, 1895) set the standard for scholarship focused on artistic personalities. The chronology and authorship of the corpus of painted Attic vases, a genre not well attested in the literary tradition, were authoritatively established by John Davidson Beazley (1885–1970), whose principles of connoisseurship were adopted for other fabrics. Furtwängler had recognized the importance of photography for stylistic analysis, and the medium was soon adopted for major projects publishing corpora of sculpture, vases, and other categories of artifacts that served as points of reference for scholarship.

The later nineteenth and twentieth centuries brought significant challenges to the paradigms established by the ancient literary tradition. Large-scale excavations at Troy (from 1870), Mycenae (from 1874), Knossos (from 1900), and other sites gave material dimension to the once legendary Bronze Age (c. 3000–1100 BCE), and the Kerameikos cemetery at Athens (from 1870) provided key evidence for art of the Protogeometric and Geometric periods (c. 1050–700 BCE). This work placed the study of early Greek art on a historical basis; similarly, the study of Orientalizing and Archaic art of the seventh and sixth centuries BCE began to approach questions of Eastern and Egyptian influence in terms of cultural interactions within a wide zone encompassing the western and eastern Mediterranean and the Near East. The study of Greek art of historical times expanded beyond an Athenian focus to include regional developments, and the valorization of Classical culture gave way to positive evaluations of Archaic and Hellenistic art.

The independence and value of Roman art were asserted by the Austrian art historians Franz Wickhoff (1853–1909) and Alois Riegl (1858–1905), preparing the way for new approaches to the corpus of painting, sculpture, and decorative arts that had long been regarded as mere imitations of Greek work. Research on the art of the Etruscans and other cultures of the Italian peninsula also contributed new perspectives on the formation of Roman art. The Italian archaeologist Ranuccio Bianchi Bandinelli (1900–1975) was influential in the study of Italic and Roman art, bringing a Marxist approach to analyzing links between the forms of art and its social function. Though traditional approaches to classical art and architecture continued, developments in other fields such as structuralist and poststructuralist thought, feminism, semiotics, critical theory, and visual culture strongly influenced research agendas and methodologies.

Twenty-first Century Practices and Prospects. Large- and small-scale excavations, including salvage projects, continue to expand the corpus of art and architecture even as uncontrolled recovery and illicit trade in antiquities remain problematic and intensive tourism and environmental degradation pose dangers to monuments. Increasing international pressure for the repatriation of works of art has encouraged museums to expand cooperative efforts like traveling exhibitions and exchange programs; the critique of traditional practices of collecting also reflects growing interest in cultural history, historiography, and the reception of classical antiquity. Contemporary concerns over globalization now help shape studies of cultural interactions such as trade, migration, and colonization. Scientific analyses are playing an ever greater role in identifying sources of raw material and understanding techniques of production, and they contribute substantially to both the study of ancient materials and their conservation.

Emerging technologies of digital imaging have had a significant effect on the recording and reconstruction of architecture and artifacts. Electronic publication of monographs, corpora, catalogs, periodicals, archives, and bibliographic tools has expanded greatly; although these resources have vastly increased access to scholarship and have made possible the continuous updating of information, the presentation of visual materials continues to pose challenges, and legitimate scholarship is sometimes hard-pressed to compete with the abundance of unreliable information available on the Internet.

[*See also* Antiquarianism; Archaeology, *subentry* Historical Overview; Architecture; Art Market; Dilettanti, Society of; Museums; Pompeii and Herculaneum; Sculptural Copies and Copying; *and* Vitruvius.]

BIBLIOGRAPHY

Brendel, Otto J. *Prolegomena to the Study of Roman Art.* New Haven, Conn.: Yale University Press, 1979. This analysis of the problem of defining Roman art and of the solutions attempted in the late nineteenth and twentieth centuries remains a fundamental contribution to the historiography of ancient art.

De Grummond, Nancy Thomson, ed. *An Encyclopedia of the History of Classical Archaeology.* 2 vols. Westport, Conn.: Greenwood Press, 1996.

Grossman, Janet Burnett, Jerry Podany, and Marion True, eds. *History of Restoration of Ancient Stone Sculptures.* Los Angeles: J. Paul Getty Museum, 2003. Essays on the theory, history, and practice of a significant aspect of the European reception of classical sculpture.

Haskell, Francis, and Nicholas Penny. *Taste and the Antique: The Lure of Classical Sculpture, 1500–1900.* New Haven, Conn.: Yale University Press, 1981. Provides an overview of European engagement with ancient art and individual discussions of significant works of sculpture.

Mattusch, Carol C., A. A. Donohue, and Amy Brauer, eds. *Common Ground: Archaeology, Art, Science, and the Humanities.* Oxford: Oxbow, 2006. Summaries of papers delivered at an international conference offer an overview of current interdisciplinary approaches to the material culture of classical antiquity, including art and architecture.

Pollitt, J. J. *The Ancient View of Greek Art: Criticism, History, and Terminology.* New Haven, Conn.: Yale University Press, 1974. A fundamental overview and analysis of the surviving ancient literary tradition on the arts; texts and translations provide the basis for discussions of individual terms in the ancient critical vocabulary.

Sichtermann, Hellmut. *Kulturgeschichte der klassischen Archäologie.* Munich: C. H. Beck, 1996. An overview of the study of classical art in Europe beginning in Roman times, with emphasis on German contributions in the eighteenth through twentieth centuries in their cultural and intellectual contexts.

A. A. Donohue

CLASSICAL TRADITION

[*This entry includes three subentries, on classical influences on Western art, music, and film and television.*]

Classical Influences on Western Art

Ancient art, literature, history, and culture never became irrelevant after the fall of the Roman Empire. Their memory and achievements survived in Constantinople, in the monastic libraries of Europe and England, and at the courts of a number of ambitious rulers. Charlemagne, aspiring around 800 CE to create what became the Holy Roman Empire, encouraged the production of classicizing manuscripts and ivory carvings. Rulers of the Macedonian dynasty in tenth-century Byzantium nurtured classical scholarship and the manufacture of artworks inspired by ancient models, from books to vases fashioned from hard stones. Frederick II Hohenstaufen, Holy Roman emperor and king of Sicily, sponsored a revival of classical culture and art in the first half of the thirteenth century, especially fostering the carving of gems, highly prized by the ancients. Elsewhere, too, much of medieval Christian art was based on ancient prototypes.

The idea of the golden age of Rome—and the political, social, and cultural gains to be attained through its return—motivated many rulers and intellectuals in the Middle Ages and later. Rome remained a crowning model well into the eighteenth century, when Europeans began to travel to Greece, study its monuments, and make a distinction between Greek and Roman art. But in each epoch Rome meant something different and was portrayed in different ways.

There were a number of renaissances before the fifteenth century, but the pace and consistency of engagement with antiquity increased dramatically at that time as artists began to emulate and creatively reinterpret classical models. The shift was deliberate. Medieval Europeans had seen antiquity as a natural extension of their own time. The fourteenth-century Italian poet Petrarch postulated a radical break between the glorious Roman era and the Dark Age in which he was condemned to live. Once Petrarch and his followers perceived a difference between themselves and the ancients, and decided that reviving that bygone culture would revitalize their own, they began to scrutinize classical arts with a new sense of purpose and commitment. Artists set out to imitate ancient works so as to learn from and surpass classical masters. In the succeeding centuries, artists looked not only at ancient prototypes but also at classicizing works of their more recent predecessors, and antiquity was refracted through its Renaissance, Baroque, Enlightenment, Romantic, and other reincarnations.

Each age created its own antiquity. In the Middle Ages and in the fifteenth century, antique subjects were often depicted in non-antique styles: in French and Netherlandish manuscripts, such as the Alexander romances, and in Netherlandish tapestries illustrating the Trojan War and other Greek and Roman stories, men and women in contemporary costumes and settings act out ancient histories. Eighteenth-century Europeans, imbued with Enlightenment ideals, favored dramatically staged depictions of heroic deeds of the Romans sacrificing themselves for the benefit of the fatherland. The rise of middle-class collectors in the nineteenth century, coupled with the birth of systematic archaeological excavations of classical sites, stimulated the production of paintings and sculptures of everyday life that seemed tangible and understandable to their viewers. The ways in which antiquity was understood and presented changed with the preoccupations of a given age. But from the fifteenth to the nineteenth century, interest in the classical past never waned, even as it formed just one of many intellectual and aesthetic currents. The classical past still remains a point of reference for us today. The following survey can examine only a few examples of the influence of Greek and Roman arts on those from the Renaissance to the present. The topic is vast and can be studied indefinitely in its many permutations.

Fifteenth Century. Artists such as Nicola Pisano (d. c. 1284), Giovanni Pisano (d. c. 1315), and Giotto (d. 1337) began to take inspiration from ancient art, and particularly Roman sarcophagi, well before the fifteenth century. Their efforts were unique in their day; only in the 1400s (the Italian *quattrocento*) did the engagement with ancient models become widespread. Filippo Brunelleschi and Donatello traveled from their native Florence to Rome to scrutinize ruined buildings and fragmentary statues so as to learn directly from the ancients. Returning home, they produced innovative works. At the church of San Lorenzo in Florence, Brunelleschi revived the Roman-style basilica with three aisles divided by elegant columns and crowned by a coffered ceiling. On the facade of the Ospedale degli Innocenti (Foundling Hospital, Florence) he re-created the ancient colonnaded portico. Brunelleschi employed a rigorous system of mathematical proportions, which constituted another kind of return to ancient principles. Seeking clarity and harmony, he kept to a minimum the decorative elements on his buildings and drew attention to the vocabulary of antique architecture—the columns, pilasters, and entablatures.

Donatello, meanwhile, imbibed the lessons of Roman sculpture. In casting the equestrian bronze portrait of the military commander Erasmo da Narni in Padua, he looked to the statues of Marcus Aurelius in Rome, the Regisole in Pavia, the four horses on the facade of San Marco in Venice, and portraits of statesmen on Roman coins. The result is an eloquent Renaissance re-creation of Roman *virtus*—the courage, steadfastness, and wisdom of a noble soldier.

Antiquity provided models not only for artists but for their patrons, who sought to ennoble themselves through comparison with Roman statesmen and intellectuals. When King Alfonso V of Aragon finally gained the throne of Naples after a twenty-year struggle, he celebrated his victory with a triumphal procession modeled on those staged by Roman generals; then he erected a marble arch (1443) at the entrance to his Castel Nuovo to commemorate the event in perpetuity—as the Romans did. Alfonso also gathered a library of ancient texts, collected ancient coins, and commissioned the artist Pisanello to cast a portrait medal. Ancient coins, amassed by collectors as historical records of Roman rulers, gave birth to the art of the Renaissance medal, and Pisanello became its preeminent practitioner.

The most archaeological painter of the fifteenth century was Andrea Mantegna. For the Gonzaga court in Mantua he created a series of nine panels, the *Triumphs of Caesar*, detailing with painstaking care the look and feel of Roman processions. The Gonzaga rulers were steeped in the study of antiquity and apparently used these paintings as theatrical backdrops for performances of plays by Plautus and Terence.

Not all fifteenth-century artists took classical revival to such levels. Sandro Botticelli painted a number of mythological works such as *Venus and Mars* and *Calumny of Apelles*, but he favored a courtly European manner. Many *cassoni*—wedding chests in which the bride kept her trousseaux—were

decorated with scenes from Roman history rendered in a Gothic style. Lorenzo Ghiberti, who had journeyed to Rome and was mesmerized by ancient sarcophagi, gave his figures on the Gates of Paradise—a set of bronze doors for the Baptistery of Florence—a classicizing air and placed them in spaces ruled by linear perspective. Yet the final product is an amalgam of the antique and the Renaissance.

The humanist Leon Battista Alberti both designed ancient-style architecture and wrote a treatise called *De re aedificatoria* (1452; published 1485)—modeled on *De architectura* of the Roman architect Vitruvius—elucidating how contemporary architects should make use of the vocabulary of ancient structures. In his Tempio Malatestiano (begun 1450), a cathedral church and monument to the lord of Rimini, Alberti applied his own theories by invoking Roman triumphal arches and aqueducts. For the church of San Andrea in Mantua (begun 1470) he used a barrel vault over the doorway framed by colossal pilasters rising through three stories, thus recalling the grandeur of Roman baths and basilicas.

The fifteenth century also initiated the passion and fashion for collecting ancient artifacts, not just as aesthetic objects, but as material witnesses to the past. Among the pioneers of this new approach was the merchant, traveler, and antiquarian Cyriacus of Ancona (or Ciriaco de' Pizzicolli). Thanks to his trading activities around the Mediterranean, Cyriacus was able to access not only Roman but also Greek monuments—nearly three centuries before they were rediscovered by other Europeans—assiduously sketching ruins into his notebooks and sharing them with artists and humanists: he is the first person after antiquity known to have drawn and described the Parthenon. In addition to his notes and drawings, Cyriacus also brought back from his travels manuscripts of ancient authors, small sculptures, coins, and gems.

The most famous and discriminating collector of the century, Lorenzo de' Medici, assembled a spectacular gathering of ancient cameos and intaglios, hard-stone vases, sculptures, and archaeological artifacts. He made his objects available for study by the artists in Florence, thus fostering the development of arts based on ancient exemplars.

Sixteenth Century. Rome became the center of classically inspired arts in the first two decades of the sixteenth century thanks to two ambitious popes: Julius II (r. 1503–1513) and Leo X (r. 1513–1521). Keen to demonstrate their power and immortalize themselves, they attracted to the city the best artists, ordering them to rebuild Saint Peter's, refurbish the Vatican palace, and embellish other parts of the city. Their works used ancient models extensively for both formal and spiritual guidance—as well as reused blocks from ancient buildings around the city—and in their turn became canonical for subsequent revivers of the classical style.

Raphael, a native of Urbino, arrived in Rome in 1508 at the invitation of Julius II and was at once commissioned to fresco a suite of rooms in the Vatican palace intended to serve as the pope's private library. In the first of these rooms, the judicial chamber known as the Stanza della Segnatura, Raphael painted *The School of Athens* (1508–1511), an idealized gathering of leading ancient and modern thinkers in a vast domed hall reminiscent of the Baths of Caracalla and the Basilica of Constantine— which also inspired Raphael's friend Donato Bramante in his new design for Saint Peter's. At the center of the composition, Raphael placed Plato with his book *Timaeus* and Aristotle with his *Ethics*, the two philosophers representing two paths to knowledge—idealism and empiricism—that also embodied qualities of the High Renaissance: a combination of direct observation of bodies and spaces with their idealization based on ancient models.

Raphael was not only an enthusiastic student of ancient art but also its official overseer, for in 1515 the pope appointed him Keeper of Inscriptions and Remains of the city of Rome. In this capacity Raphael scrutinized the finds unearthed around the city and tried to document and reconstruct the shape of ruined buildings—an attempt that went back to fifteenth-century efforts by Leon Battista Alberti and Flavio Biondo, the author of *Roma instaurata* (Rome Restored, 1444–1446), who sought to relate surviving remains to the evidence preserved in ancient texts.

A number of exciting discoveries at the turn of the sixteenth century galvanized the artistic and intellectual community. In the 1490s a statue of Apollo (now known as the Apollo Belvedere) came to light somewhere in the environs of Rome and was acquired by Cardinal Giuliano della Rovere, the future Julius II. In January 1506 a late Hellenistic group depicting the Trojan priest Laocoön and his sons was found on the Esquiline near the so-called Baths of Titus and was identified by Michelangelo as a work described by Pliny the Elder. Placed in the Cortile del Belvedere, behind the Vatican, these and other recent finds—the Sleeping Ariadne (interpreted as the dying Cleopatra), Venus Felix, and Hercules and Antaeus—were displayed in niches or above fountains to evoke the gardens of the ancients. Arousing universal admiration, these statues inspired generations of painters and sculptors. The papal outdoor exhibition itself set an example for other rich collectors around Rome. And so artists began to flock to the city to study what became for three centuries the canon of ancient art. Equally formative were the frescoes of the recently unearthed Golden House of Nero: their "grotesque" decorations informed Raphael's designs at the loggias in the Vatican and at the villas Farnesina and Madama and became a must in other High Renaissance residences. The fame of these sculptures and paintings was further disseminated through prints, thus achieving wide circulation and emulation.

Michelangelo, too, was deeply affected by ancient art, borrowing ancient prototypes for his paintings and sculptures, though making his figures more muscular and imposing. His *Creation of Adam* fresco on the Sistine Chapel ceiling transformed a delicate Victory on the Arch of Titus into the majestic God the Father, and the statue of the river Nile in front of the Palazzo dei Senatori in Rome became Adam. For the structural organization of the ceiling Michelangelo looked at the Arch of Constantine, absorbing its lessons on how to articulate a blank wall with pilasters, columns, bas-reliefs, medallions, and large-scale figures. And he was deeply affected by the Laocoön group. The power and bodily tension of its figures found reflection in many of Michelangelo's paintings and sculptures, such as the Libyan Sibyl on the Sistine ceiling and his *Slaves* for the unfinished tomb of Julius II. Meanwhile Michelangelo's *Bacchus* directly imitated an antique type, even holding an Etruscan bowl. And his *David* revived the heroic classical nude.

The Venetian painter Titian was attracted more by ancient myths than by ancient forms. He painted *Bacchus and Ariane* (1520–1523), *Danaë* (1553), the *Rape of Europa* (1575–1580), and other such scenes in a style that favored vivid color and sensual figures over classical idealization. His paintings appealed to their patrons with their ancient subject matter, while titillating them with their eroticism—antiquity serving both to ennoble and to delight.

In Florence, the Medici grand dukes promoted not only painting, sculpture, and architecture but also the ancient art of hard-stone carving, greatly esteemed by the Romans. Giovanni Antonio de Rossi's onyx cameo depicting Cosimo I, dressed in Roman-style armor and accompanied by his wife and children (1559–1562), evoked Roman imperial gems. Cosimo's son Francesco, who continued his father's efforts, attracted to the city three outstanding carvers from Milan, the brothers Ambrogio and Stefano Caroni and Giorgio Gaffurri, and built a workshop for them in his private residence, the Casino of San Marco, so as to have them nearby and closely associated with his court. Soon hard-stone carving and inlay became Florentine arts par excellence. Francesco especially favored *pietre dure* mosaics with geometric designs that showed off the colors and veins of stones and emulated ancient inlaid floors and marble wall paneling.

The Medici family also nurtured the art of small bronze sculpture, another classical revival. The court sculptor Giambologna fashioned for them highly refined and coolly elegant figures such as *Venus*, produced in many versions and poses, and *Mercury*, poised on one foot and raising one arm heavenward in a gesture borrowed from classical rhetoric.

Sixteenth-century armorers, too, looked to ancient statuary for inspiration. Bartolomeo Campi of Pesaro executed a Roman-style parade armor for Guidobaldo II della Rovere, the duke of Urbino and a famous condottiere of his day. Campi's harness replicated the muscled cuirasses ubiquitous on Roman triumphal arches, columns, and reliefs and likened its wearer to a victorious Roman general.

Architects and their patrons studied both surviving buildings and the writings of ancient authors for ideas and guidance. Andrea Palladio conjured up the grandeur of Roman imperial baths in the interior of the church of Redentore in Venice, opening up the walls by means of arches and niches and decorating them with columns and pilasters. Having scrutinized the surviving monuments of Rome, Palladio wrote a guide to them entitled *Le antichità di Roma* (1554), and he elucidated his ideas on classically inspired construction methods in *I quattro libri di archittetura* (1570), which became the most popular architectural treatise after Vitruvius.

The fashion for villas in the sixteenth century was stimulated by ancient writers, especially Pliny the Younger, who left a detailed account of his country estates in Tuscany and Laurentum. The picturesque remains of Hadrian's Villa at Tivoli also provided evidence for High Renaissance builders, as did other ruins. Bramante designed several Roman-style villas for the city's elite. In the Cortile del Belvedere he created the gardens and courtyards with exedrae, nymphaea, elaborate waterworks, and staircases leading to different levels—the last derived from the temple of Fortuna at Praeneste, approached by a series of ramps, stairs, and colonnades.

Pirro Ligorio, a native of Naples who came to Rome in 1534 and succeeded Raphael as superintendent of ancient monuments, conducted excavations at Hadrian's Villa and used what he learned in his designs for the Villa d'Este at Tivoli, where he created nymphaea and unusually shaped pools decorated with statues brought from Hadrian's estate. He also published an influential map of ancient Rome, *Antiquae Urbis Imago* (1561).

Giuliano da Sangallo kept a notebook with both drawings of ancient structures and copies of those by others, including the sketches of the buildings of Athens and Constantinople made by Cyriacus of

Ancona. Sangallo used these depictions as study guides and models for his own creations; later architects consulted them for instruction and inspiration as well. For Lorenzo de' Medici, Sangallo built a villa at Poggio a Caiano, apparently using Cyriacus' drawing of the Propylaia on the Athenian Acropolis as a basis for the facade.

Classical revival could take more whimsical forms, well illustrated by the architecture and painting of Raphael's pupil Giulio Romano at the Palazzo Te in Mantua. This pleasure retreat of the Gonzaga rulers was located outside the city and was meant to enchant them with its countryside setting and its playful decorations. In the courtyard of the palazzo, Giulio Romano used the vocabulary of classical architectural to entertain his patrons: over the heavily rusticated walls, pieces of architrave slip down from their places taking triglyphs with them, metopes go missing, and a pediment over the doorway is weighed down by the architrave rather than rising above it. Inside the palazzo the walls are frescoed with various mythological scenes: in the room depicting the *Fall of the Giants* the ceiling seems to topple and the walls to collapse as the Greek gods defeat the Giants. The subject matter is antique, but the execution is Baroque.

Sixteenth-century collectors, such as the Gonzaga and their peers, contributed to the dissemination of knowledge about antiquity and the continuing fascination with it. Cardinal Alessandro Farnese's palazzo in Rome—a veritable museum with a superb library, a picture gallery, and an unmatched assemblage of antiquities, from colossal marble statues to coins and gems—became a study center for Italian and foreign artists and humanists for two centuries.

Seventeenth Century. Seventeenth-century Rome continued to be a magnet for artists eager to imbibe ancient monuments as well as the masterpieces of Raphael, Michelangelo, and other High Renaissance masters. Taking back home what they had learned, these foreigners popularized classicism in their native lands. The rise of national academies, whose canon was Roman sculpture and sixteenth-century paintings, further codified these works as the highest forms of art.

The Bolognese painter Annibale Carracci was invited to Rome by Cardinal Odoardo Farnese—a nephew of Alessandro, whose collection of antiquities he inherited—to decorate the Palazzo Farnese and especially its great gallery displaying the family's Roman statues. Annibale crowned the room with a vast panorama of paintings, illusionistic sculptures, and seemingly live figures—all illustrating ancient myths—taking inspiration from the statues below as well as from Michelangelo's Sistine Chapel ceiling and Raphael's frescoes in the Villa Farnesina (c. 1511–1517).

The French painter Nicolas Poussin spent most of his life in Rome, studying ancient artworks as well as texts. He read ancient history, Ovid, and the Stoics, and he favored moral and philosophical subjects for his works. Poussin arrayed his figures in clear compositions, placing them in frieze-like planes parallel to the foreground—akin to reliefs on Roman sarcophagi. He constructed his scenes with the help of wax figures grouped on small stages to achieve perfectly balanced and emphatic arrangements such as the *Rape of the Sabine Women* (c. 1633). But he also created more lyrical pictures inspired by ancient mythology, such as *Landscape with Orpheus and Eurydice* (1648); this picture has Castel Sant'Angelo, originally the tomb of Hadrian, in the background. Poussin's classicism exercised a profound influence on generations of painters including Jacques-Louis David, Paul Cézanne, and Pablo Picasso.

Poussin's friend Claude came from Lorraine and likewise settled in Rome. He made landscapes and seascapes his specialty, and though he included figures and structures in his pictures, he was chiefly concerned with rendering nature, changes in light, and atmospheric effects at different times of the day. Claude's paintings did have classical subject matter, most often taken from classical mythology, with classicizing buildings augmenting antique settings. His *Landscape with the Father of Psyche Sacrificing at the Milesian Temple of Apollo* (1663) presented a typically idealized vision of the past— pastoral, poetic, and serene.

Peter Paul Rubens is best known for his exuberant Baroque canvases, but he was a keen antiquarian.

He spent eight years in Italy (1600–1608), taking full advantage of opportunities to "study at close quarters the works of the ancient and modern masters," and he became a collector of ancient statues, coins, and gems. His paintings were informed by his knowledge of ancient history and art. The *Triumphant Entry of Constantine into Rome* (1622–1623), one of twelve oil sketches for a tapestry series devoted to the emperor Constantine's portrayal, echoes the equestrian statue of Marcus Aurelius, which was long thought to represent Constantine. Here the helmeted Roma welcomes the emperor in front of a triumphal arch probably modeled on that of Constantine in Rome. Rubens painted numerous historical and mythological subjects, though he was also affected by the works of Michelangelo, Titian, and Carracci.

Gian Lorenzo Bernini, like Rubens, both absorbed the lessons of ancient and modern masters and created out of them his own unique style: vivid, vigorous, and emotionally charged. His sculptural groups of *Aeneas, Anchises, and Ascanius* (1619), *Pluto Abducting Persephone* (1621–1622), and *Apollo and Daphne* (1622–1625) were probably inspired by such Hellenistic works as the Laocoön group, for they show figures in complex twisting motion and offer virtuoso renditions of textures from smooth flesh to wild hair and fingers turning into branches.

With the establishment of the Académie Royale de Peinture et de Sculpture in Paris in 1648 and the Académie Royale d'Architecture in 1671, classicism became the official language of France, embodying rationalism and order and providing lofty aesthetic and moral models for contemporary artists and society. Academy students learned by copying works of old masters, antique sculptures, and plaster casts. Charles Le Brun, one of the founders of the Académie Royale de Peinture et de Sculpture, the First Painter to King Louis XIV, and the director of the Gobelins factory for the manufacture of tapestry and furniture, had studied in Rome and revered the works of Raphael and Poussin. His classicism was shaped to a large extent by their versions of it, and his views became the Académie standard. The highest prize for the students was the Prix de Rome, a four-year scholarship that sent them to the Académie Française in Rome to further their training in ancient and High Renaissance art. The French Academic system and canon influenced art education across Europe for the next two centuries.

Eighteenth Century. The allure and pursuit of classical art were augmented in the eighteenth century by several developments: the popularity of the so-called grand tour of Italy and its monuments, the excavations of Pompeii and Herculaneum, the rediscovery of Greece by Europeans, and the work of Johann Joachim Winckelmann, who wrote the first modern history of ancient art. These and other advances gave new materials and approaches to artists. Neoclassicism was also an expression of the Enlightenment: classical forms were seen to embody reason and order, corresponding to the prevalent philosophical and social outlook. And neoclassicism had an ideological component of instilling ancient Greek and Roman virtues into civic life.

The grand tour of Italy was de rigueur for eighteenth-century aristocrats, especially those from England. They stopped in Venice and admired the architecture of Palladio, in Rome they examined the art treasures ancient and modern, and in Naples they sought out the newly unearthed cities buried by the eruption of Vesuvius in 79 CE. They returned with stories of what they observed and their own pieces of antiquity—statues, gems, ceramic vases—furthering an interest in the past.

In 1734 a group of alumni of such journeys formed a club to encourage at home "a taste for those objects which had contributed to their entertainment abroad." They named themselves the Society of Dilettanti (from the Italian *dilettare*, to delight) and devoted much time to honoring Dionysus and Eros, ancient gods of wine and love—in other words, to drinking and carousing. But they also underwrote archaeological expeditions to Greece, Turkey, and the Middle East—regions then largely unknown to the Europeans—and published accounts of ancient monuments and sites in those lands. In the 1750s the society sponsored a three-year voyage of James Stuart and Nicholas Revett to study the antiquities of Attica. Their findings, published in *Antiquities of*

Athens Measured and Delineated (1762–1794), familiarized Europeans with the remains of ancient Greece, helped develop the science of archaeology, and fostered the Greek revival in contemporary arts. The book became instrumental in promoting the primacy of the Greek artistic ideal over the Roman. As travel to Greece became easier in the eighteenth century, more Europeans went there to examine ancient monuments, and in the spirit of Enlightenment, Greece came to be extolled as home of the arts and an exemplar of reason.

Stuart applied the lessons he had learned in Attica (as well as in Italy before that) to his architectural and design projects, modifying the homes and gardens of his English patrons in the Greek style. One of his clients was George Lyttelton, in whose Hagley Park, in Worcestershire, Stuart built an imitation of the temple of Theseus in Athens (Hephaisteion). He used fluted, baseless Doric columns that later became popular in buildings on both sides of the Atlantic.

In addition to Stuart, the architects William Chambers and Robert Adam also promoted the Greek style in Britain. Adam ran a successful practice together with his brother James, designing complete schemes for decorating and furnishing houses—often in the popular Palladian manner, although Robert also evolved a new, more flexible style that incorporated Greek and Roman elements with an admixture of Byzantine and Baroque. Adam's work was enormously influential, and in North America the Federal style evolved to a large extent on the basis of his creations.

Meanwhile excavations at Herculaneum, begun in 1738, and at Pompeii, rediscovered a decade later, introduced Europeans to Roman domestic decorations and artifacts and spurred their emulation by contemporary artists. The Bourbon royal family, under whose auspices the excavations were conducted, restricted visits to the sites and publications of their finds, making them known only in a limited deluxe edition of *Le antichità di Ercolano esposte* (The Antiquities Discovered in Herculaneum, 1755–1792) produced by the Accademia Ercolanese, founded in 1755. But cheaper editions appeared in England (1773), Germany (1778), France (1780), and Rome (1789). These books with extensive illustrations of the finds quickly popularized the arts of Pompeii and Herculaneum and inspired architecture, sculpture, painting, and design across Europe.

At the same time, ancient painted vases unearthed in South Italian tombs brought a whole other set of motifs to the eyes of artists and collectors. Sir William Hamilton, British ambassador to the court of Naples from 1764 to 1800, became fascinated with these objects and formed an extensive collection of them. He then engaged Pierre-François Hugues d'Hancarville to produce a lavish illustrated catalog so as to popularize this ancient art form and make it a lucrative commercial item. Among those who were smitten with Hamilton's vases was the English potter Josiah Wedgwood. A savvy businessman, he saw the potential of the new fashion for ancient ceramics and initiated a line of jasperware pottery that both reproduced Hamilton's pieces and created their modern versions: classicizing white figures posed against sky blue or sage green. Wedgwood called his ceramics factory "Etruria Works"—because Greek vases, found in Etruscan tombs, were thought to be Etruscan—and gave it a motto: "The Arts of Etruria Are Reborn." John Flaxman, who worked as a modeler for Wedgwood, translated the images on Greek vases into designs for pottery and prints, and his line drawings illustrating the works of Homer and Aeschylus became tremendously popular throughout Europe, further fueling the Greek revival.

Giovanni Battista Piranesi (1720–1778), in his turn, made Rome even more alluring to visitors through his picturesque etchings of the city's surviving ancient structures, evocative ruins, and sculptural remains. Fascinated from boyhood by Roman history, Piranesi championed Roman over Greek art—a polemic that raged among the cognoscenti, with the British and French antiquarians arguing that the Romans learned everything from the Greeks, and Piranesi, through his prints and treatises, defending and propagating the creative genius of the Romans. Piranesi's prints became internationally fashionable. Using dramatic shading and atmospheric effects, he made his views seem alive and emotionally charged—inspiring similar portrayals of monuments by other artists recording the ruins in Greece, Asia Minor, and Egypt. Although he investigated ancient remains with meticulous care, Piranesi and his imitators filtered them through their romantic imagination, making ancient structures appear more grandiose and consequential. Many tourists who had seen his images were disappointed to discover that Rome actually looker duller. Piranesi also collected, restored, and dealt in antiquities, publishing illustrated catalogs of his wares, and his designs for chimneypieces, furniture, and interior decorations in the antique style were widely emulated.

Another decisive force in the propagation of classicism in the eighteenth century was J. J. Winckelmann, the author of the first modern history of Greek art—at a time when no proper distinction was made between Greek and Roman works. In his *Gedancken über die Nachahmung der griechischen Wercke in der Mahlerey und Bildhauerkunst* (Reflections on the Imitation of Greek Works in Painting and Sculpture, 1755), Winckelmann asserted that "the one way for us to become great, perhaps inimitable, is by imitating the ancients." He then went on to establish a chronology based on stylistic analysis, and emphasized Greek art as the origin of perfection. He argued that the "noble simplicity and quiet grandeur" of Greek works stemmed from the political system under which they were created, postulating in his *Geschichte der Kunst des Alterthums* (History of Ancient Art, 1764) that art "is born, flourishes, and declines with the civilizations in the midst of which it develops." He divided Greek art into four groups: antique or archaic style; the sublime, grand, or elevated style of Phidias; the beautiful style of Praxiteles; and the decadent style of the first century BCE and Roman era. Winckelmann's interpretation was flawed, for he based his observations on gems and sculptures that he saw in Rome—where he arrived from Prussia in 1755 and eventually received a post as prefect of papal antiquities. He never traveled to Greece, and many of the statues that he took to be Greek were actually

Roman and Hellenistic. But his writings proved to be tremendously influential for art history, archaeology, painting, sculpture, literature, and philosophy and further spurred the neoclassical movement.

Three other proponents of the classical ideal contributed decisively to its widespread circulation. Jacques-Louis David embraced it from the time that he was a student in France, and his admiration for antiquity grew even stronger during his sojourn in Italy on the Prix de Rome in 1775–1780. David returned to Rome in 1784 to paint Roman subjects on their native soil and produced the *Oath of the Horatii* (1784), a declaration of the unity of men in the service of a political ideal—a theme of particular relevance for a Frenchman on the eve of the Revolution. David's *Death of Socrates* (1787) showed the philosopher, having just drunk hemlock, calmly discussing the immortality of the soul amid his grieving friends and students, presenting an ancient moral exemplar for modern times.

Gavin Hamilton, a Scottish painter who spent most of his life in Rome, executed many large canvases devoted to Greek and Roman history and literature. His cycle of six paintings illustrating Homer's *Iliad*, engraved by Domenico Cunego, were widely circulated and admired. Hamilton also dealt in art and antiquities and undertook excavations at Hadrian's Villa to procure marbles for resale. Excavating other sites around Rome, he provided finds to people on the grand tour and to such notable collectors as Charles Townley and William Petty, Earl of Shelburne.

Antonio Canova was born near Venice and began his career there, fashioning Baroque works. But having visited Rome in 1779 and 1781, studied antiquities there, and come under the influence of Gavin Hamilton, his style changed. He began to carve physically idealized and emotionally detached figures that recalled ancient heroes and gods. His first opus in the new manner, *Theseus and the Dead Minotaur* (1781–1782), showing the hero calmly savoring his victory, brought Canova immediate and widespread fame. In 1820 he was even commissioned to produce a statue of George Washington attired in Roman armor for the capitol of the state of

North Carolina. (The statue perished in a fire ten years later.) After Canova's death, the Danish sculptor Bertel Thorvaldsen emerged as the leading master of neoclassicism, his figures more stiff and formal than Canova's and his themes mostly drawn from Greek myths.

Another facet of eighteenth-century neoclassicism was the surge of interest in engraved gems. Greatly prized by the ancients, intaglios and cameos had been eagerly pursued by rulers, nobles, and humanists from the Middle Ages onward. With the rise of "universal" histories in the eighteenth century, gems came to be gathered into encyclopedic collections—comprising actual stones as well as their replicas in plaster, sulfur, and glass impressions—documenting the progress of ancient art history, the full range of classical mythology, and various other aspects of the past. James Tassie of Edinburgh, a dealer in gem casts, assembled a stock of nearly sixteen thousand ancient and modern stones. A number of artists—including Anton (Antonio) Pichler and his sons Giovanni, Giuseppe, and Luigi; Edward Burch; and Nathaniel Marchant—created modern versions of classical gem carvings for collectors across Europe, typically depicting antique subjects, famous Roman sculptures, and portraits of notables. But ancient gems remained the most desirable, and to satisfy a steady demand for them, some carvers, such as Thomas Jenkins, produced forgeries "authenticated" with signatures of Greek and Roman artists.

Like d'Hancarville's publication of Hamilton's vases, books with engravings of gems, as well as those illustrating newly discovered archaeological sites and artifacts unearthed in Italy, Greece, Syria, Lebanon, and the Dalmatian coast, disseminated their fame. These publications made innumerable classical antiquities available as models for artists and further nurtured the fashion for things Greek and Roman among their patrons.

Nineteenth Century. Neoclassicism remained popular into the nineteenth century, though it also evolved. The academies propagated heroic style and subject matter; paintings presented dignified and grave protagonists, placed centrally and posed amid grand public spaces, sacrificing themselves with emphatic gestures for the public good. Sculptures showed noble ancients portrayed with cool detachment. Architecture expressed civic virtues through classical vocabulary. But as the century progressed, a new viewing public emerged: the new middle-class patrons preferred portraits, landscapes, and genre scenes to large didactic paintings, and they desired household decorations elegantly fashioned in antique styles. Inspired by new archaeological finds and by Victorian historical novels set in antiquity, such as Edward Bulwer-Lytton's *The Last Days of Pompeii* (1834), these new customers craved scenes and objects reflecting the daily life of the Greeks and the Romans. Excavations in Italy and elsewhere brought to light such artifacts, popularized by books and archaeology columns in general periodicals. And archaeology itself developed as a systematic discipline that recorded and interpreted a full spectrum of finds, thus significantly expanding the understanding of antiquity. History, too, came to be written in new ways, covering more than major political events and key actors, paying attention to a variety of social and cultural phenomena.

At the beginning of the century, with neoclassicism still serving the propagandistic purposes of ruling elites, Napoleon deployed imperial Roman symbols to communicate both his ascent as the emperor and also the glory of France under his rule. He ordered Charles Percier and Pierre-François Léonard Fontaine to design the triumphal arch at the Carrousel du Louvre and Jean-François Chalgrin to create one at the Champs-Élysées (both begun in 1806). He also redecorated the former royal residences with furniture, porcelain, and tapestries showing Greek and Roman motifs. Napoleonic style, called Empire, became fashionable across Europe and influenced American architecture, particularly the United States Capitol building, although on American soil this visual language was taken to express the republican values of sobriety and balance.

Thomas Jefferson believed strongly that architecture ought to convey the ideals of the new nation. Having studied the classics and traveled in Europe, he designed several state capitol buildings, such as the one in Richmond, Virginia (c. 1790), based on the Roman temple at Nîmes, France. After the revolutions in France and America, the new governments favored neoclassical architecture as an evocation of Greek democracy and Roman republicanism. During the course of the nineteenth century a number of American architects received their training at the École des Beaux Arts in Paris—which evolved out of the Académie Française—and continued to teach classicism as the highest form of visual expression. Returning home, they built edifices that blended Greek, Roman, and High Renaissance elements, as the firms of McKim, Mead, & White did at the Boston Public Library (1888–1895) and Carrère and Hastings did at the New York Public Library (1897–1911).

A major paradigm shift in the perception of ancient art occurred with the arrival in London in 1806 of the Elgin Marbles—sculptural decorations from the Parthenon in Athens. At first their reception was mixed because they did not conform to the prevalent notion of Greek art, based as it was on Roman and Hellenistic sculptures. But their fame grew swiftly, multiplied by plaster casts ordered by clients across Europe, and soon Greek creations were extolled as preeminent models for Western art and civilization. By 1830 the Elgin Marbles replaced the Apollo Belvedere as the foremost exemplar for students in the academies, and they remained a paragon into the twentieth century, with artists such as Edgar Degas, Georges Seurat, Auguste Rodin, and Pablo Picasso copying their plaster versions.

Jean-Auguste-Dominique Ingres, having studied with David in Paris, won a Prix de Rome in 1801. Once in Italy, he was deeply impressed with the works of Raphael, Etruscan vases, and outline engravings of John Flaxman, was moved by the casts of the Elgin Marbles and sketched them repeatedly, and made no drawings of the Apollo Belvedere. Ingres's monumental *Jupiter and Thetis* (1811) and *Apotheosis of Homer* (1827) reflected his adherence to the Greek revival, although they were poorly received at the Paris Salon, for Romantic painting was by then ascendant. Alexandre Cabanel, though still painting in the academic style, achieved greater success by making his mythological scenes sensual and erotic. His *Birth of Venus* (1863) was an immediate hit at the Paris Salon and was purchased by Napoleon III for his private collection.

Thomas Couture sought to make a larger didactic point with his visions of antiquity. An Academic painter, he adhered to the view of history painting as a bearer of a moral message. Thus his 1847 masterpiece *Romans in the Decadence of the Empire* was based on a line from the Roman poet Juvenal: "Crueler than war, vice fell upon Rome and avenged the conquered world." But Couture's canvas was also a critique of contemporary French society and its corruption under the July Monarchy of Louis-Philippe.

A lighter and more popular re-creation of the past emerged from the brush of Sir Lawrence Alma-Tadema, a Dutchman who made a thriving career in England, catering to the taste of the new middle-class clientele. His meticulously detailed and archaeologically accurate scenes of the lives of the ancients were set amid opulent marbled interiors or balconies overlooking the blue Mediterranean Sea. Alma-Tadema was less concerned with the moral message of his paintings than with their material veracity. Smitten with Pompeii during his honeymoon, he took much of his inspiration from the buildings and finds unearthed there and assembled an extensive photographic archive of ancient artifacts and structures that he used to replicate precisely that physical world. His paintings later served as source material for Hollywood films such as D. W. Griffith's *Intolerance* (1916) and the several versions of *Ben-Hur* (1926, 1959), *Cleopatra* (1934, 1963), and especially Cecil B. DeMille's *The Ten Commandments* (1923, 1956), as well as Ridley Scott's *Gladiator* (2000). Alma-Tadema represented both Roman and Greek (as well as Egyptian) antiquity with such canvases as *A Roman Art Lover* (1870), *Phidias Showing the Frieze of the Parthenon to His Friends* (1868), and *The Finding of Moses* (1904).

Thomas Hope gave clients their own means of reliving Greek and Roman luxury by designing interiors and artifacts in antique styles for the residences of the fashionable well-to-do. Hope had gone on a ten-year grand tour of Europe, Greece, Turkey, and Egypt, accumulating a broad knowledge of arts, sketches of what he had seen, and artifacts both antique and modern. Having bought a house designed by Robert Adam, he remodeled it with rooms devoted to different period styles: a vase room containing Greek vases purchased from William Hamilton and an Egyptian room combining ancient and contemporary Egyptian artworks. He also commissioned pieces from John Flaxman and Bertel Thorvaldsen. In his own words, he made himself "master of *The Spirit* of the Antique." Hope opened the house to the public in order to improve modern taste and published a sourcebook, *Household Furniture and Interior Decoration* (1807), with black-and-white illustrations that could be adapted by others; it became a bible for designers. Hope's creations are known as English Regency.

Three generations of the Castellani family in Rome catered to the vogue for archaeological jewelry inspired by examples excavated at Etruscan, Roman, and Greek sites. Their pieces combined finely wrought gold with enamel, carved gems, and miniature mosaics. Fortunato Pio Castellani, the founder of the firm, also rediscovered the art of granulation—the application of tiny granules of gold to an object's surface in decorative patterns. The Etruscans had perfected granulation in the ninth to fourth centuries BCE, but their technique had been lost. Castellani's jewelry, patronized by the Roman and foreign aristocracy, allowed women both to show their cultivation and to acquire pieces akin to the ones they saw in the city's museums. But Castellani sought more than material success. By reproducing the exquisite craftsmanship of the Romans and the Etruscans, he wanted to improve Italian craft and design. This was part of the rising nationalism that led to the unification of Italy in 1860. Castellani aimed to promote Italy's cultural importance at a time when Europe was dominated by French and English taste.

Twentieth and Twenty-First Centuries. Classical art continued to fascinate artists into the twentieth and twenty-first centuries, although the variety of responses to it became much wider, ranging from serious to ironic, from direct quotation to abstraction. The new genre of cinema explored the ancient world in a multitude of ways as well, ranging from earnest large-scale productions such as Joseph L. Mankiewicz's *Cleopatra* (1963) to *300* (2007),

Raphael's *School of Athens*. Fresco, Stanza della Segnatura, Vatican. VATICAN MUSEUMS AND GALLERIES/GIRAUDON/THE BRIDGEMAN ART LIBRARY

a movie based on Frank Miller's graphic novel about the Battle of Thermopylae that sought to replicate the imagery of a comic book. Television series have included the campy *Xena: Warrior Princess* (1995–2001)—a progressive feminist retelling of Greek myth—and the realistic historical drama *Rome* (2005–2007).

In the first half of the twentieth century many artists incorporated ancient motifs, figures, and buildings into their works, using them as metaphors of nostalgia or social disorder, as ideological statements, or as reflections of the subconscious. The century's two world wars, Sigmund Freud's psychoanalytical theories, reaction against previous artistic movements, and the birth of new art genres gave classical references new purposes and forms of expression. Franz von Stuck, a German Symbolist and Art Nouveau painter, sculptor, and engraver, for example, often depicted mythological characters: the *Sphinx* (1901, 1904), *Pluto* (1909), and *Hercules and Nessus* (1927) in painting, and *Helen* in a bronze statuette (1909). Like other Symbolist artists, von Stuck sought to evoke through these figures the world of the imagination and dreams as a reaction against the naturalism and realism of nineteenth-century painting.

For the Greek-Italian surrealist painter Giorgio de Chirico antiquity was a long-lost land and time, and classical allusions informed many of his paintings. In *Ariadne* (1913) he quoted the Vatican sculpture Sleeping Ariadne, posing her next to a Roman aqueduct; in *Love Song* (1914) he included the head of the Apollo Belvedere. His *Disquieting Muses* (1916) reenvisioned Greek sculptures, evoking a dreamy and nostalgic place. But de Chirico placed his ancient references in stark modern settings, linking nostalgia with alienation.

Pablo Picasso conducted a continual dialogue with antiquity. As a boy he drew plaster casts as well as live models. After World War I he went through a neoclassical phase, painting numerous monumental female figures inspired by ancient prototypes. The Minotaur became a repeated motif in his creations in the 1930s, most famously in *Guernica* (1937), expressing the horrors of war. Max Beckmann, too, used classical myths to articulate the agonies and traumas of war and of the Nazi regime, as in the *Perseus* triptych (1941).

Ancient art was one of the ways by which Nazi Germany promulgated its ideology of racial purity. The Nazis saw themselves as the heirs of the Greek and Roman civilizations and made frequent use of ancient sculpture in their propaganda. Because they placed great emphasis on physical conditioning and strength, they linked themselves deliberately to ancient Greek supermen. This association is explicit in Leni Riefenstahl's film *Olympia*, made to document the 1936 Berlin Olympic Games: it included such images as Myron's Discobolus (Discus Thrower) coming to life as a German athlete. The Italian Fascists, meanwhile, drew on Roman antiquity for their symbols of power: the Esposizione Universale Roma (EUR) district of Rome (begun in 1935) reinterpreted Roman architecture in a modernist idiom,

Giovanni Lorenzo Bernini's *Apollo and Daphne*. GALLERIA BORGHESE, ROME/LAUROS/GIRAUDON/THE BRIDGEMAN ART LIBRARY

and the Foro Italico sports complex (1928–1938), built as the Foro Mussolini, updated the forum Romanum.

Salvador Dalí turned to antiquity after World War II, and in such works as *Leda atómica* (1949) he commented on the damage and distress caused by the atomic bomb, as well as on Albert Einstein's theory that body and mass represent energy. Dalí was fascinated with dematerialization, creating an ironic juxtaposition: in ancient art the body is the principal artistic subject, whereas Dalí seeks to dematerialize it. Surrealists such as Dalí were also profoundly influenced by Freud's theories, wherein antiquity stood for the subconscious and deeply buried traces of thoughts and feelings that could be uncovered through painting as if through an archaeological excavation. Freud himself collected ancient art.

Twentieth-century architecture continued to play off antiquity. In Spain, Ricardo Bofill's Teatre Nacional de Catalunya (1991–1996) updates an ancient temple: it has a peristyle, a pedimental roof, and a glass facade that makes the building modern

yet clearly in a dialogue with the classical past. Charles W. Moore's Piazza d'Italia in New Orleans (1976–1979) recalls the Forum of Trajan in Rome. The American architect Thomas Gordon Smith defines himself as a "leader in contemporary developments of classical architecture." He constructs private residences, such as Vitruvian House in South Bend, Indiana (1990), civic and ecclesiastical structures, and educational edifices, such as the Bond Hall of the School of Architecture at the University of Notre Dame in Indiana, achieving strength, functionality, and beauty by using the elements of Greek, Roman, and Renaissance design.

In the second half of the twentieth century more ironic uses of antiquity emerged. The Russian-born artists Vitaly Komar and Alexander Melamid based their painting *The Origin of Socialist Realism* (1983) on Pliny the Elder's story of the origin of painting in the desire of a young woman to capture her lover's silhouette on the wall. In their *Portrait of Ronald Reagan as Centaur* (1981) they commented wryly on the superhuman status of the popular American president.

Virginia State Capitol, Richmond. PRINTS AND PHOTOGRAPHS DIVISION, LIBRARY OF CONGRESS

The comic-book genre, reinvented as the "graphic novel," took up antiquity as a subject and updated ancient stories for modern readers. Eric Shanower created the *Age of Bronze: The Story of the Trojan War* (from 1998) graphic novels using Homer and other Greek and Roman writers as his sources. He also drew on medieval retellings of the war and on Shakespeare's *Troilus and Cressida*, as well as on archaeological data uncovered in excavations at Mycenae, Knossos, Pylos, and Troy. Yet the final product is a self-consciously twenty-first-century artifact.

Finally antiquity has been the subject of a number of blockbuster movies in the early twenty-first century, as in earlier decades. *Gladiator* (2000), *Troy* (2004), and *Alexander* (2004) all sought to re-create the glory and the gore of ancient Greece and Rome. They took liberties with the historical material and frequently diverged from myths and recorded sources, often deliberately. But they have also spurred an interest in the past in a new generation of viewers and thus, like earlier classicizing works, have contributed to the perpetuation of fascination with the classical world.

[*See also* Apollo Belvedere; Archaeology; Art Market, *subentry* Legal Issues; Classical Scholarship, *subentry* History of the Study of Ancient Art and Architecture; Collectors and Collections; Dilettanti, Society of; Elgin Marbles; Equestrian Monuments; Hadrian's Villa; Hamilton, William; Laocoön; Pompeii and Herculaneum; Vitruvius; *and* Winckelmann, Johann Joachim.]

BIBLIOGRAPHY

Barkan, Leonard. *Unearthing the Past: Archaeology and Aesthetics in the Making of Renaissance Culture.* New Haven, Conn.: Yale University Press, 1999.

Belozerskaya, Marina. *To Wake the Dead: A Renaissance Merchant and the Birth of Archaeology.* New York: W. W. Norton and Company, 2009.

Bober, Phyllis Pray, and Ruth Rubinstein. *Renaissance Artists and Antique Sculpture: A Handbook of Sources.* London: Harvey Miller; Oxford: Oxford University Press, 1986.

Burke, Janine. *The Sphinx on the Table: Sigmund Freud's Art Collection and the Development of Psychoanalysis.* New York: Walker & Co., 2006.

Dacos, Nicole. *La découverte de la Domus Aurea et la formation des grotesques à la Renaissance.* London: Warburg Institute; Leiden, The Netherlands: E. J. Brill, 1969.

De Sanna, Jole, ed. *De Chirico and the Mediterranean.* New York: Rizzoli, 1998.

Du Prey, Pierre. *The Villas of Pliny from Antiquity to Posterity.* Chicago: University of Chicago Press, 1994.

Greenhalgh, Michael. *Classical Tradition in Art.* London: Duckworth, 1978.

Haskell, Francis, and Nicholas Penny. *Taste and the Antique: The Lure of Classical Sculpture, 1500–1900.* New Haven, Conn.: Yale University Press, 1981.

Honour, Hugh. *Neo-Classicism.* Harmondsworth, U.K.: Penguin, 1968.

Jenkins, Ian, and Kim Sloan. *Vases and Volcanoes: Sir William Hamilton and His Collection.* London: British Museum Press, 1996.

Meulen, Marjon van der. *Petrus Paulus Rubens Antiquarius: Collector and Copyist of Antique Gems.* Alphen aan den Rijn, The Netherlands: Canaletto, 1975.

Panofsky, Erwin. *Renaissance and Renascences in Western Art.* London: Paladin, 1970.

Parslow, Christopher Charles. *Rediscovering Antiquity: Karl Weber and the Excavation of Herculaneum, Pompeii, and Stabiae.* Cambridge, U.K., and New York: Cambridge University Press, 1995.

Payne, Alina, et al., eds. *Antiquity and Its Interpreters.* Cambridge, U.K., and New York: Cambridge University Press, 2000.

Redford, Bruce. *Dilettanti: The Antic and the Antique in Eighteenth-Century England.* Los Angeles: J. Paul Getty Museum, 2008.

Scobie, Alexander. *Hitler's State Architecture: The Impact of Classical Antiquity.* University Park: Pennsylvania State University Press for the College Art Association, 1990.

Soros, Susan Weber, ed. *James "Athenian" Stuart, 1713–1788: The Rediscovery of Antiquity.* New York: Bard Graduate Center for Studies in the Decorative Arts, Design, and Culture; New Haven, Conn.: Yale University Press, 2006.

Soros, Susan Weber, and Stefanie Walker, eds. *Castellani and Italian Archaeological Jewelry.* New York: Bard Graduate Center for Studies in the Decorative Arts, Design, and Culture; New Haven, Conn.: Yale University Press, 2004.

Swanson, Vern G. *Sir Lawrence Alma-Tadema: The Painter of the Victorian Vision of the Ancient World.* London: Ash and Grant, 1977.

Tavernor, Robert. *Palladio and Palladianism.* London and New York: Thames & Hudson, 1991.

Vermeule, Cornelius. *European Art and the Classical Past.* Cambridge, Mass.: Harvard University Press, 1964.

Watkins, David, and Philip Hewat-Jaboor, eds. *Thomas Hope: Regency Designer.* New York: Bard Graduate Center for Studies in the Decorative Arts, Design, and Culture; New Haven, Conn.: Yale University Press, 2008.

Weiss, Roberto. *The Renaissance Discovery of Classical Antiquity.* 2nd ed. Oxford: Basil Blackwell, 1988.

Wilton-Ely, John. *The Mind and Art of Giovanni Battista Piranesi.* London: Thames & Hudson, 1978.

Marina Belozerskaya

Music

The civilization of ancient Greece and Rome has provided inspiration and subject matter for Western composers since the Renaissance. Themes for many musical genres—predominantly opera, but also orchestral and chamber music, song, ballet, popular music, operetta and musical, and film score—have been taken either from Greek and Roman mythology or history (usually heavily fictionalized), with an occasional glance at the barbarian fringe.

Although the earliest opera composers tried to imitate the role of music in the ancient world and even the way in which that music used the human voice, almost no composer who followed them did: their music was the music of their time and place. The languages of opera texts were not Latin or classical Greek, but modern languages, such as Italian, French, German, or English. Composers might use ancient themes as vehicles to reflect on modern concerns, sometimes with little interest in or fidelity to ancient sources. Baroque composers and librettists made praise and flattery of rulers central to many operas. In *Lysistrata, or The Nude Goddess* (2005; dates accompanying titles of musical works are dates of first performance) Mark Adamo used Aristophanes' characters as starting points to reflect on war and society in the twenty-first century. Stage directors, set designers, and costume designers might give a work on an ancient theme a modern setting that ignores antiquity entirely.

Reference to the ancient world in medieval secular music was rare and brief. The motet "De se debent bigami" from the Montpellier Codex (c. 1280) quoted Ovid's *Ars amatoria* (2.13) to the effect that "Non minor est virtus, quam quaerere, parta tueri" (Virtue is no less to guard possessions than to seek them). Francesco Landini (c. 1325–1397) worked references to four mythological musicians—Orpheus, Philomel, Amphion, and Marsyas—into his madrigal "Sy dolce non sonò con lir' Orfeo" (Not even Orpheus played his lyre as sweetly).

Opera from the Renaissance to Mozart. The earliest operas were written in Florence in the late sixteenth century. Earlier composers had provided musical *intermedi* (interludes) for dramatic works, such as Angelo Poliziano's *Orfeo* in Mantua in 1472; the *intermedi* themselves were more lyrical than dramatic. A century later, interest in the place of music in ancient society led to the writing of dramatic pieces having music as an integral part.

Renaissance musical theorists were familiar with Aristotle's notion that music, by representing states of feeling and moral qualities, "has the power of producing a certain effect on the moral character of the soul" (*Politics* 1339a–1342b). They assumed that the ancients had melded music and voice, without knowing exactly how (no one would until some lines from Euripides' *Orestes* accompanied by musical notation were published in 1892). They sought a union of the arts that would marry music and community ethos in order to encourage civic virtue as they assumed the Greeks had done in their dramatic festivals. This myth of ancient origins gave opera a patrimony and genealogy that encouraged the use of ancient subjects. Vincenzo Galilei (c. 1520–1591) argued that the Greeks emphasized the intelligibility of the text and that their music was therefore monodic rather than polyphonic. The composer Jacopo Peri described "a new way of singing," called recitative; he "thought that the ancient Greeks and Romans—who, in the opinion of many, sang the entire tragedies on stage—used a kind of harmony which, going beyond ordinary speech, remained so far below the melody of song that it constituted an intermediate form" (preface to

Euridice, 1600; quoted in Weisstein, *The Essence of Opera*, p. 20). Peri and other composers therefore preferred recitative, singing that followed the rhythms of speech; furthermore, the text of operas, the libretto, was dominant over the musical score.

The first continuously sung pastoral, *Dafne*, with libretto by Ottavio Rinucci and music by Jacopo Corsi (Peri composed some of the recitatives), was performed in Florence in 1598; the music is lost. Under the patronage of a learned society, the Camerata, the first opera, *Euridice*, with a libretto by Rinucci and music by Peri, premiered in Florence in 1600; most of the music is lost; it had an ancient theme and attempted to follow Galilei's theory in emphasizing recitative. The first opera for which the complete score survives was *La favola d'Orfeo* (The Fable of Orpheus; Mantua, 1607) with libretto by Alessandro Striggio and music by Claudio Monteverdi. Over thirty years later, Monteverdi produced a second opera, *Il ritorno d'Ulisse in patria* (The Return of Ulysses to His Fatherland, 1640) and turned to Roman history for the subject of his last opera, *L'incoronazione di Poppea* (The Coronation of Poppea, 1643).

The earliest operas were sponsored and staged by learned academies in Italy, whose membership included nobles and intellectuals; a public opera house opened in Venice in 1637. But princely, royal, and imperial patronage supported the writing and performance of most opera through the seventeenth and eighteenth centuries and, not surprisingly, operas dealt with themes that appealed to noble patrons, intellectuals, and a knowledgeable public. Incidents from mythology and history—with themes of military valor, clemency, and good rule—appealed to rulers. Operas and ballets celebrated military victories, weddings (for example, Jean-Philippe Rameau's *Platée*, 1745), and coronations (for example, Wolfgang Amadeus Mozart's *Clemenza di Tito*, 1791). Audiences loved magnificence and spectacle, and noble patrons were willing to pay for extravagant pageantry, ballet, and elaborate stage machinery. An emphasis on Latin over Greek in the syllabi of the schools in which most men of the upper classes were educated ensured familiarity

with Roman history and a predominance of Roman themes, although the librettos were in modern languages.

Mythological themes and stories from history dominated opera in the century after Monteverdi. Elaborate music matched elaborate effects, which Charles de Saint-Évremond (c. 1614–1703) compared unfavorably to ancient practice: "The Greeks fashioned good tragedies with intermittent song; whereas the Italians and the French make bad ones, where all is sung"; he denounced opera as "a bizarre mixture of poetry and music where the writer and the composer, equally embarrassed by each other, go to a lot of trouble to create an execrable work" (*Letter to the Duke of Buckingham*, 1677; quoted in Weisstein, pp. 33–34). The requirement of a *lieto fine* (happy ending) and a portrayal of virtuous rule led to ludicrous misrepresentation of history; Domenico Gisberti's libretto for *Caligula delirante* (Mad Caligula, 1672; music by Giovanni Pagliardi), for example, ends with Caligula's recognition of the evils of his reign and his vow to reform: he becomes after all a good ruler. Jean-Baptiste Lully wrote mythological operas and ballets for the court of Louis XIV, among them *Ariane et Bacchus* (1659), *Alceste* (1674), and *Atys* (1676). Louis himself portrayed Apollo in *Le ballet de la nuit* in 1653 and danced in other ballets until 1670. Henry Lawes supplied the music to John Milton's masque *Comus* (1634); Thomas Arne in 1738 and George Frideric Handel in 1745 also wrote incidental music for it. Many of Handel's operas featured ancient themes set to Italian texts, among them *Giulio Cesare in Egitto* (1723–1724), *Scipione* (1726), *Alessandro* (a rare move into Greek territory; 1726), *Tolomeo* (another Greek subject, Ptolemy; 1728), *Berenice* (1737), *Serse* (Xerxes, a "barbarian" subject; 1738), and *Semele* (1743). In the eighteenth century, Rameau composed *Hippolyte et Aricie* (1733), *Castor et Pollux* (1737), and *Platée* (1745) for the court of Louis XV of France.

The domination of words over music is clearest in the career of Pietro Metastasio, whose first libretto, *Didone abbandonata* (Dido Abandoned), appeared in 1724; his career lasted for nearly fifty years.

His librettos were set by noted composers to the end of the century: *Adriano in Siria* (Hadrian in Syria) by Giovanni Battista Pergolesi; *Antigono* and *Il Parnasso confuso* (Parnassus in Turmoil) by Christoph Willibald Gluck; *La clemenza di Tito* (The Clemency of Titus) by Gluck and (in an adapted version) by Mozart; *L'olimpiade* by Pergolesi and Antonio Vivaldi; *Ezio* (Flavius Aetius) by Handel and Gluck; *Il ré pastore* (The Shepherd King) by Gluck and Mozart; and *Il sogno di Scipione* (The Dream of Scipio) by Mozart. Metastasio was the master of opera seria, with its pattern of three-part aria, duet, and chorus, often with *lieto fine*.

Reform—rejection of the complications and improbabilities of Metastasio's librettos and the overdecorated music that accompanied them—came in the 1760s, largely in the operas of Gluck. In *Orfeo ed Euridice* (1762; French version, 1774; libretto by Raniero de Calzabigi), *Alceste* (1767; Calzabigi), *Paride ed Elena* (Paris and Helen, 1770; Calzabigi), *Iphigénie en Aulide* (1774; libretto by Marie François Leblanc du Roullet), *Armide* (1777; Philippe Quinault), and *Iphigénie en Tauride* (1779; Nicholas-François Guillard), Gluck placed the dramatic emphasis in the music rather than in Metastasian dialogues and lessened the emphasis on the alternation of individual set pieces such as arias and duets. Gluck's works also mark the subordination of librettist to composer that has obtained to the present. Gluck's body of work marks a shift to Greek rather than Roman themes. In the same period, Mozart composed operas and theatrical works to many themes and settings, among them *Mitridate, Rè di Ponto* (Mithradates, King of Pontus, 1770; a barbarian theme), *Lucio Silla* (Lucius Sulla, 1772), *Idomeneo* (1781; the aftermath of the Trojan War), and *La clemenza di Tito* (1791).

The Nineteenth Century. The beginnings of industrial society and the political changes that followed the French Revolution had little immediate impact on opera; few operas on ancient themes were composed between 1789 and 1815, however, despite revolutionary and Napoleonic fascination with ancient Rome. After 1815, monarchs continued to subsidize opera and other performing arts, but an urban and bourgeois ticket-buying public seemed less fascinated with the doings of gods and emperors and more interested in the origins and workings of the nation-state. Romantic literature—including opera librettos—emphasized sentiment, the mysterious, and the supernatural, and favored the Middle Ages and the early modern period rather than antiquity as a proxy for the modern world.

Aside from Hector Berlioz, nineteenth-century composers evinced little interest in the ancient world as inspiration. Luigi Cherubini's *Médée* (1797) is a notable exception. Ludwig van Beethoven reused a theme from his ballet *Die Geschöpfe des Prometheus* (The Creatures of Prometheus, 1801) in his Third Symphony. Among composers of songs, Franz Schubert wrote the largest number relating to antiquity, all to verses by German poets. One of Gioacchino Rossini's operas, *Zelmira* (1822), was set in ancient Lesbos; he based *Semiramide* (1823) on the Greek legend of Semiramis, foundress of Babylon. Vincenzo Bellini looked to the clash of Druids and Romans for the setting of *Norma* (1831), but he neither attempted to reconstruct nor to reimagine the ancient world and its music; the characterization, orchestration, arias, duets, and choruses were very much in the bel canto style of the Romantic period, and *Norma* still offers more a vehicle for soprano display than any enlightenment about antiquity. Another tale of Romans and barbarians, Giuseppe Verdi's *Attila*, premiered in 1846. Jacques Offenbach mined ancient stories for comedy in two operettas, *La belle Hélène* (1864), a bedroom farce, and *Orphée aux enfers* (Orpheus in the Underworld, 1858; revision 1874), in which Orpheus is delighted to leave Eurydice behind in a hell where she is happy not to have to listen to his violin playing. Camille Saint-Saëns's *Rouet d'Omphale* (Omphale's Spinning Wheel, 1871) demonstrates the difficulty of attaching any musical idea to a specific ancient allusion, since it could illustrate any spinning; from 1937 to 1954 it was used as the theme for the American radio mystery series *The Shadow*.

Among Berlioz's cantatas on ancient themes, only *La mort de Cléopâtre* (The Death of Cleopatra, 1829;

text by Pierre-Ange Vieillard) is much performed any more. His *Les Troyens* (The Trojans) is the fullest operatic realization of an ancient theme between Gluck and Richard Strauss. He composed the opera, for which he wrote the libretto, between 1856 and 1860; it was never performed complete in Berlioz's lifetime (the first complete performance was in 1969 in Glasgow). The work, which concerns the destiny that draws the Trojans to Italy, is in two parts: *La prise de Troie* (The Sack of Troy, 1890), dominated by the suicide of Cassandre (Cassandra) and the escape of Énée (Aeneas), and *Les Troyens à Carthage* (The Trojans at Carthage, 1863), dominated by the love between Énée and Didon (Dido) and the suicide of Didon.

None of the operas of Richard Wagner deal with the ancient world. Venus, in *Tannhäuser* (1845; revision 1861), is more a figure of German legend than of Mediterranean mythology. In *Art and Revolution* (1849) Wagner denounces those who considered opera as entertainment and aimed to make it the expression of the community's values and aspirations. Like the ancient Greeks and like the earliest composers of opera, Wagner sought to create a *Gesamtkunstwerk*, a total work of art in which music, words, sets, costumes, and stage business would work together to a single effect and bring about a revolution in social attitudes and behavior. Greek tragedy provided the model of a community-based drama that would put Germans in touch with their tales of gods and heroes just as the *Oresteia* did the ancient Athenians. He structured his four-part cycle *Der Ring des Nibelungen* on the model of a three-play festival cycle—*Die Walküre*, *Siegfried*, and *Götterdämmerung*—preceded by satyr play, *Das Rheingold*. In 1872 he began the construction of a theater in Bayreuth, Germany, specifically fitted to his aesthetic; the complete *Ring* premiered there in 1876. Friedrich Wilhelm Nietzsche's *Die Geburt der Tragödie aus dem Geiste der Musik* (1872; English trans., *The Birth of Tragedy from the Spirit of Music*) celebrated Wagnerian music drama as the rebirth of tragedy that engaged its audience after the model of the ancient Greeks, a position that Nietzsche himself later rejected.

The Twentieth Century. Social, political, and technological upheavals in the twentieth century ensured that ancient stories would be stories like any other, touching or entertaining on their own merits, or employed as mirrors to the modern world. Monarchies and the domination of the nobility disappeared in Central and Eastern Europe after World War I and their influence lessened elsewhere; government subsidies from ministries of culture responsible to parliamentary majorities replaced royal and noble patronage; classical education and the teaching of Latin were much reduced. Film, especially after introduction of recorded sound in the late 1920s, and other media competed with music for the attention of mass audiences.

Strauss turned to ancient myth for the stories of five of his operas, three of them to Hugo von Hofmannsthal's intricate librettos. The music of *Elektra* (1909)—the story was based on the *Oresteia*—was stark and strident, but after *Elektra*, Strauss's idiom became more lush, with thick orchestrations far removed from any imitation of ancient music. *Ariadne auf Naxos* (1912; revision, 1916) presented a witty confrontation between ancient and modern (both the eighteenth century and the twentieth century) in the characters of the opera soprano who sings Ariadne and the commedia dell'arte figure Zerbinetta, who counsels her in the ways of love. Hofmannsthal writes in the preface to *Die ägyptische Helena* (The Egyptian Helen, 1928), "Some kind of curiosity had taken hold of my imagination; it was centered on these mythological figures as upon living people whose lives one knows in part" (quoted in Weisstein, p. 301), and suggested to Strauss that he should "take everything as if it had happened two or three years ago, somewhere between Moscow and New York. . . . It would take only minor changes to remove all the mythical elements" (ibid., p. 305). Strauss composed two operas to librettos by Joseph Gregor, *Daphne* (1938) and *Die Liebe der Danae* (The Loves of Danae, 1944).

In *Oedipus Rex* (1927), based on Sophocles' *Oedipus Tyrannus*, Igor Stravinsky made no attempt to imitate imagined ancient music. The libretto by Jean Cocteau was translated into an idiosyncratic modern Latin (neither classical nor church Latin), marked by oddities of syntax and pronunciation, by Jean Daniélou (later a Jesuit priest, patristics scholar, and cardinal). The work falls somewhere between a cantata or oratorio and an opera; its effect is stark and emotionally powerful; the Latin, although unfamiliar to the audience, lends an austere and remote quality to the work.

Stravinsky's *Apollon musagète* (Apollo, Leader of the Muses) was choreographed by George Balanchine as *Apollo* in 1928. The work presents Balanchine's high regard for ballet over music and lyric: Apollo dances with three muses, choosing Terpsichore as the most important. The revisions to the production over the years also demonstrate that modern music may have little connection to the ancient world: the costumes in the earliest staging were identifiably ancient, but by the 1960s Balanchine had reduced them to leotards and the sets were starkly abstract. Likewise, Léon Bakst's sets and costumes for the premiere of *Prelude to the Afternoon of a Faun* (music by Claude Debussy) in 1912 were classical, but classical allusion could be dispensed with, as Jerome Robbins did in his 1953 version, which concerned two dancers in a ballet rehearsal studio.

Reference to the ancient world was not limited to the "serious" forms of opera, ballet, and concert music. Broadway musicals followed the example of Offenbach in seeing the comic side. The musical *The Boys from Syracuse* (book by George Abbot, music by Richard Rodgers, lyrics by Lorenz Hart; 1938) was based on William Shakespeare's *Comedy of Errors*, which was based on *Twin Menaechmi* by Plautus. The story of a department store window dresser who falls in love with a mannequin of Venus in Kurt Weil's *One Touch of Venus* (1943; lyrics by Ogden Nash and book by Nash and S. J. Perelman) owes more to Pygmalion than to any tale of Venus. *My Fair Lady* (1956; book by Alan Jay Lerner, music by Frederick Loewe) offers a modernized version of the Pygmalion story based on George Bernard Shaw's play *Pygmalion* (1913). Stephen Sondheim based *A Funny Thing Happened on the Way to the Forum* (1962; book by Burt Shevelove and Larry Gelbart) on Plautus' *Pseudolus*.

Oedipus Rex. Performance of the opera-oratorio by Igor Stravinsky, Juilliard School, New York City, 1948. Photograph by Gottscho-Schleisner, Inc. PRINTS AND PHOTOGRAPHS DIVISION, LIBRARY OF CONGRESS

Music for toga-and-sandal films usually features much brass and tympani to produce fanfares and marching tunes for armies. Lack of knowledge about what ancient music sounded like bedeviled film composers as it had composers in other genres. Miklós Rózsa, who wrote the score for *Ben Hur* (1959), recounted trying to imagine what Roman music must have been like while standing on the Palatine Hill: "I began to whistle scraps of ideas and to march about excitedly and rhythmically. Two young girls looked at me in terror and fled, muttering 'pazzo' [madman]" (from the obituary in the *New York Times*, 29 July 1995); his scraps of ideas won the Academy Award for best score in 1959. Despite thick orchestral textures that looked for inspiration more to the late nineteenth century than to Apollo and the Muses, film and television composers felt more restrained by a striving for authenticity than composers of opera or concert music: the fanfares for the television series *I, Claudius* (1976), for example, were played on reconstructed ancient instruments.

Composers and audiences maintained their interest in the ancient world throughout the late twentieth and early twenty-first century. Benjamin Britten's *Rape of Lucretia* (1946) carries a strong element of Christian moralizing. Priam's decision not to kill Paris and to allow Helen to remain in Troy is the theme of Michael Tippett's *King of Priam* (1962). The world premiere of Samuel Barber's *Antony and Cleopatra* opened the new Metropolitan Opera House in New York City in 1966. Hans Werner Henze based *The Bassarids* (1966) on Euripides' *Bacchae*; his *Phaedra* had its premiere at the Berlin State Opera in 2007.

[*See also* Atreus, House of; Euripides; *and* Music.]

BIBLIOGRAPHY

There is no book-length study of how the ancient world is interpreted in modern music, but the following works contain scattered discussions of the topic.

Conrad, Peter. *A Song of Love and Death: The Meaning of Opera*. New York: Poseidon, 1987.

Farrell, Joseph. *Latin Language and Latin Culture: From Ancient to Modern Times*. Cambridge, U.K.: Cambridge University Press, 2001. Includes a brief discussion of Daniélou's translation of the libretto for Stravinsky's *Oedipus Rex* (pp. 117–123).

Millington, Barry, ed. *The Wagner Compendium: A Guide to Wagner's Life and Music*. New York: Schirmer Books, 1992. Two articles deal with Wagner's interest in Greek drama: "Wagner and the Greeks," by Hugh Lloyd-Jones, and "Bayreuth and the Idea of a Festival Theater," by Stewart Spencer. See also Richard Wagner's *Art and Revolution*, translated by William Ashton Ellis, published in *Prose Works* (London: Kegan Paul, Trench, Trübner, 1893–1912), reprinted in *The Art-Work of the Future, and Other Works* (Lincoln: University of Nebraska Press, 1993).

Smith, Patrick J. *The Tenth Muse: A Historical Study of the Opera Libretto*. New York: Alfred A. Knopf, 1970. The best and fullest discussion of opera texts and stories.

Taruskin, Richard. *The Oxford History of Western Music*. 6 vols. New York and Oxford: Oxford University Press, 2005. A general overview of the history of music, with reference to and analysis of many individual works.

Weisstein, Ulrich, ed. *The Essence of Opera*. New York: Free Press of Glencoe, 1964. The source of most of the quotations from composers, librettists, and critics included in this article.

Stephen Wagley

Film and Television

The study of film and television productions that depict, excavate, and even reinvent classical antiquity has become a significant and rewarding critical subfield within the study of the classical tradition. Joanna Paul recently observed that "successfully—and fruitfully—the study of classics and cinema has asserted itself as a leader in the field of reception studies" (*Classical Review* 55, no. 2 [2005]: 688). Films and television programs re-create the ancient Greek and Roman worlds in a variety of different ways, and filmmakers and television producers use many different classical sources as their artistic inspiration. These various creative processes are well documented in a comprehensive book by Jon Solomon that surveys all the many different types of films about the ancient world. Screen re-creations can essentially be divided into two separate, but not always completely distinct, categories: first, films and television productions set directly in antiquity—what Solomon calls "ancients" (a term modeled on the designation used for the film genre of "Westerns")—and second, films and television productions that use classical mythological and literary plots, themes, and archetypes.

Productions Set in Antiquity. The most obvious re-creations of the ancient Greek and Roman worlds occur in films and television productions set in the ancient world: these productions are often labeled "epic" and categorized within the genre of epic film. Successful re-creations of this type include films such as Ridley Scott's Academy Award–winning motion picture *Gladiator* (2000) and Zack Snyder's blockbuster hit *300* (2007); particularly lavish in time and money expended in production was the 2005–2007 HBO-BBC television series *Rome*. These re-creations—whether set in actual historical antiquity or something more akin to a generalized mythological past—transport the viewers directly back into the ancient world, because the best ones exhibit immense amounts of historical research and careful attention to visual detail. The best re-creations not only offer the modern audience an impressive display of what is readily familiar and admired about ancient Greek and Roman culture, but also invite the audience to enjoy the glamour and excitement inherent in viewing the "otherness" of a bygone time and place. Yet however meticulous the re-creation, some classicists and historians regularly become exasperated over what they consider unforgivable inaccuracies, historical anachronisms, and the replaying of tired old stereotypes. But a broad understanding of the artistic intent and commercial imperatives of films and television productions set in the ancient world should never be lost in this critical discourse, and scholars should keep in mind what nonacademic viewers can plainly see: that these on-screen re-creations set in the ancient Greek and Roman worlds are intended primarily as rousing popular entertainment and not as historical documentaries or illustrated university lectures.

Early Period. From the very beginnings of the cinema in the early twentieth century, the genre of films set in the ancient Greek and Roman worlds dominated the screen, offering multiple opportunities for representing the alluring spectacles of battles, chariot races, triumphal processions, magnificent banquets, and sumptuous costumes. Throughout the hundred-plus-year history of films and television productions that portray the ancient world, those set in Roman antiquity have been more prevalent than those set in Greek antiquity. This is most likely because of the relatively greater familiarity that the modern Western world has with ancient Rome, and—as the historian Maria Wyke has suggested—perhaps also because of the nascent aspirations of the powerful Italian and American film industries to identify their national projects with the classical, and especially imperial, Roman past. The birth of the ancient epic film is usually traced to 1908 and the Italian producer Arturo Ambrosio's successful feature film *Gli ultimi giorni di Pompeii* (*The Last Days of Pompeii*). There followed the fertile golden age of Italian silent cinema, which produced such important and influential films as Enrico Guazzoni's *Quo Vadis?* (1912) and Giovanni Pastrone's *Cabiria* (1914). These two films set the artistic cinematic gold standard followed by all subsequent filmmakers: the epic film set in the ancient world should be a production of massive scale, elaborate special effects, and evocative historical details. In the United States, pioneering filmmakers also began to produce films set in classical antiquity—with a narrative predilection for biblical or religious themes—starting with the first film version of *Ben-Hur* (1907), directed by Sidney Olcott.

Other notable American films of this early period include J. Gordon Edwards's *Cleopatra* (1917), starring Theda Bara, and his *Nero* (1922), as well as the second film version of *Ben-Hur* (1925), directed by Fred Niblo for the newly merged Metro-Goldwyn-Mayer (MGM) studios. The 1920s saw the rise of the greatest director of the genre of epic film, Cecil B. DeMille, whose films set in antiquity include *The King of Kings* (1927); in the sound era, DeMille produced the scandal-causing *The Sign of the Cross* (1932), set during Nero's reign, and the conspicuously opulent *Cleopatra* (1934) starring Claudette Colbert. It was during this period that the Production Code of 1930 (also called the Hays Code) focused its prurient eye on the more titillating elements of films set in the ancient world, such as the infamous dance scene in *The Sign of the Cross* or Colbert's seductive milk bath in *Cleopatra*.

Rise and Fall of the Golden Age.

Next came a fallow interlude during the later 1930s and early 1940s in which few films set in antiquity were produced, a result of the extreme financial exigencies exerted by the Depression and World War II, as well as of the gloominess of the European and American national moods. But the postwar economic boom and an upsurge in popular interest in the classical world led to the reinvigoration of the genre of ancient epic, especially in the Hollywood film industry. Starting in the early 1950s the golden age of the Hollywood ancient epic "toga" film was spurred on by viewer demand. An even more crucial factor was the pressure of competition coming from the new medium of television, which began drawing paying customers away from the movie theaters. Hollywood responded with a host of extravagant epic spectaculars set in classical antiquity and mainly shot on location in Greece and Italy, including many of the most popular and recognizable film titles of the era. These include such films as MGM's vigorous version of *Quo Vadis?* (1951), directed by Mervyn LeRoy and starring Robert Taylor and Deborah Kerr; Twentieth Century–Fox's *The Robe* (1953), directed by Henry Koster, the first CinemaScope film shown in widescreen projection, and soon followed by *Demetrius and the Gladiators* (1954), directed by Delmer Daves; United Artists' *Alexander the Great* (1955), directed by Robert Rossen and starring Richard Burton; and Warner Brothers' *Helen of Troy* (1955), directed by Robert Wise. But the undeniable zenith of the gilded decade was reached with MGM's luminous remake of *Ben-Hur* (1959), directed by William Wyler and starring the Oscar-winner Charlton Heston. Wyler's *Ben-Hur* was a critically and commercially successful film that scored eleven Academy Awards and initiated a new generation of films set in antiquity.

During the 1950s a number of Italian films set in the ancient world were also produced on location around the Mediterranean and seen by American audiences, including *Due notte con Cleopatra* (*Two Nights with Cleopatra*, 1953), a comedy directed by Mario Mattoli and starring Sophia Loren, and *Ulisse* (1954, released in the United States in 1955 as *Ulysses*), directed by Mario Camerini and starring Kirk Douglas. From the venerable studios in Cinecittà, Rome, came the wildly entertaining action epic *Hercules* (1957), directed by Pietro Francisci and starring the American bodybuilder Steve Reeves: this film spawned the immensely popular and prolific genre of Italian sword-and-sandal films that flourished well into the middle of the next decade.

In the post–*Ben-Hur* era, a few American-made epic films set in antiquity tried valiantly to keep the genre alive, including Universal Studios' *Spartacus* (1960), directed by Stanley Kubrick and starring Kirk Douglas, perhaps one of the most groundbreaking and important films ever made; Fox's *The 300 Spartans* (1962), directed by Rudolph Maté; and Columbia's *Jason and the Argonauts* (1963), directed by Don Chaffey and enlivened by the visual effects of the legendary master Ray Harryhausen. But the genre of ancient epic was dealt a fatal blow from the financial and critical fiasco of Fox's *Cleopatra* (1963), directed by Joseph L. Mankiewicz and starring the real-life romantic couple and controversy-magnets Elizabeth Taylor and Richard Burton.

After that catastrophe it was clear that American viewers were finished with the four-hour, multimillion-dollar spectacular set in antiquity, and Paramount's critically hailed but prophetically titled *The Fall of the Roman Empire* (1964), directed by Anthony Mann, never found a contemporaneous audience. What the popular mood of the time did respond to were satires of the epic genre, including United Artists' rowdy film version of the Broadway play *A Funny Thing Happened on the Way to the Forum* (1966), directed by Richard Lester, and the British-produced farce *Carry on Cleo* (1964; released in the United States in 1965), directed by Gerald Thomas. Much later the satiric impulse to ridicule ancient epics on-screen was expertly resurrected in the controversial film *Monty Python's Life of Brian* (1979), directed by Terry Jones and starring the members of the British comedic troupe Monty Python in several different roles; Mel Brooks produced, directed, and starred in another manic spoof of the epic genre, *History of the World, Part I* (1981).

Made-for-television Productions. Although the serious, theatrically released feature film set in antiquity languished in the period from the late 1960s through the 1970s and 1980s, a major popular development occurred when the industry's focus turned to producing made-for-television films or "miniseries" aimed specifically at television audiences. The most outstanding early example of this entertainment trend was the BBC's production of the thirteen-episode miniseries *I, Claudius* (1976), directed by Herbert Wise, a critically hailed adaptation of the novels of Robert Graves that was shown in the United States on the PBS network. This was soon followed by several more extended made-for-television films or miniseries, such as Franco Zeffirelli's eight-hour *Jesus of Nazareth* (1977), Boris Sagal's six-hour *Masada* (1981), Peter Hunt's six-part *The Last Days of Pompeii* (1984), and Stuart Cooper's twelve-episode *A.D.* (1985), a pricey yet unexceptional miniseries that curbed the genre for the next several years. During the heyday of these television miniseries, their financial success prompted the production of a handful of feature films, such as MGM's *Clash of the Titans* (1981), directed by Desmond Davis, with visual effects by Ray Harryhausen, and starring Laurence Olivier, and another Italian version of *Hercules* (1983), directed by Luigi Cozzi and starring the American muscleman Lou Ferrigno.

The made-for-television genre was robustly revived in the 1990s with the rise of cable television, with a new crop of syndicated series aimed at younger audiences. The most lucrative was the multifaceted *Hercules* project conceived by the filmmaker Sam Raimi, who produced five made-for-television films (all in 1994) starring Kevin Sorbo as Hercules, and followed this with the hugely successful television series *Hercules: The Legendary Journeys* (1995–1999). The series ran for six seasons and spawned a spin-off also set in the ancient mythological world, the popular cult series *Xena: Warrior Princess* (1995–2001). It is likely that this profitable revival of the Hercules figure on television inspired Walt Disney Pictures to produce one of its all-time most successful animated feature films, *Hercules* (1997). Encouraged by these achievements, the American company Hallmark Entertainment produced three made-for-television miniseries at the end of the decade: the Emmy Award–winning *The Odyssey* (1997), directed by Andrei Konchalovksy and starring Armand Assante; *Cleopatra* (1999), directed by Franc Roddam; and *Jason and the Argonauts* (2000), directed by Nick Willing.

Temporary Rebirth of Ancient Epics. The release of Ridley Scott's *Gladiator* in 2000, from the partner studios DreamWorks and Universal, not only signaled the rebirth of the ancient-epic feature film but also triggered a new wave of scholarly investigation into the enduring influence of the ancient world on modern popular culture. The colossal critical and commercial success of *Gladiator*, starring Russell Crowe in an Oscar-winning performance, also made it safe for Hollywood producers to reach back once again to hallowed antiquity for their subject matter. Warner Brothers soon released two ancient-world epics for the new millennium: first *Troy* (2004), directed by Wolfgang Petersen and starring Brad Pitt, based loosely on Homer's *Iliad*, and then *Alexander* (2004), directed by Oliver Stone and starring Colin Farrell as the Macedonian king and general. Although *Troy* eventually matched the financial success of *Gladiator*, *Alexander* was considered a box-office failure, and neither film accrued the critical acclaim of the earlier film.

Not to be deterred, Warner Brothers released another ancient epic, *300* (2007), directed by Zack Snyder and starring Gerard Butler. A sleek, high-tech film adaptation of Frank Miller's graphic novel narrating the Spartans' last stand at Thermopylae, *300* broke numerous box-office records and was enormously profitable, yet it was not without controversy for some of its alleged political subtexts. Two films in the same era explored the end of late Roman antiquity in fifth century CE Britain: Antoine Fuqua's *King Arthur* (2004), starring Clive Owen, and Doug Lefler's *The Last Legion* (2007), starring Colin Firth.

On television, the ancient world continued to be popular in the early years of the new millennium. The cable network TNT produced the Emmy-nominated miniseries *Julius Caesar* (2002), directed by Uli Edel. Soon after, ABC produced two low-budget and poorly reviewed miniseries: *Helen of Troy* (2003), directed by John Kent Harrison, and *Empire* (2005), directed by John Gray and Kim Manners. In stark contrast—in terms of its historical authenticity, rich production values, and exceptional writing—was the creator Bruno Heller's series *Rome* (2005–2007), produced jointly by the BBC, the American cable network HBO, and the Italian public broadcaster RAI. *Rome*, shown in two separate seasons of twelve and ten episodes, established a new and higher production standard for forthcoming film and television productions set in the ancient world.

Classical Plots, Themes, and Archtypes. The other major way in which the cultures of ancient Greece and Rome are re-created on-screen occurs when filmmakers and television producers take ancient themes, narratives, and myths and adapt them into plots set in the modern day or in another temporal setting far removed from antiquity. This process is elucidated in a 2001 collection of essays on the subject edited by Martin Winkler. Classical literary plots and ancient mythological archetypes have been successfully used in many contemporary films, including Clint Eastwood's Iliadic meta-Western *Unforgiven* (1992) and Joel and Ethan Coen's Odyssean romp *O Brother, Where Art Thou?* (2000). Modern television has also used the classical hero archetype in programs such as *Buffy the Vampire Slayer* (which ran from 1997 to 2003) and *Heroes* (which premiered in 2006).

Such films and television productions tend to satisfy even the most accuracy-obsessed classicists. Viewing these films and television programs, the audience enjoys the essence of an ancient literary work or myth distilled to its most basic narrative and archetypal elements, those that resonate most powerfully with the modern world. At the same time, scholarly viewers are heartened to witness the core evidence of what keeps the field of classics alive: these films and television programs demonstrate what makes a "classic" myth or work relevant to new generations of spectators. And because these films are not bound by any obligation to re-create actual ancient settings or precise historical context, the filmmaker or television producer can take a more modern, innovative approach to the timeless themes and characters.

Early Period. In the early days of cinema, as Italian filmmakers focused their energies on producing ancient historical epics, filmmakers in France showed a preference for more literary, theatrical, and mythological themes. These early productions helped to initiate and develop a creative cinematic process for adapting and revising ancient themes into nonancient settings. The pioneering French director Georges Méliès filmed hundreds of short films from 1895 to 1913, including a number of mythological titles such as *Pygmalion et Galathée* (1903) and *L'île de Calypso* (1905). From the film company Pathé came a series of films adapted from ancient topics, including the contemporary battle story *Hercules in the Regiment* (1909) and one of the first cinematic explorations of Orpheus, *The Legend of Orpheus* (1909). In the United States, a handful of updated mythological films were made in this early period, including Theodore Wharton's modernized fantasy *Neptune's Daughter* (1912) and Gilbert P. Hamilton's comedy *The Golden Fleece* (1918), introducing a present-day Jason. The 1920s saw few revisions of ancient myth: one notable exception was Alexander Korda's comical romance *The Private Life of Helen of Troy* (1927), a well-reviewed domestic satire set in contemporary vernacular.

With the sound era in the 1930s came a new range of cinematic possibilities, including the movie musical. The director Frank Tuttle's time-traveling musical *Roman Scandals* (1933), starring Eddie Cantor as a modern-day American who journeys back to ancient Rome, featured several elaborate production numbers choreographed by Busby Berkeley. The 1940s saw a wartime development of viewer interest in dramatic adaptations of ancient literary works, including RKO's film adaptation of Eugene O'Neill's 1931 play *Mourning Becomes Electra* (1947), directed by Dudley Nichols, an updated version of Aeschylus' tragic *Oresteia* trilogy set during the American Civil War. Musical adaptations on film of mythological subjects remained popular in the 1940s, such as Columbia Pictures' musical comedy *Down to Earth* (1947), directed by Alexander Hall and starring Rita Hayworth as the Muse Terpsichore interfering with a modern Broadway play. This film was later remade by Robert Greenwald as *Xanadu* (1980), starring Olivia Newton-John.

Explorations of Serious Contemporary Issues. In the 1950s, filmmakers employed ancient mythological themes to explore more serious contemporary issues and concerns. One of the most significant and influential films in the history of cinema is the French director Jean Cocteau's *Orphée* (1950), an existential transformation of the ancient Greek myth of Orpheus into a profound modern statement about poetry, death, and immortality. In the same decade another French director also delved into the Orpheus theme: Marcel Camus' Academy Award–winning *Orfeu Negro* (*Black Orpheus*, 1959) was an equally revolutionary film. Filmed in Rio de Janeiro during Carnival week, starring mostly Brazilian actors, and scored by groundbreaking music, *Black Orpheus* breathed new lyrical life into the ancient myth. In the 1960s and 1970s, European master filmmakers produced several provocative and often controversial films adapted from ancient literature, including Federico Fellini's *Fellini Satyricon* (1969), a dreamlike adaptation of Petronius' fragmentary novel, and Pier Paolo Pasolini's metahistorical film versions of the Greek tragedies *Edipo Re* (1967) and *Medea* (1970).

Also emerging in this period were artistically avant-garde films of ancient myths or dramas retold in modernized settings. These include the American director Jules Dassin's *Phaedra* (1962) and *A Dream of Passion* (1978), both updates of Greek tragedies starring his wife, Melina Mercouri; Russ Meyer's *Faster, Pussycat! Kill! Kill!* (1966), a violent, campy Hollywood retelling of Aeschylus' *Eumenides*; and

Classic Film. Francis X. Bushman (*left*) and Ramon Navarro (*right*) re-create their roles in the 1925 film *Ben Hur*, directed by Fred Niblo. NEW YORK WORLD-TELEGRAM AND THE SUN NEWSPAPER PHOTOGRAPH COLLECTION/PRINTS AND PHOTOGRAPHS DIVISION, LIBRARY OF CONGRESS

Liliana Cavani's *Year of the Cannibals* (1971), featuring a futuristic but still rebellious Antigone. Arthur Allan Seidelman directed a contemporary comic-action reworking of the Hercules myth, *Hercules in New York* (1970), starring a then-unknown Austrian bodybuilder named Arnold Schwarzenegger. *Winds of Change* (1978), directed by Takashi, was a Japanese fantasy animation that re-created five stories from Ovid's *Metamorphoses* set to contemporary rock music.

Reinventions. Within the dominant medium of television starting in the 1960s and 1970s, ancient mythological and literary themes and archetypes manifested themselves more subtly in the narratives of made-for-television programs. The most outstanding example was the original science-fiction series *Star Trek* (1966–1969), created by Gene Roddenberry, which evinced a deep and abiding interest in adapting classical motifs into its futuristic setting. More recent made-for-television genres of fantasy and science fiction tend to exhibit ubiquitous classical and mythological allusions, from programs such as the space fantasy *Battlestar Galactica* (1978–1979, and launched again in 2004) to the adventure series *Lost* (which first aired in 2004).

Feature films since the late twentieth century have also reinvented ancient literary motifs and plots by situating them in more modern contexts. Themes and images from Homer's *Iliad* can be traced in Ridley Scott's dystopian *Blade Runner* (1982), Oliver Stone's Vietnam War drama *Platoon* (1986), and Clint Eastwood's *Unforgiven* (1992); characters and episodes from Homer's *Odyssey* can be found in Victor Nuñez's poetic film *Ulee's Gold* (1997), Joel and Ethan Coen's *O Brother, Where Art Thou?* (2000), and Anthony Minghella's Civil War tale *Cold Mountain* (2003). Greek tragic themes have continued to inform cinematic explorations of weighty social issues, including the Sophoclean *Antigone* plot developed in Tim Robbins's capital-punishment drama *Dead Man Walking* (1995) and the thematic elements from Euripides' *Bacchae* that punctuate Neil Jordan's surprise-ending thriller *The Crying Game* (1992). The Orpheus theme remains well-suited to the musical film and found articulation in, for instance, Baz Luhrmann's operatic *Moulin Rouge* (2001). At the start of the twenty-first century, film and television productions represent some of the most visible, omnipresent, and compelling expressions of the classical tradition.

[*See also* Classical Tradition, *subentries* Classical Influences on Western Art *and* Music.]

BIBLIOGRAPHY

Burgoyne, Robert. *The Hollywood Historical Film.* Malden, Mass., and Oxford: Blackwell, 2008.

Cartledge, Paul, and Fiona Greenland, eds. *Responses to Oliver Stone's "Alexander": Film, History, and Cultural Studies.* Madison: University of Wisconsin Press, 2009.

Cyrino, Monica S. *Big Screen Rome.* Malden, Mass., and Oxford: Blackwell, 2005.

Cyrino, Monica S., ed. *Rome, Season One: History Makes Television.* Malden, Mass., and Oxford: Blackwell, 2008.

Elley, Derek. *The Epic Film: Myth and History.* London: Routledge & Kegan Paul, 1984.

Joshel, Sandra R., Margaret Malamud, and Donald T. McGuire, eds. *Imperial Projections: Ancient Rome in Modern Popular Culture.* Baltimore: Johns Hopkins University Press, 2001.

Nisbet, Gideon. *Ancient Greece in Film and Popular Culture.* Exeter, U.K.: Bristol Phoenix Press, 2006.

Pomeroy, Arthur J. *"Then It Was Destroyed by the Volcano": The Ancient World in Film and on Television.* London: Duckworth, 2008.

Solomon, Jon. *The Ancient World in the Cinema.* Rev. ed. New Haven, Conn.: Yale University Press, 2001.

Winkler, Martin M. *Cinema and Classical Texts: Apollo's New Light.* Cambridge, U.K.: Cambridge University Press, 2009.

Winkler, Martin M., ed. *Classical Myth and Culture in the Cinema.* Oxford: Oxford University Press, 2001.

Winkler, Martin M., ed. *"Gladiator": Film and History.* Malden, Mass., and Oxford: Blackwell, 2004.

Winkler, Martin M., ed. *"Spartacus": Film and History.* Malden, Mass., and Oxford: Blackwell, 2007.

Winkler, Martin M., ed. *Troy: From Homer's "Iliad" to Hollywood Epic.* Malden, Mass., and Oxford: Blackwell, 2007.

Wyke, Maria. *Projecting the Past: Ancient Rome, Cinema, and History.* New York and London: Routledge, 1997.

Monica S. Cyrino

CLAUDIAN

(Claudius Claudianus, c. 370–c. 404 CE), bilingual poet. Claudius Claudianus flourished in Italy in the last years before Alaric's sack of Rome in 410. Born in Alexandria and educated bilingually, he began his career as an itinerant Greek poet writing verse panegyrics in praise of imperial officials and cities in the eastern Roman Empire. Except for fragments of a *Gigantomachy* (Battle of the Giants) and some epigrams, his Greek poetry is lost. Claudian left the Greek East and sought his fortune in Rome, where he delivered his first verse panegyric in Latin (395), establishing himself as the poetic heir to the epic tradition of Virgil, Ovid, and Statius. In the same year, he became panegyrist for the child emperor Honorius and his regent Stilicho and moved to Milan, the western imperial capital, where he became "tribune and notary" and held a senatorial title. The pinnacle of success came five years later (400), when a bronze statue of Claudian was erected by imperial decree in the Forum of Trajan. Its inscription praises the poet for combining the mind of Virgil with the muse of Homer (*Corpus Inscriptionum Latinarum* 6.1710). He probably died in 404, after delivering his last consular panegyric for Honorius in Rome.

Claudian composed eighteen books of epic (over ten thousand hexameters), elegiac prefaces to his epics, the beginning of a Latin *Gigantomachy*, and over fifty shorter poems, including panegyrics, epistles, and epigrams on a variety of themes. His first commission in Rome was to celebrate the consulship of the juvenile brothers Olybrius and Probinus (January 395), scions of Rome's most prominent Christian family, the Anicii. For the occasion, Claudian invented a new kind of panegyrical epic that wove the topics of a laudatory speech (as formulated by rhetoricians such as Aphthonius and Menander) into the narrative format of a short historical epic. In the opening scene the goddess Roma appears to the emperor Theodosius, after he has defeated the usurper Eugenius, and justifies why her foster children Olybrius and Probinus deserve the consulship. Claudian did not mention that his patrons (or the emperor) were Christians, but praised them in traditional classical terms. Augustine and Orosius disapproved of Claudian as pagan, but the Christian elite of Rome valued his literary culture, as did the Christian court in Milan, which charged Claudian to commemorate the consulship of Honorius in 396 in the same way. Claudian wrote six consular panegyrics, including three for Honorius (396, 398, 404), one for Mallius Theodorus (399), and a three-book masterpiece for Stilicho (400), in which the Vandal general is commended to Rome as its savior against foreign threats and guarantor of imperial peace and unity As court poet, he also composed epic invectives (two books each) against Rufinus (397) and Eutropius (399), archenemies of Stilicho in the eastern court of Constantinople. These works not only adapted a rhetorical pattern that was the inverse of the panegyric but also drew on the tradition of Roman satire for their vituperation of moral vices. Claudian authored two short war epics—one commemorating Stilicho's protection of Rome's grain supply against the rebel Gildo (*De bello Gildonico*, 397), the other his defense of Italy against Alaric the Goth (*De bello Getico*, 402)—and an epic as wedding poem for the dynastic marriage of Honorius with Stilicho's daughter Maria (398).

Apart from his official poetry, Claudian worked ambitiously on a mythological epic about the rape of Persephone or Proserpina (*De raptu Proserpinae*), three of whose four proposed books he finished, and which became his most popular work in the Middle Ages. He rewrote the Greek myth, already told twice by Ovid (cf. *Metamorphoses* 5 and *Fasti* 4), in the tradition of Latin mythological epic, but gave it the stamp of late-antique aesthetics by subordinating narrative continuity to rhetorical speeches and ekphrases (detailed descriptions of an artwork, place, or person) in which words are patterned like differently colored jewels or mosaics to highlight their brilliance. Such literary artistry is evident in the ekphrasis of a cosmic tapestry embroidered by Proserpina (at the end of book 1), depicting the creation of the world's different realms and foreshadowing Proserpina's abduction to the Underworld by Pluto. Claudian also reinterprets the myth allegorically to address contemporary fears and hopes about the division of the Roman Empire into an eastern and western realm ruled separately by the brothers Arcadius and Honorius after the death of Theodosius I in 395. The epic begins with Pluto, ruler of the Underworld, marshaling an army of monsters, Furies, and Titans to make war on his brother Jupiter because he alone was unmarried. Jupiter averts war by arranging the marriage of Proserpina to Pluto, and the second book closes with the novel scene of the Underworld celebrating in courtly fashion a dynastic wedding. If the reconciliation between Jupiter and Pluto was intended to suggest a political program for imperial peace and unity, the discontinuation of the epic—which breaks off with the grief and anger of Ceres over her lost daughter—may point to Claudian's loss of faith in this ideal.

[*See also* Christianity; Ovid; Panegyric; *and* Poetry, Latin, *subentry* Epic.]

BIBLIOGRAPHY
Works of Claudian
Claudian. Translated by Maurice Platnauer. 2 vols. Loeb Classical Library. Cambridge, Mass.: Harvard University Press, and London: Heinemann, 1956.
Claudian's In Rufinum: An Exegetical Commentary. Edited by Harry L. Levy. Cleveland, Ohio: American Philological Association, 1971. Appendix contains author's 1935 edition of text with introduction and textual commentary.
Claudii Claudiani Carmina. Edited by John B. Hall. Leipzig, Germany: B. G. Teubner, 1985.
De raptu Proserpinae. Edited by Claire Gruzelier. Oxford, Clarendon Press; New York: Oxford University Press, 1993. Includes translation.
Panegyricus de sexto consulatu Honorii Augusti. Edited by Michael Dewar. Oxford, Clarendon Press; New York: Oxford University Press, 1996. Includes translation.

Secondary Works
Cameron, Alan. *Claudian: Poetry and Propaganda at the Court of Honorius.* Oxford: Clarendon Press, 1970.
Long, Jacqueline. *Claudian's In Eutropium: Or, How, When, and Why to Slander a Eunuch.* Chapel Hill: University of North Carolina Press, 1996.

Stephen Wheeler

CLAUDIUS

(Tiberius Claudius Nero Germanicus, 10 BCE–54 CE), emperor 41–54 CE. Tiberius Claudius Nero Germanicus, the younger brother of Germanicus, was the only Julio-Claudian emperor who did not belong to the Julian clan either by birth or by adoption. His father, Drusus (the Elder), was the son of the empress Livia's first husband; his mother, Antonia Minor, was Mark Antony's daughter and Augustus' niece.

Claudius almost certainly suffered a mild form of cerebral palsy. He shook, limped, and spoke oddly, and it was assumed that his disability extended to his mental capacity. He was not allowed to enter the course of public offices as would have been appropriate for a young man of his ancestry. Augustus found him an embarrassment. Tiberius belittled him, and Caligula (Gaius) ridiculed him. Despite being marginalized within the family, he was useful because his marriages could be used to solidify political connections. He was betrothed twice and married four times.

Claudius became emperor by a "marvelous fluke" (*mirabili casu*, Suetonius *Claudius* 10.1). When his nephew, the emperor Caligula, was assassinated in 41, Claudius fled from the mayhem that followed and hid in the palace complex. Discovered by an ordinary soldier, he was hurried to the praetorian camp, where he was hailed emperor. He rewarded his captors handsomely, the first emperor to make a cash gift at the time of his accession. It is probable that the guard had sought him out intentionally, and Claudius himself may have been privy to the conspiracy that murdered Caligula.

Reign. Claudius' position was precarious from the beginning because of his irregular elevation. His response to Caligula's assassination was ambiguous, for he could not succeed if perceived as heir to an erratic predecessor nor could he seem to applaud tyrannicide. In a compromise he punished the ringleaders but granted amnesty to the senators who had tried to displace him during the brief interregnum. To strengthen his claim among the Julian emperors, he emphasized his connection with

Augustus, declared his grandmother Livia divine, and granted public honors to the memory of his father and mother, Drusus and Antonia. He gave public recognition to Germanicus and even to his grandfather Mark Antony. Claudius understood, as Caligula evidently had not, that it was necessary to maintain the pretense that the senate and emperor were equal partners. He showed it formal respect, but this effort did little to improve relations.

Claudius had reason to feel threatened, for in 42 the generals who commanded legions in the frontier provinces tried to dislodge him. Their uncoordinated attempt failed, but their challenge could only increase his unease. The next year, 43, perhaps in reaction to this crisis, Claudius sought the missing military credentials so necessary for an emperor. He successfully invaded Britain, accomplishing what had evidently been conceived by Caligula, and his generals quickly subdued the less organized British tribes. Claudius visited the island briefly, led a force into their chief town, and was saluted *imperator*, conquering general. Despite minimal personal involvement, he could claim a genuine achievement, the addition of Britain to the empire.

Claudius involved himself in the business of Rome's governance with great attention to detail. He fostered legislation through the senate, a tactic that maintained the pretense of respect, but he also ruled directly through edicts. Many measures were sensible or made governance more efficient. Conservative by nature, he sponsored regulations that upheld the traditional stratification of Roman society. Even when he advocated permission for Gallic senators to stand for office in Rome, he looked to precedent for justification. His speech in favor of their candidacy is preserved, not only by Tacitus (*Annals* 11.24) but also on a bronze tablet found at Lyons in France. Claudius took a special interest in the law courts, instituting reforms in their operation and personally ruling on cases, both directly and on appeal. In his zeal he tried many cases in his own court, and his reputation suffered from the secrecy of the proceedings and because it was said that he judged after hearing only one side of a case. He initiated public works by reconstructing aqueducts and establishing a new port for Rome near the mouth of the Tiber.

Claudius' conservative bent led him to renew neglected institutions and religious practices. He revived the censorship, an office that allowed him as censor to control the membership of the senate and equestrian order. In 47 he recalled Augustus' program by producing Secular Games, a festival intended to occur only once in a person's lifetime. This brought ridicule on him because the celebration had taken place as recently as 17 BCE. Antiquarian interests also informed his writings, which were largely historical. Claudius' physical limitations did not impair his intellect. He wrote numerous books, including one on the history of the alphabet.

Claudius' tenure as emperor was of sufficiently long duration (thirteen years) and took place long enough after Augustus had become sole ruler to contribute to making the principate an accepted entity. It has been suggested that Claudius authored a "policy of centralization" (Momigliano), but this impression results less from intention than from the simple accumulation of individual actions that caused responsibility to fall increasingly on the emperor. Claudius relied on the freedmen of his household, now imperial freedmen, to assist in the details of governing. He seems to have used their help effectively, but their conspicuous presence made it appear that they were in charge of both the emperor and Rome itself.

Claudius' wives similarly provoked the impression that it was they who controlled him and the state. He was married to the last two of his four wives while he was emperor. He married Messalina, a cousin descended from his mother's sister, probably in 37. They had a daughter, Octavia, and a son, who would be called Britannicus after the conquest of Britain. As Claudius aged, Messalina came to fear what would happen to her and to her son after her husband died. In 48 she divorced Claudius unilaterally and married Gaius Silius, consul elect for the following year. The plan was evidently that she would have a new protector and that Britannicus would become emperor in time. The plot failed and both lost their lives.

Messalina's execution made room for Agrippina the Younger, a daughter of Germanicus and so Claudius' niece. Once a decree removed the impediment of incest, she and Claudius were married. She brought to the marriage her son by a previous marriage, a boy a few years older than Britannicus, whom Claudius adopted, giving him the name Nero Claudius Caesar. Once Nero was legally an adult, Agrippina, fearing that Claudius might change his mind about her son's priority for succession, allegedly poisoned her husband. Claudius died on 23 October of 54, whether murdered or from natural causes, and Nero became emperor.

Reputation. Despite Claudius' efforts with the senate and his relatively sensible governance, he gained a reputation as a bloodthirsty fool. His qualities of stupidity and cruelty are present in a satire that circulated shortly after he died. Evidently written by Seneca, philosopher and tutor to Nero, the *Apocolocyntosis*, or "pumpkinification" of Claudius ridiculed his rash temper, uncouth behavior, and inappropriate speech, but emphasized his cruelty even more strongly. The perennial strain of succession uncertainties, lingering insecurity about his own accession, and a series of suspected conspiracies resulted in the execution of thirty-five senators and more than three hundred knights (Suetonius *Claudius* 29.2). The historian Tacitus and the biographer Suetonius record his absentminded detachment and drunkenness. These traits together with his physical awkwardness did much to disqualify him as an emperor, a role that had come to require dignity. But the conquest of Britain remained to his credit and earned him a place among the acceptable emperors of the early principate.

[*See also* Caligula; Emperor; Germanicus; Julio-Claudian Emperors; Messalina; Nero; *and* Praetorian Guard.]

BIBLIOGRAPHY

Primary Sources

Seneca. *Apocolocyntosis*. Edited and translated by P. T. Eden. Cambridge, U.K., and New York: Cambridge University Press, 1984.

Suetonius. *Works*. Vol. 2, *Lives of the Caesars*. Translated by John C. Rolfe. Loeb Classical Library, 1914. Rev. ed. Cambridge, Mass.: Harvard University Press, 1997–1998.

Tacitus. *Works*. Vol. 4, *Annals*. Translated by John Jackson. Loeb Classical Library. Cambridge, Mass.: Harvard University Press, 1998–2003.

Secondary Works

Griffin, M. T. "The Lyons Tablet and Tacitean Hindsight." *Classical Quarterly* n.s. 32 (1982): 404–418.

Levick, Barbara. *Claudius*. New Haven: Yale University Press; London: Batsford, 1990.

Momigliano, Arnaldo. *Claudius: The Emperor and His Achievement*. Translated by W. D. Hogarth. 2nd ed. Cambridge, U.K.: Hefer, 1961; New York: Barnes and Noble, 1962.

Wiedemann, T. E. J. "Claudius." In *Cambridge Ancient History*, 2nd ed. vol. 10, *The Augustan Empire*, edited by Alan K. Bowman et al., pp. 229–241. Cambridge, U.K., and New York: Cambridge University Press, 1996.

Donna W. Hurley

Claudius. Statue of Claudius I (r. 41–54 CE) in the guise of Jupiter. Museo Pio Clementino, Vatican Museums. PHOTOGRAPH BY ROBERT B. KEBRIC

CLEOPATRA VII

(69–30 BCE), queen of Egypt (51–30 BCE). The daughter of Ptolemy XII (nicknamed Auletes) and Cleopatra V (also known as Tryphaena), Cleopatra VII furthered her father's friendly relations with the Romans, though this was controversial in Egypt. Initially she ruled as co-regent with her brother/spouse Ptolemy XIII. Their differences concerning Rome led to war, and after his defeat the king drowned in the Nile. In 48 she was host to Julius Caesar, who came to Egypt in pursuit of his own defeated rival, Pompey (Gnaeus Pompeius Magnus). By the time Caesar departed three months later, her power had been consolidated and she was pregnant with his child. Between 47 and 44 BCE Cleopatra shared the throne with her youngest brother, Ptolemy XIV Theos Philopator II, with whom she traveled to Rome (46 BCE) as Caesar's guest. Caesar's assassination in 44 BCE caused them to return hastily and again threatened her power at Alexandria, where her absence had renewed conflict at court.

Ptolemy XIV's death by poisoning (at her behest) led to the accession of her infant son, Ptolemy XV, as nominal co-regent. Supposedly the son of Caesar, he was known as Caesarion ("little Caesar"). In effect, however, Cleopatra functioned as monarch, her power bolstered by Roman connections. Having thrown in her lot with Caesar's supporters after his death, she was summoned to Tarsus in 41 BCE to meet with its leader, Mark Antony. There began their liaison, which developed further when Antony spent the winter of 41–40 BCE in Egypt. Their union produced twins named Alexander Helios and Cleopatra Selene II. These names, like that of their third child, Ptolemy Philadelphus, suggest a desire to recreate the glories of the early Ptolemies. As wedding gifts Antony presented her with Khalkís (Chalcis), as well as parts of Cilicia and Phoenicia in 37 BCE, and three years later he proclaimed her "Queen of Kings." Other eastern Mediterranean lands were allocated to Caesarion and to their own children, in ways that scandalized the Roman establishment. Antony now abandoned his Roman wife, Octavia (Octavia Thurina Minor), sister of his great rival Octavian (later called Augustus), whom he had married in 40 BCE as part of a political alliance. Cleopatra presented herself publicly as the new Isis (Plutarch *Life of Antony* 54).

At a time when growing tensions between Antony, Octavian, and Marcus Aemilius Lepidus threatened the Second Triumvirate, her close association with Antony engendered conflict with Octavian. This was decided on 2 September 31 BCE in Octavian's favor at the Battle of Actium, close to Antony's naval headquarters in northwestern Greece. The defeat, spearheaded by Octavian's lieutenant Marcus Vipsanius Agrippa, led to Antony's suicide on 1 August 30 BCE. Cleopatra's own death followed eleven days later, when Octavian refused her offer of joint rule. On Octavian's orders Caesarion was put to death while trying to escape.

Cleopatra's death is celebrated by Horace (65–8 BCE) in *Odes* 1.37: though the poem makes no mention of her name, it does reveal some grudging admiration even though Horace in the first instance presents her as a mark of Antony's shame. By the same token, Sextus Propertius (c. 50–c. 15 BCE) dismisses her as the "prostitute queen of incestuous Canopus," thus referring to a notoriously dissolute town in the Nile delta (*Elegies* 3.11.39). In such contemporary accounts her foreignness receives emphasis, even though she was in fact of Greek descent, part of the Ptolemaic dynasty that dated all the way back to Alexander the Great's campaign and the foundation of Alexandria. She was reputedly the first Ptolemy to learn the Egyptian language.

With the conquest of her kingdom the Ptolemaic dynasty effectively came to an end, and the Romans added the last corner of the Mediterranean to their empire. Egypt was also the last of the Hellenistic kingdoms to succumb to Rome. It is thus no accident that Roman literary texts and coins fixated on the battle of Actium and Cleopatra's demise as the moments inaugurating the *pax Romana*. In the victors' discourse Cleopatra was essentially a foreign queen and a threat to the Roman order. Thus the queen who had been in Rome as Caesar's guest returned in 29 BCE as a wax model, complete

Cleopatra. Silver coin, before 30 BCE. NATIONAL MUSEUM, COPENHAGEN, DENMARK/VROMA: ANN RAIA, 2008

with model asp, in the triumphal procession of his successful political heir. Her surviving children by Antony were brought to Rome to take part in the procession, symbolically wearing chains.

Artistic representations of Cleopatra on Egyptian coins and marble busts—notably the Berlin Cleopatra—give little sense of her famed physical beauty. For Plutarch (c. 46–after 119 CE), it was her intelligence that explained her political impact. Rather, she is most evident in Roman sources as a touchstone for the decadence overcome by Octavian/Augustus. Thus, Pliny the Elder (23–79 CE) recounts a competition between her and Antony to see who could spend more on a dinner party: she won by dissolving a particularly large pearl in vinegar (*Natural History* 9.119–121).

While she is not subject to her own biography by Plutarch—in fact, no woman is—she does feature prominently in his *Parallel Lives* of Julius Caesar and Antony. Other ancient sources include Cicero (106–43 BCE; letters) and Dio Cassius (c. 150–235 CE). While Octavian's image-making has left an indelible impression, there is independent Egyptian evidence. The temple at Dendera dedicated to her and Caesarion contains reliefs of the co-regents in Pharaonic guise. A papyrus of 33 BCE is thought by some to contain her handwriting, by which she confirms tax exemption for an associate of Antony, but this is disputed.

It is not surprising that such an eventful life should exercise such fascination for later generations, whether as Rome's ally-turned-enemy or as queen-cum-femme fatale. Plutarch's *Life of Antony* was the main version of her life known to William Shakespeare, via Sir Thomas North's translation (1579, from a French version), as the source for his *Antony and Cleopatra*. It was, however, in the Romantic period that Cleopatra became the seductress of popular thought, partly in response to the heightened European interest in Egypt following Napoleon's expedition (1798–1801) and more recently reinforced by the cinema (for example, Joseph L. Mankiewicz's *Cleopatra* of 1963). Another strand of her popular reception is as a symbol of women's (and especially African American women's) beauty and power.

[*See also* Egypt *and* Mark Antony.]

BIBLIOGRAPHY

Chauveau, Michel. *Cleopatra: Beyond the Myth*. Translated by David Lorton. Ithaca, N.Y.: Cornell University Press, 2002.

Jones, Prudence J. *Cleopatra: A Sourcebook*. Norman: University of Oklahoma Press, 2006.

Plutarch. *Life of Antony*. Edited by C. B. R. Pelling. Cambridge, U.K.: Cambridge University Press, 1988.

Walker, Susan, and Peter Higgs, eds. *Cleopatra of Egypt: From History to Myth*. London: British Museum, 2001.

Wyke, Maria. *The Roman Mistress: Ancient and Modern Representations*. Oxford: Oxford University Press, 2002. See especially pages 206–243.

Grant Parker

CLERUCHY

See Delian League.

CLIENTS

See Patronage.

CLIMATE

See Environment.

CLODIA

(c. 95 BCE–?), Roman aristocrat. Clodia Metelli, the daughter of Appius Claudius Pulcher (consul in 79 BCE), married her first cousin Caecilius Metellus Celer by 62 and was widowed in 59. According to Plutarch and Quintilian, Clodia became notorious for her profligacy, her beauty, and her liaisons with influential men.

Clodia is questionably identified with the "Lesbia'" (a reference to the famous poet Sappho of Lesbos) celebrated by the poet Catullus. His lyrics immortalized "Lesbia" as a beautiful, educated, and intelligent beloved who was also a demanding, manipulating, and unfaithful mistress.

Cicero, whom Plutarch says Clodia once offered to marry, mentions her in his letters from 60 onward. Her infamous affair with Cicero's protégé Caelius Rufus lasted about two years. In 56 Cicero gave a vivid portrayal of Clodia in his oration *Pro Caelio*, a defense of Caelius, alleging that Clodia was behind the accusations against him, including a supposed conspiracy to murder. Cicero depicts Clodia as licentious, a "bargain-basement Clytemnestra" and "Medea of the Palatine," who allegedly poisoned her late husband and had an incestuous relationship with her brother, the tribune Clodius Pulcher, Cicero's archenemy.

Cicero's speech discredited Clodia as a competent witness and impaired her political influence. Thereafter, Clodia, formerly an astute political manipulator with access to public criminal courts, retreated from the limelight. Cicero mentions her again in 45 in connection with real estate negotiations. Despite Cicero's public defamation of her character, Clodia had continued to participate in Roman public life. Apparently this femme fatale remained independent, wealthy, and influential.

[*See also* Catullus; Cicero; and Clodius.]

BIBLIOGRAPHY

Bauman, Richard A. *Women and Politics in Ancient Rome*. London and New York, Routledge, 1992.

Skinner, Marilyn B. "Clodia Metelli." *Transactions of the American Philological Association* 113 (1983): 273–287.

Wiseman, Timothy P. *Catullus and His World: A Reappraisal*. Cambridge, U.K., and New York: Cambridge University Press, 1985.

Maridien Schneider

CLODIUS

(Publius Clodius Pulcher, c. 93–52 BCE), Roman politician. Clodius Pulcher, a patrician, was the youngest son of Appius Claudius Pulcher (consul in 79). During the Mithradatic War Clodius instigated mutiny against his brother-in-law Lucullus at Nisibis in Mesopotamia in the winter of 68/67. He subsequently commanded the Cilician fleet of Marcius Rex, was captured by pirates, and on release incited another revolt in Syria.

In 65 Clodius prosecuted Catiline for extortion, allegedly procuring his acquittal. In 64 he served in Gaul as military tribune. Clodius became notorious in 62, when he was discovered trespassing at the Bona Dea rites, disguised as a female harpist. He was prosecuted for sacrilege, but acquitted by a narrow margin. Cicero, who had disproved his alibi, became his archenemy, while Crassus, who had bribed the jury, anticipated future political cooperation with Clodius.

A shrewd operator and independent political opportunist, Clodius courted both *optimates* and urban plebs. On returning from his quaestorship in Sicily (61), Clodius sought plebeian status to qualify as candidate for the tribunate. Caesar as *pontifex maximus*, and Pompey as augur, procured Clodius' adoption into the family of Publius Fonteius in 59. Elected tribune for 58, Clodius—having adopted a populist spelling of his Claudian name—challenged senatorial authority and secured popular favor. His legislation included free grain distribution to the plebs; restriction of censors' power to expel senators without judicial authorization; prohibition of magistrates from obstructing public business on religious grounds; restoration of private clubs (*collegia*), which he later exploited as sources of gang violence; and the dispatch of Cato the Younger, a possible political opponent, as envoy to Cyprus.

Clodius took vengeance on Cicero, first invoking the Gracchan law condemning anyone who had executed Roman citizens without trial, then by exiling Cicero and confiscating his property. Clodius had Cicero's house on the Palatine destroyed, dedicated a shrine to Libertas on the site, and opposed Cicero's recall from exile with armed force. On his return, however, Cicero persuaded the pontifices that Clodius' actions were invalid. By a vote of the senate Cicero was compensated and the site deconsecrated. Clodian supporters relentlessly threatened Cicero, hindered the reconstruction of his house, and set fire to the property of Cicero's brother, Quintus.

While Caesar was campaigning in Gaul in 58, Clodius turned against his and Caesar's former ally, Pompey: he helped Pompey's prisoner the Armenian prince Tigranes to escape from custody at Rome and threatened Pompey with arson and murder, the latter retreating to the safety of his house for months. Next, Clodius attacked the validity of Caesar's land acts of 59.

Continual gang-warfare between Clodius and his political rival Titus Annius Milo, a powerful Pompeian adherent, kept Rome in turmoil. In 56, when aedile, Clodius impeached Milo for public violence. In 55, after the conference at Luca that renewed the triumvirs' alliance and secured their respective immediate political objectives, Clodius, by agitation, and still opposing senatorial interests, helped to bring about the joint consulship of Pompey and Crassus. Relations between Caesar, Pompey, and Crassus deteriorated during 54, and rioting prevented consular elections from being held for 53. In 52, when Milo and Clodius stood for consul and praetor respectively, Milo's supporters killed Clodius in an armed clash on the Appian Way near Bovillae. Subsequently Clodian followers burned his body in the senate house, which went up in flames. As an active and influential politician and a popular leader among the urban plebs, Clodius stressed the significance of both popular interests and the important role of the tribunate in late Republican politics.

[*See also* Clodia; Lucullus; *and* Rome, *subentry* Early Rome and the Republic.]

BIBLIOGRAPHY

Lintott, Andrew W. *Violence in Republican Rome.* 2nd ed. Oxford and New York: Oxford University Press, 1999.

Millar, Fergus. *The Crowd in Rome in the Late Republic.* Ann Arbor: University of Michigan Press, 1998.

Rundell, W. M. F. "Cicero and Clodius: The question of credibilty." *Historia* 28, no. 3 (1979): 301–328.

Tatum, W. Jeffrey. *The Patrician Tribune: Publius Clodius Pulcher.* Chapel Hill and London: University of North Carolina Press, 1999.

Maridien Schneider

CLOTHING

Clothing and personal adornment were essential means of constructing individual identities in ancient Greece and Rome. In these so-called face-to-face societies, it was imperative to ascertain the identity of an individual visually, without any initial verbal communication. Although the social functions of dress have received increased scholarly attention since the landmark study of Roman costume edited by J. L. Sebesta and L. Bonfante, many aspects of Greek and Roman dress remain poorly understood.

Evidence for Clothing. Greek and Roman clothing is difficult to interpret in large part because of the nature of the evidence. Few complete garments have been recovered outside of Egypt. Hence, scholars have relied upon representations of garments in sculpture and painting in order to reconstruct their appearance. The most detailed visual evidence is large-scale sculpture in the round. Unfortunately, as has been demonstrated for the Archaic Greek *korai*, for example, the statues do not always replicate the actual details of dress. In addition, the colors and decoration of sculpted garments were rendered in paint, which rarely survives (though some recent scientific analysis by Vincenz

Brinkmann has recovered the polychromy on many famous works of Greek and Roman sculpture). The polychromy of garments is best preserved in Hellenistic and Roman wall painting and in Greek white-ground vase painting. Black-figure and red-figure vase painting depict a wider variety of garments than is represented in sculpture and may be stylized to a greater or lesser degree. In general, we cannot take visual representations of Greek and Roman dress at face value.

Although complete garments are rare in the archaeological record, important evidence for dress has been recovered in the form of fasteners such as pins, fibulae, and buckles, usually of bronze but sometimes of gold or silver. Because of their intrinsic value, these items were often dedicated in sanctuaries. Objects recovered from graves give important evidence as to where on the body they were worn. Leather shoes have also been preserved archaeologically, most famously at the Roman fort at Vindolanda, in present-day Northumberland. The finds at Vindolanda have proved especially important for understanding social life on the Roman frontier: in addition to men's military footwear, a significant number of women's and children's shoes have been recovered, suggesting that families were in residence at the fort.

The visual and archaeological evidence for clothing is often difficult to reconcile with the literary evidence, which is extensive. Many varieties of garments are named in Greek and Latin literature, though the nomenclature changes over time and according to genre. In addition, clothing often features prominently in the narrative (the rags of Odysseus; the poisoned peplos of Medea). Although it often proves difficult to match garments named in the literary sources with those represented in the visual evidence, literature gives important indications as to the social functions of dress, which might otherwise be lost to us. For example, in Greek tragedy, characters often express shame by covering themselves with their garments. And although Roman women are never represented in art wearing the toga, several authors identify that garment as the distinctive attire of adulteresses and prostitutes.

Types of Greek and Roman Garments. In general, Greek and Roman garments are draped as opposed to fitted. In contrast, the garments of barbarians are generally bifurcated and sleeved. Some garments were shared by men and women; others were gender specific. Children's garments were generally smaller versions of adult garments, though they were often belted or fastened differently. The names of Greek and Roman garments are conventional: we cannot be confident in every case that the name employed by modern scholars is the ancient term. Many types of garments named in the Brauron clothing catalogs cannot be identified in the visual sources. The following list contains only the most prevalent types of Greek and Roman garments.

Greek Clothing. Kore from Chios. Marble, Archaic Greek, c. 520 BCE. ACROPOLIS MUSEUM, ATHENS, INV. 675/SCALA/ART RESOURCE, NY

Chiton. The chiton was likely a Near Eastern import to early Greece. A full-length garment made of linen with wide, billowing sleeves, it was evidently a status item. In Homer, the chiton is a man's garment. However, according to the visual, archaeological, and literary sources, women adopted the chiton at some point in the late seventh or early sixth century BCE, after which time only wealthy, older men continued to wear the long chiton. Younger men wore a shortened version known as the *chitoniskos* underneath their armor. Another variation of this short garment, known as the *exomis*, dispensed with the sleeves and was fastened over one shoulder only, leaving the opposite arm free for manual labor. Still another variation of the chiton was the *xystis*, which was also sleeveless but extended to the feet; it was often worn in ritual contexts by priests.

Peplos. The peplos is conventionally identified as a sleeveless woolen garment fastened at the shoulders with pins. In Homer, it is worn exclusively by women. If we can trust the sources, the peplos seems to have been replaced by the chiton in the early Archaic period. When it reappears in art and literature of the Classical period, it seems to be a reference to the historical or mythological past. Male characters in Greek tragedy sometimes wear the peplos, but only in exceptional circumstances to indicate their feminization; males are not represented in the visual sources wearing the peplos. The garment identified as the peplos in Greek sculpture and vase-painting is represented either with or without an overfold (sometimes wrongly identified as the *apoptygma*, which was simply a name for a section of drapery), over or under which it is usually belted with a *zone*. As a heavy, enveloping garment that obscured the shape of the female body, it is a popular type for severe-style sculpture through the Roman period. The peplos enjoyed a special role in several cults, and was the central feature of the Panathenaia at Athens.

Himation. The himation was worn by both men and women. In early Greek art it appears as kind of long woolen wrap worn over the man's chiton. When men stopped wearing the chiton in the sixth century BCE, the himation became their primary garment. A properly arranged himation reflected good breeding and proper order; a himation in disarray reflected a kind of lapse (such as at the revelry following the symposium). When women adopted the chiton, they also wore a type of diagonal himation over one shoulder. The himation was endlessly malleable and could be rearranged at a moment's notice, to be used as a veil, for example.

Chlaina (chlamys). The *chlaina* and *chlamys* are difficult to distinguish from one another in the visual and literary sources, and may in fact refer to the same garment: a man's short woolen cape or cloak that was draped over both shoulders and secured across the chest with a pin. As a practical garment that provided protection from the elements, it was typical of travelers and may have had its origins in northern Greece.

Strophion. The *strophion* was a type of breastband or brassiere. It appears in Greek vase painting and literature starting in the Classical period, but is more common in Hellenistic and Roman art, especially in erotic scenes and images of Aphrodite. Its function is unclear: although it presumably supported the breasts, it does not seem to have been regular feminine attire. The *strophion* seems to have carried erotic connotations and may have been a "special occasion" garment.

Diazoma (perizoma). *Diazoma* and *perizoma* are both names for undergarments in the form of a loincloth or briefs. Several Greek authors claim that such garments were worn only by foreigners in athletic competitions. Indeed, the few images of male athletes wearing the *diazoma* or *perizoma* in Greek vase painting seem to have been intended for a foreign market. Girls wearing briefs in a few images have been identified as athletes or acrobats.

Spargana. *Spargana* refers to infant swaddling cloths, which also functioned as diapers. According to Plato, children must be properly swaddled in order for their limbs to develop properly (*Laws* 7.789). Infants, especially boys, are frequently depicted without any garment whatsoever in order to display their sex.

Toga. The toga, the national garment of the Romans, is treated in a separate entry. Like the

Greek himation, the toga was a draped garment, usually worn over the *tunica*. A vast expanse of (usually white) wool, it was woven in a semi-round shape. The *toga praetexta*, decorated with purple stripes, was worn by those of high status and as a protective garment for freeborn children of both sexes. Although both the literary and the visual sources suggest that the toga was regularly worn by Roman citizens, it has been argued that the toga functioned more as a symbol for *romanitas* than as an everyday garment.

Tunica. Similar to the Greek chiton, the sleeved *tunica* was the primary garment for both men and women in the Roman period. Made of two panels of white or light-colored cloth sewn or otherwise fastened together at the shoulders, it was usually belted at the waist. The man's tunic generally extended to the middle of the calf, the woman's to the feet, and children's to the knee. Men of the equestrian and senatorial classes had two vertical purple stripes (*clavi*) woven into the fabric: the width of the stripe reflected the status of the wearer.

Pallium. The pallium was the Roman equivalent of the Greek man's himation. Because of its Greek associations, it was typically worn by philosophers.

Stola. The Roman *stola* was a sleeveless garment not unlike the Greek peplos. It is sometimes represented with straps over the shoulders. The *stola* was worn over the tunic by Roman matrons to indicate their married status. It seems to have been most popular during the Republic, and fell out of favor by the end of the first century CE.

Palla. The Roman woman's *palla* was similar in concept and function to the Greek himation. It was employed by Roman women as a veil.

Headgear. In general, Greek and Roman men did not cover their heads except in religious contexts. Exceptions include special hats such as the Greek *petasos*, a wide-brimmed hat worn by travelers for protection against the elements, and the *pilos*, a kind of close-fitting cap worn by workers. In contrast, women regularly covered their heads with veils (such as the himation or *palla*). Women's hair was usually bound up: Greek women tied their hair in a fillet and covered it with a *mitra* (similar to a

Roman Clothing. Dancer, from the Villa dei Papiri, Herculaneum. Bronze, first century BCE. MUSEO ARCHEOLOGICO NAZIONALE, NAPLES, ITALY/THE BRIDGEMAN ART LIBRARY

turban) or *sakkos* (a type of snood); Roman women employed woolen bands called *vittae*. Hairnets are represented in both Greek and Roman art; golden hairnets have been preserved archaeologically. Wreaths composed of plants and flowers were employed by both sexes in festal contexts.

Footwear. A wide variety of sandals, slippers, clogs, shoes, and boots were worn by Greek and Roman men and women. Some types were particular to social role (soldier, senator, patrician) or social context (indoors, outdoors, public baths). Styles seem to have changed over time, so that artistic representations of footwear can be employed to date sculpture in particular. Socks were commonly worn in the Roman period. As in our own culture, footwear seems to have held erotic connotations.

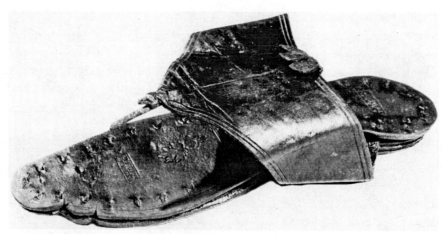

Shoe. Sole and strap of a woman's sandal, stamped with the initials of the maker, Lucius Aebutius Thales. © VINDOLANDA TRUST

Assessment. Greek and Roman dress was not static, but changed over time and according to region (though certainly not as rapidly as contemporary fashion). Despite such developments, certain garments do survive from antiquity in the form of Christian liturgical vestments. For example, the alb, derived from the chiton or *tunica*, later developed into the wide-sleeved surplice; likewise, the archbishop's *pallium* is the same as the ancient himation or *pallium*.

Given the richness of the evidence for Greek and Roman dress, it is unfortunate that modern cinema and television perpetuate inaccurate reconstructions of ancient garments. Far from the nondescript white bed sheets usually represented, ancient dress was colorful and dynamic and was a significant aspect of ancient social life.

[*See also* Adornment, Personal; Jewelry; Nudity; Textiles; Toga; Weapons and Equipment, Greek; *and* Weapons and Equipment, Roman.]

BIBLIOGRAPHY

Brinkmann, Vinzenz, and Raimund Wünsche. *Gods in Color: Painted Sculpture of Classical Antiquity.* Exhibition at the Arthur M. Sackler Museum, Harvard University Art Museums, in cooperation with Staatliche Antikensammlungen and Glyptothek, Munich, and Stiftung Archäologie, Munich, 2007.

Cleland, Liza. *The Brauron Clothing Catalogues: Text, Analysis, Glossary and Translation.* Oxford: John and Erica Hedges, 2005.

Cleland, Liza, Glenys Davies, and Lloyd Llewellen-Jones, eds. *Greek and Roman Dress from A to Z.* London: Routledge, 2007.

Cleland, Liza, Mary Harlow, and Lloyd Llewellen-Jones, eds. *The Clothed Body in the Ancient World.* Oxford: Oxbow, 2005.

Croom, Alexandra. *Roman Clothing and Fashion.* Stroud, U.K., and Charleston, S.C.: Tempus, 2002.

Lee, Mireille M. "Evil Wealth of Raiment: Deadly Peploi in Greek tragedy." *The Classical Journal* 99, no. 3 (2004): 253–279.

Llewellyn-Jones, Lloyd. *Aphrodite's Tortoise: The Veiled Woman of Ancient Greece.* London and Swansea: Classical Press of Wales, 2003.

Llewellyn-Jones, Lloyd, ed. *Women's Dress in the Ancient Greek World.* London and Swansea: Classical Press of Wales, 2002.

Roccos, Linda J. *Ancient Greek Costume: An Annotated Bibliography, 1784–2005.* Jefferson, N.C.: McFarland, 2006; http://www.library.csi.cuny.edu/roccos/greek costume.

Sebesta, Judith L., and Larissa Bonfante, eds. *The World of Roman Costume.* Madison: University of Wisconsin Press, 1994.

Mireille M. Lee

CLUBS AND ASSOCIATIONS, GREEK

Ancient Greek "clubs and associations" are difficult to identify in the absence of a standard comprehensive terminology. All are arguably instances of a *koinon* or *koinonia*, but these terms are applicable to almost any grouping. Nor does the English "voluntary association" capture all "clubs and associations," because in many a city-state, alongside such private organizations, the municipal segmentations of territory and citizen body were also internally organized as sorts of nonvoluntary "public associations." Scholars therefore must resort to the piecemeal collection of more or less organized and enduring groups sharing a common purpose and embedded within or segmenting the city-state's people or territory.

At Athens, by far the best documented and understood case, a law of Solon, the archon in 594 BCE, declares that the internal acts of "a *dēmos* (village) or *phratores* (brothers) or *orgeōnes* (votaries) or shippers or messmates or members of a burial society or revelers or groups going abroad for plundering or commerce" are to be valid among the members unless prohibited by the written statutes of the people (Gaius *Digest* 47.22.4, as emended). A generation earlier, an *hetaireia* (fellowship) is ascribed to the revolutionary Cylon by Herodotus (5.71.1), and by the end of the fifth century conspiratorial societies played a role in the overthrow of the democracy (Thucydides 8.54.4). But notices of this kind are rare in literary sources, and we must rely upon the surviving contemporary epigraphic records of the clubs and associations themselves on matters of name and number, membership, geographic distribution, internal organization, and activities. Among Solon's Athenian examples, conspicuous in these documents are the *phratores* (collective *phratria*) and *orgeōnes*, to which may be added the *gennētai* (collective *genos*), various extramural regional associations organized around a cult center, and arguably the philosophical schools—the Academy, Lyceum, and Cynosarges, all with a cultic orientation and situated on the periphery of the town.

Meanwhile, the principal segments of the city's own municipal organization, the *phylē* or phyle (often misleadingly translated "tribe") and *dēmos* or deme (already recognized in Solon's law), doubled as inclusive "public" associations of their own. Though the phyle association, meeting on or near the Acropolis, served largely ceremonial purposes, the deme association, based in an often distant rural seat, maintained a robust schedule of communal activities independently of the urban, government-dominated culture of the town. Nonetheless, the demarch represented the state's interests and policies in his village, and the association, by its scrutiny of age and legitimacy, served as gatekeeper to the citizenship (as did the phratry in policing its own citizen membership). Additional light on association versus state relations, as well as other relevant matters, is shed by the utopian and revisionist commonwealths—in varying degrees reflecting the realities of contemporary Athens—created by the philosophers Plato (*Republic, Critias,* and *Laws*) and Aristotle (*Politics*).

Again at Athens, a major watershed is marked by the decline of free government initiated by the Macedonian takeover in 322/1 BCE, soon after which a wide range of private, voluntary, and mostly cultic associations make their first appearance in contemporary epigraphic records. Among these are the *eranistai* (dining associates), independent *thiasotai* (revelers), votaries serving a particular deity, associations based on a shared ethnicity, profession, or commercial interest, and all-female groups. We may thus continue to recognize a class of Hellenistic associations overlying the still-functioning Classical networks, with the major difference that, whereas the Classical associations seem to have been open only to citizens (free adult males), the post-Macedonian associations welcomed females as well as males, slaves as well as free, nonresidents as well as citizens, non-Greeks as well as Greeks. Beyond Athens, similar groups, characterized by social activities thinly cloaked by religious name or title, calendar, and ceremony, are especially conspicuous at the trading centers of Delos, Rhodes, and Egypt. Standing out among the considerable variety of specific orientation are the commercial associations (shippers, merchants, and warehousemen), guilds of coworkers in a given craft or profession, and the well-documented Artists of Dionysus.

Several synoptic studies concentrating on the voluntary Hellenistic associations appeared through the turn of the twentieth century: Paul François Foucart, *Des associations religieuses chez les Grecs: Thiases, éranes, orgéones* (Paris, 1873); Erich Ziebarth, *Das griechische Vereinswesen* (Leipzig, Germany, 1896); and Franz Poland, *Geschichte des griechischen Vereinswesen* (Leipzig, Germany, 1909). These are now being superseded by monographs, book chapters, and articles focused on a particular association or groups of associations, locale, or major epigraphic document.

[*See also* Clubs and Associations, Roman; Family and Kinship, Greek; *and* Phratry.]

BIBLIOGRAPHY

Jones, Nicholas F. *The Associations of Classical Athens: The Response to Democracy.* New York and Oxford: Oxford University Press, 1999.

Lambert, S. D. *The Phratries of Attica.* Ann Arbor: University of Michigan Press, 1993.

Whitehead, David. *The Demes of Attica 508/7–ca. 250 B.C.: A Political and Social Study.* Princeton, N.J.: Princeton University Press, 1986.

Nicholas F. Jones

CLUBS AND ASSOCIATIONS, ROMAN

Romans had a long tradition, allegedly going back to the legendary king Numa, of organizing themselves in clubs or associations. People who, for instance, shared the same trade, who had a particular interest in the worship of a specific god, or who had the same ethnic origin could set up a club, or a club could be established for the purpose of burial—this primarily for people who did not have relatives to take care of their funerals. Although clubs were commonly established for the purpose of supporting and helping fellow merchants, religious worship was always a very important part of the club's life— just as central as social gatherings and the burial of deceased members. The terms that the Romans used for such a club or association were *collegium, sodalitas, corpus, ordo,* or *cultores.* It is not possible to distinguish among the different terms used for clubs, although the term *cultores* (worshippers) most frequently seems to refer to religious clubs.

The members of the club would refer to each other as *collegae, sodales, amici* or *amicae* (friends), and *fratres* or *sorores* (brothers, sisters).

Membership and Organization. Most of our evidence comes from funerary inscriptions: *Corpus Inscriptionum Latinarum (CIL)* 6.5475 dating from the middle of the first century CE commemorates Statilia Auge, called sister of Bebryx, Hyacinthus, and Glaphyrus. It is not likely that four biological siblings remained together in one household. The same is true of *CIL* 6.8441, in which Aegyptus, a slave of Barbarus, an imperial clerk, is commemorated by three *fratres* called Eutychus, Peculiaris, and Symmachus. In both cases we must assume that the individuals were commemorated as members of a *collegium* and not in a familial context.

Depending on the economic standing of the club, a club could own a meeting hall (*schola*) with dining facilities and a burial plot or *columbarium* reserved for members of the club and their relatives, if they had any. A club could even own slaves. Although members of clubs came primarily from the lower classes, including slaves, the hierarchy of clubs reflected that of society in general. At the top of this hierarchy was a *patronus* or a *patrona,* who could be of the equestrian or senatorial class or, in provincial towns, the local aristocracy. The highest official in a club was the *magister quinquennalis* or *quinquinnalis.* Originally this term meant "president who served for five years," but the term seems to have changed meaning over time and came to mean "president" without any implication of the length of time that the *quinquinnalis* served. Just below came the *curator.* A *quaestor collegii* was responsible for the finances of the club. One or more *scribae* (singular *scriba,* "clerk" or "secretary") were also attached to the club, and the lowest officials of a club were called *decuriones* (singular *decurio*), the same word applied to the highest officials of a *municipium* (town), who frequently appeared as *patroni* of a *collegium.* Ordinary members of a club were referred to as *plebs.*

Club members paid an entrance fee and an annual contribution. A club official could be rewarded with an exemption from this contribution and would be referred to as *immunis*. Both men and women could be members and officials of a *collegium*. *CIL* 6.10363 is an epitaph put up by Antonia Chariessa, an *immunis* of a *collegium*, to her husband, Marcus Antonius Myrtilus, and to one Marcus Antonius Boethus, a *decurio*. And women as well as men could be patrons of a *collegium*. *CIL* 9.5368 is an epitaph put up to the freeborn Alliena Berenice by her husband and son, both named Gaius Vettius Polus. She was the *patrona* of the local *collegium fabrum et centoniariorum*—presumed to mean *collegium* of carpenters and textile merchants.

Slaves and freedmen of aristocratic houses in Rome frequently organized burial clubs. These were set up like *collegia* with officials in charge of the funeral and of allotting burial spots. The presence of these household *collegia* is evidenced in, for example, the monuments of Livia and Marcella and the monument of the Statilii. The following examples are taken from the monument of the Statilii: *CIL* 6.6215 was erected to the memory of Statilia Ammia by her husband, Cerdo, who was an apartment-block caretaker, and by Bathyllus, an atrium caretaker; Musaeus, a doorkeeper; Eros, an apartment-block caretaker; and Philocalus, a masseur. They describe themselves as members of the *collegium* of *commorientes*, "those who die together." Thus there is no doubt that the purpose of this *collegium* was primarily of funerary character. We meet more members of the *collegium* of the familia Statilia in other inscriptions. In *CIL* 6.6217 we learn that Musaeus and Eros were *decuriones* of the *collegium*. Cerdo was eventually manumitted, and in *CIL* 6.10414 he greets his *commorientes* from the tomb. The burials of these household *collegia* almost always took place in subterranean *columbaria*. It is interesting to observe that each *collegium* seems to have developed its own formulaic style. The members of the *collegium* from the household of Sergia Paullina seem always to have included the formula *collegium quod est in domo Sergiae Paullinae*, "the club that is in the household of Sergia Paullina."

The Clubs in Politics. Although members of *collegia* in the municipalities of the empire seem to have been happy to adapt to the social hierarchy of their local society and to use their position to make social progress, the situation in Rome itself was different. During the last century of the republic, clubs and associations were increasingly used as tools by ambitious politicians. Crowds or "mobs" of working-class Romans should probably not be seen as voters but rather as potentially violent gangs—called *operae*, *turbae*, *urbana plebs*, *infima plebs*, *vulgus*, *Clodiani* (used of the gangs of Publius Clodius Pulcher), *Miloniani* (used of the gangs of Titus Annius Milo)—that could be called on when needed.

In an attempt to prevent street violence the senate in 64 BCE decreed that all *collegia* that were deemed subversive should be closed. The decree also prohibited the celebration of the Ludi Compitalicii, the venerable games in honor of the "ancestors of the crossroads." These *ludi* were held annually in the city's neighborhoods, the *vici*, and were seen as dangerous occasions during which shops would be closed and people would be in the streets celebrating and possibly rioting. Not all clubs and associations were closed down—only those considered dangerous to the public order. The weak position of the senate was shown when Clodius in his tribunate of 58 BCE had the law repealed and encouraged the formation of more *collegia*. One of the reasons that clubs and other associations became so powerful in the last years of the republic was probably the influx of immigrants looking for work in Rome. These immigrants were usually young men. In Rome their closest associates would be their friends and coworkers, with whom they would naturally share *collegium*. The commemorative pattern for young men in Rome differs markedly from that found in the provincial towns of Italy. There young men were normally commemorated in a familial context, whereas in Rome most young workingmen were more closely connected with their club than with their family. Given this rootlessness, politicians like Clodius or Milo had more opportunity to engage them in violent gang behavior.

In 57, Clodius' gang physically attacked Pompey during a trial. Pompey had good reason to fear for his life. After this incident the senate passed a law against such political violence, a law aimed at both

Clodius and his gang. Cicero mentions in a letter to his brother (*Epistulae ad Quintum fratrum* 2.3.5) that the decree ordered the disbanding of the political clubs and caucuses. This law has (probably erroneously) been seen in connection with another from 55, the *lex Licinia de sodaliciis* proposed by Marcus Licinius Crassus. Our main source for this law is Cicero's defense speech *Pro Plancio* from 54. Gnaeus Plancius had been accused of *ambitus* (illicit solicitation of votes) according to the *lex Licinia de sodaliciis*, but the *sodalitates* in which he was involved seem unconnected with Clodius' gangs, or with respectable *collegia* for that matter. Whereas Clodius had successfully influenced shopkeepers and artisans by directly paying them to close their shops and gather at his summons whenever he needed a violent crowd to exert political pressure, the law that Plancius was accused of breaking was aimed at *sodalitates* consisting of members of the elite organizing electoral bribery (*ambitus*). Thus the *lex Licinia* was aimed not at violence but at bribery. Cicero argues that Plancius' *sodalitates* were nothing but political friendships, *amicitiae*, intended for mutual support during an election campaign. Although *amicitiae* were central for Roman politics in the late Republic, *ambitus* was illegal. Thus it was also illegal to establish an association, *sodalitas*, for the purpose of bribing as many

African Association. Banquet of the sodalities of the amphitheater. Roman mosaic from a house near the amphitheater at El Djem, Tunisia. First half of the third century CE. MUSÉE NATIONAL DU BARDO, TUNIS, TUNISIA/GILLES MERMET/ART RESOURCE, NY

voters as possible. The *lex Licinia* was directed at any *sodalitas* using *ambitus* to secure election of its candidate.

Roman clubs and associations were active in many spheres of life. They could be formal with rules and officials or they could be less formal. Occasionally we meet these informal clubs in the inscriptions in the form of a list of names indicating individuals who seem to have nothing in common except agreeing to buy a plot of land as a shared burial space. It is unclear whether such individuals would have considered themselves members of a small club or simply friends or neighbors.

[*See also* Cemeteries; Clodius; Clubs and Associations, Greek; Death, *subentry* Death and Burial in the Ancient World; Elections and Voting; Patronage, *subentry* Social Patronage; *and* Priesthoods, Roman.]

BIBLIOGRAPHY

Caldelli, Maria Letizia, and Cecilia Ricci. *Monumentum familiae Statiliorum: Un riesame.* Rome: Quasar, 1999.

Lintott, Andrew W. *Violence in Republican Rome.* 2nd ed. Oxford and New York: Oxford University Press, 1999.

Mouritsen, Henrik. *Plebs and Politics in the Late Roman Republic.* Cambridge, U.K., and New York: Cambridge University Press, 2001.

Nijf, Onno van. *The Civic World of Professional Associations in the Roman East.* Amsterdam: J. C. Gieben, 1997.

Waltzing, Jean Pierre. *Étude historique sur les corporations professionnelles chez les Romains depuis les origines jusqu'à la chute de l'Empire d'Occident.* 4 vols. Louvain, Belgium: C. Peeters, 1895–1900.

Hanne Sigismund-Nielsen

CNIDUS

Cities named Cnidus (Cnidos) occupied two separate locations on a long peninsula, between the islands of Cos (Kos) and Rhodes in the extreme southwest of Asia Minor (ancient Caria). The first of these, the Archaic and Classical city, has been identified with the substantial archaeological remains found near Burgaz/Datça. Across the bay to the east, excavations have also uncovered the remains of a temple to the Doric deity Apollo Karneios, at Emecik.

According to Herodotus (1.174), Cnidus was a colony of Sparta, and together with the communities of Halicarnassus, Cos, Ialysus, Lindus, and Camirus it formed one of the six cities of the Dorian Hexapolis. The chief sanctuary of this group, even after Halicarnassus left and the union became a pentapolis, was that of Apollo Triopios located near Cnidus (Herodotus 1.144; Thucydides 8.35.3). Cnidus, jointly with Corcyra, founded colonies of its own at Lipara and also at Corcyra Nigra in the Adriatic in the sixth century BCE and was one of the cofounders of the Hellenion at the Pan-Hellenic settlement of Naucratis on the Nile Delta.

As the Persian forces under Harpagus advanced through Ionia and Caria, the Cnidians attempted to defend themselves by digging a channel through the peninsula at its narrowest point, thereby making their territory an island. They were unable to complete this project, and the city fell to Persian rule after 546 BCE (Herodotus 1.174). Around 467, Cimon mustered the Athenian and allied fleet here before sailing on to victory at the battle of Eurymedon. From this date onward, Cnidus came under Athenian rule until it left the Delian League to support Sparta in 412. In 394, in the waters off Cnidus, the Athenian Conon led a Persian-funded fleet against the Spartans under Peisander. The decisive Spartan defeat and the death of Peisander in the battle of Cnidus marked the end of a brief period of Spartan naval supremacy. This marked the return of Athens as the dominant sea power in the Aegean, but also a return to Persian control for Cnidus and the whole Carian and Ionian region (Xenophon *Hellenica* 4.3.10–12).

From the fourth century BCE onward, the Hellenistic, Roman, and Byzantine city was located on the very tip of the Datça peninsula. Here a sandy isthmus divides two bays, and the larger, south harbor is enhanced by two moles. The ruins are extensive and include an agora, odeum, and temples to Dionysus and Aphrodite. In this latter temple Praxiteles' famous Aphrodite was housed, and even though the

---

Ctesias of Cnidus

Ctesias was physician to King Artaxerxes II Mnemon, from 404 to 398/97 BCE; it is not known precisely how he first came to be held in the Persian court. Not only was he a doctor, but he also served as a diplomat and compiled a 23-book *History of the Persians.* He had a role in the negotiations that assembled the victorious fleet at the battle of Cnidus. As a writer of histories he had insider knowledge of the Persian court and customs and he claimed to correct lies told by Herodotus. However, his reliability as a source is questionable, and Plutarch is disparaging of him. He was a contemporary and possible inspiration for Xenophon, but his many works are known only from later reworkings and from fragments. See *Fragmente der griechischen Historiker* 688.

---

statue itself has long since disappeared, numerous copies and images of it survive, including on the coinage of the city itself. The city retained its importance into Roman times and is mentioned in the Bible (Acts 27.7; 1 Macc. 15.23).

The city was famous for its trade in wine and for its school of medicine, the Asclepiads, which was second in reputation only to that on Cos, the home of Hippocrates. The city was home to many significant thinkers including the physician and historian Ctesias, and Sostratus, who constructed the Alexandria Pharos. Eudoxus of Cnidus was a student of Plato and a famed mathematician, second only to Archimedes himself.

[*See also* Caria.]

BIBLIOGRAPHY

Berges, Dietrich. *Knidos: Beiträge zur Geschichte der archaischen Stadt.* Mainz, Germany: Verlag Philipp von Zabern, 2006.

Newton, Charles T. *A History of Discoveries at Halicarnassus, Cnidus, and Branchidae.* London: Day & Son, 1862.

Alan M. Greaves

CNOSSOS

See Knossos.

COINS AND COINAGE

Although they are sometimes overlooked or undervalued as evidence, coins have been recognized as a vital primary source for the Greek and Roman world since the Renaissance humanists first began to collect, catalog, and study ancient coins as a corollary to their renewed interest in their classical heritage. In their primary aspect as money, coins chart the economic vicissitudes of city-states, kingdoms, and empires. Their types and inscriptions featuring deities, rulers, and allusion to historical events also render the coins as political documents that can supplement and in some cases even correct the literary sources. In addition, coin iconography can be an important tool for the interpretation of Greek and Roman art, including the proper restoration of fragmentary or completely lost sculptural and architectural works. Lastly, because of their easy loss and frequent ability to be dated within relatively short periods, coins can provide crucial chronological evidence when found in the strata of archaeological sites.

Greek Coinage. The account of Herodotus and a foundation deposit in the temple of Artemis at Ephesus indicate that the earliest coinage was produced by the kings of Lydia and the Greek coastal cities of western Anatolia around 600 BCE. These coins were struck in electrum, an alloy of gold and silver, and normally carried an obverse type depicting an animal emblem, such as the lion-head badge of the Lydian kings, the seal of Phocaea, and the recumbent lion of Miletus, as well as an incuse punch-marked reverse. The earliest examples actually lack a proper obverse type, but are marked with striations from the surface upon which they were struck. Occasionally an inscription naming the issuing authority appeared in conjunction with the obverse type. Several Lydian names have been read, and one series from Halicarnassus or Ephesus has its obverse type proclaim in Greek: "I am the badge

Stater of Phanes. Electrum trite minted at Ephesus or Halicarnassus (?), c. 600 BCE. 10 millimeters, 4.72 grams. Obverse: Stag grazing; Greek inscription naming Phanes. Reverse: Two incuse punches. PHOTOGRAPH COURTESY OF GORNY AND MOSCH GIESSENER MÜNZHANDLUNG

Athenian Tetradrachm. Silver tetradrachm minted at Athens, c. 460–413 BCE. 24 millimeters, 17.12 grams. Obverse: Head of Athena, wearing crested Attic helmet. Reverse: Owl standing, head facing; in left field, olive spray and crescent; in right field, Greek epichoric ethnic naming the Athenians. PHOTOGRAPH COURTESY OF HERITAGE WORLD COIN AUCTIONS

of Phanes." It was long thought that the first Lydian coins were struck from naturally occurring electrum found in the Pactolus River near Sardis, but recent analysis has shown that the alloy was carefully controlled and therefore man-made.

The reason for the sudden appearance of electrum coinage is unclear, because the requirements of trade were already fulfilled by the long-standing use of weighed-out bullion, known today by the German terms *Hacksilber* and *Hackgold*. The use of regulated weight standards and stamps to guarantee the metal has led to the conclusion that the earliest coinage was probably invented as a simplified method of making uniform high-value payments. Mercenary soldiers are most commonly thought to have been the original recipients of electrum coins from the Lydian kings. The coins then entered circulation when their owners exchanged them for their bullion value in goods and services.

Archaic and Classical Coinage. By the mid-sixth century a true bimetallic coinage of silver and gold had replaced the earlier electrum issues, although Cyzicus, Phocaea, and Mytilene continued to strike coins in this alloy primarily for the Black Sea trade well into the fourth century. The motive for separating coinage metals probably lies in the expansion of Persian rule over the Lydian kingdom and western Anatolia. The Persians had no tradition of using electrum for payments and preferred their precious metals unmixed. They initially produced gold and silver coins at Sardis bearing the type of confronted bull and lion foreparts, traditionally attributed to King Croesus in the sixth century.

With the advent of pure gold and silver coins, the use of coined money crossed the Aegean, where it was quickly adopted by the cities of Athens, Aegina, and Corinth, as well as in silver-rich Thrace and Macedonia. By circa 530–525 BCE, coin production had spread from Greece to the Greek colonies in Italy, Sicily, Spain, and France. At the close of the sixth century the form of coinage also began to change: the traditional punched reverse was gradually replaced with a pictorial type often accompanied by a city ethnic (name), and types in general became more standardized. The famous Athenian "owls" and Corinthian "colts," so named for their respective depictions of Athena's bird and Pegasus, emerged in this period. In the fifth and fourth centuries the owls became the dominant trade coin in the East and the colts became the dominant trade coin in the West. Mints continued to appear at smaller Greek cities during the fifth and fourth centuries, while exposure to Greek coins led to the opening of native mints in Etruria, Punic North Africa, Phoenicia, Palestine, and southern Arabia.

Greek coin systems were based on the silver stater, which depending on the city and region of production was normally divisible into four, three, or two smaller coins known as drachmas (*drachmai*, singular *drachmē*). The drachma in turn could be divided into six or eight silver obols. The weights for

Tetradrachm of Alexander the Great. Silver tetradrachm minted at Amphipolis, c. 336–332 BCE. 26 millimeters, 17.19 grams. Obverse: Head of Hercules, wearing lion skin. Reverse: Zeus enthroned, holding eagle and scepter; in left field, prow; in right field, Greek inscription naming Alexander. PHOTOGRAPH COURTESY OF CLASSICAL NUMISMATIC GROUP, WWW. CNGCOINS.COM

Tetradrachm of Ptolemy I Soter. Silver tetradrachm minted at Alexandria, c. 295/4–293/2 BCE. 27 millimeters, 14.28 grams. Obverse: Diademed bust of Ptolemy I, wearing aegis. Reverse: Eagle standing on thunderbolt; in left field, monograms; around, Greek inscription naming King Ptolemy. PHOTOGRAPH COURTESY OF GORNY AND MOSCH GIESSENER MÜNZHANDLUNG

these denominations were determined according to various official standards. Some standards tended to promote only local or regional circulation, but others had wide recognition.

Silver was the preferred metal for most Greek coins, but gold was sometimes used in emergencies, as at Athens during the disastrous last years of the Peloponnesian War. The only regularly issued gold coin of the late Archaic and Classical periods was the Persian daric, supposedly named for the Persian king Darius I (d. 486) and frequently blamed for its undue influence on Greek politics during and after the Peloponnesian War. At Sardis, the Persian king also issued silver sigloi (Semitic "shekels") to pay the Greek mercenaries in his service, while his satraps in Anatolia and Egypt struck imitations of the Athenian tetradrachm in order to pay the Greeks under their command.

The late fifth century saw the first production of bronze coins by the cities of Thurii and Acragas in Magna Graecia. This event represents the earliest development of a fiduciary currency in which the value of a coin hinged on the combination of official guarantees and public trust rather than on the content of precious metal. The idea was not always popular, as evidenced by the Athenian response to a proposal for bronze coinage brought by Dionysius Chalcus in the fifth century and a third-century law of Gortyn enforcing the use of local bronze coins. Nevertheless the production and use of bronze coinage spread throughout the Greek world until it became a standard feature of Greek coinage systems. Large bronze denominations tended to replace small silver coins, while smaller bronze coins represented fractions of the smallest silver piece. These were often based on a unit known simply as the "bronze" (*chalkous*), whose weight and number to the obol could vary by region.

Hellenistic Coinage. The Greek tradition of coinage struck by individual city-states was deeply affected by the coinage policies of Alexander the Great (r. 336–323 BCE), whose conquests extended from Greece to the Indus and who commanded immense wealth in gold and silver through the output of the Pangaean mines in Macedonia and captured Persian treasuries. The mines had already provided bullion for the influential Macedonian coinages of Alexander's father, Philip II, but Alexander established a network of mints throughout the Near East to produce a unified imperial coinage in his own name. His types and the Attic standard that he preferred survived his death in the Successor kingdoms that formed in Antigonid Macedonia, the Seleucid Near East, and Thrace under Lysimachus. In contrast, Ptolemy I adopted a lighter standard for Egypt in 305 BCE as a means of reducing the loss of bullion from his silver-poor kingdom. In circa 188–180 BCE, Eumenes II of Pergamum looked to this Ptolemaic model when he introduced the long-lived cistophoric tetradrachm (named for its type featuring the *kistē* or *cista mystica*, a sacred basket used in the rites of Dionysus), which contained only three drachmas' worth of silver but had the face value of four.

As in earlier periods, the types used for Hellenistic coins were primarily religious or otherwise symbolic of the issuing authority. However, the rise of monarchies based on the personal power of the ruler led to the increased appearance of portraits on coinage. The earliest coin portraits appear on issues from Persian satraps and Lycian dynastic coins of the fifth and fourth centuries, but portraits of living rulers did not become commonplace until the early third century when Demetrius Poliorcetes, Ptolemy I, and Seleucus I began to issue coins with their own images rather than that of the deified Alexander.

Royal coinages often took precedence over the emissions of the cities, but civic coinage continued to be produced. Coins were also struck for intermediate political units between kingdom and city, such as the federal states of the Achaean and Arcadian leagues and the Cretan tribal states. Occasionally coinage was also produced for units smaller than the city, including the temple and the guild. The origin of the festival coinages can be traced back to fifth-century issues of Delphi and Olympia. Local types and standards were normally employed for coins intended for local use, while the established types and standards of Alexander, Lysimachus, and Rhodes were adopted for coins struck by the cities for international trade. In about 166 BCE, Athens remodeled its tetradrachm in the so-called New Style and introduced a reduced Attic weight standard. This coin, known as the *stephanophoros* for the wreath border on its reverse, became an important trade coin and sparked the emission of numerous civic and royal "wreathed" tetradrachms in the second century.

Coin production and use continued to expand in the West and the East during this period. The issues of Alexander and especially Philip II inspired numerous imitative coinages struck by the Celtic peoples of Europe and Britain into the first century BCE, while increased exposure to the Greek cities of Italy in the late fourth century resulted in the earliest Roman coinage (see below). Likewise the Eastern satrapies of the former Persian Empire were gradually monetized as the Seleucid kings established mints in Iran and Central Asia. The process was continued through the second century by the breakaway rulers of Bactria, who also exported Greek coinage traditions into northwestern India with the establishment of an Indo-Greek kingdom in about 187 BCE.

Technology and Production. Except for the cast-bronze issues of Olbia in Thrace and the native Italian mints, Greek coinage was generally produced by striking a metal blank between two dies. The dies were made of hardened bronze or iron, and each carried a design engraved in negative (*intaglio*) to be impressed onto the surface of the blank. It is thought that gemstone engravers may also have served as die cutters because they were the professionals with the skills to produce detailed incuse designs on very small surfaces. The obverse or anvil die normally carried the most complicated design and was sunk into an anvil. The reverse die, also known as the hammer or punch die, usually carried a somewhat simpler design than the obverse did. In the Archaic period this die was literally a punch used to create an incuse pattern and force the metal of the blank into the obverse die. Later this die was often reserved for full-figure depictions of deities, rulers, or animals, as well as for the name of the issuing authority. Some dies were executed extremely well and were signed by their engravers. This practice is especially well attested in Sicily in the early fourth century. Gold and silver blanks, also known as flans or planchets, were cast from molds or produced by flattening globules of metal. Bronze blanks were frequently cast from molds or cut from the ends of rods. Old coins were also reused, with or without the erasure of their original types, as flans for new coins.

Once the dies and blanks had been created, it was then possible to strike the coinage. Using tongs, a workman would first place a metal blank on the obverse die. In some cases the blank was

Roman Republican Didrachm. Anonymous silver quadrigatus didrachm minted in Rome, c. 225–215 BCE. 22 millimeters, 6.42 grams. Obverse: Laureate head of Janus. Reverse: Fast quadriga, carrying Victory and Jupiter brandishing thunderbolt and holding scepter; beneath, ROMA on tabula. PHOTOGRAPH COURTESY OF CLASSICAL NUMISMATIC GROUP, WWW. CNGCOINS.COM

Roman Republican Denarius of Julius Caesar. Silver denarius minted in Rome by the moneyer P. Sepullius Macer in 44 BCE. 17 millimeters, 3.95 grams. Obverse: Laureate head of Julius Caesar; in left field, star; in right field, CAESAR IMP. Reverse: Venus standing, holding Victory and scepter; around, P SEPVLLIVS MACER. PHOTOGRAPH COURTESY OF CLASSICAL NUMISMATIC GROUP, WWW.CNGCOINS.COM

probably heated beforehand in order to make it more malleable. A second workman held the reverse die over the blank, while a third struck the top of this die with a hammer or mallet. The force of the hammer blows impressed the obverse and reverse designs onto the blank, thereby creating the coin. This process was repeated many thousands of times to fill the requirements of a particular issue. Large issues involved multiple die sets, as well as several teams of workmen striking coins at the same time. In a recent experiment replicating ancient mint conditions, an obverse die was able to strike 10,638 silver coins before it became unusable, while an obverse die striking bronze

coins managed only 5,380. Reverse dies had to be replaced more frequently because they received the full force of the hammer blow and sustained damage more quickly.

Coin production was a laborious and time-consuming task, probably relegated to slaves. The same modern experiment showed that a mint team could strike a little more than five hundred coins in a day. This rate could be reduced by damaged dies, injuries to workers, and the need to correct production errors. Some attempts were made to streamline the process through the use of fixed reverse dies, as well as through the rapid striking of cast blanks while they were still attached to each other by the mold runner.

Roman Coinage. Despite early Roman connections to the cities of Etruria, some of which had produced Greek-style local coinages in the fifth century BCE, the Romans struck no true coins of their own until the late fourth century BCE. Prior to this time, payments were made in Rome using weighed-out lumps of unworked bronze (*aes rude*). As victories in the Samnite wars extended Roman power into Campania, the Romans were increasingly exposed to the coinage produced by the Greek city-states of southern Italy. A small bronze coinage inscribed *PΩMAIΩN* (*RŌMAIŌN*, or "of the Romans") was struck at Neapolis after its liberation from Samnite control in 326 BCE. This was followed around 310–300 by an issue of silver didrachms following the Campanian model.

Although the utility of using coined silver rather than great quantities of weighed bronze to make large payments must have been readily apparent at the end of the fourth century, Rome's Greek-style didrachms were not struck again until the 260s when the conquest of the cities of Magna Graecia increased Roman stocks of precious metals and involvements with the Greek cities of the south made coins necessary. From this point the production of Roman silver coins remained constant as Roman responsibilities in Italy expanded. These coins were produced alongside large cast-bronze coins known as *aes grave* (heavy bronze) and currency bars described by scholars as *aes signatum*

Roman Imperial Sestertius of Nero. Orichalcum sestertius minted in Rome, c. 64 CE. 36 millimeters, 27.56 grams. Obverse: Laureate bust of Nero; around, NERO CLAVDIVS CAESAR AVG GERM P M TR P IMP P P. Reverse: Arch of Nero flanked by S C. PHOTOGRAPH COURTESY OF NUMISMATICA ARS CLASSICA

Roman Imperial Antoninianus of Caracalla. Silver antoninianus minted in Rome, 215 CE. 22 millimeters, 4.49 grams. Obverse: Radiate, draped, and cuirassed bust of Caracalla; around, ANTONINVS PIVS AVG GERM. Reverse: Jupiter enthroned, holding Victory and scepter; at feet, eagle; around, P M TR P XVIII COS IIII P P. PHOTOGRAPH COURTESY OF CLASSICAL NUMISMATIC GROUP, WWW.CNGCOINS.COM

(marked bronze), representing the continuation of the old Roman system of valuation according to the bronze *as* unit (plural *asses*).

The early phases of the Second Punic War (218–201) placed an immense financial strain on Rome. In an attempt to cope with the crisis, the weight of the cast-bronze coinage was reduced until its value became fiduciary, while the didrachm was debased and ultimately discontinued by 212 BCE. The silver coin was replaced shortly thereafter by the *denarius* (piece of ten; plural *denarii*), which was valued at ten bronze asses. The cast-bronze coinages were also discontinued in favor of a struck token coinage.

Republican Coinage. Production of the new silver denarius with its associated bronze and gold denominations was overseen by an annual college of moneyers, normally consisting of three young men at the beginning of their political careers. The bullion for the denarius coinage was derived primarily from booty in precious metals brought back by the expansion of Roman power in Italy and in the eastern Mediterranean, as well as from important mines acquired in Spain and Macedonia. This vast wealth in silver resulted in massive production of denarii through the later second and first centuries BCE, but the token bronze coinage was poorly maintained in the same period. To make change, it was necessary to use the worn bronze issues of the late third and early second centuries, as well as various unofficial issues that circulated in central Italy. The continued circulation of these coins was assisted by an increase in the face value of the denarius to sixteen asses in 141 BCE. These old bronze coins were occasionally supplemented by new bronze emissions and fractional silver coins such as the *quinarius* (plural *quinarii*) and the *sestertius* (plural *sestertii*), but a regular Roman bronze coinage was not restored until the reforms of Augustus.

Because it smacked too much of kingship, until the first century BCE, gold was generally considered an inappropriate metal for regular Roman coinage, although emergency issues of staters and denarius multiples had been struck during the Second Punic War. The civil wars that began to tear apart the Roman Republic in the 80s BCE made gold coinage a necessary tool for retaining the loyalty of the army. Sulla struck the first *denarius aureus* (gold denarius; plural *aurei*) in 84 BCE to support his second march on Rome. This precedent deeply influenced later Roman dynasts, including Julius Caesar, who converted the gold booty from his Gallic and British victories into the single largest emission of aurei struck before the imperial period. The rival triumvirs who survived him also coined quantities of gold in order to maintain their armies, thereby establishing a custom of gold military donatives that continued until the end of the Roman currency system.

The late Republican descent into civil war also involved the intense politicization of the coinage. Already by the 150s, Roman moneyers had been

Roman Imperial Solidus of Constantine I. Gold solidus minted in Antioch, c. 335–336 CE. 20 millimeters, 4.46 grams. Obverse: Pearl diademed, draped, and cuirassed bust of Constantine; around, CONSTANTINVS MAX AVG. Reverse: Victory advancing, holding trophy and palm branch; around, VICTORIA CONSTANTINI AVG; in right field, VOT XXX; in exergue, SMAN. PHOTOGRAPH COURTESY OF NOMOS

regularly signing the emissions produced during their tenures and adorning them with reverse types related to Republican cult and history or to personal ancestors. But during the civil wars the coin types and legends became vehicles for partisan politics, presenting the images and ideologies of the various contenders for power. Octavian (Augustus from 27 BCE), the sole surviving leader of the civil wars, transferred the use of coin types and inscriptions as a political tool wholesale to the coinage of the imperial period.

Imperial Coinage. Around 23 BCE, Augustus reformed the Roman currency and gave it the character that it maintained well into the third century CE. The Augustan system established a ratio of one gold aureus to twenty-five silver denarii and ended production of silver fractions. A new *aes* (bronze) coinage was also introduced, which included large sestertii and *dupondii* (singular *dupondius*) struck from a copper and zinc alloy known as *orichalcum*, bronze asses and semises, and copper quadrantes.

The reforms of Augustus remained largely unchanged until 64 CE when Nero reduced the weight and fineness of the denarius, as well as the weight of the aureus. The aureus remained intact at the Neronian standard until 215, but the denarius almost immediately began a roller-coaster ride of debasement

and reform. For most of the second century the reduction of the coin's silver fineness was gradual and was frequently predicated upon costly wars or other major expenses. Such reductions were evidently seen as emergency measures to be reversed when the imperial finances improved.

The excesses of Commodus (r. 180–192) and the return of civil war increased the velocity of the denarius' debasement, as placating the army became the paramount concern of would-be emperors. Under the Severan dynasty (193–235) the weight of the aureus was reduced and the silver content of the denarius dipped as low as 46 percent. In 215, Caracalla introduced a larger silver denomination known to modern scholars as either the *antoninianus* or the *radiatus* (radiate) for its depiction of the emperor wearing a radiate crown. This new coin contained the silver content of about one and a half contemporary denarii but is believed to have had a face value of two. These modifications made it possible to stretch stocks of precious metal while increasing the pay of the soldiers. Further debasements dragged the silver content of both the denarius and the antoninianus even lower than the Severan levels, ultimately turning them both into billon coins, that is, coins made of a silver-bronze alloy less than 50 percent silver. By the mid-third century the antoninianus had replaced the denarius as the primary coin of the Roman Empire. Still, the denarius managed to live on as a sporadically produced billon or bronze piece until 293 and as a unit of account (the *denarius communis*) into the early fifth century.

The debasement of the silver created inflation, which in turn had serious repercussions for the system of token aes coinage. By the reign of Marcus Aurelius (r. 161–180), the semis and quadrans fractions of the as had already ceased production. Under Maximinus I Thrax (r. 235–238) and Gordian III (r. 238–244) the weights of the sestertius and dupondius were reduced, and under Philip the Arab (r. 244–249) their Augustan orichalcum composition was replaced with a less expensive alloy of leaded bronze. Despite public desire for aes coins, by the 270s these had become so costly to produce in comparison to the increasingly overvalued antoninianus that the mints largely ceased to strike them except for a few special issues.

Aurelian attempted to arrest this crisis by reforming the currency in 274. He replaced the debased antoninianus, in which the public had lost all confidence, with a heavier radiate coin with higher silver content that modern numismatists call the *aurelianianus*. This denomination was marked *XXI* or, in Greek, *KA* probably as a ratio, 20:1, indicating the copper-to-silver content, although it has also been suggested that this was a value mark indicating 20 sestertii to the aurelianianus. Billon and leaded bronze fractions of Aurelian's new coin were also produced to fill the void created by the collapse of the denarius and the aes coinage. These measures lent some greater stability to the Roman coinage and were generally respected by Aurelian's immediate successors. The silver content of the aurelianianus was even raised to 10 percent (indicated by the mark *XI* or, in Greek, *IA*) for a brief period in 276.

In 293, Aurelian's improvements were replaced by sweeping reforms instituted by Diocletian. These set the weight of the aureus (renamed the *solidus*), which had been issued on a bewildering variety of standards in the later third century, at about 5.5 grams. He also replaced the radiate aurelianianus with a billon coin bearing a laureate portrait known as the *nummus* (plural *nummi*). Diocletian also introduced a new pure silver denomination— the *nummus argenteus*—that replicated the standards of the Neronian denarius, but its role was limited in what had essentially become a bimetallic system of gold and billon/bronze denominations. Despite this complete overhaul of the coinage, Diocletian's reforms failed to win the confidence of the public because from the beginning the nummus was greatly overvalued in terms of its silver content. It lost further popularity when its value and those of Diocletian's other denominations were officially doubled twice in 301.

The civil war that ensued upon Diocletian's abdication in 305 spelled disaster for his reforms as imperial rivals began anew the tiresome cycle of debasement and reform. The argenteus disappeared until it was resurrected by Constantine I in 324 along with multiples like the *miliarensis*, but these suffered repeated weight reductions. Likewise, more robust billon denominations, such as the *maiorina* and *centennionalis* introduced by Constantius II and Constans and the unnamed heavy coins of Julian the Apostate (r. 361–363), were habitually debased and ruined by the expense of civil and foreign wars. At last the emperors Valentinian I and Valens outlawed billon coinage entirely in 371, replacing it with bronze nummi and multiples. These were repeatedly devalued and reduced in weight until the fifth century when only the smallest *nummi minimi* circulated.

By the fifth century the Roman coinage system of the East and the Mediterranean had become completely and inconveniently bimetallic, based on the gold solidus—along with its popular fraction, the *tremissis*, demanded by the army and barbarian rulers alike—and the small bronze nummus. Silver coinage tended to survive only in western and northern Europe largely because of the taste for it among the barbarian rulers of these regions. The gulf between the solidus and the nummus was filled only in 498 when Anastasius terminated the late Roman system and established the reformed currency of the Byzantine monetary system.

Provincial Coinage. When the Roman Republic expanded its authority in the East and reorganized the Greek world into provinces, Rome inherited a multiplicity of long-standing local and regional systems of coinage. These were not immediately abolished and replaced with the denarius and aes denominations. Roman denominations did not begin to have much impact on provincial systems until the first century BCE. Instead the Roman authorities fostered the major regional coinages—namely, the Attalid cistophoric tetradrachm, the reduced Attic tetradrachm of Seleucid Syria, and the token coinage system of late Ptolemaic Egypt—as stable money. Over time these survivals of Hellenistic coinages were romanized in their appearance better to reflect their status as provincial coins. In addition to the silver and billon coinages produced at the provincial mints at Ephesus, Cappadocian Caesarea, Antioch, and Alexandria, numerous cities of the Greek East also struck vast numbers of bronze coins for use in quotidian transactions. As in the Hellenistic period, these coins were produced primarily for use within the territorial limits of the issuing city, but some regional issues were also struck. Together these provincial and civic issues are sometimes called "Greek imperials," although this usage has fallen out of vogue.

Most provincial and civic coinage carried the image of the emperor with his titles on the obverse and an image celebrating the tutelary deities, mythological past, or current honors of the issuing city. Some denominations replaced the imperial portrait with the head of a deity or a personification of the city's *dēmos* or senate. In earlier scholarship, coins lacking the imperial portrait are often described as being "pseudo-autonomous" on the erroneous assumption that such coins represented elevated civic status.

Much as the imperial silver denarius and the aes coinage became progressively debased in the second and especially the third centuries, so, too, did the coinage of the provinces. The silver content of the Egyptian tetradrachm, which had been billon since the time of Ptolemy XII in the mid-first century BCE, was drastically reduced already in the late reign of Marcus Aurelius, and the weight and fineness of the Syrian tetradrachm began a precipitous fall with the reforms of Caracalla in 215. Likewise, the provincial and civic bronze coinages were increasingly debased with lead in this period as a method of reducing the cost of their production. The decline in the silver content of the antoninianus and the gradual development of a network of imperial mints outside Rome ultimately made it unprofitable for the Eastern cities to continue issuing their own coins. With the exception of Alexandria, which continued to issue coinage for the closed economy of Egypt until 296/7, all other civic and provincial mints had ceased production by circa 275.

In contrast to the Greek East, which assimilated Roman monetary ways relatively slowly, Western provinces like Spain and Gaul embraced the Roman denarius and the associated aes denominations early on. This phenomenon may be accounted for by the comparatively young traditions of local coinages in these regions. Local denarius and bronze imitations were not uncommon in the West and seem to have been encouraged to some degree by the Roman authorities. Nevertheless, the Western provincial coinages all came to an end by circa 45 CE, probably because they had already become economically and politically superfluous.

Technology and Production. Roman methods of producing cast and struck coinage were essentially the same as those outlined for Greek coinage. The only major differences pertain to flan treatment in the Republican and late imperial periods. Some denarii of the second century BCE had their edges marked with chisel cuts, earning them the modern appellation of *denarii serrati*. It was once thought that these cuts may have served as a primitive anti-counterfeiting device or an indicator of superior metal quality, but the discovery of denarii serrati with bronze cores has shown that either this form of edge treatment was a failure against the wiles of ancient forgers or, more likely, the serrated edges had some other function.

Much more important was the development of chemical processes to enrich the surfaces of a coin. Through the use of acidic solutions it was possible to remove copper from the surface of a coin blank containing minimal silver. The loss of the copper left the silver on the surface, and the action of striking flattened it out, thereby giving the appearance of a good silver coin even when the precious metal content was as little as 33 percent. Surface-enrichment techniques were used on a large scale for the heavily debased antoniniani of Valerian I and continued in use until the end of Roman billon coinage. Surface-enriched billon coins initially provided substantial savings to the state by allowing it to pay its debts with a pseudo-silver coin of highly inflated value, but such coins also became problematic by eroding public faith in the money. Losses were also incurred by the state when enterprising individuals discovered that chemical processes could also be employed to extract the silver from the coin, leaving them with the value of the bullion, as well as with the coin.

The Romans also added orichalcum to the traditional repertoire of metals regularly employed for coinage. Following its experimental usage for a series of dupondii struck by the prefect Gaius Clovius in 45 BCE, orichalcum was adopted as the standard metal for sestertii and dupondii issued under Augustus and later emperors until the reign of Philip I. Orichalcum was also employed for some issues struck by the Roman mint expressly for provincial use.

In the early Republican period, Roman coinage was primarily struck at Rome in the temple of Juno Moneta, but in the first century BCE, mints tended to be established wherever and whenever they were needed by rival leaders and their armies, whether in Italy or abroad. By the end of the first century CE, production of Roman coinage was again focused entirely on Rome. The capital remained the sole regular source of imperial currency until 240 CE when Antioch began to coin antoniniani in order to pay the army of Gordian III. Additional imperial mints were opened in the provinces over the course of the late third century, until there was a network of fifteen at the beginning of the fourth century.

Many of the provincial coinages were struck at mints located in the issuing cities, although there is also evidence to suggest that smaller cities may have had their coins produced by facilities in the larger cities. As mentioned above, some provincial issues were struck at Rome and then transported to the provinces in which they were intended to circulate. Even when individual cities took responsibility for production, many had their dies cut by the same workshops of engravers located in major provincial centers.

Later Influence. After the collapse of the Western empire and the introduction of the Byzantine monetary system, the influence of the preceding Roman imperial coinage continued to be strong. Byzantine emperors were depicted on some bronze and gold denominations in the traditional late Roman manner (diademed, draped, and cuirassed bust facing right) until the late seventh century, and their titulature was still given in Latin until the introduction of full Greek legends in the eighth century. These same design features were transmitted to the new barbarian rulers of western Europe and North Africa through direct exposure to the coins of the last Roman emperors and to the continued use of this form for the Byzantine tremissis. Thus the numismatic images of Gothic kings and early Anglo-Saxon rulers all have the appearance of late Roman emperors.

Roman denomination names also survived the end of the empire to influence later coinage. The use of the term *denarius* to refer to a silver coin was inherited by the Frankish king Charlemagne (r. 768–814), whose *denier* became the cornerstone of medieval European coinage. The Carolingian reinterpretation of the denarius led to the adoption of this term for similar silver coins produced by other medieval states. It also lies behind the English penny, which, despite its Germanic name (from Old English *penig, penning*, akin to Old High German *pfenning*), continues to be signified by the abbreviation "d." for *denarius*. This Roman coin denomination was also adopted by the Islamic world as the *dinar*, but because this term always refers to a gold coin, it must ultimately derive from the gold denarius (*denarius aureus*) rather than the silver denarius.

[*See also* Economy and Economic Theory, Greek; Economy and Economic Theory, Roman; Mines and Mining; Trade and Commerce, Greek; *and* Trade and Commerce, Roman.]

BIBLIOGRAPHY

Balmuth, Miriam S., ed. *Hacksilber to Coinage: New Insights into the Monetary History of the Near East and Greece.* New York: American Numismatic Society, 2001.

Burnett, Andrew M., Michel Amandry, and Pere Pau Ripollès. *Roman Provincial Coinage.* 2 vols. London: British Museum Press; Paris: Bibliothèque Nationale de France, 1992–1999.

Crawford, Michael H. *Roman Republican Coinage.* 2 vols. London: Cambridge University Press, 1974.

Duncan-Jones, Richard. *Money and Government in the Roman Empire.* Cambridge, U.K.: Cambridge University Press, 1994.

Gitler, Haim, and Matthew Ponting. *The Silver Coinage of Septimius Severus and His Family (193–211 AD):*

A Study of the Chemical Composition of the Roman and Eastern Issues. Milan: Ennerre, 2003.

Harl, Kenneth W. *Coinage in the Roman Economy, 300 B.C. to A.D. 700.* Baltimore: Johns Hopkins University Press, 1996.

Head, Barclay V. *Historia Numorum: A Manual of Greek Numismatics.* 2nd ed. Oxford: Clarendon Press, 1911.

Howgego, Christopher, Volker Heuchert, and Andrew Burnett, eds. *Coinage and Identity in the Roman Provinces.* Oxford: Oxford University Press, 2005.

Jenkins, G. K. *Ancient Greek Coins.* 2nd rev. ed. London: Seaby, 1990.

Jones, John R. Melville. *Testimonia Numaria: Greek and Latin Texts Concerning Ancient Greek Coinage.* 2 vols. London: Spink, 1993–2007.

Kraay, Colin M. *Archaic and Classical Greek Coins.* London: Methuen, 1976.

Le Rider, Georges. *La naissance de la monnaie.* Paris: Presses Universitaires de France, 2001.

Lorber, Catharine. "A Revised Chronology for the Coinage of Ptolemy I." *Numismatic Chronicle* (2005): 45–64.

Mattingly, Harold, et al. *The Roman Imperial Coinage.* 10 vols. London: Spink, 1926–2007.

Mørkholm, Otto. *Early Hellenistic Coinage from the Accession of Alexander to the Peace of Apamea (336–188 B.C.).* Cambridge, U.K.: Cambridge University Press, 1991.

Ramage, Andrew, and Paul Craddock. *King Croesus' Gold: Excavations at Sardis and the History of Gold Refining.* Cambridge, Mass.: Archaeological Exploration of Sardis, Harvard University Art Museums, 2000.

Rutter, N. K., ed. *Historia Numorum: Italy.* London: British Museum Press, 2001.

Schaps, David M. *The Invention of Coinage and the Monetization of Ancient Greece.* Ann Arbor: University of Michigan Press, 2004.

Walker, D. R. *The Metrology of the Roman Silver Coinage.* 3 vols. Oxford: British Archaeological Reports, 1976–1978.

Oliver D. Hoover

COLLECTORS AND COLLECTIONS

By definition collecting is a form of consumption characterized by the accumulation of related objects. As a recognizable phenomenon, collecting originated in classical antiquity, at the royal courts in Alexandria and Pergamum. Both during antiquity and in the modern period collecting evoked long-term memory, prestige, and the value of objects, but differences between ancient and modern collecting practices are more obvious. First, ancient collecting was usually strongly associated with cultic practice and religious belief. Apart from some parallels with medieval collections, particularly those of church relics, religion played no part in European collecting of classical antiquities, which began during the early Renaissance. Second, issues such as national identity, the legitimation of power, and social seclusion—that is, class—which were important motivations behind the collecting of ancient art in modern Europe and America, played no significant role in the formation of ancient collections. Third, the Romans were avid collectors of Greek artworks. Greek art was not collected seriously again—with notable exceptions, such as the Elgin Marbles—until the advent of grand-scale excavations in Greece and Asia Minor during the nineteenth centuries and the formation of national museums in Europe and America. Finally, even though it is possible to identify some Roman collectors, few individuals stand out. Individualism and eccentricism, however, play a key role in modern collecting. Anthropological and psychoanalytical approaches have played an important role in the study of modern collecting. Recently, however, there has been focus on the diversities of collections (and of individual collectors) and the concept that material culture should be understood within specific socioeconomic, historic, and political contexts.

Bearing in mind the role that collecting of classical antiquities has played in the shaping of classical archaeology as an academic discipline, three main chronological periods stand out (the Renaissance, the eighteenth century, and modern times), and five important scenarios impacted the process of collecting: (1) European "cabinets of curiosities"; (2) Renaissance Italy; (3) the Bay of Naples; (4) the grand tour and eighteenth-century England; and (5) European and American grand public museums.

The international trade that followed along with the discovery of the New World during the early

Renaissance caused a new focus on physical objects and materiality. The emergence of cabinets of curiosities (*Wunderkammern* or *studioli*)—referring to the secluded architectural space in which these collections were kept—across Europe during the fifteenth and sixteenth centuries was basically an attempt to understand and explain the world through objects. The most famous collections were those of Ferrante Imperatore (Ferdinand II) in Naples, Athanasius Kircher in Rome, Isabella d'Este in Mantua, Ole Worm in Copenhagen, and Samuel von Quicchelberg in Amsterdam. Such early collections represented the first serious attempts at understanding the past by way of material objects, rather than solely through classical authors. The main purpose of these early collections was to present the widest representation in a small space, thus transforming the macro cosmos into a micro cosmos.

These so-called cabinets also served a didactic purpose. Objects were displayed in a tripartite classification system of *naturalia*, *artificialia*, and *instrumenta*, which represented a new way of perceiving the world, served as an important precedent for modern museums, and was a precursor to modern, empirical rationalistic research. Simultaneous with the cabinet collections and focusing attention on the classical past as a formative aesthetic for European art and identity, sculpture in particular served as an appropriate backdrop for an aristocratic lifestyle. Large collections of sculpture—as well as inscriptions, vases, coins, and medals—were assembled in Italy by aristocratic families. The transfer of Pope Julius II's private collection of sculptures (including the Apollo Belvedere) to the Vatican and its placement in the newly constructed Belvedere Court (begun in 1503) commenced a long tradition of collecting at the Vatican. Most of the sculptures collected were newly discovered in or near Rome, and were largely divided between the Vatican and the city of Rome for the Capitoline Museums, which marked the beginning of institutional collecting. Much of the sculpture was displayed by aristocratic families in Rome, Florence, and Venice in the palaces of the Medici, Farnese, Giustiniani, and Borghese families.

In the rest of Europe, however, classical sculpture was found at the royal courts.

The wider diffusion of classical art only began in the eighteenth century as a consequence of extensive traveling, the vast excavations at villa sites around Rome, the excitement of the discovery of the ruins at the Bay of Naples, the sale of a number of the Italian Renaissance collections, and through the writings of Johann Joachim Winckelmann on classical art, which were formative in the emergence of neoclassicism. The trade in antiquities became systematized by dealers, and by the third quarter of the eighteenth century there were more Roman sculptures furnishing the interiors of Britain's country houses than anywhere except for Italy. There were many and varied personal motives behind the acquisition of sculpture collections, which became indicative of leisure life in the countryside of the English gentry. A sculpture collection was the

Director of the Louvre. Ennio Quirino Visconti (1751–1818), curator of antiquities at the Louvre from 1799. Portrait by Féréol Bonnemaison, 1812. PHOTOGRAPH COURTESY OF GALLERIA W. APOLLONI–ROMA

characteristic of a true connoisseur and it made him stand out from the rest of society. By the end of the eighteenth century the use of classical antiquities as a class indicator was was no longer an issue and the Napoleonic Wars anyways put an end to the trade. The ninetenth century, which has been referred to as the "Museum Age," saw the start of grand scale institutional collecting and the formation of the large public museums in Europe and America. Founded for the benefit and education of the general public, these museums through their concepts of display, taxonomies, and restoration of objects have had a strong impact on studies of Greek and Roman art. Ancient art was also used to make political, nationalistic, or imperialistic statements. At the core of Napoleon's Louvre were sculptures from collections in occupied Italy; and objects removed from excavations in Greece and Asia Minor by, for example, British and German expeditions entered the national museums in these countries. Vast acquisitions by museums and private collectors in America and Europe during the nineteenth and twentieth centuries led to heated discussions of property rights associated with ancient art. The UNESCO convention of 1970, signed and now ratified by most countries, was intended to stop illicit trade in antiquities with uncertain provenance.

[See also Classical Tradition, subentry Classical Influences on Western Art; Elgin Marbles; and Museums.]

BIBLIOGRAPHY

Assmann, Aleida, Monika Gomille, and Gabriele Rippl, eds. Sammler, Bibliophile, Exzentriker. Tübingen, Germany: Narr, 1998.

De Benedictis, Cristina. Per la Storia del Collezionismo Italiano. 2nd ed. Florence: Ponte alle Grazie, 1998.

Coltman, Viccy. Fabricating the Antique: Neoclassicism in Britain, 1760–1800. Chicago: University of Chicago Press, 2006.

Elsner, John, and Roger Cardinal, eds. The Cultures of Collecting. Cambridge, Mass.: Harvard University Press, 1994.

Jane Fejfer

COLOGNE

Cologne on the Lower Rhine was established by Augustus for the Ubii, a Germanic group who had been allies of Rome since Julius Caesar's Gallic wars in the mid-first century BCE. Their ancestral home lay east of the Rhine in the Lahn river valley, but pressure put on their territory by a large confederation of the Germanic Suebi forced them in the last decades of the first century BCE to migrate westward with the sanction of Rome. The new urban focus of their west-bank lands, the Oppidum Ubiorum, or town of the Ubians, was built at the turn of the millennium on unoccupied land and connected with the main Roman roads leading north, south, and west. Its strategic location and fertile hinterlands quickly attracted a mixed population of Mediterranean Romans and Gallic and Germanic merchants and traders, as the many surviving inscriptions from the cemeteries outside the city walls indicate.

This civitas or territorial capital was laid out according to a Roman plan, with a regular grid of streets and a central forum. Monumental stone architecture dating to this early phase includes the governor's palace (praetorium), as well as a sanctuary of the imperial cult, focusing on a central altar (ara Ubiorum) of supraregional importance. Here Germanic chieftains held priestly offices. When Roman plans for a province of Germania on both banks of the Rhine came to an abrupt end following a crushing Roman defeat at the hands of a Germanic alliance led by the Cherusci in 9 CE, the river became the permanent frontier of Roman territory, and Cologne's role as an administrative and political center increased in importance in this militarized zone.

The Ubian capital was promoted to a veteran colony under Claudius in 50 CE and thereafter bore the name Colonia Claudia Ara Agrippinensium. Within the hierarchy of newly created Roman towns on the Lower Rhine, Cologne's status was further elevated around 85 CE to that of capital of the new province of Germania Inferior. New investments in the provincial capital included the construction of an aqueduct bringing fresh water from the Eifel, a hilly region fifty-six miles (ninety kilometers) away.

From the early first century CE, detachments of Roman legions maintained a winter base south of the town, and under Claudius this base became the main headquarters of the Roman fleet on the Rhine, the *Classis Germanica*. Because of the existence of the fleet base and other legionary and auxiliary forts along the Rhine, as well as the secondment of army personnel to the provincial governor, a military presence remained a constant factor throughout the history of the town. The last troops associated with the city were posted in Divitia, a bridgehead fortress built in 310–315 CE by Constantine opposite Cologne to defend the frontier against the Franks. Visible remains today include parts of Cologne's city wall and towers, a stretch of the sewer, and the foundations of the governor's palace. The Römisch-Germanisches Museum displays important artifacts from Cologne's Roman and Frankish past.

[*See also* Colonies and Colonization, Roman, *and* Germans.]

BIBLIOGRAPHY

Carroll, Maureen. "The Genesis of Roman Towns on the Lower Rhine." In *The Archaeology of Roman Towns: Studies in Honour of John S. Wacher*, edited by Pete Wilson, pp. 22–30. Oxford: Oxbow Books, 2003.

Carroll, Maureen. *Romans, Celts, and Germans: The German Provinces of Rome*. Stroud, U.K.: Tempus, 2001.

Maureen Carroll

COLONIES AND COLONIZATION, GREEK

Migration has been a constant feature of Greek history because the underlying causes have remained broadly constant: Greece is made up of landscapes containing unequal distributions of natural resources, often of poor quality, and is located on the doorstep of a sea that is generally highly welcoming to travel. These two *longue durée* (long duration) factors, which together encouraged interregional contact and exchange, have done much to shape Greeks into a people characterized by their

movement and acquisitive zeal. The first millennium BCE, from the Dark Age to the Hellenistic period (traditionally dated to c. 1100–31 BCE), represents an important phase of Greek migration history. In roughly the first half of this millennium, numerous Greek settlements were established at first in the Aegean Sea basin, and later, in the eighth to sixth centuries BCE, they were joined by five hundred or more settlements, of various shapes and sizes, all around the Mediterranean's shores (the latter figure representing somewhere between about one-third and one-half of the total number of ancient Greek city-states estimated in the Archaic and Classical periods). In the second half of this millennium, various Greek empires built on and expanded the lands of migration, especially in the former Persian (or Achaemenid) Empire located in Egypt, western Asia, and central Asia. At the root of all these migratory movements was the desire to acquire spaces and resources lacking at home, undertaken at first by individuals and/or individual city-states and thereafter by fewer but larger states usually employing colonization as imperialism's tool to centralize and control these spaces and resources.

Since the Renaissance, scholars interested in these migrations have normally used the terms "colonies" to describe the settlements founded outside Greece and "colonization" to describe the process by which they came to be established. Such terminology readily brings to mind ways of conceiving of the ancient Greek past that resonate with Roman and modern European colonialism. Classical antiquity provided inspiration to Europeans, who, like their ancient counterparts, spread their unquestioned higher culture to less developed peoples, using colonies and colonization as the arm of innovative and dynamic centers. As a result, classical and modern societies became entangled into a single whole. While we know of ancient Greek cases in which an extra-regional authority regulated the sending out and control of a veritable colony (see below), it is clear today that before 500 BCE most Greek colonies, and colonization itself, were far more haphazardly established and usually not controlled by a distant metropolis. The state infrastructure to do so was poorly developed or nonexistent, and much private individual initiative has also to be allowed in these early migrations. The terms "colonies" and "colonization" are used here, therefore, purely out of convention, especially for history before 500 BCE, but they are problematic terms. Alternatives, using ancient Greek terms and modern coinages based thereon would be better: the ancient Greek word *apoikia* (pl. *apoikiai*) for "colony" and the modern coinage "apoikiazation" for the process leading to an independent settlement, and the ancient Greek word *klēroukhia* and the modern coinage "kleroukhiazation" for the process leading to a dependent (more properly colonial) settlement.

The foregoing problem is also related to the nature of the ancient written sources (literature and inscriptions, particularly so-called foundation decrees), which, for the first five hundred years of migratory history discussed here, are generally not contemporary with the matters they discuss, or which, if contemporary as in the next five hundred years of migratory history, depict practices current at the time, and so are certainly not representative of this millennium of migration as a whole. Practices did seem to have largely changed in this second period, as already noted: colonization had often become truly colonialist and imperialistic in nature. Caution, therefore, needs to be exercised in handling these written sources. An important source of evidence to help determine the character of pre-Classical overseas settlements, and even Classical and Hellenistic settlements for that matter, has been archaeology, whose growth and development, especially since the end of World War II, has once and for all revealed the complexities of ancient Greek migratory history, at the same time filling out and challenging the ancient written sources. The combination of both written and material sources has taught us that all colonization has to be viewed as multifunctional, regardless of any initial motivation a colony is said or thought to have had.

Dark Age and Archaic Period. The idea that ancient Greeks ventured little from home in the so-called Dark Age (c. 1100–750 BCE) has come under increasing scrutiny in recent years. While the Greeks certainly had less contact with the outside world than in the preceding Bronze Age, there is evidence to show that some contacts were maintained both with parts closer to home and parts further away. Stories abound in ancient literature of migrations and settlements within the Aegean Sea basin by Greeks in the Dark Age, following the collapse of Mycenaean palatial society. Such stories are seen as credible, for there is contemporary material evidence in many of these regions, especially on the west coast of Asia Minor, to support these stories in a general way. Beyond the Aegean Sea basin, movement to and from Greece is also suggested by the small quantities of Greek pottery finds in the Near East and Italy and by imports from these same regions found in Greece, at such sites as Lefkandi and Olympia. Older generations of scholarship tended also to use stories in ancient literature about wandering Greek heroes after the Trojan War as further evidence of settlement in regions beyond Greece. However, such viewpoints have largely fallen out of favor. On the whole, however, it is rather improbable that Greeks left their homes without some idea of what they might expect at their destination, and the storytelling no doubt went hand in hand with the development of their overseas exploration and settlement.

Classical Greeks who wrote about the migrations that happened during the Dark Age and later Archaic period (c. 750–480 BCE) did not make a terminological distinction between these migrations, whereas modern scholarship has made a clear one, although the reasons are no more than conventional. For both migrations the sources often contain, besides the same terminology, a common vision as to how their settlements were founded. A group of settlers, led by a founder, the *oikistēs* in ancient Greek (pl. *oikistai*), worked together consciously and collectively. A visit was also customarily made to the oracle at Delphi to gauge the venture's propitiousness and in particular to get the blessing of the god Apollo, one of whose many roles was that of *archēgetēs* (leader of expeditions). Laws and customs were also brought from the homeland, and on arrival in their new homes the settlers organized their living space, with plots of land parceled out to each of the settlers. The *oikistēs*, moreover, was worshipped after death for his efforts in leading and coordinating the foundation, which, at this point, could technically be said to have finished. Again, it is difficult to know how far this ideal framework can be extended, in part or in whole, to earlier periods, yet we can be certain that Classical practices would not have emerged wholesale. Evidence in fact exists to suggest that some of these practices occurred earlier: the organization of space can be traced archaeologically to the early Archaic period, and the worship of *oikistai* to the end of the Archaic period. While it is only logical to think that settlers brought other cultural baggage with them from their homeland, the long-term outcomes of colonization show that allowance must also be made for the development of new cultural forms as a result of encounters with different physical environments and populations, both Greek and non-Greek, who lived in the vicinity or on the very sites Greeks wished to settle.

It used to be pretty much exclusively thought that Greeks, on the whole, were politically, militarily, and intellectually superior to their neighbors, and that they overran them through violence and conquest. Such scenarios, while they should not be dismissed altogether, are partly supported by analogy with modern European colonization and imperialism, whereas in reality the cultural and technological gulf between ancient Greeks and their preexisting neighbors was never as wide as in modern times. In consequence, there was also much integration, leading to the creation of multicultural communities and hybrid forms. At any rate, scenarios of domination need to be set alongside ones in which we know of Greek colonies controlled by "barbarians" (the term the Greeks used for foreigners, which gradually acquired, starting already in antiquity, the negativity associated with it today), such as Naucratis in Egypt, the port of trade founded in the mid-seventh century BCE under the watchful eye of the pharaoh Psammetichus I (Psamtik I), and the Greek colonies of the Thracian Black Sea,

which paid tribute to the Odrysian kingdom from at least the fifth century BCE.

A handful of Greek states were the most active colonizers in the Archaic period. These migrations coincided with state formation in Greece, an upturn following the Dark Age, that pushed Greeks, through political and economic pressures, to seek spaces and resources beyond their Aegean homeland. Particular Mediterranean regions were often focused on by particular Greek groups. Italy and Sicily seem to have been the first major regions settled by Greeks in the eighth century BCE, especially by Chalcis and Eretria (on the island of Euboea), Achaea, Megaris, Corinth, Rhodes, Crete, Locris, and Sparta. Two of the best known of these settlements are Pithekoussai on the island of Ischia in the Bay of Naples and Megara Hyblaia in southeast Sicily. The former is recorded in ancient sources as having been founded by Chalcis and Eretria, but archaeological evidence suggests a more complex picture of a settlement whose size, complexity (an estimated 5,000–10,000 people living on about 100 hectares or 247 acres), and multicultural makeup of native Italians, other Greeks, and Levantines extended well beyond the character and capabilities of its two founding Euboean towns. Both agriculture and trade were Pithekoussai's mainstays: the island's thick and rich volcanic soils, as well as its proximity to Etruscan metal resources in central Italy, ensured this. At Megara Hyblaia, we have evidence of a mixed population living side by side and, from the start, of a well-organized settlement, which essentially was a large open village with houses and ritual spaces for the first century, later followed by the construction of public buildings. This is a pattern commonly found in many of the early Greek settlements overseas where known: urban development and monumentalization occurred gradually, as time was needed to establish economic and cultural systems.

The next major area settled by Greeks was the northern Aegean (especially the Chalcidice and Thrace) and the Black Sea and its approaches. The settlement of these regions was carried out by various Greek states, mainly Chalcis, Eretria, Corinth,

Miletus, Megaris, Paros, Clazomenae, and Teos, resulting in such important foundations as Thasos, Byzantium, Cyzicus, and Sinope. These regions offered access to western Eurasia's extensive agricultural, mineral, and human (slave) resources, as well as securing strategic locations for the redistribution of their fruits to Greece. Three more regions were settled by Greeks in the Archaic period: the Adriatic (spearheaded chiefly by Corinth), Libya (led by Thera and resulting in Cyrene), and southern France (undertaken by Phocaea and represented mainly by Massalia, today Marseilles).

Classical and Hellenistic Periods. By 500 BCE most of the best sites for settlement had already been occupied by Greeks or other Mediterranean peoples, and as the landscape filled in, there emerged the unprecedented increase in political competition and centralization. Colonies and colonization of the Classical period (c. 480–323 BCE) tended to become ways of controlling conquered peoples and territories, and hence came under the jurisdiction of states, now more fully developed. In the fifth century, this can be best seen in the actions of an imperialistic Athens, which had surpassed its ability at home to supply itself with the foodstuffs and timber it required. Thus we find the establishment of Thurii in southern Italy (444/43 BCE) and Amphipolis in the northern Aegean (437/36 BCE) as footholds in strategic and resource-rich areas to ensure the survival of this naval empire's basic needs. Athens was at this time also at the head of the so-called Delian League and often punished rebellious members (for instance, Chalcis, Aegina, and Lesbos) with the establishment of *klēroukhiai* in their territories. These *klēroukhiai* were made up of Athenian citizens, who, while maintaining their citizenship in Athens, were given land in these subject territories and acted as garrisons that kept an eye on the rebellious population. A similar use of colonies and colonization occurred in the fourth, third, and second centuries BCE in connection with the conquests of Greece and the Persian Empire by the Macedonian Empire established by Philip II of Macedon and his son Alexander the Great.

Greek Colony. Archaeological remains of the Greek colony at Gela, Sicily, sixth to fifth century BCE. THE BRIDGEMAN ART LIBRARY

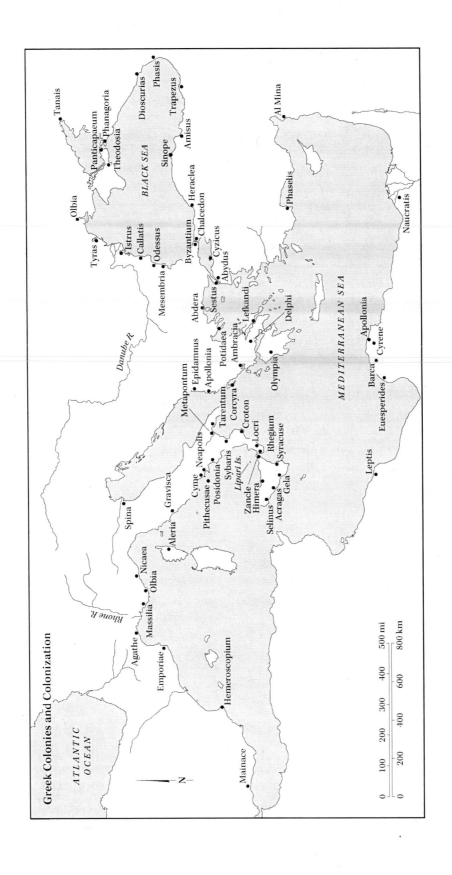

Greek Colonies and Colonization

ATLANTIC OCEAN

MEDITERRANEAN SEA

BLACK SEA

Rhone R.

Danube R.

—N—

Agathe
Massilia
Emporiae
Olbia
Nicaea
Aleria
Spina
Gravisca
Hemeroscopium
Mainace

Cyme
Neapolis
Pithecusae
Posidonia
Sybaris
Lipari Is.
Zancle
Himera
Selinus
Acragas
Gela
Croton
Locri
Rhegium
Syracuse

Metapontum
Epidamnus
Apollonia
Tarentum
Corcyra
Potidaea
Ambracia
Olympia
Lefkandi
Delphi

Leptis

Euesperides
Barca
Cyrene
Apollonia

Naucratis
Phaselis
Al Mina

Mesembria
Tyras
Istrus
Callatis
Odessus
Byzantium
Chalcedon
Cyzicus
Abydus
Sestus
Abdera
Heraclea

Olbia
Tanais
Panticapaeum
Phanagoria
Theodosia
Dioscurias
Phasis
Trapezus
Amisus
Sinope

0   100   200   300   400   500 mi
0   200   400   600   800 km

These monarchs set up strategically placed garrison towns (sometimes on preexisting settlements) to settle veterans and guard their conquests, often naming these settlements after themselves, such as Philippi in eastern Macedonia and Alexandria in Egypt. Alexander the Great's Hellenistic successor kingdoms (the Antigonids, the Ptolemies, and the Seleucids; c. 323–31 BCE) ruled his large but ultimately unwieldy empire in more regional blocks, in which they too employed colonies in similar ways both within and at the edge of their kingdoms. Antioch in northwest ancient Syria (today in modern southeastern Turkey) was perhaps the Seleucids' most successful foundation, located at the intersection of important land and water routes. It is best known archaeologically in the subsequent Roman period, when it became an important regional hub home to impressive public buildings, which are presumed for the preceding period too. Perhaps the best known Seleucid foundation is Ai Khanoum in ancient Bactria (today northern Afghanistan). It was established at the intersection of two important rivers, a site previously occupied by an Achaemenid fortification. Here was a Greek-style town, with public spaces, theater, sanctuary, gymnasium, stoas, and fortifications, as well as architecture, including temples, of Achaemenid styles. Archaeologists have also uncovered there Greek writing on papyrus and stone, the latter containing Delphic maxims, which, fittingly, bring us back to an important center in Greece for colonies and colonization. But Ai Khanoum's population was mixed, and the Greek dimension was but one side of it.

Rome conquered the Greek world during the third to first centuries BCE, but the widespread nature of Greek culture, brought about in large part through a millennium of migration, ensured that it would survive and become an integral part of the Roman Empire that followed.

[*See also* Colonies and Colonization, Roman; Greece, *subentries* The Archaic Age *and* The Classical Age; Interstate Relations; Slavery, *subentry* Slavery in Greece; *and* Trade and Commerce, Greek.]

BIBLIOGRAPHY

Billows, Richard A. *Kings and Colonists: Aspects of Macedonian Imperialism.* Leiden, The Netherlands: E. J. Brill, 1995.

Boardman, John. *The Greeks Overseas: Their Early Colonies and Trade.* 4th ed. London: Thames and Hudson, 1999.

Cargill, Jack. *Athenian Settlements of the Fourth Century B.C.* Leiden, The Netherlands: E. J. Brill, 1995.

De Angelis, Franco. "Colonies and Colonization." In *The Oxford Handbook of Hellenic Studies,* edited by George Boys-Stones, Barbara Graziosi, and Phiroze Vasunia, pp. 48–64. Oxford and New York: Oxford University Press, 2009.

Dougherty, Carol. *The Poetics of Colonization: From City to Text in Archaic Greece.* New York: Oxford University Press, 1993.

Fraser, Peter M. *Cities of Alexander the Great.* Oxford: Clarendon Press, 1996.

Karageorghis, Vassos. *The Greeks Beyond the Aegean: From Marseilles to Bactria.* New York: Alexander S. Onassis Foundation, 2002.

Tsetskhladze, Gocha, ed. *Greek Colonisation: An Account of Greek Colonies and Other Settlements Overseas.* 2 vols. Leiden, The Netherlands: E. J. Brill, 2006.

Tsetskhladze, Gocha, and Franco De Angelis, eds. *The Archaeology of Greek Colonisation.* Oxford: Oxford University Committee for Archaeology, 2004.

Franco De Angelis

COLONIES AND COLONIZATION, ROMAN

Colonization was central to the diffusion of Roman power and cultural influence throughout Italy and the provinces. Historians have traditionally viewed colonization as highly formalized and structured, driven by the Roman state, but recent studies and new archaeological evidence suggest a much more diverse and fluid process.

Foundations. The earliest colonies may date to a very early phase of Rome's expansion (sixth–fifth centuries BCE)—although supporting archaeological evidence is slight—but by the fourth century BCE, foundation of colonies on conquered territory was a regular event. Between 338 and 218 BCE small groups (about three hundred people) of Roman settlers were settled at sites in Latium and Campania, often—although not exclusively—in coastal centers such as Antium (Anzio) and Tarracina (Terracina). These were mostly added to existing communities, and land allocations were relatively small.

Many early colonies were close to Roman territory and were too small to form independent communities. Colonists retained their Roman citizenship, and the communities were designated as Roman-citizen colonies, but they adopted local administrative systems based on that of Rome—typically two annually elected magistrates (*duoviri*) and a senate to run their internal affairs. Other colonies were designated as Latin colonies (*coloniae Latinae*) and differed in some important respects. These were self-governing communities with Latin status and were larger settlements. Latin colonies were frequently new communities, often founded in areas with low levels of urbanization, although some, such as Paestum (founded 273 BCE), were additions to existing settlements.

A central feature of colonization before 90 BCE was a requirement for most colonies to provide troops to assist Rome, and contingents from both Latin and Roman colonies were an important part of the Roman army. A possible exception were colonies designated as *coloniae maritimae*, which may have been exempt because of their role in protecting the coastline, but the status of such colonies and the nature of their exemption is unclear. In any event the juridical distinction between different types of colonies is not clear-cut, and there is a considerable degree of blurring between categories.

Colonial foundations continued into the second century BCE, but with some changes. Around 177 BCE, the foundation of Latin colonies was abandoned and citizen colonies became larger—from about two thousand to about five thousand colonists—and were new communities. In the 180s large-scale colonization in northern Italy imposed Roman-style urbanization on a region that was newly conquered and provided defense against Gallic incursions. Colonies at Bononia (Bologna), Parma, Mutina (Modena), and Aquileia established Roman urban settlements in the region. After 90 BCE when Roman citizenship was extended to the rest of Italy south of the river Po, the distinction between Latin and citizen colonies disappeared, and colonization became more closely linked with military settlement. Sulla, Julius Caesar, Mark Antony, and Augustus all founded significant numbers of colonies, which were largely composed of discharged troops who received land grants as a reward for service and were added to existing communities.

The first colony outside Italy was Junonia, founded at Carthage in 122 BCE by Gaius Sempronius Gracchus. There was strong senatorial opposition and its charter was later revoked, but the settlers remained, and subsequent provincial colonies at Narbo Martius in Gaul (Narbonne, France; 118 BCE) and other sites in Africa and southern France were successful. Overseas colonization remained infrequent until the late first century BCE when Caesar, Antony, and Octavian (later Augustus) regularly settled Roman colonists in the provinces, as well as in Italy. Some of these colonists were from the civilian population, but the majority were discharged troops. This process continued during the Principate, using colonial settlement as a means of controlling and Romanizing key areas of the empire. The higher civic status enjoyed by colonies became sought after, particularly in the eastern empire. By the reign of Hadrian this reached its logical conclusion. After that date, grants of the title *colonia* were enhancements of civic status and were not accompanied by settlement of colonists.

Motivations. Roman motives for colonial foundation, particularly during the conquest of Italy, are a matter of debate. Ancient writers associate colonies directly with extension of Roman power (Velleius Paterculus 1.14–15). Cicero describes colonies as "bulwarks of empire" (*De lege agraria* 73), and Livy suggests that they were founded by Rome to increase its number of citizens (Livy 27.9.11). A letter of Philip V of Macedon to the city of Larissa (215 BCE; *Sylloge Inscriptionum Graecarum*, vol. 3, 543) states that colonization was a key to Roman success, and other sources note that colonies were used to control territory and protect it from incursions (Cicero *Pro fonteio* 5.13; Appian *Civil Wars* 1.7).

Colonies were often founded at vulnerable locations or on newly conquered territory to provide a core Roman presence. This is most apparent in the foundation of *coloniae maritimae*, which were situated along the coast of Italy, possibly to defend against pirates and control formerly threatening coastal cities such as Antium, which was defeated by Rome in 338 BCE after a fierce struggle. It seems unlikely, however, that Rome—particularly at an early date—had a political system that could generate long-term planning in foreign policy, and recent research has questioned whether Republican colonization was driven by a conscious policy of imperial expansion. From the first century BCE onward, and particularly in the Roman provinces, there is a much stronger link between colonization and military activity. In the era after the Social War, colonies were mostly composed of discharged soldiers, thus linking settlement much more closely with military needs.

Ancient writers present the foundation of a colony as a structured process that took place according to rituals that reflected important aspects of Rome itself. Where the colony was a new settlement, the auspices were taken by a magistrate and a ritual boundary was established to separate the urban center from its territory. Key cults were founded, the land was surveyed and distributed to the colonists, and new forms of civic administration were established. Civic organization of the colonies was based, like that of Rome, on a local senate and annually elected magistrates, usually a board of two *duoviri* (sometimes four *quattuorviri*), although details differed from place to place. Some adopted internal subdivisions named after areas of Rome, such as the vicus Esquilinus found at Cales (*Inscriptiones Latinae Selectae* 8567). However, most sources for foundation rituals, and for other forms of colonial organization, date to the first century BCE or later. They may reflect later practices or a conflation of foundation rituals from different contexts and periods.

Early colonies in particular may have been the result of individuals settling bands of their own supporters, clients, or troops in a much more ad hoc manner, and they may have involved all-male groups that intermarried into the local population.

The status of the original inhabitants in early colonies is problematic. There are cases, such as Antium, where the colonists and precolonial inhabitants seem to have formed parallel communities with separate administrations that did not merge until a later date, but the details are unclear. In other cases—for example, Ferentinum (Ferentino) in 195/4 BCE—the inhabitants were explicitly barred from taking the status of the new colony (Livy 34.42.5–6). By the first century BCE, however, colonial organization was more standardized. Adoption of a colonial charter setting out details of the administration of the community, such as the colonial charter found at Urso (Osuna) in Spain (44–47 BCE; *Corpus Inscriptionum Latinarum* II, vol. 2, 5.1022), became common practice, as did the Roman-style constitution of *duoviri* and *ordo decurionis*.

Roman Colony. View of the Capitolium, Thugga, North Africa (now Dougga, Tunisia), late second century CE. GIRAUDON/THE BRIDGEMAN ART LIBRARY

Colonization could alter social structure of a community profoundly. Sulla, for instance, settled colonies in communities that had opposed him, such as Pompeii, where about two to three thousand colonists were settled. The colonists seem to have rapidly supplanted the Pompeian elite in the senior magistracies of the city and dominated positions of social and political influence. It is possible, although not certain, that the Pompeians also suffered some loss of political rights (Cicero *Pro Sulla* 60–62).

Colonies undoubtedly assisted the dissemination of Roman culture and Roman forms of urban life. Ancient authors assert that colonies were replicas of Rome, particularly in terms of their laws and customs (Aulus Gellius *Noctes Atticae* 16.13.8–9), as well as in their physical form. They adopted Latin as an official language and constructed specifically Roman types of building. Capitolia—temples of Jupiter Capitolinus, the central cult of the Roman state—were constructed in many colonies. Curia/comitia buildings, which housed meetings of the *ordo* and political gatherings, were common in colonies in Republican Italy, and most colonies were organized around a regular street grid and a rectangular forum. Other structures associated with colonial settlement include amphitheaters, which are often found in veteran colonies.

Despite these similarities, the extent to which colonies in the pre-Augustan era were deliberately and closely modeled on Rome is debatable, particularly given the unplanned development of Rome itself. Excavation of colonies such as Fregellae, Alba Fucens, Cosa, and Paestum has established that although foundation of a colony led to significant changes in the organization and physical layout of urban space, the colonies show less uniformity of planning and less reliance on Rome as a model than was previously believed. However, it is undeniable that the colonies from the Augustan period onward were an important feature in the dissemination of Romanization.

[*See also* Citizenship, Roman; Interstate Relations; Latins; Romanization; *and* Rome.]

BIBLIOGRAPHY

Bispham, Edward. "*Coloniam Deducere*: How Roman Was Roman Colonization?" In *Greek and Roman Colonization: Origins, Ideologies, Interactions*, edited by Guy Bradley and John-Paul Wilson, pp. 73–160. Swansea: Classical Press of Wales, 2006.

Bradley, Guy. "Colonization and Identity in Republican Italy." In *Greek and Roman Colonization: Origins, Ideologies, Interactions*, edited by Guy Bradley and John-Paul Wilson, pp. 161–188. Swansea: Classical Press of Wales, 2006.

Brunt, Peter. *Italian Manpower, 225 BC–AD 14*. Oxford: Clarendon Press, 1971.

Keppie, Lawrence. *Colonisation and Veteran Settlement in Italy, 47–14 B.C.* London: British School at Rome, 1983.

Mouritsen, Henrik. "Pits and Politics: Interpreting Colonial Fora in Republican Italy." *Papers of the British School at Rome* 72 (2004): 37–67. See also the response by Filippo Coarelli in *Papers of the British School at Rome* 73 (2005): 23–30.

Salmon, Edward T. *Roman Colonization under the Republic*. London: Thames & Hudson, 1969.

Sherwin-White, Adrian N. *The Roman Citizenship*. 2nd ed. Oxford: Clarendon Press, 1973.

Kathryn Lomas

COLOR

Color was an integral part of Greek and Roman art and architecture. Buildings could employ materials of different colors as well as painted architectural ornament; wall paintings and mosaic or *opus sectile* (cut stone) floors lent color to interiors. Most sculpture of wood and stone was painted or gilded; statues could be carved of colorful marble; bronze statuary was enhanced with inlays of differently colored metal, stone, and glass; chryselephantine (gold and ivory) statues were further decorated with glass; and terra-cotta sculpture of all sizes was painted. On a smaller scale there were panel paintings, elaborate furniture and textiles, painted and glazed pottery and glass vessels, and colorful jewelry and gemstones.

Less permanent than the stone itself, the original coloration of many ancient monuments has left few traces, allowing Classical architecture and sculpture to be whitewashed by neoclassical ideals. Ancient writers occasionally hinted at the role of color in art, as was first shown by Antoine-Chrysostome Quatremère de Quincy in *Le Jupiter olympien* (Paris, 1815). Intensified investigation of ancient sites in the nineteenth century revealed architectural and sculptural remains with significant traces of paint, resulting in a lively debate on polychromy that was followed in the earlier twentieth century by a period of disregard. The increased application of scientific technologies since the 1970s has provided the material basis for a fresh evaluation of the role of color in Greek and Roman art and architecture.

Archaic Greek temples and other buildings were crowned by molded terra-cotta decoration, mostly painted in black and red, with some white. Architectural terra-cottas were especially popular in South Italy and Sicily, as well as in Etruria and early Rome. With the introduction of marble as a prime building material in sixth-century Greece, white temple exteriors became standard. The limestone columns and walls of the temple of Aphaea on Aegina (c. 500–475 BCE) were coated with white stucco. Painted architectural ornament lent rhythm to the building, with red used for horizontal elements and black and blue for vertical ones. Greek temple architecture could also employ colorful stones. On the Erechtheum (Athenian Acropolis, c. 421–406 BCE), dark bluish limestone formed the background of the figural frieze, and glass inlays embellished carved ornaments. From the second and first centuries BCE the use of colored marbles became increasingly common in Rome, a prime example being the Pantheon (c. 118–125 CE). Different kinds of marble were chosen for their visual effects, sumptuousness, and exotic origins, reflecting the extent of the Roman Empire. Already in the fourth century BCE, Greek building interiors imitated monumental ashlar masonry with colorful stucco and paint, eventually leading to the illusionistic wall decorations seen in Pompeian houses.

The Archaic statuary from the Athenian Acropolis and the architectural sculpture of the Siphnian Treasury at Delphi (c. 525 BCE) and the temple of Aphaea on Aegina preserve extensive remains of paint. This evidence suggests that Archaic and early Classical marble sculpture was entirely painted, with individual colors applied to well-defined fields and linear details. The palette included various reds, blues, yellows, and greens. The background color of reliefs changed from red to blue to white over the course of the Archaic and Classical periods. More than twenty different pigments were used to color the so-called Alexander Sarcophagus from Sidon (c. 320 BCE), which shows the sophisticated shading and highlights characteristic of painting at the transition to the Hellenistic period. In the Hellenistic period a preference for pastel colors may be observed.

More research is needed on the polychromy of Roman sculpture. The statue of Augustus from Prima Porta and the head of Caligula in Copenhagen indicate that imperial marble portraits could be painted, including flesh tones for the skin. Other statuary was partly or entirely gilt, or was decorated in a combination of techniques; reduced coloration was probably a result of the prestige of white marble. The intrinsic colors of different marbles were exploited in works such as the kneeling barbarians associated with Augustus' Parthian monument (c. 20 BCE). Color symbolism underlay the use of polychrome marble for representations of barbarians and Dionysiac figures and of porphyry for imperial imagery.

The colors of most painted Greek pottery were restricted to earth tones applied before the firing process; the minimalist color scheme of Attic red-figure vases probably had both visual and practical appeal. Written sources and the few examples of Greek polychrome painting surviving on white-ground pottery, grave markers, and the walls of tombs—including the hunt frieze from Vergina dating to the fourth century BCE—illustrate the main tendencies in wall and panel painting. Archaic and early Classical paintings were characterized by clearly delineated fields and geometric patterns executed in bright, mostly unmixed and often contrasting colors. The later Classical period saw the introduction of shading (*skiagraphia*), of modeling with light and shades, and of highlights. In a parallel development, mixing of colors became more common, referred to with negative undertones as *phthora* (literally, "destruction"). The rendering of light and shade unified compositions and led to new concerns for the overall tone and harmony of a painting. The four-color palette, restricted to white, yellow, red, black, and their mixtures (Pliny *Natural History* 35.50) and exemplified by the Alexander Mosaic (a first century BCE adaptation of a Greek painting), was one possible solution. The later Hellenistic and Roman Odyssey Landscapes (c. 50–40 BCE) and wall paintings at Pompeii built on these earlier trends and made use of expensive pigments in luxurious domestic settings.

Ancient pigments were mainly of mineral origin, including yellow ochre and red iron oxides, the bright-red mercury sulfide cinnabar (vermillion), copper carbonates such as green malachite and blue azurite, and the artificially produced Egyptian blue. Pliny (*Natural History* 35.30) distinguished the "florid" *colores floridi*, including cinnabar, malachite, ultramarine, and the organic indigo and purple, from the "austere" *colores austeri*, mostly earth tones. Some pigments were appreciated for their rarity, and some colors conveyed prestige or carried symbolic associations. Most remarkable, however, is the shift from conventional color to color modulated by light and shade. This artistic practice corresponds to the notion expressed in the Peripatetic treatise *On Colors* that pure colors cannot be seen, because the perception of colors is impacted by neighboring colors and by light and shadows (793b).

[*See also* Architecture; Mosaics; Painting; *and* Sarcophagus.]

BIBLIOGRAPHY

Bradley, Mark. "Colour and Marble in Early Imperial Rome." *Cambridge Classical Journal* 52 (2006): 1–22.

Gage, John. *Color and Culture: Practice and Meaning from Antiquity to Abstraction.* Boston: Little, Brown, 1993. See especially chapters 1–3.

Panzanelli, Roberta, with Eike D. Schmidt and Kenneth Lapatin, eds. *The Color of Life: Polychromy in Sculpture from Antiquity to the Present.* Los Angeles: J. Paul Getty Museum and Getty Research Institute, 2008. The essays by Vinzenz Brinkmann and Jan Stubbe Østergaard give an overview of recent research on polychrome statuary in Greece and Rome.

Tiverios, Michalis A., and Despoina S. Tsiafakis, eds. *Color in Ancient Greece: The Role of Color in Ancient Greek Art and Architecture (700–31 B.C.).* Thessaloníki, Greece: Aristotle University, 2002.

Susanne Ebbinghaus

COLOSSEUM

The Colosseum is an amphitheater constructed in Rome during the Flavian dynasty. Brilliant in form but infamously brutal in function, it remains awe-inspiring even in ruins. However inaccurately, its popular associations with gladiatorial massacres, debased crowds, deranged despotism, and glorious martyrdom have darkened the image of Rome for almost two millennia.

Gladiatorial and beast shows took place in the Forum and the Circus Maximus at Rome for centuries before the introduction of the amphitheater. Some scholars credit the invention of the amphitheater to Campania, an area of southern Italy associated with gladiatorial training schools and amphitheaters, including the early example of circa 70 BCE at Pompeii, but it is now argued that the proto-amphitheater form—an elliptical arena with seating on all sides, and especially if complete with subchambers—emerged first with temporary wooden structures in the Roman Forum itself. Titus Statilius Taurus, Augustus' associate, built Rome's first stone amphitheater in 30 BCE, and Nero built a wooden version in 57 CE, but fire destroyed both venues in the Campus Martius in 64 CE.

Designed by a brilliant but unknown architect, the Flavian Amphitheater became known as the Colosseum in medieval times because the Colossus of Nero (121 feet, or 37 meters, tall), a statue of Nero as the sun god, stood nearby. Vespasian (r. 69–79 CE) began constructing this specialized, purpose-built, monumental stone facility early in his reign, and work continued under his son Titus. By placing the amphitheater centrally and strategically on the site of Nero's artificial lake (in the gardens of his Golden House), Vespasian was declaring that he was

Ludus Magnus

When the emperors took control of the arena games and banned from Rome privately owned gladiatorial schools, four imperial gladiatorial training schools—Ludus Magnus, Ludus Dacicus, Ludus Matutinus, and Ludus Gallicus—were established near the Colosseum, possibly under Augustus and definitely by the time of Domitian (r. 81–96). Each was managed by an equestrian procurator and staffed by trainers, armorers, slaves, and even doctors. The largest of the schools, the Ludus Magnus, was adjacent to and connected by a subterranean tunnel to the Colosseum. Its elliptical arena—about 204 by 135 feet (62 by 41 meters)—was used for exercises, practice fights, and rehearsals, spectator seating areas arose above storage areas, and a rectangular portico on all sides housed gladiators in cells similar to those of the *ludus* at Pompeii. Training and care in such facilities increased the gladiators' chances of fighting well and possibly surviving in the Colosseum.

returning the site to the people to house entertainments for them. The oval structure—about 617 by 512 feet (188 by 156 meters) and about 171 feet (52 meters) high—rested on massive concrete foundations about 39 feet (12 meters) deep around outer walls. In travertine stone, the exterior included three stories of arches and engaged half-columns (in the Tuscan and then the Ionic and Corinthian orders), topped by an attic story with Corinthian pilasters, windows, and gilded shields. Arches on the second and third stories held statues of Greek gods and heroes.

Titus dedicated the nearly complete facility in 80 CE with extravagant spectacles spread over some one hundred days, and Martial's *Spectacula* (On the Spectacles) applauds the wild-beast hunts and shows, gladiatorial and infantry combats, some sort of ship battle (*naumachia*), and theatricalized and mythologized (but fatal) executions of criminals, who were dressed in costumes and often mauled by wild animals.

A showplace of imperial generosity and power, the Colosseum housed violent entertainments, but the shows and spectators were to be orderly. Reinforcing the hierarchical nature of Roman society, the seating areas included five tiered levels. The podium, a high platform about 13 feet (4 meters) directly above the sanded wood floor of the elliptical arena (253 by 151 feet, or 77 by 46 meters), had special seats for the imperial family, priests, Vestal Virgins, senators, and dignitaries, all kept safe from beasts by a system of nets and rollers. The level above was assigned to *equites*, the next to male citizens, and the next to noncitizens and slaves, and women sat on wooden stands at the topmost level. About the Colosseum's paved perimeter, upright stone standards secured barriers for crowd control as some forty-five to fifty thousand spectators entered through seventy-six numbered arches; four unnumbered grand entrances on the axes were for dignitaries and processions. A triumphal arch, surmounted by a chariot group, decorated the entrance leading to the imperial box on the west end of the minor axis. Tokens indicated which entrance to use, and spectators followed circular arcades, staircases, and tunnel exits to the proper level and section of the stands (*cavea*). Crowds were provided with fountains, lavatories, and perfumed sprays to refresh themselves. Contingents of troops formed a security force, and to provide shade, sailors could spread an elaborate awning (*vela*) from masts seated on corbels on the exterior of the top level.

Added or enlarged by Domitian (r. 81–96), subchambers (about 23 feet, or 7 meters, deep) on two levels under the arena provided room for cages, lifts, and ramps for beasts, cells for prisoners, and storage space for equipment, machinery, props, and scenery. Exotic beasts might appear suddenly in an arena spectacularly decorated with artificial landscapes of hills, woods, and pools. A large, specialized workforce, from beast handlers to musicians, worked expeditiously to put on memorable spectacles, and emperors spared no expense in trying to surpass earlier shows in numbers, novelties, and special effects. An architectural triumph and a compelling symbol of Roman power and order, the Colosseum

The Colosseum. Interior of the Colosseum. Photograph by the Moffett Studio, 1909. Prints and Photographs Division, Library of Congress

inspired some two hundred other amphitheaters, both grand and modest, as markers of romanization in Europe and North Africa, although fewer arose in the Greek East.

[*See also* Amphitheaters and Arenas; Colossus; Flavian Family and Dynasty; Gladiators and Gladiatorial Games; *and* Rome, *subentry* The City of Rome.]

BIBLIOGRAPHY

Gabucci, Ada, ed. *The Colosseum.* Translated by Mary Becker. Los Angeles: J. Paul Getty Museum, 2001. A lavishly illustrated, large-format study of the architecture and function of the Colosseum. Noted Italian scholars thoroughly discuss the spectacles and gladiators, the origins, form, archaeology, and operation of the facility, and also its later history from antiquity to the present.

Hopkins, Keith, and Mary Beard. *The Colosseum.* Cambridge Mass.: Harvard University Press, 2005. A concise, lively, and accessible discussion by two major scholars of the construction, design, and later centuries of the amphitheater; clarifies misconceptions while discussing the spectacles, combatants, spectators, and emperors associated with the Colosseum.

Welch, Katherine E. *The Roman Amphitheatre: From Its Origins to the Colosseum.* Cambridge, U.K.: Cambridge University Press, 2007. Magisterial archaeological study of the rise of arena games, amphitheatrical architecture at Rome and in Italy during the Republic and the early Empire, and the amphitheater's reception in the Greek world.

Donald G. Kyle

COLOSSUS

The term "colossus," from the Greek *kolossos,* originally simply meant "statue" but eventually came to mean a gigantic statue. Herodotus used the term only in reference to Egyptian sculpture. Although there were many colossi in the ancient world, the only one named as such was the colossus of Rhodes, a statue of the god Helios, one of the Seven Wonders of the ancient world. Although there are no extant colossi from the Bronze Age, in myth the Trojan horse would certainly have ranked as one. Colossal statuary is fairly common in the Archaic and Hellenistic periods but is reserved for cult images during the Classical period. For the purposes of this essay a "colossus" is defined as a figure more than ten feet (three meters) tall.

The earliest and best-known Archaic colossus is that of Apollo on Delos, circa 600 BCE, which now is preserved in two huge pieces of Naxian marble (chest and buttocks). Resembling the common statuary type known as the kouros, it originally stood 28 feet (8.5 meters) tall outside the temple of the god. The next-tallest kouros, that discovered on the island of Samos in 1980, is more than 15 feet (4.5 meters) tall and was dedicated to Hera circa 570 BCE by an individual named Ischys. Some marble colossi have been found abandoned unfinished in their quarries, like the bearded male on Naxos that is 35 feet (10.7 meters) tall. The Ram-bearer, found in pieces in the sanctuary of Apollo on Thasos, stands 11.5 feet (3.5 meters) tall and also was never finished. Pausanias (3.18–19) reports an approximately 46-foot (14-meter) statue of Apollo at Amyclae near Sparta, probably made of sheets of bronze over a wooden core.

During the Classical period the Athenian sculptor Phidias is best known for his colossal chryselephantine (gold and ivory) cult statues: the standing Athena Parthenos in Athens, 38 feet (11.6 meters) tall, and the enthroned Zeus at Olympia, 42 feet (12.8 meters) tall. His first commission, however, was a colossal standing bronze statue of Athena that stood outdoors on the Acropolis; the tip of her spear could be seen by ships rounding Cape Sounion.

The late fourth-century sculptor Lysippus brought colossal sculpture back into vogue. For the city of Tarentum he made colossal bronzes of Zeus (60 feet, or 18.3 meters) and a seated Heracles. His most copied statue was the twice life-size Resting Heracles of which the best-known copy (Naples) was made for the Baths of Caracalla. In 1960 a colossal version of the Heracles Epitrapezios ("at the table") by Lysippus was unearthed at Alba Fucens in central Italy.

Lysippus' pupil Chares of Lindos created the largest colossus ever recorded, the Helios of Rhodes, which measured 110 feet (33.5 meters) tall. Cast in bronze circa 280 BCE, it stood next to (not astride) the harbor of Rhodes until 224 BCE when it was toppled by an earthquake. In Roman times it became customary to erect colossal statues, usually on tall bases, at the entrances of harbors; such statues are recorded at the harbor of Caesarea built by Herod the Great in 22–20 BCE, at Ostia the port of Rome, and at Patras in the Peloponnesus, to name a few.

The most famous Roman colossus is that which gives its name to the Colosseum, the gilded bronze statue of Nero fashioned by the Greek sculptor Zenodorus circa 64–66 CE. Reputedly 102 or 120 feet (31 or 36.6 meters) tall, it was converted to a statue of Sol (Helios) after Nero's death when it was hauled by twenty-four elephants from the entrance to his Golden House to the west end of the Flavian Amphitheater.

No doubt imperial Rome was filled with colossal statuary in antiquity. Among those that survive are a twice life-size seated female (called Minerva but her aegis is modern) whose dress is made of yellow Numidian marble (first century BCE to first century CE), two 12-foot (3.7-meter) standing gods (Hercules and Bacchus) of metallic green stone from Egypt found in the audience chamber of the Domitianic palace on the Palatine (now in Parma), and some Parian marble hand fragments of a six times life-size male statue standing in the elaborate Hall of the Colossal Statue of the Forum of Augustus. In the provinces one also encounters colossal marble images of emperors (Titus from the Flavian temple at Ephesus) and empresses (Faustina the Elder at the temple of Artemis at Sardis). One of the last colossal statues to be carved in Rome was that of Constantine the Great, which was set up in the apse of his basilica; the marble head (Capitoline) alone is 8.5 feet (2.6 meters) high, suggesting that the seated statue was almost 50 feet (15.2 meters) tall.

In addition to freestanding sculptures, colossal groups were also fabricated in antiquity. At Lycosura in Arcadia, the cult group of the Great Goddesses, Despoina and Demeter, was made of local marble by Damophon of Messene circa 200–150 BCE. Extant fragments of this group suggest that the seated goddesses were about 14 to 15 feet (4.3 to 4.6 meters) tall. At Claros in Ionia the temple of Apollo housed statues of the Delphic triad, a seated Apollo flanked by standing figures of Artemis and Leto some 25 feet (7.6 meters) tall. In western Turkey at the site of Nemrud Dagh, a high peak of the Taurus Mountains, Antiochus I of Commagene erected a shrine to himself circa 64–38 BCE. It consisted of two terraces with rows of limestone statues more than 10 feet (3 meters) tall that depicted various gods in a hybrid style that combined Hellenistic with Near Eastern traits.

A modern, classically inspired colossus recalling the Helios of Rhodes is the Statue of Liberty, which like its predecessor is bronze, wears a radiant crown, and stands next to a harbor. At 142 feet (43.3 meters) tall, not counting her pedestal, she is taller than the Helios, but not by much.

[*See also* Colosseum; Cult Images; Lysippus; Phidias; Rhodes; *and* Seven Wonders.]

BIBLIOGRAPHY
Clayton, Peter A., and Martin J. Price. *The Seven Wonders of the Ancient World*. New York: Routledge, 1988.
Dickie, Matthew W. "What Is a *Kolossos* and How Were *Kolossoi* Made in the Hellenistic Period?" *Greek, Roman, and Byzantine Studies* 37 (1996): 237–257.
Roux, Georges. "Qu'est-ce qu'un *kolossos*?" *Revue des Études Anciennes* 62 (1960): 5–40.

Jenifer Neils

COLUMELLA

(Lucius Junius Moderatus Columella, first century CE), Roman writer. During his youth in Spain, Columella learned about farming and estate management from his uncle who had an estate near Gades. He then left Spain for Rome and, presumably, a career, about which we know nothing. He was roughly contemporary with Seneca the Younger (4 BCE/1 CE– 65 CE), also a Spaniard. The *De re rustica* was initially composed in nine books, covering all the practicalities of agriculture on an Italian estate. At the request of Publius Silvinus and Claudius Augustalis, a tenth book in hexameters on kitchen gardens was written, filling a gap Virgil had consciously left in the *Georgics*. Then Columella added two more books on the responsibilities of the bailiff and his wife. A separate and earlier work, the *De arboribus*, concerns crops and trees, the subjects treated at greater length in books 1 and 2 of the *De re rustica*. From his work we know that Columella had substantial landholdings in Italy, was actively involved in the work of his estate, and, as his friends were confident he could emulate Virgil, was thought to be something of a *littérateur*. He is not interested in court flattery, and writes nothing like the panegyric to Augustus that opens Vitruvius' treatise on architecture. Although he indulges in elaborate Hellenistic allusiveness in book 10, he avoids any reference to the emperor or the state even there, and holds strictly to his subject.

Columella laments the decline of morals in his day, and praises the farmer's character—praise that is heavily dependent on Cato's republican ideology and Xenophon's *Oeconomicus* in Cicero's translation. He is appalled not just by the neglect of farming by the noble and freeborn, but by their attempts to blame diminishing harvests on exhausted soil and bad weather. Columella holds estate owners' ignorance of agricultural principles responsible for bad crop yields and observes with indignation that there were schools of oratory and philosophy, but not of agriculture. His comprehensive treatise was written, with Silvinus' encouragement, in response. His style is elegant, clear, and superbly well organized for practical instruction. In particular, each book begins with reference to the previous book's subject, and ends with an indication of the subsequent topic to be addressed. Such clear organizational sign-posting is a major reason why Columella's work survived complete into the modern era. Silvinus read the early books to an audience, and book 4 shows that some of them then disputed theories of vine-planting with Columella as though with a philosopher-teacher. Book 10, in homage to Virgil, was, among other things, a pointed demonstration that literary accomplishment was compatible with intelligently managing one's estates. Columella's extensive knowledge of his predecessors (including Virgil) is far from uncritical, but his frequent citation indicates the tremendous authority Virgil's texts had already acquired. Columella himself rightly became an authority, quoted extensively by technical writers from Pliny (first century CE) to Isidore (seventh century CE). He was a natural teacher, and his love of his subject is unmistakable.

[*See also* Agricultural Treatises.]

BIBLIOGRAPHY
Works of Columella
On Agriculture. 3 vols. Translated by Harrison Boyd Ash. Cambridge, Mass.: Harvard University Press, 1941.

Secondary Works

Baldwin, Barry. "Columella's Sources and How He Used Them." *Latomus* 22 (1963): 785–791.

Gowers, Emily. "Vegetable Love: Virgil, Columella and Garden Poetry." *Ramus* 29, no. 2 (2000): 127–148.

Henderson, John. "Columella's Living Hedge: The Roman Gardening Book." *Journal of Roman Studies* 92 (2002): 110–133.

C. M. C. Green

COLUMNS, COMMEMORATIVE

Commemorative columns were used in both Greece and Rome to honor ancestors and achievements and to magnify the status of the ruler. Some of the largest and most famous, such as the columns of the emperors Trajan and Marcus Aurelius, have survived in a relatively well-preserved state.

Greece. Columns were one of the many forms of stone tomb markers used in Greece in the sixth and early fifth centuries BCE. The flat surface of the square abacus of a Doric column capital was inscribed at times with an epitaph for the deceased. The smooth, faceted, or fluted shaft of a column of any order could also serve as a ground for a funerary epigraph. The inscriptions often use language and meter reminiscent of Homer. Funerary columns in ancient Greece usually commemorate men who died young. In a few cases marks on top of the capital show that the columns once supported tripods from athletic victories, or metal vases or urns.

The Greeks of the Archaic (800–480 BCE) and Classical periods (480–323 BCE) also used columns to support statues or offerings to the gods. Rather than being strictly commemorative, votive columns are the testaments of a vow fulfilled, though at times they were dedicated on the occasion of a significant event, such as an athletic victory or a windfall. Either the column capital or the shaft may bear an inscription in the form of a dedicatory epigraph naming the donor, the god or other recipient, or the reason for the gift. In the Hellenistic period (323–31 BCE) commemorative portraits were erected on columns. After noting that the Greeks invented the convention of placing statues on top of columns,

Pliny the Elder remarks that the Athenian governor Demetrius of Phaleron (c. 350–after 297 BCE) had more statues dedicated to himself than did any other statesman (*Natural History* 34.27). Pliny implies that some of these statues must have been supported by columns. At Delphi a monument made up of two Ionic columns supporting an entablature served as a base for four statues of family members dedicated by a woman in the early third century BCE.

Rome. During the Roman Republic and the Empire, statues on columns became a standard form of commemoration, especially for military victories. The oldest Roman use of the form may have been the Columna Minucia, mentioned by Pliny (*Natural History* 34.21) and erected in Rome in honor of the semilegendary Lucius Minucius Augurinus (prefect in 439 BCE). This column is first represented on coins of 129 BCE, so it may have been set up long after the death of the man it honored. Columns were used to commemorate naval victories, as with the Columna Maenia, set up in 338 BCE in honor of Gaius Maenius, the victor of the battle at Antium (Pliny *Natural History* 34.20). A specific form of column for a naval victory was the *columna rostrata*. The bronze prows (*rostra*) of the ships of a captured navy could be either attached to the column, like the *columna rostrata* in honor of the consul Marcus Aemilius Paullus, erected on the Capitoline Hill in 255 BCE, or melted down and recast in the form of a metal column, as was done with the prows of the Nile fleet that Octavian defeated at Actium in 31 BCE. Cleopatra's fleet was so large that Octavian was able to cast four columns from the ships' bronze prows (Virgil *Georgics* 3.28–29).

Roman commemorative columns could also serve a funerary purpose. Such columns were incorporated into family grave monuments and compounds in Pompeii and other Roman towns. Suetonius (*Divus Iulius* 85) notes that a solid column of Numidian stone was set up in the Roman Forum in honor of Julius Caesar shortly after his death, cremation, and burial there in 44 BCE.

The most famous and artistically innovative commemorative columns in Rome were those of the emperors Trajan and Marcus Aurelius. Trajan's column was planned at the north end of his forum complex and dedicated in 113 CE. The column, possibly designed by Apollodorus of Damascus, was composed of seventeen drums of Luna marble and was one hundred Roman feet (125 feet, or 38 meters) in height, including the base. The interior was hollow, and a spiral staircase of 185 steps led to the top. The column was supported by a cubic base of seventeen feet (five meters) on each side. The base eventually housed the ashes of the emperor and his wife. Trajan's column may have been intended as both a victory and a funerary monument from its conception. A statue of the emperor in bronze overlaid with a thin surface of gold once stood on the capital.

The exterior of the base of Trajan's Column bears relief sculpture of arms and armor and a dedicatory inscription above the door. A sculptured historical narrative spirals around the column in relief, commemorating the victories of the emperor's Dacian campaigns. There are 155 scenes involving some 2,500 figures. The frieze is 3 feet high and 670 feet long (about one meter high and two hundred meters long) and curves around and up the column in twenty-three turns. The individual scenes depict Roman military activities, from the building of forts and bridges to battles that conclude with the surrender of captives and the deportation of women and children. With a tomb at its base and a gilt statue at its summit, the column alludes to Trajan's death, ascent, and deification. The sculptural program thus represents the emperor's *res gestae* (achievements).

The emperor Marcus Aurelius and his co-ruler Lucius Aurelius Verus set up a monumental column in honor of their adoptive parents, Antoninus Pius and Faustina, in 161, the year of Marcus' ascendancy. This Column of Antoninus Pius (now lost) was an undecorated monolithic shaft of red granite, half the height of Trajan's Column, supported by a white marble base. It stood in the Campus Martius and faced the *ustrinum* (funerary pyre structure) of the Antonines. The carved face of the surviving pedestal represents the apotheosis of Antoninus and Faustina. The imperial couple is transported heavenward on the back of a winged genius and is flanked by eagles. Below them, personifications of the Campus Martius and the city of Rome witness the ascent. A *decursio*, the circular parade of cavalry who honor the deceased, decorates two opposite faces of the base.

Close by, Commodus commissioned a column modeled on that of Trajan in honor of his own father, Marcus Aurelius, as part of a temple complex on the Campus Martius. According to a building inscription found nearby, the column was completed in 193. A spiraling frieze in low relief circles the column twenty times, showing scenes from Marcus Aurelius' German and Sarmatian campaigns. The narrative again shows military events including sacrifices, the *adlocutio* (the emperor or general's address to his troops), and pitched battles resulting

Trajan's Column, Rome. MERILYN THOROLD/THE BRIDGEMAN ART LIBRARY

in the deaths of barbarians and the emigration of survivors, but it depicts fewer moments of Roman engineering and ingenuity and more scenes of divine intervention than does Trajan's Column. Marcus Aurelius' army seems less secure than Trajan's, and the emperor is less a leader of troops than a symbol of imperial power, surrounded only by close staff. The column's base is not preserved.

Late Roman commemorative columns at Constantinople, where Constantine established his capital in 324, include a 121-foot (37-meter) porphyry Corinthian column dedicated circa 328 in the Forum of Constantine, as well as those erected by Theodosius I (r. 379–395) and his son Arcadius (r. 395–408). The last two both bore spiraling narrative friezes that documented imperial achievements. Theodosius claimed descent from Trajan and sought to legitimize his rule and reinforce Constantinople's imperial status by building a forum based on Trajan's, complete with temple, basilica, and column.

[See also Sculpture, Architectural.]

BIBLIOGRAPHY

Bassett, Sarah. The Urban Image of Late Antique Constantinople. Cambridge, U.K., and New York: Cambridge University Press, 2004.

Cichorius, Conrad. Trajan's Column: A New Edition of the Cichorius Plates. With introduction, commentary, and notes by Frank Lepper and Sheppard Frere. Gloucester, U.K., and Wolfboro, N.H.: Alan Sutton, 1988.

Davies, Penelope J. E. Death and the Emperor: Roman Imperial Monuments from Augustus to Marcus Aurelius. Cambridge, U.K., and New York: Cambridge University Press, 2000.

Keesling, Catherine M. "Patrons of Athenian Votive Monuments of the Archaic and Classical Periods." Hesperia 74 (2005): 395–426.

Kleiner, Diana E. E. Roman Sculpture. New Haven, Conn., and London: Yale University Press, 1992.

McGowan, Elizabeth P. "Tomb Marker or Turning Post: Funerary Columns in the Archaic Period." American Journal of Archaeology 99 (1995): 615–632.

Steinby, Eva Margareta, ed. Lexicon topographicum urbis Romae. 6 vols. Rome: Quasar, 1993–1999.

E. P. McGowan

COMEDY, GREEK

[This entry includes three subentries, on Old, Middle, and New Comedy.]

Old Comedy

Kōmōidia (comedy) is an original Greek term that the Greeks themselves explained with three different etymologies: (1) from kōmos (procession of festive revelers), (2) from kōmē (village), (3) from kōma (sleep). The first two etymologies are already found in Aristotle (Poetics 3.1448a 30–34), in his reporting the competing claims of Dorians and Athenians to be comedy's inventors. Out of this, Hellenistic scholars constructed an antithesis between city dwellers and village dwellers: the latter, being despised by the former, retaliated with mocking chants against them (see, e.g., Koster, ed., Prolegomena de comoedia, 3, p. 7, lines 1–5). The third etymology was sometimes combined with the second: these chants first took place under the cover of darkness at sleeping time (e.g., in Prolegomena de comoedia, 4 and 12b).

Apart from such speculation there is little reliable evidence about comedy's origins. The Marmor Parium, an Attic inscription from the middle of the third century BCE, names the poet Susarion as the first producer of a "comic chorus" in the Attic deme Icaria in the middle of the sixth century BCE (Kassel and Austin, eds., Poetae Comici Graeci [PCG], Susarion test. 1); later testimonies (PCG, Susarion test. 8 and 10) claim him as a Megarian—that is, Dorian—poet. The few extant verses ascribed to Susarion are clearly a later invention.

Modern research has judged the first etymology above to be the most plausible one: chorus-like kōmoi are depicted on Greek vases dating from the early seventh century BCE, then in the sixth century so-called padded dancers appear on Corinthian vases and groups in animal costumes appear on Attic vases looking already like animal choruses of later Old Comedy. There are also depictions of processions centering on gigantic phalli (as symbols of fertility), which again Aristotle (Poetics 4.1449a10f) connected with the beginning of comedy.

Early Comedy Outside Athens. Still in the sixth century, comedy-like forms of play developed not only in Athens but elsewhere in the Greek world. The thriving and mostly Doric Greek colonies in Sicily and southern Italy proved especially fertile ground for such plays. Hellenistic scholars like Sosibius Lacon (*Fragmente der griechischen Historiker* [*FGrH*] 595 F 7) and Semus of Delos (*FGrH* 396 F 24) still had evidence for widely disseminated popular Doric farces with many local variants.

Among these, two cities are particularly prominent. On the Greek mainland the inhabitants of Megara—reputedly Susarion's hometown—claimed that their own form of comedy was older than the Attic one, and Attic comic poets in fact liked to ridicule "more primitive" Megarian jokes (*PCG*, Eupolis fragment 261, Ecphantides fragment 3; Aristophanes *Wasps* 57). In Sicily, Epicharmus was considered by his fellow citizens of Megara Hyblaea to be earlier than the earliest Attic comic poets, Chionides and Magnes (see Aristotle *Poetics* 3.1448a31–34); some sources regard Epicharmus as the real inventor of comedy (*PCG*, Epicharmus test. 1, 18). He presented his plays—which he himself called *dramata*, not *kōmōidiai*—in Syracuse, the biggest city of Sicily, and again already Aristotle (*Poetics* 5.1449b5–7) ascribed to Epicharmus, as well as to other Sicilian poets, an important influence on the development of Attic comedies (e.g., those of Crates). Epicharmus' plays apparently lacked a very important ingredient of Attic Old Comedy, however: the chorus.

The Two Phases of Attic Old Comedy. The most significant and momentous development of Greek comedy—for later antiquity and the whole Western world—took place at Athens. The first phases of Attic comedy cannot be securely traced back beyond the beginning of the fifth century BCE, although there might be a kernel of truth in the entry of Marmor Parium concerning Susarion (see above). The early development of Attic comedy is best explained as a combination of popular farce—featuring individual actors, as in Doric regions, see above—and phallus-honoring *kōmoi* (as predecessors of choruses); in this way the curious double

nature of Old Comedy, which comprises both individuals and a prominent group, is best accounted for (see Körte, p. 1221).

The first securely attested Athenian comic poets appear in the 480s and 470s BCE. In 486, Chionides was the victor of the first comic contest officially organized by the Athenian state at the Great Dionysia (*PCG*, Chionides test. 1); in 472, Magnes celebrated his first of eleven victories at such a contest (*PCG*, Magnes test. 5). All in all, the names of forty-five poets of Old Comedy are known. For Aristophanes, Magnes was the quintessential successful poet (see *Knights* 520–525), but none of Magnes' plays—written between 486 and 455—survived to Hellenistic Alexandria. Information becomes more plentiful after Cratinus—the oldest of the three poets (the other two are Eupolis and Aristophanes) who later embodied the essence of Old Comedy—began to write in the 450s. Cratinus wrote at least twenty-eight plays and was nine times victorious in comic competitions; he is credited with significant innovations (*PCG*, Cratinus test. 19), and he is the first poet in whose plays one of Old Comedy's main characteristics—namely, its penchant for political satire and invective—becomes prominent: some of his favorite targets were the great Pericles and his wife Aspasia. Cratinus also wrote travesties of famous myths (his *Odyssēs* distorted the famous Cyclops episode of book 9 of the *Odyssey*), sometimes combining them with contemporary politics (his *Dionysalexandros* makes the origins of the Trojan War a mirror image of those of the Peloponnesian). In his last and most famous play, *Pytinē* (Bottle), he even poked fun at himself, letting personified Madame Comedy berate him for drinking too much wine.

During Cratinus' time—about 440—a second publicly organized comic contest was added at the Lenaea festival. In Cratinus' last years, a younger generation of comic poets began to write (from about 429 onward), most notably represented by Phrynichus, Eupolis, and Aristophanes. Eupolis quickly became Aristophanes' most serious rival in the Athenian comic contests in the 420s and 410s. He produced between fourteen and seventeen plays and was seven times victorious, which probably made him the most successful comic poet of his age. Among his memorable plays were *Colaces* (421), which satirized the wealthy Callias and his intellectual toadies, among them the Sophist Protagoras; *Taxiarchoi* (probably mid-420s), in which the gruff Athenian general Phormion had as one of his recruits the theater god Dionysus himself; *Baptai* (416 or 415), which ridiculed a strange orgiastic cult and also poked fun at the mighty Alcibiades; and *Dēmoi* (412), in which great Athenian statesmen of the past were recalled from Hades to assist troubled Athens in its current severe crisis. Soon after this play Eupolis was apparently killed in a naval battle in the Hellespont, thus ending his great rivalry with Aristophanes. Phrynichus wrote at least ten plays and was at least three times victorious; with his last known play, *Musai* (405), he finished second after Aristophanes' *Frogs* while presenting a similar theme: a poetical contest between (probably) the dead giants Sophocles and Euripides. His *Monotropos* of 414 may have been something like a forerunner of Menander's *Dyskolos*.

Characteristics of Attic Old Comedy. Firmly grounded in the political, cultural, and religious realities of their time, the poets of Old Comedy expressed their opinions about contemporary developments and people so explicitly and sometimes even outrageously that Athenian politicians at least twice tried to curb such outbursts of comic free speech (Morychides 440/39–437/36; Syracosius about 415). Another danger was lawsuits: Aristophanes was taken to court by the demagogue Cleon, though somehow he got away unharmed. Nevertheless comic poets kept presenting comically distorted images of Athens' most powerful and famous people: generals, such as Lamachus in Aristophanes' *Acharnians*; politicians, such as Pericles in Cratinus' *Thrattae* and *Chirones*, Hyperbolos in Eupolis' *Marikas*, Alcibiades in Eupolis' *Baptai*, Nicias in Phrynichus' *Monotropos*, and Cleophon in Plato Comicus' *Cleophon*; and intellectuals, such as Euripides in Aristophanes' *Acharnians* and *Thesmophoriazusae* and Sophists in Eupolis' *Colaces*. Nobody prominent in Athenian life was safe.

Remarkably, these phenomena of real life are often mixed with surreal and fantastic elements: hedonistic utopias (the first of which is presented in Cratinus' *Plutoi*), flights into heaven on most improbable vehicles (like the giant dung-beetle in Aristophanes' *Peace*), the return of famous dead men from the underworld (apparently Solon in Cratinus' *Chirones*, and Solon, Aristides, Miltiades, and Pericles in Eupolis' *Dēmoi*). The "normal" logic of space and time is easily suspended, and the absurd is lurking just around the corner, as in the hostage-taking of coals or wineskins in Aristophanes' *Acharnians* and *Thesmophoriazusae*.

Some Old Comedy poets like Crates (on him, see Aristotle *Poetics* 5.1449b6–9) and Pherecrates developed another, less politicized and less aggressive kind of play with more self-contained, fictional plots, which in fact led the way into comedy's future. Crates began to produce plays—between seven and nine are attested—around 450 BCE; he is reputed to have been the first to present drunken people on the stage (in *Geitones*). Pherecrates apparently started writing plays—between seventeen and nineteen—in the later 440s and probably was the first poet to give prominence to hetaerae: in four of his plays (*Koriannō, Epilēsmōn ē Thalatta, Ipnos ē Pannychis, Petalē*) these Athenian call-girls were title characters and thus probably occupied center stage. There was, of course, no sharp dividing line between the two sorts of plays: Cratinus wrote mythical plays that could be either pervasively political, like *Dionysalexandros*, or far removed from contemporary issues, like *Odyssēs*; in Pherecrates' *Automoloi*, a winged ship seems to ascend into heaven, his *Metallēs* presents a fantastic underworld, and in his *Tyrannis* men grapple with the establishment of women's political rule. Plays with mythical themes naturally tended to have a more tightly structured plot than plays like *Acharnians*, with its more loosely connected scenes.

The Chorus. One of Old Comedy's most conspicuous elements is its exuberant and boisterous choruses. They take diverse shapes: for instance, animals—wasps, birds, fish, goats—and not rarely extravagant personifications, including Attic villages in Eupolis' *Dēmoi*, allied cities of Athens in Eupolis' *Poleis*, and isles of the Aegean in Aristophanes' *Islands*. The chorus regularly disrupts the comic play itself, as when in the so-called parabasis (stepping aside) they suddenly step out of their costumes and, sometimes, their roles and address the audience with themes dear to the poet himself, such as his relationship with the audience or his rivalry with other poets.

Dramatic Structure. The chorus's parabasis often divides the play in the middle. Before it, the conflict between the hero and his opponents—either other individuals or the chorus—often is central and is visualized as a great scene of altercation (the so-called agon). This conflict can continue into the second part after the parabasis (as in Aristophanes' *Knights*), but more often the second part demonstrates the consequences of the victory that the hero has won in the first part—for example, in a sequence of shorter parallel scenes that sometimes depict some drastic action, such as someone getting soundly thrashed. In the end the hero is shown triumphant and often reveling in hedonistic pleasures.

Costumes and Language. Both optically and linguistically, Attic Old Comedy was an exuberant, lavish spectacle. Choruses are clad in extravagant costumes and masks, individual actors sport tights (covered by a short chiton) with exaggeratedly padded bellies and behinds and—most conspicuously—an erect and oversize phallus (highlighting the prominence of sexual themes). The language of the plays covers an astonishingly wide range of idiom and register—from the high-flown lyrical to the downright vulgar and obscene—combined with a wealth of different rhythms and meters. Sadly, all trace of the accompanying music is lost. Linguistic and thematic parody of other genres—Homeric and other epics (as in Cratinus' *Odyssēs*), lyric songs, but most of all contemporary Attic tragedy—is very common; comic poets reused motives, scenes, and even whole plays by their tragic counterparts, and thus, willy-nilly, tragedy contributed to the further development of comedy.

[*See also* Aristophanes.]

BIBLIOGRAPHY

Primary Works

Kassel, Rudolf, and Colin Austin, eds. *Poetae Comici Graeci (PCG)*. 8 vols. Berlin and New York: de Gruyter, 1983–2001. The fundamental edition of Greek comic fragments.

Koster, Willem J. W., ed. *Prolegomena de comoedia*. Scholia in Aristophanem, part 1, fascicle 1A. Groningen, The Netherlands: Bouma, 1975. A collection of ancient and Byzantine texts on the history of Greek comedy.

Olson, S. Douglas, ed. *Broken Laughter: Select Fragments of Greek Comedy*. Oxford: Oxford University Press, 2007. A new translation of selected fragments with notes.

Secondary Works

Harvey, David, and John Wilkins, eds. *The Rivals of Aristophanes: Studies in Athenian Old Comedy*. London: Duckworth, 2000.

Kerkhof, Rainer. *Dorische Posse, Epicharm, und Attische Komödie*. Munich: K. G. Saur, 2001.

Körte, Alfred. "Komödie (griechische)." In *Paulys Realencyclopädie der classischen Altertumswissenschaft*, vol. 11.1, pp. 1207–1275. Stuttgart, Germany: Druckenmüller, 1921.

Kyriakidi, Natalia. *Aristophanes und Eupolis: Zur Geschichte einer dichterischen Rivalität*. Berlin and New York: Walter de Gruyter, 2007.

Nesselrath, Heinz-Günther. "Komödie." In *Reallexikon für Antike und Christentum*, edited by Theodor Klauser et al., vol. 21, pp. 330–354. Stuttgart, Germany: Hiersemann, 2005. Especially useful on etymologies of the term "comedy" and on the reception of comedy in later antiquity.

Seeberg, Axel. "From Padded Dancers to Comedy." In *Stage Directions: Essays in Ancient Drama in Honour of E. W. Handley*, edited by Alan Griffiths, pp. 1–12. London: Institute of Classical Studies, 1995.

Storey, Ian C. *Eupolis: Poet of Old Comedy*. Oxford: Oxford University Press, 2003.

Storey, Ian C., and Arlene Allan. *A Guide to Ancient Greek Drama*. Malden, Mass.: Blackwell, 2004.

Heinz-Günther Nesselrath

Middle Comedy

Old Comedy ended around 405 BCE, more or less simultaneously with Athens' catastrophic defeat in the Peloponnesian War. Aristophanes' *Frogs* is the last extant play that fully fits the standard features of Old Comedy. In Aristophanes' last two plays—*Ecclesiazusae*, staged around 392, and *Wealth*, staged in 388—the role of the chorus was already considerably reduced. In *Wealth*, only the chorus' entrance (*parodos*) is still found in the text as a fully developed scene; at all later places where the chorus had to act, there is just the short stage direction *chorou*, and this became the rule. In Menander's plays, *chorou* is still the normal sign for the division between acts even though the chorus is no longer in the plays.

From Old to Middle Comedy. Thus the years around 400 BCE saw significant changes in Attic comedy, although many poets who had written plays before (Aristophanes among them) continued to do so. Various reasons have been offered for these changes: a general turning away from politics after Athens' disastrous defeat in the Peloponnesian War; the disappearance of great (and thus well worth mocking) political figures; a disillusionment and loss of conviction on the part of the poets that they were really able to influence their city's political course. This time is often referred to as the epoch of "Middle Comedy," a term probably coined by Hellenistic scholars in Alexandria, who—because of their vast library resources—had an excellent grasp of the whole development of Attic comedy. Unfortunately the exact time of these changes remains rather obscure to us because of the extreme scarcity of sources. Apart from Aristophanes' last two plays, not a single play is entirely preserved until Menander, although no fewer plays were produced in these two generations than in the preceding ones: the production of just two poets, Antiphanes and Alexis, comprised several hundred plays for each, and all in all, fifty-seven poets are attested as being active during these decades (see Koster, ed., *Prolegomena de Comoedia*, 3, p. 10, line 45). Of all their plays, only a jumble of fragments—the majority of them rather short—and hundreds of titles of plays have been preserved.

Still, all these bits and pieces enable us to recognize some lines of development. After a transitional phase of several decades, Middle Comedy proper can be limited to the years between 380 and 350, followed by another transitional phase—until about 320—in which the characteristics of New Comedy gradually take shape.

Myths on the Stage. In the first decades of the fourth century (until about 370/60), there is a notable preference for mythical subjects in comic plays; the very last—and not preserved—plays of Aristophanes, *Cocalus* and *Aeolosicon*, shared this preference. Fragments of these plays show that comic poets liked to draw on tragedies dealing with the same subject matter, but they systematically de-heroicized tragedy's plots and its actors. Mythical kings, heroes, even gods were now depicted just like the bourgeois and all-too-human figures of everyday Athenian life. In Antiphanes' *Ganymēdēs*, for instance, the story of Zeus' abduction was set into a very Athenian-looking city street, with Laomedon's palace looking like the house of just a wealthy citizen; in Anaxandrides' *Tereus*, the title figure was not changed into a bird at the end, but rather was just called "bird" because he let himself be henpecked by cheeky females; and in Eubulus' *Procris*, the famous mythical hunting dog Laelaps was turned into a pampered pet.

After the middle of the fourth century this tendency to de-mythicize mythical themes had run its course, and everyday Athenian life and happenings—as compared to the often fantastic plotlines of Old Comedy—were now definitively established as the backbone of Athenian comedy. Comedy thus experienced a reduction of imaginative scope; a similar reduction took place in the realm of language and verse composition. For a certain time there was still a penchant for linguistic and metrical parody of higher poetic genres, made all the more glaring by putting such parody into the mouth of rather unlikely people; thus lowly slaves and cooks were presented as spouting long speeches in dithyrambic language and anapaestic dimeters. But by the middle of the fourth century these curious recitatives were gone as well. There remained, with a few exceptions, just two sorts of spoken verse: iambic trimeter and—to mark some slightly more agitated scenes—trochaic tetrameters. Comic language at this point almost totally consisted of a slightly elevated version of everyday Attic speech.

Gone, too, were the metatheatrical escapades and disruptions of dramatic illusion of Old Comedy, apart from some short addresses to the audience in actors' monologues. Nothing obscene titillated the eyes and ears of spectators; language became very well-behaved, and at a certain point (although exactly when still escapes us) Old Comedy's tights and phallus vanished from the stage. Sexuality may still have played a certain role, but probably not a much larger one than in New Comedy, where pregnancies induced by a sexual assault often are the foundation for the action played out in the comedy itself. Homosexuality, a very visible part of Old Comedy, was usually eschewed by later (Middle and New) comedy. Athenian politics was sometimes still present but usually only in narrowly circumscribed passages.

New Character Types. Middle Comedy was not, however, characterized simply by what post-Aristophanic comedy reduced or totally lost of Old Comedy. It also developed new elements, most conspicuously with regard to people presented on the stage. Although Old Comedy often placed real people (more or less distortedly, of course) on its stage, and although its heroes (at least in their Aristophanic variety) had some characteristics in common, these did not amount to full-blown character types. Such types were developed in the course of the fourth century, though, and by the middle of this century a distinct cast of characters became recognizable. First of all there usually was the son of a well-to-do bourgeois family; typically this character was likable, in love, a bit timid with regard to his father, and sometimes a bit lacking in wit and intelligence. The cast would likely also include his father—more or less severe and always striving to prevent the son from getting into trouble—and sometimes his resolute wife. The play might also incorporate a second family of similar makeup.

These bourgeois characters were counterbalanced by less bourgeois figures, who usually provided the "comic" element(s) of these comedies: the clever slave, often an important helper of his young master, not least against his master's father; the hetaera, always a temptation for the bourgeois son and sometimes for his father as well; the blustering (mercenary) soldier, who commonly vies with the bourgeois son for the hetaera's favors; the cook, often hired for the marriage feast with which these plays commonly end, a professional who is endlessly self-praising, deadeningly garrulous, and insatiably nosy; the rapacious pimp, normally a really evil character; and last but not least the parasite, often the obsequious retainer of a blustering soldier, and having to bear the whims—and sometimes even a sound thrashing—of the people he courts to fill his always empty belly.

By the time of Menander these types were fully developed and were represented by an extensive range of subtly differentiated comic masks, evidence for which is provided both by an extensive catalog in the imperial Greek writer Pollux (4.143ff.) and by terra-cotta models found on the island of Lipari. These types were put into self-contained fictional plots, which may already have been organized along the five-act structure that became standard in New Comedy.

BIBLIOGRAPHY
Primary Works
Kassel, Rudolf, and Colin Austin, eds. *Poetae Comici Graeci (*PCG*).* 8 vols. Berlin and New York: de Gruyter, 1983–2001. The fundamental edition of Greek comic fragments.
Koster, Willem J. W., ed. *Prolegomena de comoedia.* Scholia in Aristophanem, part 1, fascicle 1A. Groningen, The Netherlands: Bouma, 1975. A collection of ancient and Byzantine texts on the history of Greek comedy.
Olson, S. Douglas, ed. *Broken Laughter: Select Fragments of Greek Comedy.* Oxford: Oxford University Press, 2007. A new translation of selected fragments with notes.

Secondary Works
Nesselrath, Heinz-Günther. *Die attische Mittlere Komödie.* Berlin and New York: de Gruyter, 1990.
Nesselrath, Heinz-Günther. "Myth, Parody, and Comic Plots: The Birth of Gods and Middle Comedy." In *Beyond Aristophanes: Transition and Diversity in Greek Comedy*, edited by Gregory W. Dobrov, pp. 1–27. Atlanta: Scholars Press, 1995. On plays with certain mythological themes in the transition phase from Old to Middle Comedy.

Nesselrath, Heinz-Günther. "Parody and Later Greek Comedy." *Harvard Studies in Classical Philology* 95 (1993): 181–195. On borrowings of comedy from tragedy regarding plot structure.

Nesselrath, Heinz-Günther. "The Polis of Athens in Middle Comedy." In *The City as Comedy*, edited by Gregory W. Dobrov, pp. 271–288. Chapel Hill and London: University of North Carolina Press 1997.

Storey, Ian C., and Arlene Allan. *A Guide to Ancient Greek Drama*. Malden, Mass.: Blackwell, 2004.

Heinz-Günther Nesselrath

New Comedy

Starting in 321 BCE with the plays of Menander, Attic comedy began to appear in a form that is markedly different from comedies of earlier times, most of all those of Old Comedy, and thus was named "New Comedy" (in Greek, *kōmōidia nea*). Presumably Alexandrian scholars named it such, thereby further developing the notion of "new" and "old" comedies—*kainos* versus *palaios* in Greek—already found in Aristotle's *Nicomachean Ethics* 4.8.1128a22f.

Poets and Themes. Playwrights of New Comedy were just as productive as their predecessors were: the three most important ones—Menander, Diphilus, and Philemon—wrote about a hundred plays each. Both Philemon, who apparently started presenting plays somewhat earlier than Menander, and Diphilus, who started presenting plays more or less contemporaneously with Menander, apparently liked to place figures with reliable comic potential at the center of their plays: blustering soldiers (Philemon in *Stratiōtēs*; Diphilus in *Hairēsiteichēs*, later restaged as *Eunuchos ē Stratiōtēs*), cooks (Philemon in *Pareisiōn* and *Stratiōtēs*; Diphilus in *Apoleipusa* and *Zōgraphos*), hetaerae (Diphilus in *Synōris*), parasites (Philemon in *Metiōn ē Zōmion* and *Pareisiōn*; Diphilus in *Synōris*, *Telesias*, and *Parasitos*), and pimps (Philemon in *Adelphoi*; Diphilus in fragment 87 of *Poetae Comici Graeci*, of an unknown play). Philemon seems also to have liked to poke fun at philosophers (in *Pyrrhus* and *Philosophoi*), and in his depiction in *Sardion* of a likable slave who cares about his young master, he seems to come close to similar slaves presented by Menander in, for example, *Aspis*.

The plays of both Philemon and Diphilus were as much reused by the Roman comic poet Plautus as Menander's were; in contrast, playwrights like Caecilius Statius and Terence markedly preferred Menander. Plautus took Philemon's *Emporos*, *Thēsauros*, and *Phasma* and made *Mercator*, *Trinummus*, and *Mostellaria* out of them; he converted Diphilus' *Klērumenoi* into *Casia*, *Schedia* into *Vidularia*, and an unknown play into *Rudens*. Terence incorporated a scene from Diphilus' *Synapothnēskontes* in his *Adelphi*.

During their (overlapping) lifetimes, Diphilus and Philemon were at least as successful in comic contests as Menander was; according to Aulus Gellius (*Noctes Atticae* 17.4.1), Athenians rather often even preferred Philemon's plays to Menander's, and it was only after his death that Menander advanced to the position of classic and finally sole representative (the "lone star") of Attic New Comedy. Other major poets of New Comedy—they wrote sixty-four plays altogether (as attested by Koster, ed., *Prolegomena de comoedia*, 3, p. 10, line 53)—were Apollodorus of Carystus, an emulator of Menander's style, and Posidippus of Cassandrea.

New Comedy—as is most conspicuously shown by Menander's plays, less so by those of his rivals, because his rivals profited far less than Menander did from major papyrus finds, so their plays can be known only from a number of mostly short fragments and some Roman adaptations—likes to depict problems within the bourgeois family of the Greek city-state, usually Athens, as well as clashes of this family with marginal figures of bourgeois society such as pimps, hetaerae, and soldiers. Politics is conspicuously absent, as are mythological or surreal elements. Plots are constructed from the interactions of the various typical roles that poets had developed in the preceding decades. These roles were now so much taken as fixtures of comic drama that Menander could proceed to reindividualize them—so that we can observe in his plays such walking contradictions as likable soldiers with gentle sentiments and noble hetaerae with an urge to improve the lot of their fellow human beings. It is, however, hard to say whether Menander's rivals followed similar trends. If we may judge from some extant Roman adaptations of their plays, New Comedy poets seem rather to have opted for preserving the comic potential of these well-defined types, and this may explain why they had at least as much or even greater success on the stage than Menander did.

End and Afterlife. New Comedy's creative phase ended around the middle of the third century BCE; already by then poets like Menander and Philemon had acquired the status of classics, poets whose plays were often revived on the stage. Still, new plays continued to be written as well: we know the names of more than fifty poets from the third century BCE, of more than thirty from the second century BCE, of at least ten from the first century BCE, and of a further six from the next three centuries. But of these authors, few play titles and almost no fragments have been preserved. Comic contests continued to go on, too (there is substantial inscriptional evidence, for example, for the second century BCE), not only in Athens but in other places as well. Although such contests are still attested even for the Imperial Age, and although in the time of Dio Chrysostom (Dio of Prusa, late first and early second century CE; see his *Orationes* 19.5) whole comedies still seem to have been performed, other types of play, such as mimes and pantomimes, became vastly more popular on the stages of the Roman Empire, and comic texts had come to be used for higher literary education or to be the subject of recitals at banquets and symposia or of private reading. (Menander was still read by Sidonius Apollinaris and his son in the fifth century CE: see his *Epistulae* 4.12.1f.)

Before Greek New Comedy finally withdrew into the private sphere, however, it had its greatest impact on the history of theater by being transferred into Roman culture and the Latin language. In 240 BCE, Lucius Livius Andronicus presented the first Latin adaptation of a Greek comedy to a Roman audience, and in the following hundred years Roman comic poets—of whom Plautus and Terence are only the best known because their plays are extant—produced a great number of comic plays by translating and adapting Greek originals, usually from poets of New Comedy. These Roman plays are called *comoediae palliatae* because the actors appeared dressed in the pallium, a Greek kind of cloak. The most important "suppliers" were New Comedy's big three—Menander, Philemon, Diphilus—but there were others as well, such as the somewhat older Alexis, and even rather obscure ones, such as Demophilus, who nowadays is known only because his *Onagos* was used by Plautus to write *Asinaria*.

The relationship between the Greek originals and their Roman adaptations has been the subject of much discussion since the late twentieth century, with one side wanting to reduce Greek influence to a minimum and the other regarding the Roman plays as faithful copies—which fact was obscured by textual tampering through later restaging—of their Greek models. The truth probably lies somewhere in between. In any event, it must be taken into account that in almost every case the Greek original of a Roman adaptation has been lost, thus making assessments of their relationship very difficult and always precarious; many elements that today are considered typically Roman might have been prefigured in the Greek original. Regardless of the actual nature of the relationship between originals and adaptations, there is no denying that Greek New Comedy was essential in establishing a tradition of literary comedy at Rome that then became the basis for all later Western comic writing. Oscar Wilde's *The Importance of Being Earnest* (1895) is only one well-recognizable descendant of the witty and charming plays of Greek New Comedy.

[*See also* Comic Theater, Roman; Menander; Plautus; *and* Terence.]

BIBLIOGRAPHY
Primary Works
Kassel, Rudolf, and Colin Austin, eds. *Poetae Comici Graeci (PCG)*. 8 vols. Berlin and New York: de Gruyter, 1983–2001. The fundamental edition of Greek comic fragments.

Koster, Willem J. W., ed. *Prolegomena de comoedia.* Scholia in Aristophanem, part 1, fascicle 1A. Groningen, The Netherlands: Bouma, 1975. A collection of ancient and Byzantine texts on the history of Greek comedy.

Olson, S. Douglas, ed. *Broken Laughter: Select Fragments of Greek Comedy.* Oxford: Oxford University Press, 2007. A new translation of selected fragments with notes.

Secondary Works

Antonsen-Resch, Andrea. *Von Gnathon zu Saturio: Die Parasitenfigur und das Verhältnis der römischen Komödie zur griechischen.* Berlin and New York: de Gruyter 2004. Stresses the closeness of Roman comedies to their Greek models.

Benz, Lore, and Eckard Lefèvre, eds. *Maccus barbarus: Sechs Kapitel zur Originalität der Captivi des Plautus.* Tübingen, Germany: Narr, 1998. Minimizes Plautus' dependence on Greek models.

Hunter, Richard L. *The New Comedy of Greece and Rome.* Cambridge, U.K.: Cambridge University Press, 1985.

Lefèvre, Eckard, Ekkehard Stärk, and Gregor Vogt-Spira, eds. *Plautus barbarus: Sechs Kapitel zur Originalität des Plautus.* Tübingen, Germany: Narr, 1991. Minimizes Plautus' dependence on Greek models.

Nesselrath, Heinz-Günther. "Menander and His Rivals: New Light from the Comic Adespota on Papyri?" In *Culture in Pieces: The Proceedings of a Conference in Honour of Peter Parsons,* edited by Dirk Obbink and Richard Rutherford. Oxford: Oxford University Press, forthcoming.

Stärk, Ekkehard. *Die Menaechmi des Plautus und kein griechisches Original.* Tübingen, Germany: Narr, 1989. Denies the derivation of Plautus' play from a Greek model.

Storey, Ian C., and Arlene Allan. *A Guide to Ancient Greek Drama.* Malden, Mass.: Blackwell, 2005.

Zwierlein, Otto. *Zur Kritik und Exegese des Plautus.* Vols. 1–4. Stuttgart, Germany: Steiner, 1990–1992. Stresses the closeness of Plautus' plays to their Greek models.

Heinz-Günther Nesselrath

COMIC THEATER, ROMAN

Plautus' popularity in the second century BCE often obscures the fact that Roman theater included both other important Italian playwrights who composed Latin adaptations of Greek comedies (*fabulae palliatae,* plays in Greek clothing) and also native Italian forms of entertainment, unscripted dramatic spectacles that acquired literary form by the first century BCE. What remains from these plays are only titles and fragments cited by grammarians, encyclopedists, and lexicographers.

The origin of the Hellenizing fashion in Roman playwriting is linked with Livius Andronicus, from Tarentum in southern Italy, Gnaeus Naevius, and Caecilius Statius. Naevius, from Campania in west-central Italy, wrote at least thirty comedies in the late third century BCE, some of which seem to have insulted various noble Roman families. Periplectomenus, an old man in Plautus' *Miles Gloriosus* (The Boastful Soldier), makes a joke at lines 210–212 that has been taken to imply Naevius' imprisonment because of his abusive comments. From Terence's *Andria* (lines 9–21) we surmise that Naevius did not keep closely to his Greek originals; this is also the impression we get about Caecilius, writing between 180 and 168 BCE. Caecilius comes first—with Plautus second and Naevius third—in the list of the ten best playwrights compiled by Volcacius Sedigitus (first century BCE), and Varro commends Caecilius for his plot construction. Some of the titles attributed to Caecilius (*The Heiress, The Fraud, The Marriage, The Abducted Maiden, The Courtesan, The Token*) show a close affinity with motifs of Greek New Comedy, and twenty of the forty-two titles attributed to Caecilius correspond closely to works by Menander, but the comparison that Aulus Gellius (2.23) made in the second century CE between three passages of Caecilius' *Plocium* (The Necklace) and the corresponding thirty-two lines of its original, Menander's *Plokion,* demonstrates that Caecilius lowers the tone and alters the ethos of his Greek original by inserting crude jokes such as the complaint of the old man about the bad breath of his rich, ugly, and arrogant wife. Caecilius' farcical style in adapting Menander resembles more Plautus' than Terence's approach to drama.

Contemporary with, if not earlier than, the *fabulae palliatae* were performances of *fabulae togatae,* called "toga clad" because they involved Italian, probably masked, characters in fictional intrigues. The playwrights Titinius (second century BCE), Afranius (Lucius Afranius, second century BCE), and

Atta (Titus Quintus Atta, d. 77 BCE) seem to have derived at least their inspiration from Greek New Comedy: their casts comprise slaves, prostitutes, and parasites, and family affairs seem to have been vital to the plots. But differences did exist: in the fourth century CE the grammarian Donatus (on Terence *Eunuchus* 57) implies that the master-slave relationship was not subverted in the *togata*, and Quintilian (10.1.100) rebukes Afranius for the pederastic affairs of his plays—a motif unattested in the *palliatae*.

Obscenity is strong also in the literary *fabula Atellana*, which seems to have evolved from largely improvised farces performed in the Oscan dialect of Campania by amateur actors (Livy 7.2; Valerius Maximus 2.4.4). Plays in the Oscan language may still have been performed alongside plays in Greek and in Latin during Caesar's and Augustus' times. Composed in the meters of the *palliata* and the *togata*, the plays of Lucius Pomponius and Novius—both writing in the 90s and 80s BCE—seem to have dealt with lowlife situations couched in equally low language. Five stock characters—Bucco the blockhead, Dossennus the hunchback, Maccus the fool, Manducus the glutton, and Pappus the graybeard—starred in comic situations (for example, *The Adopted Bucco, Pappus' Jug, Maccus the Maiden, The Two Dosenni*). Others were parodies of mythological scenes known from tragedy (*The False Agamemnon, The Dispute over the Armor*). Cicero (*Epistulae ad familiares* 9.16.7) implies that Atellane farces were traditionally performed after tragedies, and this might explain the mythological content; he also implies that it was currently fashionable to have low mimes rather than *Atellanae* as afterpieces (*exodia*).

Mime as a dramatic form in Rome covered any kind of theatrical spectacle that did not belong to masked tragic and comic drama, and it took shape both through the (perhaps unscripted) shows of Italian mime actors—possibly of Greek origin—as early as the third century BCE and also through the native Italian (Greek-language) mime tradition, which had flourished in southern Italy and Sicily for centuries in the comedies of Epicharmus, the prose mimes of Sophron (both fifth century BCE),

and the burlesque plays of Rhinthon (fourth century BCE). But in the mid-first century BCE, playwrights such as the Roman knight Decimus Laberius and the Syrian freedman Publilius gave mime literary qualities that it may not have had until then. Sources portray Laberius as a witty and outspoken man who was not afraid to confront Cicero and Caesar in public, was fond of coining neologisms and playing with Latin morphology, and did not spare philosophical sets such as the Pythagoreans and the Cynics. The titles of plays attributed to Laberius suggest that he targeted mythology (*Anna Peranna, Lake Avernus, Necromancy*), low professions (*The Seamstress, The Fireman, The Painter, The Fuller, The Fisherman, The Rope-maker, The Salt-seller*), popular religious festivals (*Compitalia, Parilicii, Saturnalia*), people of various ethnic origins (*The Cretan, The Etruscan, The Gauls*), and character types (*The Forgetful, The Flatterer*).

Both Laberius' and Publilius' literary mimes, composed in verse and performed in theaters, should be contrasted with the so-called popular mimes, enacted in streets, squares, theaters, and private houses and featuring adulteries, mock weddings, staged trials and shipwrecks, and grotesquely rendered false deaths. These popular mimes had scenarios rather than fixed scripts. Mime, with its imitation of base things and worthless characters, was the genre of crude realism in antiquity: maskless actors or actresses, usually slaves or freedmen or freedwomen, would expose themselves to the public gaze and satirize important people and contemporary events with inelegant and uncouth words. Political abuse, shamelessness, and violence—both simulated and real—abound in mime plays. The nude bodies of mime actresses seem to have been a stereotypical source of entertainment, especially in the obscene festival traditionally associated with the mimes, the Floralia, instituted in or after 173 BCE. Names of mime playwrights are also attested for the late imperial period, but nothing survives from their works.

[*See also* Comedy, Greek; Mime; Music; Pantomime; Plautus; Satire, Latin; Satyr Play; Terence; *and* Theatrical Production, Roman.]

BIBLIOGRAPHY
Primary Works

Frassinetti, Paolo, ed. *Atellanae fabulae.* Rome: In Aedibus Athenaei, 1967.

Daviault, André, ed. and trans. *Comoedia togata: Fragments.* Paris: Belles Lettres, 1981. Latin text with French translation.

Panayotakis, Costas, ed. *Decimus laberius: The Fragments.* Cambridge, U.K.: Cambridge University Press, forthcoming.

Warmington, Eric H., ed. and trans. *Remains of Old Latin.* Vol. 1 (Caecilius) and vol. 2 (Livius and Naevius). Loeb Classical Library. Cambridge, Mass.: Harvard University Press, 1935–1940.

Secondary Works

Coleman, Kathleen. "Fatal Charades: Roman Executions Staged as Mythological Enactments." *Journal of Roman Studies* 80 (1990): 44–73.

Fantham, Elaine. "Mime: The Missing Link in Roman Literary History." *Classical World* 82 (1989): 153–163.

Goldberg, Sander. "Plautus on the Palatine." *Journal of Roman Studies* 88 (1998): 1–20.

Jory, John. "Publilius Syrus and the Element of Competition in the Theatre of the Republic." In *Vir bonus discendi peritus: Studies in Celebration of Otto Skutsch's Eightieth Birthday,* edited by Nicholas Horsfall, pp. 73–81. London: University of London, Institute of Classical Studies, 1988.

Panayotakis, Costas. "Women in the Greco-Roman Mime of the Roman Republic and the Early Empire." *Ordia Prima: Revista de Estudios Clásicos* 5 (2006): 121–138.

Rawson, Elizabeth. "Theatrical Life in Republican Rome and Italy." *Papers of the British School at Rome* 53 (1985): 97–113. Also in Rawson, *Roman Culture and Society: Collected Papers* (Oxford: Clarendon Press, 1991), pp. 468–487.

Wright, John. *Dancing in Chains: The Stylistic Unity of the Comoedia Palliata.* Rome: American Academy, 1974.

Costas Panayotakis

COMITIA

See Political Structure and Ideology, Roman.

COMMERCE

See Trade and Commerce.

COMMODUS

(Lucius Aelius Aurelius Commodus; 161–192 CE), Roman emperor from 180 to 192. The only surviving son of Marcus Aurelius, Commodus took the throne in 180 at the age of only eighteen and was murdered in 192, leading to civil war and the end of the dynasty. His autocratic style of rule and reliance on court favorites were seen by contemporaries as breaking the Antonine tradition of elite consensus rule and created a highly unfavorable historical reputation.

Except for a British war ending in 184, Commodus' reign was relatively quiet militarily, but it was turbulent internally. After a botched aristocratic coup in 182 and a subsequent purge of the senate, politics were dominated by a series of non-senatorial ministers who held power by controlling access to the emperor. Notable are the Praetorian prefect Sextus Tigidius Perennis (182–185) and the freedman Cleander (185–190), promoted to Praetorian prefect after Perennis' death.

In spite of hints of popularity among soldiers, provincials, and Christians, our view of Commodus comes mostly from hostile senators who portray him as lazy, stupid, and finally delusional. Particularly striking are his self-identification with Hercules, which is attested in art and coins, and his passion for gladiatorial performance. Contemporary literary portraits of him are similar in spirit, if not in detail, to the monster portrayed by Joaquin Phoenix in the 2000 film *Gladiator.*

Although some recent scholarship has detected in Commodus' actions a coherent new scheme of imperial self-presentation, by late 192 his behavior was increasingly bizarre: he renamed all twelve months and the city of Rome after himself and went on public animal-killing sprees in the Circus. This evidence of critical instability finally led members of his own inner circle to have him killed on 31 December and replaced by the senior senator Publius Helvius Pertinax.

[*See also* Antonine Family and Dynasty *and* Marcus Aurelius, *subentry* Life and Career.]

BIBLIOGRAPHY

Birley, A. R. "Hadrian to the Antonines." In *The High Empire, A.D. 70–192*, edited by Alan K. Bowman, Peter Garnsey, and Dominic Rathbone, pp. 186–194. Cambridge Ancient History, vol. 11. 2nd ed. Cambridge, U.K.: Cambridge University Press, 2000.

Hekster, Olivier. *Commodus: An Emperor at the Crossroads*. Amsterdam: J. C. Gieben, 2002.

Adam M. Kemezis

CONCORD

See Values and Virtues, Roman.

CONCRETE

Concrete or *opus caementicium* developed in central Italy by the end of the third century BCE. This concrete is different from modern concrete in that it consists of fist-sized pieces of aggregate (*caementa*) set in abundant mortar. Unlike modern concrete, which is poured into place, the *caementa* and mortar were typically laid by hand with the aid of a trowel and tamped down to increase solidity. Though Greeks knew of lime mortar, the Roman material was especially strong and durable because of the addition of the local volcanic ash, ranging from powder to the size of a pea, known today as pozzolana, which takes its name from the town of Pozzuoli on the Bay of Naples where there are large deposits. Rome also had its own plentiful sources of pozzolana from the Alban Hills. When mixed with the lime and water, the soluble silica and alumina in the pozzolana created a chemical reaction that allowed the mortar to harden under water and increased the strength to up to eight times more than that of simple lime mortar. In areas where pozzolana was not available, builders often added crushed terra-cotta to the lime mortar, which created a similar chemical reaction resulting in a stronger lime mortar for concrete construction and a waterproof mortar for cisterns and aqueducts. Given the great quantities of water required for concrete, the early development of concrete was probably aided by the supply of water provided by the Roman aqueducts, beginning with the aqua Appia in 312 BCE.

Concrete provided a number of advantages over cut-stone construction. Laying the concrete required less skill than carving precisely shaped stones. Concrete construction was faster because many masons could be distributed along opposite sides of a given wall and raise the wall all at once, whereas a stone structure had to be laid block by block in a given order using heavy-lifting equipment. Given the heterogeneous nature of concrete, the suppliers could be much more diversified: many different individuals could supply the lime, pozzolana, and *caementa*, thus allowing for larger projects to be built in a shorter period than if a single quarry was supplying the majority of the material.

Roman concrete walls were always faced with either small stones or brick. Vitruvius (*De architectura* 2.8.1) notes the two most common techniques in his day, the second half of the first century BCE: *opus incertum*, which he notes was by then old-fashioned, and *opus reticulatum*. Indeed the earliest concrete walls in Rome and Latium are faced with randomly laid small stones of *opus incertum* creating a smooth face (Sanctuary of Fortuna, Palestrina, second half of the second century BCE). *Opus reticulatum*, which appeared by the late second century BCE, consists of small, square-pyramid-shaped blocks set in a diagonal grid pattern, as at the Theater of Pompey (55 BCE). The development of *opus reticulatum* has been related to a shift in demographics and labor organization in Rome during the second century BCE, when the slave population increased dramatically because of Roman conquests abroad. A division of labor would have been possible: the newly acquired unskilled slave could form the pyramidal blocks while more skilled workers (free or slave) put them in place. Once brick was produced on a large scale in Rome by the first century CE, it became the most common facing for concrete walls (*opus testaceum*).

Concrete also provided the opportunity to grade the *caementa* so that it was heavier and more resistant in the lower part of the structure and lighter at

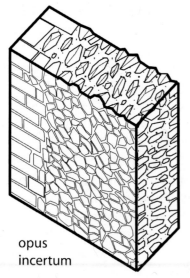
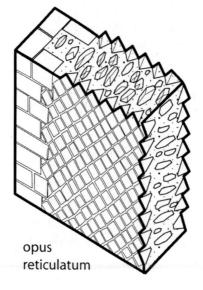
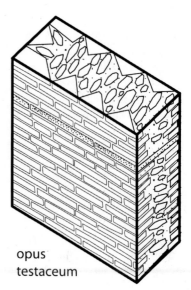

opus
incertum

opus
reticulatum

opus
testaceum

Wall Types. COURTESY OF LYNNE LANCASTER

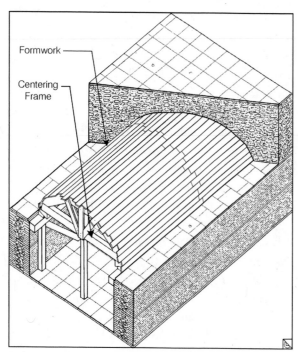

Formwork

Centering
Frame

Centering. COURTESY OF LYNNE LANCASTER

the top. With the large-scale production of brick, concrete was combined with structural elements such as arches and vaulting ribs in order to reinforce particular parts of the structure. Such developments were particularly important in the ability to create large structures such as the Pantheon, where lightweight volcanic *caementa* was used at the crown of the dome to reduce the outward thrust, and then brick arches within the concrete walls served to channel loads through the structure.

Concrete is an amorphous material that had to be laid on a wooden form until it hardened and gained its strength. This allowed for the creation of more dynamic shapes, the only limitation being the carpenter's ability to build the desired form in wood. Some of the most adventurous vaulting can be seen at Hadrian's villa at Tivoli (second century CE). Ultimately this material changed the aesthetic expectations within Roman culture and led to design innovations in architecture throughout the empire.

[*See also* Architecture; Building Materials and Construction; Engineering; *and* Vaults and Vaulting.]

BIBLIOGRAPHY

Adam, Jean-Pierre. *Roman Building: Materials and Techniques.* Translated by Anthony Mathews. London: Batsford, 1994.

Lancaster, Lynne C. *Concrete Vaulted Construction in Imperial Rome: Innovations in Context.* New York: Cambridge University Press, 2005.

Torelli, Mario. "Innovazioni nelle tecniche edilizie romane tra il I sec. a.C. e il I sec. d.C." In *Tecnologia, economia, e società nel mondo romano*, pp. 139–161. Como, Italy: Banca Popolare Commercio e Industria, 1980. An English translation is available in Mario Torelli, *Studies in the Romanization of Italy*, edited and translated by Helena Fracchia and Maurizio Gualtieri (Edmonton: University of Alberta Press, 1995), pp. 213–238.

Lynne C. Lancaster

CONSOLATION LITERATURE

The challenge of comforting others upon the loss of a loved one or other misfortune inspired an extensive corpus of literature in the ancient world that usually took the form of a letter to an individual, though the length and formality of some works imply the author had a wider audience in mind. Some works are clearly directed to a group. The writer of a sympathy letter nowadays would have to be well read in philosophy, poetry, history, myth, and religion to match many of the consolatory works that survive from antiquity. Their authors employed combinations of commonplaces, philosophical approaches, and religious and mythical precepts, as well as literary and historical examples that sometimes defied logic. Writers of consolation literature drew from all forms of oral and written communication dealing with hardship or death, and flexibility was of paramount importance, as the goal was to comfort rather than to argue for a specific view. The ancients did not conceive of "stages of grief" as we know them today, but writers were aware that one should not try to alleviate grief too soon and that the passing of time was a necessary part of the healing process. The most frequent occasion for consolation was death; others included exile, poverty, political failure, illness, shipwreck, and old age.

Consolation literature as a distinct literary type, the *paramythikos logos* or *consolatio*, and, in verse form, the *epicedium* (funeral ode), began in the Classical period and flourished throughout the Hellenistic and Roman periods. Archaic epic, lyric, and classical tragedy contained consolatory themes that became traditional in the genre, as did funeral orations, epitaphs, and inscriptions offering praise for the dead and solace and encouragement to the living. Homer's *Iliad* provided an archetype of consolation in Achilles' response to Priam's grief over the death of his son Hector (24.518–551), emphasizing the inevitable suffering shared by all humans and the futility of grieving.

In the fifth and fourth centuries BCE, sophists and philosophers took a more direct approach to consolation. The Attic orator Antiphon, for example, wrote *The Art of Eliminating Grief* (no longer extant) and set up a booth in the agora of Corinth to counsel those in emotional distress. Perhaps the most influential Greek letter of consolation was *On Grief*, written about 300 BCE by the Academic philosopher Crantor, composed for a friend whose children had died. Crantor's work (which survives only in fragments) brought together all previous methods and philosophical stances on death and grieving.

Cicero, who admitted his debt to Crantor, wrote a consolation to himself in 45 BCE following the death of his daughter Tullia. This work was also a significant influence on later authors, and although it is no longer extant, much of its content appears in Cicero's *Tusculan Disputations*, which set forth philosophical views on death and the emotions. The collection of his letters contains several consolations, perhaps the most notable being Servius Sulpicius Rufus' letter to Cicero on the death of his daughter (*Epistolae ad Familiares* 4.5).

Consolatory letters loosely adhere to a sequence of structural and thematic elements. The author first expresses sympathy by recounting the details of the misfortune and sharing in the recipient's sorrow. This lament is often followed by or mingled with praise for the family and life of the deceased, further justifying lamentation but also comforting the bereaved by acknowledging the magnitude of the loss. Verse consolations often dwell longer on lament and eulogy than do those in prose. The recipient is sometimes praised as well, strengthening ties between consoler and bereaved while instilling confidence in the recipient that he or she can and will endure. In poetic consolations a description of the death and funeral often precede or follow praise of the deceased.

The final component is the consolation itself, which varies according to the circumstances. The primary goal is to convince the recipient to change his or her perception of the event: to see that the misfortune was not really so bad after all, or that excessive grief would not be a useful and appropriate response. The most common themes, especially in consolations concerning death, are that no one can escape death or misfortune, and so we should be prepared for these in advance; that nothing is accomplished by grieving to excess; that time heals, but the use of reason can expedite the process; and that death is not an evil, rounded out by admonitions to "count your blessings" and to honor the deceased through remembrance. Often the recipient is encouraged to attend to responsibilities and maintain a noble demeanor and to be aware that the deceased would not want the survivor to suffer prolonged sorrow. Consolations often cite historical examples of others who bravely endured similar hardships and quote commonplaces and earlier literature to support these arguments.

Excessive grieving is of paramount concern in consolatory works. All writers acknowledge the inevitability and necessity of mourning soon after a misfortune, but take various approaches to ease sorrow if it lingers too long. Prose writers (especially Stoics and Platonists such as Plutarch) sometimes scold the mourner for weakness and "womanish" behavior, reminding the reader of the importance of image and reputation, and pointing out that excessive grief is inappropriate and unnecessary, for it benefits neither the living nor the dead.

Belief in the afterlife plays a large role in condolence, drawing from philosophy, religion, and myth. Cicero found great comfort in the belief that the soul is immortal (an idea derived largely from Plato), and, as he expressed in letters to his friend Atticus (*Epistulae ad Atticum*), he even wanted to build a shrine for his daughter, following the premise that those who are exceptional in some way can be honored among the gods or heroes after death. The Roman poet Statius in the *Silvae* (about 91 to 95 CE) portrayed vivid images of the deceased in Elysium and present with the bereaved in spirit or in dreams, or possibly to be reincarnated.

Christian consolations usually emphasize belief in a life after death, and include prayer as well as citations from scripture, while often also incorporating pre-Christian philosophy, commonplaces, and examples. While pre-Christians usually qualified their assertions concerning the afterlife with statements such as "if what they say is true," Christians proclaimed it with surety. Jerome's *Letter* 60 to Heliodorus (late fourth century) is one of the longest and most poignant of early Christian consolatory literature. Boethius' *Consolation of Philosophy* (about 525), portraying a dialogue in both prose

Consolation of Philosophy. Philosophia and the Muses visit Boethius in prison. *De consolatione philosophiae* (Ghent: Arend de Kaysere, 3 May 1485). PRINTS AND PHOTOGRAPHS DIVISION, LIBRARY OF CONGRESS

"Endure, and do not grieve stubbornly in your heart. For you will do nothing for your son by mourning, nor will you bring him back to life sooner than you will suffer another misfortune." (Homer *Iliad* 24.549–551)

"At the loss of a friend may our eyes be neither dry nor overflowing. We must weep but not wail." (Seneca to Lucilius, *Letter* 63.1)

"The strongest drug for the alleviation of pain is reason (*logos*), and the use of reason prepares us for all the changes encountered during our lives." ([Plutarch], *Consolation to Apollonius* 103F)

"The achievements of the general will live on, and so will the hard-earned glory of his deeds. This remains, this alone escapes the greedy funeral pyre." ([Ovid], *Consolation to Livia on the Death of Her Son Drusus*, 265–266)

Philosophy as Therapy; *and* Plutarch, *subentry* Philosophical Writings.]

BIBLIOGRAPHY

Baltussen, Han. "Personal Grief and Public Mourning in Plutarch's Consolation to His Wife." *American Journal of Philology* 130, no.1 (March 2009): 67–98. In-depth discussion of Plutarch's letter, interpreting his philosophical approach as an ancient form of psychotherapy with comparison to modern therapeutic techniques; history of psychology and consolation literature. Bibliography includes primary and secondary sources for consolation literature and ancient psychology.

Cicero, Marcus Tullius. *Cicero on the Emotions: Tusculan Disputations 3 and 4.* Translated and with commentary by Margaret Graver. Chicago: University of Chicago Press, 2002. Includes appendix on "Crantor and the Consolatory Tradition." A good source for the various philosophical stances on death and grieving.

Fern, Sister Mary Edmund. *The Latin Consolatio as a Literary Type.* St. Louis, Mo.: n.p., 1941. Analysis with some text and translation of pre-Christian Latin consolations; bibliography of primary and secondary sources.

Scourfield, J. H. D. *Consoling Heliodorus: A Commentary on Jerome, Letter 60.* Oxford and New York: Oxford University Press, 1993. Excellent overview of the history of consolatory literature with bibliography of primary and secondary sources; text, translation, and commentary on *Letter* 60.

Andrea L. Purvis

and verse between the imprisoned author and Lady Philosophy, relies largely on Platonic thought, stressing the notion that human happiness comes from within and should be independent of external circumstances. Philosophy consoles Boethius with a hope of reward beyond death, for there is a highest good (*summum bonum*) and virtue does not go unrewarded. Despite its lack of specifically Christian themes, Boethius' treatise assured the survival of consolation literature into the Middle Ages.

[*See also* Boethius; Cicero, *subentry* Philosophy of Cicero; Death, *subentries* Death in Literature *and* Explanations of and Attitudes toward Death; Funeral Oration, Greek; Funeral Oration, Latin;

CONSTANTINE

(Flavius Valerius Constantinus; c. 272/3–337), emperor. Constantine was proclaimed emperor at York in Britain on 25 July 306. Born at Naissus (modern Niš, Serbia), near the Danube, he had previously served as a junior military officer with the emperors Diocletian and Galerius in the Eastern provinces. Eventually he had joined his father, the emperor Constantius I, in northern Gaul and Britain. At Constantius' death the army hailed Constantine, his eldest son. To enhance the legitimacy of his imperial rule, Constantine negotiated with Galerius, the senior emperor in the Eastern provinces, and he married a daughter of Maximian, a former emperor.

He also gradually eliminated his imperial rivals. Maxentius, the son of Maximian, had been proclaimed emperor at Rome in 306. In 312, Constantine invaded Italy, and on 28 October he defeated Maxentius outside Rome at the battle of the Milvian Bridge. Afterward he formed an alliance with the emperor Licinius (Valerius Licianus Licinius). After skirmishes between the two during 316–317, Constantine acquired control of the Balkans. On 18 September 324, Constantine defeated Licinius in northern Asia Minor and took control of the Eastern provinces. With this victory he had reunited the empire under his rule.

Christianity. Throughout his reign Constantine advertised his religious beliefs. Initially panegyrics, coins, and dedications associated him with Jupiter and Hercules; in 310 in a vision at a temple in Gaul he saw himself as Apollo. Before the battle against Maxentius in 312 he had, he later claimed, a vision of a cross in the sky, followed by a dream of a conversation with Jesus Christ, who instructed him to construct a military standard in the shape of a cross (the so-called labarum). Constantine himself recounted these stories about the vision and the dream, but only much later in his reign. The audience for his memories included Eusebius, bishop of Caesarea in Palestine, who subsequently enshrined the stories in an account of the battle in his *Life of Constantine*. Eusebius' recasting of these stories as a moment of religious conversion has been powerfully influential.

Early in 313, Constantine and Licinius agreed on a joint declaration that promoted the "highest divinity" and extended freedom of worship "to both Christians and everyone." But involvement in the theological controversies that consistently disturbed Christian congregations made it difficult for Constantine to live up to his own recommendation. In North Africa, churchmen were still arguing ferociously over the aftermath of the recent persecutions. The immediate accusations focused on the surrender of the Bible for burning; the larger concerns highlighted the continuing value of martyrdom and the importance of ritual purity. Already in late 312, Constantine intervened on behalf of

Caecilianus, bishop of Carthage, by describing him as the leader of "the catholic church," and he soon referred petitions to the bishop of Rome, who convened a council of Italian and Gallic bishops that exonerated Caecilianus and condemned his rival Donatus. The supporters of Donatus, known as Donatists, appealed again to the emperor. This time Constantine presided in person at a council of bishops at Arles in 314. After the Donatists likewise rejected this verdict, the emperor eventually ordered repression and the confiscation of their churches. Constantine ended his intolerance only as he anticipated his coming war with Licinius. But as a result of his opposition, Donatists could now represent themselves as the authentic heirs of the martyrs who had confronted pagan emperors in the early empire. As the true "church of the martyrs," Donatist Christianity flourished in North Africa, and by 330 its supporters had even seized a church that Constantine had built at Cirta in Numidia. All the emperor could do was rant against the "heretics and schismatics" and offer to construct another church for the "catholics."

After defeating Licinius in 324, Constantine inherited another ecclesiastical dispute in the Eastern provinces. This dispute concerned a fine point of Trinitarian doctrine about defining the relationship between God the Father and Jesus Christ. Some theologians, including Arius, a priest at Alexandria, emphasized that the Son was subordinate to the Father, both after in time and inferior in essence. Others stressed the coordination, coexistence, and identity of Father and Son. Constantine's primary concern was to prevent his recent unification of the empire from imploding in ecclesiastical discord. In June 325 he presided over sessions of an ecumenical council of bishops at Nicaea that pointedly rejected Arian doctrines and defined Father and Son as "identical in essence." After the council, however, Constantine seemed to waver in his doctrinal preferences, often preferring Arian (or Arianizing) churchmen who temporized over strict proponents of Nicene theology. He offered reconciliation to Arius himself, he flattered Eusebius of Caesarea, a supporter of Arius, and he once exiled Athanasius, bishop of Alexandria and an inflexible advocate of Nicene theology.

Legislation. One distinguishing feature of Constantine's imperial decisions was his increasingly overt support for Christianity and its clerics. Immediately after his victory at Rome in 312 he sent letters to magistrates and churchmen in North Africa ordering the restoration of property to churches and the distribution of imperial funds. He also announced that clerics were immune from having to assume the financial burdens of holding municipal offices and serving on municipal councils, and he enhanced the authority of bishops by allowing them to hear civil cases. Membership in the clergy soon became so attractive that he eventually tried to limit the recruitment of members of municipal councils. Nevertheless, virtually all the known bishops from the fourth century were from the class of municipal notables. Constantine's legislation hence contributed to a rise of episcopal power, an increase in ecclesiastical wealth, and the gradual takeover of municipal functions by churchmen. One constitution included an explicit preview of the future: "it is necessary for the poor to be supported by the wealth of the churches" (Theodosian Code 16.2.6).

Constantine's decisions also reflected older, more traditional concerns. In his legislation about families and inheritance law he was concerned primarily to protect the rank, status, and property of aristocrats. In one edict, for instance, he abolished the penalties on the unmarried and childless that had been imposed long before by the emperor Augustus. This decision made it easier for wealthy aristocrats, such as the senators at Rome, to transfer property within their families. At the same time he expanded the application of imperial law to respond to the common practices of ordinary provincials. Some of his decisions endorsed a traditional code of conservative moral behavior, even implicitly accepting the exposure of infants, while others condemned the practice of abduction marriage. In this legislation concerning both aristocrats and ordinary provincials the values of Christianity had a limited impact. Even as Constantine overturned some earlier imperial legislation, he tended to support ancestral customs.

In the early fifth century more than three hundred of Constantine's rescripts and edicts were collected in the Theodosian Code. Much of his legislation consisted of responses to issues and questions brought to his attention by letters from imperial magistrates or by petitions from communities and individuals. As a typical Roman emperor, Constantine still had to rely on the goodwill of the magistrates, great aristocrats, and municipal notables who were expected to respect and implement his decisions. As a patron of Christianity, however, he also had to negotiate with prominent bishops, all of whom had their own agendas.

Empire, Frontiers, and Capitals. Like his immediate predecessors, Constantine was a military emperor. By the end of his reign he had renewed his victory titles over the Germans four times, the Goths twice, and the Sarmatians twice. These titles commemorated his successful campaigns on the Rhine frontier against the Franks primarily during the early years of his reign, and in the Balkans primarily during the later years. He built bridges across the Rhine and the Danube, and he even claimed to have recovered Trajan's lost province of Dacia north of the Danube. Constantine complemented these victories by accelerating some important reforms of the Roman army. He enlarged the mobile central field army (*comitatenses*)—in part by mobilizing frontier detachments, in part by raising more units recruited from barbarians—and he put it under the command of professional generals (*magistri*). He separated the military hierarchy from the civil administration, and he transferred the command of the troops stationed in forts along the frontiers (*limitanei*) to career military officers (*duces*). Constantine's first concern was always the loyalty and success of his soldiers.

Constantine spent most of his reign on or near the extended northern frontier that stretched from Britain along the Rhine and Danube rivers to Thrace. His important residences included Trier in northern Gaul, Milan in northern Italy, Sirmium and Serdica in the Balkans, and Nicomedia in northwestern Asia Minor. Despite reigning for more than thirty years, he never visited the provinces

Arch of Constantine, Rome. PRINTS AND PHOTOGRAPHS DIVISION, LIBRARY OF CONGRESS

along the southern edge of the Mediterranean from Spain through North Africa and Egypt to Palestine, and he made only one round trip through central Asia Minor to Antioch in Syria. Constantine was fundamentally a northern emperor, and his reign seems to preview the rising importance of continental Europe during the medieval period at the expense of Mediterranean Europe.

In this upside-down empire even Rome had become a peripheral city. Constantine visited Rome three times: in late 312 when he entered in triumph after his victory over Maxentius, in summer 315 to celebrate the tenth anniversary of his accession, and in summer 326 to celebrate the twentieth anniversary. These were all short visits, totaling about five months of his long reign. His visits nevertheless noticeably influenced the monumental appearance of the capital. On his initial arrival he erected a statue of himself (perhaps the colossal statue whose fragments are now displayed on the Campidoglio). He renovated the Circus Maximus and claimed credit for completing the construction of the huge basilica Nova (or basilica of Maxentius and Constantine). In 315 the senate and people

dedicated in his honor the grand victory arch that still stands next to the Colosseum. These monuments inserted him into the long sweep of imperial traditions at Rome. But Constantine also patronized the construction of churches at Rome. The most important were the Church of Saint Peter located on the Vatican Hill and the Church of Saint John Lateran on the southeastern edge of the city. By presenting many expensive gifts and endowing both churches with estates, Constantine initiated the gradual transformation of Rome into a papal city.

Almost immediately upon acquiring control of the Eastern provinces in 324, Constantine decided to found a new capital at the minor city of Byzantium. Located at the intersection of the Aegean Sea and the Black Sea, Byzantium was at the eastern end of the long northern frontier, with ready access to the Balkans and the eastern frontier in Armenia and Syria. Constantine now commenced the rapid enhancement of its amenities and privileges. He planned walls, a palace, a senate house, and a hippodrome, as well as numerous churches. He diverted some of the grain from Egypt that had previously gone to supply the doles at Rome. He provided this new capital with an instant antiquity by importing souvenirs of Greek and Roman history, such as the Serpent Column from Delphi that had memorialized a famous victory of the Greeks over the Persians and a bronze statue that had commemorated Augustus' victory at Actium. He began to import biblical relics. At its official dedication on 11 May 330, this new capital could claim a place in Greek, Roman, and ecclesiastical history. Initially Constantine called the city New Rome or Second Rome (Altera Roma); soon it was known as Constantinople, "Constantine's city."

Constantine's military career had drawn him away from the Mediterranean core of the Roman Empire, first to the northern frontier, then to the eastern frontier. At the end of his life he was planning to invade the Middle East in a campaign against the Persian Empire. His funeral emphasized again these new priorities. The internment in Rome both of his mother, Helena, in a mausoleum attached to the basilica of Saints Marcellinus and Peter and also of his two daughters in a mausoleum next to the basilica of Saint Agnes may imply that Constantine was likewise planning his own eventual burial in Rome. In fact, as a military emperor he had never been comfortable at Rome. Upon learning about his death, the senate and people erected a portrait that depicted Constantine reclining in heaven, presumably in anticipation of performing the usual ritual of consecration. But when they heard that he was to be buried in Constantinople, they were deeply upset. Constantine was credited with having "renewed" Rome; now, however, he was buried in New Rome.

Emperorship. A Christian emperor was difficult to imagine, simply because the possibility was so unexpected. Earlier models of emperorship were often more complicating than relevant. During his visits to Rome, Constantine had behaved like a conventional "Republican emperor," deferential toward the fiction that emperors had restored the traditions of the old Republic, respectful toward the senate that served as the guardian of those traditions. He erected a dedication in which he claimed to have "restored the senate and the Roman people to their original liberty and nobility"; he furthermore promoted senators from Rome to high offices again. But this sort of Republican emperorship also entailed service as a priest in pagan cults, and during one of his visits Constantine offended the people of Rome by his failure to celebrate a traditional festival on the Capitoline Hill.

The Tetrarchic emperors, his immediate predecessors, offered another model of emperorship. Diocletian had formed a consortium of four co-emperors, each nominally with equal authority but in fact ranked by seniority and prestige. To cope with this tension between hierarchy and harmony the emperors had identified themselves with gods, in particular Jupiter and Hercules. Constantine adopted a different solution to managing the conflicts between

Constantine. Head of the colossal statue of the emperor Constantine from the Basilica of Maxentius and Constantine, 313 CE. Palazzo dei Conservatori, Musei Capitolini, Rome. PHOTOGRAPH BY ROBERT B. KEBRIC

co-emperors by gradually eliminating his rivals. But he retained the linkage, even identification, of emperors and deities. The problem now was to define the correlation between Christian emperor and Christian God.

Churchmen had not anticipated the appearance of a truly Christian emperor, and they had not developed any distinctive Christian political philosophy. Instead their contemporary disputes over theology had to substitute. The debates over Donatist Christianity and Arian Christianity had significant implications for defining a Christian emperor. One involved the limits of interference by emperors in ecclesiastical affairs. Because their appeals were typically unsuccessful, Donatists soon concluded that Christians should not mix with emperors and that bishops should not visit the palace. Their opponents, who had benefited from Constantine's patronage, argued instead that the church was inside the Roman Empire, which in turn protected clerics. A second implication focused on the divinity of the emperor. By highlighting the subordination of Jesus Christ the Son to God the Father, Arian Christianity seemed to leave open the possibility that a Christian emperor might be an analogue of Jesus. In contrast, by firmly insisting that only the Son shared the same essence with the Father, Nicene Christianity clearly demoted the standing of the emperor enough that already during Constantine's reign some bishops were prepared to confront his authority. Church and state, rulers and God: the political implications of these theological controversies thus defined many of the issues for subsequent medieval, Byzantine, and even modern debates over religion and society.

Constantine's own contribution to the making of theology included his promotion of a distinctive Holy Land in Palestine that memorialized important events in the life of Jesus Christ. After the Council of Nicaea he funded the building of the Church of the Holy Sepulcher to commemorate Jesus' crucifixion and burial at Jerusalem. He also assisted the building of the Church of the Nativity at Bethlehem and the Church of the Ascension at the Mount of Olives. With these memorials Constantine had constructed a life of Jesus in which he had a place as both patron and likeness. He presented the twelve columns commemorating the twelve apostles that encircled the apse of the Church of the Holy Sepulcher. In his own mausoleum at Constantinople he likewise placed his sarcophagus in the middle of twelve empty tombs. Lest the correspondence be overlooked, at the end of his life Constantine hoped to imitate the Savior by being baptized in the Jordan River.

Constantine prepared for succession by combining his three surviving sons—Constantine II, Constantius II, and Constans—with his nephew Dalmatius, as a "tetrarchy" of Caesars, junior emperors, and assigning them to particular regions of the empire. After his death on 22 May 337, however, troops at Constantinople massacred many collateral members of the family, including Dalmatius. On 9 September only the three sons were hailed as emperors. Not surprisingly, Bishop Eusebius of Caesarea immediately described their joint reign as a "trinity."

Afterlife. Constantine is one of the best documented of Roman emperors. The most important source is Eusebius' *Life of Constantine*, which was simultaneously a biography, a panegyric, a dossier of imperial documents, an anthology of oral traditions, and a scrapbook of recycled opinions. It was also a theological treatise, because Eusebius represented the emperor in such a way as to support his own particular theology. In fact, every source offered a distinctive construction of the emperor. Panegyrists were trying to fit a Christian emperor into classical terminology. Christians such as the rhetorician Lactantius and the bishop (later Saint) Optatus of Milevis were trying to fit a Christian emperor into biblical terminology. Petitions from communities, subsequently erected in public inscriptions, were hoping to elicit favorable responses through flattery. Even Constantine himself, in his letters and one surviving sermon, was contributing to the formation of *Constantin imaginaire*.

Already in late antiquity historians sensed that Constantine's reign had marked a significant transition. Ecclesiastical historians characterized him as the first Christian emperor, who had converted after his vision of the cross in the sky. Other historians emphasized political and military changes by claiming that he had been the first emperor to found a city named after himself and the first to have appointed barbarians as consuls, or by holding him responsible for the collapse of the frontiers. In post-Roman western Europe many barbarian kings, in particular the kings of the Visigoths, Ostrogoths, and Lombards, adopted Constantine's family name of Flavius as a royal title. In the Eastern Roman Empire subsequent emperors wanted to be complimented as "New Constantines." For centuries images of Constantine continued to define Christian rulership.

[*See also* Christianity; Church Buildings; Constantinople; Helena; Jerusalem; Rome: The Empire; *and* Tetrarchy.]

BIBLIOGRAPHY

Barnes, Timothy David. *Constantine and Eusebius.* Cambridge, Mass.: Harvard University Press, 1981.

Demandt, Alexander, and Josef Engemann, eds. *Konstantin der Grosse: Ausstellungskatalog.* Trier, Germany: Konstantin-Ausstellungsgesellschaft; Mainz, Germany: von Zabern, 2007. Catalog of an exhibition held in Trier in 2007.

Demandt, Alexander, and Josef Engemann, eds. *Konstantin der Grosse: Geschichte, Archäologie, Rezeption.* Trier, Germany: Rheinisches Landesmuseum, 2007.

Drake, H. A. *Constantine and the Bishops: The Politics of Intolerance.* Baltimore: Johns Hopkins University Press, 2000.

Eusebius. *Life of Constantine.* Introduction, translation, and commentary by Averil Cameron and Stuart G. Hall. Oxford: Clarendon Press; New York: Oxford University Press, 1999.

Evans Grubbs, Judith. *Law and Family in Late Antiquity: The Emperor Constantine's Marriage Legislation.* Oxford: Clarendon Press, 1995.

Grünewald, Thomas. *Constantinus Maximus Augustus: Herrschaftspropaganda in der zeitgenössischen Überlieferung.* Historia Einzelschriften 64. Stuttgart, Germany: Steiner, 1990.

Hartley, Elizabeth, Jane Hawkes, Martin Henig, and Frances Mee, eds. *Constantine the Great: York's Roman Emperor.* York, U.K.: York Museums and Gallery Trust; Aldershot, U.K.: Lund Humphries, 2006.

Lenski, Noel, ed. *The Cambridge Companion to the Age of Constantine.* Cambridge, U.K.: Cambridge University Press, 2006.

Lieu, Samuel N. C., and Dominic Montserrat, ed. *Constantine: History, Historiography, and Legend.* London and New York: Routledge, 1998.

Odahl, Charles M. *Constantine and the Christian Empire.* London and New York: Routledge, 2004.

Van Dam, Raymond. *The Roman Revolution of Constantine.* Cambridge, U.K.: Cambridge University Press, 2007.

Raymond Van Dam

CONSTANTINOPLE

[*This entry includes two subentries, on the history and on the archaeology of Constantinople.*]

History

Septimius Severus (r. 193–211) laid the foundations for Constantine's development of an imperial capital at the ancient city of Byzantium. Although he did not rebuild the city walls that had resisted his armies for three years, Septimius Severus did leave a circus; what one source calls a hunting theater (*kynēgesion*); a new forum—the Tetrastoon—surrounded by four stoas at the point where two colonnaded streets, or *emboloi*, came together; a basilica just west of the Tetrastoon; a great bath house; and a large area with some sort of military use, the Strategion (*Chronicon Paschale*, p. 495).

Constantine (r. 306–337) decided to establish a dynastic capital in the East after his defeat of Licinius I in 324. Although later tradition held that he was inspired to select Byzantium by a divine vision—previously he had been thinking of using the site of Troy for this purpose—and that the Christian God also showed Constantine where to establish his new circuit of walls, it is likely that his choice was made for more mundane reasons (Sozomen *Church History* 2.3). Educated in Nicomedia, Constantine knew the region well, and presumably he desired a new venue in which he could reveal his conception of imperial power.

One notable difference between his capital and earlier tetrarchic capitals is that he placed his mausoleum just inside the circuit of the new city wall, about a mile west of the old circuit, and just off the northern wing of the main street, the Mese. The mausoleum showed that, contrary to the practice of Diocletian and Galerius, whose tombs were in long-prepared "retirement palaces," there would be no retirement palace for Constantine—and, consequently, no abdication.

Aside from his mausoleum, the bulk of Constantine's building activity was concentrated on the port facilities and to the immediate south or west of the Severan forum. The new palace was attached to the circus, or Hippodrome, that was enlarged and fitted with an imperial box. The Tetrastoon, renamed the Augusteion, was enhanced with an image of the emperor's mother, Helena, on a small porphyry column. A new church, the Church of the Holy Wisdom (Hagia Sophia), was constructed on the north side of the forum, and a monumental gate, the Chalke, linked the forum to the palace on the southeast side. Hagia Sophia was balanced by two new temples, one of Cybele and one of Tyche, placed in front of the basilica. A monumental gateway to the west of the forum, in the area of the golden milestone that listed distances to other major cities in the empire, led to a new forum, this one just outside the old city wall. This forum became known as the Forum of Constantine and was centered on a porphyry column, once intended for a tetrarchic monument at Rome, that supported a colossal statue of the emperor. The city was further embellished with works of art from other cities. Some were donated by cities that wished to illustrate their devotion to the regime, as was the case with Miletus, which sent a statue of its great citizen Theophanes, friend of Pompey. Delphi sent the Serpent Column, erected to commemorate the Battle of Plataea in 479 BCE, to decorate the *spina*, or central barrier, of the Hippodrome; Nicopolis sent an Augustan victory monument; and Rome sent several ancient works of art, including the statue of the wolf suckling Romulus and Remus.

The date of the inauguration of the new capital, 11 May 330, marks the likely end of work on the improved Hippodrome, for the event was celebrated by a parade in that building. It is possibly at this time that three temples on the ancient acropolis—those of Apollo, Artemis, and Aphrodite—were deprived of their revenues but not destroyed, even as a new church, that of Saint Irene, was rising there (John Malalas *Chronicle*, p. 324). The center of government, however, remained Nicomedia, perhaps because other buildings were incomplete; Hagia Sophia, for instance, was not inaugurated until 15 February 360.

Constantine, who saw the city as a celebration of himself rather than as a rival to Rome, did not found a new senate; rather he enhanced the existing city council by inviting wealthy men to move to the city and become members of that body, which met in a big new council house near his new forum. It was Constantine's son, Constantius II, who converted the mausoleum of Constantine into the Church of the Holy Apostles and, in 340, declared Constantinople to be the "New Rome" as he transformed the town council into a senate on an equal footing with Rome's (Theodosian Code 6.4, 5, 6; Philostorgius *Church History* 3.1). It was also during Constantius' reign that the bishop of Constantinople obtained patriarchal status on a par with that of the bishops of Rome, Alexandria, and Jerusalem. In the realm of civic administration, Constantius created three, later five, praetorships, to finance public works (including games), and in 359 he appointed the first urban prefect, who was charged with the maintenance of order in the city. The main stress to that order, in addition to the usual sorts of urban mayhem, arose out of theological disputes—especially when one or the other side found assistance from the inhabitants of the monasteries in and around the city—and out of disputes between partisans of the two main circus factions, the "Blues" and the "Greens." We do not know when the people of the city began to distinguish themselves as "Blues" or "Greens," but it possible that this predated Constantine.

Although all emperors added to the cityscape, the two principal periods of urban development after the time of Constantine were the reigns of Theodosius II

Constantinople. Relief from the obelisk of the emperor Theodosius I, erected in the Hippodrome, fourth century. VANNI/ART RESOURCE, NY

(r. 408–450) and Justinian (r. 527–565). From the reign of Theodosius II comes the snapshot of the city provided by the *Notitia Urbis Constantinopolitanae*: according to this list Constantinople was divided into fourteen regions, encompassed by the new wall that Theodosius II had built a mile (a kilometer and a half) west of the walls of Constantine. The attractions of the city included five palaces, fourteen churches, six palaces of the empresses, eight baths, two basilicas, four forums (one each for Arcadius and Theodosius II in addition to those of Constantine), two senate houses (the original council house and the one built by Constantine), two columns hollowed out so that one could walk to the top, one big porphyry column, five butcher shops, five granaries, four public fountains, twenty public bakeries, 120 private bakeries, 4,388 noble houses, and one hippodrome. Estimates of the city's population range from a quarter of a million to a million; lower estimates are more likely.

Justinian's building projects in the heart of Constantinople were occasioned by the massive destruction of that area in the Nika riot of 532. The most famous and longest-lasting product of this phase was the new Church of Hagia Sophia, itself replacing the church of the same name that had been dedicated in 415 to replace the Constantinian church, which was destroyed during a riot in 404. After the capture of the city by the Ottoman Turks on 29 May 1453, Hagia Sophia was transformed into a mosque. On that day, too, Constantine XI, the last emperor of Rome in the line reaching back to Augustus, died in battle.

[*See also* Byzantium; Constantine; Justinian; *and* Septimius Severus.]

BIBLIOGRAPHY

Bassett, Sarah. *The Urban Image of Late Antique Constantinople.* Cambridge, U.K.: Cambridge University Press, 2004.

Dagron, Gilbert. *Naissance d'une capitale: Constantinople et ses institutions de 330 à 451.* Paris: Presses Universitaires de France, 1974.

Fowden, Garth. "Constantine's Porphyry Column: The Earliest Literary Allusion." *Journal of Roman Studies* 81 (1991): 119–131.

Kazhdan, Alexander P., ed. *The Oxford Dictionary of Byzantium.* New York: Oxford University Press, 1991.

David S. Potter

Archaeology

Situated on a hilly peninsula that juts into the Sea of Marmara at the confluence of the Golden Horn and the Bosporus, the city developed in three major phases: as Byzantium (seventh century BCE to second century CE), as Colonia Antonina (second to fourth century CE), and finally as New Rome or Constantinople (fourth to sixth century CE). Archaeological investigation of the city has been and remains limited. The Ottomans showed little interest in the city's past, and the building campaigns of the Turkish sultans, who built over much of ancient Constantinople, together with the dense population of the modern city, have meant little systematic excavation. Thus although a general imprint of the city's ancient grid can be seen in the street plan of modern Istanbul, most of the city's infrastructure is known from fragmentary archaeological evidence, graphic records of European travelers, and literary sources.

Historical Development. Byzantium, which took its name from the legendary founder Byzas, was established as a colony from the Greek city of Megara around 660 BCE. Little is known of this early city's physical disposition or the chronology of its development. An acropolis on the high ground at the tip of the peninsula included temples dedicated to Artemis, Aphrodite, and Apollo. Lower down the slopes there was a temple to Poseidon. Two harbors provided port facilities in the waters of the Golden Horn, and a military parade ground to the west of the acropolis probably served as the original forum. Theaters, baths, and residential quarters rose on the hills sloping down to the sea, and a fortification wall ran from the Golden Horn on the north to the Marmara shore on the south.

Under Septimius Severus (r. 193–211 CE), Byzantium underwent radical transformation when, in the aftermath of a civil uprising against the emperor, the city was razed, given a new name—Colonia Antonina, in honor of the emperor's own dynastic line—and refurbished with a set of new buildings in the area southwest of the old acropolis. This monumental construction, which was left incomplete at the death of Septimius Severus, included three colonnaded streets the most important of which was the Mese, a forum known as the Tetrastoon, a basilica complex, a public bath known as the Zeuxippus, and a hippodrome. Evidence suggests that the buildings conformed to planning and construction traditions prevalent in western Asia Minor and the East.

The Severan construction set the stage for the city's last major phase of development, providing the armature around which all late Roman construction and planning grew. This rebuilding and expansion took place first under the direction of Constantine and the members of his dynasty (324–363). Constantine refounded Byzantium in 324 and dedicated the city in 330 as Nova Roma (New Rome). The name "Constantinople" was established in popular usage by the end of the fourth century. At the foundation the emperor extended the city limit west and with it the fortifications: a new land defense was built from the Golden Horn to the Sea of Marmara, and the existing seawalls were extended to join with the new land defenses.

Completion of the Severan projects in the center of the city created an imposing monumental core. New buildings were also introduced into this armature: the Great Palace of the Byzantine emperors, the church of Hagia Eirene, and the Milion, a tetrapylon arch at the confluence of the major streets. Later Constantine's son and successor Constantius II (r. 337–361) added the first church of Hagia Sophia to this group.

Constantine also oversaw the westward expansion of the city. These territories, which were enclosed between the old Severan wall and the new Constantinian defense, grew up around the extension of the Mese and its northern spur. At the juncture of the Mese and the ruined Severan wall, he built the Forum of Constantine. The forum straddled the Mese and marked the boundary between the old city and the new territories. Further west at the bifurcation of the Mese he erected a Capitolium, itself near a space known as the Philadelphion. On the Mese's northern extension an imperial bath, the Thermae Constantinianae, and Constantine's mausoleum—later incorporated into the Church of the Holy Apostles by Constantius—stood as the major imperial monuments in neighborhoods that were otherwise residential. Integral to this development was the display of sculpture, much of which was robbed from the cities and sanctuaries of the Greco-Roman world for display in the capital.

After a hiatus during the reign of Julian (360–363), Theodosius I (r. 379–395), his son Arcadius (r. 395–408), and his grandson Theodosius II (r. 408–450) made the development of Constantinople a priority.

Public areas within the old Severan walls were restored and newly decorated. The territory west of the Forum of Constantine saw the construction and aggrandizement of a new series of monumental civic spaces along the western stretch of the Mese, the Forum of Theodosius and the Forum of Arcadius prime among them. Finally, during the reign of Theodosius II the city itself was enlarged with the construction of a new defensive wall about two miles (three kilometers) to the west of the Constantinian circuit. Construction of this wall

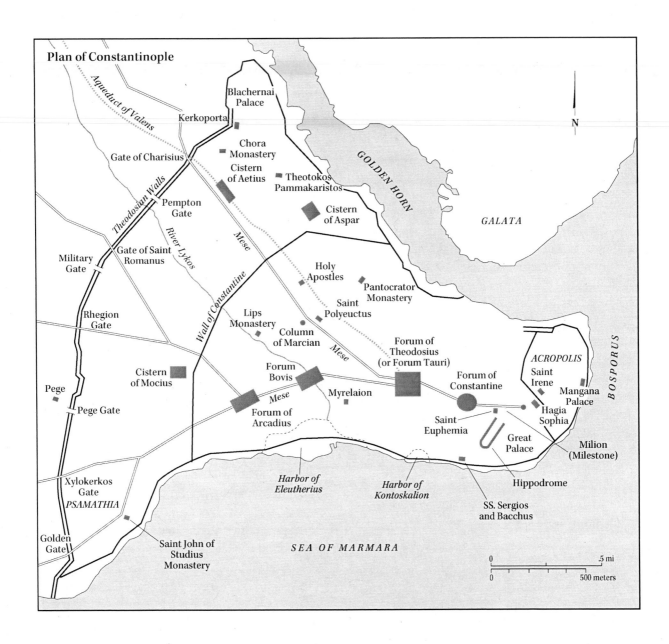

Plan of Constantinople

represented the last major expansion of the city and effectively served as its western boundary until the twentieth century. The Theodosians also oversaw a good deal of church building, including the renovation of Hagia Sophia in 403.

The period around the sixth-century reign of Justinian (r. 527–565) represents the last major ancient construction phase. Although no significant alterations were made to the plan, fires attendant upon the Nika riot of 532 afforded the emperor opportunities for both the development of new projects and the renovation of old. As with the Theodosians, Justinian's major contribution to the city's development was in the realm of church building, including the reconstruction of Hagia Sophia in 532–537.

Extant Monuments. Only a handful of monuments survive from this long period of development. These include structures related to defense (sea-walls, Theodosian landwall), commerce (port facilities), and the water-supply system (Aqueduct of Valens, cisterns). Evidence for public spaces also remains. The hippodrome preserves its substructures and three of the monuments from the central barrier: the Serpent Column or the Plataean Tripod, the Theodosian Obelisk, and the Built Obelisk. The Column of Constantine marks the place of the Forum of Constantine, and remains of a triumphal arch stand at the Forum of Theodosius. Another honorific column dedicated to Marcian (r. 450–457) also survives, as do the fragmentary remains of the Great Palace, the Palace of Antiochus (later the church of Hagia Euphemia), and the Palace of Lausus. Evidence of church building includes the ruined structures of Saint John Studius (fifth century) and Saint Polyeuktos (sixth century), as well as the surviving Justinianic projects—the church of the saints Sergius and Bacchus and the Magna Ecclesia (Great Church), Hagia Sophia.

[*See also* Archaeology, *subentry* Sites in Turkey, *and* Church Buildings.]

BIBLIOGRAPHY

Bassett, Sarah E. *The Urban Image of Late Antique Constantinople*. Cambridge, U.K.: Cambridge University Press, 2004.

Mango, Cyril. *Le développement urbain de Constantinople (IVe-VIIe siècles)*. Paris: Diffusion de Boccard, 1985.

Mathews, Thomas F. *The Early Churches of Constantinople: Architecture and Liturgy*. University Park: Pennsylvania State University Press, 1971.

Müller-Wiener, Wolfgang. *Bildlexikon zur Topographie Istanbuls*. Tübingen, Germany: Wasmuth, 1977.

Sarah E. Bassett

CONSTITUTIONS

See Democracy; Oligarchy; Polis; *and* Tyranny.

CONSUL

The consuls were the chief magistrates of the Roman Republic. In the imperial period the office, often held by the emperors themselves, remained the most significant in the hierarchy of the Roman state.

In the generation of Cicero (106–43 BCE), the period in which evidence for Republican institutions is most robust, a consul must have held the praetorship no less than three years previously. He was elected by vote of the centuries in the *comitia centuriata* and was required to wait ten years before he could hold the office again. If for some reason the consul did not complete his year in office, he would be replaced in a special election by a *consul suffectus*. If a consul was not present in Rome to conduct a consular election, or had failed to complete the election for a new consul prior to leaving office, the election would be conducted by an *interrex*, appointed by senators of patrician descent. The *interrex* would hold office for five days, during which time he would select one consul, who would then preside over the election of his colleague. The first of the two consuls elected each year ran the business of the state in odd-numbered months; the second man elected was in charge during the even-numbered months. The two consuls who opened the year in office gave their names to the year as *consules ordinarii*.

While acting in his official capacity, the consul sat in a curule chair, wore a toga with a purple border (*toga praetexta*), and was preceded by twelve assistants, lictors, who bore the bundle of rods around an axe—the *fasces*—that symbolized his authority. When he left Rome to command an army he wore the military cloak, the *paludamentum*. While in Rome the consul had a variety of administrative and legal duties. On the administrative side he ran meetings of the senate, conducted elections, and, in times of emergency, conducted the appointment of a dictator. The legal duties of a consul included the ability to preside over adoptions, manumissions, and the emancipation of children. In addition, although he would not ordinarily preside over court cases, he might conduct special investigations. In some instances a consul could employ *coercitio*, the power to force a citizen to stop doing something. Forms of *coercitio* could also including flogging, fines, imprisonment, sale into slavery (usually for refusal of military service), the destruction of a house, or relegating an individual or group to a specific distance from Rome. In time of special emergency the consul could ask the senate to give him the power to "take whatever action was necessary to ensure that the state did not come to harm."

The generation of Cicero was the first in which eligibility for the consulship was governed under the *lex Cornelia Annalis* of 81 BCE. The *lex Cornelia* set the minimum age for the quaestorship as the thirtieth year, for the praetorship as the thirty-ninth year, and for the consulship as the forty-second year if a plebeian and as the forty-first year if a patrician. Minimum ages for office had previously been governed by the *lex Villia Annalis* of 180, which required that a man hold first the quaestorship and then the praetorship prior to the consulship—assuming that ten years' military service, beginning at age seventeen, would be completed before the quaestorship—and required a two-year interval between offices. These norms could be ignored under special circumstances, as when Marius succeeded himself four times between 105 and 100 BCE, or when Pompey, who had held no previous office, was elected consul for 70 BCE.

The Early Consulship. In Cicero's day it was also believed that the first consuls after the expulsion of the kings in 509 BCE were Lucius Junius Brutus and Publius Valerius Publicola. This appears to have been a vast oversimplification.

An immensely archaic-sounding document cited by Varro from the *Consular Commentaries* (presumably a collection of documents relating to the duties of the consul) offers a formula for summoning the citizen army in which the chief magistrates are called the *iudices*, "judges" (*On the Latin Language* 6.88). Other evidence coming from texts that appear to date to the fifth or fourth century suggests that the chief magistrates were also known as "praetors," from the verb *praeire*, "to lead the way." Indeed the Greek term for consul, *stratēgos hupatos*, "highest general," is simply a translation of the Latin *praetor maximus*, "highest praetor," and is well established in second-century Greek inscriptions, suggesting that the term had been in common usage for some time. Livy's statement that "in that time [the fifth century BCE] it was not yet the custom to call the 'judge' 'consul' rather than 'praetor' " (*History of Rome* 3.55.12) may be result of confusion over the terminology; it is quite possible that the chief magistrate was called *iudex* in the domestic sphere and "praetor" in the military. The term "consul," which Romans derived from the verb *consulere*, "to consult," is first attested in the epitaph of Lucius Cornelius Scipio Barbatus, consul of 298, who says that his father was also consul, which may place the beginning of the use of the word in the mid-fourth century.

The proto-consulship that emerges from the earliest evidence shows that the office combined sacral, judicial, and military functions that may previously have been concentrated in the office of *rex*. The potential involvement of an *interrex* in selecting the highest magistrate suggests that this was actually the case.

The priestly aspect of the proto-consulship is embodied in the power to take the *auspicia*—which enabled the control of public business—the initiation of military action, and the requirement for a consul to preside over the Feriae Latinae at Alba (a requirement that continued past the Augustan Age). The military aspect seems initially to have been as commander of one of the two legions that appear to have existed in the early period; if it is correct to see the triumph as a very early ceremony, then the symbolic linkage of the victorious general with Jupiter is a reflection of the close connection between the religious and secular aspects of the position. In fact, the functional linkage between religious duties and other duties—one could not act without taking the *auspicia*—suggests that a formal distinction between religious and secular activities would not have occurred to a Roman of the time.

In the earliest period there was no requirement that a holder of the highest office have held previous office, nor was there a legal restriction on self-succession. The earliest consular lists include repeated consulships by Publius Valerius Publicola in 509–507, by Gaius Plautius Decianus in 329–328, by Lucius Papirius Cursor in 320–319, and by Manius Curius Dentatus in 275–274. Although Publicola's career was the object of fictionalized reconstruction, the repeated consulships of the late fourth and early third centuries were all during periods of intense warfare and represent a break with tradition that may have stemmed from administrative necessity. The one restriction on eligibility for office that appears to have developed in the course of the fifth century was that both chief magistrates had to be from patrician families. The consulship was opened to plebeians in the Licinian-Sextian reforms of 367, which also created a praetor who was junior to the chief magistrates. In 342 the *lex Genucia* required that one of the consuls be plebeian. In 172 BCE both consuls were plebeian for the first time.

Among the many unanswered questions about the history of the proto-consulship is why, from the middle of the fifth century onward, it was periodically replaced by a board of five officials, called "military tribunes with consular authority." There is no record of struggle over the creation of this position, and it is possible that it resulted from a need for more officials at a time when Rome confronted multiple enemies and when the judicial functions of

the consulship may have required that a person with consular authority remain in Rome.

The Consulship of the Imperial Period. The Augustan Age saw the beginning of radical transformation in the consulship and the senatorial career as a whole. The most important of these changes were the number of offices available between praetorship and consulship, the number of consuls each year, and the circumstances under which a person became consul. The number of consuls increased because Augustus made persistent though irregular usage of suffect consulships. Elections changed because Augustus played a significant role in selecting candidates. Although the matter remains controversial, it appears that under the Augustan system there were three sorts of candidates for offices below that of consul: "candidates of the emperor," who were guaranteed the office; men "nominated" by the emperor, who still had to compete for election but did so with a powerful advantage; and candidates who had to canvass for the office without imperial support. It appears that by the time of Augustus' death, consular candidates were always "nominated" (Cassius Dio 52.19.4; 53.21.7). Another significant change was in the age at which the earlier offices could be held. The minimum age for the quaestorship was lowered to a man's twenty-fifth year, and the praetorship to his thirtieth. An additional reduction in age was possible for men who, in accordance with the Augustan marriage laws, had three children. Patricians could become consul in their thirty-second or thirty-third year, while plebeians tended to obtain office between their thirty-eighth and forty-second years.

The duties of the consuls were little changed from the Republican period, though major trials involving members of the aristocracy now came to be held in the senate, at whose sessions the consul presided. Otherwise consuls concentrated on civil affairs, mostly letting contracts for public services (including the collection of some taxes), running meetings with the senate, tending to refer serious business to the emperor before allowing the senate to pass a motion. Over time the succession of suffect consuls became regularized so that in the Julio-Claudian period the consuls who opened the year tended to resign mid-year; in the Flavian and Antonine periods the consuls who opened the year tended to resign after four months, allowing time for two more pairs of suffect consuls, each pair also with a four-month term, to follow. Occasional anomalies, usually occasioned by political unrest, resulted in the appointment of additional suffects. The record was twenty-five in 190 CE. Under the Julio-Claudians, elections for suffect consuls were held at the same time as those for the *consules ordinarii* who opened the year in office. In the Flavian period, it appears that the election of suffects was moved to 12 January of the year in which they would hold office. At some point, possibly also in the Flavian period, all consular elections were moved to the senate, though it appears that into the third century the assemblies were summoned to ratify the senate's selections. Tiberius had moved elections for magistrates without *imperium* to the senate in 14 CE.

For a senator the consulship still remained the pinnacle of a career, and the ability to gain one was an indication that he had proven his worth in the years after his praetorship. Unlike during the Ciceronian era, when a former praetor expected to govern only one province before running for consul, men now expected substantial careers after their praetorship, and their conduct determined their future. Fewer than half of all praetors advanced to the consulship, and very few consuls obtained the distinction of governing one of the two major provinces whose governors were chosen by lot rather than by the emperor—Africa and Asia. On very rare occasions, a man who had earned particular imperial favor might be honored with a second or even a third consulship. To be selected as *consul ordinarius* and thus to give one's name to the year remained a great honor.

Although throughout the imperial period the consulship remained the mark of the highest social and political distinction, in the second half of the third century CE the capstone of a senatorial career became the urban prefecture of Rome. At the same time, careers in imperial service seem increasingly to have begun rather than ended with the consulship.

The years before the consulship seem usually to have been filled by localized administrative positions in Italy as military and provincial commands were increasingly given to men of equestrian status.

In the fourth century, when there were multiple imperial courts, the ability to appoint consuls was an important imperial prerogative, so much so that emperors tended to reserve ordinary consulships for themselves and family members. With the decline in political influence, as well as with the great cost that came to be associated with the games that were expected of men who held the office, the consulship gradually declined in both desirability and significance. This was especially true of the suffect consulship, whose holders were often young men in their teens. Still, in the West, where the last consul was Flavius Paulinus in 534, the consulship endured longer than did the emperors. In the East the last imperial subject to hold the consulship was Anicius Faustus Albinus Basilius in 541.

[*See also* Magistrates and Officials, Roman; Patricians; Plebeians; Political Structure and Ideology, Roman; *and* Rome, *subentries* Early Rome and the Republic *and* The Empire.]

BIBLIOGRAPHY

Bagnall, Roger S., et al. *The Consuls of the Later Roman Empire.* Atlanta: Scholars Press for the American Philological Association, 1987.

Broughton, T. Robert S. *Magistrates of the Roman Republic.* 2 vols. with supplement. Atlanta: Scholars Press for the American Philological Association, 1951–1952; 1960; 1986.

Lintott, Andrew. *The Constitution of the Roman Republic.* Oxford: Clarendon Press, 1999.

Mommsen, Theodor. *Römisches Staatesrecht.* 3rd ed. 3 vols. in 5. Leipzig, Germany: S. Hirzel, 1887–1888.

Talbert, Richard J. A. *The Senate of Imperial Rome.* Princeton, N.J.: Princeton University Press, 1984.

David S. Potter

CONTRACEPTION

See Birth and Reproduction.

CONTRACT

See Law, Greek, *and* Law, Roman.

COOKING

See Food.

COOKS AND COOKBOOKS

The Greek *mageiros* or "cook" originally specialized in sacrifice and preparing the resulting meat for feasts. The term was later applied to butchers who sold surplus meat from sacrifices, as well as to professional cooks who were hired to prepare elaborate meals unconnected to a sacrifice. A more technical term for a "chef" (*opsopoios*) also appears, but in the classical period *mageiros* is most frequently used. The evidence from Attic Middle and New Comedy and from Athenaeus suggest that these cooks were most often freeborn or former slaves; despite their low status as tradesmen (Cicero *De officiis* 1.150 describes the profession as disgraceful), they are usually depicted in comedy as arrogant and boastful of their talents (Athenaeus *Deipnosophists* 9.377ff.). The pretentious cook was adopted as a stock character in Roman comedy (*coquus*), although Plautus and Terence depict the cook as a household slave to reflect Roman practice.

With the rise of gastronomy in western Greece in the late sixth through the fourth centuries BCE, South Italian and especially Sicilian cooks became famous for their sophisticated and luxurious creations. A heightened interest in cooking is reflected in the rise of gastronomic literature, especially poetry on food by authors such as Philoxenus, Lynceus, Matro, and most famously, Archestratus (early to mid-fourth century BCE), whose *Hedupatheia* (Life of Luxury) became a byword for Sicilian gastronomic excess. Preserved almost exclusively through quotations in Athenaeus' *Deipnosophists*, the poem appears to be in the tradition of Hesiodic catalog and didactic epos on the topic of fine living through dining. Among discussions of the best sources for various delicacies in the Greek world, Archestratus also offers methods of preparation, particularly for rare species of expensive fish. That the poem was known in the Roman world as early as the late third century BCE may be inferred by a few fragments of Quintus Ennius' Latin adaptation of the poem, entitled *Hedyphagetica*. Prose cookbooks in Greek, probably concise lists of ingredients and cooking methods, do not survive, although as early as Plato's *Gorgias* (518b) a cookbook by a Sicilian Mithaecus is mentioned. Athenaeus 12.516c gives a list of seventeen cookbook authors, including Mithaecus, although the dates and texts of the other authors are unknown. Doctors also recorded recipes for therapeutic diets; Galen's works include many preparations for food and drink including an entire essay on the use of barley porridge as a medicine.

Cooks and cookbooks arrived in Rome in the second century BCE as part of an increased interest in Greek culture. Livy (39.6) records that the first slaves who specialized in preparing lavish meals arrived with Gnaeus Manlius Vulso's army after victories in the Greek East in 187 BCE. Livy's account describes the inflated prices for these slave cooks and the new regard for their skills as indicative of a growing corruption by foreign luxury in Rome. This information echoes the contemporary evidence of Cato the Elder, who famously complained that a cook cost more than a horse; Pliny the Elder (*Natural History* 9.67) caps this by declaring that in the current day, a single fish costs more than Cato's cook! Cato's *De agri cultura* (On Agriculture) provides a store of information and advice for landowners, and the recipes may derive from a handbook kept on the property by the *vilicus*, or estate manager, as Pliny the Elder describes in *Natural History* 2.15. The text also contains a number of traditional recipes for preserving food and remedies for animal and human ailments. The inclusion of recipes in agricultural handbooks continues in later texts such as Marcus Terentius Varro's *De agri cultura* (late second to first century BCE) and Columella's *De re rustica* (mid-first century CE).

Despite the opposition of conservatives like Cato, Roman appetites grew with the expanding empire, and dining increased in status and complexity. Cooking continued to be the domain of specialized domestic slaves, further subdivided into a team consisting of the head chef (*archimagirus*), a sous chef (*vicarius supra cocos*), and assistants (*coci*); slaves were even trained in serving and especially carving, as in Petronius' *Satyrica*. Relying on their expert staff, Roman gourmets competed to present the most elaborate and expensive dishes to their guests. The most famous cookbook of antiquity, the *De re coquinaria* (On Cooking) transmitted under the name "Apicius," reflects the culture of expertise and conspicuous consumption that defined Roman imperial tables. "Apicius" was the cognomen of several Roman gourmets, beginning in the early first century BCE, and probably became attached to the text as an indicator of luxury as there is no evidence that any of the historical individuals were authors. The best attested Apicius, Marcus Gavius Apicius (*Prosopographia Imperii Romani Saeculi*[2] G 91), was a wealthy gourmet who lived under the emperors Augustus and Tiberius. In a notorious anecdote about this Apicius, upon discovering his fortune had dwindled to a mere 10 million *sestertii*, the gourmet committed suicide rather than curtail his gastronomic expenditures (Seneca *Ad Helviam* 8; Martial 10.73). The Apician text is first attested in 400 CE and the earliest manuscripts date from the ninth century CE. This compilation of recipes seems to derive from the late first century CE onward, and probably started as a nucleus of recipes translated from Greek cookbooks; the language is concise and nonliterary, indicating a functional purpose for experienced but only moderately literate kitchen staff.

Many of the recipes feature strongly flavored sauces composed of various crushed herbs (rue, lovage, mint) and expensive imported spices (black pepper, asafetida) pounded with grape derivatives such as must or vinegar, and the ubiquitous Roman condiment, *liquamen* or *garum*, a pungently salty liquid extracted from fermented fish. Especially elaborate dishes, such as the *patina Apiciana*, incorporate a variety of exotic ingredients through intricate cooking techniques: the recipe calls for highly seasoned sows udder, fish, chicken, and breasts of songbirds ground to a forcemeat and layered with egg and thin crepes, and finally recommends an expensive silver platter for optimal presentation (Apicius 4.141)!

[*See also* Food and Drink, Roman.]

BIBLIOGRAPHY
Primary Works
Apicius. *De re coquinaria*. Translated by Christopher W. Grocock and Sally Grainger. Totnes, U.K.: Prospect, 2006. Latin text, English translation and commentary.
Athenaeus. *The Deipnosophists*. 7 vols. Translated by Charles Burton Gulick. Cambridge, Mass.: Harvard University Press, 1927–1941. Loeb Classical Library.
Athenaeus. *The Learned Banqueters*. 2 vols. Translated by S. Douglas Olsen. Cambridge, Mass.: Harvard University Press, 2006–. Loeb Classical Library. Updated edition and new translation of Athenaeus, still in progress.
Cato, Marcus Porcius. *On Agriculture*. Translated by William Davis Hooper. Revised by Harrison Boyd Ash. Cambridge Mass.: Harvard University Press, 1934. Loeb Classical Library.
Columella, Lucius Junius Moderatus. *On Agriculture*. 3 vols. Translated by Harrison Boyd Ash, Edward Seymour Forster, and Edward Hoch Heffner. Cambridge, Mass.: Harvard University Press, 1941–1955.
Galen. *Galen: On Food and Diet*. Translated by Mark Grant. New York and London: Routledge, 2000. Translation of selections from Galen's works.
Olson, S. Douglas, and Alexander Sens, eds. *Archestratos of Gela: Greek Culture and Cuisine in the Fourth Century BCE*. New York and Oxford: Oxford University Press, 2000. Text, translation, and commentary.
Varro, Marcus Terentius. *On Agriculture*. Translated by William Davis Hooper. Revised by Harrison Boyd Ash. Cambridge, Mass.: Harvard University Press, 1935. Loeb Classical Library. Combined in a single volume with Cato, *On Agriculture*.

Secondary Works
Berthiaume, Guy. *Les rôles du mageiros: étude sur la boucherie, la cuisine, et le sacrifice dans la Grèce ancienne*. Leiden, The Netherlands: Brill, 1982.
Dalby, Andrew. *Siren Feasts: A History of Food and Gastronomy in Greece*. London and New York: Routledge, 1996.
Dalby, Andrew, and Sally Grainger. *The Classical Cookbook*. Los Angeles: J. Paul Getty Museum, 1996.

Introductory essay on ancient cooking; recipes adapted from classical texts.

Lowe, J. C. B. "Cooks in Plautus." *Classical Antiquity* 4 (1985): 72–102.

Salza Prina Ricotti, Eugenia. *Dining as a Roman Emperor: How to Cook Ancient Roman Recipes Today.* Rome: "L'Erma" di Bretschneider, 1995.

Wilkins, John. *The Boastful Chef: The Discourse of Food in Ancient Greek Comedy.* New York and Oxford: Oxford University Press, 2000.

Wilkins, John, David Harvey, and Mike Dobson, eds. *Food in Antiquity.* Exeter, U.K.: University of Exeter Press, 1995. Diverse collection of essays on specialized topics in ancient food.

J. Mira Seo

COPTIC ART

See Christian Art, *subentry* Egypt.

CORINTH

Ancient Corinth occupied a territory of immense strategic and commercial value, straddling the western portion of the isthmus joining the Peloponnesus to the rest of mainland Greece and controlling the fertile plain along the northeastern Peloponnesian coast. The region was settled in the Neolithic and Bronze ages, but only achieved its strategic potential after Dorian occupation in the post-Mycenaean period (tenth century BCE and later). By the eighth century BCE, the early Dorian settlements consolidated into a polis centered at the base of the Acrocorinthus, a steep hill 1,887 feet (575 meters) in height. The Acrocorinthus was too inaccessible to serve as the center of civic or religious life, as did the Acropolis in Athens, but it did provide an excellent vantage point and a defensible place of refuge in time of war.

Corinth established harbors on both her Saronic Gulf and Gulf of Corinth coasts; Cenchreae in the east and Lechaeum in the west. The polis was eventually able to construct a paved road across the narrowest portion of its territory on the isthmus, the *diolchos*, which became the preferred transit route from the Aegean Sea to the Gulf of Corinth and the seas beyond, avoiding the long and sometimes treacherous circumvention of the Peloponnesus. Passengers and cargo could disembark at one of the ports, cross the *diolchos*, and continue their journey on the other side of the isthmus. Though disputed by scholars, it may even have been possible to transport fully loaded cargo vessels across the *diolchos*, or at least empty warships—penteconters and triremes.

The Early Polis. Monarchy may have survived into the earliest period of Corinth's existence as a polis, but was forcibly ended around the middle of the eighth century BCE by the aristocratic Bacchiad clan, an association of several hundred families linked by marriage. In this period, Corinth emerged as one of the most dynamic early poleis. The size of the settlements in Corinthian territory grew rapidly, indicating substantial population growth. Corinth succeeded in expanding its territory on the isthmus by seizing land, including the sacred Perachora Peninsula, from its neighbor to the north, Megara. Early Corinthian pottery is attested throughout the Mediterranean, evidence of an active and growing commerce. From the middle decades of the eighth century, Corinth also established a number of colonies, including Corcyra (modern-day Corfu) in the Ionian Sea and Syracuse in Sicily. The sum of these developments was the establishment of Corinth as a leading center of commerce. Its consequent wealth is attested in its major temples and public buildings. Corinth remained an important commercial center throughout its history, though gradually eclipsed by Athens.

The domination of the Bacchiads was abruptly ended by the rise of one of Greece's earliest tyrannies, that of Cypselus. Himself a Bacchiad, though probably not from one of the more powerful families, Cypselus rallied the discontented elements in the state to establish his rule. During a seventy-year period of dominance by Cypselus and his son, Periander, Corinth's commercial wealth and influence continued to grow. As was the pattern with tyrannies elsewhere, the Cypselids eventually fell in the third generation, and a narrow oligarchy was established. This government proved remarkably stable, producing few leaders of note, but avoiding the destructive internal conflicts that plagued many poleis in the sixth and fifth centuries BCE.

The major threat to early Corinth's political independence was the large and powerful neighboring polis of Argos. The Argive tyrant Pheidon made several abortive attempts to conquer Corinth in the seventh century. In the sixth century, Corinth allied itself with more distant Sparta, as a counterweight to Argos, thus becoming part of Sparta's anti-Argive alliance system, eventually known as the Peloponnesian League. Corinth's wealth and naval prowess made it a valuable member of the league. Within the Peloponnesus, Corinth's and Sparta's strategic interests usually coincided—avoiding war; supporting narrow, oligarchic regimes; and isolating Argos. Beyond the Peloponnesus, Corinth's interest in naval commerce often conflicted with Sparta's agrarian and isolationist tendencies. Despite differences in their economies and cultures, however, Sparta's and Corinth's strengths complimented each other, and, with few exceptions, they remained reliable allies until the early fourth century BCE.

Classical Corinth. Corinth participated in the Hellenic League formed to meet the threat of Persian invasion in the 480s, contributing forty ships to the major naval engagements at Thermopylae and Salamis, the second-largest contingent after that of Athens, and five thousand troops to the Spartan-led army at Plataea. Corinth and the other Peloponnesian League states withdrew from the Hellenic League as the Persian threat receded, leaving Athens a clear field to pursue the war into Persian territory and organize the liberated Greek poleis into the Delian League. By the 460s, Corinth began to view Athens and the Delian League as a threat to its own colonial and commercial interests. It spent the remainder of the fifth century pressuring Sparta and its other allies to take a stand against Athenian expansion, and was instrumental in bringing about the first and second Peloponnesian Wars, pitting the Peloponnesian League against the Athenian Empire.

These wars proved extremely costly to Corinth and did not bring about any lasting improvement of her position vis-à-vis her archrival, Athens. As a result, Corinth's long-standing oligarchy and its loyalty to Sparta were shaken. In the early fourth century Corinth joined an anti-Spartan coalition that included her longtime enemies, Argos and Athens, triggering the so-called Corinthian War against Sparta and its remaining allies. Soon after, the Corinthian oligarchy was overthrown by democratic elements supported by Argos and Athens, and steps were taken toward the unification (*isopoliteia*) of Corinth and Argos. The King's Peace, brokered by Persia, put a swift end to Corinth's democracy and its union with Argos, and Corinth returned to its status as a Spartan ally. Corinth was not a factor in the subsequent conflicts of fourth-century Greece, but was repeatedly thrust into the limelight by its strategic location.

Corinth in Hellenistic and Roman Times. After his victory at Chaeronea in 338 BCE, Philip II of Macedon garrisoned the Acrocorinthus and consolidated his

Temple of Apollo, Corinth. PHOTOGRAPH BY ROBERT B. KEBRIC

control of Greece by convening the Greek states at Corinth and forming the League of Corinth. In 243 BCE, Aratus of Sicyon ended the Macedonian occupation and brought Corinth into the Achaean League. The Roman conquest of Greece in 196 BCE restored Corinth's independence, but in 146 BCE the Roman general Lucius Mummius made an example of Corinth by destroying the city for its role in resisting Roman rule. The site was abandoned until a Roman colony was established there a century later.

[See also Greece; Peloponnesian League; Peloponnesian Wars; and Peloponnesus.]

BIBLIOGRAPHY

O'Neill, J. G. Ancient Corinth, with a Topographical Sketch of the Corinthia. Part I: From the Earliest Times to 404 B.C. Baltimore: The Johns Hopkins Press; London: H. Milford, 1930–.

Salmon, J. B. Wealthy Corinth: A History of the City to 338 B.C. Oxford: Clarendon Press; New York: Oxford University Press, 1984.

Will, Edouard. Korinthiaka: Recherches sur l'histoire et le civilisation de Corinthe des origines aux guerres médiques. Paris: E. de Boccard, 1955.

Ronald P. Legon

CORINTHIAN LEAGUE

See Greece, subentry Classical Age; and Philip II.

CORINTHIAN WAR

The Corinthian War (395–386 BCE) arose out of Spartan hubris, grievances of other Greek states, and Sparta's belligerence toward the Persian Empire. The Spartans after their victory in the Peloponnesian War unwisely pursued dominance on the mainland and in the Aegean, overextending their limited demographic and economic power. Their behavior alienated their former allies Corinth and Thebes, while their hereditary rival Argos sought to humble Sparta, and Athens yearned to become a major power again. The Spartans also provoked the Persian king Artaxerxes II, first by supporting the king's brother Cyrus in a rebellion against the king and then by sporadic anti-Persian military campaigns on the coast of Anatolia.

An aggressive campaign there by the new Spartan king Agesilaus was the last straw. The Persians mobilized a large navy under the Athenian admiral Conon to seize control of the Aegean from the Spartans, while Persian financial support incited factions in Thebes, Argos, Corinth, and Athens to form an anti-Spartan coalition. The defeat and death in Boeotia of Lysander, author of Sparta's victory over the Athenians in the Peloponnesian War, led to general war in 395 BCE.

The Spartans recalled Agesilaus' army to help them deal with the mainland crisis; before its return, the opposing armies fought a major hoplite battle near Corinth at Nemea in 394 BCE in which the Spartans outflanked and rolled up their opponents' battle line. Agesilaus' army fought the allies in a bloody battle at Coronea near Thebes in which, ominously for Spartan power, the Theban phalanx broke the Spartan battle line after the Spartans had routed the other allied forces. Thereafter the land war became a stalemate as the anti-Spartan coalition fortified and defended the Isthmus of Corinth. In 390 BCE light-armed peltast mercenaries under the Athenian Iphicrates nearly wiped out two regiments of Spartans, negating Spartan gains elsewhere.

In 394 BCE the Persian fleet smashed Sparta's fleet near the island of Cnidus, ending Spartan control of the Aegean. Conon used Persian funds and the Persian fleet to rebuild Athens' long walls and to start rebuilding an Athenian empire; when Persian support waned, the Athenians achieved considerable success on their own. Athens' growing power and its foolish aid for a Cyprian rebellion against Persia led Artaxerxes to turn against Athens; Athens' subsequent naval defeat and the specter of Persian support for Sparta forced the anti-Spartan allies to accept the King's Peace of 386 BCE. Its terms gave Anatolia to Persia and mandated that other Greek poleis become autonomous. Sparta initially interpreted this provision in its own interest—and then nakedly flouted it.

The war did end Sparta's foolish aspiration for an Aegean empire, but Agesilaus still sought to dominate mainland Greece, sowing the seeds for Sparta's downfall. The war also saw Thebes' emergence as Sparta's rival in land warfare, the increased importance of mercenaries and light-armed troops, and the ability of Persian kings to shape and direct Greek affairs for their own purposes. These trends continued until the rise of Macedonia.

[*See also* Agesilaus; Athens; Cnidus; Corinth; Phocis; *and* Sparta.]

BIBLIOGRAPHY

Cartledge, Paul. *Agesilaos and the Crisis of Sparta*. Baltimore: Johns Hopkins University Press, 1987. Excellent topical treatment of Agesilaus and Sparta's decline by the foremost scholar on Sparta.

Hamilton, Charles D. *Sparta's Bitter Victories: Politics and Diplomacy in the Corinthian War*. Ithaca, N.Y.: Cornell University Press, 1979. The most detailed account of the war in English.

James M. Williams

CORNELIA

(c. 190–102 BCE), daughter, wife, and mother of famous Romans. The mother of the Gracchi, Cornelia became famous in her own right. Her much older husband, Tiberius Sempronius Gracchus, was an established political figure at the time of their famously happy marriage, and they had twelve children together. Widowed, Cornelia devoted herself to her surviving children, only three of whom lived to be adults. She saw to it that they were educated by leading intellectuals. She married her daughter Sempronia to a relative, the famous Scipio Aemilianus (Scipio the Younger), and ignited the political ambitions of her sons Tiberius Sempronius Gracchus and Gaius Sempronius Gracchus, the brothers known as "the Gracchi."

Legends, many of them obvious political fabrications, surround the stages of Cornelia's life: her betrothal to Gracchus senior (until then an enemy of her father), his readiness to die in her place, her wish to be known as "mother of the Gracchi" rather than daughter or mother-in-law of famous generals, her put-down of a Campanian woman who was displaying her jewelry with the comment that Cornelia's children were her jewels, her refusal of an offer of marriage from the Ptolemaic king of Egypt, and her withdrawal to her villa on the Bay of Naples, where she spent her old age reminiscing proudly to other celebrities about the deeds of her dead father Scipio Africanus and her sons.

Such legendary anecdotes, together with examples of her sayings and her prose, circulated for generations after her death in the final years of the second century BCE. The biographer Cornelius Nepos has preserved a letter supposedly from Cornelia to her son Gaius warning him against copying his brother's radicalism in further political agitation (Horsfall, trans., pp. 41–43). A statue to her with the inscription "Cornelia daughter of Scipio mother of the Gracchi," placed in the Porticus Octaviae by the emperor Augustus' regime, was later described by Pliny the Elder and may have been (or been based on) one erected by Gracchan supporters in the second century BCE. Even orators like Cicero, who deplored the politics of the Gracchi, admired Cornelia for her Latin, and she was upheld by successive writers into Christian times as a model of Roman motherhood, of prose style, and of dignified endurance of grief.

[*See also* Empresses and Imperial Women; Gracchi; Scipio Aemilianus; Scipio Africanus; Widows, Roman; *and* Women, *subentry* Women in Rome.]

BIBLIOGRAPHY

Dixon, Suzanne. *Cornelia, Mother of the Gracchi*. London and New York: Routledge, 2007.

Horsfall, Nicholas, trans. *Cornelius Nepos: A Selection, Including the Lives of Cato and Atticus*. Oxford: Clarendon Press; New York: Oxford University Press, 1989. Includes introductions and commentary.

Plutarch. *Roman Lives: A Selection of Eight Roman Lives*. Translated by Robin Waterfield. Oxford: Oxford University Press, 1999. See the lives of Tiberius Gracchus and Gaius Gracchus.

Suzanne Dixon

Cos

The island of Cos lies off the southeastern corner of modern Turkey (ancient Asia Minor). Long and narrow in shape, it covers about 112 square miles (290 square kilometers). A low spine of hills runs along its southeastern edge. The island is fertile and agriculturally productive; its wine was exported.

The political history of Cos is poorly attested. Cos was settled by Dorians—according to Herodotus (7.99.3), specifically by people from Epidaurus—and belonged to the Dorian hexapolis or pentapolis. According to Homer the Coans at one time ruled the neighboring islands of Calymnos and Nisyros. Tyrants, possibly supported by the Persians, are attested for the early fifth century. Cos had entered the Delian League by 451/0 and remained under Athenian authority until perhaps 411, when a revolt has been inferred. The island seems to have been under the sway of the Hecatomnid satraps of Caria in the fourth century, and it participated in the Social War against Athens in 357–355. Cos remained under Persian/Carian authority until Alexander's conquest of the Persian Empire. With the death of Alexander the Great and the emergence of the Hellenistic kingdoms, southeastern Asia Minor became a contested region. In 309–308, Ptolemy I Soter used Cos as a base for his efforts to recover southwestern Asia Minor; his wife Berenice gave birth on the island to Ptolemy II Philadelphus in 308. This circumstance led to close connections between Egypt and Cos in the years when the island was under Ptolemaic suzerainty, namely from about 280 to 197. Cos enjoyed considerable autonomy under Ptolemaic rule and was praised by the court poets Theocritus and Callimachus. Cos is the setting for a number of the mimes of Herodas.

In the Archaic and Classical periods the island supported more than one polis. Two are attested for certain. Astypalaea, situated on the northwestern end of the island, was the home to the cult of Asclepius before the *synoikismos* (see below). Cos Meropis was located at the site of the later town of Cos (the modern Chora) at the northeastern tip of the island. Its chief god was Apollo Cyparrisius, whose sanctuary—known epigraphically from the fifth century BCE—occupied the site later usurped by Asclepius. There is some ambiguous evidence for additional poleis on Cos before the *synoikismos*. Halasarna, an important deme site in the Hellenistic and Roman periods, is a candidate; it was occupied from at least the sixth century BCE and had a temple perhaps dedicated to Apollo Pythios.

In 366/5 BCE the Coan poleis underwent a *synoikismos* or synoecism, that is, a unification that terminated the political independence of Astypalaea and any other poleis on the island and created a single island-wide political entity. The transformation was marked by the refoundation of Cos Meropis as simply Cos. The exact circumstances that led to this change remain debated, but in general it seems likely that the Coan decision to synoecize was influenced by Mausolus' establishment of Halicarnassus as his capital with enforced migration of inhabitants from the towns of the Halicarnassian peninsula. On Cos some population movement must have occurred to create the new city, but epigraphic evidence and archaeological work demonstrates that the old urban centers continued to be inhabited. They became demes (*dēmoi*) in the new Coan political structure, and a persistent local identity can be seen in inscriptions of the Hellenistic and Roman imperial period. This is especially true of the former polis of Astypalaea, which was now known as Isthmos but exhibited an internal structure of three tribes (*phylai*), a peculiarity that may be explained as a remnant of an earlier polis organization.

Cos was famous for its wine, flavored with seawater. Although attested prices suggest that the Coan product did not figure among the high-quality wines, it was widely exported. Coan wine is attested explicitly as early as the fourth century BCE, but it seems to have enjoyed increasing appeal in the second and first centuries, spreading out of the eastern Mediterranean into Italy. Coan amphorae with their distinctive double-barreled handles have been found throughout the Mediterranean and even in India; they seem to have served as the model for the Dressel 4 amphorae produced in the west. However, both the handle type and the wine were also a regional product.

In cultural and religious terms the most important Coan contribution to the larger Greco-Roman world was surely its worship of Asclepius and its school of medicine. After the *synoikismos* the cult of Asclepius was established at the sanctuary of Apollo Cyparissius, which lay a few miles from the town of Cos nestled against a low set of hills with a spectacular view of the sea and the mainland. The Hellenistic period saw an expansion of the sanctuary with the construction of numerous buildings and the articulation of a terraced setting. Unlike at Epidaurus in the Argolid, the site of another major sanctuary for Asclepius, there is no indication on Cos of incubation cures. Instead, the Coan medical school promoted the tenets of Hippocratic medicine, emphasizing natural causes for disease and treatment by diet, exercise, and other human interventions. Coan-trained doctors were much in demand. The most famous was perhaps Gaius Stertonius Xenophon, personal physician to the emperor Claudius; Tacitus implicates him in the emperor's assassination by poisoning.

[*See also* Aegean Sea; Asclepius; Caria; Dorians; *and* Epidaurus.]

BIBLIOGRAPHY

Hansen, Mogens Herman, and Thomas Heine Nielsen, eds. *An Inventory of Archaic and Classical Poleis.* Oxford: Oxford University Press, 2004. See pages 752–754.

Sherwin-White, Susan M. *Ancient Cos: An Historical Study from the Dorian Settlement to the Imperial Period.* Hypomnemata 51. Göttingen, Germany: Vandenhoeck & Ruprecht, 1978.

Gary Reger

COSA

Cosa was a Latin *colonia* founded in 273 BCE on land north of Rome confiscated from the Etruscans after the defeat of Vulci in 280 BCE (Velleius Paterculus 1.14.7; Livy *Periochae* 14; Strabo 5.2.8). Located on a hill now known as Ansedonia rising over the coast,

Cosa was easily accessible both from the sea and from the Via Aurelia. The lagoons that flanked the site made fishing an important resource, although otherwise the colony was not particularly prosperous. Apart from its great polygonal walls, there is little evidence for its occupation in the third century BCE. New settlers arrived in the beginning of the second century, which is probably the date of the town plan. Destroyed around 70 BCE, perhaps after an attack by pirates, Cosa was later refounded under Augustus. As early as 80 BCE, however, Cosa seems to have been almost deserted. It was revived under the emperor Caracalla (r. 211–217), during whose reign the portico around the forum and the odeum were restored, a Mithraeum (place of worship for the followers of the mystery cult of Mithraism) was constructed in the basement of the *curia*, and a sanctuary to Liber was erected at the southeast end of the forum.

The new town did not last long, however, and by the fourth century only the sanctuary of Liber was periodically visited. In the early sixth century some occupation of the ruins is attested by pottery, and the remains of a church have been found built onto the basilica. Perhaps at the same time the *arx* or citadel was occupied by a fortified farm, subsequently transformed into a small fortified outpost under Byzantine control. This was abandoned in the late sixth or early seventh century. That the occupation of the town was intermittent may have been because, already in the early Empire, malaria was hyperendemic on the coast of Tuscany. One of the last textual references to Cosa comes from the work of Claudius Rutilius Namatianus. In his *De reditu suo*, describing a coastal voyage made in 417, the author remarks that the site was in ruins.

Excavations of Cosa were carried out from 1948 to 1998 under the auspices of the American Academy in Rome, directed by Frank Edward Brown. His excavations (1948–1972) traced the city plan, the temples of the *arx*, and the buildings of the forum. Subsequently Russell T. Scott excavated a number of houses. In the 1990s excavations by Elizabeth Fentress aimed at understanding the history of the site between the imperial period and the Middle

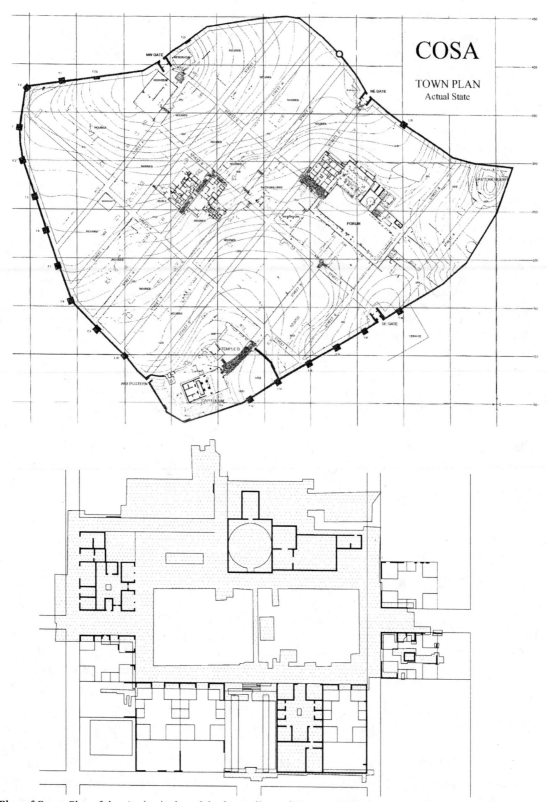

Plan of Cosa. Plan of the city (*top*); plan of the forum (*bottom*). PLAN BY F. E. BROWN WITH MODIFICATIONS BY ELIZABETH FENTRESS

Ages. Sample excavations took place over the whole site, with larger excavations on the eastern height and around the forum.

Within the irregular city walls the plan of the site represents a subtle adaptation of an orthogonal plan to the complicated topography of the hill. The forum was found on a saddle between two heights, with the sacred area, the temple of the Capitoline Triad, linked to it by a broad processional way. One side of the forum was devoted to public buildings, including a basilica, a *curia-comitium* complex, and a temple with a polygonal podium attributed by Brown to Concordia, although its terra-cottas indicate that it was more likely dedicated to Demeter or the Cereres. Brown's supposition that the other three sides of the forum were given over to buildings that he called *atria publica* has been demonstrated false by the excavation between 1995 and 1999 of the House of Diana on the southwest side of the forum (see Fentress). This was a much larger house on a standard atrium plan, very similar to that of the House of Sallust in Pompeii. Built around 170 BCE, it was entirely rebuilt in the Augustan period, from which we have a fine series of frescoes and mosaics. In the 50s it seems to have become the house of Lucius Titinius Glaucus Lucretianus; a small sanctuary to the goddess Diana was added in the rear garden.

[*See also* Archaeology, *subentry* Sites in Italy; *and* Latins.]

BIBLIOGRAPHY

Brown, Frank E. *Cosa, the Making of a Roman Town.* Ann Arbor: University of Michigan Press, 1980.

Brown, Frank Edward, Emeline Hill Richardson, and L. Richardson Jr. *Cosa III: The Buildings of the Forum.* Memoirs of the American Academy in Rome, vol. 37. University Park: Pennsylvania State University Press, 1993.

Fentress, Elizabeth, et al. *Cosa V: An Intermittent Town, Excavations 1991–1997.* Memoirs of the American Academy in Rome, supplementary vol. 2. Ann Arbor: University of Michigan Press, 2004.

McCann, Ann Marguerite, Joanne Bourgeois, et al. *The Roman Port and Fishery of Cosa: A Center of Ancient Trade.* Princeton, N.J.: Princeton University Press, 1987.

Elizabeth Fentress

COSMOGONY AND COSMOLOGY

See Causation, Theories of; Creation Myths; *and* Teleology.

COSMOPOLITANISM

In ancient Greece and Rome, many people claimed to live as citizens of the world, as "cosmopolitans." They did not all mean the same thing by this claim. Few of them meant that they were literally citizens of a world-state; even Rome at its greatest extent did not suggest to many that a Roman citizen was automatically a world citizen. But there are various ways to conceive of "citizenship" as a metaphor.

For each of these ways, there can be negative and positive sides to the cosmopolitan's claim. On the one hand, the cosmopolitan might mean to deny that he is an active citizen of any local community. On the other hand, he might mean to insist that he shares some sort of "citizenship" with human beings outside his native community. Of course, the cosmopolitan might wish to do both these things simultaneously. It is often difficult to determine whether a particular cosmopolitanism is merely negative (rejecting local ties), merely positive (embracing fellow cosmopolites as well as, implicitly, local compatriots), or both (embracing fellow cosmopolites and rejecting local compatriots).

One might say that one is a "citizen of the world" primarily to record that one does not give much attention to being an active citizen of the local city, without suggesting that one is giving special political attention elsewhere. So Anaxagoras, who preferred quiet contemplation, is said to have defended his withdrawal from the local city by claiming attachment to the cosmos (Diogenes Laertius 2.7). Other wandering intellectuals, including Democritus of Abdera (fragment 247 Diels and Kranz), seem to have been considered citizens of the world, perhaps more for their comfort in many places than for their intellectual devotion to the cosmos (cf. Diogenes Laertius 9.35). But it is not clear how much positive commitment to fellow cosmopolites such cosmopolitans showed, even if they did establish a widespread community of fellow intellectuals.

One might also say that one is a "citizen of the world" when one is thinking of citizenship as a politically engaged project of pursuing a common good with other human beings. There were several ways of doing this. First, Socrates developed an unusual way of engaging in politics by examining people and thereby helping them (Plato *Apology* 36c3–5 and *Gorgias* 521d6–8), and he shared this with foreigners (Plato *Apology* 23b4–6 and 30a3–5), out of love of humanity (Plato *Euthyphro* 3d5–9), instead of limiting his conception of political action to traditional engagement to support Athenians alone. Early followers of Socrates such as Diogenes the Cynic (Diogenes Laertius 6.63 and 6.38) and Aristippus the Cyrenaic (Xenophon *Memorabilia* 2.1.13) rejected active citizenship in a local community more explicitly, although their commitment to forge a common good with fellow cosmopolites is less clear.

Later followers of Socrates, the Stoics reconciled cosmopolitan aims with traditionally local engagement. They clearly favored serving human beings as such through traditionally local political engagement (Diogenes Laertius 7.121), perhaps by emigrating to another location and working to advise political rulers there (Plutarch *Contradictions of the Stoics* 1043b–d; Seneca the Younger *On Tranquility of Mind* 4.4). But the Stoics did not all agree about whether they owed special service to their compatriots in addition to helping humanity more generally. Nor did they agree about whether citizenship in the cosmos is a special achievement of the wise, who live by right reason, or is a common characteristic of all humans, who possess reason.

The Epicurean community of likeminded folk open to people from throughout the Greek world suggests still another kind of cosmopolitan political engagement, fostering a common good with fellow humans outside a traditional political community. The *Republic* of the founding Stoic Zeno of Citium might have called for a similarly countercultural political community of cosmopolites.

Yet another way of tying cosmopolitanism to politics would be to work for a world-state, perhaps by imperialist means (cf. Herodotus 7.8). Some have thought that cosmopolitanism motivated Alexander the Great (Plutarch *Moralia* 329a–329c), though the evidence for this is slim. It would be natural to find the marriage of cosmopolitanism and imperialism in Roman Stoic texts, such as Cicero's *On Duties* or Marcus Aurelius' *Meditations*, but however much they hint at, they do not develop the notion. In fact, Roman belief that Rome was suited to rule the world (cf. Virgil *Aeneid* 6.851–853) was only sporadically linked to the vocabulary of cosmopolitanism (e.g., Aelius Aristides *To Rome* p. 207, lines 27–29 Jebb).

In addition to the intellectually contemplative cosmopolitans and the various politically engaged cosmopolitans, later antiquity gives us the Christian ideal of fellow citizenship in the City of God (so Augustine; see also Ephesians 2:19). The relation between this cosmopolis and earthly politics was contested for hundreds of years to come.

[*See also* Citizenship, Greek; Citizenship, Roman; *and* Stoicism.]

BIBLIOGRAPHY

Baldry, H. C. *The Unity of Mankind in Greek Thought.* Cambridge, U.K.: Cambridge University Press, 1965.

Brown, Eric. *Stoic Cosmopolitanism.* Cambridge, U.K.: Cambridge University Press, forthcoming.

Konstan, David. "Cosmopolitan Traditions." In *A Companion to Greek and Roman Political Thought*, edited by Ryan K. Balot, pp. 473–484. Chichester, U.K., and Malden, Mass.: Wiley-Blackwell, 2009.

Eric Brown

COSMOS

See Causation, Theories of; *and* Creation.

COUNCIL

The *boulē* was the council in the ancient Greek state. Its name derives from the verb "to will, want," that is, the *boulē* facilitated decision making in the assembly by giving counsel and assisting deliberation. As an institution it dated back to Homeric times, when it referred to councils of nobles whose duty was to advise the king, as with Agamemnon in *Iliad* books 1–2; the king does not appear to have been bound by the advice of the *boulē*.

Most Greek states had a *boulē*. Its power within the state varied, depending on whether its city was democratic or oligarchic. In oligarchic Sparta, the *gerousia*, or council of elders, was limited in membership to thirty (including the kings) and to men over sixty who were full Spartan citizens. Membership was for life, and it is said that election to the *gerousia* was the highest honor any Spartan could attain while living. The *gerousia* was also quite powerful; in addition to the usual function of advice, it served as a check on both royal power and the power of the Spartan *apella* or assembly, as the highest criminal court, as an arbiter of customs and laws, and may also have had significant influence on foreign policy via its counsel to the ephors. The *boulē* of a democratic city, by contrast, would be open to more citizens, have a limited term of office, and prepare legislation for the assembly rather than dictate to it.

Our best evidence is for the Athenian *boulē*. The original Athenian *boulē* was a council of former archons, or the chief magistrates of the state. Membership was for life and was not elective; the number of *bouletai* or councilors was not restricted. This council, called the Areopagus, also served as the highest court in Athens, especially for murder cases. Solon may have added a second, more popular council during his reforms in the 580s BCE in order to provide the function of counsel to the assembly prior to a vote on a decree (the process was called *probouleusis*), but the evidence for this second council is not contemporary. If he did create such a *boulē*, it consisted of four hundred men, one hundred drawn from each of the four tribes.

Cleisthenes reformed the *boulē* in 508 by changing the membership to five hundred, fifty from each of his ten tribes. Representation within the tribe was proportional to the size of the tribal demes. All the properted classes were eligible except the lowest class of *thētai* (wage-earners), ensuring that the *boulē* reserved some power for the moneyed classes in Athens. Over the next two hundred years the Cleisthenic *boulē* underwent some reforms

(selection by lot from a preelected pool, a term limit of a year with no more than two terms of service in a lifetime), but except for two brief hiatuses in 411 and 404/3, when Athens was governed by an oligarchy, it remained largely as he had established it.

In 462/1, Ephialtes removed many of the powers of the Areopagus Council, and those powers devolved onto the *boulē*. The *boulē* now regulated state finances, the armed services, religious matters, public funds and buildings, day-to-day administration, and audited officials after their term of office expired, or even impeached them in office. It became essential to the daily functions of the democratic government, meeting daily except for holidays. To envision democratic Athens without the *boulē* produced by Ephialtes' reforms is nearly impossible: some administrative body was required to set an agenda for the assembly, which was open to all adult male citizens and thus needed a set agenda, and to govern the city in the interim periods between assembly meetings.

In addition to its selection by lot, the *boulē* served as an equalizing force in Athens in other ways. Each tribe held its presidency once during the year, and individuals from that tribe were selected by lot to be the actual president for a day. By the end of the fifth century, councilors were paid, an attempt to encourage the lower classes, who could now serve, to do so. The rich, however, always tended to predominate, making the *boulē* a conservative and stable force in democratic Athens, although the popular assembly was always sovereign.

The *boulē* continued to be a feature of the Greek city into Hellenistic and Roman times. Greek federal leagues, such as the Boeotian, Achaean, and Aetolian leagues, also used *boulai* as well as assemblies in their federal systems. The councilors were drawn from the various cities within the league.

[*See also* Archon; Areopagus; *and* Polis.]

BIBLIOGRAPHY

Larsen, J. A. O. *Representative Government in Greek and Roman History*. Berkeley: University of California Press, 1955.

Rhodes, P. J. *The Athenian Boule.* Oxford: Clarendon Press, 1972.

Rhodes, P. J., and David M. Lewis. *The Decrees of the Greek States.* Oxford: Clarendon Press, 1997. See pp. 11–28, 475–501.

Sarah Bolmarcich

COURTESANS

Prostitution was a familiar feature of the ancient urban landscape. A broad spectrum of individuals engaged in commercial sex: males, females, foreigners, slaves, and freed persons. They worked under the control of others, or functioned as independent contractors. In a world of sharp social divisions, the prostitute, whether courtesan or brothel slave, was considered the antithesis of the respectable citizen wife. The distinction revolved in part around classical attitudes toward the body: by law a free person's body, male or female, could not be assaulted with impunity, unlike that of a slave. Within the realm of prostitution, however, both the Greeks and the Romans differentiated between courtesans and other types of prostitutes. The Greek word *hetaira* (companion) referred to a woman who was maintained by one or two men alone in exchange for sexual favors and companionship at dinner parties and public events. Often she began her career as a brothel slave or *pornē*, but, after buying her freedom, she could amass great wealth, enough to finance a public benefaction, such as a large-scale dedicatory offering. Courtesans were known for their beauty, erudition, and conversational skills as well as for their ability to bewitch men with their charms. Women such as Aspasia, Phrynē (born Muesarete), and Lais were linked to illustrious men and were portrayed as exerting a powerful influence over them.

The Romans also differentiated high-status courtesans from their brothel counterparts. The Latin word *meretrix* (from *mereo*, "earn") denoted the named courtesans of Roman comedy, who functioned as the objects of romantic intrigue and individual passion. The term *scortum* (hide), in contrast, designated the anonymous brothel prostitute, male or female, who might walk the streets or participate in temporary liaisons at dinner parties. As in the case of the Greek terminology, the dividing line between the *meretrix* and other lower-order prostitutes is sometimes blurred, although both types of women are set over against the virtuous *matrona* (Horace *Satires* 1.2). By the early second century BCE, Greek and Roman courtesans plied their trade in Italian cities. The Roman historian Livy praises the courtesan Hispala Faecenia for her role in helping to suppress the Bacchanalian conspiracies of 186 BCE (Livy *History of Rome* 39.9–19). Volumnia Cytheris, a slave actress with the stage name of Lycoris who earned her freedom, may have also been a courtesan. Such women could enter into private contracts with individual men, by which they guaranteed exclusive sexual access in exchange for material support, or *merces annua* (annual wage). Roman courtesans were also the only women not forbidden to consort with elite men by Augustus' *lex Julia* of 18–17 BCE, a law that attempted to regulate the sexual behavior of the upper classes. Indeed, the Roman historian Tacitus states that Vistilia, a woman of senatorial class, registered as a prostitute to avoid prosecution for adultery under this law (Tacitus *Annals* 2.85).

No first-person memoirs of courtesans survive from classical antiquity, although authorship of erotic manuals is attributed to a few. While ancient sources, including letters and dialogues, historiography, philosophy, oratory, and law codes, offer vivid fictive depictions of courtesans, they yield little concrete evidence for the realities of their lives. Courtesans begin to appear regularly as literary characters in the genres of Greek Middle and New Comedy, and in Attic oratory during the second half of the fourth century BCE. In *Against Neaira*, a private law court speech delivered by Apollodorus, the courtesan Neaira is prosecuted for transgressing Athenian marriage laws in order to defame her lover, Stephanus, the orator's rival. In Menander's *Samia*, an Athenian citizen threatens to cast off the title character, a former courtesan, because he mistakenly suspects her of bearing a child to his son. The ambiguity of the courtesan's status in this play and elsewhere (she is called a *hetaira*, a concubine and a wife interchangeably) made her indispensable to comic plots of mistaken identity. The playwrights Plautus and Terence adapted this genre to the Roman stage and retained the stock character of the courtesan, along with her Greek name, yet placed her in a distinctly Roman context. Another major source is book 13 of Athenaeus' second-century CE work *Dining Sophists*, which provides an extensive collection of literary quotations relating to courtesans from all periods. In addition to the genres mentioned above, he quotes Hellenistic treatises on courtesans that chronicled their names and nicknames, their various lovers, and their witticisms at table. Also popular during the imperial Roman period were the humorous psychological sketches of courtesans as found in the fictional works of the Greek writers Lucian and Alciphron.

[*See also* Aspasia; Menander; *and* Prostitution, Greek.]

BIBLIOGRAPHY
Primary Works
Apollodorus. *Apollodoros Against Neaira: (Demosthenes) 59*. Edited and translated by Christopher Carey. Warminster, U.K.: Aris & Phillips, 1992. Greek text along with commentary and translation.
Athenaeus of Naucratis. *The Deipnosophists*. Vol. 6, *Books 13–14.653b*. Edited and translated by Charles Burton Gulick. Loeb Classical Library 327. Cambridge, Mass.: Harvard University Press; London: W. Heinemann, 1927–1941. Reprinted 1993.
Lucian. *Chattering Courtesans and Other Sardonic Sketches*. Translated by Keith Sidwell. London and New York: Penguin Books, 2004.
Menander. *Menander*. 3 vols. Edited and translated by W. G. Arnott. Loeb Classical Library. Cambridge, Mass.: Harvard University Press, 1979–2000. Volume 3 includes *Samia*.
Menander. *Plays and Fragments*. Translated by Norma Miller. London and New York: Penguin, 1987.
Plautus. *Asinaria: The One about the Asses*. Edited and translated by John Henderson. Madison: University of Wisconsin Press, 2006. Latin text, commentary, and an English translation.

Secondary Works
Davidson, James. *Courtesans and Fishcakes: The Consuming Passions of Classical Athens*. New York: St. Martin's Press, 1998. An entertaining account of prostitution in classical Athens and its social and political implications for citizen men.
Faraone, Christopher A., and Laura K. McClure, eds. *Prostitutes and Courtesans in the Ancient World*. Madison: University of Wisconsin Press, 2006. A collection of essays that explores prostitution from ancient Mesopotamia through the early Christian period.
Hamel, Deborah. *Trying Neaira: The Story of a True Courtesan's Scandalous Life in Ancient Greece*. New Haven, Conn.: Yale University Press, 2003. A reconstruction of the life of the historical courtesan Neaira, from her brothel childhood in Corinth to her trial at Athens.
Henry, Madeleine M. *Prisoner of History: Aspasia of Miletus*. New York: Oxford University Press, 1995. Examines the tradition surrounding Aspasia, the famous concubine of the Athenian statesman Pericles.
Krenkel, Werner A. "Prostitution." In *Civilization of the Ancient Mediterranean: Greece and Rome*, edited by Michael Grant and Rachel Kitzinger, pp. 1291–1297. New York: Scribners, 1988. A frequently cited essay on prostitution in the Greco-Roman world.
McGinn, Thomas A. J. *The Economy of Prostitution in the Roman World: A Study of Social History and the Brothel*. Ann Arbor: University of Michigan Press, 2004. Explores the physical venues of Roman prostitution, such as brothels, circuses, and private houses, and their economic impact.
McGinn, Thomas. *Prostitution, Sexuality, and the Law in Ancient Rome*. Oxford: Oxford University Press, 1998. The first detailed study of prostitution in the Roman world, with emphasis on the laws governing female prostitution.

Laura K. McClure

CRAFTS AND ARTISANS

One means of understanding ancient Greece and Rome is through the study of archaeological remains—namely, objects made by human hands. These objects include both the monumental arts (such as architecture, painting, and sculpture) and more mundane, crafted objects that are used in daily life (such as knives and hair combs), along with practically everything in between. Any attempt to define exactly what constitutes an ancient craft is fraught with problems, however. Ever since the Renaissance period in Italy, the hierarchical division between art and craft—and artist (genius) and artisan (skilled worker)—has been set. In part this hierarchy is attributable to Giorgio Vasari, who elevated Italian Renaissance artists to a quasi-divine status in his influential multivolume *Lives of the Artists* (first published in 1550 and enlarged in 1568). The creations of artists were, and continue to be, distinguished over and above crafts and their anonymous makers.

Although these values have been entrenched for more than six hundred years, it is important to bear in mind that what we may identify as a craft, as opposed to art, may not have been sharply defined in ancient Greece and Rome. In fact, the word *technē* in Greek and *ars* in Latin were used to refer to both art and craft interchangeably. Likewise the term *technitēs* could be used in Greek to describe a skilled laborer as well as an artist, and in Latin the terms *faber* or *artifex* could describe the same. For the present purpose, "crafts" will be broadly defined so as to include the making of any handmade durable object, which may or may not have had an aesthetic value. Crafts therefore encompass the whole range of man-made objects, from paintings, sculptures, and buildings to ceramics, textiles, glassware, furniture, and utilitarian objects.

Artists and Artisans. This is not to suggest that ancient artisans should be equated with artists, in our modern use of the term, or that artisans enjoyed prestige in their respective societies. In fact, with few exceptions, ancient writers denigrate artisans, many of whom came from servile stock. In Greece skilled laborers, whether free or slave, could also be referred to as *banausos* (a rather insulting term for a craftsman or artisan, with the meaning also of vulgarity or bad taste), meaning that in the eyes of the more elite segment of society these laborers were thought to belong to an uneducated underclass, existing only on the margins of society. A similar sentiment prevailed in ancient Rome as well, with artisans often described as sordid and lowly.

Two passages, among the hundreds that survive on this topic, will serve to illuminate just how ignoble artisans were perceived to be. Plutarch, writing in the early second century CE about famous Classical Greek masterpieces (fifth century BCE) and their makers, sharply observes, "It does not necessarily follow that if a work is delightful because of its gracefulness, the man who made it is worthy of our serious regard. . . . No one, no gifted young man, upon seeing the Zeus of Pheidias at Olympia or the Hera of Polykleitos at Argos ever actually wants to be Pheidias or Polykleitos" (Plutarch *Pericles* 2.1, from Burford, p. 12). According to Plutarch, even the most revered sculpture of ancient Greece does not elevate the status of its maker. Likewise Cicero, in his discussion of occupations suitable for noble aristocrats, makes clear that no Roman of any standing would engage in manual crafts. He writes, "All craftsmen, too, are engaged in vulgar activities, for a workshop or factory can have nothing noble about it" (Cicero *De officiis* 1.42). The only craft that Cicero isolates as having any possible merit is architecture, which requires intelligence over manual skill and therefore would be an appropriate profession for someone of middle rank, though not of the aristocracy. Nonetheless, Cicero—and Pliny the Elder in the *Natural History*—do praise good craftsmanship and their own abilities to recognize it, much like an art connoisseur in our modern use of the word.

Despite the rhetoric of Plutarch and Cicero, among many others, it is important to bear in mind that the wealthy members of ancient Greek and Roman society who scorned artisans also voraciously consumed the goods made by them. Although most artisans remain anonymous, these same individuals made the plates and vessels from which others ate and drank, wove the cloth that adorned others, carved the statues that decorated public spaces, and built the ships that sent goods abroad, among the myriad other possibilities. More specifically, the very objects made by "vulgar" hands were the same objects that could confer prestige upon the owners of the objects.

For example, the bronze statue of the Charioteer at Delphi, part of a larger sculptural ensemble that dates to the Classical period (c. 470 BCE), celebrates an individual's victory in a chariot race. Part of the inscription at the base of the sculpture proclaims,

"Polyzalos [a tyrant of a Greek colony in Sicily] dedicated me." The statue, displayed publicly at Delphi, would have stood as a visual testimony to the achievements of the winner and, equally important, to his social standing as a wealthy aristocrat capable of commissioning a monumental bronze sculptural ensemble (included in the grouping would also have been a horse, a chariot, and possibly a groomsman). The artisans responsible for creating the sculptural ensemble remain anonymous and nearly invisible, however. The historical focus when studying this ensemble is on the owner of the object, not on its maker.

Likewise, the hoard of 118 silver vessels recovered from the House of Menander at Pompeii, buried by Mount Vesuvius' eruption in 79 CE, undoubtedly procured prestige for the owners as they displayed their enormous wealth to guests at banquets, which could be rather extravagant affairs. The silver vessels were adorned with a whole range of finely executed imagery, including animal and vegetal motifs and hunting and mythological scenes. Our modern-day interest in the vessels focuses primarily on the owners of the objects and on what the objects can tell us about the lives of the city's wealthy individuals. The artisans responsible for creating these vessels remain frustratingly silent.

Artisans and the Gods. Although artisans tended to be slaves, former slaves, or foreigners, their skills and their crafts were integral to the shaping of the economic, political, social, and material life of ancient Greece and Rome. Society thus depended on artisans and their technical (manual) skills to produce the objects that individuals desired but could not create for themselves. In fact, so integral were artisans in the workings of Greco-Roman society that even gods could be closely associated with crafts. Hephaestus (Roman Vulcan) was the god of fire, smiths, and metalworking, and his creations are celebrated in ancient literary sources. For example, he produces the arms for the gods in the Gigantomachy, and in Homer's *Iliad* (18.373–379 and 614–615) he fabricates all kinds of wonderful objects, including Achilles' new shield and automata (such as self-propelled tripods). On Greek vases the smith god is often portrayed at his forge completing the new armor for Achilles with Thetis, Achilles' mother, standing by—as depicted, for example, in the interior of the Berlin Foundry Cup. An attribute of Hephaestus in Greek art is the exomis, or short chiton, worn with one shoulder bare—the typical garb of workers.

For all his admired work, Hephaestus, like his mortal counterparts, was seen as marginalized, an outsider among the pantheon of gods. Most notably, he is represented as lame. Vases also depict Hephaestus on muleback, unable to walk on his own, as he, having been expelled from Mount Olympus, is readmitted on account of his unsurpassed skill in metalworking. In Roman depictions of Vulcan, the god's physical maladies tend to be downplayed. Instead Vulcan is often depicted wearing the *pilleus*, a cap typically associated in daily life with Roman freedmen and artisans. This attribute unequivocally reinforces the god's marginal status. Vulcan is portrayed as a typical Roman artisan, hard at work at his craft and largely undistinguishable as a god.

Athena (Roman Minerva), the preeminent patron goddess of crafts and war, also occupies a rather ambiguous place in Greco-Roman thought, despite her central position as the patron deity of Athens. The story of her birth sets the stage for her paradoxical nature. Athena was born from the head of Zeus, with the likely assistance of Hephaestus himself. Homer describes her as skillful in weaving—hence the epithet Ergane (*erganē* means "worker")—and as fearless in battle (*Iliad* 5 passim). With her dual-gendered nature, highly unusual in Greek and Roman thought, she was integral to the lives of both young men and women. It is in her role as Athena Ergane, however, that she has fame, both as the divine weaver (Homer *Iliad* 5.734f; later in Ovid *Metamorphoses* 6.5–54 and 129–145) and also as the inventor of weaving (Plato *Symposium* 197B). In the Panathenaea, a yearly festival celebrated in honor of Athena, the denizens of the city came together to honor their patron goddess. Part of the festivities included a procession to the Acropolis for the ritual adornment of a wooden cult statue of the goddess in a peplos, a woven garment created by a select group of elite women who dedicated a year to Athena and the weaving of her peplos. This ritual thus reenacted and reinforced Athena's role as the patron goddess of crafts.

Male and Female Spheres. In daily life, too, weaving was constructed as an activity to be done by the ideal wife in ancient Greek society. The connection between weaving and the goddess of crafts is made explicit within sanctuaries dedicated to Athena, at which women dedicated various offerings to the goddess, including loom weights and spindles. In addition, vases depicting domestic scenes often include an image of a loom or a basket for weaving accoutrements, signifying that this particular craft belongs to the female realm. This is not to suggest, however, that Greek women who were engaged in these activities would have been considered artisans (*technitai*). For the most part women do not receive mention in ancient discussions of crafts and artisans per se, because ideally women did not make a living from their weaving activities, but rather were engaged in that craft at a rather modest level in the home (and therefore not in a workshop setting). Indeed, spinning thread and weaving cloth, when done to sustain the household (*oikos*), were viewed as virtuous female activities. As is well known, Homer exploits this notion in his depiction of Odysseus' wife Penelope, who, as she patiently awaits Odysseus' return, works industriously at the loom by day, only to undo her work at night in an attempt to keep her suitors at bay (*Odyssey*). Despite the cunning ruse, however, Penelope's work at the loom enables her to maintain her wifely virtue. The association of women, weaving, and virtue continues throughout the Roman period: numerous epitaphs describe the virtuous matron, with weaving being cited as an important attribute. One excerpt of an epitaph praises a matron's virtues: "She kept the house, she made the wool" (*Corpus Inscriptionum Latinarum*, 2nd ed., 1.1211 = 6.15346).

For the most part, *technē* and *ars* thus belong to the male sphere; most of our evidence comes from this realm, even though domestic weaving and women's work can—and probably should—be talked about in terms of crafts. Our evidence for Greek women as artisans is therefore rare. An unexpected exception to this statement comes from an image adorning the shoulder of a hydria attributed to the Leningrad Painter (c. 450 BCE). The scene depicts a potter's studio in which various artisans work diligently as they adorn vessels of various sizes and shapes. Athena is present in her role as the patron deity of crafts and artisans. She crowns the largest figure of the group, seated on a high-backed chair (*klismos*), in recognition of his skill; presumably he is the head of the workshop. On either side of him an artisan, shown in smaller scale, sits on a stool, also engaged in his craft. In each case a winged Nike crowns the artisan. The unexpected, unusual detail appears at the far right of the composition: a woman is depicted within the studio as she works on a vessel herself. She is isolated from the male figures and does not receive the crown of victory that her male colleagues receive. Although she works in a studio setting, her activities seem removed from the realm of *technē*.

Depictions of Craftsmen and Craft Making. Other types of craft making activities appear on a number of vases, and these can be useful in offering glimpses of Greek artisans—shoemakers, potters, smiths, and carpenters—at work, whether alone or in a workshop setting. Typically historians use these types of images as a means of recognizing the tools, processes, and products of the various crafts, with relatively little attention devoted to the artisans themselves. For example, the exterior of the Berlin Foundry Cup (the interior contains the aforementioned image of Hephaestus manufacturing the arms of Achilles) displays an image of a bronze workshop, showing the production of statuary in various stages of completion. This image appears in numerous publications on ancient bronze statuary, with the focus being on the process and the final product. Indeed, on one side the cup shows workers constructing a statue, the head of which lies at the feet of one of the artisans. At the forge a smith prepares his rod for soldering the parts of the statue together. On the other side two artisans are putting the finishing touches on a bronze warrior by smoothing its surfaces. Two large-scale figures frame this scene and have been variously interpreted as the owners of the workshop, the sculptors or designers, or onlookers.

An observer who wonders what this scene might tell us about the artisans cannot help but notice first the nudity, or relative nudity, of the artisans at work, a fact whose meaning is a source of debate. Perhaps the nakedness of some of the artisans reflects the realties of harsh working conditions and the need for mobility. Some historians have more optimistically suggested that the naked body is to be understood as a type of "heroic nudity" that glorifies the artisan's body in a manner analogous to the depicted nudity of Greek youths of higher social standing. In this later interpretation the naked body of the artisan would be, not the subject of contempt—as it usually is portrayed in literary sources—but rather elevated within a scene of idealized work (for the relative status of these workers see Cuomo, pp. 9–10; Burford, pp. 70–71; and Neils). In any case many Greek workers and slaves are shown semi-nude, with only a mantle around their waists; in contrast aristocrats wore mantles in a way that impeded any manual labor.

Images of workshops in Roman art also tend to make sharp distinctions in dress as a means of distinguishing between workers and the owners of workshops. Depictions of semi-nude workers usually connote servile status. A Pompeian painted shop sign of a clothing manufactory, belonging to Verecundus, illustrates this distinction. At left, two seated figures work at a table carding wool. At the center of the composition four semi-nude male figures make felt, which required workers to stand at a furnace to press together wool and animal hair by means of a warm binding agent. At the far end of the picture Verecundus displays the finished product, a piece of double-striped clothing, for passersby. The hard, physical labor of felt making is distinguished from the less labor-intensive activity of carding wool: the felt makers are shown without much clothing, perhaps out of necessity. In a society in which outward appearances were to signal social standing, however, the lack of clothing on these individuals probably also signified low rank, possibly servile status. Although both Verecundus and his workers engage in the craft of textiles, Verecundus has been careful to distinguish himself as the owner of the enterprise and not as one of the workers. Even so, an electoral appeal above the image announces: "The felt workers want Vettius Firmus as aedile." This slogan asserts solidarity among these artisans and their potential collective impact on local affairs (Clarke, pp. 105–112).

Although our primary consideration has been on crafts as objects of consumption and on their makers as seen through the eyes of the elite, for whom artisans were considered lowly and practically invisible, we have also seen how reality was far more complex. We do, in fact, possess some perspectives from the artisans themselves, which add another layer to an understanding of craftspeople in ancient society. Inscribed on a bronze strigil (a scraper used by bathers), for example, the artisan responsible for making this rather mundane object signed it, "Lucilius made me," suggesting that this Roman artisan might have had pride in his craft (*Corpus Inscriptionum Latinarum*, 2nd ed., 1.2.2437 / *Inscriptiones Latinae Selectae* 9444). In Athens, vase painters were in fierce competition with each other as they sought to entice buyers through excellent design and workmanship. Vase painters occasionally signed their work, but this notion of competition and pride is particularly brought to the fore on one amphora (now in the Staatliche Antikensammlungen, Munich). Decorating one side of the vessel are three semi-nude revelers, twisting and turning in space as they dance about. The inscription could not be more pointed. It proclaims, "Euthymides painted me," but then adds the jab, "as never Euphronios"—a phrase that has traditionally been interpreted as meaning that Euthymides' rival painter Euphronios could never achieve anything as fine as this painting. Plainly, good workmanship could be a source of pride and reputation—and income.

In the funerary realm of both the Greek and the Roman world, enough evidence survives to suggest that despite all of the elite-authored rhetoric, well-to-do artisans commemorated themselves for

Artisans. Producing bronze statues in a foundry. Detail from the shell of an Attic red-figure kylix (drinking cup) from Vulci, 490–480 BCE. ANTIKENSAMMLUNG, STAATLICHE MUSEEN ZU BERLIN/BILDARCHIV PREUSSISCHER KULTURBESITZ/ART RESOURCE, NY

perpetuity by their crafts. From Athens the funerary stele of one Xanthippus (now in the British Museum) shows the deceased seated upon a high-back chair (klismos) and holding in his right hand a cobbler's last (a metal or wooden model of a foot for making shoes), thus making visible his craft: he was a shoemaker. From Ravenna, Italy, a Roman shipbuilder, Longidienus, commemorates his work on a funerary stele by showing himself, not holding the tools of his trade, but engaged earnestly in building a ship. Indeed, one of the inscriptions declares that Longidienus is "busy at work" (Clarke, pp. 118–121). He undeniably uses his body to make a living. But here, and elsewhere in Greece and Rome, artisans celebrate their crafts, reminding us just how central craftsmen could be in the workings of their respective societies.

[*See also* Vase Painters.]

BIBLIOGRAPHY

Burford, Alison. *Craftsmen in Greek and Roman Society.* Ithaca, N.Y.: Cornell University Press, 1972.

Clarke, John R. *Art in the Lives of Ordinary Romans: Visual Representation and Non-elite Viewers in Italy,* *100 B.C.–A.D. 315.* Berkeley: University of California Press, 2003.

Cuomo, Serafina. *Technology and Culture in Greek and Roman Antiquity.* Cambridge, U.K.: Cambridge University Press, 2007.

DeRose Evans, Jane. "Recent Research in Roman Crafts (1985–1995)." *Classical World* 91, no. 4 (1998): 235–272.

Joshel, Sandra R. *Work, Identity, and Legal Status at Rome: A Study of the Occupational Inscriptions.* Norman: University of Oklahoma Press, 1992.

Lexicon Iconographicum Mythologiae Classicae. 8 vols. Zurich, Switzerland: Artemis Verlag, 1981–1997.

Mattusch, Carol, ed. *The Fire of Hephaistos: Large Classical Bronzes from North American Collections.* Cambridge, Mass.: Harvard University Art Museums, 1996.

Neils, Jenifer. "Who's Who on the Berlin Foundry Cup?" In *From the Parts to the Whole: Acta of the 13th International Bronze Conference,* edited by Carol C. Mattusch, Amy Brauer, and Sandra E. Knudsen, vol. 1, pp. 75–80. Portsmouth, R.I.: Journal of Roman Archaeology, 2000.

Painter, Kenneth S. *The Insula of the Menander at Pompeii. Vol. 4: The Silver Treasure.* Oxford: Clarendon Press, 2001.

Robertson, Martin. *The Art of Vase-Painting in Classical Athens.* New York: Cambridge University Press, 1992.

Strong, Donald, and David Brown, eds. *Roman Crafts.* London: Duckworth, 1976.

Zimmer, Gerhard. *Antike Werkstattbilder*. Berlin: Mann, 1982.

Zimmer, Gerhard. *Römische Berufsdarstellungen*. Berlin: Mann, 1982.

Lauren Hackworth Petersen

CRASSUS

(Marcus Licinius Crassus, c. 115–53 BCE), Roman politician and financial magnate. The son of Publius Licinius Crassus (consul in 97), Crassus escaped the proscriptions of Marius (87) and went into exile in 85. Upon the deaths of first Marius and then the surviving consul, Cinna, Crassus raised a private army in Spain (84) and joined the opposition forces of Sulla in Africa. In Italy he secured a final victory for Sulla at the battle of the Colline Gate (82) and subsequently made a fortune from the acquisition of proscribed property. An accomplished orator, Crassus entered the senate in 81. Concurrently he provided fire-ridden Rome with fire brigades and skilled slaves so as to profit enormously from repairing and buying fire-damaged properties. Investments in silver mining and tax farming and loans to ambitious clients gave him powerful political leverage, as described in Plutarch's *Life of Crassus*.

Between 77 and 73 Crassus was elected successively quaestor, aedile, and praetor. As propraetor with consular imperium, Crassus defeated Spartacus, leader of the slaves' revolt, in two engagements (72–71) and had six thousand slaves crucified along the road from Capua to Rome. Pompey, who caught up with the fugitives, claimed credit for ending the war. This offended Crassus, who received only an *ovatio* and laurel crown for his accomplishments while Pompey triumphed. Formal reconciliation between Crassus and Pompey secured their joint consulship for 70. They restored power to the tribunes, but retained Sulla's administrative reforms.

By 67, while Pompey was voted special military commands, Crassus strengthened his political following. Elected censor (65) Crassus attempted to enlist the Transpadanes as citizens and have Egypt annexed. His colleague Quintus Lutatius Catulus strongly disagreed, and both were forced to resign.

Next, Crassus allegedly supported Catiline's candidacy for consul (63) and, together with Julius Caesar, promoted the land redistribution bill of Publius Servilius Rullus. In 62 Crassus aided Caesar financially, thus enabling him to leave for his province in Further Spain. On his return, his debts cleared, Caesar was able to stand as candidate for consul, and by 60 he persuaded Crassus to join himself, together with Pompey, in an alliance, subsequently termed the First Triumvirate. In turn, to secure Crassus' business ventures, Caesar as consul for 59 passed a law that reduced Asian taxes, and so procured a tax legislation that Crassus had previously tried to obtain from the senate. For the next three years rivalry between Crassus and Pompey continued, with Crassus trying to outmaneuver both of his colleagues: he allegedly supported the tribune Clodius, who harassed Pompey; welcomed Cicero on his return from exile; and opposed Pompey's efforts to win a command that would give him control of Egypt (56). However, when Caesar's position was compromised in his absence from Rome, and the power of the triumvirs became seriously threatened, Crassus informed Caesar of the present danger. Pompey was then summoned to Luca where the triumvirs renewed their coalition, and Crassus and Pompey became consuls for a second time in 55. Each of the men received special commands for the next five years. This political victory earned Crassus both the governorship of Syria and an opportunity to invade Parthia.

In 54 Crassus campaigned across the Euphrates and was hailed *imperator* (commander) for an initial success. During his next venture into the Mesopotamian desert Crassus suffered defeat at the battle of Carrhae (53), and his legions were captured with their standards. Taken prisoner and forced to parley with the Parthian commander Surenas, Crassus was executed. Crassus' death upset the precarious power balance in the Late Roman Republic and was a harbinger of the civil war of 49–45.

[*See also* Julius Caesar; Persian Wars; Pompey; Rome, *subentry* Early Rome and the Republic; Spartacus; Sulla; *and* Triumvirs]

BIBLIOGRAPHY

Adcock, Frank E. *Marcus Crassus, Millionaire.* Cambridge, U.K.: Heffer, 1966.

Marshall, B. A. *Crassus: A Political Biography.* Amsterdam: Adolf M. Hakkert, 1976.

Ward, Allen M. *Marcus Crassus and the Late Roman Republic.* Columbia: University of Missouri Press, 1977.

Maridien Schneider

CREATION

The earliest extant Greek accounts of human origins are in Hesiod's *Theogony* and *Works and Days*. In the *Theogony* the origin of men is not explained, but we are told that Hephaestus and Athena, at the instigation of Zeus, designed and created Pandora, the first woman, as a punishment for the trickery of Prometheus (570–602). In *Works and Days* a similar story of the creation of Pandora is told (59–105), but we are also told that Zeus and the other Olympians created a succession of races of declining quality (109–201), from the golden, silver, and bronze races down to the current iron race. No explanation is given of why they did this.

Origin of Humans. Many other mythological sources describe humans, or individual heroes, growing from the earth autochthonously—for instance, Erechtheus (or Erichthonius) from the soil of Attica, Pelasgus from the soil of Arcadia. Other accounts say that humans are somehow related to the Titans or the Giants: either we were molded from clay by Prometheus (e.g., Ovid *Metamorphoses* 1.82–83), or we were born from the blood of the slain Titans or Giants (e.g., Ovid *Metamorphoses* 1.156–162). A variant may be preserved in Hesiod's *Theogony* at line 50: "the race of men and of powerful Giants."

Brief reports of the theories of Anaximander (A11 and A30 DK [Diels and Kranz]) indicate that he argued either that humans had originally been fish-like creatures or that they were originally born from fish, and hence they had survived in an originally watery world. Few details are recorded, but it is unlikely that he was thinking of the gradual evolution of fish into humans.

According to Empedocles, humans and animals were created by Love (Aphrodite), who constructed organs and limbs and then joined them in random combinations to assemble creatures (Strasbourg fragment a(ii).23–30 and B57, B59, B61, and B71 DK). Most creatures were wrongly assembled—for instance, man-headed ox creatures, double-fronted creatures, and so on—and so died out, but some were, by chance, correctly assembled and so went on to found a species. This has been seen as a forerunner of Charles Darwin's theory of natural selection, but the picture is complicated by Empedocles' description of Aphrodite intelligently designing organs such as the eye, a description that has recently led one leading scholar to classify Empedocles as a creationist (Sedley, pp. 52–62).

The role of chance in Empedocles' theory was, however, certainly an important influence on the Epicurean anti-creationist theory of the origin of species presented by Lucretius (5.837–877). He argues that in the beginning all possible varieties of creatures grew up from the earth without any purpose, design, or pattern. Although none was a hybrid like Empedocles' creatures, most were unviable monsters, being, for instance, without hand or eyes, or with limbs not properly formed. A few arose by chance with a viable constitution, and these went on to found species. Species were further refined by another round of natural selection in which creatures competed in a struggle for survival. Thus lions survived because of their strength, foxes because of their cunning, and deer because of their speed. Humans survived because they developed altruism and cooperative abilities (5.1011–1027).

One of Lucretius' main targets in his criticism of creationist theories is Plato's *Timaeus*. In the most detailed and fully worked up creationist theory of antiquity, Plato argues that the world was created by a craftsman god (demiurge) as a copy of an eternal model that exists in the world of the forms. The world is itself a living animal endowed with soul and intelligence and is based on a model that includes all possible animal forms. There are four main types of living creatures: the stars (fiery gods), creatures of the air, land animals, and sea creatures. The gods create men, but they leave the development of other creatures to a process of devolution from the ideal mortal creature, the male human. Men who behave badly are reincarnated as women, and the other creatures are produced from them according to a process of metamorphosis caused by behavior (41d–42d). Birds were formed from light-minded people, land animals from people who had no use for philosophy, and fish from the most stupid of humans (91a–92c). The theory seems to be a blend of mythological accounts of species origins by metamorphosis and of Pythagorean transmigration of souls, and—paradoxically given that it is a creationist account—it is the only extant ancient scientific theory in which species are not fixed, apart, perhaps, from Anaximander's.

Progress or Decline? Hesiod again supplies the earliest Greek account of the direction that humanity is taking and of the relative moral value of past, present, and future. His story of the decline of humanity through the metallic races in *Works and Days* (109–201) was widely influential. The first race was a race of gold; the people of this race were loved by the gods and lived lives free from toil or misery in a state of bliss. They were succeeded by the silver race, people who committed crimes against each other and refused to worship the gods. The violent bronze race followed until the people wiped each other out. Then came the race of heroes, seemingly from a different tradition, and finally the current iron race: now there is no justice at all, humans must labor and suffer, and only might is right. This primitivistic thinking, however, exists in Hesiod alongside a more optimistic idea that progress is at least possible, even if the gods are grudging and hostile to humans. Prometheus steals fire from the Olympians in order to aid suffering mortals (54–58), and Hesiod encourages his errant brother Perses with a description of a city of the just according to which it seems almost that a golden age can be regained (225–237). The road to excellence, he says, is steep and hard at first, but it becomes easier as you approach the top (289–292). So Hesiod displays both primitivist and progressivist thinking, and this is quite common.

Both primitivism and progressivism developed over time. Accounts of the golden age became more moralized, as in Empedocles (fragments 128 and 130), where we find a golden age of vegetarian sacrifices and harmony between humans and animals, and in Aratus, where the golden age is the age of justice (*Phaenomena* 96–136) when the maiden Justice herself lived among humans; as humanity declines through the metallic ages, so Justice retreats into the hills, and then finally leaves earth forever when people eat her oxen.

In contrast progressivist (or antiprimitivist) accounts picture the first age of humanity as a miserable time when people had no technology, not even fire, nor clothes to protect them, and were lashed by storms and attacked by wild animals, or even ate each other (e.g., Aeschylus *Prometheus Bound* 447–506; *Homeric Hymn to Hephaestus* 1–7; Moschion in *Tragicorum Graecorum Fragmenta* 1.97 fragment 6; Diodorus Siculus 1.8.7). We have been rescued from this beastlike life by the acquisition of technology and culture. According to some sources, culture has been granted to us as a gift by the gods; Zeus granted justice (Plato *Protagoras* 320c ff.), Hermes fire (*Homeric Hymn to Hermes* 3), and so on. Others stress the role of human culture heroes such as Pelasgus, who gave the Arcadians acorns as food and huts for houses (Pausanias *Tour of Greece* 8.1.4–6). Prometheus as a culture giver often occupies an ambiguous position as variously a Titan, a god, or a personification of human intelligence: in the "Ode to Man" in Sophocles' *Antigone* (332–375) arts and technologies traditionally attributed to Prometheus are invented by humans themselves.

For some it does not appear to matter much whether a culture giver was divine or human (e.g., Pliny *Natural History* 7.57), yet for others it was of great importance. In the myth in Plato's *Protagoras*, for example, Plato is happy enough for humans to invent all other arts themselves, so long as justice is a gift of the gods. One particular tradition of anthropological thought, beginning with Democritus, does away with the need for culture heroes altogether and stresses the role of the application of human ingenuity over time, inventing culture by trial and error with necessity as a spur and often with nature as teacher: humans learned weaving from spiders, building from swallows, and singing from swans and nightingales (Democritus fragment 154). This makes the development of culture more of a "democratic," bottom up, rather than top down, process that owes nothing either to the intervention of the gods or to outstanding individual culture givers, and makes all humans Promethean. This tradition finds its fullest expression in Lucretius' account of culture history (5.772–1457). Lucretius' main task is to show that humans and animals were not created or designed by the gods, and to show how humans developed culture themselves without any aid from the gods; the first humans lived a wandering beastlike life without any culture or technologies, and they gradually developed these first by learning directly from nature and then by applying reason to what they had learned. There was no need for any original inventor of any art. Despite this progressivist outline, Lucretius also invests his account of prehistory with an attractive primitivistic coloring; the first humans, although they had nothing, were better off in some ways than modern humans because there was no warfare, greed, money, or politics to disturb them. In fact it turns out that Lucretius does not consider modern civilization as the pinnacle of human achievement, but rather locates the Epicurean ideal in a simpler stage of human culture in the first village societies, before the rise of cities and civilization and the horrors that they bring.

[See also Barbarians; Creation Myths; Golden Age; and Human Nature.]

BIBLIOGRAPHY

Blundell, Sue. The Origins of Civilization in Greek and Roman Thought. London: Croom Helm, 1986.

Campbell, Gordon Lindsay. Strange Creatures: Anthropology in Antiquity. London: Duckworth, 2006.

Campbell, Gordon Lindsay. "Zoogony and Evolution in Timaeus, the Presocratics, Lucretius, and Darwin." In Reason and Necessity: Essays on Plato's "Timaeus," edited by M. R. Wright, pp. 145–180. London: Duckworth; Swansea: Classical Press of Wales, 2000.

Cole, Thomas. Democritus and the Sources of Greek Anthropology. Atlanta: Scholars Press, 1990.

Lovejoy, Arthur O., and George Boas. Primitivism and Related Ideas in Antiquity. Baltimore: Johns Hopkins University Press, 1935.

Sedley, David. Creationism and Its Critics in Antiquity. Berkeley: University of California Press, 2007.

Gordon Lindsay Campbell

CREATION MYTHS

The Greeks had various myths about the creation of the universe (cosmogony) and the creation of the gods (theogony). The early stories were composed for the purpose of entertainment and, perhaps, instruction, but they were not intended to be sacred texts connected with ritual observance.

The earliest and most influential text comes from the Hesiodic tradition, a seventh century BCE poem in hexameter verse called the Theogony. The poem begins with an invocation and hymn to the Muses, then turns to the origins of the universe. Chasm (chaos) comes into being first, followed by Gaia (Earth), Tartarus (Underworld), and Eros (Desire), each arising spontaneously within the formless space of Chasm. Darkness and Night emerge from Chasm, and Gaia creates Sky (Uranus) and Mountains and Sea (Pontus). After this, children are born through the sexual unions of Gaia with Uranus, Pontus, and Tartarus, and subsequent generations are born from other unions (Darkness and Night producing their opposites Bright Air and Day, and so on). Hesiod does not explain what he means by chaos and shows no concern with the reason for its appearance. Rather, he concentrates on the four basic divisions of the world: earth, sky, sea, and underworld. By personifying these natural elements as male and female, Hesiod quickly turns cosmogony into theogony with a "sacred marriage" between gods and goddesses.

The Theogony arranges the different gods into families and details some of their myths. Most important is the story of how Zeus comes to power, a succession myth that has strong parallels in Near Eastern mythology. Uranus, apparently in continual intercourse with his mother, hates his children (the Titans) and pushes them back into Earth as soon as they are born, but Gaia enlists the aid of one son, Cronus, who castrates his father. This causes the separation of Earth and Sky. Cronus mates with his sister, Rhea, to produce the Olympian gods, but to avoid his father's fate, he swallows each child as it is born. With the help of Earth and Sky, Rhea bears Zeus on the island of Crete, and at the birth she gives Cronus a swaddled rock to eat. Zeus grows up, tricks Cronus into vomiting up the other Olympians, and deposes his father as king. Zeus survives various challenges to his authority, finally defeating the Titans and the monster Typhoeus to establish his rule. He hurls the Titans down to Tartarus, portions honors for the gods, and mates with various women to produce other gods and heroes. Informed by a prophecy from Earth and Heaven, Zeus swallows his first wife, Metis, to prevent a continuation of the succession struggle.

Near Eastern Parallels. Hesiod's account was undoubtedly influenced by Near Eastern traditions, although how and when the connections developed remains unclear. Unlike Hesiod's text, these Eastern myths are closely tied to cult, but their similarities with the Greek tradition are clear evidence of influence at an early stage. A Hittite myth details the battle of gods in heaven in which Kumarbi bites off the genitals of the sky god Anu, spits out two gods, and then swallows a stone to destroy the weather god still within him. This fails, and the third god emerges to gain victory. A similar succession myth is preserved in the Babylonian *Enuma Elish*, which like Hesiod's text begins with cosmogony. The universe is formless, with saltwater and freshwater mingled, and no earth or sky yet divided from them. Apsu (freshwater) begets children who remain in their mother, Tiamat (saltwater), and whom he hates. Ea, a cunning god like Cronus, tricks Apsu and deposes him. In her anger, Tiamat produces monsters who, along with her, are ultimately defeated by Ea's son, Marduk. Marduk then creates the world from the body of Tiamat and creates mankind.

Egyptian creation myths vary in their details, but all agree that the universe began with the primordial elements of water, darkness, eternity, and air, represented by four gods and their consorts. In one account, these gods produce an egg that, when opened, reveals Ra, the sun god and lord of eternity, who creates the world and its inhabitants. The account in Genesis also has similar elements, without the great struggle between generations. The world is formless and empty with darkness over water, but God, by speaking a word, creates light and divides it from the dark. He likewise divides sky and sea and earth, and, ultimately, he creates mankind. Here, unlike in the other accounts, creation is in the hands of an intentional creator from the start.

Other Greek accounts provide a counterpoint to the Hesiodic text. Homer (*Iliad* 14.200, 244, 301) alludes to a tradition closer to the Near Eastern versions in which the sea gods Oceanus and Tethys were the primeval parents instead of Earth and Sky. The *Homeric Hymn to Hermes* follows the Hesiodic tradition with one exception in a brief theogony sung by Hermes. Whereas Hesiod begins his poem with the Muses, Hermes honors their mother, Mnemosyne, first. No details of the theogony are given except that Hermes honors the gods according to their order of birth, presumably placing himself in the prominent last position. Like Hesiod's *Theogony*, these early hexameter poems are not interested in questions of cosmogony but focus instead on the gods of myth and are intended to entertain.

Alternative Traditions. Pherecydes of Syros, a mid-sixth century BCE prose writer, represents a shift from traditional myth-telling to the beginnings of rational speculation about the causes of creation. Our evidence for his cosmogony is fragmentary and includes late sources, but it provides a clear alternative to the literary traditions that predate it. Pherecydes describes three preexisting figures: Zas (Zeus), Chronus (Time), and Chthonie (She within the Earth). Chronus produces fire, wind, and water and places them, presumably with two other elements, in five "nooks." From these nooks a second generation of gods emerges. Zas and Chthonie marry, and when Zas fashions a robe embroidered with the ocean and earth and presents it to his bride, she takes the name Earth.

The myth includes a struggle between Chronus, now called Cronus, and a serpent figure; Cronus defeats the monster and his descendants, much as Zeus defeated Typhoeus. Zeus succeeds Cronus (peacefully), assigns domains to the gods—keeping the sky for himself—and banishes the conquered to Tartarus, where the souls of men who have shed blood pass through to be born again. Pherecydes assumes familiarity with the Hesiodic tradition even as he contradicts it. For him, Time plays a primary role, Zeus creates as well as orders the world without a succession struggle, and the rebirth of souls is important. Pherecydes thus provides a point of transition between pure mythology and the beginnings of philosophy that were developing in the works of Anaximander and the Milesian school.

Orphic Theogony. Cosmogonies attributed to Orpheus began to develop in the seventh and sixth centuries and were collected in a late canonical version called the *Rhapsodies* that influenced the Stoics, Platonists, and many later authors. These accounts, though based on the Hesiodic model of theogony, are connected with mystery rituals in a way that the early poems were not, and they place Dionysus as the successor to Zeus. In one account Chronus (Time) is the first element, and from him come Aither, Chaos, and Erebus. In the Aither, Chronus forms an egg from which springs Phanes, the creator of the gods, also called Protogonus, Eros, and other names. With his daughter, Night, Phanes produces Uranus and Gaia. The usual succession myth of Cronus and Zeus is included, with the detail that Zeus swallows Phanes and re-creates the world a second time. He mates with Rhea/Demeter to produce the goddess Persephone, then with Persephone to produce Dionysus, who is killed and eaten by the Titans. Zeus blasts them with a lightning bolt, and from their ashes mankind is born with a divine soul derived from Dionysus, who is himself reborn. The creation of man from the conquered divinity recalls the Babylonian *Enuma Elish*.

The Derveni Papyrus, discovered in 1962, partially preserves an allegorical interpretation of a sixth-century Orphic theogony and includes quotations from that poem. The text is fragmentary and scholars do not agree on its details, but unlike most creation myths, the poem clearly begins with Zeus, whereas prior generations and the first creation appear as a flashback in the narrative. Creation begins with Night, whose son, Uranus, is connected with the first appearance of light. Like Hesiod's account, the poem seems to include the castration of Uranus by Cronus, who is succeeded by Zeus. Zeus receives prophecies from Night, as Zeus did from Earth in Hesiod, and apparently swallows the phallus (the same motif that appears in the Kumarbi myth). This interpretation is not certain in the papyrus, which may instead refer to the swallowing of Phanes/Protogenus that appears in other Orphic accounts.

A parody of these Orphic views appears in Aristophanes (*Birds* 690–702), making clear that the public of the fifth century understood the basics of the Orphic view. The cosmogony begins with Chaos, Night, Erebus, and Tartarus, all primordial figures of darkness. Night places an egg in Erebus, and Eros is born. Eros mates with Chaos to produce the birds and only later brings the other elements together to produce Sky, Ocean, Earth, and the other gods.

Creation of Man and Woman. Unlike for Near Eastern and other cultures, evidence for a Greek myth about the creation of man appears relatively late. A fragment of Sappho mentions the creation of men by Prometheus, and a tradition in which Prometheus forms man from clay is preserved in Aesop, Plato, and others. In the *Works and Days*, Hesiod includes a myth of the five generations of mankind beginning with the so-called golden generation during the rule of Cronus. Here he says only that "at the very first the immortals made a golden race of mortal men" (lines 109–110), but the myth focuses on the deterioration of the human race rather than on its creation.

In Hesiod the myth of Prometheus focuses on a time when man already existed and regularly feasted with the gods. The *Theogony* tells how, at one such feast, Prometheus divided the portions unevenly, tricking Zeus into choosing the inferior portion. As punishment Zeus denied fire to mankind, but Prometheus stole it back in a fennel stalk and gave it to man. Zeus then ordered the smith god, Hephaestus, to craft a woman who, Hesiod says, is the source of evil for mankind. He amplifies this part of the story in the *Works and Days*, where we learn that the woman is called Pandora (All Gifts) because each of the gods gave her a gift. Before this, man lived free from toil and pain, but Pandora opens the lid of a jar she carries and lets these evils out into the world. Only Hope is caught under the rim and kept in the jar. This myth provides two *aetia*: one for the origin of fire, the other for the origin of evil in the world.

[*See also* Creation; Golden Age; Mythography; *and* Orphism.]

BIBLIOGRAPHY

Betegh, Gábor. *The Derveni Papyrus: Cosmology, Theology, and Interpretation.* Cambridge, U.K.: Cambridge University Press, 2004.

Gregory, Andrew. *Ancient Greek Cosmogony.* London: Duckworth, 2007.

Laks, André, and Glenn W. Most, eds. *Studies on the Derveni Papyrus.* Oxford: Clarendon Press, 1997.

Schibli, Hermann S. *Pherekydes of Syros.* Oxford: Clarendon Press, 1990.

West, M. L. *Early Greek Philosophy and the Orient.* Oxford: Clarendon Press, 1971.

West, M. L. *The Orphic Poems.* Oxford: Clarendon Press, 1983.

Susan C. Shelmerdine

CRETE

[*This entry includes three subentries, on the history of ancient Crete, on Cretan mythology, and on the archaeology of ancient Crete.*]

The History of Ancient Crete

The history of Crete was influenced by its geographical position: simultaneously Crete had relative isolation from the Greek mainland and was in a central position on the traditional routes from Greece to Cyprus, the Levant, and Egypt.

From the Bronze Age to the Dark Age. In the Bronze Age, known as the "Minoan period" after the mythical Cretan king Minos, Crete was inhabited by a pre-Hellenic population of unknown origins. The chronology of this period depends on the dating of the volcanic eruption of Thera (also known as Thíra and Santorini), which occurred sometime between circa 1620 BCE and circa 1450 BCE. The Prepalatial period (c. 3000–2000) is marked through technological developments (metallurgy, stone vases, pottery), improved exploitation of the natural resources, small organized settlements connected in local networks, and contacts with the Aegean islands and Egypt.

Luxury items, architecture, rituals, and the use of seals all reflect a complex social structure and the emergence of an elite class of producers, warriors, and priests. As the increasing specialization in complementary economic activities required new structures, large administrative centers—called "palaces" by the late nineteenth-century British archaeologist Arthur Evans, a designation that is misleading but that has endured—were created around 2100 or 2000 BCE (starting the so-called Palatial period, dated circa 2100/2000–1450? BCE). The Minoan palaces, or palatial complexes, were large, unfortified two- or three-story building complexes consisting of magazines, workshops, residential areas, administrative areas, and cult spaces, arranged around a central court and connected with processional ways, corridors, and staircases.

Several palaces of various sizes—at Knossos (Cnossus), Phaestus, Malia, Zakros, Archanes, Galatas, Petras Sitias, and Monastiraki—collected, controlled, and redistributed the resources of large areas of the island. The rituals performed there guaranteed the support of divine beings and represented the authority of the elite. Regional centers such as Gournia and so-called villas such as Agia Triada, Amnisus, and Zominthos fulfilled analogous tasks. A hieroglyphic script was introduced circa 2000 BCE; it was soon replaced by a syllabic script, Linear A. The language in which these texts are written is unknown.

There is evidence for a complex social structure at this time, including an elite, soldiers, ritual experts, and probably slaves. Women were prominent as participants in public rituals, but this does not justify the assumption of a matriarchy. The achievements of this high culture include a monumental architecture, elaborate art styles, technical specialization, music and songs, and an advanced polytheistic religion in which female divinities of nature and fertility (Diktynna, Britomartis), along with their young divine consorts, played a prominent role. The economy was based on the production of surplus used in international trade with Egypt and the Near East. The fleet exercised direct or indirect control of Aegean islands such as Thera and Cythera, as well as of coastal sites in mainland Greece.

Around 1800 BCE the palaces were destroyed by an earthquake, but they were rebuilt and the administrative structure did not change. A second natural disaster, perhaps circa 1520–1450 BCE and perhaps connected with the volcanic eruption of Thera, seems to have intensified a preexisting crisis and put an end to the traditional order. Only the palace of Knossos remained in use, but in its last phase (c. 1450–1380?) its occupants were Greeks, possibly Achaeans. Immigrants from Mycenaean Greece, which had long been under Minoan influence, gained control over Crete or part of the island. The new rulers adopted the Minoan script for their administration (Linear B), and this script, deciphered in 1955, turned out to be an early form of Greek.

The Linear B documents provide information concerning place-names, the cult of gods with Greek names, the monarchical rule of a *wanax*, the social structure (elite warriors, landowners, slaves), the army, and the economy. Mycenaean Crete had contacts with mainland Greece, the Aegean islands, Egypt, the Levant, Asia Minor, and Sicily. Around 1380 BCE or possibly later the palace of Knossos was destroyed by fire. The Linear B script continued to be used for a certain period in an administrative center in Cydonia. The archaeological finds suggest a process of decentralization, with strong regional centers. Around 1200 BCE some settlements were abandoned or destroyed; part of the population moved to naturally protected sites inland, and the contacts with other areas were limited.

A period of four centuries with no written sources, the so-called Dark Age, brought substantial changes. The homogeneous administrative structure was abandoned, resulting in economic decline, limited trade, and insecurity. Crete was affected by waves of migrations and raids (c. 1200–1000 BCE). The latest immigrants were Dorian groups. Small, naturally protected settlements in the highlands indicate a feeling of insecurity. The economy was primarily oriented toward subsistence, with small-scale exchanges of surplus and only limited trade with areas outside Crete.

The Orientalizing, Archaic, and Classical Periods. Signs of stability and growth appear around 1000 BCE. The cultural growth from about 900 to 650 is closely connected with the presence of Phoenicians, who were possibly craftsmen, traders, or settlers. Visible signs of cultural influence from the Near East include motifs, techniques, and stylistic features in art—causing circa 710–630 to be called the "Orientalizing period"—and the adaptation of the Phoenician alphabet circa 800.

Under Oriental influence, Cretan artists developed various innovations, especially the making of life-size stone sculpture; these innovations, which revolutionized Greek art, were associated with the legendary sculptor Daedalus and thus called "Daedalic art." Archaeological finds at the Idaean Cave, Eleutherna, and Simi Viannou (c. 900–600 BCE) attest complex social institutions such as elite warriors and transition rites performed by ephebes. In the eighth century the erection of temples and the emergence of large cemeteries indicate the concentration of population in urban centers—early poleis—with citadels, temples, market spaces, and different quarters. A decree of Dreros forbidding iteration in office (c. 650–600 BCE) uses the term "polis" with the meaning "citizen-body." Crete was known as *hekatompolis* (the island of one hundred poleis), and about forty to sixty city-states are attested in different periods. If there had been kings, their rule was replaced with that of an aristocratic elite by the seventh century BCE. Cretans participated in the foundation of Gela jointly with Rhodians.

This cultural and economic growth came to an abrupt end around 630–600 BCE. Trade and craftsmanship lost their innovative power. Although Crete was never isolated from the rest of Greece and participated in the transit trade among Athens, the Peloponnesus, and North Africa, the contacts with other Greek areas were not impressive. The economy was oriented toward subsistence. Many legal documents treat constitutional matters, the administration of justice, family law, property law (debts, the economic rights of women), the rights of foreign craftsmen, and cult. The longest and best preserved is the Law Code of Gortyn (c. 450 BCE). These early laws aimed at preventing conflicts by setting out strict rules for the exercise of political power, defining social and legal positions, and delimiting the rights and privileges of citizens, foreigners, women, landowners, dependent farmers, dependent communities, and various categories of slaves.

Despite differences in details, the general social and political order of the numerous poleis seems to have been the same, possibly the result of an artificial homogenization (c. 600 BCE). The citizen-body consisted of warriors who owned land that was divided into lots and cultivated by an unfree population. Requirements for citizenship included legitimate birth in a family of citizens, participation in social and military training, membership in a military unit (tribe or *startos*), membership in a men's group, and attendance of common meals (*syssitia*) in so-called men's houses (*andreia*), funded through contributions by the citizens, the serfs, and public revenue.

The poleis were ruled by boards of ten *kosmoi*, who had the military leadership, presided over the assembly, and supervised the administration of justice; they were elected from the same tribe for one year. The tribes rotated in the leadership of the community. The citizen assembly had the right to accept or reject the proposals of the magistrates, but it lacked the right to make its own proposals or to discuss the motions. A council (*bola*, *preigeia*), consisting of old men (perhaps former magistrates) who served for life, oversaw the magistrates. The Cretan constitution had an aristocratic character, with a few prominent families alternating in power.

The political history of Crete in the Classical period is unknown, except for a civil war in Knossos (early fifth century BCE) and conflicts within the ruling elites in Aristotle's lifetime. The Cretans did not participate in the Persian Wars, but Cretan mercenaries served in the Peloponnesian War, in the army of the Persian prince Cyrus (the "ten thousand"), and in Alexander's army.

Hellenistic Crete. Hellenistic Crete was dominated by wars: wars between poleis for the control of land and resources, mercenary service, and raids of pirates in the Aegean islands and along the coast of Asia Minor. *Asylia* (inviolability) treaties reflect the raids of Cretan pirates, which culminated in two wars with Rhodes (206–204 and 155–153 BCE). The raids were organized both by poleis and by private individuals; treaties deal with the division of booty. These raids made Crete an important center of slave trade. Cretan mercenaries played a prominent part in the major Hellenistic armies, and many of them settled in their area of service, such as Ptolemaic Egypt or Miletus.

Large-scale commercial activities increased but were primarily limited to transit trade and trade in war booty and slaves. Social conflicts were caused by the increasing number of indebted individuals and citizens without land; the results were migration, mercenary service, raids, internal colonization, and wars. Bilateral treaties reveal a tendency toward military and economic cooperation. With an isopolity treaty, any two Cretan cities mutually granted citizenship to those citizens who were willing to make use of it, allowing them to settle in the partner city and develop their economic activities there. Treaties also regulated the relations between the poleis and their dependent communities, which received autonomy and land in exchange for tribute and other services.

The political history is characterized by the continual antagonism of Gortyn and Knossos for hegemony, interventions of Hellenistic kings (Philip V, the Ptolemies), and the expansion of a few major cities, which by the end of the second century BCE had absorbed the territories of most of their small neighbors. The leadership of a *koinon* (federation) of Cretan cities was disputed between Knossos and Gortyn. This federation lacked citizenship, army, and magistrates, but it had a council and probably a federal court (*koinodikion*) and had developed a procedure for the resolution of conflicts. The most important among the numerous local wars was the war against Lyttos (c. 222–219), caused by Lyttos' refusal to join the *koinon* under the leadership of Knossos and Gortyn and resulting in civil wars and the dissolution of the *koinon*. A new alliance under the leadership of Gortyn allied itself with Philip V of Macedon from about 217 to 201 BCE and supported his military activities, with raids against the islands of the Dodecanese and coastal cities of Asia Minor.

Crete remained the theater of local wars circa 205–114 BCE, caused by the antagonism between Knossos and Gortyn and by territorial disputes. Repeated arbitrations by the Romans remained ineffective. In the course of these wars many cities were destroyed. The influence of Ptolemaic Egypt increased in the second century when an Egyptian garrison was established in Itanos (c. 165–145 BCE). A final arbitration by Rome (118–114 BCE) led to a delimitation and a general peace (110 BCE). The major cities of Crete—Gortyn, Knossos, Lyttos, Hierapytna, Cydonia—were now in control of large territories.

The last phase of the Hellenistic period (110–70 BCE) is characterized by intensive raids of Cretan pirates, limited mercenary service, and trade in slaves and other booty. The relations between Crete and Rome deteriorated in the early first century BCE because of the presence of Cretan mercenaries in the army of Mithradates VI and because of the raids of pirates. After an unsuccessful attack by Marcus Antonius Creticus in 71 BCE and fruitless negotiations, in 69–67 Quintus Caecilius Metellus Creticus defeated the Cretan army; some cities were destroyed, others were damaged, and Crete was subdued.

Roman Domination. Under the Republic, Crete and Cyrene were joined in a single province. Cretan mercenaries were recruited by Pompey, Cassius, Brutus, and Mark Anthony, and the island was used for the settlement of veterans. Mark Anthony, who controlled Crete from 42 BCE, donated it to Cleopatra (36 BCE), but after the Battle of Actium (31 BCE), Crete was finally integrated into the Roman Empire.

The coming of Rome meant the establishment of a provincial government and the extinction of the traditional social and political order. The many competing cities were united under a single administration. Immigrants (Italian traders, Roman colonists, Jews from Cyrenaica) came to Crete and contributed to its economic, social, and cultural integration in the Roman Empire. Crete formed together with Cyrenaica a senatorial province, governed by a proconsul of praetorian status with his seat in Gortyn. The governor and his staff (quaestor, *legati*) were responsible for the administration of justice, finances, public works, and the resolution of border disputes. An imperial procurator, a member of the equestrian order, represented the emperor's economic interests. The emperor possibly owned land on Crete, and he was involved in the delivery of medicinal plants to Rome. Only fifteen or sixteen poleis retained the status of free cities; the most prominent were Gortyn, Knossos, Lyttos, and Hierapytna. The only Roman colony, Colonia Iulia Nobilis Cnossus, was governed by *duoviri* and aediles and had a council of *decuriones*.

Under Roman influence, other cities introduced boards of possibly four *kosmoi* presided over by a *protokosmos*. The free cities were members of the new League of the Cretans (*Koinon ton Kreton*). The *koinon* was responsible for the imperial cult, organized athletic and music competitions every five years, and issued coins. The Roman army was not stationed on Crete, but Cretans served in the *cohortes sagittariorum* and *cohortes Cretum* in the Danube *limes* and in Jordan (first–fourth centuries CE). Agrarian production was reoriented to more profitable branches such as the massive production of wine (*passum*) and oil for export. The rule of aristocratic families was replaced by the rule of a new oligarchy of wealth.

The integration of Crete into the Roman Empire resulted also in new forms of architecture (aqueducts, theaters, amphitheaters, baths, new types of funerary monuments) and new cults (Egyptian gods, Theos Hypsistos). Cults in traditional sanctuaries such as the Ideaean Cave and Diktynnaion revived in association with the Cretan *koinon* and remained strong until the late fourth century CE. The sanctuary of Asclepius in Lebena attracted large numbers of pilgrims. The slow process of Christianization started with the apostle Paul in 61 CE and his disciples. Many Christians were killed in persecutions in 250 and 304.

Late Antiquity. Diocletian's administrative reforms of the late third century separated Crete from Cyrenaica and made it part of the diocese of Moesia. First it was governed by a *praeses* of equestrian rank, then, after Constantine, by a *consularis*. From the late fourth century, Crete belonged to the Eastern Roman Empire, although until the eighth century its church was subject to the authority of the pope in Rome and of his *vicarius* in Thessalonica. The social changes of late antiquity must have affected Crete, but written sources are lacking. In the fourth and fifth centuries, bishops are attested in several cities, but the earliest of the about seventy basilicas was built only around 450 CE in Eleutherna.

In late antiquity, Crete lived in relative prosperity and had close trade contacts with Cyprus and Palestine. It did not suffer under the raids of barbarian tribes, except for isolated raids of the Goths (268 CE), the Vandals (457 CE), and the Slavs (612? and 623 CE). Far more destructive were earthquakes, especially in 365 CE, the ultimate result of which was that the western part of the island rose and the eastern part sank into the sea. The Arab conquest of Egypt in 642 CE turned Crete into one of the frontiers of the Eastern Roman Empire and initiated a series of Arab raids that ultimately led to the conquest of Crete by the Arabs circa 820.

[*See also* Evans, Arthur; Gortyn; and Knossos.]

BIBLIOGRAPHY

Chaniotis, Angelos. *Das antike Kreta.* Munich: Beck, 2004.

Chaniotis, Angelos. *Die Verträge zwischen kretischen Poleis in der hellenistischen Zeit.* Stuttgart, Germany: Steiner, 1996.

Chaniotis, Angelos, ed. *From Minoan Farmers to Roman Traders: Sidelights on the Economy of Ancient Crete.* Stuttgart, Germany: Steiner, 1999.

Dickinson, Oliver. *The Aegean Bronze Age.* Cambridge, U.K.: Cambridge University Press, 1994.

Dickinson, Oliver. *The Aegean from Bronze Age to Iron Age: Continuity and Change between the Twelfth and Eighth Centuries BC.* London and New York: Routledge, 2006.

Effenterre, Henri van. *La Crète et le monde grec de Platon à Polybe.* Paris: E. de Boccard, 1948.

Link, Stefan. *Das griechische Kreta: Untersuchungen zu seiner staatlichen und gesellschaftlichen Entwicklung vom 6. bis zum 4. Jahrhundert v. Chr.* Stuttgart, Germany: Steiner, 1994.

Myers, J. Wilson, Eleanor Emlen Myers, Gerald Cadogan, eds. *An Aerial Atlas of Ancient Crete.* Berkeley: University of California Press, 1992.

Perlman, Paula. "Crete." In *An Inventory of Archaic and Classical Poleis*, edited by Mogens Herman Hansen and Thomas Heine Nielsen, pp. 1144–1195. Oxford: Oxford University Press, 2004.

Sanders, I. F. *Roman Crete: An Archaeological Survey and Gazetteer of Late Hellenistic, Roman, and Early Byzantine Crete.* Warminster, U.K.: Aris & Phillips, 1982.

Willetts, R. F. *Aristocratic Society in Ancient Crete.* London: Routlege and Paul, 1955.

Angelos Chaniotis

Cretan Mythology

Crete was inhabited in the Neolithic and supported a unique Bronze Age civilization that mirrored, however, practices from the Near East and Egypt. The period from circa 2700 to circa 1450 BCE is called Minoan, after a coinage by Arthur Evans, who excavated Knossos (Cnossus) beginning in 1900.

Minoans and Greeks. The Minoans were of unknown language and race, though ties with Anatolia are strong. The Greek occupation of Knossos after 1450, and absorption of Minoan culture including syllabic writing for accounting, establishes a direct historical connection between the Minoans and the classical Greeks, who told many stories about ancient Crete. Are these stories based in Minoan culture? Does Minoan culture explain these stories?

Evans took the name Minoan from the legendary Minos, and the relationship between classical stories about Crete and the society that Evans uncovered remains a case study in correlating literary tradition with archaeological finds. There is no Cretan myth as such, but only myths about Crete, popular already in the Archaic period (especially the story of the Minotaur), but well preserved in literary versions only in the Latin authors. Ovid loved the Cretan stories and emphasized the bizarre or humorous sexual elements in them. Athens plays a special role in these stories and must have been important in their early transmission, but is there a historical connection between Athens and Bronze Age Crete? Did Crete once rule Athens, who broke away?

We can never be sure of answers to such questions because archaeological evidence about Bronze Age Crete is opaque or puzzling. Two early writing systems from the second millennium (Middle Minoan), so-called Cretan Hieroglyphic (whose characters can be pictorial) and Linear A, are undeciphered because of the scarce material, lack of any bilingual document, and ignorance of the underlying language or languages. These writings were in any event used mainly for economic purposes, as was initially their Mesopotamian model. The deciphered (1952) Linear B, whose abundant tablets encode Greek, prove that circa 1400 BCE Mycenaean Greeks were ruling parts of the island and creating economic documents similar to the Minoans whose land they had occupied. We must start from these deciphered tablets in our efforts to untangle the relationship between Cretan reality and classical myth, remembering that the tablets are in Greek and not in the unknown language of the Minoans.

Gods and Divine Figures. Gods important in classical Greece existed in Mycenaean Greece and their names appear as recipients of offerings along with gods of whom we know nothing. From tablets at Knossos we find Potnia ("mistress"), Potnia of Atana ("Athena"), Ares?, Enyalios (a war-god in Homer c. 800 BCE), Paionos (= classical Apollo or a hymn attached to Apollo), Poseidon, Enosidas (= Enosigaios, "earthshaker"), Zeus, Diwia (female Zeus), Diktynna? (lady of Mount Dikte?), Potnia of the Labyrinth (syllabic DA-PU-RI-TO-JO), Eleuthia

(= classical Eileithyia, goddess of childbirth, worshipped in a cave at Amnisos mentioned by Homer), Erinys? (a classical cult epithet of Demeter). From the Pylos tablets comes a more Hellenized selection: Potnia, Sphagianeia? (local goddess), Hippeia ("she of the horses"?), Aswia (local goddess), Newopeos (?), Upoios (?), Poseidon, Posidaieia (female counterpart of Poseidon), Zeus, Diwia, Hera (with Zeus on one tablet), Artemis, Hermes?, Ares?, Dionysus (or someone named after the god), Peleia?, Iphimedeia (in myth, mistress of Poseidon and mother of the giants Otos and Ephialtes), Manasa (?), Trisheros ("triple hero"), Despotas? ("lord"), Mater theia ("mother goddess"), Wanasoi ("the two Queens"?), Dipsioi ("thirsty ones"?).

Divine figures unknown to the classical era, about half of these, prove how the traditional religion will change by the time of Socrates, as we would expect. Striking in the Knossos tablets is the lack of correspondence with the archaeological finds: no snake goddess, like the idols found in the palace at Knossos; no "horns of consecration" or double-ax, two ubiquitous religious symbols; and about half the deities are male, whereas in Cretan art female deities are predominant by far. Already in the Bronze Age the Greeks have imposed their own traditions, and we cannot be at all clear about the Minoan contribution.

The Labyrinth. Prominent in myths about Crete is the Athenian Daedalus, master craftsman who designed the wooden cow in which Pasiphae had intercourse with a bull to beget the monstrous Minotaur ("bull of Minos"), then built the labyrinth in which to imprison it. Later Daedalus was imprisoned in it with his son Icarus, a story not attested until the fourth century BCE. The word "Daidaleion" appears on a Knossos tablet, but we are not sure what is meant by it, perhaps a sanctuary. By the time of Homer (c. 800 BCE), the hero Daedalus has become the eponym for Daidaleion: Homer says that Daedalus built the dancing-place for Ariadne (*Iliad* 18.591). In fact dancing-places surrounded Cretan tholoi as part of the cult of the dead already in the third millennium; in Cretan cult, to judge from representations, dancing was always important.

It is startling to find "labyrinth" in Linear B. A late commentator explains *labrys* as a Cretan word for "double-ax," so that labyrinth should mean "house of the double ax," a conspicuous symbol at Knossos. Because sacrifice was the principal act of ancient religion, many think that the *labrys* was the special ax used to kill the sacrificial bull, as Theseus killed the Minotaur. The bull-games painted on frescoes must have ended in just such killing. Was Labyrinth the name of the palace at Knossos, where the killing took place? Is Mistress of the Labyrinth on the Knossos tablet the protective female spirit of the palace at Knossos?

Certainly the immense palace that Evans found at Knossos is labyrinthine in our own understanding and not only decorated with bulls and double axes, but frescoes suggest that in the large open court a deadly game was played in which young men and women somersaulted over a charging bull. According to the myth, seven Athenian youths and seven maids were regularly given to the monster. Is this dangerous game the origin of the story of the sacrifice, or does the story suggest rather the Near Eastern practice of burning children in the fire to the bull-god Baal-Moloch, as some think? There is evidence for Cretan human sacrifice. An earthquake circa 1700 BCE, perhaps the one that destroyed the early palace at Knossos, destroyed a shrine south of Knossos in which four bodies were found, one a young man trussed on an altar and evidently already slaughtered when the building collapsed. From a second period of crisis circa 1450 BCE, when the new palaces were destroyed, come over three hundred bones from several dismembered children, cooked and eaten, from a burned deposit near Knossos. No human remains come from the numerous peak sanctuaries, where a fire cult was celebrated, but clay parts of human bodies and animals were thrown into the sacrificial fire to an unknown power. The practice of Cretan human sacrifice may be remembered in the myth, but no other detail of the story accords with archaeological finds.

Female Goddesses and Cave Cults. On the basis of Cretan art we know that female goddesses associated with trees and plants and bulls played an important role in Cretan religion. The ubiquitous "horns of consecration," a stylized two-pronged symbol, are usually taken to represent horns (as of bulls sacrificed in cult), but imitate the Egyptian hieroglyph for "horizon" over which the new sun rises every day and could have carried some such meaning. Greek myth represents the bull-god Zeus abducting Europa and begetting Minos, the king of Crete. He has the same name as the first pharaoh in Egypt MN (Menes) and Minos may have been a Cretan title like pharaoh. But even if bulls were important in ritual and sacrificed in cult (as many other animals certainly were), there is no sign of a Cretan bull-god. Pasiphae's intercourse with a special bull resulting in the Minotaur suggests the Near Eastern rite of sacred marriage, and we might imagine a priest wearing a bull's mask to have intercourse with a priestess; there are, however, no sexual symbols in the Minoan finds.

Seals, or small designs on sealing rings, represent a woman with upraised arms, a position designating a deity in epiphany, seated on an animal, but the animals are horses or fantastic beings, never a bull swimming in the water, the Europa and the bull favored in classical art. Other seals show bizarre, half-human, half-animal creatures, but never a bull-man or a labyrinth. In medieval times the "Tomb of Zeus" was shown near Knossos, suggesting an ancient story about a dying god of the Near Eastern type: In fact the "Tomb" was one of many peak sanctuaries. If such sanctuaries celebrated the sky god, as they did in Greece and in the Near East, we have no evidence.

Striking in Minoan religion is the prominence of cave cults, unusual elsewhere, reminding us of the story that Hesiod tells about the infant Zeus (*Theogony* 453–506): Because of Cronus' hostility to his offspring, Rhea traveled to Crete and there gave birth to Zeus, where he was raised in a cave. Later tradition reports that nymphs nourished him with goat's milk and honey and that the Couretes ("youths") banged their spears against their shields outside the cave to keep Cronus from hearing the infant's cries. The finds in the caves are sometimes pottery, but in the great cave off the high

Cretan Snake Goddess. From the Palace of Knossos. Faience, c. 1500 BCE. ARCHAEOLOGICAL MUSEUM OF HERAKLEION, CRETE, GREECE/LAUROS/GIRAUDON/THE BRIDGEMAN ART LIBRARY

mountain-encircled Lasithi plain in central Crete, often claimed to be the cave where Zeus was born, were found model daggers, double-axes, and human and animal votives unconnected to any cult of Zeus. Many animals were burned here, cattle, sheep, pigs, and goats. The animal figures and in one cave the drawing of a Mistress of the Animals makes likely that the caves were wombs from which sprang the wealth of the natural world, with a little help from ritual behavior. The cave at Amnisos, mentioned by Homer as belonging to the birth goddess Eileithyia (*Odyssey* 19.198), certainly had this function; a well-worn stalagmite in it, surrounded by a wall, had magical power. But "Eileithyia," which appears on a tablet from Knossos, is a name of Greek not Minoan formation, "the one who comes," a cry of the Greek woman in childbirth. The Curetes' dancing and banging is an Anatolian ritual attached to the mother goddess in classical times, and no sign

shows that they or the Near Eastern dying god formed any part of Minoan religion.

Bulls, the Labyrinth, human sacrifice, caves, dancing—these elements appear to have roots in the Minoan Bronze Age, but myths are stories, and the Cretan stories are folktales sprung from the brains of poets who lived long after ashes lay on Knossos. Theseus is the man on a quest who must defeat a dragon of chaos, a myth powerful in Mesopotamian stories where such stories explicate the creation of the world. He would have perished had not the daughter of the evil king fallen in love, who provided the trick of the clew by which the beast was overthrown. Ariadne, "very holy one," may have been a Greek epithet for a Minoan goddess, but in the story she is a woman dewy-eyed in love, resentful of treachery, and the wife of Dionysus, god of fertility.

[*See also* Evans, Arthur; Linear B; *and* Theseus.]

BIBLIOGRAPHY

Burkert, Walter. *Greek Religion.* Translated by John Raffan. Cambridge, Mass.: Harvard University Press, 1985.

Gantz, Timothy. *Early Greek Myth: A Guide to Literary and Artistic Sources.* Baltimore: Johns Hopkins University Press, 1993.

Marinatos, Nanno. *Minoan Religion: Ritual, Image, and Symbol.* Columbia: University of South Carolina Press, 1993.

Nilsson, Martin P. *The Minoan-Mycenaean Religion and Its Survival in Greek Religion.* 2nd rev. ed. Lund, Sweden: C. W. K. Gleerup, 1950.

Nilsson, Martin P. *The Mycenaean Origin of Greek Mythology.* Berkeley: University of California Press, 1932.

BARRY B. POWELL

Archaeology of Crete

Crete, one of the largest islands in the Mediterranean, has produced evidence for continuous phases of ancient civilizations from the Neolithic to late Roman times. Although recent investigations have revealed earlier human presence on the island, the first known permanent settlement has been identified at Knossos (c. 7000 BCE). Over the course of the

Neolithic period (c. 7000–3500 BCE), especially the later part, additional sites appeared, including settlements, burials, and shrines in caves, as well as open settlements.

The Bronze Age. Minoan civilization, named after the legendary king Minos, was divided by Arthur Evans into Early, Middle, and Late Minoan (EM, MM, LM) on the basis of pottery styles.

The Prepalatial Period. By around 3000 BCE a large number of relatively small organized settlements, made up of groups of houses frequently separated by paved streets or courtyards or both, had been founded at sites such as Myrtos Fournou Korifi, Vasilike, and Trypeti, with much larger settlements perhaps at Knossos and Phaestus. Caves or rock shelters, *tholos* tombs (aboveground circular built structures), and house tombs, as well as rock-cut pits, were used for burial in the Prepalatial period (EM I–III and MM IA; c. 3500–1900 BCE). Cult ritual was commonly practiced in caves, on hilltop shrines ("peak sanctuaries"), and sometimes in small shrines within the settlements. This period is also characterized by the widespread use of bronze, developments in ceramic technology, and increases in agriculture, including the first cultivation of olives and grapes, specialized craftsmanship (ivory carving, stone vessels, seal carving, and metalwork, including tools, weapons, and jewelry), and foreign contact and trade, as well as in general prosperity and social complexity. Over the course of the Prepalatial period these changes culminated in the centralization of power and accumulation of wealth (in the palaces) seen in the next period.

The Protopalatial Period. In the Protopalatial period (MM IB–II; c. 1900–1700 BCE) the first Minoan "palaces" were founded at Knossos, Phaestus, and Malia, and similar large buildings were constructed at sites like Petras. Each palace served important political, economic, and administrative functions for a specific region, including the collection, storage, and distribution of produce, as well as the import and export of goods; they may also have played a role in religion and contained living quarters for the rulers. Specialized workshops were based in these buildings, and the Protopalatial period saw continued advances in metalwork (especially gold jewelry), ivory, seal carving, and pottery, including the introduction of the fast wheel and a fine polychrome style known as Kamares ware. In addition, the first wall paintings appeared during this period, containing primarily abstract and floral motifs. The administration of the palaces was supported by the development of two systems of writing: Cretan hieroglyphs and Linear A (found on clay tablets, seal impressions, and pottery).

Foreign contact and trade also increased during this period, with Minoan products found not only throughout the Cyclades and Greek mainland but also in Egypt, Cyprus, and the Near East. Many new settlements, as well as commercial harbor towns (e.g., Poros and Kommos), appeared, each under the control of its respective regional palace. Peak sanctuaries (e.g., Juktas and Petsofa) and caves (e.g., Kamares), as well as small rural sanctuaries, continued to be used for religious rituals, with small terra-cotta human and animal figurines typically left as offerings; in addition, *tholos* tombs and house tombs were still present, though burials inside pithoi (large storage jars) and larnakes (chests) became more common. The Protopalatial period ended with destructions seen across the island, possibly the result of a large earthquake or multiple earthquakes.

The Neopalatial Period. Following the large destructions the palaces were rebuilt, often with different plans, and new palaces were built, as at Zakros and Galatas. The palaces of the Neopalatial period (MM III to LM IB; c. 1700–1450 BCE) were multistoried buildings of ashlar masonry, organized around a central court, with many storerooms and an elaborate drainage system. The early part of the Neopalatial period is in many ways the height of Minoan civilization, with Minoan influence abroad at its greatest extent. Developments continued to be made in specialized craft production; figural wall paintings—including scenes such as bull leaping, processions, and rituals—are well known from this period, and certain symbols, such as horns of consecration, bulls, and double axes, are prominent in religious art.

Although the palaces continued to serve as bureaucratic administrative centers, they also took on a much more significant role in religion and ritual, with peak sanctuaries less frequently visited. Settlements like Palaikastro and Gournia flourished in this period, and new types of buildings appeared, including so-called villas (e.g., Vathypetro and Tylissos), which had architectural features similar to those of the palaces and may have served administrative, production, storage, and economic functions, while still ultimately being dependant upon the palaces. Most of the previous burial forms continued during this period, and the rock-cut chamber tomb made its first appearance.

Many sites were abandoned, destroyed, or significantly decreased in size at the end of LM IA, perhaps as a result of the volcanic eruption at Thera. This event marks the beginning of a general decline in Minoan civilization, and political instability may also have ensued. By the end of the Neopalatial period the majority of palaces and large villas, except for Knossos, had been destroyed by fire, perhaps because of natural disasters, military activity, or a combination of both.

The Postpalatial Period. At the beginning of the Postpalatial period (LM II–IIIB; c. 1450–1200 BCE) the palace of Knossos remained in use as an administrative center—though at a reduced scale—and a limited number of sites, such as Kommos and Cydonia (Chania), flourished. Although the extent of Mycenaean physical presence on the island is uncertain, the influence of Mycenaean Greeks is potentially visible at many sites in the appearance of the Linear B script, new wall paintings with motifs like shields in the palace at Knossos, and Mycenaean architectural features and pottery shapes, as well as in the presence of so-called warrior graves—which typically contained numerous bronze weapons, jewelry, and pottery—and a more Mycenaean-style belowground *tholos* tomb (e.g., Armenoi, Archanes, Knossos).

The palace at Knossos was finally destroyed in the second half of the Postpalatial period. At this time the ruins of buildings at abandoned or destroyed sites were sometimes reused for small-scale habitation or as shrines (e.g., the Shrine of the Double Axes in the Knossos palace). In addition, a new type of domestic shrine, called the "bench shrine," also appeared and typically contained terra-cotta female goddesses with upraised arms (as at Gournia and Hagia Triada). Although a few new settlements were founded during this period, overall a general decline is seen throughout the island. By the end of the twelfth century, many sites had been destroyed by fire or abandoned (e.g., Mochlos, Pseira), a trend also seen across the eastern Mediterranean.

The Early Iron Age. The Early Iron Age (c. 1200–700 BCE; covering the LM IIIC, Subminoan, Protogeometric, Geometric, and Early Orientalizing periods) has also been referred to as the Dark Age because monumental architecture, writing, centralized authority, and specialized craft production temporarily disappeared. The Early Iron Age is characterized by the widespread use of iron. Gradually across the island, new sites sometimes called "refuge settlements" were founded far from the coast, typically on mountaintops (e.g., Karphi, Kavousi Kastro, Vrokastro). This change in settlement location may have been a response to the political instability created after the final collapse of the palatial system, in connection with fear from an outside threat such as piracy or possibly climatic changes.

At the beginning of the period, settlements tended to be small, with only minor distinctions in building size and architecture. This suggests limited social stratification, though the settlements may have been organized around a chief or "big man." Continuity in cult is visible in the presence of community shrines containing female goddesses with upraised arms (e.g., Chalasmenos, Kavousi Vronda, Vasiliki Kephala). Small *tholos* tombs and rock-cut chamber tombs were typical at the beginning of the Early Iron Age, though by the end of the period, pit, cist, and pithos burials (especially with cremations) were more common. Around 1000 BCE many small sites were abandoned, their populations presumably moving to other nearby sites that expanded in size and show indications of rebuilding or reorganization, with planned, more regular architecture. This gradual development of nucleated settlements, together with an increasingly complex sociopolitical structure and the rise of an elite, put in place at certain sites the foundation for the polis or city-state, which is commonly believed to have developed on Crete by the end of the period. In addition, an increase in foreign contacts and imported goods occurred over the course of the period, with Orientalizing figural motifs—those inspired by the Near East and Egypt—appearing in Crete much earlier than in the rest of Greece.

The Orientalizing and Archaic Periods. Overall the seventh century was a flourishing period throughout the island, with Crete again becoming a center for trade across the Mediterranean. During the Orientalizing period (c. 700–600 BCE), Orientalizing art continued, with stone and terra-cotta sculpture in the Daedalic style commonly found; in addition, fine metalwork may reveal not only the influence but also the physical presence of foreign, especially Phoenician, craftsmen working on the island. City-states were forming and growing, as at Knossos, Eleutherna, Prinias, and Gortyn, and the earliest stone stelae with legal inscriptions (e.g., Gortyn, Dreros, Lato) also come from this the Archaic period (c. 600–480 BCE). Furthermore, early forms of stone temples with impressive sculptures were built (e.g., Dreros, Prinias, Gortyn), and known shrines continued (e.g., Idaean Cave, Kato Symi), often with rich votive deposits. Burial in urns and pithoi in organized cemeteries was also typical in the seventh century. Until recently, few remains (other than inscriptions) from the sixth century had been identified on Crete, leaving a gap in the archaeological record; new excavations at Azoria, however, have revealed a large thriving settlement that shows a high degree of urban planning, with large complexes of public buildings and a shrine. Nevertheless, by the end of the century a decrease in commercial activity is visible throughout the island, and rivalry between city-states seems to have been significant, as revealed in inscriptions and perhaps by the violent fiery destructions observed at sites like Azoria in the early fifth century.

The Classical and Hellenistic Periods. Although imported—especially Attic—pottery continued to be put at many grave sites (e.g., Phalasarna, Cydonia, Eleutherna) at the beginning of the fifth century BCE, Crete was in a sense cut off from the rest of the Greek world in the Classical period (480–323 BCE), playing no significant role in events like the Persian or Peloponnesian wars. Few settlements of this period have been excavated, and most are known primarily through inscriptions or from cemeteries (rock-cut tombs or cist graves), reuse of sanctuaries (e.g., Demeter at Knossos; Zeus at Amnisos), or scant remains mostly obscured by later occupation. Life on Crete in the Classical period continued to be centered on the city-states (e.g., Lyttos, Hierapytna, Itanos, Gortyn), which likely increased in size, though this was a period of growing intercity rivalry and fighting. A wide variety of coinage representing individual cities also appeared at this time, illustrating the cities' wealth and economic recovery.

The period after the conquests of Alexander the Great brought new prosperity to the island. During the Hellenistic period (323–69 BCE) city-states were still dominant, though the rivalries among them intensified, with many sites ultimately being destroyed and with alliances being sought with foreign powers. Cities were often built up and fortified, as at Aptera, where large fortification walls, sanctuaries, and a theater are thought to date to this period; houses, shops, *prytaneia* (public buildings), and *bouleutēria* (council buildings) are other new types of buildings. Large barrel-vaulted tombs, as well as simple cist graves, have been excavated at several sites (e.g., Cydonia, Hierapytna, Gortyn, Polyrrhenia), with terra-cotta figurines, jewelry, glass vessels, and pottery commonly found. In addition, an even greater variety of Cretan coins is found from this time. Crete's central location again allowed the island to play a significant role in trade for the eastern Mediterranean, as a result of which coastal settlements or emporia and harbor towns (e.g., Mochlos, Phalasarna) thrived. Finally, though many previous religious practices were maintained, the worship of Asclepius was introduced, and several important sanctuaries have been excavated (e.g., Asclepius at Lissos and Lebena; Hermes and Aphrodite at Kato Symi).

The Roman Period and After. The Roman general Quintus Caecilius Metellus invaded the island in 69 BCE (and subdued it in 67), and Crete became a Roman province with its capital at Gortyn. The Roman period was a time of prosperity and peace not seen since the Minoan era: cities flourished, and large public buildings (typically of Roman brick-faced concrete), such as amphitheaters, temples, odea, circuses, and baths, as well as roads, aqueducts, and cisterns, were constructed at many sites (e.g., Gortyn, Aptera, Knossos). Rural villas (e.g., Villa of Dionysus at Knossos), not commonly seen in the Hellenistic period, were characteristic of the Roman era, and most Hellenistic tomb types continued in use. The general wealth of the period, as well as links to mainland Greece and Rome, is visible in, for example, sculpture that tends to represent copies of Classical Greek works or portraits of emperors. Mosaic floors also became popular during the later Roman period; they were installed in public buildings, fountains, and wealthy villas. Traditional Cretan divinities (such as Diktynna and Britomartis) continued to be worshipped, in addition to the Greek pantheon and certain Egyptian deities (Isis and Serapis) acquired by the Romans.

Christianity gradually spread across the island, especially after 330, the year of the founding of Constantinople. In 330–824 CE (known as the Late Roman or Early/First Byzantine period), many Christian basilicas (churches) were built: approximately seventy are known, including at Gortyn, Panormus, Chersonesus, and Olous. The influence of Christianity can also be seen in a change in burial practices, with simple cist graves, often without offerings, becoming the primary type.

In 824 the island was captured by Saracen Arabs from North Africa, who destroyed many cities, including Gortyn the capital and churches, which were sometimes converted into mosques. A new fortified capital, Chandax ("moat"; now Herakleion), was founded, though only a few coins and sections of fortification walls remain from this period. In 961 the Byzantine general (and later emperor)

Nicephorus Phocas took back the island and renewed contact with Constantinople. In 961–1204 (known as the Second Byzantine period), many basilicas were built or rebuilt, often with painted frescoes, and monasteries were founded; numerous towns, including Chandax, were also restored, often with fortification walls. After the Byzantine Empire collapsed, the island of Crete was ultimately taken over by the Venetians.

The Venetian period (1204–1669), although plagued by numerous uprisings against the foreign administration, is characterized by the construction of many castles (e.g., Grambousa, Francocastello), defensive walls, churches with elaborate frescoes (e.g., Panagia Kera at Kritsa), and monasteries (which often acquired large libraries), as well as arsenals, harbors, fountains, other civic buildings, and country villas. The city of Candia—the Venetian name for Chandax—became a center for copying Greek manuscripts brought from Constantinople after its destruction in 1453, and a famous school of Cretan icon painting was developed, in which tradition El Greco (1541–1614) began his career. In addition, many ancient ruins—which often no longer survive—were recorded by Italian travelers, such as Onorio Belli in the sixteenth century. At the same time, unfortunately, many remains were systematically removed and taken to Venice, just as the Ottomans later also carried finds to Constantinople. Finally, many signs remain of the turbulent period in which the Ottoman Turks controlled the island (1669–1898), such as mosques, fountains, houses, cisterns, baths, castles, and city walls.

Although limited investigations were conducted earlier, archaeological excavations, especially by foreigners, began in earnest in the years immediately following the island's independence from the Ottomans in 1898. Early twentieth-century excavations include those by Americans (Harriet Boyd Hawes at Gournia, Kavousi Vronda, Kastro, and Azoria; Richard Seager at Pseira, Vasilike, and Mochlos; and Edith Hall at Vrokastro), Britons (Arthur Evans at Knossos and Juktas; Richard Dawkins, Robert Carr Bosanquet, and John Myres at Palaikastro; John Pendlebury at Karphi; David

Hogarth at Zakros; and Humphrey Payne at Eleutherna), Italians (Frederico Halbherr at Phaestus, Gortyn, and Prinias and Luigi Pernier at Phaestus and Prinias), French (Pierre Demargne at Lato, Dreros, and Malia; Fernand Chapouthier at Malia; and Hubert Gallet de Santerre, Andre Dessenne, and Jean Deshayes at Itanos), and Greeks (Joseph Hazzidakis at Malia and Tylissos; Stephanos Xanthoudides at Gortyn and Dreros; and Spyridon Marinatos at Dreros and Vathypetro). Investigations continue to this day at nearly all of these sites, for which the archaeologists are too numerous to name individually. Additional sites of significance that have recently been investigated include Myrtos Fournou Korifi (Peter Warren), Trypeti (Antonis Vasilakis), Chalasmenos (Metaxia Tsipopoulou and William Coulson), Galatas (Georgos Rethemiotakis), Kommos (Joseph Shaw), Petras (Metaxia Tsipopoulou), and Chania (Yannis Tzedakis and Carl-Gustaf Styrenius).

[See also Archaeology, subentry Sites in Greece; Evans, Arthur; Gortyn; Knossos; and Phaestus.]

BIBLIOGRAPHY

Betancourt, Philip P. The History of Minoan Pottery. Princeton, N.J.: Princeton University Press, 1985.

Betancourt, Philip P. Introduction to Aegean Art. Philadelphia: INSTAP Academic Press, 2007.

Cadogan, Gerald. Palaces of Minoan Crete. London: Barrie and Jenkins, 1976.

Cavanagh, W. G., and M. Curtis, eds. Post-Minoan Crete: Proceedings of the First Colloquium on Post-Minoan Crete held by the British School at Athens and the Institute of Archaeology, University College London, 10–11 November 1995. London: British School at Athens, 1998.

Chaniotis, Angelos, ed. From Minoan Farmers to Roman Traders: Sidelights on the Economy of Ancient Crete. Stuttgart, Germany: F. Steiner, 1999.

Cullen, Tracey, ed. Aegean Prehistory: A Review. Boston: Archaeological Institute of America, 2001.

Detorakis, Theocharis E. History of Crete. Iráklion, Crete, Greece: Detorakis, 1994.

Dickinson, Oliver. Aegean from Bronze Age to Iron Age: Continuity and Change between the Twelfth and Eight Centuries B.C. London: Routledge, 2006.

Fitton, J. Lesley. Minoans. London: British Museum Press, 2002.

Hägg, Robin, and Nanno Marinatos. The Function of the Minoan Palaces: Proceedings of the Fourth International Symposium at the Swedish Institute in Athens, 10–16 June, 1984. Stockholm, Sweden: Svenska institutet i Athen, 1987.

Harrison, George W. M. The Romans and Crete. Amsterdam: A. M. Hakkert, 1993.

Immerwahr, Sara A. Aegean Painting in the Bronze Age. University Park: Pennsylvania State University Press, 1990.

Krzyszkowska, O., and L. Nixon, eds. Minoan Society: Proceedings of the Cambridge Colloquium 1981. Bristol, U.K.: Bristol Classical Press, 1983.

Myers, J. Wilson, Eleanor Emlen Myers, and Gerald Cadogan. The Aerial Atlas of Ancient Crete. Berkeley: University of California Press, 1992.

Nowicki, Krzysztof. Defensible Sites in Crete c. 1200–800 B.C. (LM IIIB/IIIC through Early Geometric). Aegaeum 21. Liège, Belgium: Université de Liège, 2000.

Preziosi, Donald, and Louise A. Hitchcock. Aegean Art and Architecture. Oxford: Oxford University Press, 1999.

Sanders, Ian F. Roman Crete: An Archaeological Survey and Gazeteer of Late Hellenistic, Roman, and Early Byzantine Crete. Warminster, U.K.: Aris & Phillips, 1982.

Shelmerdine, Cynthia W., ed. The Cambridge Companion to the Aegean Bronze Age. Cambridge, U.K.: Cambridge University Press, 2008.

Warren, Peter, and Vronwy Hankey. Aegean Bronze Age Chronology. Bristol, U.K.: Bristol Classical Press, 1989.

Whitley, James. The Archaeology of Ancient Greece. Cambridge, U.K.: Cambridge University Press, 2001.

Melissa Eaby

CRIME

See Law, Greek and Law, Roman.

CRONOS

See Gods, Greek, subentry Lesser Greek Gods.

CULT IMAGES

A cult image is a sculptural representation of a divinity that served as the earthly substitute for a god or goddess and as a focus of worship and cult activities. Cult images were considered the most sacred of cult objects, imbued with even greater sanctity if their origins were deemed miraculous or attributable to the distant past.

In Greek a cult image was called *eidos*, *agalma*, *xoanon*, or *bretas*, though sometimes in epigraphic texts a cult statue was referred to simply as "the god" (*theos*). The word *xoanon* was used variously by ancient authors and in epigraphical texts to refer to divine images, either cult images or dedicatory statues, made of wood or other materials. In Latin a cult image was called *statua*, *simulacrum*, *signum*, *imago*, or *effigies*.

Greek and Roman cult images were most often anthropomorphic, though there were contemporaneous examples of aniconic idols that were objects of divine worship, such as logs or rocks. The nature or special properties of a divinity were embodied in anthropomorphic cult images through identifying characteristics such as the seated or standing pose (frontality is the general rule in all periods), position of the arms, dress, coiffure, ornaments, and especially the sacred symbols or attributes held by or accompanying the divinity (e.g., scepter, snake, thunderbolt, owl).

Cult images were generally distinguished in function from other sculptural representations of deities, such as dedicatory statues, by their special role in religious ceremonies. Temples were arguably built as sacred homes (*oikoi*) of the gods and to house the anthropomorphic cult image of a god. Anthropomorphic cult images were typically positioned on raised bases or podiums, often at the rear of the cella (inner chamber) in a temple or in another architectural setting such as beneath a baldachin, though the settings of cult images show some regional and chronological variations; some were worshipped outdoors. In the canonical Greek sanctuary—in which the temple faced an altar—sacrifices were carried out in view of the god in the form of the cult statue. Offerings and prayers were directed to the divinity by worshippers in front of the cult image. Votive gifts were presented to the divinity and were often housed in or around the temple; sometimes these took the form of clothing, jewelry, or other ornaments intended to adorn the statue. Smaller cult images were often carried in processions, and some were washed and fed in rituals whose origins can be traced to the Near East and Egypt.

In Greek and Roman cult practice a single image usually represented the divinity, though there are examples at a single shrine of multiple cult images of the same deity. Sometimes an old venerable statue was replaced by a newer image that stood alongside the old or in another nearby temple—for instance, the gold and ivory Athena Parthenos and the wooden Athena Polias on the Acropolis. Cult statue groups, often family groups, such as Zeus and Hera or the Capitoline Triad (Jupiter, Juno, and Minerva), were common.

For the most part early Greek cult images from the eighth and seventh centuries BCE were rather small statues, but by the sixth century BCE and through the Classical, Hellenistic, and Roman periods larger-than-life and colossal cult statues were preferred. A change is apparent in attitudes toward cult images in the Classical and Hellenistic periods when impressive new cult images were designed to bring more attention and financial rewards to the sanctuary and to display the prosperity of the polis or regional authority controlling the cult or sanctuary.

The earliest Greek cult images, beginning in the eighth century BCE, were mostly made of wood, sometimes gilded or painted, or of hammered bronze (*sphyrēlaton*). By the Classical period wooden cult images became anachronistic, and cult statues were more typically made of bronze or stone, especially marble, or of mixed materials, either acrolithic (with head and limbs of stone and body of a different material) or chryselephantine (gold and ivory).

Beginning in the late Archaic period the names of sculptors responsible for the creation of cult images were recorded, and sculptors became famous for these highly visible and important works. Phidias was renowned for his famed chryselephantine cult images of Athena Parthenos at Athens and of Zeus at Olympia; Agoracritus was well known for his marble Nemesis at Rhamnus. Several Hellenistic sculptors and families of sculptors who specialized in the making of cult statues—for instance, Damophon of Messene—are attested in statue bases, literary sources, and surviving statues.

In the Hellenistic period new cult images with Greek and foreign iconographic syncretism entered the repertoire, such as the Egyptian gods Isis and Serapis. With the introduction of the ruler cult and the deification of the Successors of Alexander the Great, idealized statues representing these ruler gods were created. The settings of these new cult images varied, sometimes sharing temples with deities—such as the cult statue of Attalus III in the temple of Asclepius at Pergamum—or placed outdoors, such as the colossal image of Antiochus I of Commagene at Nemrut Dag.

Out of this ruler cult tradition came the establishment in the Roman imperial period of the cult of the deified emperor. Cult statues of deified emperors and empresses were official state-sanctioned images—usually idealized portraits amalgamated with or in the guise of a divinity (e.g., Jupiter, Ceres, or Venus), with suitable dress (often semi-draped males), headgear (e.g., lunate diadem, star), and attributes.

For the conventional gods, Roman tradition records that the first cult image in Rome was a painted terra-cotta statue made by an Etruscan sculptor, Vulca of Veii (Pliny the Elder *Natural History* 35.45.157), and the Romans credited the Etruscans with the innovation of worshipping gods in the form of cult images. Sculptors of Republican Roman cult images, however, looked to Greek models for their conservative iconography and types, though the styles are eclectic and hark back to various periods. The sculptors of many cult images for temples in Italy from the third through the first century BCE were probably Greek, such as the sculptors of the second century BCE acrolithic cult statue heads from the sanctuary of Diana at Lake Nemi, now in Copenhagen, Nottingham, and Philadelphia.

Republican cult statues were made of wood (e.g., the cypress wood image of Veiovis on the Capitoline Hill, mentioned in Pliny the Elder 16.79.216), bronze (e.g., the second century BCE Hercules Victor from

Cult of Athena. Modern version of the statue of Athena Parthenos by Phidias, constructed between 1982 and 1990 by Alan LeQuire. The statue is 41 feet 10 inches tall; its weight is estimated at 12 tons. The statue of Nike in Athena's hand is 6 feet 4 inches tall. THE PARTHENON, NASHVILLE, TENNESSEE

the forum Boarium, now in the Museo Conservatori, Rome), or stone, especially limestone and imported Greek marble. Later, with the exploitation of the quarries at Carrara in the first century BCE, Roman cult statues were also made of indigenous marble. Roman imperial cult images were most commonly made of marble or bronze, though Pliny in the first century CE records that gold and silver cult images were popular in his time (35.45.157). With the expansion of the marble trade in the imperial period, colored marbles in various combinations were used for cult images.

[*See also* Colossus; Imperial Cult, Roman; Phidias; Religion, *subentry* Roman Religion; Sculpture; Temples; *and* Terra-cotta Figurines.]

BIBLIOGRAPHY

Damaskos, Dimitris. *Untersuchungen zu hellenistischen Kultbildern.* Stutttgart, Germany: F. Steiner, 1999.

Guldager Bilde, Pia. "The Sanctuary of Diana Nemorensis: The Late Republican Acrolithic Cult Statues." *Acta Archeologica* 66 (1995): 191–217.

Martin, Hans G. *Römische Tempelkultbilder: Eine archäologische Untersuchung zur späten Republik.* Studi e Materiali del Museo della Civiltà Romana 12. Rome: L'Erma di Bretschneider, 1987.

Ridgway, Brunilde S. "Images of Athena on the Acropolis." In *Goddess and Polis,* edited by Jenifer Neils, pp. 119–142. Hanover, N.H.: Hood Museum of Art; Princeton, N.J.: Princeton University Press, 1992.

Romano, Irene Bald. "Early Greek Cult Images and Cult Practice." In *Early Greek Cult Practice: Proceedings of the Fifth International Symposium at the Swedish Institute at Athens,* edited by Robin Hägg, Nanno Marinatos, and Gullög Nordquist, pp. 127–133. Stockholm, Sweden: Svenska Institutet i Athen; Göteborg, Sweden: Paul Aströms Förlag, 1988.

Vermeule, Cornelius C. *The Cult Images of Imperial Rome.* Rome: G. Bretschneider, 1987.

Irene Bald Romano

CUPID

See Cupid and Psyche *and* Venus.

CUPID AND PSYCHE

Though it occurs first in figurative art as early as the fourth century BCE and later often on sarcophagi, sometimes as a symbol of love transcending death, the story of Cupid and Psyche is primarily known from a substantial inserted tale in the second-century CE Latin novel *Metamorphoses* or *The Golden Ass* by Apuleius.

Apuleius' version tells of Psyche, a princess feted for her great beauty, who thereby incurs the wrath of Venus and is told by an oracle that she would marry a terrifying winged monster. Exposed on a rock and expecting death, she is taken away to the luxurious palace of Cupid, who has fallen in love with her. Cupid visits her bed nightly but forbids her to see him face to face or to ask his identity. Psyche asks for her sisters to visit; they, jealous, make her curious and trick her into finding out who her husband is; on the discovery he leaves her. Psyche, now pregnant, searches for Cupid in laborious wanderings, while Venus, still hostile, harries her and sets her a number of arduous tasks. Psyche completes these tasks through indirect help from Cupid, but in the course of the final task, involving descent to the Underworld, Psyche is again overcome by her curiosity and almost perishes on her return journey; she is rescued by Cupid and admitted to the company of gods, where the pair, reconciled with Venus, live happily ever after, and have a daughter, Pleasure.

Within Apuleius' novel this episode covers approximately one-fifth of the text and is literally and metaphorically central, providing a mirror of the novel's main plot (*mise en abyme*), where the protagonist Lucius similarly gets into trouble for his curiosity and is rescued by a divine power (Isis). Its character as an extensive inserted narrative recalls the epic tales of Odysseus in *Odyssey* 9–12 and Aeneas in *Aeneid* 2–3, suitably transformed for a lower novelistic context, and Psyche's descent to the Underworld clearly echoes Aeneas' descent in *Aeneid* 6. The speaking names of its protagonists, the centrality of curiosity, and several literary echoes of Platonic dialogues on love (*Phaedrus* and *Symposium*) suggest some link with Platonic doctrine on Love and the Soul, but it is hard to establish a thoroughgoing philosophical allegory, or indeed an allegory of religious initiation, as some have argued.

This playful obscurity of message is matched by a playfully complex narrative frame. Within the novel, the story of Cupid and Psyche has three levels of narrator: the anonymous old woman who tells the story, Lucius-ass who retails it within the novel, and the final writer Apuleius. The first of these tells it to calm a tense kidnap victim (Charite), presumably aiming to induce her to believe that all will turn out well for her as for Psyche in the tale; the second of these re-tells it as a mere "pretty story," ironically concealing the more subtle purposes of the third. The embedding of narrative levels and the mythical nature of the story suggest Platonic literary color, but not necessarily Platonic ideology: the ending of the tale in the birth of Pleasure may simply be a hint that the narrative aims at readers' enjoyment rather than ideological edification.

Cupid and Psyche has often been pointed to as evidence for Apuleius' engagement with folktale in his novel. Although its story-patterns find parallels in standard fairy-tales (e.g., Beauty and the Beast), it seems likely that these similarities are owed to classically educated folktale collectors such as Charles Perrault and the brothers Grimm who had read Apuleius, and Cupid and Psyche as a whole shows much more concern with intertextual reworking of the classics of Greek and Roman literature than with popular or oral narrative.

The reception of Apuleius' story in literature, music, and art has been extensive. Cupid and Psyche was popular on its rediscovery in the Italian Renaissance, giving rise to a number of poetic versions, dramas, and operas, and famous cycles of frescoes narrating the story were produced by Raphael for the Villa Farnesina in Rome and by Giulio Romano for the Palazzo del Te in Mantua. The tale was also used in nineteenth-century literature, in John Keats' *Ode to Psyche*, some paraphrases by Elizabeth Barrett Browning, a version in Walter Pater's novel *Marius The Epicurean*, and in extensive poetic treatments by William Morris and Robert Bridges, and in art, ranging from classicizing sculpture (Antonio Canova, Bertel Thorwaldsen) and painting (Sir Edward Coley Burne-Jones, John William Waterhouse) to splendid sets of Paris-manufactured wallpapers.

[*See also* Aphrodite; Apuleius; Eros; *and* Venus.]

BIBLIOGRAPHY

Kenney, E. J., ed. *Cupid and Psyche / Apuleius.* Cambridge, U.K.: Cambridge University Press, 1990.

Fehling, Detlev, ed. *Amor und Psyche.* Mainz, Germany: Akademie der Wissenschaft und der Literatur Wiesbaden, Germany: Franz Steiner, 1977.

Zimmerman, M., et al., eds. *Aspects of Apuleius' Golden Ass II: Cupid and Psyche.* Groningen, The Netherlands: E. Forsten, 1998.

Stephen Harrison

CYBELE AND ATTIS

Matar kubeleya (the mountain mother) was the principal deity of the Phrygians in west central Anatolia. By at least the seventh century BCE the cult of the goddess Kubelē—the Phrygian epithet treated as a proper name—was known in the Greek world, not only in Ionia but also in mainland Greece and the colonies of southern Italy. Although her alternative Greek name, Kubēbē, was evidently borrowed from a quite different divinity, the Neo-Hittite Kubaba, protectress of Carchemish in northern Syria, the Greeks always thought of Kubelē as the Phrygian goddess.

They called her "the Great Mother," *megalē mētēr*, and her characteristics are already attested in the *Homeric Hymns* of the sixth century BCE: "Clear-voiced Muse, daughter of great Zeus, sing me the Mother of all gods and all human beings; she takes pleasure in the joyful sound of castanets and drums and the din of pipes, the howl of wolves and roar of bright-eyed lions, the echoing mountains and the wooded glens" (14.1–5).

The din of percussion and baritone Phrygian pipes enabled her worshippers to achieve the trance-like state of being *mētrolēptos*, "possessed by the Mother," and the cult often took the form of nocturnal initiation into her mysteries. But she was more than a goddess of the wild; the fifth-century Athenian democracy had a Mētrōon (Mother-cult site) in the Agora that was used as the state archive.

The goddess's consort Attis is first attested in the fourth century BCE, and in Greece; though her Phrygian priests were often called Attis, the god of that name was never part of the Phrygian cult. Callimachus in the third century BCE provides the earliest evidence for the Galli (Galloi in Greek), the goddess's cross-dressing eunuch priests, who hymned their mistress in the headlong galliambic meter and danced in frenzy, tossing their long hair like bacchic maenads. Also third century are the earliest of the various myths of Cybele and Attis, of which the best known is an etiological tale of love, jealousy, and self-castration.

In 205 BCE, when Hannibal was still undefeated in Italy after twelve years, the Romans were told by the

Sibylline Books that the enemy could be driven out and conquered if the Idaean Mother were brought to Rome. Delphi advised the Romans to apply to King Attalus III of Pergamum, and the king was prevailed on to yield to them the stone in which the goddess's power was believed to reside. Pergamum was an important center of the goddess's cult, and Attalus' realm included Ilion at the site of Troy, where she was worshipped as Idaia. Since Mount Ida was where Aeneas was born, and where he collected the refugees after the fall of Troy, in this particular manifestation the goddess was, in a sense, the mother of Rome.

Cybele (as we may now call her, in Latin) was received with great ceremony in 204, and housed in the temple of Victory on the Palatine until her own temple, also in the precinct of Victory, was completed in 191 BCE. Her title was *Mater deorum magna Idaea*, the Great Idaean Mother of the Gods, and the new temple was at the historic heart of Rome, directly above the Lupercal, where the she-wolf suckled the twins, and close to the preserved hut that was believed to be that of Romulus. Archaeological exploration of the temple has revealed the importance of Attis in the Roman cult: many terracotta figurines, deposited as votive offerings, have been found from the earliest level of the temple, and ninety-four are of Attis against just eleven of the Great Mother herself.

Every April the aediles put on stage performances in her honor, called Ludi Megalenses after the Greek for "great mother." The steps of the temple on its high podium served as the auditorium for the shows, which were performed on a temporary stage in the small triangular piazza immediately in front of it. Incorporated into the steps was a substantial lustral basin, evidently used for the ritual washing (*lavatio*) of the goddess. At a later stage, when the temple was rebuilt after a fire in 111 BCE, the piazza was extended at a higher level, covering the basin along with the lower range of steps. It may have been from this date that the *lavatio* ceremony was transferred to the river Almo outside the Porta Capena, with the goddess's image being carried along in a joyful, noisy procession through the streets of Rome. Ovid attributes the washing of the goddess in the Almo to the occasion of her arrival in 204 BCE, and comments on the noisy involvement of the Galli: "The attendants shriek, the mad pipe blows, and effeminate hands beat the bull-skin drums."

The Galli were also prominent at the theater games, as we know from a stray quotation from one of Varro's satires: "When I got there I saw a crowd of Galli in the temple, raving about and singing their hymn in zealous confusion, while the aedile was putting on the statue the crown he had brought from the stage-show." That evidently refers to the restoration of the symbol of the Great Mother which had represented her presence at a separate performance away from the temple, probably at the Lupercal directly below.

A passage in Dionysius of Halicarnassus, probably taken from Varro's *Divine Antiquities*, insists that the public cult of the Great Mother was carried out according to traditional Roman standards, "rejecting all fabulous claptrap" such as stories of self-castration, mystic initiations, ecstatic frenzies, and promiscuous all-night festivals. "The priest and priestess are Phrygians. . . . But it is contrary to the law and the Senate's decree that any native Roman should process in a spangled robe begging alms to the music of the pipes, or celebrate the Goddess's orgies in the Phrygian manner." However, the Galliambic hymn written by Varro's contemporary Catullus shows how powerful an effect the Galli, and the myth of Attis that explained their condition, could have on even the most sophisticated Romans.

In the 30s BCE the young Caesar, who would soon become Augustus, chose to build his house and his new temple of Apollo right next to the precinct of Victory, which contained the temple of Magna Mater. Virgil shows how the goddess could be assimilated to the new ruler's more puritanical outlook: he makes much of the Great Mother in her capacity as the helper and supporter of Augustus' ancestor Aeneas, even associating her with the walls of Rome in the prophetic context of *Aeneid* book 6. When the temple was burned down again— evidently in 3 CE, when his house was also

Cybele. Hellenistic statue of Cybele seated on a throne flanked by two lions; the name of the donor, Virius Marcarianus, is inscribed on the base. MUSEO ARCHEOLOGICO NAZIONALE, NAPLES, ITALY/ALFREDO DAGLI ORTI/BILDARCHIV PREUSSISCHER KULTURBESITZ/ART RESOURCE, NY

destroyed—Augustus rebuilt it with his own name on the architrave.

The republican and Augustan celebrations of Magna Mater were in early April. At some later stage (John Lydus attributes it to Claudius, though it may have been a gradual development in the first and second centuries CE), a series of festivals in March associated the goddess and her consort with the spring equinox. On 22 March a pine tree (Attis castrated himself beneath a pine) was borne in procession to the Palatine; the "day of blood" on 24 March, marked by the Galli slashing their arms in mourning for the dead Attis, was followed the next day by the celebration of his return, like the sun, at the Hilaria; 26 March was a rest day (Requietio), and then came the traditional bathing of the goddess at the Almo, evidently brought forward from its previous April date to 27 March. A surviving Roman calendar shows that these rites were still important in the life of the city in 354 CE.

[*See also* Eunuchs *and* Mythology, Roman.]

BIBLIOGRAPHY

Lane, Eugene N., ed. *Cybele, Attis and Related Cults.* Leiden, The Netherlands: E. J. Brill, 1996.

Roller, Lynn E. *In Search of God the Mother: The Cult of Anatolian Cybele.* Berkeley: University of California Press, 1999.

Simon, Erika. "Kybele." In *Lexicon Iconographicum Mythologiae Classicae* 8, no. 1 (1997): 744–766.

Vermaseren, Maarten J. *Cybele and Attis: The Myth and the Cult.* Translated by A. M. H. Lemmers. London: Thames and Hudson, 1977.

Vermaseren, M. J., ed. *Corpus Cultus Cybelae Attidisque.* 7 vols. Leiden, The Netherlands: E. J. Brill, 1977–1989.

T. P. WISEMAN

CYCLADES

The Cycladic archipelago in the southern Aegean played an important role in Greek history. This chain dotting the sea surrounded by mainland Greece, Asia Minor, and Crete includes large and small islands varying in size from more than 155 square miles (400 square kilometers) to less than one square mile. Ancient writers defined the Cyclades as a ring around Delos, emphasizing the political and religious importance of the great sanctuary of Delian Apollo. Mineral resources contributed to the prosperity of these mountainous islands. For example, Siphnos discovered extensive silver veins in the sixth century BCE, which were used to fund a magnificent treasury building at Delphi. Winds and currents also influenced developments by creating alternate periods of open and closed sea-lanes. Island connectivity is a major theme of Cycladic history.

A distinctive Cycladic civilization emerged in the Early Bronze Age (third millennium BCE). Many of the earliest villages were coastal locations facilitating communication and providing a livelihood through fishing. Islanders soon began building fortified towns, of which the best known is Kastri on Syros. It is situated on a hilltop overlooking the sea and has a strong circuit wall with projecting semicircular bastions. Of roughly the same date is the fortified town on the Greek mainland at Lerna, suggesting cultural contact. Communication routes are also responsible for the wide distribution in the Aegean of obsidian, for which the island of Melos is the only source. In addition Cretan architectural and artistic influences at Akrotiri on Thera may signal a commercial connection, unless the later myth of a Cretan sea empire under King Minos has any validity.

Much of what is known of prehistoric Cycladic cultures, however, comes from tombs. The largest excavated cemetery at Chalandriani on Syros, from circa 2000 BCE, had more than six hundred burials. The richest were provided with bronze knives and daggers, anthropomorphic marble figurines, and characteristic Cycladic stone and ceramic vessels. The schematic marble figurines have attracted much attention as works of art. Although they come in many forms, the canonical type is a female subject with folded arms. Many were painted, and some even bore tattoos. Unfortunately, tomb looting has resulted in the loss of essential information about the role of these objects in funerary rituals.

The Cyclades were hit hard by the collapse of Aegean palatial centers and trade routes. Many islands were deserted or depopulated in the eleventh century, but then, according to tradition, Ionians resettled most of the northern chain, while Dorians from the Peloponnesus occupied a few southern islands, including Melos and Thera. Archaic city-states established control over entire islands or divided the resources of the largest into two or more autonomous states. Native marble sources enabled Paros and Naxos to take leading roles in Archaic Greek architecture and sculpture. During the Persian Wars many Cycladic islands submitted to Persia and contributed vessels to the Persian fleet. Few thereafter recovered their autonomy, and most became tributary members of the Athenian Empire in the fifth century. The Cyclades frequently changed hands in the struggles between Hellenistic kingdoms and became part of the Roman province of Asia in 133 BCE.

[*See also* Aegean Sea; Delos; Greece, *subentry* Prehistory to the End of the Bronze Age.]

BIBLIOGRAPHY

Barber, R. L. N. *The Cyclades in the Bronze Age.* London: Duckworth, 1987.

Broodbank, Cyprian. *An Island Archaeology of the Early Cyclades.* Cambridge, U.K.: Cambridge University Press, 2000.

Constantakopoulou, Christy. *The Dance of the Islands: Insularity, Networks, the Athenian Empire, and the Aegean World.* Oxford: Oxford University Press, 2007.

Brice Erickson

CYCLOPS

See Homer.

CYNICS AND CYNICISM

Ancient Cynicism was an ideological identity adopted by a series of self-fashioning figures, mostly men but also one notable woman, who made it a goal to live "in accordance with nature," usually in voluntary poverty, and to flaunt social convention, probably for the purpose of instructing others about the difference between nature and convention. Cynicism arose in classical Athens in the fourth century BCE and spread through Greek cities during the Hellenistic period and then to Rome. It remained a visible mode of resistance to culture and power until at least the time of Julian, late fourth century CE, and it is attested until the sixth century. The Cynics probably had no school, doctrine, leadership, or formal succession, but can be identified by a core set of valued behaviors, strategies, and ideas. Later in their history, Cynics maintained their identity by invoking their long-dead predecessors as their models. The status of Cynicism as a "philosophy" rather than just a lifestyle was debated in antiquity (e.g., Diogenes Laertius 1.18–20), and this controversy shows that Cynicism had an ethically serious component, even while its practice often takes the form of antics critical and mocking of dominant discourses, including, prominently, philosophy itself.

The Name "Cynic." In all likelihood, the Cynics took their name from the Greek word for "doglike,"

kynikos. Diogenes Laertius equates this etymology with the scurrilous humor of the Cynics: like dogs, they took no shame in public behavior that would be outrageous by polite standards, not only verbal behavior such as their "biting" one-line repartees to figures commanding respect, but also, as it seems from the anecdotes, bodily functions including sex, eating, and spitting. According to the late antique philosophical commentator Elias (of the Neoplatonic school in Alexandria, sixth century CE), there were four reasons to say the Cynics were "doglike": they were indifferent to conventions about value, but took their values from nature; they were shameless in their outspokenness; they were guardians or watchdogs of philosophy and virtue; and, like the discerning dogs mentioned by Plato, they knew how to distinguish and drive off persons "foreign" to philosophy and how to admit those "at home" there. It is clear from Aristotle (*Rhetorica* 1411a24–25) that someone in his time circa 340 BCE, probably Diogenes of Sinope (c. 412/403–c. 324/321), was known by the nickname "the dog"; Antisthenes of Athens (c. 445–c. 365), a disciple of Socrates, was called in later times, if not already by his contemporaries, the "simple dog" (Diogenes Laertius 6.13); and other permutations of this name were applied to other individual Cynics. An alternative ancient etymology connects the name "Cynics" to the precinct of an Athenian temple of Heracles, the Cynosarges, where Antisthenes allegedly taught. While it is not impossible that Antisthenes sometimes held forth in this spot, it is unlikely that this was the location of an institutionalized Cynic School. Diogenes of Sinope, meanwhile, lived his frugal life with few possessions and no fixed home, like a dog in this way, dividing his time between Athens and Corinth, where he probably mingled with the populace in public urban settings, just as Socrates had done in the Athenian marketplace.

Cynics and Their Motives. Ancient histories of philosophy derive the Cynic tradition from Socrates (c. 470–399 BCE) by way of his disciple Antisthenes, who in turn taught Diogenes of Sinope, the quintessential, original Cynic. Although this succession story has been denied in modern scholarship, there can be no doubt that it is true in a broad sense. Socrates, perhaps following the lead of other Athenian intellectuals in his time, refused to accept received convention as the grounding for any moral value, whether for public virtues such as justice or private ones such as courage and piety. He sought to find, and help others find, the real nature of such values. Whereas other figures of his time, mostly the foreign Sophists working in Athens, took money in exchange for their services as teachers and intellectuals, Socrates refused to do so, not because poverty was his goal, but because he was indifferent to luxury and he refused to compromise his personal freedom to associate with whomever he wished, whether rich or poor. According to Xenophon, he practiced an ethics of asceticism, which was connected to his "self-sufficiency" (*autarkeia*), for which many of the illustrative anecdotes are drawn from military settings, where denial of bodily pleasure was in accord with necessity or a greater good.

Antisthenes was a loyal Socratic disciple, who became convinced that his lifetime should be committed to becoming wise and promoting the good rather than making money or pursuing gratification from society, and he was also a disillusioned Athenian, who either was barred from full citizenship by a low birth or, more likely, was alienated by bad decisions of the Athenians, such as the execution of Socrates and obedience to the demagogues through the tumultuous period of the Peloponnesian Wars and oligarchic revolutions (431–403 BCE). His life after the death of Socrates was probably devoted to private conversations, reading, and writing, and he left a corpus of texts (now lost) whose titles can be compared both with Plato's and with those of some Stoics. Because he seems to have been a serious intellectual, owned property, and lived a more or less conventional life, he has seemed not to fit the template of a Cynic forefather. But the fragments of his writings have a pervasive countercultural and counterintuitive thrust, and his interest in certain technical aspects of language and logic might have been directed toward defending a fundamentally rhetorical, social nature of language against tendencies among other Socratic successors, mainly

Plato, to formalize language in directions that led toward the demonstrative logic of Aristotle. His views of ethical value, meanwhile, remained firmly based in nature (if also indefinable), as they did for the Cynics as well.

Diogenes of Sinope was the first to adopt the radical Cynic lifestyle, living in the open during the warm seasons and taking shelter in a barrel for the winter, owning only a drinking cup but discarding even that when he recognized that it was unnecessary, masturbating in public because he was self-sufficient, and sparring verbally with others at every opportunity. Yet he also probably wrote dialogues and tragedies, and he attracted responses from mainstream philosophers. It is reported that he argued formally, if only against certain opponents, and to prove disruptive or self-refuting theses (Diogenes Laertius 6.72). His motive for the Cynic life is traced in ancient tradition to his exile from his native city Sinope, where his father, a banker, was caught defacing the coinage, or "revaluing the currency" (*paracharattein to nomismai*). Diogenes was effectively expelled and fled to Athens, where, story has it, he became a disciple of Antisthenes and began to imitate Socrates.

Whether this episode was the real inspiration for Diogenes' lifelong Cynic mission to "revalue the currency" of conventional norms of belief and behavior or a fiction fashioned later to explain it, Diogenes' status as an exiled, transient noncitizen in Athens was closely related to his Cynic mission. To ingratiate himself as a foreigner in a new community would have required forfeiting aspects of his self-determination. Moreover, as Athens recovered itself through the mid-fourth century from the turmoil of the oligarchic revolutions, it became increasingly rigid and institutional in various social aspects: the moneyed economy, officers and legalism of the government, the philosophical schools, and perhaps a neo-aristocratic identity among some families. Diogenes, perhaps an aristocrat in his own land, might have tried to reproduce in this new time the Athens he knew from the period of its "radical democracy" (c. 460–403 BCE), before constitutional "law" was protected from the ephemeral decrees of the citizens, when the outspokenness or *parrhesia* of every citizen was encouraged, and when Socrates walked the streets reminding the citizens of their ethical responsibilities. Even when, according to a popular series of later anecdotes, Diogenes was sold into slavery, he retained his freedom to assent with his condition and a superior virtue and happiness sufficient to instruct his captors. Or so he claimed. This indifference to circumstance (*apatheia*) has close parallels to Stoicism and was said in antiquity to be a major source for the Stoic notion of virtue.

Unlike Antisthenes, Diogenes is credited with inspiring an array of disciples (Diogenes Laertius 6.82–93). The most important of these was Crates of Thebes (c. 368/65–288/85 BCE), a member of the Theban aristocracy who renounced his wealth, who is credited also with multiple disciples. One of these, Hipparchia the Cynic of Maroneia, renounced her dowry and arranged marriage to consort with Crates: according to anecdote, the two "mixed" in public, thus demonstrating that what was good behind closed doors was also good in the open. By the third century BCE, Cynicism had spread to urban centers all over the Greek world, such as Alexandria, Ephesus, and back to Sinope, and it seems, from literary references, as well as portraits in statue and wall paintings, if not from a lot of famous individual examples, that the presence of Cynics was ubiquitous until the end of the Roman Empire.

It is clear from the cases of Crates and Hipparchia, and the spread of Cynicism in the late fourth century, soon after the Greek city-states had come under the power of the Macedonian empire, that the motivation for Cynicism could no longer be personal circumstance such as low birth or exile—if these ever were the motivations. Rather, Cynicism was a principled renunciation of socially constructed value, not only money, property, luxury, and civic status, but also manners, modes of wisdom and education, and intellectual pretension. A widespread set of anecdotes preserving outspoken replies to Alexander the Great shows most directly the Cynic mission to "speak the truth to power" (to borrow a phrase from the modern Quakers), and a similar pattern recurs under the Roman Empire,

when Demetrius the Cynic clashes with Nero and Vespasian. The principles claimed were those "according to nature" and are, roughly speaking, universal: historically independent movements, such as the American hippies of the 1960s, share essential features with the Greek Cynics. What gave the Cynics their distinct identity in antiquity was the enduring memory of Diogenes, who was available in a living tradition of literature and lore as the type of subject devoted to bashing open the consciousness of humans who had lost touch with what being a human really was.

Cynic Literature, and Cynics in Literature and Visual Arts. From at least the time of Crates, Cynics performed their role not only in person but also by writing dialogues and poetry that either created the mimesis of older Cynic characters at work or revalued prestigious Greek literature, especially through parody. It is likely that the writings of Diogenes and some of those by Antisthenes could be classified in similar ways; but evidence is scant. Substantial fragments survive from Crates, Bion of Borysthenes (c. 335–c. 255 BCE), and Teles (c. 235 BCE), and we know Menippus of Gadara (early third century BCE) well from reputation (especially from Varro and Lucian of Samosata), even if we have little direct evidence of his writings. Cercidas of Megalopolis (c. 290–220 BCE) was both a statesman and a moralizing poet. The poetry and prose of these writers is distinguished by parody of Homer and others (especially Crates and Bion), moralizing and often riling dialogue between a wise teacher and a disciple whose education is in progress (especially Teles), and inflation of pretension to a point where it bursts itself (suggested in many titles, and probably typical, of Menippus). Menippus was recognized for boldly mixing genres, and even mixing poetry with prose. Both the moral themes and the confrontational, intertextual, and revisionist tactics of this literature became common territory in the Hellenistic period, and many Hellenistic poets, such as Phoenix of Colophon and Leonidas of Tarentum, can be called "Cynicizing" even if they would not have identified themselves as Cynics by living a Cynic lifestyle.

In addition to these probably unified and artful works, Cynics seem to have collected anecdotes about the adventures of Diogenes and others and recorded them, often in the form of brief sayings or one-line replies to challenges put to them. These were considered "useful" examples, and called *chreiai.* The Stoic founder Zeno of Citium is credited with a work called "Chreiai of Crates," who, according to tradition, was among Zeno's teachers. Most of these anthologies, so to speak, which are likely to be the origins of most surviving anecdotes about Diogenes of Sinope, were probably sympathetic to their Cynic subjects, but it is clear from Diogenes Laertius that there were also hostile traditions, some arising from rivalries between Cynics and established philosophical schools of the fourth and third centuries such as Aristotle's Peripatos.

In later centuries, under the Roman Republic and Empire, both positively Cynicizing literature and literature attacking the Cynics continued with vigor. Varro, Horace, and Petronius show or claim the influence of Menippus. Gaius Musonius Rufus, Epictetus, and Seneca the Younger bear comparison with Teles, and exemplify at times what some scholars call "Cynic diatribe," as if in imitation of the sermons delivered by real Cynics on the streets. A collection of letters addressed by famous older Cynics to their likely interlocutors was probably compiled in early imperial times from Cynic commonplaces and anecdotes. Dio Chrysostom uses Diogenes of Sinope as his heroic protagonist; Lucian uses Diogenes and other early Cynics as one guise for his intellectual hero. At the same time, Lucian, Athenaeus, and others point out the ease with which Cynicism can be faked and exploited to gain false glory or other unearned rewards: both present Cynic parasites at cultured dinner parties, where their behavior is boorish and disruptive for no higher purpose. Lucian attacks a character named Peregrinus for charlatanry in his staged suicide at the Olympics. Julian, in opposing derelict Cynicizers of his time, distinguishes the "real" Cynics of the olden days, who practiced what they preached in their rigorously ascetic lives.

In the visual arts, as probably in life, the Cynic was recognizable from his long, unkempt hair and beard, his simple clothing, a cloak folded double in place of the more elaborate layering of tunic and woolen cloak, his lack of shoes, his staff of authority, and his beggar's purse, in which he carried his food and everything he owned. His gaze was directed not upward in contemplation, as in other philosophical portraiture, but toward the viewer in engagement or confrontation, or sometimes into the distance, in disengagement from the human world.

[*See also* Diogenes the Cynic; Religion, *subentry* Philosophical Criticism; Philosophical Schools; *and* Socrates.]

BIBLIOGRAPHY

Primary Works

Giannantoni, Gabriele, ed. *Socratis et Socraticorum Reliquiae.* 4 vols. Naples, Italy: Bibliopolis, 1990. Fragments of the Cynics are in volume 2, pp. 135–589, and bibliographical notes in volume 4, pp. 195–583.

Laertius, Diogenes. *Lives of Eminent Philosophers*, edited by Robert Drew Hicks. Book 6. Cambridge, Mass.: Harvard University Press; London: Heinemann, 1938.

Malherbe, Abraham, ed. *The Cynic Epistles: A Study Edition.* Missoula, Mont.: Scholars Press, 1977.

Secondary Works

Billerbeck, Margarethe. *Die Kyniker in der modernen Forschung: Aufsätze mit Einführung und Bibliographie.* Amsterdam: B. R. Grüner, 1991.

Branham, R. Bracht, and Marie-Odile Goulet-Cazé, eds. *The Cynics: The Cynic Movement in Antiquity and Its Legacy.* Berkeley: University of California Press, 1996.

Dudley, D. R. *A History of Cynicism from Diogenes to the Sixth Century A.D.* London: Methuen, 1937. Reprint, Chicago: Ares, 1980.

Susan H. Prince

CYNOSCEPHALAE, BATTLE OF

Cynoscephalae, fought in Thessaly in spring 197 BCE, marked the decisive and final battle of the Second Macedonian War. It forced the defeated Macedonian king Philip V to enter peace negotiations with Rome. He agreed to withdraw his garrisons from Greece and to pay an indemnity of one thousand talents to Rome over a ten-year period, ending more than one hundred years of Macedonian rule in Greece.

Polybius' description of the battle survives (18.18–27), but the context needs to be supplemented by Livy 33.1–18, based on Polybius. By winter 198, Philip had lost control of much of southern and central Greece in spite of holding onto key garrisons such as Corinth. Early in 197, Titus Quinctius Flamininus, commander of the Roman forces, after wintering in Phocis, took steps to emphasize Philip's growing isolation by winning over the Boeotian League. He then acquired troops from the Aetolians and headed northward to Thessaly, where Philip was still strong. The two armies approached Pherae, where they encamped within ten miles (sixteen kilometers) of each other, learning of the other's presence through scouts. Flamininus' choice of Pherae may have been intended to cut Philip off from his garrisons at Phthiotic Thebes and Demetrias in southeastern Thessaly; certainly that was the effect.

The terrain, however, was unsuited for a battle, and the armies moved westward, separated by the Karadagh range. Possibly the move was precipitated by Philip, who according to Polybius was in need of supplies that he intended to get from the territory of Scotussa. When the battle did occur, it was almost by accident. In misty conditions advance forces of each met unexpectedly on the ridge itself, the resulting skirmish escalating into a full-scale battle. Philip was said to have been reluctant to commit his forces because of doubts about the suitability of the land but was led to do so by reports that the Romans were in difficulties—"the barbarians are fleeing," messengers told him.

Philip's defeat highlighted the limitations of the Macedonian phalanx when confronted by the adaptable Roman legion (cf. Polybius 18.28–32). The Aetolians, however, were widely perceived by Greeks to have played a crucial role in the Roman victory, as is evident from their prominence in the contemporary epigram by Alcaeus (Plutarch *Flamininus* 9). Of the twenty-five thousand Macedonians who fought, eight thousand died and five thousand became prisoners; the Roman dead numbered seven hundred. Although Philip requested a truce to collect the dead (Livy 33.11), bodies were still said to have been there when Antiochus arrived six years later

and very deliberately prepared an impressive funeral (Appian *Syrica* 16).

The hills where the battle took place were known as Cynoscephalae—literally, the "dog heads"—presumably named after their appearance. Because the hills' position is uncertain, scholars have variously located the battle both east and west of Scotussa, the latter most recently advocated by N. G. L. Hammond. It was also the scene of an earlier battle in 364 between Jason of Pherae and the Thebans in which the Theban general Pelopidas died.

[*See also* Flamininus, Titus Quinctius; Macedon; *and* Macedonian Wars.]

BIBLIOGRAPHY

Hammond, N. G. L. "The Campaign and the Battle of Cynoscephalae in 197 bc." *Journal of Hellenic Studies* 108 (1988): 60–82.

Hammond, N. G. L., and F. W. Walbank. *A History of Macedonia Vol. 3: 336–167 B.C.* Oxford: Clarendon Press, 1988. See pages 429–443.

Walbank, F. W. *A Historical Commentary on Polybius. Vol. 2: Commentary on Books VII–XVIII.* Oxford: Clarendon Press, 1967. See pages 572–601.

Andrew Erskine

CYPRUS

Strabo described Cyprus as "second to none of the islands of the Mediterranean: it is rich in wine and oil, produces grain in abundance and possesses extensive copper mines…." (14.6.5). Geographical proximity placed Cyprus within the orbit of the Levant; currents and winds situated the island in the flow of peoples and ideas between the Aegean and eastern Mediterranean. But at the same time, Cyprus' insularity and large size fostered idiosyncratic developments. This tension—between native and imported ideas, and invention in a middle ground—informs studies of ancient Cyprus.

Sources and Historical Outline. Archaeology plays a primary role in our understanding of ancient Cyprus, even in the historical periods. Writing first appeared on Cyprus at the start of the Late Bronze Age (1650–1050 BCE), but the script—a curious mixture of Aegean and Near Eastern traits—has not yet been deciphered. The cuneiform, Phoenician, and Cypro-Syllabic, and many Greek and Latin inscriptions of the Archaic, Classical, and Roman periods offer names, places, organizations, and formulae, but in total only a few sentences of narrative. No internal accounts of Cypriot ancient history exist. References to the island or its inhabitants in external texts offer only glimpses of the island's affairs. Nevertheless, they provide the framework of a political history: Cyprus' incorporation into the Assyrian empire (707 BCE) and a brief period of Egyptian rule (c. 570–526/25) during the Archaic period; unsuccessful uprisings against Persian rule (525–333); its submission to Alexander and eventual annexation (294) into the Ptolemaic kingdom; its appropriation by Rome in 58; a brief interval again in the Ptolemaic orbit (presented to Cleopatra VII first by Julius Caesar, then Mark Antony); and incorporation into the Roman Empire after Actium, first as part of the province of Syria, and then as a senatorial province in 22, a status it held until 395 CE, when Cyprus was allocated to the eastern half of the Roman Empire. *Pax Romana* was marred only by a violent Jewish uprising in 115–116 CE and major earthquakes in 15 BCE and 76/77 CE.

Ancient Cyprus was never directly part of the Greek political world. Cimon failed in his attempt to make it so in 450/49. Athens formally renounced all claims in the King's Peace (Antalkidas, 387/86), in which she acknowledged Persian sovereignty over Asia and Cyprus. Nevertheless, Hellenic influence looms large from at least the eleventh century, when an influx of Greek immigrants can be identified in the archaeological record. Despite Assyrian, Egyptian, and Persian rule, Greek is the predominant language of Archaic and Classical inscriptions and it continued to be the lingua franca of Ptolemaic Cyprus and the Roman East. Pottery, sculpture, the iconography of coins, the names and images of Cypriot deities all indicate continuing and strong ties with the Aegean throughout the long *durée* of Cypriot ancient history.

Bronze Age through Archaic. The Late Bronze Age is characterized by the first appearance of monumental architecture, urban settlements, and burials wealthy with imported exotica. In exchange, Cypriots exported copper and ceramics and served as a conduit for raw materials and finished goods. Mycenaean ceramics, Cretan architectural features, and aspects of the writing system indicate strong Aegean connections. The archives of Egypt, Syria, and Anatolia make evident that Alashiya (a toponym accepted by most scholars as referring to all or part of Cyprus) was fully integrated into the network of diplomatic and economic interrelationships of the eastern Mediterranean littoral.

That entire system crashed circa 1200 and the havoc wreaked elsewhere affected Cyprus, too. Widespread abandonments and destructions of the twelfth century are often attributed to the "Sea Peoples," a shorthand designation for a constellation of causes and refractions whose nature continues to be elusive. The first substantial wave of Greek immigrants may have come to Cyprus at this time.

Certainly they arrived in the eleventh century. As elsewhere, the "Dark Age" of Cyprus is turning out not to have been so dark. It was, rather, a period of new technologies, new overseas ties, new settlements. Greek myth attributes these new foundations to heroes of Troy, stopping en route home. And certainly there is evidence for ties with Greece, most fundamentally in the adoption of the Greek language. As in the case of Cyprus' Bronze Age script, with its Aegean affinities, the association of native Iron Age script (Cypro-Syllabic) with the geographically distant Greek Arcadian dialect is an interesting puzzle, given the proximity of Cyprus to the Levant and the expanding Phoenicians.

The earliest indisputable evidence for Phoenician presence on Cyprus is a tomb inscription dating to circa 850. By 800, Phoenician inscriptions are common especially at Kition, and by the fifth and fourth centuries they are widely distributed. Many are dedications and from them we learn names not only of individuals but also of divinities worshipped on Cyprus, for example, Astarte, Baal, and Melqart. Bilinguals are important indicators of associations made across cultures, for example,

Aphrodite-Astarte and Apollo-Reshef. Archaeology fills in the wider context of inscriptions; burials, pottery, architectural spaces, and religious offerings in stone and terracotta form the basis for discussions of Phoenician presence and interaction with other populations on the island.

Phoenicians may have facilitated economic and political relations between Cyprus and Assyria. A stele of Sargon II found at Kition signifies that Cyprus was under Assyrian political control by the end of the eighth century. Assyrians are traditionally portrayed as a ruthless military power but recent reevaluations of texts and archaeological materials suggest that Assyrian control of Cyprus may have been indirect and not inordinately onerous, for the seventh century was a period of prosperity for the island. The relationship continued until the fall of Nineveh (c. 612).

An inscription (673/72) erected by the Assyrian king Esarhaddon lists ten Cypriot rulers and later texts add two more names. These twelve city-kingdoms remained the basis for Cypriot political organization until the Hellenistic period. Numismatic, epigraphic, architectural, and funerary evidence suggests that the political divisions were also cultural: for example, Salamis had Greek associations, whereas inscriptions and tombs at Amathus indicate a strong native (Eteocypriot) presence, and Kition had long-standing ties with Phoenicia.

Contact with Egypt spiked during the reign of Amasis (Ahmose II; r. 570–526) when Herodotus (2.182.2) reports that the Egyptian pharaoh "seized Cyprus, the first man to do so, and compelled it to pay tribute." Certain inscriptions and texts can be interpreted as confirming Herodotus' account, but the relationship may have been less hostile than he portrays. Artistic styles and iconography, such as Egyptianizing Hathor-head capitals found on the island, indicate lively exchange among artisans of the two cultures.

Classical and Roman Periods. Whatever the formal association with Egypt, it came to an end circa 526/25, when Cyprus was made part of Persia's fifth satrapy. Cyprus paid tribute to Persia, but Persian interference with internal affairs was apparently minimal. Cypriot coins, first minted at this time, were all based on the Persian weight standard, but each city-kingdom had its own mint and the iconography and script of their distinctive issues varied greatly. Identifiable Persian influences are rare in the archaeological record. Conversely, freedom of movement within the empire intensified contact with the wider Greek world and Greek influences are easily perceived in the art, architecture, and religion of fifth- and fourth-century Cyprus. In collaboration with Greeks, Cyprus several times revolted against Persian rule. Kings of Salamis played particularly active roles, Onesilos in 499 and Evagoras from 411 to 380.

Coins issued in 306 commemorate Demetrius I Poliorcetes' defeat of Ptolemy, but from 294 Cyprus became firmly incorporated into the Ptolemaic kingdom and cultural sphere. As never before, a foreign power invested in formal symbols of authority. The city-kingdoms ceased to exist. Administration was organized as a military command under overall control of a *stratēgos*, with a garrison posted at each town. Nea Paphos, the closest port of call for ships sailing from Egypt, was made capital and remained so through the end of the Roman period. The mints (now reduced to four) issued coinage at the behest of Ptolemaic authority, their individual marks of identity reduced to subsidiary symbols. Inscriptions attest to the busy activities of the Koinon of Cypriots, an organization dedicated to promoting worship of the ruling Ptolemy. Arsinoë II, wife of Ptolemy II, was particularly popular. Archaeological finds add depth and nuance to the information provided by coins and inscriptions. Alexandrian influences filtered into common culture, but did not overwhelm the existing amalgam of Phoenician, Greek, and native features. So, for example, the cult of Aphrodite at Soloi incorporated Serapis (or Sarapis), but at Tamassos Aphrodite continued to be linked with Astarte and Cybele, and worship at Kaphizin remained centered on a local deity.

Roman Cyprus has traditionally been characterized as a region of stagnant isolation. But theoretical and archaeological approaches have shifted. Now the peripheries and intersections are privileged. Thus studies of the sanctuaries, tombs, civic and private architecture, sculptures, mosaics, jewelry, and pottery of Roman Cyprus currently flourish, adding vitally to the continuing questions of Cypriot cultural history: defining native, foreign, and local, and their shifting interfaces within the island.

[See also Coins and Coinage; Diadochi and Successor Kingdoms; Egypt, subentry Ptolemaic Egypt; Levant; Persia, subentry Achaemenid Persia; Phoenicia; and Ptolemies.]

BIBLIOGRAPHY

Iacovou, Maria, and Demetrios Michaelides, eds. Cyprus, The Historicity of the Geometric Horizon. Nicosia: The Archeological Research Unit, University of Cyprus, 1999.

Mitford, Terence B. "Roman Cyprus." In Aufstieg und Niedergang der römischen Welt (ANRW) 2.7.2 (1980): 1,285–1,384.

Reyes, Andres T. Archaic Cyprus: A Study of the Textual and Archaeological Evidence. Oxford: Clarendon Press, 1994.

Steel, Louise. Cyprus before History: From the Earliest Settlers to the End of the Bronze Age. London: Duckworth, 2004.

Tatton-Brown, Veronica. Ancient Cyprus. 2nd ed. London: British Museum, 1997.

Nicolle Hirschfeld

CYRENAICS

See Socratics, Minor.

CYRENE

The Greek city Cyrene, modern Shahat in Libya, was founded around 630 BCE by settlers from the island of Thera. The account by Herodotus (4.150–8) is the most complete information about the establishment of a Greek city, outlining issues such as the divine sanction, the choice of the site, and the several missteps before the location was actually settled upon. The city was situated about seven miles (twelve kilometers) inland and over two thousand feet (six hundred meters) above sea level, one of the most remote of Greek cities, lying between Egypt and Carthage and influenced by both. It controlled perhaps more territory than any other Greek city, with a large indigenous population with whom relations varied and were, at first, often hostile. Eventually, however, there was extensive intermarriage, and Cyrene became one of the most multicultural of Greek cities, with a racially mixed territory and a prosperous economy that included not only the traditional Greek commodities such as vines and olives, but especially horses and the exotic herb silphium. Its location at the southwestern extremity of the Greek world meant that it was an outlet for remote trade routes from sub-Saharan Africa: in fact, practically everything the Classical Greeks knew about the interior of the continent was received via Cyrenaean sources.

Like that of most Greek cities, its history is one of political instability. Kings descended from the founder Battus ruled into the fifth century, except for a period of Persian control after 525: little is known about the republican government that came to power around 440. The city submitted to Alexander III and was then annexed by Ptolemy I in 322, who gave it a new constitution (Diodorus 18.21). Despite provisions for permanent Ptolemaic control, Ptolemy's governor Ophellas ruled independently with visions of a Cyrenaean empire spreading across North Africa. He attacked Carthage around 308, with the collusion of Agathocles, tyrant of Syracuse, which resulted in a revolt at Cyrene, the death of Ophellas, and the collapse of the imperial plans (Diodorus 20.40–43). The stepson of Ptolemy I, Magas, took charge, and eventually claimed the title of king of Cyrene on Ptolemy's death in 283, ruling as such until his own death in 250. Late in life, however, he decided that a reconciliation with the Ptolemies would be wise, and married his daughter Berenice III to the heir-apparent Ptolemy III; when the latter came to the throne of Egypt in 246, Cyrene became permanently part of the Ptolemaic empire. The Egyptian court took on a distinct Cyrenaean tilt, with Berenice as queen and the Cyrenaean intellectuals Callimachus and Eratosthenes in residence, the latter Librarian at Alexandria from 246 until around 205 and the originator of the discipline of geography: it seems no accident that such a person should come from a remote heterogeneous city.

The latter Hellenistic period saw younger or less-favored members of the Ptolemaic family sent to Cyrene to rule as local king, most notably Ptolemy VIII (at Cyrene from 163 to 145), who willed the territory to Rome, the first major example of that familiar Hellenistic phenomenon, but in this case not implemented. The city flourished in Hellenistic times, with major building programs, significant art collections, and notable citizens. In addition to Callimachus and Eratosthenes, Cyrenaean intellectuals included Aristippus, who was a student of Socrates, his grandson of the same name, who probably founded the Cyrenaean school of thought, and Carneades, director of the Academy in Athens in the second century BCE.

The last king of an independent Cyrene was Ptolemy Apion, son of Ptolemy VIII. When he died in 96 he also willed the kingdom to Rome, and this time Rome acted, diffidently and over a twenty-year period, first annexing only the royal estates (Livy *Summary* 70). But by 74 a Roman governor was in residence and the territory became a Roman province, although in 36 Mark Antony gave it to his daughter Cleopatra Selene (Diodorus 49.32.4–5); she held it, unrecognized by Rome, until her death thirty years later.

Cyrene is a major archaeological site that has been under excavation for over a century. As might be expected, most of the visible remains are Roman, but the Roman city reflects a Hellenistic urban plan, with an agora and stoas. Portions of the extensive Hellenistic city walls survive. Most of the major sanctuaries were Ptolemaic or earlier in origin, especially the important precinct of Apollo, which was begun in the sixth century. In the vicinity of the agora are other early remains, perhaps including a precinct sacred to the founder Battus.

[*See also* Archaeology, *subentry* Sites in North Africa; Callimachus of Cyrene; Eratosthenes; Ptolemies; *and* Thera.]

BIBLIOGRAPHY

Hölbl, Günther. *A History of the Ptolemaic Empire*. Translated by Tina Saavedra. London: Routledge, 2001. Translation of *Geschichte des Ptolemäerreiches*, first published 2000. The best available history of the Ptolemaic world, with much about Cyrene.

Jones, A. H. M. *Cities of the Eastern Roman Provinces*. Oxford: Clarendon Press, 1937, pp. 351–362.

White, Donald. "Cyrene." In *Princeton Encyclopedia of Classical Sites*, edited by Richard Stillwell, pp. 253–255. Princeton, N.J.: Princeton University Press, 1976.

Duane W. Roller

D

See Balkans.

DAEDALIC ART

Art historians of the early twentieth century coined the term "Daedalic" to describe the most characteristic style for human figures in Greek art of the seventh century BCE. The famous Cretan architect and sculptor Daedalus clearly belongs to the realm of myth (Homer *Iliad* 18.592 associates him with Ariadne), but some Roman authors (e.g., Apollodorus mythographus *Bibliotheca* 3.15.8–9, first century CE) credit Daedalus with the invention of Greek sculpture, hence the connection of his name with the earliest Greek statues. In fact, Greek artists appropriated the style from Syria-Phoenicia during the phase of intense Greek interest in Levantine ideas and images known as the Orientalizing period (c. 700–600 BCE).

Daedalic figures are strictly frontal. The top of the head is flattened, and the face has the shape, more or less, of an inverted triangle. The forehead is low with a straight hairline. The hair falls in front of the shoulders either in a mass with horizontal divisions (the *Etagenperücke*) or as thick, vertically divided locks. The eyes are large. When represented, the ears lie at right angles to the face on top of the hair. The features of the body are not so diagnostic, but many Daedalic figures hold their arms straight down against their sides, and both males and females wear wide belts. The hairstyle reflects the strong Egyptianizing current in Phoenician art.

Daedalic Style. The main elements of the Daedalic style occur in Syrian and Phoenician ivory carvings of the ninth and eighth centuries BCE, some of which have been excavated in Greece, most importantly in the Idaean Cave on Crete. About the same time that the Daedalic style emerged, Greeks learned the Levantine technique of using molds to manufacture terra-cotta relief plaques. This technique permitted the mass production of cheap, portable votive objects that rapidly proliferated the Daedalic style through Greece and into Etruria. It has been suggested that casts taken from imported ivory carvings were used as molds for generating terra-cotta copies. Crete was certainly an early and influential region for Daedalic works; large deposits of Daedalic terra-cottas have been found at Gortyn, Axos, and Siteia. Other important Daedalic centers were Rhodes, Sparta, and Corinth, but examples of Daedalic art, executed in wood, bronze, ivory, gold, and stone as well as in terra-cotta, can be found in most areas of Greece in the Orientalizing period.

The dating of Daedalic works depends largely on stylistic analysis and links to Protocorinthian vases with three-dimensional Daedalic heads

(Louvre CA 931 aryballos, c. 650 BCE). In the earliest phase, Proto-Daedalic (c. 700–675 BCE), elements of the Syro-Phoenician models are rendered with strong echoes of the previous Geometric period (900–700 BCE), as in the angular bronze statuette dedicated by Mantiklos to Apollo at Thebes (Boston Museum of Fine Arts 03.997). Early Daedalic figures (c. 675–655 BCE) have long triangular faces, but the chin is softened into a U-shape; a well-known example is the small ivory sphinx from Perachora (Athens NM 16519). In Middle Daedalic (c. 655–630 BCE), faces like that of the limestone architectural relief from Mycenae (Athens NM 2869) are shorter and wider with squarer chins. The final phase, Late Daedalic (c. 630–600 BCE), can be seen in the kneeling ivory youth from the Sanctuary of Hera on Samos (Samos Vathy Museum E 88); here the face is almost as wide as it is long, and the head has a higher and more rounded crown. Daedalic vestiges, especially the thick, vertical side locks, continue after 600 BCE, but the strong regional styles of Greek art in the sixth century BCE replace the relative homogeneity of many seventh-century works.

Developments. Several developments crucial for later Greek art come in the Middle Daedalic period. Perhaps the earliest marble sculptures in Greece are the *perirrhantēria* (stands with large, shallow basins) from Sparta (Sparta Museum 3362), Samos (Berlin, Staatliche Museum 1747), and Isthmia (Isthmia Museum). On a circular or quadratic base, Daedalic female caryatids stand on or beside reclining lions, the whole ensemble carved from a single block. The caryatids supported a large marble basin that could be more than a meter in diameter. A few pre-Daedalic limestone sculptures are known from Crete, but the large-scale Cretan limestone works of the mid-seventh century BCE are the earliest Greek freestanding statues in stone. These include the top half of a female figure from Astritsi (Heraklion 407) and the bottom half of a seated female from Gortyn (Heraklion 380), as well as the smaller but more famous standing figure from Auxerre (Louvre 3098). Crete has also furnished the earliest Greek examples of architectural sculpture. A limestone relief from Gortyn that shows two

almost life-size nude female figures flanking a central male (Herakleion 379) seems like a much enlarged terra-cotta relief and is paralleled by a clothed triad in an ivory relief from Sparta. About the same time (c. 630 BCE), a lintel (horizontal beam) from an ambitious temple at Prinias depicts two large seated females on top with reliefs of animals and standing females on the sides and soffit (underside); a frieze from this building depicts mounted warriors (Herakleion 231).

The first Greek freestanding statues in marble were made in the Cyclades not long after the appearance of large limestone sculptures on Crete. A Naxian woman named Nikandre dedicated an over-life-size marble female in the Sanctuary of Artemis on Delos (Athens NM 1, c. 640 BCE). The November 2000 discovery on Thera of a giant marble female statue—7.6 feet (2.3 meters) tall—is a spectacular addition to the repertory of Daedalic works. The Thera statue is quite close in style to the statuette from Auxerre and provides a connection between the limestone sculpture of Crete and the marble statues of the Cyclades.

Just as the Daedalic female statues presage the long sequence of sixth century BCE Archaic *korai* (maidens), Daedalic male figures establish the characteristic type for the Archaic male statue. The first fully developed kouros (young man) has been recognized in the small bronze statuette from Delphi (Delphi Museum 2527, c. 630 BCE), nude except for a belt, hands clenched at the thighs, and the left leg slightly advanced. He is soon followed by life-size and larger marble kouroi from Delos and Thera.

The technique of creating statues from sheets of hammered bronze (*sphyrēlata*) was used on Crete in the late eighth century BCE for three small cult statues from Dreros (Herakleion 2445–7). A century later, three larger (about 4 feet, or 1.2 meters, high) hammered bronze female figures found at Olympia probably represent Late Daedalic Cretan work. A major advance in bronze-working technology came around the middle of the seventh century with the first Greek examples of hollow-cast bronzes made with the lost-wax process. A hollow-cast bronze Daedalic head of circa 640 BCE from Olympia

(Karlsruhe, Badisches Landsmuseum F 1890), about one-third life size, may have supported a cult basin.

[*See also* Greece, *subentry* The Archaic Age and Sculpture.]

BIBLIOGRAPHY

Adams, Lauren. *Orientalizing Sculpture in Soft Limestone from Crete and Mainland Greece.* Oxford: British Archaeological Reports, 1978.

Jenkins, R. J. H. *Dedalica: A Study of Dorian Plastic Art in the Seventh Century B.C.* Cambridge, U.K.: Cambridge University Press, 1936.

Kaminski, Gabriele. "Dädalische Plastik." In *Die Geschichte der antiken Bildhauerkunst,* vol. 1: *Frühgriechische Plastik,* edited by Gabriele Kaminski and Caterina Maderna-Lauter, pp. 71–95. Mainz am Rhein, Germany: Verlag Philipp von Zabern, 2002.

Matz, Friedrich, ed. *Dädalische Kunst auf Kreta im 7. Jahrhundert v. Chr.* Mainz am Rhein, Germany: Verlag Philipp von Zabern, 1970.

Morris, Sarah P. *Daidalos and the Origins of Greek Art.* Princeton, N.J.: Princeton University Press, 1992.

Jane B. Carter

DAEDALUS

See Crete, *subentry* Cretan Mythology.

DALMATIA

See Balkans.

DANAIDS

The Danaids were the fifty daughters of the Egyptian king Danaus, who claimed a connection to Greece as a descendant of Io. Danaus promised his daughters in marriage to their cousins, the fifty sons of his brother, Aegyptus. Strongly objecting to the marriage, the Danaids fled with their father to Argos, where they were received as suppliants by the king Pelasgus. In the version of the story presented in Aeschylus' dramatic trilogy about the Danaids, Pelasgus agrees to protect them from the sons of Aegyptus, who arrive in hot pursuit and attempt to drag the Danaids from the altar where they have taken refuge. Although the first and only extant play in the trilogy, *Suppliants,* ends with Pelasgus' successful effort to protect the women, fragments of the ensuing plays indicate that the sons of Aegyptus manage to overpower Pelasgus and force the Danaids into marriage. The Danaids, however, urged by Danaus, plot to kill their husbands on their wedding night; only one daughter, Hypermestra, spares her husband, Lynceus. She then becomes the ancestor of later Argive kings. The other Danaids, according to Pindar (*Pythian* 9.111–116), eventually remarry and are honored in Argive tradition as benefactors.

The love of Hypermestra for Lynceus, which was probably already a factor in the Aeschylean drama, became a favorite theme for Roman poets, especially Horace (*Odes* 3.11) and Ovid (*Heroides* 14). Roman writers such as Ovid (*Metamorphoses* 4.462–63) popularized a different ending that became proverbial, in which in Hades the Danaids are condemned to carry water in leaky vessels perpetually.

[*See also* Aeschylus.]

BIBLIOGRAPHY

Keuls, Eva. *The Water Carriers in Hades.* Amsterdam: Hakkert, 1974.

Zeitlin, Froma. "The Politics of Eros in the Danaid Trilogy of Aeschylus." In *Innovations of Antiquity,* edited by Ralph Hexter and Daniel Selden, pp. 203–252. New York: Routledge, 1992.

Jennifer Clarke Kosak

DANCE

Dance was an integral part of the musical culture of early Greece, an essential component in that unity of music, movement, and word that the Greeks called *mousikē.* The pleasures of song and dance are vividly depicted in the city at peace on the shield of Achilles: young men and girls of marriageable age dance together, hands clasped at the wrist in a pose familiar from early Greek vases, while two tumblers lead them from the middle, the whole spectacle bringing joy to all who watched (Homer *Iliad*

Dancing Maenads. Marble relief, Roman, first century CE. MUSÉE NATIONAL DU BARDO, LE BARDO, TUNISIA/LAUROS/GIRAUDON/THE BRIDGEMAN ART LIBRARY

18.590–606). Similarly Alcinous' entertainment of Odysseus on the island of Phaeacia includes a display of dancing by young men in the first bloom of youth, culminating in an acrobatic performance by the two most skillful, while their companions beat time around them (Homer *Odyssey* 8.367–384). Throughout the *Odyssey* song and dance typify the life of pleasure associated with the feast.

The gods, too, delight in dancing. Apollo rejoices in the dancing of his worshippers on Delos (*Homeric Hymn to Apollo* 142ff.); he himself leads the Graces and the other goddesses as they dance on Olympus while Zeus and Leto look on (*Homeric Hymn to Apollo* 182–206); and the nine Muses, the archetypal heavenly chorus, are dancers as well as singers (Hesiod *Theogony* 1–10, 62–71). Human pleasure in dancing is mirrored by that of the gods, hence dance is seen as a form of communication with the divine. According to Plato (*Laws* 653c ff.) song and dance, *choreia*, was a gift from the gods to console human beings for the miseries of life, and the picture we are given in early Greek poetry certainly corroborates this view.

Dance as Ritual. No less important than the pleasure inherent in dance is its ritual function. From earliest times dancing together in a group was a central feature of religious worship, which also served to bind the group together. So, for example, Dionysus was honored with dithyrambs, Apollo was honored with paeans, and Artemis was honored in maiden dances such as the *partheneia* performed by the choruses of young girls at Sparta for which the poet Alcman was famous. The development of complex meters in the choral lyric poetry of the Archaic period seems to reflect the rhythms of music and dance, and most scholars agree that as a general rule choral performance includes both song and dance, even if we cannot be certain in individual cases. Particularly controversial are Pindar's epinicia (victory odes), but the references to dance (e.g., *Olympian* 14.15–17; *Pythian* 1.2), together with the fact that his other compositions were for choral performers, suggest that some, if not all, of his epinicia were also performed by a chorus of singers and dancers. The song-dance culture continued into the Classical period, and in Athens participation in a chorus was part of a citizen's education. Greek drama was said to have originated in choral singing and dancing, and the importance of dance in tragedy and comedy is well known: dramatists were not just poets but also composers of music and choreographers of dance. Aeschylus is said to have invented many dances, and Sophocles himself was an accomplished dancer.

To dance is to live, and Hades is imagined as a place without wedding song, lyre, or dance (Sophocles *Oedipus at Colonus* 1221–1222). Dancing was ubiquitous in Greek life, at weddings and funerals, at harvests, sacrifices, and festivals, in mystery cults and initiation rites, at victory celebrations, and in preparation for war. We also find dancing for entertainment in the more private context of the symposium, such as that so graphically described in Xenophon's *Symposium*. One of the most famous stories about solo dancing concerns Hippocleides, who, Herodotus tells us (6.127–130), was one of the suitors of the daughter of Cleisthenes, tyrant of Sicyon. On the day that he was to declare his choice, Cleisthenes organized a great banquet at which the suitors competed in music and in speaking. Hippocleides was emerging as the winner until, as more and more wine was consumed, he began dancing to the music of an aulos, finally standing upside down on a table, waving his legs in the air in time to the music. This was too much for Cleisthenes, who declared that Hippocleides had danced away his marriage. The story is repeated much later by Athenaeus (628c–d), who interprets it as an illustration of the relationship between dance and character: Hippocleides' vulgar dancing mirrored the vulgarity of the man.

Dance as Education. The ethical dimension of dance is evident from Plato's *Laws*, a primary source for our understanding of the cultural and religious significance of dance in Greek life. In the city that Plato envisions, the entire community—men, women, and children—will be involved in choral performances, which will reinforce the values of the polis and create social cohesion among its members. Choral dance and education are one and the same thing: *choreia* is *paideia*, and the uneducated person is one who cannot take part in a chorus (*Laws* 654a). Plato assumes that dance is both a natural human activity and one that connects us with the gods: humans are the only creatures who have perception of rhythm and harmony. Music and dance are the principal means of bringing order into human life, instilling the ethical qualities necessary for individuals and society and affecting both body and soul.

But there are bad as well as good forms of dancing: one type represents the graceful movement of beautiful bodies, the other the unsightliness of ugly bodies, both expressing the characters of the dancers. The appropriate types for citizens to perform are the war dance (the *pyrrhichē*), which promotes courage and a fine physique, and the peaceful moderate dancing termed *emmeleia*. All Bacchic dancing such as that which allegedly imitates the drunken behavior of satyrs and sileni is to be discouraged. As for the lewd dances of comedy, these will be staged by slaves and foreigners for the benefit of citizens who need to know about ugly and ridiculous behavior in order to avoid it, but citizens must not engage in such dances themselves (814e–816d).

Post-Classical and Roman Dance. After the Classical period and the demise of the song culture, dance became separated from music and song, lost its central role in education, and became increasingly the activity of the professional rather than the gentleman. Later writers—notably Lucian, whose treatise *On Dance* is the only such work to survive, and Athenaeus (14.628c–631e)—build on Plato's discussion and preserve traditions about the history of dance and its various classifications. Among the most important are the *hyporchēma*, a broad category of choral dance with song; three types of dramatic dance, the *emmeleia* of tragedy, the *kordax* of comedy, and the *sikinnis* of the satyr play; and the *pyrrhichē*, danced everywhere but particularly associated with the military society of Sparta. A belief in the primordial status of dance is reflected in Lucian's claim that dance came into being with the cosmogonic Eros with whom the universe began (*On Dance* 7). Even the infant Zeus owed his life to dance: the Curetes (young, divine Cretan warriors) saved him from being devoured by his father by dancing around him in warlike fashion, clashing their swords against their shields—hence the association between dancing and warfare (*On Dance* 8).

The Romans, too, had their solemn dances, notably those performed by the priesthood of the Salii in honor of Ares (Lucian *On Dance* 20). But dance had less prestige in Roman society than in earlier times: Cicero could even remark that no man dances when sober unless he is mad (*Pro Murena* 6.13). The wild and ecstatic dancing that came to Rome with the arrival of Oriental cults such as those of the great mother goddess Cybele reinforced this disapproval of dance among moralists (though wild Bacchic dancing existed in Greece, too: witness Plato's disapproval). But as a form of entertainment dance had its place in the *convivium*, the dinner party, where guests would enjoy performances by professionals, often slaves.

The popularity of dance reached new heights in Rome with the arrival of the pantomime, in which the solo dancer took center stage. Traditionalists objected that the enjoyment of such displays was beneath the dignity of a freeborn gentleman, whereas apologists looked back to the long history of dance in ancient Greece to defend its value. According to Plato (*Laws* 816a) dance originated in the gestures (*schēmata*) that naturally accompany vocal expression, and Lucian, recalling this, declares that because dance is an art of imitation and portrayal, it is the dancer's task to know what is appropriate in every case and to express it by the clarity of his gestures (*On Dance* 36). But bodily gestures are inextricably linked with the soul, hence dance, unlike the other arts, combines both body and soul (71) and is the perfect means of educating its spectators in the harmonious concord of the two.

[*See also* Meter, Greek; Meter, Latin; Muses; Music; *and* Pantomime.]

BIBLIOGRAPHY

Lonsdale, Stephen H., *Dance and Ritual Play in Greek Religion*. Baltimore: Johns Hopkins University Press, 1993. Explores the place of dance in the cults and festivals of Greece in the Archaic and Classical periods in conjunction with Plato's *Laws*.

Naerebout, F. G. *Attractive Performances: Ancient Greek Dances*. Leiden, The Netherlands: J. C. Gieben, 1997. Provides a detailed survey of the history of scholarship on Greek dance and a critical discussion of the ancient sources; includes an extensive bibliography.

Penelope Murray

DANTE

(1265–1321), Italian poet. Not only is Dante the greatest poet to write in Italian: he also was the greatest Latinist of his age. This is clear both from the many works that he wrote in Latin and also from the deep understanding implicit in the allusions to Latin poetry in the *Commedia* (known in English as the *Divine Comedy*). Dante Alighieri had an unsettled life during his years of exile from his native Florence—from 1302 until his death in Ravenna— but nevertheless his learning and his command of Latin and Latin poetry were immense and evident not only in the *Divine Comedy* but in all of his major works: the *Vita nuova* (New Life), the *Convivio* (Banquet), *De vulgari eloquentia* (On Eloquence in the Vernacular), his Latin letters, and most dramatically in book 2 of his *Monarchia* (Monarchy).

Of Latin poets his knowledge and appreciation of Virgil—Virgil of the fourth ("Messianic") *Eclogue* and the *Aeneid*—went deepest and are most evident. In the *Divine Comedy*, Virgil is Dante's guide down through the nine circles of Hell and, with significant disorientation, in the ascent of the seven terraces of the Mount of Purgatory to the terrestrial paradise at its summit. As a pagan, Virgil is unable to enter Paradise but must return to the choice company of his fellow pagans in Limbo. Virgil disappears abruptly and returns to Limbo at the moment that Dante catches sight of Beatrice across the river dividing them (*Purgatorio* 30). When he registers Virgil's disappearance, Dante calls out to him three times in imitation of the passage in Virgil's *Georgics* where Orpheus calls out to Eurydice (*Purgatorio* 30.43–54; *Georgics* 4.525–527).

Dante twice asserts his appreciation of Virgil as something new in Italy: first when he initially encounters the Virgil of his *Divine Comedy* and describes him as someone who "seemed hoarse from long silence" (*Inferno* 1.63)—meaning that Virgil, who died in 19 BCE, could now speak to Dante at the beginning of the fourteenth century CE; second when Dante suggests to Cavalcante dei Cavalcanti that his son, the great poet of the vernacular Guido Cavalcante, "might have held Virgil in contempt"

(*Inferno* 10.61–63). But Dante is not subservient to Virgil. He creates his own Virgil for his *Divine Comedy*. When he protests Virgil's advice that he must descend into Hell, Dante says: "I am not Paul, I am not Aeneas" (*Inferno* 2.32). Despite this profession of humility, Dante ultimately proves himself to be much more than Paul, who—according to a tradition based on 2 Corinthians 12—ascended only to the third sphere of Heaven, and Aeneas, who did not actually enter Tartarus. By penetrating deeper into Hell and higher into Heaven, Dante surpassed both Virgil's Aeneas and Paul.

Dante took as a model for his *Inferno* Aeneas' descent into Hell in *Aeneid* 6—as Virgil had taken *Odyssey* 11 as his model. But the remarkable thing about Dante's imitation of Virgil is that aspects of Virgil's underworld are distributed in the *Purgatorio* and the *Paradiso* as well. Dante recalls Virgil's description of the Elysian fields in his description of the Valley of the Princes (especially in *Purgatorio* 7.73–77) and in his meeting with his great-great-grandfather Cacciaguida in *Paradiso* 15–17—a scene that imitates Aeneas' encounter with his father, Anchises, in *Aeneid* 6.

As his guide, Virgil is very generous to Dante and his understanding of the *Aeneid*, at one point saying that Dante knows his "high tragedy by heart" (*Inferno* 20.112–124). That claim must be true. One proof of this is that when Francesca da Rimini recalls her past joys with her lover, Paolo, she says to Dante:

> There is no greater sorrow
> than thinking back on a happy time
> in misery—as your teacher knows. (*Inferno* 5.121–123)

Dante here transforms Aeneas' words to his discouraged companions in *Aeneid* 1.203: "At some time it might give us pleasure to recall these troubles."

Dante not only knew the *Aeneid* by heart; he also understood, in his own way, the intimations of the pagan prophecy of Christian truth that are inaugurated in Virgil's fourth *Eclogue*, that continue in Ovid's *Metamorphoses* and the epic poetry of Lucan and Statius, and that culminate with Dante's own *Divine Comedy*, where the emperor Justinian's vast history of the Roman eagle (in *Paradiso* 6)—that is, Dante's history of the manifest destiny of the Roman Empire—is another version of Dante's conception of God's plan for mankind united by a universal Roman emperor. (Unfortunately, Dante's hopes came to an end with the death of the Holy Roman Emperor Henry VII on 24 August 1313.) This conception is also revealed in the second book of Dante's *Monarchy*, where he speaks of "pagan scripture" and the "miracles" of Roman history. Dante's *Monarchy* offended the Vatican and was placed on the *Index Librorum Prohibitorum* in 1585.

Dante's choice of Italian as the language of his *Divine Comedy* offended many Latinists, but Dante made his Tuscan dialect the national language of a unified Italy and made his pagan learning accessible to the speakers of a language that cries *mamma* and *babbo* for mother and father (*Inferno* 32.9).

[*See also* Classical Scholarship, *subentry* The Middle Ages and the Renaissance; *and* Virgil.]

BIBLIOGRAPHY

Brownlee, Kevin. "Dante and the Classical Poets." In *The Cambridge Companion to Dante*, edited by Rachel Jacoff. Cambridge, U.K., and New York: Cambridge University Press, 1993.

Davis, Charles Till. *Dante and the Idea of Rome*. Oxford: Clarendon Press, 1957.

Diskin Clay

DAPHNIS AND CHLOE

Composed in the late second or early third century CE by an otherwise unknown author named Longus, *Daphnis and Chloe* became one of the most popular ancient Greek novels. Johann Wolfgang von Goethe, for instance, enthusiastically praises it in his conversations with Johann Peter Eckermann, recommending that one read the work each year to "learn from it again and again and sense anew the impression of its great beauty" (20 March 1831).

In the absence of external evidence, scholars must rely on internal clues to date the text (see Hunter, pp. 1–15): the novel's style in particular, and its playful interaction with the literary tradition, strongly speak in favor of regarding it as a product of the second-century intellectual movement known as the Second Sophistic. Its title appears in several versions, the most common form being *poimenika ta peri* [or *kata*] *Daphnin kai Chloen* ("shepherd stories about Daphnis and Chloe"), to which one manuscript adds *Lesbiaka erōtika* ("erotic stories from Lesbos"). Inscriptions attest the presence of Pompeii Longi in Lesbos (see Conrad Cichorius, *Römische Studien* [Leipzig, Germany: Teubner, 1922], pp. 321–323), the island where the plot is set, and the suggestion that the author may have been a member of that Greco-Roman family is, though unprovable, not without plausibility. It should, however, be noted that one of the two primary manuscripts, F, gives the author's name as Logos, which gave rise to the (mostly discredited) theory that *Longos* is, in fact, a corruption originating from a heading (*logos a* = book 1).

Spanning a period of almost two years, the four books of *Daphnis and Chloe* relate the story of a teenage goatherd and shepherdess who gradually discover the nature of love and sexuality with charming innocence and naïveté. Exposed as babies by their urban parents, Daphnis and Chloe are raised by poor foster families in rural surroundings. They are suckled by, respectively, a she-goat and a ewe, which explains their profound attachment to these animals and nature in general. Even after the discovery of their true identities, which is followed by their wedding and sexual union at the end of the novel, the two protagonists renounce the luxury of city life and prefer to spend most of their time in the countryside.

The first book opens with the *ekphrasis* of a painting that the narrator claims to have encountered in a grove sacred to the nymphs. The painting depicts the entire story of *Daphnis and Chloe* and inspires in him a desire (*pothos*) to compete with the pictorial representation by means of his verbal art (on the preface *see* Zeitlin, pp. 430–436). This idea of an agon between the two media, programmatically staged at the outset of the novel, is indicative of the narrative style of Longus, who, as befits a Second Sophistic author, excels in the art of description and frequently makes use of a whole panoply of rhetorical devices to evoke stunning landscape scenes before our eyes. Longus' linguistic skill and sophistication stand in clear contrast to the simplicity and naturalness of his characters and their surroundings. At the same time, however, his style bears all the marks of the rhetorical mode characterized as *glukutēs* (sweetness) by ancient handbooks and is thus in harmony with the "sweetness" of the novel's subject matter (on language and style *see* Hunter, pp. 92–98).

At the heart of *Daphnis and Chloe* lies the dichotomy between art (*technē*) and nature (*phusis*), which finds a parallel in the opposition of city and country. Although preference is given to the rural life of the protagonists, Longus also makes it clear that nature is to be refined by art. The extent of Chloe's beauty, for example, is revealed only when she appears washed, combed, and properly dressed (4.32). And even though the two teenagers are seized by a mutual longing, they are in need of both theoretical and practical instruction in the art of love to remedy their erotic "sickness."

Through the intervention of an old man called Philetas (on his association with the Hellenistic poet of this name *see* Bowie), who tells them about his encounter with Eros (2.3–7), Daphnis and Chloe first come to realize that they are in love, but for a long time they do not know how to satisfy their physical desire. In one of the novel's most hilarious scenes, Daphnis tries to mimic copulating goats by making Chloe stand up and embracing her from behind—all in vain (3.14.5). Though Daphnis is initiated in the deeds of love by Lycaenion (3.16–18), a young woman from the city who is married to an elderly farmer, Chloe will have to wait until the very end of the work to learn that "what happened at the edge of the wood was but shepherds' games" (4.40.3). Had it not been for Lycaenion's warning about the pain of defloration (3.19), Daphnis would immediately have shared his newly acquired knowledge with the beloved. Ironically, it his only his hesitation to hurt Chloe that helps her preserve the virginity that she is—contrary to other novelistic heroines—desperately trying to lose (for Chloe's sexual education *see* Winkler and Goldhill).

All in all, *Daphnis and Chloe* can be characterized as a generic experiment in that it combines the erotic novel with pastoral poetry. Teeming with allusions to Theocritus and other bucolic poets (*see* Effe), it offers amusing variations on novelistic themes and substitutes relatively harmless threats for the grave dangers typically faced by the lovers: at 1.28–31, for instance, Daphnis is kidnapped by pirates, but she is saved when the stolen cattle jump overboard on hearing Chloe play the flute. Instead of traveling to exotic countries, the two protagonists set out on a sexual discovery voyage; theirs is, as B. P. Reardon has observed, "a journey not in space, but in time" ("The Greek Novel," *Phoenix* 23 [1969]: 301). Thus the four seasons play a major role in structuring the novel, and their succession parallels the gradual development of Daphnis and Chloe's love.

[*See also* Eros; Novel, Greek and Latin; Poetry, Greek, *subentry* Pastoral; *and* Second Sophistic.]

BIBLIOGRAPHY

Primary Works

Longus. "Daphnis and Chloe." Translated by Christopher Gill. In *Collected Ancient Greek Novels*, edited by B. P. Reardon, pp. 285–348. Berkeley: University of California Press, 1989. An English translation.

Longus. *Daphnis and Chloe.* Translated by John R. Morgan. Aris & Phillips Classical Texts. Oxford: Aris & Phillips, 2004. An English translation with introduction and commentary; the included Greek text is that of Reeve's Teubner edition.

Longus. *Daphnis et Chloe.* Edited by Michael D. Reeve. 3rd ed. Stuttgart, Germany: B. G. Teubner, 1994. An edition of the Greek text.

Longus. *Daphnis and Chloe.* Translated by George Thornley, revised and augmented by J. M. Edmonds. Loeb Classical Library. London: W. Heinemann; Cambridge, Mass: Harvard University Press, 1916. A Greek text with a parallel English translation.

Secondary Works

Bowie, Ewen L. "Theocritus' Seventh Idyll, Philetas, and Longus." *Classical Quarterly* 35 (1985): 67–91.

Bretzigheimer, Gerlinde. "Die Komik in Longos' Hirtenroman *Daphnis und Chloe.*" *Gymnasium* 95 (1988): 515–555.

Effe, Bernd. "Longus: Towards a History of Bucolic and Its Function in the Roman Empire." In *Oxford Readings in the Greek Novel*, edited by Simon Swain, pp. 189–209. Oxford: Oxford University Press, 1999. An English translation of "Longos: Zur Funktionsgeschichte der Bukolik in der römischen Kaiserzeit" (*Hermes* 110 [1982]: 65–84).

Goldhill, Simon. *Foucault's Virginity: Ancient Erotic Fiction and the History of Sexuality.* Cambridge, U.K.: Cambridge University Press, 1995. See especially chapter 1, pages 1–45.

Hunter, Richard. *A Study of "Daphnis and Chloe."* Cambridge, U.K.: Cambridge University Press, 1983.

MacQueen, Bruce D. *Myth, Rhetoric, and Fiction: A Reading of Longus's "Daphnis and Chloe."* Lincoln: University of Nebraska Press, 1990.

McCulloh, William E. *Longus.* New York: Twayne, 1970.

Winkler, John J. "The Education of Chloe: Hidden Injuries of Sex." In his *The Constraints of Desire: The Anthropology of Sex and Gender in Ancient Greece*, pp. 101–126. New York and London: Routledge, 1990.

Zeitlin, Froma I. "The Poetics of Erôs: Nature, Art, and Imitation in Longus' *Daphnis and Chloe.*" In *Before Sexuality: The Construction of Erotic Experience in the Ancient Greek World*, edited by David M. Halperin, John J. Winkler, and Froma I. Zeitlin, pp. 417–644. Princeton, N.J.: Princeton University Press, 1990.

Regina Höschele

DARK AGE

See Greece, *subentry* The Dark Age.

DEAD SEA SCROLLS

The Dead Sea Scrolls are ancient Jewish manuscripts that were discovered between 1947 and 1956 in eleven caves on the northwestern shore of the Dead Sea in and around Qumran. Written in Aramaic, Hebrew, and Greek, the approximately nine hundred manuscripts date from the third century BCE through the first century CE. The scrolls have significantly increased understanding of the diversity of early Judaism and of Christian origins.

From 1951 to 1956 archaeologists under the leadership of Father Roland de Vaux of the École Biblique in Jerusalem excavated the ancient settlement in the immediate vicinity of the caves. Vaux concluded that Khirbet Qumran served as the community center of the group now associated with the scrolls, a hypothesis that has since been corroborated by most archaeologists. The community first occupied the site around the year 100 BCE, and the settlement was destroyed by the Romans in 68 CE. Based on archaeological evidence the sect must have been modest in size and may not have included more than a hundred and fifty to two hundred inhabitants at any moment. The scrolls do not reveal the identity of the group or that of the group's leader, the Teacher of Righteousness, though most scholars hold that the group was a radical offshoot of the Essenes, an ancient Jewish group whose description by Philo and Josephus agrees significantly with the self-depiction of the Qumran group that is found in the sectarian documents.

The state of preservation of the Dead Sea Scrolls varies greatly. The longest is the Temple Scroll from cave 11, measuring about twenty-six feet (eight meters). Most manuscripts are badly fragmented, however. Cave 4 alone, the richest cave, yielded thousands of fragments. Based on their content, the Qumran texts can be divided into six categories:

1. Biblical scrolls. Of the nine hundred Dead Sea manuscripts, about 222 are biblical scrolls. Manuscripts of all the books of the Hebrew Bible (the Old Testament) were discovered at Qumran, most in multiple copies, with the exception of the book of Esther, which is not attested. Leading the list is the Psalter, with thirty-nine copies. The biblical manuscripts, some of which predate previously known manuscripts by a full millennium, provide scholars with invaluable new information about the genesis and history of the biblical text.

2. Biblical commentary. Members of the Qumran sect spent one-third of each night as well as a portion of each day studying Scripture. There is hardly a text among the scrolls that is not affected by biblical interpretation. Biblical commentary takes various forms at Qumran, from the paraphrasing or retelling of the book of Genesis in the Genesis Apocryphon to the verse-by-verse explication of Scripture in the Pesharim.

3. Legal texts. Some of the foundational compositions that indicate the structure and theology of the community fall under this category. The Damascus Document, so called because it repeatedly refers to Damascus as the place of residence of the community, consists of two parts: an extended admonition to follow the ways of God and a legal part that covers a wide range of topics. The Community Rule, at times called "a constitution of the Qumran community," sets out much of the sect's rules and regulations. The Halakhic Letter or 4QMMT is a letter from the head of the Qumran community to the high priest in Jerusalem in which he outlines some of the group's differences with the Temple hierarchy that led to the division. The Temple Scroll is a retelling of the legal sections of the books of Exodus and Deuteronomy.

4. Calendars, liturgical and poetic texts, and prayers. These texts are concerned with the religious holidays that are marked by liturgies and prayers and that are regulated by the sect's distinctive calendar. The calendar, a subject of considerable dispute in early Judaism, was of central importance. The Qumran community strictly followed a 364-day solar (as opposed to a lunar) calendar, in which the third, sixth, ninth, and twelfth months consisted of thirty-one days, and all other months consisted of thirty days. The liturgical and poetic texts include the Songs of the Sabbath Sacrifice, a cycle of thirteen angelic hymns, and the Hodayot, or Songs of Thanksgiving.

5. Wisdom texts. A number of texts follow the sapiential tradition known from the Bible from books such as Proverbs. In 4QInstruction a sage instructs a student on issues such as finances, society, and family.

6. Eschatological texts. The members of the Qumran community believed that they were living in the final age and that God would intervene at any moment to bring history to an end.

The War Scroll provides an account of the eschatological battle between the Sons of Light and the Sons of Darkness. The New Jerusalem Text describes the Heavenly Jerusalem in its apocalyptic proportions.

[*See also* Bible, *subentry* Jewish Scripture and Other Writings; Jerusalem; Jews and Judaism; *and* Judaea, *subentry* The Roman Province of Judaea.]

BIBLIOGRAPHY

Primary Works

The official publication series is titled *Discoveries in the Judean Desert* (Oxford: Clarendon Press, 1955–). See also Florentino García Martínez and Eibert J. C. Tigchelaar, eds., *The Dead Sea Scrolls Study Edition* (2 vols.; Leiden: Brill, 1997–1998), and Géza Vermès, ed. and trans., *The Complete Dead Sea Scrolls in English* (rev. ed., London and New York: Penguin, 2004).

Secondary Works

Cross, Frank Moore. *The Ancient Library of Qumran.* 3rd ed. Sheffield, U.K.: Sheffield Academic Press, 1995.

Magness, Jodi. *The Archaeology of Qumran and the Dead Sea Scrolls.* Grand Rapids, Mich.: Eerdmans, 2002.

Schiffman, Lawrence H., and James C. VanderKam, eds. *Encyclopedia of the Dead Sea Scrolls.* 2 vols. New York and Oxford: Oxford University Press, 2000.

VanderKam, James C., and Peter Flint. *The Meaning of the Dead Sea Scrolls: Their Significance for Understanding the Bible, Judaism, Jesus, and Christianity.* San Francisco: HarperSanFrancisco, 2002.

Matthias Henze

DEATH

[*This entry includes three subentries:* Death and Burial in the Ancient World, Explanations of and Attitudes toward Death, *and* Death in Greek Literature.]

Death and Burial in the Ancient World

Death, dying, and commemoration are shaped by social order and values and norms. What is problematic for the historian, however, is that although we may have an understanding of the social order, its real values and particular norms may remain opaque. Caution rightly dictates that we not speculate too much as to the nature of the values and norms that may generate specific death and burial practices. But to avoid any type of informed speculation would reduce scholarship on this matter to mere catalog. In the following overview, therefore, the catalog is unavoidable, and speculation must be limited to trends rather than to exceptions. Considerably more is known about the process of death and of dying in Rome than in Greece. And much more is known about the deaths of the elite than of the poor. The higher literacy levels of ancient elites skew the evidence, leaving us ignorant of burial practices for the *lemures*—the majority of poor Greeks and Romans.

Death Rituals. The rituals accompanying death in Greece and Rome are broadly similar. In Greece burial was something carried out by the deceased's family, and in Athens, at least, the responsibility was taken so seriously that a family member who neglected this duty could be barred from holding public office (Lysias 31.20–23). It follows, therefore, that publicly funded burial was rare and was restricted to deaths of great civic significance, as described in Pericles' funeral oration for the Athenian dead after the first year of the Peloponnesian War (Thucydides 2.35–46). Civic interference in burial seems to have remained minimal, except for occasional laws to limit funeral spending. Such restrictions were enacted in more democratic periods presumably so as to limit destructive and dangerous competition between wealthy aristocratic families. In Greek as in Roman contexts, burials were normally outside the city and often along the main roads. This would have been the practice, at any rate, for the wealthier members of a civic entity.

Greece. The ritual process of preparation for burial exhibited marked similarities in Greece and Rome. In Greece, on the first day after death, the body was laid out for viewing (the so-called *prothesis*). This took place after the body had been washed, anointed, wreathed, and normally had had a coin placed in the mouth—to pay Charon to ferry the spirit of the dead person into the Underworld. The viewing proper occurred on the second day after death. Female relatives provided the "accompaniment" with dirges, hair tearing, and self-beating.

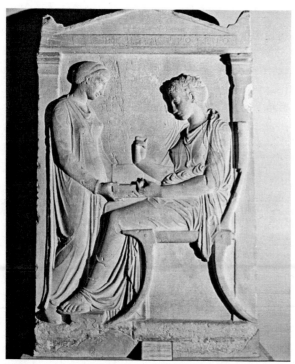

Funerary Stele of Hegeso. Athenian, c. 410–400 BCE. NATIONAL ARCHAEOLOGICAL MUSEUM, ATHENS/ANCIENT ART and ARCHITECTURE COLLECTION LTD./THE BRIDGEMAN ART LIBRARY

On the third day the body was taken out for burial in a predawn procession (the *ekphora*).

Rome. The comparable process is better known in Rome from our greater textual and archaeological evidence. At the time of Augustus, Rome was a metropolis of more than one million people. As with the Greeks, however, the surviving evidence relates mostly to the upper-class funeral. The Roman postmortem rituals seem to have begun with the traditional closing of the deceased's eyes. Ritual lamentation (*conclamatio*) was performed by the female members of the household. Subsequently the corpse was washed, anointed, provided with Charon's coin, and laid out in full dress—of a type appropriate to the deceased's status—on a bed in the forecourt of the aristocratic house. The deceased was laid out in this manner for viewing for up to a week (the *collocatio*), the amount of time doubtless depending on the season. During this period the aristocratic house was considered to be *funesta* (in a condition of ritual impurity). Potential visitors were warned of this condition by the presence of cypress or pitch-pine boughs hung outside the door. The *domus* remained in this condition of ritual impurity until after the funeral. To symbolize the end of this unclean period, the deceased's heir formally swept away the impurity with a dedicated broom. The cleansing was also marked by two feasts, the *silicernium*, or funeral feast, which occurred soon after the funeral, and then the *cena novendialis*, or nine-day feast. Thus ended both the period of mourning and the period of the ritual impurity of the house.

Little of this process applied to the poor, who lived in cramped tenement houses (the so-called *insulae*) or above their shops. Freed slaves, though possibly resident in *insulae*, were still technically part of their former owner's *familia* and may therefore have received their funerary rites as part of the household. For those without such helpful connections there were burial societies or clubs (*collegia*). The burial clubs were required if the state-appointed contractors (*libitinarii*) were to be paid the fee (*lucar Libitinae*) for their services. The poor were as concerned for proper burial as the rich were. Without proper burial, as Rüpke notes, "the dead cannot live, and the living can enjoy no peace" (p. 235). For the desperately poor and those without family, no such ritual was possible. Death by the wayside and removal to a public burial pit (*puticulus*)—which formed part of the vast cemetery on the Esquiline and which were, presumably, maintained by public slaves—can have been all that they might hope for. The sight of the unclaimed dead or portions of the bodies of the unclaimed dead must have been common both within and without Roman cities.

There was a Roman goddess of burials, Libitina, at whose grove on the Esquiline burials were registered (Dionysius of Halicarnassus *Antiquitates Romanae* 4.15.5). Servius Tullius, king of Rome in the sixth century BCE, is said to have been the first to set up temples to Libitina that housed all the equipment necessary for funerals, as well as housed the gravediggers. Her temples also usually contained the registers of the dead. One gate of the Colosseum is said to have been dedicated to Libitina for all the gladiators who died within.

Greek Burial Practices. The modes of ancient burial vary considerably. In the late Bronze Age Aegean, for example, group inhumation in chamber tombs was preferred. From 1100 BCE individual inhumation came to displace the group practice except at Athens, where cremation was the norm and remains were placed in an urn. By 700 BCE cemeteries of large scale and of a relative paucity of grave goods became usual in Greece. Simplicity in burial became increasingly common during the fifth century. It is hard not to discount the influence of democracy and even the egalitarianism of military tactics, such as the hoplite phalanx, here. Such burials were completed sometimes even without tombstones, and inhumation continued to be the preferred mode of disposal. Cremation seems to have been associated with heroic or warrior status. The aristocratic penchant for extravagance becomes visible once again in the fourth century, concomitant with a swing from democratic to aristocratic institutions. The warlike, aristocratic Macedonians built extravagant vaulted tombs with painted walls and very rich grave goods—evident in the tomb at Vergina thought to be that of Philip II and other kings of Macedon.

Roman Burial Practices. By contrast with its Greek colonies, Rome seems to have preferred cremation during the Republic and early Principate, although some families, such as the Cornelii, continued the practice of inhumation until 78 BCE (Cicero *De legibus* 2.57). Before about 100 BCE burials were simple affairs. Interment was not allowed within the city precinct, the *pomerium*. Thus as in Greece, the roads leading to Rome were lined with tombs. Aristocratic burials, especially in later years, became an elaborate process with processions and actors masked as representatives of the family, followed by a spectacular cremation. For the poor there was neither cremation nor procession. Their remains were thrown into public cemeteries into *puticuli* to rot (Varro *De lingua Latina* 5.25; Horace *Satires* 1.8). These "common pits or fosses," as Lanciani explains, "covered an area on the Esquiline one thousand feet long, and three hundred feet deep, and contained many hundred *puticuli*, or vaults, twelve feet square, thirty deep" (p. 65).

Whereas burial in Greece was family-driven, in Rome the *collegia*, or self-help societies, came into being to provide for proper burial. Lists of *collegia* members survive in, for example, *Inscriptiones Latinae Selectae* 6174–6176 and 7225–7227. People with sufficient funds could join one of these *collegia* and have their burial taken care of by the society. Such societies were particularly important for those who lacked family support—the *pietas* that mandated the care of old parents—or the benevolence of a patron or fellow freedman. Perhaps most affected by the need for such *collegia* were working-class men between the ages of about eighteen and thirty who had outgrown their own families but had not yet established new households.

Between 170 and 300 CE the Roman aristocracy turned from cremation to inhumation, perhaps adopting the custom of their Greek colonies, where inhumation had persisted essentially since the seventh century BCE. In one of the more striking turnarounds to occur in the ancient world, this practice of ritual inhumation spread throughout the empire by the third century CE. The reasons for this change are uncertain. The change is not usually attributed to Christianity, democracy is out of the question, and to attribute the change merely to the colonized Greek influence seems unlikely. There may be some connection between a new valuation of the status of the individual—evident in the explosion of funerary memorialization in the first century CE—and this apparently new respect for the body of the deceased.

The values that shaped burial practices are also reflected in the manner by which the remains of the dead were laid to rest. Private monumental tombs were uncommon in Greece until the fourth century BCE when wealthy Athenians began to build elaborate aboveground walled tombs—called "household" tombs by the Romans—that were furnished with sculptures and inscriptions. Indeed the practice seems designed to provide a postmortem landscape to match that of the living.

The two dominant modes of burial for wealthy and middle-class Romans were the so-called household tombs and the *columbaria* (literally "dovecotes"). The former were financed and maintained by the Roman elite; the latter were for those who had less money. Household tombs typically line the roads leading from the major cities, though cemeteries like the one at Isola Sacra, serving Ostia, also existed. This form of tomb was designed to house, intergenerationally, a whole Roman *familia* of wealthy masters and their children, their slaves, and their freedmen and freedwomen. In the period from 100 BCE to 100 CE household tombs contained funerary urns for the ashes of the deceased. In the following centuries they also contained sarcophagi (the Greek term means "flesh eaters"), stone coffins that could be kept above ground in such family tombs.

Columbaria were mass burial sites, housing from 150 to several thousand dead in rows of small niches (the "dovecotes" or *columbaria*) that were constructed one above another. These structures were designed primarily for urns, though some sarcophagi may be found. Places in these *columbaria* seem to have been bought and sold. Accordingly, they were the normal destination for members of the burial *collegia*. Sarcophagi became popular in Rome with the increased preference for inhumation, though much earlier Greek examples can be found. Perhaps the most famous examples are Etruscan, dating from the fifth and fourth centuries BCE, often showing a rather self-satisfied-looking married couple reclining for a funerary banquet.

Catacombs were another mode of burial in later antiquity. So named from the Greek *kata kumbas*, "at the hollows" (perhaps directions to a particular cemetery on the Via Appia), catacombs were passages built underground. They are found in a number of ancient cities and are associated with Jews and Christians. The catacombs in Rome extend along roads but also in labyrinthine manner for up to more than three hundred miles (more than five hundred kilometers). Bodies in shrouds were placed into *loculi* (niches) within the catacombs, which closely resemble the *columbaria*, except that because of inhumation they required much more space. The niches usually identified the dead, and the walls were sometimes painted. The third and fourth centuries saw the greatest use of catacombs. The acceptance of Christianity thereafter allowed burial to be associated with churches. Nevertheless the practice continued until the sixth century. Christian preference for inhumation is certainly in part the result of the Christian stress on the importance and responsibility of the individual. The early Christians rejected cremation and preferred burial perhaps in imitation of the burial of Christ. They believed that the body itself was holy and, along with the soul, would in due course be resurrected into eternal life. Cremation would negate bodily resurrection (a view shared by the Jews).

Rituals Surrounding Burial. The rituals surrounding burial are of particular interest. Once again, more is known of Roman than of Greek practices, and what is known has the usual elite demographic bias.

The dead were commemorated, or celebrated, in various fixed and unfixed annual festivals. One such was the Rosalia (Festival of Roses), an unfixed festival of private commemoration. Families apparently met at the tombs of their dead and decked them with roses. The dead were venerated as the *manes* or *di manes*, which means, according to Festus, something like the "holy spirits of the dead" or even the "good ones." They were believed to have joined an undifferentiated group or collectivity, also termed the *di parentes* or the *inferi*, that is, "deified ancestors" or "those who dwell below" (Varro *De lingua Latina* 6.13). Note that although in the Classical period the dead were said to be thought of as an undifferentiated group, they were nonetheless discretely commemorated at quite differentiated sites. That paradox in itself indicates how very little we understand these matters.

There was also the fixed festival of the Parentalia (13–21 February) for the *di manes*, at which families, for all but the last day of this period, celebrated their family dead. On the final day a public ceremony, the Feralia, was held (Ovid *Fasti* 2.532ff.). Ovid lists the grave offerings provided on such occasions by the family: garlands, grains of wheat, salt, bread softened with wine, a few violets (*Fasti* 2.537–539). These gifts were believed to appeal to these undifferentiated *manes*. On 22 February, the day after the Feralia, there followed the Caristia, or Cara Cognatio (a festival for the "dear kin"), at which the living members of the family joined together to celebrate a banquet (*Fasti* 2.617). Such activities, however, cannot have been common for the poor of cities such as Rome. Significantly there was also the festival of the Lemuria (9, 11, 13 May), when the "lemurs," the ghosts of the unburied who lacked family or collegial connections, haunted houses and demanded appeasement through some form of feeding (*Fasti* 5.419ff.). These were the ghosts of the very poor. The existence of the *puticuli* must have prevented for most the postmortem fate of becoming a lemur. Or did it? In large, violent, unpoliced, and poverty-stricken cities such as Rome, the number of lemurs on the prowl in early May must have been considerable indeed.

[*See also* Catacombs; Cemeteries; Deification, Greek; Deification, Roman; Festivals, Roman; Funeral Oration, Greek; Funeral Oration, Latin; Funerals, Roman; Funerary Art; Mummies; Purification and Pollution; Religion; Sarcophagus; Suicide, Greek; Suicide, Roman; Tombs; Urns, Cinerary; *and* Widows, Roman.]

BIBLIOGRAPHY

Edwards, Catharine. *Death in Ancient Rome.* New Haven, Conn.: Yale University Press, 2007.

Garland, Robert. *The Greek Way of Death.* 2nd ed. London: Bristol Classical Press, 2001.

Humphreys, S. C., and Helen King, eds. *Mortality and Immortality, the Anthropology and Archaeology of Death: Proceedings of a Meeting of the Research Seminar in Archaeology and Related Subjects Held at the Institute of Archaeology, London University, in June 1980.* London and New York: Academic Press, 1981.

Kurtz, Donna C., and John Boardman. *Greek Burial Customs.* London: Thames & Hudson, 1971.

Lanciani, Rodolfo. *Ancient Rome in the Light of Recent Discoveries* (1888). New York: Blom, 1967.

Morris, Ian. *Death-Ritual and Social Structure in Classical Antiquity.* Cambridge, U.K., and New York: Cambridge University Press, 1992.

Nock, Arthur D. *Conversion: The Old and the New in Religion from Alexander the Great to Augustine of Hippo.* Oxford: Clarendon Press, 1933.

Reece, Richard, ed. *Burial in the Roman World.* London: Council for British Archaeology, 1977.

Rüpke, Jörg. *Religion of the Romans.* Translated and edited by Richard Gordon. Cambridge, U.K.: Polity, 2007.

Toynbee, J. M. C. *Death and Burial in the Roman World.* Ithaca, N.Y.: Cornell University Press, 1971. Reprint, Baltimore: Johns Hopkins University Press, 1996.

Walker, Susan. *Memorials to the Roman Dead.* London: British Museum, 1985.

Peter Toohey

Explanations of and Attitudes toward Death

In many cultures, people explain why death exists by referring to a primeval mistake or transgression. Claude Lévi-Strauss recorded a story from South America according to which, in spite of having been warned by their creator-god, the first humans stupidly embraced Death, who arrived among them disguised as a pleasant-looking man in a canoe. The book of Genesis traces death to Eve's curiosity and to Adam's inability to resist Eve. In contrast, the peoples of ancient Greece and Rome have left behind no such explanations of why death exists. The South American story may remind us of Hesiod's tale of Pandora—whom Epimetheus stupidly embraced and who subsequently, like Eve, allowed her curiosity to get the better of her, thereby releasing evils upon the world—but this is not a tale about the origin of death per se; rather, Pandora releases all manner of "grievous cares" upon humanity, including the diseases that might bring death, but not only those (Hesiod *Works and Days* 55–106). This story, moreover, as familiar as it may be to us, was not canonical in antiquity: we hear very little about Pandora and her jar in later sources.

Nor, unlike many other cultures, did the Greeks and Romans create myths to explain the rituals through which they cared for the dead. These rituals were validated simply by the insistence that they had always been performed. If the ancients thought mythically about death at all, it was only to reiterate its inescapability: Orpheus failed to retrieve Eurydice and died himself in the aftermath; Protesilaus' wife learned to her regret that bringing back the dead was a mistake.

What the Greeks and Romans did expend thought upon was how to control the effects of the inevitable as much as they could: they invented rituals to ensure a good afterlife for oneself and one's family, as well as rituals to keep the potentially unpleasant dead at bay or at least under control. The first requirement for achieving all of these things, as in most cultures, was to dispose of the body properly. Both cremation and interment were practiced by the Greeks and Romans—the choice depending on place, time, and personal preference. Those whose bodies were not disposed of properly or who were not given adequately elaborate funerals were likely to become restless, angry ghosts (on which see below). Those who were happy with their funerals became helpful ancestors, aiding their descendants and their cities. So-called heroes were members of the dead who had been particularly powerful or significant during life and who subsequently received special cult after death, usually by an entire city or other group rather than by just their own family members; the most famous example is Heracles. Many of these figures were well developed in myth; in cult, it is sometimes hard to discern the differences between heroes and gods.

The living—especially family members of the deceased—were expected to continue caring for the dead even after the funeral; typically, libations and other offerings (including clippings of hair, a sign of survivors' devotion to the deceased) were deposited at the grave rather frequently during the year immediately after death and then annually thereafter at certain festivals: in Greece the Genesia, for example, and in Rome the Rosalia and the Parentalia. After a few generations the individual dead merged into a more or less anonymous collective, called Tritopatores (the "thrice-ancestors") in some parts of Greece, for example, and called the *maiores* (the "older ones") in Rome. These groups, too, received regular offerings during annual festivals, and they might be approached for immediate help when disaster threatened as well.

As important as it was for the living to care for the dead, in carrying out these duties the survivors did incur pollution, particularly female survivors who were expected to prepare the corpse for burial and to be especially expressive in their mourning. The pollution lasted for several days or even weeks, depending on local custom. Funerary display could get out of hand; in both Greece and Rome, attempts were made to legislate such things as the number of mourners, the luxuriousness of the goods given to the deceased and the grandeur of the grave monument, and even the time of day at which the funerary procession might take place.

The Good Afterlife. If the dead were properly cared for by their survivors, they could expect to enter the underworld without problem. In our earliest traces of beliefs concerning the afterlife (most significantly, those in *Odyssey* 11), ghosts endure an existence that is dreary and boring but not painful; they drift around in the darkness with little to do and little memory of their former lives. Only the very wicked—generally, those who offended the gods, such as Tityus—are punished, and only those with familial connections to the gods, such as Menelaus, receive the reward of eternal life in a lovely place called the White Island or Elysium. At some point, however, probably during the later Archaic period, the idea developed that one's experiences after life would reflect the way one behaved while alive—all bad deeds would be punished and good deeds rewarded (e.g., Plato *Republic* 330d–e).

Not surprisingly, at about the same time there developed rituals that promised to erase the effects of evil deeds and thus guarantee—to anyone who could pay the fee to have the rituals performed—a blissful afterlife of eating, drinking, and lolling around in sunlit meadows. The most popular of these cults were the mysteries at Eleusis in honor of Demeter and her daughter Kore and the mysteries of Dionysus or Bacchus, which were performed by itinerant priests. These cults, as well as some other mystery cults, anchored themselves in sacred texts credited to Orpheus or other mythic poets. An additional boon that was promised by the Dionysiac mysteries (and perhaps by others) was eternal memory: not only would the dead be remembered by their descendants—a universal desire, addressed by funerary cult the world over—but they themselves would be able to remember their lives and converse about them with their companions in the underworld (cf. Plato *Apology* 40c–41c.)

Roman beliefs about what would happen after death, so far as we can recover them in any explicitly articulated form (e.g., *Aeneid* 6), seem to be borrowed from Greece; the Romans also adopted Greek mystery cults. In both Greece and Rome there had also, from an early time, been philosophers who spoke against common beliefs: for example, Epicureans argued that there was no afterlife at all, because the individual atoms that composed the soul dispersed after death. Of course, it is impossible to be certain how far any given individual sincerely embraced any of the beliefs that our sources express; beliefs are never more fluid than when they concern death and the dead—inevitably so, given that the best sources of information are no longer able to communicate their experiences.

The Bad Afterlife. In addition to being punished in the afterlife for having done bad things while alive, there were three ways a departed soul might end up in trouble: if the body were not buried, if the person had died too young (before accomplishing what a person ought to accomplish in life), or if the person had died a particularly violent death, such as through murder. In any of these cases the soul would be denied entry to the underworld and be condemned to wander between the world of the living and the world of the dead, never finding rest in either. Ancient sources express the dreadfulness of this fate (e.g., *Iliad* 23.65–74). Such souls understandably were angry and resentful both toward those who were directly responsible for their situation—their murderer, or those who failed to give them a funeral—and toward those whose lives were proceeding along the path to which they had aspired (unmarried girls who died, for instance, haunted living girls of a marriageable age). Rituals were developed to appease such angry ghosts or, where appeasement was not possible, to avert them. Certain gods, such as Hecate and Hermes, were understood to be particularly good at controlling such ghosts, and they received offerings to guarantee their help.

Such ghosts might also be useful to living people who wanted to do harm to someone else. *Defixiones*—small lead tablets that were buried with corpses of people who were likely to end up as unhappy ghosts, or were buried in places such as wells, which were understood to lead to the underworld—call on the restless dead to thwart opponents in athletic and rhetorical contests, to torture a wandering lover until he or she returned, and to ensure that competing businessmen failed. These tablets also call on Hecate, Hermes, and other gods associated with the dead to guarantee that the dead would cooperate.

[*See also* Orphism *and* Underworld and Afterlife.]

BIBLIOGRAPHY

Garland, Robert. *The Greek Way of Death*. Ithaca, N.Y.: Cornell University Press, 1985.

Graf, Fritz, and Sarah Iles Johnston. *Ritual Texts for the Afterlife: Orpheus and the Bacchic Gold Tablets*. London and New York: Routledge, 2007.

Johnston, Sarah Iles. *Restless Dead: Encounters between the Living and the Dead in Ancient Greece*. Berkeley: University of California Press, 1999.

Lévi-Strauss, Claude. *The Raw and the Cooked*. Translated by John and Doreen Weightman. New York: Harper & Row, 1969. Originally published in French in 1964.

Morris, Ian. *Death-Ritual and Social Structure in Classical Antiquity*. Cambridge, U.K.: Cambridge University Press, 1992.

Toynbee, J. M. C. *Death and Burial in the Roman World*. London: Thames & Hudson, 1971.

Sarah Iles Johnston

Death in Greek Literature

Few authors have described battlefield deaths more vividly than Homer. Of the 240 deaths to which he makes reference in the *Iliad*, four—those of Hyperenor (14.518f.), Sarpedon (16.505), Patroclus (16.856), and Hector (22.362)—are described in terms of the departure from the body of the *psychē*, an obscure entity of no fixed abode. The *psychē* later became central to the concept of death, particularly in Platonic philosophy: see the *Phaedo* for Plato's proof of its immortality. In all the remaining references Homer describes the biological process that generates the onset of death—either an interruption of vital functions caused by the dispatch of the *thymos* (aptly described by Bruno Snell as the "organ of [e]

Death of Alcestis. Sarcophagus depicting the death of Alcestis. VATICAN MUSEUMS AND GALLERIES/THE BRIDGEMAN ART LIBRARY

motion") or a loss of muscular control caused by a "loosening" either of the *guia* (limbs) or of the *gounata* (knees).

Notable deaths in tragedy include that of the youthful Alcestis, who pawns her life for that of her husband Admetus (Euripides *Alcestis*); that of Oedipus, who undergoes heroization (Sophocles *Oedipus at Colonus*); that of Ajax, who commits suicide (Sophocles *Ajax*); and that of Heracles (Hercules), who perishes from inextinguishable flame (Sophocles *Women of Trachis*). We also have Plato's description in the *Phaedo* of Socrates' execution, which set a standard of philosophical calm that others, such as Cato the Younger in the first century BCE, sought to emulate. We lack, however, a single account of what, in the absence of hospitals in ancient Greece, was undoubtedly the normative type of death: in bed at home, in the bosom of one's family.

Literature and Reality. Despite being atypical and, we might add, staged, these literary accounts have much to tell us about how the Greeks confronted their last moments. Alcestis saves her relatives the trouble of washing her body and dressing it

for burial by performing these tasks herself. Then after praying to Hestia to look after her children, she places wreaths on all the altars in the house. The messenger in *Oedipus at Colonus* reports that when Oedipus realized that his last hour had come, he requested running water with which to bathe and make a libation. He then dressed "in the manner ordained by custom" and wept with his daughters. Being summoned by a mysterious voice, he committed his daughters to the safekeeping of Theseus, in whose land he was sojourning, and ordered everyone except Theseus to depart, so as not to witness his passing from life (1586ff.).

Before falling upon his spear, Ajax in Sophocles' play prays to Zeus that his brother Teucer will be the first to discover his body, to Hermes that his death will be swift, and to the Furies that the hated sons of Agamemnon will pay for his death. He then bids farewell to his homeland and to his hearth, to Athens, to his relatives, and to Troy (823ff.). Heracles, wracked with intolerable pain as his skin burns, appeals to Hades to terminate his agony as soon as possible (Sophocles *Trachiniae* 1040ff. and 1085).

Finally, Socrates, after dismissing the women to prevent any violent display of emotion attending his death, bathes before receiving the cup of hemlock. Denied permission by the jailer to make a libation, he prays that his "change of residence" (*metoikēsis*) will be blessed with good fortune. His famous last words—"Crito, we owe a cock to Asclepius, see that it is paid"—may allude to his regarding death as a "cure" for life, because Asclepius was the god of healing (*Crito* 118a).

We can deduce from this evidence that the dying (1) committed their children to the care of others (Alcestis and Oedipus), (2) prayed to Hestia (Alcestis and Ajax), (3) prayed for a safe passage to Hades (Socrates and Ajax), and (4) bade farewell to family and friends (Ajax, Alcestis, and Oedipus). From the fifth century BCE onward a coin was placed in the mouth of the deceased as payment for Charon, the ferryman of the dead. The female relatives of the deceased uttered a ritual cry of lament or *ololugē*, which was followed by a dirge sung over the dead body.

Rites of Passage. Dying was a rite of passage that involved journeying from this world (*enthade*, literally "here") to the next (*ekei*, literally "there"). Primarily because of the polluting effect of the corpse, the gods kept well clear of the dying. At the end of Euripides' *Hippolytus*, Artemis makes a hasty exit when her favorite is dying because, as she says, it was not permitted by divine law (*themis*) for a deity "either to look at the dead or to sully her eyes with the expirations of the dying" (1437f.). Though the chthonic deity Hermes Psychopompos (Leader of *psychai*) led the dead to Hades, a Greek's relationship with the Olympian gods terminated once death became inevitable. Also, that the gods were "deathless" or "undying" (*athanatoi*) meant that they lacked any comprehension of the human dilemma.

There was a belief that each individual had an allotted span of life. In Homer this finds expression in the word *kēr*, meaning "one's own personal death," or *moira*, meaning more generally "doom or destiny." Exceptional individuals could apparently accelerate or delay the onset of their death, as in the case of Achilles, who declared that "twin *kēres* are bearing me to the end of death" (*Iliad* 9.411).

If he stays to fight at Troy, he goes on to say, he will not return home but will win everlasting glory, whereas if he returns to his native land "my life will be long and the doom of death will not come quickly."

In the fifth century the notion of a death struggle or *psychorrhagia*, the process whereby the *psychē* wrenches itself with difficulty from the body, appears in both poetry and philosophy (e.g., Euripides *Alcestis* 20, 143; Plato *Phaedo* 108b). A painless death was, therefore, a gift of the gods. When the mother of Cleobis and Biton prayed to Argive Hera to reward her sons with the greatest boon that life could offer, the goddess responded by causing them to die in their sleep (Herodotus 1.31). Similarly at the end of the *Iliad*, Hecuba compares her dead son Hector to "one whom the silver-bowed archer Apollo has slain with his painless arrows" (24.759), which suggests that his death at the hands of Achilles was almost instantaneous. Though the Argive hero Argos in Euripides' *Suppliants* (1109f.) speaks scornfully of those who "try to drag out their lives with food and drink and magic spells," death for the majority would rarely in fact have been protracted.

Medicine and Memorialization. Hippocratic authors treated death with clinical dispassion. The author of *Epidemics* describes the deaths of twenty-five out of forty-two patients whose decline he observed—in some cases for months on end—without, it seems, offering any palliative. The author of *Aphorisms* enumerated the signs of impending death as follows (7.87): a chilly and withdrawn right testicle, blackening nails, toes that are cold and clenched, livid fingernails, and dark lips. He concludes with a Homeric flourish: "The boundary of death is reached when . . . the *psychē*, leaving the abode of the body, hands over the cold, mortal image [*eidōlon*] to bile, blood, phlegm, and flesh." Aristotle advanced the notion that death comes as the result of *auansis* or "loss of vital heat" (*On Breathing* 478b 28) and that it often occurred as the result of cardiac arrest (*Parts of Animals* 667a–b), whereas the Hippocratic school maintained that death was primarily the result of the cessation of brain activity.

Anticipating Horace's *dulce et decorum est pro patria mori* (*Odes* 3.2.13), the elegiac poet Tyrtaeus claimed that a "good death" occurred when a young man died in battle at the height of his physical powers, whereas it was "shameful" for an old man to meet a similar fate (Tyrtaeus fragments 6, 7 Diehl). The explanation would seem to be either that it was the exclusive responsibility of young men to give their lives to the state or that the corpse of an old man was unseemly to look upon. The Classical Athenian funeral speech, or *epitaphios logos*, delivered annually over the war dead, served a similar propagandist purpose of encouraging the young to risk their lives in battle.

A variety of literary genres, including tragedy, indicate that particular compassion was felt toward young women of marriageable years, such as Iphigenia and Antigone, who died unwed. Hence the Athenian custom of designating such women's graves with a marble *loutrophoros*, a vase used in the ceremonial bridal bath preceding the wedding. Compassion may have been intensified by the very high value that the state attached to childbearing: particular honor attached to those who died in childbirth. In Classical Athens such women were commemorated with gravestones decorated with an image of the deceased sitting on a birthing stool. Though it has been argued that the high incidence of infant mortality—perhaps as high as 25 percent—would have limited the degree of emotion that parents invested in their newborn, the deaths of older children may well have aroused considerable distress, as we see from the fact that miniature vases, known as *choes*, that were placed in the graves of toddlers were decorated with poignant scenes from childhood.

In epic the dying were believed to attain a higher plane of consciousness. Patroclus, expiring, predicts the death of Hector at the hands of Achilles (*Iliad* 16.851ff.), and Hector, expiring in turn, predicts the death of Achilles at the hands of Paris (22.358ff.). The last words of the dying were especially prized. Andromache regrets that her husband Hector failed to bequeath "some word of wisdom, on which I might have pondered day and night, shedding tears" (24.744f). The theme is taken up in Hellenistic epigrams, as in the words of a dying daughter to her mother: "Stay here with Daddy and give birth to another daughter who will be more lucky than I was and who will look after you in old age" (*Greek Anthology* 7.647). Many of the practices and beliefs of the ancients remain current in rural Greece to this day: the soul is thought to leave the body through the mouth, a young woman who dies unwed is buried in a bridal dress, laments are sung in the house of the deceased, and coins are placed in the coffin.

[*See also* Funeral Oration, Greek; Hermes; Hippocratic Corpus; Martyrs, Martyrdom, and Martyr Literature; Suicide, Greek; Underworld and Afterlife; *and* Values and Virtues, Roman.]

BIBLIOGRAPHY

Alexiou, Margaret. *The Ritual Lament in Greek Tradition* (1974). Revised by Dimitrios Yatromanolakis and Panagiotis Roilos. Lanham, Md.: Rowman & Littlefield, 2002.

Bremmer, Jan N. *The Early Greek Concept of the Soul.* Princeton, N.J.: Princeton University Press, 1983.

Danforth, Loring M. *The Death Rituals of Rural Greece.* Princeton, N.J.: Princeton University Press, 1982.

Garland, Robert. *The Greek Way of Death.* 2nd ed. London: Bristol Classical Press, 2001.

Vermeule, Emily. *Aspects of Death in Early Greek Art and Poetry.* Berkeley: University of California Press, 1979.

Vernant, Jean-Pierre, and Gherardo Gnoli, eds. *La mort, les morts dans les sociétés anciennes.* Cambridge, U.K., and New York: Cambridge University Press; Paris: Maison des Sciences de l'Homme, 1982.

Robert Garland

DECIUS

(Gaius Messius Quintus Traianus Decius; born c. 190), Roman emperor (r. 249–251). Decius challenged Philip the Arab after defeating marauding Goths and Carpi on the lower Danube in the Roman province of Moesia, and killed him in battle near Verona in northern Italy in the autumn of 249. His reign marks the beginning of the most dangerous period of the Crisis of the Third Century (also known as the Imperial Crisis, or the Military Anarchy). Long-standing internal political, military, fiscal, and social problems were revealed and exacerbated by an unprecedented number of simultaneous external threats, particularly from a renascent Sassanid Persia and from predominantly Germanic barbarians on the Rhine and the Danube. Unlike many of those who were to follow him and restore order to the empire, Decius was no reforming or "soldier emperor." By birth, marriage, and career a Roman aristocrat of the old school, he revealed his conservative leanings by adopting the name Trajan, minting coins depicting "good" emperors of earlier times, and insisting on public attestations of piety to the empire's traditional deities. Refusal was not tolerated, which led inevitably to the first empire-wide persecution of Christians—including the deaths of the bishops of Rome, Jerusalem, and Antioch—although persecution was almost certainly not Decius' initial aim. He returned to Moesia to face Goths, led by Cniva, in 250, and Decius and his co-emperor, his elder son Herennius Etruscus, were killed in battle at Abrittus in June 251. His defeat sapped imperial military strength and created major strategic weaknesses, and its psychological impact (for Christians, grimly uplifting) was intensified by Roman failure to recover his body. The empire's situation was critical, and it is hardly surprising that the reigns of his two immediate successors, Gallus (252–253) and Aemilian (253), were equally short.

[See also Philip the Arab and Rome, subentry The Empire.]

BIBLIOGRAPHY

Bowman, Alan K., Peter Garnsey, and Averil Cameron, eds. *The Cambridge Ancient History*. Vol. 12, *The Crisis of Empire*, A.D. *193–337*. 2nd ed. Cambridge, U.K.: Cambridge University Press, 2005. Indispensable: offers a full discussion of the period and a comprehensive bibliography.

Johne, Klaus-Peter, ed. *Die Zeit der Soldatenkaiser. Krise und Transformation des Römischen Reiches im 3. Jarhundert n. Chr. (235–284)*. Berlin: Akademie Verlag, 2008.

Potter, David S. *Prophecy and History in the Crisis of the Roman Empire: A Historical Commentary on the Thirteenth Sibylline Oracle*. Oxford and New York: Oxford University Press, 1990.

John F. Drinkwater

DECLAMATION

In both Greece and Rome, declamation was an educational and recreational practice that required speakers to deliver speeches based on fictional, often fantastical, legal cases (*controversiae*) and laws. In the Roman curriculum, this assignment was the culmination of a student's rhetorical education, following immediately upon the *suasoria*, a speech in which the student offered advice to a historical or mythological figure facing a difficult choice—for instance, whether the three hundred Spartans at Thermopylae should flee or fight (Seneca *Suasoriae* 2).

Greek rhetorical exercises that required the student to speak on fictional themes probably date to the fifth century BCE when Greek Sophists began to teach rhetoric in a systematic fashion. Greek teachers used the school exercise (*meletē*) to facilitate recognition of the types of issues posed by rhetorical problems (*stasis* theory). Over time, Greek teachers of rhetoric created a range of increasingly complex assignments (*progymnasmata*) that prepared students for the range of rhetorical challenges they might face in public life. The Greek assignment called the *thesis*, for example, required students to speak on both abstract and particularized philosophical questions. The most advanced forensic assignments presented fictional legal cases that increasingly came to be organized by stock narrative themes and characters that could be combined and reused (e.g., the tyrant, the stepmother, the war hero). In general, Greek rhetorical education seems to have been less preoccupied with the firm distinction that Romans drew between legal exercises (*controversiae*) and deliberative exercises (*suasoriae*).

Greek rhetoricians during the Hellenistic period debated *stasis* theory exhaustively. Their influence reached Italian shores as Rome gradually seized effective control of the Greek-speaking world in the second and first centuries BCE. Greek intellectuals in Rome were often teachers and companions of the Roman elite, who were beginning to create both Roman rhetorical theory and a rhetorical curriculum. Early Latin rhetorical works of the first century BCE—for example, the *Rhetorica ad Herennium* and Cicero's *De inventione*—assume a student's familiarity with exercises like the *progymnasmata* and indicate the influence of these Greek intellectuals upon the development of Roman education.

Declamation and classroom learning in general were but part of the repertoire of practices by which a Roman student learned the skills necessary to become an effective public speaker. Cicero speaks of the apprenticeship (*tirocinium fori*) and the memorization of famous orators' speeches (*Brutus* 304–305). These practices remained important aspects of rhetorical training even in Tacitus' day, nearly two centuries later. Roman education in Cicero's youth had not yet acquired the formal organization that characterized it when Quintilian, in the *Institutes* (after 90 CE), offered its most thorough and cogent, if idealized, description. Education in the late Republic, therefore, was a complex and changing set of processes of which declamation was one element, although an increasingly important one.

In Cicero's youth the school was just beginning to appear as a distinct Roman social institution. Even in Quintilian's day many leading citizens rejected schools, preferring to employ private tutors in the home to educate their children. Suetonius' biographies of the early teachers in *De grammaticis et rhetoribus* reveal a great degree of fluidity in educational practices in the first century BCE. By the time of Cicero's praetorship (66 BCE), a number of schools, operated by freed or freeborn teachers, had appeared in Rome. These teachers opened their schools each market day, and with their students they would declaim to an audience of proud and nervous fathers of prestigious birth and rank. Variation characterized the Roman rhetorical curriculum of the late Republic. Even the term *declamatio* had not yet taken on the specific definition that it acquired in the works of Seneca the Elder (d. c. 40 CE). The *controversiae* of Cicero's youth presented fairly specific Roman settings and practices. By Seneca's time the *controversiae* were inherently and deliberately melodramatic.

In addition to discussions by rhetorical theorists like Cicero and Quintilian, the evidence for the Roman practice of declamation during the late Republic and early Empire is quite extensive. The corpus of declamations from this era shows a regular generic form, consisting of two parts. The first part, the *controversia* proper, contains several elements: a title, a brief narrative describing a conflict, and often a statement of the law or laws that will govern the declaimer's analysis of the conflict. The second part offers excerpts and samples of declamatory responses to the *controversia*. Some texts additionally offer commentary (the *sermo* or the *divisio*) on the rhetorical challenge of the *controversia*. Students—who would already have studied Latin and Greek language and literature, as well as preliminary rhetorical exercises—wrote and memorized the declamations that they delivered orally.

The plots of the *controversiae* typically involve conflict within a family or a hero's valiant action against political and economic exploitation. The characters are broadly drawn stock figures: the adulterous stepmother, the spendthrift son, the rapacious tyrant, or the wealthy man. Declaimers typically spoke in the voice of one of the characters to the lawsuit and were allowed to supplement the facts of the case so long as they did not contradict the facts offered in the *controversiae*. In giving content to the plots and characters, students learned not simply to construct successful arguments but also to master the complex and often contradictory range of Roman social values.

The elder Seneca's collection of *Suasoriae* and *Controversiae* reveals that in addition to its function as an educational practice, declamation in the Julio-Claudian era was also a recreational pastime of the Roman elite. Fathers who attended the open-house days at their sons' schools heard their sons and their sons' teachers declaiming on the same *controversiae* that they had declaimed on in their own youth and that they still declaimed on with their friends in leisure. Seneca describes members of the Roman elite who, as orators, gave formal speeches in the Forum and senate during the day and then, in the evening, engaged in friendly declamatory competition with peers and successful rhetors—much as modern jazz musicians might play with friends at an after-hours club.

In addition to Seneca the Elder, who is a useful source for documenting the activities of Greek rhetors at Rome during his lifetime, Philostratus' *Lives of the Sophists* similarly provides evidence of the continuing importance of declamation as both an educational technique and a social activity in the Greek-speaking parts of the Roman Empire during the Second Sophistic. As the career of the Greek rhetorician Libanius (314–c. 393) suggests, the influence of declamation continued even as Christianity transformed the culture of the empire in the fourth century. In the Latin West, Ennodius' *Dictiones* (Discourses) of the early sixth century indicate that declamation retained its curricular importance as the Christian church increasingly asserted control over social institutions like the school. Declamation continued to influence the educational traditions of Renaissance humanism.

[*See also* Education; Oratory, Greco-Roman; Rhetoric; *and* Second Sophistic.]

BIBLIOGRAPHY

Primary Works

Håkanson, Lennart, ed. *Declamationes XIX maiores Quintiliano falsae ascriptae.* Stuttgart, Germany: Teubner, 1982.

Kaster, Robert A., ed. and trans. *Suetonius: De grammaticis et rhetoribus.* Oxford: Clarendon Press, 1995.

Kennedy, George A., trans. *Progymnasmata: Greek Textbooks of Prose Composition and Rhetoric.* Leiden, The Netherlands, and Boston: E. J. Brill, 2003.

Sussman, Lewis A., ed. and trans. *The Declamations of Calpurnius Flaccus: Text, Translation, and Commentary.* Leiden, The Netherlands, and New York: E. J. Brill, 1994.

Sussman, Lewis A., trans. *The Major Declamations Ascribed to Quintilian: A Translation.* Frankfurt am Main, Germany, and New York: Peter Lang, 1987.

Winterbottom, Michael, ed. and trans. *The Elder Seneca, Declamations.* 2 vols. Loeb Classical Library. Cambridge, Mass.: Harvard University Press, 1974.

Winterbottom, Michael, ed. *The Minor Declamations Ascribed to Quintilian.* Texte und Kommentare, no. 13. Berlin and New York: De Gruyter, 1984.

Secondary Works

Anderson, Graham. *The Second Sophistic: A Cultural Phenomenon in the Roman Empire.* London and New York: Routledge, 1993.

Bloomer, W. Martin. *Latinity and Literary Society at Rome.* Philadelphia: University of Pennsylvania Press, 1997.

Bonner, Stanley F. *Education in Ancient Rome: From the Elder Cato to the Younger Pliny.* London: Methuen; Berkeley: University of California Press, 1977.

Bonner, Stanley F. *Roman Declamation in the Late Republic and Early Empire.* Liverpool, U.K.: University Press of Liverpool; Berkeley: University of California Press, 1949.

Bowersock, Glen W. *Greek Sophists in the Roman Empire.* Oxford: Clarendon Press, 1969.

Fairweather, Janet. *Seneca the Elder.* Cambridge, U.K., and New York: Cambridge University Press, 1981.

Gunderson, Erik. *Declamation, Paternity, and Roman Identity: Authority and the Rhetorical Self.* Cambridge, U.K., and New York: Cambridge University Press, 2003.

Russell, Donald. A. *Greek Declamation.* Cambridge, U.K., and New York: Cambridge University Press, 1983.

MARGARET IMBER

DEIFICATION, GREEK

In antiquity, legendary heroes were honored at local shrines marking their places of burial ("hero cults"), such as Protesilaus at Elaeus. The pious worshiped and consulted these chthonic deities by means of elaborate rituals, including sacrifice. Greek mythology also features a few heroes, such as Heracles, who, upon death, were transformed into gods like the Olympians, with influence not restricted to discrete geographical regions. Greek religion's porous boundaries between humanity and divinity allowed Euhemerus (late fourth to early third century BCE) to explain all the Olympian gods as originally human sovereigns deified by appreciative subjects, a rationalizing approach known as "euhemerism." However, only during the Hellenistic period—when, not coincidentally, Euhemerus wrote—did it become common for populaces in the Greek world to worship their rulers. Although this continued under Roman rule, the Greek ruler-cult originally constituted a strategy by which traditionally self-governing Greek cities understood and acknowledged their innovative subjection to alien Hellenic kings, namely the Macedonian Alexander the Great (r. 336–323 BCE) and his Successors. The ruler cult may also have been influenced by practices from newly Hellenized eastern regions, especially Egypt, whose pharaoh was identified with various gods from the local pantheon.

Deification plays a role in ancient Christianity as well. The apostle Paul (fl. mid-first century CE) may be invoking an early creedal formula when he declares Christ to have been "descended from David according to flesh and appointed Son of God . . . by resurrection" (Romans 1:3–4). Orthodoxy ultimately insisted that Jesus was God incarnate—simultaneously human and divine—but "deification" (Greek *theōsis*) continued to be used, in the Greek East especially, as a metaphor for the believer's spiritual union with God, which the eschatological resurrection would consummate. Analogously, although the canonical gospels' insistence on Jesus' empty tomb in part aims to distinguish his worship from that of chthonic heroes, points of continuity emerge between the Greek hero-cult and the Christian cult of saints.

[*See also* Chthonic Gods; Heroes; Imperial Cult, Roman; Jesus; Mythography; *and* Religion, *subentry* Greek Religion.]

BIBLIOGRAPHY

Aitken, Ellen Bradshaw, and Jennifer K. Berenson Maclean, eds. *Philostratus's Heroikos: Religion and Cultural Identity in the Third Century C.E.* Leiden, The Netherlands: Brill, 2004.

Price, S. R. F. *Rituals and Power: The Roman Imperial Cult in Asia Minor.* Cambridge, U.K.: Cambridge University Press, 1984.

Austin Busch

DEIFICATION, ROMAN

Discussing the nature of the gods, Cicero (*De natura deorum* 2.62, 3.39–41) reports that exceptional benefactors of the human race such as Hercules, Castor and Pollux, Aesculapius, and Liber (Bacchus) were held by the Greeks to be gods, and that the Romans had added Romulus (they would also add Aeneas). All these mortals were sons of gods and became gods on their death. With the model of Alexander the Great, Roman commanders like Scipio Africanus Maior were seen as divinely inspired: typically Scipio fostered his own legend by visiting the Capitoline temple at dawn to talk with Jupiter, encouraging the tale of his mother's impregnation by the god (Livy 26.19; Silius 13.634–47) and propagating the myth that Neptune had appeared to him in a dream, promising the miraculous ebb of the lagoon at Carthago Nova (Cartagena) that enabled him to storm the city.

The ritual of the triumph had long assimilated the conquering general to Jupiter: in royal costume, with his face painted like the image of Jupiter, the general ended his parade at the Capitoline temple to enjoy intimate communion with the god. The statue of Africanus in Jupiter's shrine (Valerius Maximus 8.15.1) was probably placed there after his death.

These patterns return with Julius Caesar and Augustus. While Pompey was content to be venerated as a great man, Cassius Dio reports that Julius Caesar received a series of divine honors after his victorious return from Africa and Spain: his statue (inscribed "To the unconquered god"—*deo invicto*) was erected in the temple of Romulus-Quirinus and carried with Quirinus' statue in circus processions, his birth month, Quintilis, was given his name Julius (July), and just before Caesar's death Antony proposed himself as priest (flamen) for the new cult of Divus Iulius ("the deified Julius": Dio 44.6.4; Cicero *Philippics.* 2.110). A comet that appeared during commemorative games in 44 was hailed by Octavian as Caesar's apotheosis, and the temple of Divus Iulius was decreed and erected in the Forum.

Octavian himself, as son of the Divus (compare his denarius inscribed "Divi Filius," showing Caesar's temple and cult image surmounted by a star),

Roman, Deification. Apotheosis of Antoninus Pius and his wife Faustina. Marble relief from the base of the column of Antoninus Pius, Rome. Late first century CE. PHOTOGRAPH BY ROBERT B. KEBRIC

had over forty years of rule to accumulate divine honors, first from the eastern Greeks, then from other provinces, and finally at Rome. An alternative myth developed that his mother, Atia, was impreg-nated by Apollo. Poets were the ideal vehicle for promoting his divine destiny, accelerated by gratitude for his restoration of order in the 30s. Virgil's shepherd (*Eclogues* 1) compares the young Octavian to gods ready to give aid (*praesentes*) and promises monthly sacrifices to his benefactor; the poet's opening prayer in the *Georgics* addresses Octavian as destined to become a god, whether as protector of human cities, or of sea or sky (where the zodiac Scorpion would retract its claws to admit his sign). Horace compares Augustus to Mercury or Apollo, predicting that he will be judged a "praesens deus" (*Odes* 3.5.1), and envisions Augustus celebrated in worship of his numen (divine spirit) in both the cults of the local public lares on street altars and the libations of private homes. Such panegyric leads to imperial cult, arising partly from gratitude for social prosperity and partly as an extension of the cult paid by pious Romans to departed ancestors.

[*See also* Cult Images; Imperial Cult, Roman; *and* Religion, *subentry* Roman Religion.]

BIBLIOGRAPHY

Taylor, Lily Ross. *The Divinity of the Roman Emperor.* Middletown Conn.: American Philological Association, 1931 and various reprints.

Walbank, Frank W. "The Scipionic Legend" in his *Selected Papers: Studies in Greek and Roman History and Historiography.* Cambridge, U.K, and New York: Cambridge University Press, 1985.

Weinstock, Stefan. *Divus Julius.* Oxford: Clarendon Press, 1971.

Elaine Fantham

DELIAN LEAGUE

See Athens, *subentry* History of Athens in Antiquity.

DELOS

[This entry includes two subentries, a historical overview and a discussion of the archaeology of Delos.]

Historical Overview

Excavated by the École Française d'Athènes almost continuously since 1873, the archaeological remains of Delos, a small island at the center of the Aegean, date back to the Bronze Age. In Classical times the island became a renowned pilgrimage center because of its celebrated sanctuary of Apollo. Mythological tradition held that Leto gave birth to Apollo and Artemis beside the island's Sacred Lake. No humans could be born or die on the island; those who were ill were transported to neighboring Rheneia where a large necropolis has been excavated. Although administered until the second century BCE by local inhabitants, the sanctuary and the island were perceived as the geographical center of the Cyclades and the religious meeting place of Attic and Ionian peoples. Patronage, if not outright dominance, of the sanctuary served as an expression of authority in Aegean politics. In the seventh century BCE the people of nearby Naxos erected the famous lions of Delos, as well as the colossal statue of Apollo, and the earliest temple (the Oikos of the Naxians). From the sixth to the fourth centuries BCE the Athenians dominated the sanctuary, using it as the site for Delian League meetings and for a brief interval as its treasury depot. The three central temples of the sanctuary are presumed to have been constructed during this time. The sanctuary attained its greatest importance during the early Hellenistic era after the Delians liberated themselves from Athens, established a city-state hierarchy (with remains of a council house, the Prytaneion, the Ekklesiasterion, and altars sacred to the gods of the polis), and assumed leadership as the headquarters of the Cycladic League of Islanders. To win support of the league and wider Aegean communities, competing Macedonian dynasties graced the sanctuary with sweeping porticoes (the porticoes of Antigonus II Gonatas, Philip V, and the south portico of the Attalids), monuments, sanctuaries (the Sarapeia and Sanctuary of the Syrian Gods on Mount Cynthus), and numerous statue dedications. The priests of the sanctuary and the island inhabitants used their heightened importance to operate as a center for Aegean communications and the grain trade. Municipal growth proceeded along traditional lines with the construction of a theater, a gymnasium, a stadium, and two private palaestrae. A modest community emerged in the vicinity of the theater and the sanctuary itself became defined by an enclosure wall.

The period of Delian independence came to an abrupt end during the war between the Roman Republic in Italy and King Perseus of Macedonia (170–168 BCE). During this conflict Delian authorities, along with several other Aegean states, displayed undisguised sympathy for Perseus, despite their insistence on neutrality. For their betrayal the Roman senate expelled the island inhabitants and ceded control over the sanctuary to the Athenians, who promptly dispatched a cleruchy (that is, a settlement of Athenian citizens). The one restriction the senate imposed on the Athenians was that Delian trade be allowed to transpire duty free. Whether deliberate or otherwise, the consequence of this decision was to convert the island sanctuary into an international trading center where wealthy merchants from throughout Italy and Sicily could conduct business with similarly wealthy traders from eastern ports, such as Antioch, Laodicea, Aradus, Tyre, Sidon, Berytus, Ascalon, and Alexandria. The Athenian cleruchy was rapidly displaced by an influx of foreign traders who set the island on an unprecedented path of growth. Using landfill to expand the shore, new marketplaces (the Agora of Theophrastus, the Agora of the Competaliastai) were constructed beside the Sacred Harbor and rows of warehouses, separated from the domestic quarters by a causeway known as Road Five, extended more than two-thirds of a mile (about a kilometer) along the island's western shore. Modest houses near the theater were purchased and remodeled into palaces and development extended north of the sanctuary according to a regular Hippodamean street plan. Men's clubs, such as the Establishment of the Poseidoniastai of Berytus, the House of the Diadumenos, and the so-called Agora of the Italians, were constructed to accommodate the crush of foreign residents, who organized themselves according to religious fraternities. Although the geographer Strabo states that Delos became the center of the trans-Mediterranean slave trade, the island's internal evidence suggests that an array of luxuries were exchanged there as well. The notoriety of this wealthy foreign community made it a target for reprisal at the outbreak of the First Mithradatic War (88–84 BCE). The foreign residents were overrun twice by Cilician pirates in 87 and 69 BCE. By the time Rome had restored Mediterranean security, trading networks had moved further east eliminating the need for this harbor. The island was essentially abandoned by the imperial era.

[*See also* Aegean Sea.]

BIBLIOGRAPHY

Bruneau, Philippe, and Jean Ducat. *Guide de Délos.* 4th ed. Athens: École française d'Athènes, 2005.

Rauh, Nicholas K. *The Sacred Bonds of Commerce: Religion, Economy, and Trade Society at Hellenistic Roman Delos, 166–87 B.C.* Amsterdam: J. C. Gieben, 1993.

Reger, Gary. *Regionalism and Change in the Economy of Independent Delos, 314–167 B.C.* Hellenistic Culture and Society. Berkeley: University of California Press, 1994.

Nicholas K. Rauh

Archaeology of Delos

Delos is a small island—1.9 miles by 0.80 miles (5 kilometers by 1.3 kilometers) at its extremes, or 889 acres (360 hectares)—in the center of an Aegean archipelago known as the Cyclades. It is characterized by a semiarid climate with rainfall as the only source of freshwater, and it has little agricultural land—both unfavorable conditions for the development of a settlement. Delos was known primarily for its Panhellenic sanctuary of Apollo. Its sacred character was based on the myth that the island was the only place to accept Leto when she was pregnant by Zeus and therefore persecuted by Hera; here Leto gave birth to the twin gods Apollo and Artemis. Delos was also renowned as an international trade center.

The earliest archaeological remains consist of a small settlement from 2500–2000 BCE on Delos' highest hill, Mount Cynthus (367 feet, or 112 meters). In the Mycenaean period (1400–1200 BCE) a more important settlement developed in the plain later occupied by the sanctuary of Apollo. This included simple graves that were later venerated as hero tombs; their identification as the tombs of the Hyperborean maidens ("Theke," "Sema") that were intimately connected to Apollo's cult is, however, debated. Clear evidence of a Mycenaean cult of Apollo and its continuity into the following centuries is lacking.

The Sanctuary of Apollo. Though ceramics and expensive bronze votives testify to the veneration of Apollo in the late eighth century BCE, an architectural monumentalization of the sanctuary developed only from the seventh century BCE onward. The sanctuary is located on the plain next to the main harbor, and it had always remained both the center of the city and also the primary place where political and legal claims were made.

The first to exert noticeable influence on the sanctuary were the inhabitants of the nearby island of Naxos, who dedicated to Apollo many statues and several buildings, all made with Naxian marble. In the sixth century BCE they shaped the appearance of the sanctuary significantly by building a rectangular structure with a colonnaded porch and an internal colonnade—referred to as their *oikos*, the Oikos of the Naxians—an L-shaped stoa, and perhaps a monumental gate (propylon) between these two buildings and therefore in a location that served as the main entrance to the sanctuary throughout its history. In addition the Naxians set up a spectacular colossal statue of Apollo about thirty feet (nine meters) high. The Oikos building served either as the first temple of Apollo, perhaps housing the famous cult image of Apollo made by Tektaios and Angelion (known from literary sources), or as a multifunctional building used for assemblies, banquets, and the display of votive offerings. Finally, a unique series of at least nine monumental Naxian lions is commonly dated to the seventh century BCE. Displayed on a terrace to the north of Apollo's sanctuary, overlooking the Sacred Lake, these marble lions might originally have been dedicated to Apollo, but they were probably reattributed to Leto when her

Delos. Temple of Isis on the Terrace of the Foreign Gods at Mount Cynthus. COURTESY OF NICHOLAS K. RAUH

small temple was built in the later sixth century BCE next to the lions' terrace. It is very likely that, from the beginning, the center of Apollo's sanctuary was the so-called Altar of Horns (Keraton), reputedly erected by Apollo himself. It has been identified as an apsidal structure whose earliest remains date to the fifth century BCE and that might have replaced an ephemeral predecessor; this structure was repeatedly remodeled, and thus obviously carefully preserved, through the second century BCE.

In the later sixth century BCE the Athenians replaced the Naxians, dominating Apollo's sanctuary until 314 BCE. Athenian supremacy manifested itself in the successive construction of three temples to Apollo, located next to each other and oriented toward the Keraton: the Poros Temple (sixth century BCE), the Temple of the Athenians or Temple of the Seven Statues (c. 425–417), and the Great Temple (begun c. 475–450, completed in the third century). Athenian patronage has also been proposed for a fourth temple, dedicated to the Delphian Apollo and known as the Pythium (fourth century BCE). In a gradual expansion mainly toward the

north and east, the temples were surrounded by several buildings that were used for banquets and the display of precious votive offerings (treasuries and *oikoi*); according to inscriptions, the buildings were dedicated by different cities. Next to Apollo's sanctuary to the northwest, his sister Artemis had her own small sanctuary that developed from the sixth century BCE onward.

The sanctuary of Apollo saw another major change when Delos became an independent city (314–167/6 BCE). Through the centuries, several Hellenistic royal dynasties documented their political status and concerns, notably the constantly changing supremacy in the Aegean, with generous dedications to Apollo. Most conspicuous was the patronage of the Antigonids, who built three impressive monuments in the third century BCE: a huge stoa that was originally located outside the sanctuary of Apollo but that formed its northern boundary from the later second century BCE onward; the so-called Monument of the Bulls in the eastern part of the sanctuary, which housed a ship in commemoration of a naval victory; and another stoa that flanked and defined, together with an earlier equivalent to its east (South Stoa), the dromos (main entrance passage) of the sanctuary of Apollo.

The City. Though several civic administrative buildings at the border of Apollo's sanctuary—tentatively identified as an *ekklēsiastērion* (assembly hall), a *bouleutērion* (council-chamber), and a *prytaneion* (town hall)—date from the sixth to fourth centuries BCE, little is known of life outside this sanctuary before the period of Delian independence. The liberated Delians engaged in impressive building activity, erecting many buildings considered to be standard for a Greek city of this time. This building activity did not include the layout of a strictly orthogonal grid plan for new quarters, but it did show some concern for functional zoning and for the island's new role as a commercial center of local and regional trade with the surrounding Cycladic islands. Buildings included commercial structures in the vicinity of the harbor (e.g., the multifunctional Hypostyle Hall, the Agora of the Delians), sports facilities to the east of the Sacred Lake (e.g., the Palaestra of the Lake, the *stadion*), a theater for about sixty-five hundred spectators on a hill in the vicinity of the harbor, and sanctuaries for foreign deities on Mount Cynthus (e.g.. the three Serapea, the sanctuary of the Syrian gods). Public water supply was greatly improved by constructing huge reservoirs to store precious rainwater (e.g., the Inopos reservoir, the theater cistern). The territory outside the city was terraced, irrigated with water from reservoirs and wells, and exploited for animal husbandry and cultivation. Although it is very likely that residential quarters developed on a relatively regular street plan to the south, east, and north of Apollo's sanctuary, none of the ninety to a hundred houses currently visible can safely be dated to this period.

That Delos lacks two standard elements of a Greek city—city walls and cemeteries—is because of the island's sacred character: after purifications in the sixth and fifth centuries BCE, laws prohibited birth and burial on Delos. Thus protection against attacks that implied a high chance of casualties was not deemed necessary until the first century BCE when the sacred laws were obviously no longer respected and the Roman official Gaius Triarius protected the center of Delos against imminent assaults by building a wall. Furthermore, from 426 BCE onward, burials were displaced to the neighboring island of Rheneia.

The Romans ushered in the city's heyday by declaring Delos a free port in 167/6 BCE and handing its control back to Athens. The island developed into a booming cosmopolitan trade center with merchants coming from all over the Mediterranean world, particularly from Italy. To suit its new purpose, the city grew considerably, and most of the visible remains belong to this period: squares, quays, warehouses (five), shops (more than five hundred), new residential quarters, and clubhouses of foreign associations (at least five) were constructed, and public buildings and sanctuaries, particularly of foreign deities, were either renovated and extended or newly built. The numerous residential units are one of Delos' most intriguing and well-preserved features. They range from simple lodgings over shops and modest, often rentable apartments, to large lavish houses with colonnaded courtyards; the majority are simple courtyard houses with an average area of 1,400 to 1,650 square feet (130 to 150 square meters). The continuous enlargement and embellishment of numerous houses provide evidence of an increasingly luxurious lifestyle: many were decorated with polychrome stucco decorations, mosaics, and sculptures and were equipped with marble colonnades, lavish rooms for the reception of guests, latrines, and bathrooms.

Among the many nondomestic buildings two stand out: a synagogue on the eastern shore, built by Orthodox Jews or Samaritans before 88 BCE—and therefore the earliest surviving example from the ancient world—and the so-called Agora of the Italians, the largest building on Delos (about 87,726 square feet, or 8,150 square meters), prominently located to the north of the sanctuary of Apollo. This innovative, luxurious parklike complex with a monumental entrance (propylon), a garden, double-storied porticoes, niches for honorific statues, and a lavish bath suite with two fashionable round sweat-baths was built by the most important and powerful ethnic group of the cosmopolitan trade center, the Italians and Romans; it served to symbolize their status and wealth, as well as to reinforce their ethnic identity in the foreign environment.

Although Delos was sacked twice, first in 88 BCE by the troops of Mithradates, king of Pontus, in his war against the Romans, and again in 69 BCE by pirates, its desertion during the first century BCE was pre-dominantly due to rivalry with increasingly success-ful Roman ports like Puteoli and Ostia. As shown by inscriptions and remains of several Roman bath buildings and Christian basilicas, life in Delos did not come to an abrupt halt; instead it continued, only on a much smaller scale, until the eighth cen-tury CE. Because the island was never inhabited after this date, its ancient remains are well preserved and could be excavated on a large scale. This has been accomplished by the École Française d'Athènes (French School in Athens), which has uncovered about 24 percent (or about 23 of 95 hectares) of the ancient city since 1873.

[*See also* Archaeology, *subentry* Sites in Greece and Domestic Architecture.]

BIBLIOGRAPHY

Bruneau, Philippe, Michèle Brunet, Alexandre Farnoux, and Jean-Charles Moretti. *Délos: Île sacrée et ville cosmopolite.* École Française d'Athènes. Paris: Paris-Méditerranée, 1996.

Bruneau, Philippe, and Jean Ducat. *Guide de Délos.* 4th ed. Paris: Ecole Française d'Athènes, 2005.

Étienne, Roland. "The Development of the Sanctuary of Delos: New Perspectives." In *Excavating Classical Culture: Recent Archaeological Discoveries in Greece*, edited by Maria Stamatopoulou and Marina Yeroulanou, pp. 285–293. BAR International Series 1031. Oxford: Hadrian Books, 2002.

Exploration archéologique de Délos, vols. 1–42. Paris: École Française d'Athènes, 1909–2007. Ongoing pub-lication series.

Trümper, Monika. *Wohnen in Delos: Eine baugeschicht-liche Untersuchung zum Wandel der Wohnkultur in hellenistischer Zeit.* Internationale Archäologie 46. Rahden, Westphalia, Germany: Marie Leidorf, 1998.

Monika Trümper

DELPHI

[*This entry includes two subentries, a historical over-view and a discussion of the archaeology of Delphi.*]

Historical Overview

Delphi was a small city-state in the region of Phocis. Its historical importance derived from the presence within it of the sanctuary of Apollo Pythios, which was site of the most important oracle in Greece, and also of one of the major Pan-Hellenic festivals, the Pythian Games.

The earliest archaeological material found at the site of the settlement of Delphi is dated to c. 875 BCE, and the earliest certain evidence of dedications at the sanctuary of Apollo, in the form of tripods and figurines, comes from c. 800 BCE. There was a con-siderable increase in the quantity of dedications from c. 725 BCE, and literary evidence suggests that the wealth of the sanctuary was dramatically in-creased from c. 680 BCE with rich dedications from the Lydian king Gyges and his successors. The earli-est temple was built sometime between 650 and 600 BCE, and burned down in 548 BCE. The earliest of the sanctuary's many treasuries, built by Greek cities to house the dedications they made to Apollo, also dates from the seventh century BCE. Greek tradition dated the first Pythian Games, probably approxi-mately correctly, to 582/81 BCE. In their fully devel-oped form the games took place every two years, and included musical competition as well as athlet-ics and chariot racing.

As the wealth and importance of the sanctuary grew, from some time in the sixth century, oversight of aspects of the sanctuary became the responsibil-ity of the Delphic amphictyony, a group of neighbor-ing communities that also took responsibility for a number of sanctuaries near Thermopylae. Details of the working of the amphictyony before 346 BCE are limited, but by that time major Greek cities from farther away, including Athens and Sparta, were sending delegates to its meetings.

The sanctuary of Apollo received large numbers of dedications in the sixth century, but even more in the fifth, reflecting in particular the prestige of the oracle. Some modern writers believed that the oracle advocated support for the Persians at the time of their invasions of Greece in 490 and 480–479 BCE, but there is no evidence to support this. Herodotus reports an unsuccessful raid on Delphi by the Persians during their invasion in 480 BCE, and states that Delphi was the site of major dedications of spoils from the Greek victories of the Persians.

Through the fifth century and the first half of the fourth there were a number of attempts by the other cities of Phocis to force Delphi to join the Phocian confederation. While the Phocians were usually supported by Athens, Thebes and Sparta resisted these moves, which would have strengthened the confederation by giving the Phocians access to the wealth stored at Delphi. The so-called Third Sacred War (356–346 BCE) was the final conflict over this issue. The Phocians occupied the sanctuary at the start of the war, and in the course of it used most of the silver and gold dedicated in the sanctuary to pay for their military activity. They were eventually defeated when Philip II of Macedon intervened against them. The amphictyony was reorganized, with Philip given a major role, and the Phocians were accused of temple robbery and expelled from the organization. The loss of the wealth at Delphi, coming after the destruction of the second temple of Apollo in an earthquake in 373 BCE, appears to have contributed to a decline of the prestige of the oracle.

Macedonian kings did not retain control of Delphi, which came under the control of the Aetolian Confederacy at the start of the third century. In 279 BCE Delphi was attacked by a Gallic raiding party, who were driven off by the Aetolians and Phocians. Ancient accounts of the event are clearly modeled on the Persian raid of two centuries earlier. The Phocians once again and the Aetolians now became members of the amphicytony, and a new festival, the Soteria, was founded later to celebrate the salvation of Delphi. There were many Aetolian dedications in the sanctuary from the mid-270s BCE onward.

As early as c. 400 BCE the Roman general Camillus possibly consulted the oracle at Delphi and certainly made a dedication there. There were Roman consultations of the oracle again during the Second Punic War, the war against Hannibal (218–201 BCE). Roman military intervention in Greece began around this time, with the Romans declaring Greek cities free from Macedonian control in 196 BCE. In 190 BCE Delphi was made independent of Aetolia, but treasure was seized from there by Sulla in 86 BCE. In the following year the city and sanctuary were damaged by an Illyrian raid, and the poverty of the sanctuary in his own time was noted by Strabo, writing under Augustus.

Delphi's fortune improved a little when a number of emperors took a direct interest in the community and the sanctuary. Nero (r. 54–68 CE) performed at the Pythian Games, Domitian (r. 81–96 CE) made repairs to the temple, and Hadrian (r. 117–138 CE), who devoted a lot of attention to Greece, was twice archon of Delphi, and is recorded as having consulted the oracle himself. His reign saw an increase in other dedications and building works in the sanctuary, although this did not continue long.

Plutarch, who was from Chaeronea in Boeotia, served as priest of Apollo at Delphi in the reign of Trajan (98–117 BCE). At this time he wrote a number of philosophical essays about Delphi and the oracle. From his perspective Delphi, and oracles in general, had fallen considerably from their former position of importance, and the picture he presents of Delphi in c. 100 CE is of a quiet provincial backwater, visited by tourists rather than representatives of communities.

Nonetheless, Delphi was still honored even by Christian emperors into the fourth century CE, as is revealed by a series of dedications in the names of Constantine and his sons Constantine II and Constans from 317 to c. 338 CE, which describe Delphi as "the sacred city." The oracle appears to have ceased to function by the end of the fourth century, when the site was abandoned.

[*See also* Aetolia and the Aetolian Confederacy; Apollo, *subentry* Apollo in Greek Religion; Boeotia; Cyclades; Delphic Oracle; Greece; Phocis; and Sacred Wars.]

BIBLIOGRAPHY

McInerney, Jeremy. *The Folds of Parnassos: Land and Ethnicity in Ancient Phokis.* Austin: University of Texas Press, 1999.

Morgan, Catherine. *Athletes and Oracles: The Transformation of Olympia and Delphi in the Eighth Century BC.* Cambridge, U.K.: Cambridge University Press, 1990.

Parke, H. W., and D. E. W. Wormell. *The Delphic Oracle.* 2 vols. Oxford: Blackwell, 1956.

Sánchez, Pierre. *L'Amphictionie des Pyles et de Delphes: recherches sur son rôle historique, des origines au IIe siècle de notre ère.* Stuttgart, Germany: Franz Steiner, 2001.

Hugh Bowden

Archaeology of Delphi

The archaeology of Delphi is closely linked to the site's natural setting and geology, as well as to the history of the oracular shrine. Backed by sheer cliffs known as the Phaedriades or "Shining Ones," Delphi commands a wide view of the southern slopes of Mount Parnassus, the Pleistus river valley, and the distant Gulf of Corinth. The spectacular topography was likened in antiquity to a theater. Owing to its location astride active faults on the northern edge of the Corinthian-Saronic rift valley, Delphi exists under constant threat of earthquakes and avalanches—a motivation for the local cult of Poseidon the Earthshaker. Polygonal masonry was introduced to withstand tremors. Early inhabitants erected terraces to deal with the steep slope. Over much of the site the original ground surface is thus deeply buried beneath fill. Soft gray local limestone provided building material for Delphi's walls and monuments; marble had to be imported.

Two springs provided Delphi's water. To the east, rain and snowmelt from Parnassus emerged in the Castalia gorge, then flowed through pipes to the bathing pool of the gymnasium. Within the sanctuary of Apollo, calcium-rich waters from the Cassotis (modern Kerna) spring system coated the slopes with travertine rock. Overflow from Cassotis and runoff from the cliffs were channeled through elaborate drains to minimize erosion. Neolithic and early Bronze Age potsherds and stone axes have been unearthed in the zone of Cassotis, but without associated structures. These finds may reflect seasonal occupation by herdsmen attracted to the springs.

Ancient writers referred to a natural *chasma* or fissure beneath the crypt where the Pythia delivered the oracles of Apollo. According to Plutarch, a priest at Delphi in the early second century CE, the spring waters in or around the temple also brought an oracular *pneuma* or vapor bubbling to the surface. Recent studies by several scientific teams suggest that the ancient *chasma* was a fault running under the site and that the *pneuma* was a natural gas emitted from the bituminous limestone bedrock. Carbon dioxide, light hydrocarbons (methane, ethane, and ethylene), and benzene have been proposed as candidates for the *pneuma*. Plutarch believed the flow of *pneuma* that triggered the Pythia's trances had been weakened over the centuries by earthquakes or by exhaustion of the natural substance that produced it.

Fifteenth to Second Centuries BCE. Starting about 1500 BCE a Mycenaean town stretched from the Castalia gorge to the site of the temple of Apollo, with a detached cemetery sited farther west. In the area between the town rampart or retaining wall and the chamber tombs lay a cult center, on the spot later occupied by the oracular chamber (*adyton*) of the Classical temple. Here archaeologists found a Bronze Age sacrificial pit filled with bones, potsherds, and ash layers. Fragments of a Minoan lion-head rhyton (drinking horn) were found nearby. Directly downhill was the spring of Ge (Mother Earth), focus of a pre-Apolline cult. Its rock-cut steps are visible on a limestone outcrop north of the Athenian treasury. An important group of 175 terra-cotta figurines—some with outstretched arms, others seated on three-legged chairs or thrones—date to the thirteenth century BCE. In about 700 BCE these figurines were collected and interred in the sanctuary of Athena Pronaia. Their original Bronze Age context is uncertain.

As Iron Age tombs attest, Delphi was not abandoned at the end of the Bronze Age, but both population and ritual activity diminished. Renewed growth began in the early eighth century BCE: a massive Geometric retaining wall created a terrace

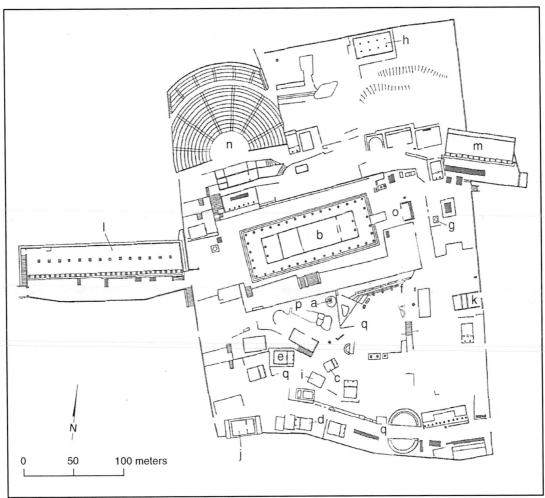

Plan of the Sanctuary of Apollo, Delphi, sixth to third century BCE. (a) Naxian column; (b) Temple of Apollo; (c) Cnidian Treasury; (d) Siphnian Treasury; (e) Athenian Treasury; (f) Stoa of the Athenians; (g) site of tripod of the Crotonians; supposed site of tripod of Plataea; (h) *Lesche* of the Cnidians; (i) Treasury of the Syracusans; (j) Treasury of the Thebans; (k) Treasury of Cyrene; (l) West Stoa; (m) Stoa of Attalus; (n) theater; (o) altar; (p) Spring of Ge; (q) Sacred Way. © OXFORD UNIVERSITY PRESS

for the sanctuary of Athena Pronaia, houses with hearths in a corner were constructed of local stone, and bronze votive offerings were deposited in the area of the sanctuary. In time the Delphians banished private dwellings from the area today enclosed by the *temenos* wall, a shift that may mark the introduction of the cult of Apollo.

The *Homeric Hymn to Apollo* relates that the first priests of Apollo came from Knossos (Cnossus), and Cretan tripods and other bronzes show links to Crete at this time. The circular *halos* or threshing floor of the original community now lay within the

sanctuary—it spanned the line of the Sacred Way in front of the later Athenian Stoa—and became the stage for pageants that reenacted Apollo's arrival and slaying of Python. By the late seventh century a small temple of Apollo was built on the present site. To the southeast stood the rectangular *thēsauros* or treasury of the Corinthians, whose influence was then particularly strong.

Delphi entered its heyday as a great Panhellenic center with the establishment of the Pythian Games and the Amphictyonic League circa 600 BCE. The upper and lower sanctuaries rapidly became

Rediscovering Delphi

In March 1486, Cyriacus of Ancona, an Italian merchant and classical scholar, found the location of ancient Delphi. During a six-day visit he noted the remains of the stadium, the theater, and a rotunda that he called the temple of Apollo (now known to be a pair of semicircular statue bases for an Argive monument). Cyriacus also copied inscriptions and described statues and tombs.

Over the next four centuries many travelers sought additional traces of the ancient site. Colonel William Martin Leake, who visited in 1802 and 1806, astutely observed that the temple of Apollo must in fact lie buried beneath the modern town of Kastri. In 1870, Heinrich and Sophie Schliemann spent two days exploring Delphi and the Castalia spring. In the 1880s the German scholar Hans Pomtow embarked on photographic documentation and Robert Koldewey, future excavator of Babylon, further studied the colonnade and inscriptions of the Athenian Stoa.

In 1830 antiquities from Delphi were displayed at Aegina in the first Greek archaeological museum; four years later local citizens petitioned for a museum at Delphi itself. In 1838 Greek scholars proposed that Kastri be relocated to permit excavation of the entire sanctuary. In 1891 the French pledged substantial financial support to shift Kastri westward to the site occupied by the modern town of Delphi. In return the Greek government granted to the École Française d'Athènes a concession for a decade to excavate the site.

Most of the monuments visible at Delphi today came to light during the Grande Fouille or "Big Dig" of 1892–1903. Théophile Homolle, veteran of excavations at the sanctuary of Apollo on Delos, directed the campaign. The team initially worked downhill from the previously exposed Athenian Stoa to reveal the Sacred Way and the treasury of the Athenians, with its sculpted metopes and its rare inscribed hymn to Apollo, complete with musical notation. The team then extended the excavated area uphill to the temple of Apollo, which they found had been stripped in antiquity of virtually all its treasures and sculptural adornments. Spectacular finds elsewhere compensated for these losses: a splendid pair of archaic kouroi, later dubbed Kleobis and Biton; a fine marble statue of Hadrian's beloved Antinous; and the famous bronze Charioteer.

Between 1898 and 1902, French archaeologists uncovered the gymnasium and practice running track below the road, the lower zone known as the sanctuary of Athena Pronaia, and the eastern necropolis. These and subsequent archaeological discoveries revealed a sequence of cultic activities and occupations that spans two millennia from the Bronze Age to the early Christian period.

---

crowded with treasuries, war memorials, and sculptural dedications from city-states as far afield as Massalia, Cyrene, and Pontic Heraclea. Some of these, like the treasury of the gold-mining Siphnians with caryatids and a Gigantomachy, rank among the finest Greek art. With space at a premium, some dedications took the form of tall pillars, like the Archaic sphinx of Naxos, the serpent column of Plataea (c. 479 BCE), and the nearly forty-three-foot (thirteen-meter) acanthus column with dancing girls that was dedicated by Athenians circa 330 BCE.

When earthquakes damaged statues and buildings the remains were reverently interred behind retaining walls or in pits. Thus archaeologists found the bronze Charioteer of Delphi behind the Ischegaon wall, the Archaic trove of chryselephantine sculpture and the silver-sheeted bull beneath the Sacred Way, and the apsidal Archaic treasury behind the polygonal wall. The temple of Apollo, a Doric building with an interior Ionic colonnade, was rebuilt each time after destructions in 548 and 373 BCE. Strong walls protected the treasures; a fortification near the stadium may date to the Sacred War of the fourth century BCE.

During the time of Alexander's successors, Delphi was eclipsed by other oracles such as Claros and

Didyma in Asia Minor, but important building projects continued. A grand pair of stoas west and east of the sanctuary commemorated two separate victories over the Celtic Galatians, one by Aetolian Greeks and the other by king Attalus I of Pergamum. In this period Hellenistic kings were honored with equestrian statues set on high pillars. The pillar of King Prusias I of Bithynia has been rebuilt. Inscriptions proliferated, including eight hundred minuscule records of freed slaves on the Athenian Stoa. A magnificent theater in white limestone replaced an older wooden theater in this period.

First Century BCE **to Seventh Century** CE. Roman rule left only a modest mark on the sanctuary of Apollo, aside from a new frieze in the theater depicting the labors of Hercules. Roman tourists came to see antiquities, not new buildings. To accommodate the influx of visitors the terraced and colonnaded so-called Roman Agora was constructed in fine brickwork outside the sanctuary gate, and the Sacred Way was repaved with corrugated slabs to prevent slipping. Hadrian's rich Athenian friend Herodes Atticus rebuilt the stadium with limestone seating for seven thousand and a triple-arched entrance behind the starting line. The Doric colonnade of Attalus' stoa was bricked up to create a reservoir for a large bath complex.

Plutarch provided lively vignettes of Roman Delphi in three essays, and the travel writer Pausanias wrote a guide to the site that still helps modern archaeologists identify various precincts and monuments. Though Domitian repaired the temple of Apollo after a fire, the Roman period was notable for losses as well. Sulla and Nero took hundreds of statues, and in about 340 CE Constantine had the Serpent Column of Plataea conveyed to his new capital at Constantinople. Its inscribed bronze shaft still stands near Hagia Sophia on the spina of the former hippodrome, while the one surviving serpent head is kept in Istanbul's Archaeology Museum. The last Delphic oracle was said to have been given to an emissary from Julian the Apostate in about 360 CE. The Pythia's references to fallen buildings and waters that had ceased to flow suggest yet another devastating earthquake.

Initially Delphi thrived under the Christians. The basilica church of the bishops of Delphi stood on the site of the modern town. Its figural mosaics are displayed near the entrance to the museum. The Geometric mosaic beside the path between the museum and the archaeological site once adorned the Byzantine church of Saint George, built near the temple from classical spoils. Slabs bearing Christian symbols have been collected in the Roman Agora. In this period many public baths, perhaps for pilgrims, were constructed at the Castalia spring and around the old pagan sanctuary. On a grimmer note, part of a new defensive wall can be seen between the gymnasium and the sanctuary of Athena Pronaia. Despite these fortifications the town seems to have fallen to invaders. Although a monastery survived above the ruins of the gymnasium, from the seventh century onward Delphi was little more than a mountain village sustained by herding and agriculture.

[See also Apollo, subentry Apollo in Greek Religion; Archaeology, subentry Sites in Greece; Delphic Oracle; and Oracles.]

BIBLIOGRAPHY

Amandry, Pierre. *Delphi and Its History*. Athens, Greece: Archaeological Guide Editions, 1984.

Broad, William J. *The Oracle: The Lost Secrets and Hidden Message of Ancient Delphi*. New York: Penguin, 2006.

Higgins, Michael Denis, and Reynold Higgins. *A Geological Companion to Greece and the Aegean*. Ithaca, N.Y.: Cornell University Press, 1996.

Parke, Herbert W. *The Delphic Oracle*. Oxford: Blackwell, 1939.

Pendazos, Vanghelis, and Maria Sarla. *Delphi*. Athens, Greece: Yiannikos-Kaldis, 1984.

Themelis, Petros. *Delphi: The Archaeological Site and the Museum*. Translated by Louise Turner. Athens, Greece: Ekdotike Athenon, 1991.

John R. Hale

DELPHIC ORACLE

Delphi was the site of the most famous oracle of Apollo, situated high up on the southern slope of Mount Parnassus; its unwelcoming situation among cliffs and gorges was often remarked on in antiquity. Together with the sanctuaries of Apollo on Delos and Zeus in Olympia, Delphi's *temenos* was one of the major sanctuaries in ancient Greece, especially during the Archaic and Classical periods. Later its oracular function was rivaled by the sanctuaries of Clarus and Didyma, and its overall splendor was rivaled by the sanctuaries dedicated to Asclepius at Epidaurus, Cos, and Pergamum.

History. The first archaeological traces of a settlement at Delphi date to the ninth century BCE, and the first dedications from the sanctuary come from the eighth century. Shortly afterward, Delphi's wealthy sanctuary with a "threshold of stone"—that is, presumably, a first stone temple—is mentioned in the *Iliad* (9.404f.). Myth attests to several consecutive early temples, of laurel, of feathers, and of bronze (Pindar *Paean* 8), or has Apollo build his temple himself, together with the heroic architects Trophonius and Agamedes (*Homeric Hymn to Apollo* 295–297). In 548/7 the temple burned down; not long after, it was replaced by a monumental one financed by the Athenian Alcmaeonids, then exiled from Athens. An earthquake in 373 destroyed parts of the sanctuary including the temple; the new temple was finished around 330 and remained upright until late antiquity. The prohibition of pagan cult by Theodosius (392/3 CE) caused its closing, and an edict of Arcadius caused its demolition.

During the Archaic and Classical periods the Delphic oracle was the most influential oracular shrine in Greece and beyond; although the historicity of many early oracles is doubtful, the sheer number of stories reflects its historical importance. It was involved in most major political developments; it sanctioned Lycurgus' constitution for Sparta and Cleisthenes' democratic reforms in Athens. It advised cities and individuals in the many colonial ventures of the Archaic period. Its fame spread beyond the Greek world: Croesus, the king of Lydia, was said to have consulted it before his disastrous attack on the Persians. Before the Persian invasions of Greece, the oracle was consulted on the best way to deal with the threat; although it infamously mostly advised nonresistance, its importance was not diminished after the wars. Before the outbreak of the Peloponnesian War in 431, the oracle encouraged Sparta; this did hinder Athenians from continuing to use it, both publicly and privately. Only the political and economic fallout of the Mithradatic rebellion against Rome in the first century BCE caused a rapid decline from which the oracle never fully recovered, despite the help of philhellenic emperors.

Many splendid dedications attested to the prominence of the oracle. Greek cities and foreign powers vied for religious self-representation, and several Archaic cities built splendid treasuries along the Sacred Way that led from the city through the *temenos* up to the temple terrace and the monumental altar dedicated by the Chians. The *temenos* also contained the navel of the earth (*omphalos*), a manifest expression of Delphic claims.

Given its importance and wealth, possession of Delphi was precious and contested; several so-called Sacred Wars were fought over it. During most of the Archaic period, Delphi was under the influence of Thessaly, the prominent power in the amphictyony, the "league of neighbors" that exercised political influence in Delphi. Later Macedonia under Philip II dominated the league, then the Aetolians. In 480 BCE the Persians tried unsuccessfully to conquer Delphi, as did marauding Gauls in 279; Sulla's armies plundered and occupied it in 87–83. The rescue from the Gauls led to the panhellenic festival Soteria and a growing number of legends of how Apollo himself saved his shrine.

The Oracle. The *Homeric Hymn to Apollo*, the earliest extensive document on the Delphic cult, gives no details on the way the oracle functioned. When trying to found his sanctuary, young Apollo was surprised by a giant snake, he killed it and let its body rot, and from its stink (*pythein*) came the other name of Delphi, Pytho. Apollo then instructed the first priests to gain their livelihood from the sacrifices brought by the oracle seekers. The Pythia, the prophetess of Apollo, is not mentioned, but there can be no doubt that from early on the Pythia communicated between Apollo and the consultants; other forms of divination such as lot oracles might have existed in Delphi as well, but these were never important.

Most of our knowledge about how the Delphic oracle functioned comes from the Delphic dialogues of Plutarch of Chaeronea, himself a Delphic priest. The Pythia was Apollo's prophetess who gave oracles while possessed by the god (*entheos*). Oracular sessions originally took place once a year, on Apollo's birthday on Bysios 7, later once a month; the possibility of additional extraordinary sessions is debated. A mantic session could take place only when the god agreed by making the victim of the initial goat sacrifice nod its head; disregarding this condition could lead to the death of the Pythia. For the session, the Pythia descended into the *adyton*, placed herself on the sacred tripod, and received the god; additional personnel must have been present, although the exact architectural arrangement is lost because of the extensive destruction of this part of the temple. This personnel included the *prophētēs* (or several *prophētai*) and the *hosioi* (consecrated men), in Plutarch's time a body of five men who assisted the *prophētēs*. The relationship between Pythia and *prophētēs* remains unclear, and any generalization is problematic, including the modern assumption that the prophet put the vocal utterances of the Pythia in verse: Plutarch attests to the coherent and often versified pronouncements of the Pythia (*De Pythiae oraculis* 22). On the other side, there were suspicions that the oracular answers were manipulated, in whatever way (Herodotus 6.63–66).

The Pythia served her entire life, but the exact conditions of this service are debated. In historical times she was an older woman who even could have had children before her service; in religious ideology, she was and had to remain a virgin, conversing only with Apollo. Mediumistic gifts must have constituted a basic condition of her selection. The exact nature of the Pythia's extraordinary state of mind during the sessions and the ways of inducing them remain equally conjectural. A legend told in Diodorus Siculus (16.26) ascribed the origin of the oracle to vapors coming from a chasm in the earth and inspiring first goats and then men to incoherent prancing and oracular utterances; this contradicts Plutarch's information on the Pythia's coherent speech and quiet demeanor during the mantic session. Christian polemicists elaborate on the vapors and their sexual stimulation. Whereas the French excavators of the sanctuary rejected the theory that some gaseous exhalation could cause the Pythia's trance, recent geological research has reopened the question, with very tentative results; if vapors played a role, they did so not by altering the Pythia's state of mind through chemical means, but as an extraneous trigger of a self-induced trance.

Dionysus and Pythian Games. Apollo shared his *temenos* with Dionysus, who was said to reside in Delphi during the winter when Apollo was absent among the Hyperboreans (Plutarch *De E apud Delphos* 398d). The east pediment of the temple represented Apollo and the Muses, the west pediment Dionysus and the thyiads (*Thyiades*), the Delphic maenads; his grave was said to be within the temple. Athens sent an annual delegation of thyiads to the *orgia* (sacred rites) on Mount Parnassus that took place every second winter. But the alternation between the two divinities might be a later theological construction; the paean of Philodamus, performed in 340/39, invoked the god to participate in the spring festival of the Theoxenia.

The Theoxenia was performed annually on behalf of all Greeks, with sacrifices and choric performances. The main Delphic festival, however, were the Pythian Games, said to have been founded by Apollo to commemorate his victory over the Pytho dragon; the games were performed every fifth year, though originally they were performed every ninth year. They were open to all Greeks and vied in splendor and importance with the Olympic games, as Pindar's victory odes demonstrate. The games were founded or reorganized in 591/0 or 58/56 BCE; the well-preserved stadium at the very top of the *temenos* is early Hellenistic. The contests comprised musical and athletic performances and a chariot race; the victors received a laurel wreath.

[*See also* Apollo, *subentry* Apollo in Greek Religion; Delphi; Oracles; *and* Prophecy.]

BIBLIOGRAPHY

Fontenrose, Joseph. *The Delphic Oracle: Its Responses and Operations, with a Catalogue of Responses.* Berkeley: University of California Press, 1978.

Johnston, Sarah Iles. *Ancient Greek Divination.* Oxford: Blackwell, 2008.

Suárez de la Torre, Emilio. Art. "Divination. C. Institutionen: Orakel. 1 Delphes," In *Thesaurus Cultus et Rituum Antiquorum*, vol. 3, pp. 16–31. Los Angeles: J. Paul Getty Museum, 2005.

Fritz Graf

DEMES

A deme was a district, village, or town in ancient Greece, which in some city-states was the basic political unit. Demes may be the oldest continuously employed political units in ancient Greece, since the word appears on the Mycenaean Linear B tablets and in Homer. The best evidence for them, especially in their political role, comes from Athens and Attica, although they also appear in many other Greek cities (for example, on Euboea and in Asia).

The deme system in Athens and Attica was the heart of the Cleisthenic reforms of 508 BCE. Cleisthenes divided the existing four tribes of Attica into ten, and further subdivided these into thirty *trittyes* and 139 demes, which covered all Attica. Cleisthenes did not attempt to regulate the size of the demes; although some were quite small, others were sizeable towns. While the motives behind Cleisthenes' reforms are much debated, what is striking about his subdivision of the tribes into demes is that he took great care not to permit the political division of Attica by locality, a situation that had led to the rise of the tyrant Peisistratus fifty years before. Presumably he hoped to forestall control by one region alone by creating political loyalty to demes and not to locales dominated by tribes. Demes were instead split up among the three geographical divisions of Attica: coast, plain, and hill country. Almost every tribe did have at least one deme in Athens herself, and it is assumed that those urban demes were to some degree the tribal "capitals." Cleisthenes' apparent altruism in these reforms is slightly suspect; one wonders how these arrangements would have benefited him and his family, the Alcmaeonidae.

The deme subsequently became essential to the political and social identity of the Athenian citizen. Membership was hereditary (even if area of residence changed) and was signified by the addition of a deme name (or *demoticon*) to the given name and the patronymic, which had been used hitherto. For instance, in the name "Alcibiades son of Cleinias from Skambonidai," Alcibiades is the given name, Cleinias the patronymic, and Skambonidai the deme name. This naming system now became standard, and a deme name was a mark of citizenship, since only citizens belonged to demes. Over time, the deme name became more commonly used than the patronymic in Athens, reflecting the transition from an aristocratic society to a democratic one. At the age of eighteen, each Athenian male registered with his deme, giving proof of his citizenship to the demarche ("leader of the deme"). Membership in a deme guaranteed his citizenship in the city as a whole.

Demes were much like the city in miniature. Each was to some degree autarkic, since remains of shops and workshops have been found in demes. There were assemblies in each deme, which appointed a "mayor" (demarche) and any other officials necessary, and passed decrees and laws, some of which are preserved on stone. Taxes were levied to support a deme treasury, and each deme had its own local cults and festivals.

[*See also* Athens and Attica, *subentry* History of Attica.]

BIBLIOGRAPHY

Traill, John S. *Demos and Trittys: Epigraphical and Topographical Studies in the Organization of Attica.* Toronto: Athenians, Victoria College, 1986.

Traill, John S. *The Political Organization of Attica: A Study of the Demes, Trittyes, and Phylai, and Their Representation in the Athenian Council.* Princeton, N.J.: American School of Classical Studies at Athens, 1975.

Whitehead, David. *The Demes of Attica, 508/7–ca. 250 B.C.: A Political and Social Study.* Princeton, N.J.: Princeton University Press, 1986.

Sarah Bolmarcich

DEMETER

The goddess Demeter was one of the five deities born from the primordial Titans Rhea and Cronus. Sister to the reigning Olympian gods Zeus, Hera, Poseidon, and Hades, she received as her share of the universe the power to promote or arrest the fertility of the earth, above all the production of life-giving grain. Through the Eleusinian mortal Triptolemus, who took her teachings around the civilized world, she taught humans how to cultivate the earth.

Demeter's beneficence was temporarily interrupted by the abduction of her daughter, Persephone (also known simply as Kore, "Maiden"), while Persephone was picking flowers in a meadow in the company of, in various versions, virginal goddesses (Athena and Artemis) and minor deities (such as the daughter of Oceanus). Persephone's father, Zeus, had promised her to his brother Hades, lord of the underworld. Sicilian myths claimed that the abduction took place at Enna in Sicily, followed by Persephone's descent to the world below at the Cyane spring near Syracuse. Demeter's mourning for her lost daughter took her away from Olympus to wander in disguise on earth.

In various versions of the myth, Demeter was helped by either mortals or immortals to discover the whereabouts of her lost child. In our earliest version, the late seventh or early sixth century BCE *Homeric Hymn to Demeter*, she took refuge in the palace of King Celeus of Eleusis, where she became nurse to a mortal child, Demophon. When her attempt to immortalize the child by anointing him with ambrosia and placing him in fire at night was discovered and misunderstood by his mother, Metaneira, Demeter abandoned the boy either to mortality or—in Orphic versions—to immediate death. She then angrily retired to a new temple that the Eleusinians built for her and created a famine by preventing the grain from growing. The gods, fearful of losing sacrifices from starving mortals, capitulated to Kore's return; Demeter taught her Mysteries to the princes of Eleusis.

In other versions the famine occurred earlier within the tale, and Demeter negotiated directly with Zeus/Jupiter. Because Persephone had eaten pomegranate seeds in the world below, she was fated to spend one-third (or in later versions, one-half) of her time with Hades as queen of the underworld and the rest of her time in the world above. Persephone's cyclic reappearances in the world above increasingly became linked to the agricultural cycle, although her spring return in the *Homeric Hymn to Demeter* does not mark the planting of grain, which took place in autumn after the fall rains began. Myths involving the withdrawal and return of fertility deities had precedents in the Near East—for example, the Sumerian-Babylonian myth of the descent of Inanna-Ishtar—but the link between goddess and daughter appears unique.

Persephone's new position as a mediator between the upper worlds of earth and Olympus and the impenetrable lower world enabled the creation of the Eleusinian Mysteries by Demeter. Initiates in the Mysteries were promised agricultural beneficence in the world above—symbolized by Demeter's child Plutus, or Wealth, who was sired by the Cretan Iasion on a thrice-plowed field—and a better life under Persephone's aegis in the world below. The goddesses' brush with the world of mortality apparently led them to pity the mortal lot and adopt a symbolical maternal role toward human beings; the second half of Demeter's name means "mother." Persephone's abduction at a nubile age also made the myth resonate with marriage. Her marriage to Hades became a metaphor for the early death of virgins, who were often called "brides to Hades," or served to express the symbolic death involved in the marriage rite itself, in which the bride figuratively dies to life in her natal family and is resurrected as wife in another.

Every Greek city worshipped Demeter, and her increasing centrality in literature and culture after the seventh century BCE reflects growing dependence on agriculture and property requirements for citizenship. The oldest of her widespread cults appears to have been the Thesmophoria, celebrated throughout the Greek world exclusively by women. In these rites women—citizen wives, and probably also some concubines—withdrew from their home life to reexperience ritually the two goddesses' withdrawal and return. Pigs, animals noted for their fertility, were thrown into pits along with cakes representing sexual organs. The rotten remains were withdrawn during the Thesmophoria and mixed with the seeds of grain before the autumn planting. Demeter's withdrawal to the world of women in the *Homeric Hymn to Demeter*, her drinking of the *kykeōn* (a special barley drink), and her ritual joking were enacted in the Mysteries, where initiates imbibed the drink and were subjected to ritual insults on their way from Athens to Eleusis; at the Thesmophoria, women shared sexual jokes about fertility. Women served as priestesses in cults of Demeter, although the Eleusinian Mysteries included hereditary roles for male priests as well.

The secrecy surrounding Eleusinian and other, lesser Mysteries perhaps explains the limited and largely fragmentary literary versions of the goddesses' myths that have survived. For example, we know almost nothing about Demeter's mysterious union as Black Demeter with the god Poseidon in Arcadia, both in the form of a horse. The Hellenistic poet Callimachus' *Hymn to Demeter* (also known as his *Hymn 6*), focuses on the anger of the goddess when the Thessalian king Erysichthon, though warned by Demeter's priestess, insisted on cutting down her sacred grove to enhance the building of his palace. Demeter, exercising once again her power over food, punished the king with insatiable hunger. He finally reduced both his family and himself to ruin. The goddess's own tendency to lose interest in eating during her mourning reemerges in Pindar's first *Olympian Ode*, where the distracted goddess makes the mistake of taking a bite of the mortal Pelops' shoulder when he is served to the gods by his unscrupulous father, Tantalus. The Roman poet Ovid retold the myth in his *Metamorphoses* (5.385–661; see also *Fasti* 4.417–620), and Claudian's unfinished *On the Rape of Proserpina* shows a new interest in the relation between Hades and his bride. Although the *Homeric Hymn to Demeter* represents Persephone's attitude to her abductor as ambivalent, Claudian's underworld god becomes a more sympathetic suitor.

[*See also* Ceres; Eleusis and Eleusinian Mysteries; and Gods, Greek, *subentry* The Olympian Gods.]

BIBLIOGRAPHY

Foley, Helene P., ed. *The Homeric Hymn to Demeter*. Princeton, N.J.: Princeton University Press, 1994.

Richardson, N. J., ed. *The Homeric Hymn to Demeter*. Oxford: Clarendon Press, 1974.

Helene P. Foley

DEMETRIUS OF PHALERON

(c. 350–c. 285 BCE), Athenian legislator, writer, and orator. Of Demetrius' background little is known. An ancient tradition that he was born a slave is probably mere invective; his well-documented relationship with Theophrastus, Menander, and the Peripatetic school hints at more prosperous origins. Demetrius entered political life at a time of great turmoil (c. 324) and gained sufficient stature to serve as an envoy when Athens conceded defeat to Macedon in the Lamian War in 322. Demetrius may have played a part in the oligarchy subsequently imposed on Athens by Antipater of Macedon; his sympathies were thus not those of his brother, Himeraeus, who was put to death under that oligarchy. Having himself survived a death sentence passed by a briefly restored democracy, Demetrius was elevated to power when Antipater's son, Cassander, seized Athens in 318/7. With Cassander's backing, Demetrius dominated Athenian politics for the decade 317–307, until Demetrius I Poliorcetes took control of Athens and expelled him. He later gained influence at the court of Ptolemy I Soter in Alexandria, but his promotion of a rival to Soter's eventual successor, Ptolemy II Philadelphus, precipitated a fall from favor and culminated in his death sometime around 285 in suspicious circumstances.

The belief, once common, that Demetrius ruled Athens as *stratēgos* (general) must be dismissed now that an inscribed statue base (*Inscriptiones Graecae*, vol. 2 [2nd ed.] 2971) attesting multiple generalships for a Demetrius of Phaleron has been shown to pertain to the homonymous grandson of our Demetrius. The ancient sources instead style him variously *epimelētēs* (overseer) and *nomothetēs* (lawgiver), and he later ranked as one of the great lawgivers of Athens. The scope of his legislation is, however, imperfectly understood; the extent to which he was a philosopher-king and the extent to which his laws were informed by his association with the Peripatetics have been matters of particular controversy. These uncertainties stem from a lack of data: a law restricting extravagance of burial and mourning practices is the only measure explicitly attributed to him in the ancient sources (Cicero *On Laws* 2.26.66). Significant curtailments of democratic processes are sometimes ascribed to him, as is a wholesale abolition of the Athenian liturgies (whereby individuals undertook certain state expenses). But much of this is insecurely attested, and Demetrius' prime concern may rather have been with a moral program to regulate the private lives of Athenian citizens—for example, through restrictions on feasts. On Demetrius' political achievements, some ancient writers return a favorable verdict; for others, his reputation remained tainted by his complicity with a foreign master and his toleration of a Macedonian garrison within Attic territory.

Demetrius enjoyed great renown also as an orator and prolific writer. Although the complete loss of his speeches and the only fragmentary survival of his treatises have now obscured his achievements in these fields, his intellectual output may have exerted a pervasive influence on Peripatetic scholarship. Demetrius' activity in Egypt may have generated a lasting legacy: late tradition credits him with the idea of creating the great Library at Alexandria and of translating the Jewish religious texts into Greek (the Septuagint).

[*See also* Athens, *subentry* History of Athens in Antiquity, and Lyceum.]

BIBLIOGRAPHY

Works of Demetrius of Phaleron
Demetrius of Phalerum: Text, Translation, and Discussion. Edited and translated by William W. Fortenbaugh and Eckart Schütrumpf. Rutgers University Studies in Classical Humanities 9. New Brunswick, N.J., and London: Transaction, 2000. Contains all direct ancient testimonia to Demetrius and fragments of his writings, with an excellent selection of essays on his life and works. For Cicero *On Laws* 2.26.66, see F53 in this edition, and for the redating of *Inscriptiones Graecae*, vol. 2 (2nd ed.) 2971, see Steven Tracy's essay on pp. 331–345.

Secondary Works
Gehrke, Hans-Joachim. "Das Verhältnis von Politik und Philosophie im Wirken des Demetrios von Phaleron." *Chiron* 8 (1978): 149–193. A fundamental discussion of the philosophical influences on Demetrius' legislation.

Green, Peter. *Alexander to Actium: The Historical Evolution of the Hellenistic Age.* Berkeley: University of California Press, 1990. A vast general work on Hellenistic history; Demetrius is treated at pp. 36–51.

Habicht, Christian. *Athens from Alexander to Antony.* Translated by Deborah Lucas Schneider. Cambridge, Mass.: Harvard University Press, 1997. First published in German in 1995. An excellent examination of Demetrius' rule within the wider context of Hellenistic Athenian history; see pp. 53–66 for Demetrius.

Lara O'Sullivan

DEMETRIUS POLIORCETES

(c. 336–c. 283 BCE), Macedonian commander and self-proclaimed king. Demetrius, nicknamed *Poliorcetes* (Besieger of Cities), was the son of Antigonus Monophthalmus, with whom he had a legendarily warm relationship.

Demetrius, celebrated for his military zeal (and notorious for his profligate sexual behavior and extravagant spending on luxuries), spent his adult life warring against other Macedonian commanders for control of the fragmented empire of Alexander III (356–323). As Plutarch describes in his Life of Demetrius, Poliorcetes' brilliant success and then devastating failure posed enduring questions about the roles of character and luck in history.

Demetrius grew up, far from his homeland, in Phrygia (central western Asia Minor), where his father governed the region for Alexander. Trained

Love between Father and Son

The ancient biographer Plutarch (c. 46–after 119 CE) reports that the family of Antigonus I Monophthalmus and Demetrius Poliorcetes was unusual for the harmony and goodwill between fathers and sons through the generations, in an age when murders for power were far from unknown in leaders' houses. Antigonus, for example, trusted his son Demetrius so completely that he let him come into his presence at court bearing his weapons. As a father, Antigonus was known to show his affection for his son with good-natured teasing, as on the occasion when Demetrius, a riotous playboy when not training for war, was said to be sick in bed with a high fever. His father went to his room to check on him, passing a beautiful woman leaving the room as he entered. When Antigonus took his son's hand (to check his temperature), Demetrius said that his fever had departed. "You're right, my boy," said Antigonus, "it bumped into me at the door on its way out." (Plutarch *Life of Demetrius* 3 and 19)

as a cavalry commander, Demetrius fought well at Paraetacene and Gabiene in Persia (317–316) in his father's campaign to dominate the Near East, but as sole commander he lost to the much more experienced Ptolemy I at Gaza in 312. Typically resilient, he bounced back to defeat another Ptolemaic army. But against Seleucus I Nicator in Mesopotamia in 311, he could not maintain his initial conquest. In 307, he succeeded in the campaign to "liberate Greece" (from Macedonian rivals). The Athenians were so enthused by his restoration of their freedom and democracy that they hailed him and Antigonus as gods. Alexander had previously claimed divinity, but this divinization of men by Greeks supported the creation of a ruler cult.

When Demetrius defeated Ptolemy's fleet at Salamis off Cyprus in 306, employing innovative naval artillery, he and his father declared themselves kings. This assertion of "personal monarchy" (they were not Alexander's heirs) led their rivals to call themselves kings, too, opening the way to Hellenistic kingship. Demetrius flaunted his new status with spectacular partying and spending. He earned his nickname for his spectacular siege of Rhodes in the eastern Aegean Sea in 305–304; he failed to take the walled city, but his multistoried wheeled siege towers firing huge catapults made him famous. Demetrius and Antigonus reestablished Philip II's alliance of Greek states at Corinth (the Hellenic League) in 302 to rally support against their rivals, but at Ipsus in Phrygia they were defeated disastrously (301), Antigonus dying on the field when Demetrius' unrestrained cavalry charge into the enemy lines left his father unprotected.

When the Athenians barred Demetrius from entering their city to regroup, he was stunned to find their goodwill false; he was now a man without even an adopted country. (His licentious ways and demands for money to satisfy his personal pleasures had alienated the Athenians.) Demetrius married his daughter to Seleucus in a short-lived alliance against the other commanders. In 295 he retook Athens, treating the city leniently but garrisoning it with his troops nonetheless. In 294 he won the kingship of Macedonia and fought for control of mainland Greece, founding a new capital in Thessaly named after himself (Demetrias). He assembled a massive force to pursue his father's dream of conquering the Near East. The enormous warships that he built foreshadowed the fabulous expenditures of Hellenistic kings on military technology. When he lost Macedonia in 287 after his troops deserted him, preferring Pyrrhus of Epirus to a Macedonian who had lost his roots, Demetrius' power eroded. He surrendered to Seleucus, who kept him captive in luxurious surroundings until he drank himself to death, leaving behind his capable son Antigonus II Gonatas to found a dynasty.

[*See also* Antigonids; Antigonus Monophthalmus; Diadochi and Successor Kingdoms; Kingship, Greek Macedon; *and* Macedonian Wars.]

BIBLIOGRAPHY

Billows, Richard A. *Antigonos the One-Eyed and the Creation of the Hellenistic State*. Reprint ed., chapters 3–5.

Berkeley and Los Angeles: University of California Press, 1990. Detailed study, including extensive descriptions of important battles, covering Demetrius' career until the death of his father in 301.

Habicht, Christian. *Athens from Alexander to Antony.* Translated by Deborah Lucas Schneider. Chapter 3. Cambridge, Mass.: Harvard University Press, 1997. In the context of the history of Athens, a brief description of the major events of Demetrius' career from the liberation of Athens in 307 to the overthrow of Demetrius' urban (but not harbor) garrison in 287.

Thomas R. Martin

DEMOCRACY

For the contemporary world no other achievement of Greek civilization overshadows the development of democracy. Greek democracy's reputation now shines brighter among historians and political theorists than at any other time in the modern age, no doubt because the late twentieth century saw democracy triumph as the sole legitimate and universal form of political organization. Its emergence in late Archaic (600–500 BCE) and Classical (500–323) Greece therefore looks like the archetype for modern political development and for just societies on a global scale.

Principles, Goals, and Beginnings. A few core principles of equality, freedom, and majority rule link democracies ancient and modern: (1) all citizens are theoretically equal before the law, (2) the law guarantees all citizens individual and collective freedoms from coercion in political and social life, (3) in exercising political self-rule, the will of ordinary citizens prevails. Even though Greek citizens practiced these principles through direct participation in government instead of through the modern alternative of representative government, in a nutshell both ancient and modern democracies achieve two goals: they empower typical citizens with popular sovereignty over the state's destiny, and they protect this privilege from encroachment by elite citizens with superior resources.

The dynamic link between the three principles and the two goals helps explain why the study of Greek democracy is today fluid and controversial, about more than just defining a set of governmental procedures guaranteeing equality, freedom, and popular sovereignty. Democracy is seen as a broad cultural enactment of the principles: a way of waging war, worshiping divinities, composing poetry and history, practicing philosophy, erecting civic monuments and adorning them with sculpture and paintings, and so on. "Democratic" also names a kind of ancient theory about society and human nature, both an ideology and a type of social identity for citizens. And because the Greek experience serves as an avatar for modern democracies, contemporary political thinkers use it as a touchstone when they debate democratic ideals and practices.

Recent controversies and disagreements raise questions about Greek democracy's origins, how widespread it was, and its life span. Did it appear as a revolutionary break with pre-democratic culture and politics? Or did it develop slowly and cumulatively without discontinuities between tradition and innovation? Its development seems to have occurred in two steps, each achieving one of its two goals. The first step secured popular sovereignty for the collective agent that is all the "people" (*dēmos*), but especially the poor (also called the *dēmos*), empowering typical members to act freely in self-interest and take responsibility for their political future. The second step used the sovereignty of law to cultivate institutions and procedures guaranteeing this agency in perpetuity, including low property qualifications and use of a lottery to fill state offices, public scrutiny of officeholders, and pay for the poor to serve on juries and councils or to attend the citizen assembly.

Aristocratic values may have dominated in Archaic Greece, but a noticeable egalitarian current surfaced in the earliest works of Greek literature, Homer's *Iliad* (c. 750) and *Odyssey* (c. 700) and Hesiod's *Works and Days* (c. 700). As city-states and federated states emerged after 770 in the Aegean, southern Italy, Sicily, and the Black Sea region, most acknowledged the theoretical equality of all male citizens. Increasing reliance on hoplite warfare in the seventh century also strengthened the need for solidarity among citizens of diverse resources; Sparta's growth during this century into a hoplite state enshrined similar values in the form of institutions like the "Great Rhetra," a written constitution guaranteeing some degree of popular control over decision making. When written statute laws appeared in many states after 650, they curtailed the abuse of weak or average citizens by their elite neighbors. From fragmentary writings, inscriptions, and other archaeological evidence, it is therefore reasonable to claim that the principles and goals of democracy emerged during the sixth century in a few states and spread slowly to a handful of others (Achaea, Elis, Metapontum, Chios, Megara, Samos) until it proliferated as a familiar form of government in the fifth century.

Athenian Democracy. Most modern historians, however, equate the history of Greek democracy with that of only one city-state, Athens, from 508 to 322 BCE. This Athenian bias results not only from the wealth of documentation in ancient sources on Athens, much of it contemporary to that democracy's flourishing, but also because historians can use these rich details to elaborate their competing models of democracy's origin as a revolutionary break versus a cumulative process, their explanations of just how the three principles worked and the two goals were secured, and their descriptions of democracy as an array of cultural practices.

The debate about how democracy emerged in Athens deserves particular attention. Three unpredictable events during the sixth century are pivotal for the model based on a revolutionary break, whereas institutional developments in the fifth and fourth centuries point to slow development without discontinuity. The first event occurred in 594 when Solon arbitrated a crisis provoked by elites who used debt to inflict a serflike status on poor citizens, requiring them to surrender one-sixth of their annual produce. Some debtors were even enslaved and sold abroad to repay debt. Solon averted civil war with a surprising series of reforms that jump-started the collective agency of ordinary citizens as a sovereign people and created institutions preserving that sovereignty through the force of law. He abolished existing debts, prohibited seizure of a debtor to repay debt, restored to the "one-sixthers" the full use of their land, and at state expense purchased back citizens sold as slaves. In one stroke this guaranteed the economic self-sufficiency of poorer citizens and also served as the precondition for their participation in a citizen assembly. Though this assembly's exact powers are unknown, Solon's written laws and constitutional reforms protected its deliberations.

The assembly's sovereignty was conditioned by two councils. The elite Council of the Areopagus, numbering in the hundreds, which probably existed before Solon, held a "guardianship of the laws" that may have permitted a veto power over the assembly's "excessive" decisions and the right to monitor the performance of state officials. The Council of Four Hundred, which Solon either created or reformed, was more popularly based and set the assembly's agenda free from elite control. It, too, may have scrutinized state officials, but it also functioned as a people's court where any citizen could bring suit against any other.

In 508/7 a second surprising event makes a stronger case for democracy's emergence. Despite Solon's efforts, resistance from elites and decades of tyrannical control by Pisistratus and his sons (c. 560–510) prevented ordinary citizens from assuming mastery of state decision making. When the last Pisistratid had been expelled and two elite factions squared off for control, Athens faced two possible outcomes that were politically and militarily problematic. Either the faction of the conservative Isagoras would prevail, but with the assistance of a Spartan military force intent on imposing an oligarchic constitution, or the faction of Cleisthenes would prevail, but only if its unofficial membership expanded to include the mass of ordinary citizens. For reasons that remain unclear, the elite Cleisthenes rewrote the rules of political rivalry by inviting ordinary citizens to join his men in controlling the state. When the Spartans seized the Acropolis on behalf of Isagoras' faction and tried to install an oligarchy, a spontaneous uprising of the masses besieged and ousted them.

If this act of resistance led to popular sovereignty, it was because Cleisthenes had planned carefully to align the masses with elites politically as well as militarily. He implemented three institutional reforms to prevent any elite faction from counteracting the will of the numerical majority:

1. All citizens now entered political life locally, in formal village units ("demes") in which neighbors approved their citizenship and engaged them in local governance; citizens entered state politics through ten new tribes whose membership mixed them into a balanced geographical and sociological cross-section of the state.

2. This tribal membership determined military service and participation in state politics, especially membership on a new Council of Five Hundred (replacing the old Council of Four Hundred), whose deliberations set the agenda for voting on decrees (laws) in the citizen assembly. Fifty members were chosen in their demes by lot each year to represent each tribe, and no citizen could serve more than twice in a lifetime, guaranteeing a high rate of participation.

3. To squelch the leadership that led to a dangerous faction or the return of a tyrant, the assembly could determine each year whether one citizen posed a threat to state welfare. Whoever's name appeared scratched on the majority of pottery shards (*ostraka*) found himself "ostracized," or banished from the territory of Athens for ten years.

It looks as though "democracy" as the "rule of the *dēmos*" (or "with the help of the *dēmos*") emerged here as an unpredictable mass military initiative but also as a plan for its long-term political extension through the sovereignty of law.

The third surprising event concerned the poorest citizens, the *thētes*, who were unable to fulfill their promised role of full participation in Cleisthenes' plan until after the Persian invasion of 480–479: then the poor, who provided most of the rowers in the Athenian fleet, enabled Athens to become "the savior of Greece." Athens' growing commitment in the 470s–460s to constructing an empire likewise strengthened the social prestige of those who manned the fleet. However, the Council of the Areopagus, with its broad powers of intervention, veto, and scrutiny of officials, had long provided elites a trump card over popular sovereignty. In 462/1, Ephialtes unexpectedly pushed through a decree depriving the council of all its powers except for the right to try certain homicide cases—and transferring the lost privileges to the assembly, the Council of Five Hundred, and law courts. Despite Ephialtes' assassination, Pericles continued paving the way for the poor to participate in government through including pay for jury service and (perhaps) for the Council of Five Hundred and through introducing a law restricting citizenship to sons of typical marriages between an Athenian father and mother.

Around 450 BCE, Athenians began exercising popular sovereignty radically and rapidly, and at this point the core democratic principles of equality and freedom began transforming the Athenians' culture as well as politics. This Periclean golden age looked to tragedy and comedy as expressions of both elite and popular values; the humanistic philosophy and rhetoric of Sophists like Protagoras and Gorgias, as well as the response of Socrates, transformed inquiry and deliberation; experiments in architecture, sculpture, and painting turned the Acropolis into a religious expression of a civic power and pride rooted in democracy and imperialism. Athens' egalitarian domestic administration and its expansionist, imperialist foreign policy did, however, coexist in an uneasy symbiosis. Not only did the democracy rely on revenue from the maritime empire to pay its bills, but the daily use of radical popular sovereignty to produce decrees generated a volatile formula for policies that veered from clear-sighted and prudent to deluded and reckless. This heady mix resulted in the protracted Peloponnesian War with Sparta and its allies (431–404) and ultimately to defeat by the Spartans.

Radical popular sovereignty ended up costing the Athenians their empire but not their democracy, which tottered briefly in the oligarchic coups of 411 and 403 only to reemerge stronger through persistent efforts in the fourth century to make democratic procedures and institutions more organized, regulated, and efficient. The resulting stability lends force to the argument that democracy truly developed in this age, not through a break or rupture with the past but through a cumulative, consistent commitment to the principles of equality, freedom, and majority rule. These efforts looked to the sovereignty of the law itself and included (1) overhauling lawmaking and the law code to eliminate contradictions and to distinguish permanent statutes from temporary decrees, (2) paying citizens to attend the assembly and to serve as specialized lawmakers and as arbitrators in private lawsuits, (3) increased use of written documents to render legislative and judicial actions more detailed and consistent, (4) streamlining the state's financial administration, and (5) restoring to the Council of the Areopagus some of its lost privileges.

Difficult as it is to pinpoint Athenian democracy's origins, it is even more difficult to mark its demise. Philip II of Macedon's victory at Chaeronea in 338 over Athens and other Greek powers, along with the victories of his son Alexander against the Persian Empire (336–323), cast long shadows over Greek freedom in the Aegean, but Athens nevertheless maintained much of its autonomy. Arguably Macedon's threat ignited the most vigorous displays of leadership in the democracy's history as statesmen and orators like Demosthenes, Aeschines, Lycurgus, Hyperides, and Demades fought bitterly over policies of opposition or accommodation to Philip and Alexander. In one sense 323–322, the year after Alexander's death, marks the democracy's terminus, when Athens rose in revolt with other Greek states in the Lamian War to throw off Macedon's yoke. This spirited defense of freedom failed, and a Macedonian garrison occupied Athens' port, the Piraeus. But in another sense the defeat only temporarily ended the democracy by imposing an oligarchic constitution for several years and stripping Athens of its fleet.

The democracy showed remarkable vitality, returning in 318 and persisting in compromised forms for the remainder of the Hellenistic Age (up to 31 BCE), still capable of governing the state and conducting relations with other states. And the brilliant democratic culture of the fifth and fourth centuries continued to prosper. The New Comedy of Menander (342–292) and his contemporaries invented new character types and plots reflecting the city's altered democratic realities, and Athens secured its position as the philosophical center of the Greek world when the schools and movements that emerged earlier in fourth century—Plato's Academy, Aristotle's Lyceum, the Cynics—were joined by the Stoics, the Epicureans, and the Skeptics.

The great exception to life in a genuinely democratic society was the Athenians' inability to act as masters of their own fate in the most vital international relations, for Macedon regularly handpicked a governor for Athens. Some of these men were vigorous leaders who maintained democratic traditions, like Demetrius of Phaleron (governor 317–307) and Demetrius I Poliorcetes ("the Besieger"; governor 307–301), but their leadership had to remain in line with Macedonian policies. Interludes of freedom did occur in 287–262 and 229–200, when Athenians exploited power struggles among the Hellenistic kingdoms to throw off a Macedonian governor or even (in 229) to oust the Macedonian military from the Piraeus (with assistance from the Ptolemies in Egypt). But Rome's growing intervention in Greek and Macedonian affairs after 216 proved decisive when Athens needed to ally itself with the Romans against Philip V of Macedon. The city escaped the worst outcomes of these struggles and continued to govern itself, but by the first century BCE its democratic institutions had waned. The victory in 31 BCE of Octavian (later Augustus) in the Roman civil wars ended recognition of the unique constitution and political rights of Athens as a democratic state unlike any other.

Democracy in Syracuse. To counterbalance the bias toward Athens in understanding Greek democracy, it helps to remember that the Athenians neither invented democracy nor monopolized its practice. Their leadership in defeating Persia (480–479) enhanced democracy's prestige among Greeks, and the Athenians regularly imposed democratic regimes on subject states in their empire, but other states developed or restored democratic constitutions on their own. The most brilliant of these was Syracuse, which threw off two decades of tyranny in 466 and established (or reestablished) a democracy that lasted until 405.

As the wealthiest and most populous Greek state in Sicily, Syracuse under its tyrants had vigorously defended Greek interests against barbarians (Carthaginians and Etruscans), and this energetic championing of Hellenism continued under the democracy, making Syracuse a double of Athens among the western Greeks. Its democracy may at first have catered to aristocratic interests, but the *dēmos* took increasing control, meting out harsh punishment to unsuccessful generals, responding to the popular rhetoric of demagogues, making laws and sometimes rash decisions, and vigorously suppressing would-be tyrants. After Syracuse crushed the Athenian invasion of 415–413, the democracy became even more radical, introducing the lot for office holding. Like the Athenians, the Syracusans under democracy sustained the remarkable cultural life they knew under their tyrants: they continued to develop a strong theatrical tradition of comedy and mime and created their own tradition of historiography, and it was in Syracuse that (according to some) the art of rhetoric originated and flourished under the clever orators Corax and Tisias. But in 406–405 a powerful Carthaginian offensive against Sicilian Greeks saw Syracuse's democracy yield to the tyranny of Dionysius I.

Greek Democracy in Contemporary Political Theory. Most contemporary political theorists endorse Greek democratic practices, some enthusiastically and others with qualified appreciation, but a few outright condemn it for basic flaws. Enthusiasts see in the common values and identity shared by democratic citizens a communitarian remedy for the splintering effects of identity politics in today's liberal, multicultural societies. They also see in citizen deliberation and collective reasoning a precursor to the ideals of deliberative democracy. And they find in the Greek citizen's commitment to participation in civic life an antidote to ways that contemporary democracies rely on elite cadres of experts and specialists to deliberate, form policy, and run their governments. As a first incarnation of Robert Dahl's "strong principal of equality," they point to the trust that Athenians had in ordinary citizens to make decisions and administer state office.

Those who qualify their appreciation look less to Greek democracy as a political constitution with its institutions and more toward the democratic culture and ideology that enabled ordinary citizens to share collective political knowledge in a unique communication network worthy of emulation today. Voices that condemn democratic practices particular to Athens call for a more objective, dispassionate assessment of the failures and civic disasters caused by its radical popular sovereignty, the poor demagogic leadership that this sovereignty at times encouraged, and the subsequent mismanagement of empire. Others disparage the historical methods used by many contemporary historians and theorists because these scholars sometimes project modern ideologies and self-interested goals onto ancient democratic realities that continue to resist clear understanding.

[*See also* Citizenship, Greek; Elections and Voting; Freedom; Oligarchy; *and* Tyranny.]

BIBLIOGRAPHY

Boedeker, Deborah, and Kurt A. Raaflaub, eds. *Democracy, Empire, and the Arts in Fifth-Century Athens.* Cambridge, Mass.: Harvard University Press, 1998. Discussion of Greek (Athenian) democracy in a broad spectrum of cultural practices. For democracy, Sophists, rhetoric, and Socrates, see the essays by R. Wallace, H. Yunis, and C. Rowe.

Euben, J. Peter, John Wallach, and Josiah Ober, eds. *Athenian Political Thought and the Reconstruction of American Democracy.* Ithaca. N.Y.: Cornell University Press, 1994. The introduction discusses the participation of ordinary citizens in decision making.

Farenga, Vincent. *Citizen and Self in Ancient Greece: Individuals Performing Justice and the Law.* Cambridge, U.K.: Cambridge University Press, 2006.

Farrar, Cynthia. *The Origins of Democratic Thinking.* Cambridge, U.K.: Cambridge University Press, 1988.

Habicht, Christian. *Athens from Alexander to Antony.* Translated by Deborah Lucas Schneider. Cambridge, Mass.: Harvard University Press, 1997. Athenian democracy from 338 to 31 BCE.

Hansen, Mogens Herman. *Athenian Democracy in the Age of Demosthenes: Structure, Principles, and Ideology.* Rev. ed. Translated by J. A. Crook. Norman: University of Oklahoma Press, 1999. The institutional and procedural changes in Athenian democracy after 403.

Lape, Susan. *Reproducing Athens: Menander's Comedy, Democratic Culture, and the Hellenistic City.* Princeton, N.J.: Princeton University Press, 2004.

Ober, Josiah. *The Athenian Revolution: Essays on Ancient Greek Democracy and Political Theory.* Princeton, N.J.: Princeton University Press, 1996.

Ober, Josiah, and Charles Hedrick, eds. *Dēmokratia: A Conversation on Democracies, Ancient and Modern.* Princeton, N.J.: Princeton University Press, 1996.

Phillips, Derek L. *Looking Backward: A Critical Appraisal of Communitarian Thought.* Princeton, N.J.: Princeton University Press, 1993.

Raaflaub, Kurt A., Josiah Ober, and Robert A. Wallace, eds. *Origins of Democracy in Ancient Greece.* Berkeley: University of California Press, 2007. For the origin of Athenian democracy in Solon's reforms, in events surrounding Cleisthenes' reforms, and in reforms by Ephialtes and Pericles, see the essays by Robert A. Wallace, Josiah Ober, and Kurt Raaflaub.

Rhodes, P. J. *Athenian Democracy and Modern Ideology.* London: Duckworth, 2003.

Roberts, Jennifer Tolbert. *Athens on Trial: The Antidemocratic Tradition in Western Thought.* Princeton, N.J.: Princeton University Press, 1994.

Robinson, Eric W. *The First Democracies: Early Popular Government outside Athens.* Stuttgart, Germany: F. Steiner, 1997.

Robinson, Eric W., ed. *Ancient Greek Democracy: Readings and Sources.* Malden, Mass.: Blackwell, 2004.

Samons, Loren J., II. *What's Wrong with Democracy? From Athenian Practice to American Worship.* Berkeley: University of California Press, 2004. Discusses Athenian democracy's civic disasters and poor leadership.

Winkler, John J., and Froma I. Zeitlin, eds. *Nothing to Do with Dionysos? Athenian Drama in Its Social Context.* Princeton, N.J.: Princeton University Press, 1990.

Woodruff, Paul. *First Democracy: The Challenge of an Ancient Idea.* Oxford: Oxford University Press, 2005. Comparison of Greek with American democracy.

Vincent Farenga

DEMOCRITUS OF ABDERA

(c. 460–c. 360 BCE), Presocratic philosopher. Democritus developed into a systematic theory the atomistic hypothesis advanced by his older associate, Leucippus, and wrote extensively on a broad range of philosophical, scientific, and cultural topics.

There is little reliable information about the circumstances of either his or Leucippus' life. Democritus' greater prominence tended to obscure the contribution of his apparent mentor, so much so that Epicurus (341–270 BCE) could later deny Leucippus' existence. However, Diogenes Laertius' third century CE catalog of Democritus' works notes that the *Great World System*, listed first among his treatises on natural philosophy, was attributed to Leucippus by Theophrastus (c. 372–c. 287 BCE) and his circle. Diogenes, though, regards this work as authentically Democritean and as one of his best. Democritus was said to have described himself in the *Little World System* as a young man when Anaxagoras (c. 500–428 BCE) was old, and the ancient authorities report that he lived to a very old age. There was also a tradition, duly recorded by Diogenes, that Democritus had early interactions with the sages of the East and that he later traveled extensively, to Egypt, Persia, the Red Sea, India, and Ethiopia, though what truth there may be in this is impossible to say. A more solid basis for some sort of Athenian sojourn is provided by his reported statement, "For I came to Athens and no one recognized me."

Democritus' writings were prodigious in both number and scope. Diogenes' catalog lists seventy treatises and reproduces Thrasyllus' arrangement of the majority of these into tetralogies, with two tetralogies on ethics, four on natural philosophy, three on mathematics, two on literary topics, and two on technical arts such as medicine. Apart from a substantial body of ethical sayings, only a paltry group of fragments from Democritus' writings remains. Fortunately, Aristotle discussed Democritus' views extensively in his own natural philosophical treatises. His testimony provides the primary basis for reconstruction of the physical theory of the early atomists, with the late Aristotelian commentators and the doxographical tradition providing additional evidence. Democritus is normally regarded as developing in a more detailed fashion the basic theory originally articulated by Leucippus, in large part by pursuing its implications into such areas as epistemology and psychology. The wide range of Democritus' interests, which clearly extended beyond atomism and its applications, shows him to have been not only the last great Presocratic philosopher but also a thinker in step with certain ambitions of the Sophistic movement as well.

Physics and Epistemology. Presocratic atomism was a theory of the physical world formulated largely in response to the monistic Eleaticism of Melissus and to Zeno's paradoxes of infinite divisibility. Aristotle, in an important stretch of *On Generation and Corruption* 1.8, characterizes Leucippus as endorsing Melissus' originally counterfactual positing of void as a necessary condition of motion while rejecting his material monism by positing instead, as the ultimate constituents of all observable phenomena, a limitless number of imperceptibly small, indivisible bodies. In imputing the attributes of plenitude, immutability, and impassivity to each of his atomic particles, Leucippus appears to have taken up the challenge implicit in Melissus' claim that "if there were many things, they would need to be of just the same sort as the one" (30B8.6 Diels and Kranz). The collisions and congregations of atoms in the void that led ultimately to the formation of macroscopic bodies and entire worlds such as our own were viewed by Democritus as purposeless processes governed primarily by necessity. More particularly, the quantitative differences at the atomic level with respect to shape, arrangement, and size he viewed as providing the ultimate basis for qualitative differences at the level of everyday observation.

Democritus appears to have been keen on exploring the problems resulting from the atomic theory's distinction between the fundamental reality of the microscopic level and, at the macroscopic level, the phenomenal properties of objects and the experiences of intellects. He notably expressed the starkness of this distinction by saying, "Conventionally sweet, conventionally bitter, conventionally hot, conventionally cold, conventionally color, but really atoms and void" (fragment 9). Perceptible qualities such as these he regarded as resulting from interactions via the sense organs between the soul-atoms of perceivers and the atomic surfaces of objects—either indirectly in sight, smell, and hearing, via films (*eidōla*) emanating continuously from these surfaces, or directly in touch and taste. Perceptible qualities are thus unique and private to each individual perceiver, are not "real" properties of objects, and yet are all that we can know of objects via the senses, given that there can be no interactionless perception.

This theory led Democritus to characterize our epistemic position in ways that can make him appear a proto-skeptic. For example, Sextus Empiricus draws the following statement from Democritus' *Confirmations*: "We in actuality have no secure apprehension, but we apprehend what befalls us according to the disposition of the body and what enters and presses against it" (fragment 9). However, unlike his fellow Abderite Protagoras, Democritus was not a complete relativist, for he thinks that there is a way the world really is, at the atomic level, independently of its relation to us. Nor is he a complete skeptic. Although he regards perception, which he calls the "bastard" form of judgment, as unable to reveal to us the actual nature and character of things, he also recognizes a "genuine" form of judgment that belongs to the reasoning mind and that, if it remains properly grounded by sensory evidence, may lead to some apprehension of the reality of things. Democritus would, in fact, want to claim that this genuine judgment has done so in his own atomic theory.

Ethical and Social Views. Democritus' views on ethics and social affairs survive primarily in two collections of sayings and brief texts that found their way into the anthology of John of Stobi (fifth century CE). Both collections are evidently the product of a long process of deformative excerpting and recasting. One collection is ascribed to "Democrates," and although this is easily regarded as a corruption of "Democritus," the authenticity of this collection has seemed less secure than that of the others. When employed with due caution, however, and supplemented by the other available evidence, together the two collections show that Democritus dealt more extensively with ethical topics than any of the Presocratics did, though perhaps in no very systematic way. There are various reports that he identified life's ultimate end or *telos* as both contentment (*euthymia*) and prosperity (*euestō*), perhaps with the intention of distinguishing internal and external conditions upon a good life. The tenor of the ethical sayings ascribed to Democritus balances between strictly pragmatic advice and more reflective concern with themes of the principal eudaemonistic theories of antiquity. The sayings emphasize how a rational governance of one's pleasures, desires, and actions enables one to avoid trouble and distress and, conversely, how one's own senselessness, rather than some external culprit, is typically responsible for one's afflictions; there is also an emphasis on the inner conditions and proper motivation characteristic of genuinely virtuous activity.

Chief among Democritus' ethical treatises was the work entitled *On Contentment*, from which two fairly substantial stretches of text survive. They advise those who would be happy against desiring things that exceed their natural capabilities, and they offer some practical guidance on how to remain content with present circumstances so as to avoid envy, jealousy, and ill-will. The views on law and social relations represented in the Stobaean collections tend to present the role of law as the external governance of those somehow incapable of proper internal governance, with a view to preventing interpersonal injury and promoting civil concord. There also appear to be traces in Diodorus Siculus and Lucretius of a Democritean theory of the origins and development of human culture, which, by emphasizing progress over decline, inaugurated a rich tradition of ancient *Kulturgeschichte*.

Influence. Although Plato never mentions Democritus by name, his presence has been detected at certain points in the dialogues, such as in the *Timaeus*' theory of vision. Like Plato, Aristotle operates with an explanatory framework almost diametrically opposed to the anti-teleological, mechanistic, and apparently reductivist framework of Democritus, and yet Aristotle devotes a good deal of attention to Democritus' physical theories, even judging them in *On Generation and Corruption* as superior to Plato's on certain points.

Democritus had followers of his own, and there was a tradition tracing his influence down to the founder of the Hellenistic school that made atomism the basis of its teaching, as follows: Democritus—Nessas—Metrodorus of Chios—Diogenes of Smyrna—Anaxarchus of Abdera—Pyrrho of Elis—Nausiphanes of Teos—Epicurus. Although Epicurus modified Democritean atomism in a number of crucial respects, including rejecting its reductivist and determinist tendencies, he evidently owed a great debt to Democritus' development of the core atomic theory, however unprepared he may have been to acknowledge it. Another of the major Hellenistic schools, the New Academy of Arcesilaus and his followers, appealed more openly to Democritus as a reputable forerunner of their own skeptical stance, and Pyrrho of Elis is also supposed to have regarded him favorably. Because only the merest scraps of Democritus' vast array of writings survive, however, we are in a poor position to know the true extent of his influence.

[*See also* Presocratics.]

BIBLIOGRAPHY
Primary Works
Diels, Hermann, and Walter Kranz, eds. *Die Fragmente der Vorsokratiker*. 6th ed. Vol. 2. Berlin: Weidmann, 1952. See §68.
Luria, Solomon, ed. *Democritea*. Leningrad: Nauka, 1970.
Taylor, C. C. W., ed. and trans. *The Atomists, Leucippus, and Democritus, Fragments: A Text and Translation with Commentary*. Toronto: University of Toronto Press, 1999.

Secondary Works
Annas, Julia. "Democritus and Eudaimonism." In *Presocratic Philosophy: Essays in Honour of Alexander Mourelatos*, edited by Victor Caston and Daniel W. Graham, pp. 169–182. Aldershot, U.K.: Ashgate, 2002.

Furley, David J. "Democritus and Epicurus on Sensible Qualities." In *Passions and Perceptions: Studies in Hellenistic Philosophy of Mind*, edited by Jacques Brunschwig and Martha C. Nussbaum, pp. 72–94. Cambridge, U.K.: Cambridge University Press, 1993.

Furley, David J. *The Greek Cosmologists*. Vol. 1: *The Formation of the Atomic Theory and Its Earliest Critics*. Cambridge, U.K.: Cambridge University Press, 1987.

Guthrie, W. K. C. *A History of Greek Philosophy*. Vol. 2: *The Presocratic Tradition from Parmenides to Democritus*. Cambridge, U.K.: Cambridge University Press, 1965. See chapter 8.

Lee, Mi-Kyoung. *Epistemology after Protagoras: Responses to Relativism in Plato, Aristotle, and Democritus*. Oxford: Clarendon Press, 2005. See chapters 8 and 9.

Warren, James. *Epicurus and Democritean Ethics: An Archaeology of Ataraxia*. Cambridge, U.K.: Cambridge University Press, 2002.

John Palmer

DEMOGRAPHY

See Population and Demography.

DEMOSTHENES

(384–322 BCE), Athenian orator. Demosthenes is recognized in modern times as the best of the ancient Greek orators. Although ten or more of the sixty speeches in the Demosthenic corpus were clearly not written by Demosthenes, he still has by far the greatest number of surviving speeches from the Classical period. Both as a political leader and as an orator, however, he had detractors in his own time, so despite his eloquence he is a controversial figure. For more than twenty years he led Athens in a losing fight against the increasing power of Philip II and Alexander the Great of Macedon, before he finally succumbed to the scandal of bribery charges and exile by killing himself.

Early Life. After studying rhetoric with Isaeus and perhaps some philosophy with Plato, Demosthenes honed his skills as an orator when in 363–362 he prosecuted the guardians of his estate for mismanaging it—his wealthy father having died when he was seven. He won the first case and was awarded

Demosthenes. © ASHMOLEAN MUSEUM, UNIVERSITY OF OXFORD/ THE BRIDGEMAN ART LIBRARY

ten talents, but a series of cases protracted the process over two years, and he never recovered his full inheritance. The speeches related to this litigation (numbers 27–31 in the Demosthenic corpus) appear rather different stylistically from his more mature speeches; his own style took some time to develop.

A great deal of legend surrounds Demosthenes' training as an orator. His natural skill is said to have been limited, so that he used various training methods to develop his craft, including practicing speaking while having pebbles in his mouth and speaking while walking uphill or on the beach, where he practiced speaking over the sound of the waves. Nevertheless, he was also criticized for his inability to speak impromptu.

Demosthenes went on to become a speechwriter (*logographos*) for others engaged in private lawsuits in Athens' public courts and then for politicians pursuing public lawsuits, such as his speeches against Androtion (number 22), against Timocrates (24), and against Aristocrates (23). He then wrote such a speech for himself, *Against Leptines* (20), in 355/4. Speechwriting appears to have been quite lucrative, for although Demosthenes was able to recover only modest amounts from his estate, he took on some expensive public services (*leitourgiai*), such as equipping a trireme and financing a theatrical chorus.

Demosthenes took to the political stage himself in the aftermath of the Social War (357–355), when Athens lost its most important allies. Athenian finances were in disastrous shape, and in a speech to the assembly, *On the Symmories* (14), Demosthenes advocated a fiscal plan for rebuilding Athens' fleet. At this time he was concerned about the threat posed by the Persian king. He also gave a speech rejecting Athens' avoidance of all but the most essential military campaigns (13). In 352 he conjured up a threat from Sparta, then woefully weak, when speaking in support of Megalopolis (16). Then he spoke on behalf of the Rhodian democrats, who were then in revolt against Caria (15). In this context, in 351, Demosthenes gave the first of his *Philippics* (4), polemical speeches against Philip II of Macedon, several years after Philip had begun his incursions on Athens' interests in the northern Aegean. Despite its losses in the Social War, Demosthenes clearly wanted to see an activist and prominent Athens, and Philip was at first only one of a number of possible targets of this activism.

In 350–349 a lawsuit brought Demosthenes' activities as a speechwriter into controversy. The ambitious young politician Apollodorus—the true author of several of the speeches in the Demosthenic corpus—brought a charge against his stepfather and guardian Phormion. Demosthenes wrote a speech in Phormion's defense (36). However, when Apollodorus subsequently brought a suit for false testimony against Stephanus, one of Phormion's witnesses, Demosthenes appears to have had a hand in writing Apollodorus' speech (45). The two speeches present opposing views of Phormion's character, bringing into question Demosthenes' ethics as a speechwriter.

Most of the private speeches of Demosthenes are not so easily dated and do not involve him in so much controversy. In one of the most famous, *Against Conon* (54), a young man offers a vivid account of how he has been brutally assaulted and is now prosecuting the father of his assailants. Other speeches written for clients involve loans for maritime trade (32–35, 56), mining rights (37), inheritance (38, 41, 44), property damage (55), and citizenship (57). Two speeches even concern the right to use a name (39–40).

Opposition to Philip. In 349, with the three *Olynthiacs* (1–3) in support of Olynthus, which had been attacked by Philip and asked Athens for help, Demosthenes began to devote more of his time to public affairs and to direct his political speeches more consistently against Philip. As in the *First Philippic*, in the *Olynthiacs* Demosthenes chastises the Athenians for their complacency and diffidence, as well as for their unwillingness to take an active part in defending their interests against the Macedonian king. The rich were unwilling to spend money to equip ships and hire mercenaries, and the poor were unwilling to engage in personal military service. One of the consequences of Demosthenes' activity was that he ran afoul of Eubulus, the most dominant politician up to this time, who advocated that the Athenians pursue interests only closer to home, such as on the island of Euboea. One of Eubulus' supporters, Midias, slapped Demosthenes in the face at the City Dionysia festival in 348, at which Demosthenes had the semiofficial role of producing a chorus. The slap became a cause célèbre concerning which Demosthenes wrote one of his most famous speeches, *Against Midias* (21), but the case probably never came to trial.

The Third Sacred War (356–346) finally drew Philip from his territorial ambitions in northern Greece into the affairs of central Greece against Athens' ostensible allies, the Phocians. The conclusion of the peace treaty that ended that war, the so-called Peace of Philocrates, is one of the central events in Demosthenes' career, and he clearly took a leading role in advocating it. But delays in the passage of Philocrates' proposal both in Athens and by the embassies that were sent to Philip—in which Demosthenes and his rivals participated—in order to negotiate the terms of the peace and then to ratify it resulted in disaster for the Phocians and, to a lesser extent, for the Athenians. Philip actively pursued his ambitions during the intervening periods of time and chose finally to exclude the Phocians from the peace, which enabled him to carry out severe punishment on them.

The Athenians had been outmaneuvered, and in a speech given in the immediate aftermath of the peace (5), Demosthenes admits as much, though he does his best to disown his participation in the peace and in what came after. Much of Demosthenes' later career was spent in defending his own actions during this time and in attacking those of his rivals, notably Aeschines. After Aeschines diverted Demosthenes temporarily with a suit against Demosthenes' associate Timarchus, in 343 Demosthenes brought a prosecution against Aeschines (19), accusing him of having collaborated with Philip during the embassies. Aeschines was only narrowly acquitted, and in a separate trial Philocrates was condemned and went into exile.

In 341, Demosthenes gave speeches about two different parts of Greece that continued to be sources of conflict between Philip and Athens. In the *Third Philippic* (9), he decries Philip's interventions on the island of Euboea, Athens' last source of strength outside Attica. In *On the Chersonese* (8), he defends Athens' claims to the trade route through the Hellespont, which brought grain from the Black Sea. Again his attempts to mobilize the Athenians met with only partial success until in 340 Philip took the unprecedented step of seizing the grain fleet itself. Now Demosthenes' diplomatic skills were called to the fore as he managed to reconcile Athens with its longtime rivals in Thebes, as well as with several other former enemies, to present a united opposition to Philip as the Macedonian king marched south again.

At Chaeronea in 338, however, the Macedonians defeated the combined Greek armies. Demosthenes fought as a foot soldier and fled when the battle was lost so that he could organize the city's defenses. Although he did not take part in the negotiations leading to Athens' surrender, he was allowed to continue participating in Athenian politics subsequently, and he was chosen to give the Athenian funeral oration that year for those who had died in the battle. Ostensibly for his participation as a commissioner for walls in the following year—but in fact for his long career of opposition to Philip, particularly in the events leading to Chaeronea—his friend Ctesiphon nominated Demosthenes for an honorific crown in 336. Before the proposal passed the assembly it was challenged by Aeschines through a suit for illegal proposal.

Aeschines' Suit and After. Aeschines' suit did not come to trial until 330. In the meantime, Philip was assassinated in 336, and Demosthenes briefly attempted to rally Greek support for a revolt against Macedon—which may explain why Aeschines delayed his suit. Demosthenes was opposed in Athens by the general Phocion, and Philip's successor Alexander the Great quickly and brutally crushed the revolt in Thebes. Alexander at first demanded the surrender of Demosthenes, among other politicians, but diplomatic intervention by pro-Macedonian Athenians saved him. For the time being, Demosthenes appears to have let his hopes of unseating the Macedonian hegemony lie with the Persians.

Little of Demosthenes' activities during the period 336–330 is known, but it seems likely that he occupied himself again as a *logographos*. There is no explicit evidence for why Aeschines delayed until 330 his prosecution against Ctesiphon and his proposal to award a crown to Demosthenes, but it seems likely that Demosthenes had kept up low-level anti-Macedonian agitation. However, with the final Persian defeat at Gaugamela in 331, Demosthenes' longtime anti-Macedonian policy appeared ultimately to have been profoundly misguided, and the essence of Aeschines' charge was that throughout his political career Demosthenes had repeatedly given bad advice to the Athenians.

Aeschines thus brought the long-delayed case to trial. However, the Athenians clearly did not share Aeschines' view. Demosthenes' speech in defense of himself and Ctesiphon, *On the Crown* (18), is the masterpiece of his rhetorical career. In it he combines both an explanation of the legal issues and a narrative of his policy decisions. His policies simply attempted to live up to Athenian traditions in defense of Greek freedom. Aeschines' prosecution failed utterly, and he retired to Rhodes in disgrace. The lively style of Demosthenes' speech is direct and unobtrusive, using the common language of Athenian politics, avoiding archaisms but sometimes interjecting words from, for example, comedy or tragedy, with an unpredictable variation in sentence length and structure.

During the period 330–324 little is known of Demosthenes' activities. He had apparently reconciled himself to Macedonian hegemony and enjoyed the economic prosperity that flowed from the leadership of Athens by Lycurgus and from the fact that Athens was no longer trying to keep itself on a war footing.

By 324, Alexander had driven to the limits of the former Persian Empire and was ready to demilitarize his new empire. His decree that all exiles return to their home cities—instead of offering themselves to potential rivals as mercenaries—caused strains on many Greek cities, including Athens. Demosthenes was again in a leading position and advocated a cautious, diplomatic response, which Alexander nevertheless rejected. The arrival in Athens at about the same time of Alexander's renegade treasurer Harpalus with seven hundred talents brought about Demosthenes' undoing. Demosthenes counseled that Harpalus be jailed and his money seized, which was done, but Harpalus escaped. When only half of his money was found, Demosthenes and several others were accused of accepting bribes to let him escape. After an investigation by the Areopagus council, Demosthenes was found guilty and fined fifty talents, but instead he fled into exile.

The death of Alexander in 323 provoked the Greeks into widespread revolt against the Macedonians and their regent Antipater. In exile Demosthenes toured other Greek cities to rouse support before, on a motion introduced by his cousin, the Athenians pardoned him. He was warmly greeted in Athens, but the revolt, known as the Lamian War, soon came to an end. Antipater defeated the Greeks at the battle of Crannon in 322 and dealt harshly with Athens: he suspended its democracy and exiled a significant part of its population. Demosthenes, among others, was condemned, fled into exile, and was hunted down. He then committed suicide.

Assessments. Would Athens have done better if it had not followed Demosthenes' advice against Macedon? Doubtless. He clearly underestimated the political and military skills of Philip and Alexander—as well as their luck—relying instead on Athens' traditions of military might and his devotion to Greek freedom. Philip may have begun as an opportune enemy against whom Demosthenes could build his career, but Demosthenes' devotion to this cause provides one of the great sagas of ancient Greek history.

The biographer Plutarch aptly compares Demosthenes with Cicero, who waged a lengthy, and also ultimately losing, battle in defense of Roman republican government. Both Cicero and Demosthenes were on the wrong side of the historical movement of their times. Indeed, Cicero himself attempted to emulate Demosthenes, referring to the series of polemical speeches that he himself delivered against Mark Antony in 44–43 BCE as *Philippics*. In Demosthenes, Cicero saw the perfect orator, whose thought and words excelled all others' in their sublimity, passion, and ornateness. Cicero's contemporary Dionysius of Halicarnassus likewise admired Demosthenes' forcefulness (*deinotēs*), and according to Hermogenes and Quintilian, two and three centuries later, Demosthenes still set the standard for oratory.

When Manuel Chrysoloras brought Greek teaching into Italy at the end of the fourteenth century, Leonardo Bruni's translations of Demosthenes and his rival Aeschines became core texts of the Renaissance humanist curriculum. Together with Cicero, Homer, and Virgil, Demosthenes remained a mainstay of higher education until World War II. Demosthenes' lack of natural talent was seen as balanced by his diligent pursuit of the craft of rhetoric. For the Peripatetic critics of Demosthenes' own time and shortly after, this combination was seen as a weakness, but it emerged in the Roman period, and ever after, as evidence of Demosthenes' strengths.

Essentially this point is made in the preface to the first printed edition of Demosthenes' works, where Aldus Manutius in 1504 quoted the Roman Valerius Maximus: *Alterum Demosthenes natura, alterum industria fecit* (Nature made one Demosthenes; hard work made the other).

[*See also* Aeschines; Oratory, Greek; *and* Speech Writing.]

BIBLIOGRAPHY

Works of Demosthenes

Speeches 18 and 19. Translated by Harvey Yunis. Austin: University of Texas Press, 2005.

Speeches 20–22. Translated by Edward M. Harris. Austin: University of Texas Press, 2008.

Speeches 27–38. Translated by Douglas M. MacDowell. Austin: University of Texas Press, 2004.

Speeches 50–59. Translated by Victor Bers. Austin: University of Texas Press, 2003.

Speeches 60 and 61, Prologues, Letters. Translated by Ian Worthington. Austin: University of Texas Press, 2006.

Secondary Works

Jaeger, Werner. *Demosthenes: The Origin and Growth of His Policy*. Berkeley: University of California Press, 1938.

McCabe, Donald F. *The Prose-Rhythm of Demosthenes*. New York: Arno, 1981.

Pearson, Lionel. *The Art of Demosthenes*. Meisenheim am Glan, Germany: A. Hain, 1976.

Pickard-Cambridge, Arthur W. *Demosthenes and the Last Days of Greek Freedom, 384–322 B.C.* New York and London: G. P. Putnam's Sons, 1914.

Plutarch. "Demosthenes." In *The Age of Alexander: Nine Greek Lives*. Translated and annotated by Ian Scott-Kilvert. Harmondsworth, U.K.: Penguin, 1973.

Sealey, Raphael. *Demosthenes and His Time: A Study in Defeat*. New York: Oxford University Press, 1993.

Worthington, Ian, ed. *Demosthenes: Statesman and Orator*. London and New York: Routledge, 2000.

Yunis, Harvey, ed. *Demosthenes: On the Crown*. Cambridge: Cambridge University Press, 2001.

David Mirhady

DERVENI KRATER

The bronze Derveni Krater is the most elaborate metal vessel of the ancient world yet known. Containing human ashes, the krater was discovered in 1962 in one of a group of seven tombs at Derveni, northeast of Thessaloníki in northern Greece. Made following a Greek vessel shape for mixing wine with water known in Athens by 470 BCE, with a slender oval body thirty-five inches (ninety centimeters) high and high volute handles, the krater is unique in being covered with figural imagery. Though its tomb could be dated by Attic ceramic finds to the late fourth century BCE, the krater was an heirloom at the time of its burial. Produced during the second quarter of the fourth century BCE, probably in Athens, it is likely to have been brought into the kingdom of Macedon during the reign of Philip II (r. 359–336 BCE) by the Thessalian whose name and patronymic is inscribed on the rim. It was found without the cast bronze stand traditionally made for vessels of this type.

Below the wide ribs hammered into the shoulder of the krater are two repoussé relief friezes. On side A, a naked reclining Dionysus takes possession of his consort Ariadne, who is fully clothed and smaller in scale, by placing an outstretched leg in her lap. Nearby sits his panther, and in the frieze below two griffins begin devouring a young deer.

Encircling the vessel around Dionysus is a *thiasos* (band of worshipers) comprising five ecstatic maenads (female worshipers of Dionysus), an ithyphallic (sexually aroused) Silenus, and a bearded male hunter wearing a single boot, a characterization of Pentheus that predates the king of Thebes described as youthful in Euripides' *Bacchae*. Two of the maenads carry a young deer between them, and another swings a young child on her shoulder. On side B a maenad twists and bends in ecstatic dance, sharing a silver snake in her lowered hand with a maenad almost naked from her frenzy who falls, exhausted, into the lap of a third, who is seated. Below, a lion and a female panther have felled a bull. Nearby, beneath the hunter's booted foot, is a young deer.

The theme of predator and prey is repeated in the parade of separately made repoussé bronze animals added to the krater's neck. Repoussé masks of four bearded gods of the underworld cover the volutes of the great cast handles: Achelous and Heracles

(Hercules) on side A, Hades and Dionysus in his underworld personification on side B. Finally, on the ribbed shoulder sit four statuettes of solid cast bronze, two on each side. On side A, a little Dionysus gestures with extended arm toward a disheveled maenad with lowered head who is falling asleep. On side B a Silenus dozes fitfully and a maenad, whose exaggerated torsion expresses total abandon, handles a silver snake.

The high tin content of the bronze alloy (14.88 percent) gives the krater a golden color. Overlays of silver, copper, bronze, and base metal form details of the major frieze. An overlaid silver garland of grape vine encircles the krater body above the figures, and one of ivy encircles the neck below the animals. Stripes in the bodies of the vipers that wind around the handle volutes are silver and copper inlays. There are silvered copper inlays in the cast-bronze foot, as well as silvered copper and crafted bronze additions to the decorative motif on the hammered mouth. Silver covers the orbs of the eyes of the volute masks. Such labor-intensive production suggests luxury ware, and the iconography indicates some religious use—perhaps cultic, possibly familial.

[See also Derveni Papyrus; Dionysus; Metals and Metallurgy; Metalwork; and Urns, Cinerary.]

BIBLIOGRAPHY

Barr-Sharrar, Beryl. *The Derveni Krater: Masterpiece of Classical Greek Metalwork*. Princeton, N.J.: American School of Classical Studies at Athens, 2008.

Beryl Barr-Sharrar

DERVENI PAPYRUS

In 1962 a grave site was uncovered in the course of construction near Derveni, not far from Thessaloníki (ancient Thessalonica or Salonica). Among much to interest historians and archaeologists—most notably a magnificent metal krater—one badly charred papyrus was also found alongside a funeral pyre. Although as difficult to separate into its different layers as any burned papyrus from Herculaneum, this text soon showed itself to be the oldest Greek papyrus ever found and the only one found in Greece itself. Its contents, moreover, even at this early stage, proved immediately intriguing: a literary text (as opposed to, say, official records) mentioning the legendary bard Orpheus, who became the object of religious veneration by the end of the sixth century. Moreover, papyrological form aside, it is also the earliest example of a lemmatized commentary.

The cremation of the papyrus along with, presumably, its owner took on some significance once the partial subject was known, for Orpheus himself was cremated and reborn. A brief preliminary announcement by Stylianos G. Kapsomenos, with the title "Der Papyrus von Derveni: Ein Kommentar zur orphischen Theogonie" (*Gnomon* 35 [1963]: 222–223), aroused great interest and promised imminent publication, with Kapsomenos as editor. This, however, was not to be. The scholarly world waited in vain for official publication. In 1982 the distinguished journal *Zeitschrift für Papyrologie und Epigraphik* printed a pirated text at the back of volume 47, based on a text that had been shown to several scholars. Totally unofficial and decried by the Greek editors (after the death of Kapsomenos in 1978, these were now George M. Parássoglou and Kyriakos Tsantsanoglou), this text opened a floodgate of literary, philological, and philosophical scholarship. A more critical text, vetted by Tsantsanoglou, was published along with the proceedings of a conference on the Derveni papyrus held at Princeton University in 1993 (edited by André Laks and Glenn W. Most). The official text was finally published in 2006, edited by Theokritos Kouremenos, Parássoglou, and Tsantsanoglou.

Because there are almost no other papyrus texts from the same time, physical means of dating the hand of the papyrus offer little. The grave site offers a terminus ante quem of about 330 BCE, and papyrologists were satisfied with a fourth-century date for the hand. Of greater interest is the date of composition. The dialect is largely Ionic, with many (normally distinct) Attic forms, but such combinations are common (they can be detected in Anaxagoras, for example). More telling are a number of forms suggesting letter forms from the later fifth century that were misunderstood when they were transcribed into the later orthography; for example, *DIEGETAI* transcribed as *diēgeitai* rather than as *diēgētai*. These suggest a late fifth-century date, as does the absence of any mention of Plato—although that could be the result of the provincialism of the Derveni Author ("Author" for short in what follows).

The Derveni papyrus is thus one of only three examples of actual texts (as opposed to citation in other authors) from the age of the Presocratics, along with the papyrus texts of Antiphon's *Truth* and Empedocles' *On Nature*. It is quite possible, therefore, that the Author is someone already known to us, although none of the many attempts to name him has won wide acceptance, in part because a convincing identification depends upon correlating the Author's beliefs with those of whoever is proposed as the Author, whose purpose and philosophical views, however, have been not easy to pin down. In part this is because all that is extant are twenty-six columns, out of an unknown number, and of these only the upper ten to fifteen lines, often quite lacunose, remain, which deprives us of a continuous run of thought.

Although Kapsomenos's original description of the papyrus as a commentary on an Orphic poem was long taken as reasonable, by the time of the Princeton conference the actual nature of the prose text that quoted epic lines of Orpheus had become a moot point. "Commentary" can stand if taken broadly, but the Author does not seem much like a disinterested scholar. Is Orpheus quoted in order primarily to explain his verses (as in a straightforward commentary), or is he quoted as part of an appeal to a sacred text in order to illustrate and exemplify what the Author himself believes? If the former, the Author proves himself to be an untrustworthy scholar, in the process giving a very bad name to the practice of allegoresis (that is, the practice of interpreting a text allegorically). If the latter, the commentary must be read more as a religious text than as a textual commentary, although as later biblical commentaries illustrate, the superficial language and basic structure remain the same: cite the text and explain its meaning, give a lemma and commentary thereon.

Moreover, because the papyrus is incomplete, the preponderance of Orpheus' verses may skew our understanding of its overall purpose. Even in what is extant, Heraclitus, Homer, and another, anonymous writer of hymns are quoted along with Orpheus, perhaps as part, not of a commentary, but of a religious-philosophical treatise on the origin of the cosmos. Orpheus, after all, was included among the "useful" (i.e., didactic) poets in Aristophanes' *Frogs*.

The first six extant columns discuss the Erinyes, here, as in Aeschylus, regarded as the same as the Eumenides. The Author gives several steps involved in their worship, including the "funeral libations in droplets," which are of "water and milk"; also sacrificed are "cakes with many knobs," which represent the multitude of souls, as well as something "birdlike." It is not clear why or for what audience the Author outlines these ritual actions, but clearly more important than this is the reason one should worship and offer prayers to the Erinyes: they are souls who have become daimones with the power to punish wrongdoers. In doing so they act as servants of Dike (Justice), just as Heraclitus said that if the sun should overstep its bounds and increase in size, "the Erinyes, servants of Dike, will find it out and punish it so that it not transgress." The Author could have (and perhaps did in the lost lines that follow) quoted those lines of Homer in which Achilles' horses, given voice, are stopped by the Erinyes.

The papyrus from this point on, however, in columns 7–26, is characterized by the Orphic quotations and their analyses; the Erinyes disappear from the text. The transition from Erinyes to Orpheus is unfortunately missing, but one notes a continuation of the idea that rites and texts alike have hidden meanings in need of explication. The first meaningful words of column 7 are "him [soon to be identified as Orpheus] speaking a sound and righteous hymn," but nothing in this column connects clearly with what preceded—except perhaps that (depending on how column 4 is restored) both Heraclitus in column 4 and Orpheus here and later are said to speak in ways not always obvious to the layman.

"Enigmatic" in one form or another is applied to Orpheus many times by the Author, so that his audience can never forget how clever he is.

From Orpheus' verses, a theogony in form, a cosmogony can be derived. These total twenty-three complete hexameter lines (some known from citations in other authors), to which can be added a number of evident paraphrases of Orpheus embedded in the Author's prose commentary. The Author proudly offers his analysis, but his philological and allegorical methods do not reassure. He tells us that two of Orpheus' lines have been transposed (column 8.6), imposes false etymologies (column 22.12–13), engages in Sophistic feats of discrimination between synonyms and homonyms (e.g., columns 10.1, 11.5), and generally engages in mad displays of philology run amok. For all this, however, a distinct theory of nature emerges that is not unlike that found in Anaxagoras or Diogenes of Apollonia. Thus column 9 reads like an Anaxagorean interpretation of the formation of material objects, even to the point of using similar language (note, e.g., in column 9.8 [*ta*] *onta sumpagēnai*), but where Anaxagoras maintains a scientific neutrality about the cosmos' purpose (for which Socrates criticized him), the Author tacitly assumes a teleology that understands the sun occupying its natural place in the center of the universe and the moon serving the purpose of enabling farmers and sailors to fit their labor to the passing of the seasons. For Anaxagoras, *nous* (mind) largely functions as the laws of the universe; for the Derveni Author, *nous* is what Socrates wanted, a god that plans for the best of all possible worlds.

Orpheus' verses, like similar Orphic and Dionysian poems previously known, present a primitive theogony in which, among other events, Zeus wrests power from his father, who if he is not the sun himself derives from the sun. For the Author, however, the sun represents elemental fire, which hinders other elements and objects from cohering (see in particular column 9). This was desirable at the beginning of the world so that things could be set in motion, but if the sun prevailed then nothing could ever cohere. Zeus, here equated with the cosmic *nous*, by controlling and keeping the sun under his control—specifically, by swallowing his penis—provides the necessary amount of desirable stability, so that the cosmos can take form and maintain its orderly cycles. The Author assures us that this is in fact Orpheus' meaning, as though Orpheus were as conscious a writer of allegory as Pherecydes and Empedocles are. To put it anachronistically, the Author treats Orpheus as if he were a Presocratic philosopher, which does not necessarily entail that he himself was not an Orphic.

[*See also* Cosmogony and Cosmology; Derveni Krater; Literary Criticism, Ancient; Orpheus and Eurydice; Orphism; *and* Papyrology.]

BIBLIOGRAPHY

Betegh, Gábor. *The Derveni Papyrus: Cosmology, Theology, and Interpretation.* Cambridge, U.K.: Cambridge University Press, 2004.

Henry, Madeleine. "The Derveni Commentator as a Literary Critic." *Transactions and Proceedings of the American Philological Association* 116 (1986): 149–164.

Janko, Richard. "The Derveni Papyrus (Diagoras of Melos, *Apopyrgizontes logoi?*): A New Translation." *Classical Philology* 96 (2001): 1–32.

Kouremenos, Theokritos, George M. Parássoglou, and Kyriakos Tsantsanoglou. *The Derveni Papyrus.* Studi e Testi per il Corpus dei Papiri Filosofici Greci e Latini 13. Florence, Italy: L. S. Olschki, 2006.

Laks, André. "Between Religion and Philosophy: The Function of Allegory in the Derveni Papyrus." *Phronesis* 42 (1997): 121–142.

Laks, André, and Glenn W. Most, eds. *Studies on the Derveni Papyrus.* Oxford: Clarendon Press, 1997.

Most, Glenn W. "The Fire Next Time: Cosmology, Allegoresis, and Salvation in the Derveni Papyrus." *Journal of Hellenic Study* 117 (1997): 117–135.

David Sider

DEVOTIO

The *devotio* (literally "consecration" or "dedication") was a battlefield ritual in which the commander of a Roman army vowed to give his own life in return for the gods' destroying the enemy force and awarding victory to the Romans. This was performed and brought victory on two known occasions: by Publius Decius Mus at the battle of Veseris against the

Latins in 340 BCE, and by his son (of the same name) commanding against the Samnites at the battle of Sentinum in 295; his grandson (also Publius Decius Mus) may have repeated the ritual against Pyrrhus of Epirus at Asculum in 279, but he seems to have survived and the battle (famous as the original "Pyrrhic victory") was indecisive. Livy (8.9 and 10.28) quotes partial reconstructions of the prayer, made to Jupiter, Mars and Quirinus, Janus, Juno and Bellona, goddess of war, and to the Manes, in the underworld invoking their anger as a curse against the enemy to take them among the dead. The legend of the ancient Athenian king Codrus, who learned of a prophecy that his people would conquer the enemy provided he was killed, and so disguised himself, tricking the enemy into killing him, reflects a similar belief.

It became a model or metaphor for acts of self-sacrifice: Cicero when recalled from exile in 57 BCE represents his own flight as an act of devotion to the republic, because he claimed to have risked his life to avoid civil bloodshed. Virgil's Turnus calls his promise to fight Aeneas in single combat *devotio*, but fails in his commitment, even begging for his life when Aeneas has him at his mercy: in Lucan's *Civil War* Cato the Younger declares that he will join the war in order to stand in the front line and be killed as an act of *devotio*. The element of cursing the enemy entailed in *devotio* distinguishes it from two similar Christian beliefs: that God sacrificed his son, Jesus, to redeem man from his sins (which did not entail any destructive force) and that the devout Christian should invite death by declaring his faith so as to become a martyr at the hands of the authorities.

[*See also* Oaths; Sacrifice; *and* Warfare, *subentry* Roman Warfare.]

BIBLIOGRAPHY

Dumézil, Georges. *Archaic Roman Religion.* Translated by Philip Krapp. Chicago: University of Chicago Press, 1970.

Scheid, John. *An Introduction to Roman Religion.* Translated by Janet Lloyd. Edinburgh: Edinburgh University Press; Bloomington: Indiana University Press, 2003.

Elaine Fantham

DIADOCHI AND SUCCESSOR KINGDOMS

Alexander the Great's unexpected death in Babylon on 11 June 323 BCE left the Macedonian domains with no designated ruler and no clear path into the future. There was no hope of a smooth transmission of power, and a constitutional crisis ensued. The so-called settlement at Babylon was hammered out—violently—over the next few weeks, but it achieved only a brief stable platform from which the leading powerbrokers could begin to oversee the dismemberment of the empire. These individuals—including Alexander's bodyguards, leading generals, and officials, also sometimes referred to as the "marshals"—came to be known as the Diadochi (Successors), and the same term is applied to the subsequent forty-year period, as well as to the kingdoms that emerged to form the political framework of the Hellenistic world.

Historical sources for the period are diffuse and fragmentary, making study of the Successors and of the evolution of their kingdoms difficult. Most ancient accounts derive from the now-lost work of the long-lived fourth-century historian Hieronymus of Cardia, who served first Eumenes of Cardia and then three generations of the Antigonid family, so he participated in many of the events he recorded. Other genres of evidence, such as coins and inscriptions, are plentiful, however, and Babylonian cuneiform documents are becoming increasingly accessible, though these are often not effectively integrated into historical reconstructions by modern scholars. Books 18–20 of Diodorus Siculus' *Bibliothēkē* (*Library of History*; first century BCE) contain the fullest extant account of the years 323–301, and this may be supplemented and extended by Plutarch's relevant *Vitae parallelae* (*Parallel Lives*)—the *Phocion*, *Demosthenes*, *Eumenes*, *Demetrius*, and *Pyrrhus*—and the generalized epitome of Pompeius Trogus' lost *Historiae Philippicae* (*Philippic History*) by Justin. Book 10 of Quintus Curtius Rufus' *De rebus gestis Alexandri magni* (*History of Alexander*) contains the most detail on the settlement at Babylon, and this may be supplemented by several palimpsests and epitomes of Arrian's lost work *Ta meta*

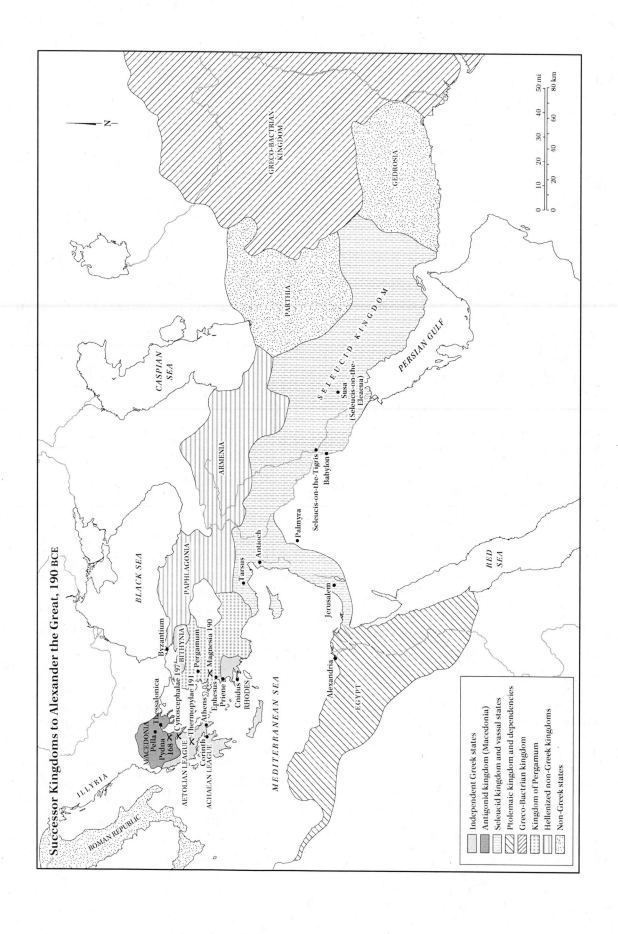

Successor Kingdoms to Alexander the Great, 190 BCE

N

GRECO-BACTRIAN KINGDOM

GEDROSIA

PARTHIA

CASPIAN SEA

S E L E U C I D   K I N G D O M

PERSIAN GULF

Susa
Seleucis-on-the-Eulaeus
(Seleucis-on-the-Eulaeus)

ARMENIA

Seleucis-on-the-Tigris
Babylon

Palmyra

Antioch

PAPHLAGONIA

Tarsus

Jerusalem

BLACK SEA

Byzantium

BITHYNIA
Pergamum
Magnesia 190
Cynoscephalae 197
Thermopylae 191
AETOLIAN LEAGUE
Athens
Ephesus
Priene
Corinth
Cnidus
ACHAEAN LEAGUE
RHODES

MACEDONIA
Thessalonica
Pella
Pydna
168

ILLYRIA

Alexandria

EGYPT

RED SEA

MEDITERRANEAN SEA

ROMAN REPUBLIC

	50 mi	80 km
	40	60
	30	
	20	40
	10	20
0		0

Independent Greek states
Antigonid kingdom (Macedonia)
Seleucid kingdom and vassal states
Ptolemaic kingdom and dependencies
Greco-Bactrian kingdom
Kingdom of Pergamum
Hellenized non-Greek kingdoms
Non-Greek states

Alexandron (*Events after Alexander*). In addition, a number of minor authors, such as Polyaenus, Cornelius Nepos, Appian, Athenaeus, and Pausanias, preserve useful historical snippets.

Fragmentation. The fragmentation of Alexander's empire into five, then eventually three, major kingdoms occurred in several stages from 323 to 281 BCE. The complex initial settlement brokered by the marshals at Babylon was made unsustainable by the absence of three important figures: Antipater, Alexander's regent in Macedonia; Craterus in Cilicia; and Antigonus I Monophthalmus (the One-Eyed), satrap of Phrygia. These players were awarded ambiguous titles in the agreement on the royal succession and centralized power structure that was eventually reached by the senior officers present. Perdiccas, a royal bodyguard and senior cavalry hipparch, and Meleager, an infantry battalion commander, emerged initially as regents for a dual kingship comprising Alexander's mentally disabled half brother, Philip III Arrhidaeus (the candidate of the infantry), and Alexander's as-yet-unborn son by Roxane, Alexander IV (the candidate of the cavalry). Although notionally a centralized government, the first actions of Perdiccas' junta were to cancel Alexander's last plans, thus preventing any further military expansion, and to distribute the satrapies among the Macedonian hierarchy, thus essentially creating a blueprint for the permanent division of the empire.

From this point the Diadochi tended to manifest either centralist or separatist ambitions, according to their oscillating fortunes in the ensuing four decades of political maneuvering and wars. Certainly Perdiccas aspired to unify the empire under his own rule, as did Antigonus after 321 and Antigonus' son Demetrius I Poliorcetes (the Besieger) until 287. Seleucus eventually came close to possessing the whole empire in 281, and it is arguable that such figures as Craterus and Leonnatus in 322, Pithon in 318, and Ptolemy I (Ptolemy Soter) from 310 also harbored hopes of preeminence.

Meleager was quickly eliminated by Perdiccas, who went on either to reward or to bribe the other marshals with the plum satrapies and offices: Ptolemy with Egypt, Pithon with Media, Peucestas with Persis, Leonnatus with Hellespontine Phrygia (until his death in 322), Lysimachus with Thrace, and Eumenes with Cappadocia. Seleucus was made chiliarch (second-in-command), while others, such as Antipater and Antigonus, were confirmed in the offices they already held. Perdiccas' ambitions and domineering personality, however, raised suspicions among the other marshals, and—in a pattern that was regularly repeated for some forty years—they formed a coalition against him. The First Diadoch War (322–320) ensued, during which Craterus was killed fighting Eumenes in Asia Minor and Perdiccas was assassinated by his own officers during an abortive invasion of Egypt in 321 or 320. This resulted in a reshuffling of power, and a second satrapy distribution, at Triparadeisus in Upper Syria. From this Antipater emerged supreme, with Antigonus as his executive with a commission to eliminate Eumenes and the remaining supporters of Perdiccas. Also at this time the two most enduring Successor kingdoms were established, with Ptolemy being confirmed in Egypt and Seleucus receiving the vital satrapy of Babylonia.

Alexander's former Greek secretary, Eumenes, displayed surprising military and political acumen, however, and on the death of Antipater in 319 the stage was set for the Second Diadoch War (319–315). This new wave of conflict saw Antigonus pursue Eumenes into Iran and saw Antipater's son Cassander rebel against Polyperchon, another of Alexander's old generals, who was the newly appointed regent in Macedonia. By 316, Antigonus not only had defeated Eumenes but also had eliminated many other ambitious potential rivals, including Pithon and Peucestas, and had driven Seleucus to take refuge with Ptolemy. At the same time, Cassander had triumphed in Macedonia in a bitter civil war against Polyperchon, Alexander's mother Olympias, and several other generals; during the war Philip III had been murdered and Alexander IV had been sequestered in Amphipolis. At this stage the power blocs of the major Diadochi were set for the next fifteen years, with Antigonus and Demetrius being arrayed against Ptolemy, Cassander, Lysimachus, and Seleucus.

The Third Diadoch War (314–311) between these antagonists ended inconclusively with the peace of 311, but in the aftermath Seleucus returned to Babylon, which he was this time able to hold against the Antigonids, and expanded his territory east to the Indian border. Meanwhile Antigonus and Demetrius fought Cassander's forces in Europe and fought Ptolemy in the Levant and Cyprus, and by 303 they had decisively gained the upper hand. Once more a coalition was formed against the most ambitious Diadoch, and in the Fourth Diadoch War (307–301), Antigonus was killed in a great battle against Lysimachus and Seleucus at Ipsus in 301, and his kingdom was divided between the victors. From this point Alexander's empire had devolved into four geographically and culturally distinct kingdoms, and any hope for reunification was extinguished.

The Remaining Kingdoms. Demetrius had survived Ipsus, and he became king of Macedonia in 294. From there he initiated the last Diadoch impulse for reunification with a massive armament buildup in 289, but once more the familiar pattern repeated itself. Lysimachus, Ptolemy, Seleucus, and Pyrrhus, the young king of Epirus, united to depose Demetrius, who was finally driven into captivity by 285. Macedonia was briefly partitioned and then was controlled by Lysimachus. One last act remained in the dance of the Diadochi: by 282 dynastic troubles had destabilized Lysimachus' kingdom, and Seleucus invaded Asia Minor. The two elderly kings met in battle in 281 at Corupedium, where Lysimachus was defeated and killed. For a few months Seleucus' kingdom extended from the Indian border to Europe, but he was assassinated by his ally Ptolemy Ceraunus later in 281, and the near reunification proved fleeting. Only three Successor kingdoms remained, and the torch passed to the next generation: Ptolemy I's younger son, Ptolemy II (Ptolemy Philadelphus), had inherited Egypt; Seleucus' son Antiochus Soter (Antiochus I) had inherited Asia; and by 276 Demetrius' son, Antigonus II Gonatas, had taken and successfully defended Macedonia against the Celtic invasions.

The unity of Alexander's empire was never likely to survive his early death: in the absence of a suitable heir, the Diadochi were never likely to agree on one of their number's inheriting the kingdom. The process of disintegration consisted of an initial division of key satrapies among a dozen prominent marshals, and the gradual emergence of five dominant Diadochi who maneuvered against each other through a combination of open war and various shifting alliances until two of the players were eliminated. By 281, Alexander's empire had devolved into the three major Hellenistic states—centered on Europe, Asia, and Egypt—that dominated the region in the next centuries.

[*See also* Antigonids; Antigonus Monophthalmus; Argeads; Attalids; Babylon; Demetrius Poliorcetes; Egypt, *subentry* Ptolemaic Egypt; Greece, *subentry* the Hellenistic Age; Ipsus, Battle of; Macedon; Ptolemies; Seleucids; *and* Syria.]

BIBLIOGRAPHY
Primary Works
Arrian. *Ta meta Alexandron*. In *Flavii Arriani quae exstant omnia*. Vol. 2: *Scripta minora et fragmenta*. Edited by A. G. Roos. Revised by Gerhard Wirth. Leipzig, Germany: Teubner, 1968.

Curtius Rufus, Quintus. *The History of Alexander*. Translated by John Yardley. Harmondsworth, U.K.: Penguin, 1984.

Diodorus Siculus. *Library of History*. Vols. 9–10. Translated by Russel M. Geer. Loeb Classical Library. Cambridge, Mass.: Harvard University Press, 1947–1954.

Diodorus Siculus. *Library of History*. Vol. 11. Translated by Francis R. Walton. Loeb Classical Library. Cambridge, Mass.: Harvard University Press, 1957.

Justin. *Epitome of the Philippic History of Pompeius Trogus*. Translated by John Yardley. Atlanta: Scholars Press, 1994.

Plutarch. *Plutarch's Lives*. 11 vols. Translated by Bernadotte Perrin. Loeb Classical Library. Cambridge, Mass.: Harvard University Press, 1914–1926. See volumes 7–9.

Secondary Works
Anson, Edward. *Eumenes of Cardia: A Greek among Macedonians*. Boston: Brill Academic, 2004.

Billows, Richard. *Antigonos the One-Eyed and the Creation of the Hellenistic State*. Berkeley: University of California Press, 1990.

Bosworth, A. B. *The Legacy of Alexander: Politics, Warfare, and Propaganda under the Successors*. Oxford: Oxford University Press, 2002.

Grainger, John. *Seleukos Nikator: Constructing a Helle-nistic Kingdom.* London: Routledge, 1990.

Hammond, N. G. L., and F. W. Walbank. *A History of Macedonia.* Vol. 3: *336–167 B.C.* Oxford: Clarendon Press, 1988.

Heckel, Waldemar. *The Marshals of Alexander's Empire.* London: Routledge, 1992.

Heckel, Waldemar. *Who's Who in the Age of Alexander the Great: Prosopography of Alexander's Empire.* Malden, Mass.: Blackwell, 2006.

Lund, Helen. *Lysimachus: A Study in Early Hellenistic Kingship.* London: Routledge, 1992.

Pat Wheatley

DIANA

Diana, whose name derives from an Indo-European root meaning "bright" or "shining," was an Italic hunting goddess identified with the moon. She had three forms: an underworld goddess (equated with the dark of the moon), the queen of heaven (the full moon), and the young huntress (the intermediate states of the moon). Her cult was a repository of knowledge about animals and plants in the wild, wounding and healing, about weather and the sky, and of course, about birth, death, and the life cycle of nature.

As the huntress, Diana was a warrior's goddess. Hunting bands were the origins of much Italic military and civic identity, and predator animals were often theriomorphic patrons of cities and peoples. In Latium, Diana's hunting cult rituals were foundations for establishing the leadership of Latin military organizations and for alliances between potentially hostile communities.

The three major cult centers in Italy were at Aricia (in the crater of an extinct volcano about 12 miles [19 kilometers] southeast of Rome), Rome (on the Aventine), and Tifata in Campania. There were other minor sanctuaries, and many wild places were sacred to Diana, but lacked cult. The penultimate king of Rome, Servius Tullius (traditionally 578–535 BCE), failed in his attempt to make the Aventine sanctuary of Diana the religious center for all Latin cities under Rome's leadership. Instead, by the late sixth century, Arician Diana had become the patron goddess of the Latin League, a variable alliance of Latin cities, led by Aricia, opposing Rome's military expansion.

Though Rome ultimately triumphed, the Arician sanctuary gradually became one of the wealthiest in Italy. By the third century Diana was equated with Artemis who became her iconographic model. The young huntress was her most popular representation, but the cult statues portrayed a regal and mature woman. The Aricians appropriated Hippolytus' Greek myth to explain their deity Virbius. Both were young hunters whom the hunting goddess loved, and brought back to life after a violent death. Similarly, they used the escape of Orestes and Iphigenia from King Thoas of the Taurians, and Orestes' purification by Diana, as the etiology for the *rex nemorensis*, Diana's Arician priest who had to be an escaped slave and kill his predecessor in combat.

To balance his own identification with Apollo in Rome, the emperor Augustus appropriated Diana as patroness of his wife Livia and his daughter Julia. The wealth of his own mother, Atia, derived in part from ceramic manufacturing and money changing in the Arician sanctuary, and this connection with priest slave-kings and trade had been a staple of political abuse of the young Octavian before Actium (31 BCE); thereafter, respectful allusions to Arician Diana are common in Augustan literature and art. By then, Diana's worship in Rome seems to have evolved into a cult primarily for slave women. At Aricia during the Principate, dedications honoring the emperors, magistrates, and freedmen, and offerings from foreign cities demonstrate the sanctuary's continued importance. The cult's large Hellenistic-style structures included a gold-roofed temple, porticoes, granaries, baths, and a theater. This was a healing sanctuary, treating humans and animals with an eclectic mixture of empirical medicine and philosophic-religious practices. Worship of Diana spread throughout the empire, and there is evident creolizing of Diana with local hunting goddesses, especially near legionary stations.

[*See also* Artemis; Mythology, Roman; *and* Religion, *subentry* Roman Religion.]

BIBLIOGRAPHY

Bilde, Pia Guldager, and Mette Moltesen. *A Catalogue of Sculptures from the Sanctuary of Diana Nemorensis in the University of Pennsylvania Museum, Philadelphia.* Rome: "L'erma" di Bretschneider, 2002.

Green, C. M. C. *Roman Religion and the Cult of Diana at Aricia.* Cambridge, U.K., and New York: Cambridge University Press, 2007.

C. M. C. GREEN

DICTATOR

During the Republic, in times of military or political crisis, Romans allowed the appointment of a dictator, a supreme magistrate who possessed nearly monarchical powers for a short term, until the crisis abated or six months elapsed (the length of a military campaigning season), whichever came first. Dictators were appointed for minor tasks as well, such as holding elections, supervising games, or performing other ritual functions. A dictator was traditionally chosen from among the former consuls by one of the consuls for the year (Livy 22.8) in an unusual ceremony that had to take place at night (Livy 9.38.14). The dictator was also called the *magister populi* (master of the people), and his second-in-command, appointed by the dictator himself, was *magister equitum* (master of the horse). These titles seem to betray the dictatorship's origin in military conflict, with the dictator himself commanding the infantry and his *magister equitum* commanding the cavalry. The dictator was preceded in public by twenty-four *lictores* (attendants) and the same number of *fasces* (rods of state), perhaps in imitation of the ancient Roman kings. Our sources disagree on whether a dictator's decision was subject to the right of appeal (*ius provocationis*), as a consul's was, or to the veto power of the tribunes of the plebs (*intercessio tribunicia*).

Modern scholars have long noted the unusual nature of this office, in that the dictator had no colleague (apart from his *magister equitum*, who in any case was clearly subordinate), had no fixed term of office, and was not elected by the people, thus contravening the basic principles of Republican Rome's system of government. Thus a considerable debate has arisen over the origin of the dictatorship. Our source tradition dates the office's origin back to the earliest period of the Republic in response to external threats but admits confusion over the precise chronology and the name of the first dictator. Livy discusses the problem (2.18.3–7) and names Titus Larcius the first dictator, probably in 501 BCE; for Dionysius (*Roman Antiquities* 5.70) the threat that provoked the appointment of the first dictator was an internal one. It is curious that Romans chose to institute an office with visibly monarchical powers so soon after expelling the kings and founding the Republic. This, along with the apparent sacral character of the dictatorship—the dictator, like the *rex sacrorum* and the Vestal Virgins, could not mount a horse (Plutarch *Fabius Maximus* 4)—has led some scholars to posit the origin of the office in the Regal period. That other Latin towns are known to have elected annual magistrates called "dictators" has encouraged the belief that the Roman dictatorship was in origin a Latin institution, or at least that Romans adopted the title of the office from their Latin neighbors. But if this was the case, the Roman dictatorship had a markedly different evolution from that of its Latin counterpart.

The dictatorship fell into disuse after 202 BCE, probably as a result of the increased appointments of promagistrates, and was revived only amid the civil wars of the late Republic, first by Sulla in 82 BCE and next by Julius Caesar in 49 BCE. The victorious Sulla made known his belief that only by reviving the office of dictator could Rome recover from the recent civil disturbances. As a consequence Lucius Valerius Flaccus, the leading senator, sponsored a law conferring on Sulla the power to pass legislation and reform the constitution (*legibus scribundis et rei publicae constituendae*) without the constraint of the customary fixed term limit (Appian *Roman Civil Wars* 1.98–99). The likely result was that Sulla was entitled to issue edicts with the force of law without recourse to senate or people. Once the constitution had been settled to his satisfaction, Sulla laid down his dictatorship at the beginning of 79.

A generation after Sulla, Caesar was appointed dictator by virtue of a law sponsored by the praetor Marcus Aemilius Lepidus for the first time in 49 (Caesar *Civil War* 2.21.5) and held the office in successive years until he was named dictator for life (*dictator [in] perpetuo*) at the beginning of 44, an event that precipitated his assassination. He used the office to fill magistracies and, like Sulla, enact legislation intended to ease the recovery from the debilitating effects of civil war. In the immediate aftermath of Caesar's death and in a spirit of accommodation for those responsible, Mark Antony sponsored a law outlawing the dictatorship forever (Cicero *Philippics* 1.2). The last word on the Roman dictatorship came in 22 BCE when Augustus declined amid a severe famine the senate's and the people's urgent requests that he take up the office (*Accomplishments of the Deified Augustus* 5.1).

[*See also* Political Structure and Ideology, Roman.]

BIBLIOGRAPHY
Primary Works
The source tradition for the Roman dictatorship is scattered throughout the works of many ancient authors. References to these ancient sources and summaries of the accomplishments of specific dictators can be found in T. Robert S. Broughton, *Magistrates of the Roman Republic*, 2 vols. (New York: American Philological Association, 1951–1952; with a third volume of corrections and additions, Atlanta: Scholars Press, 1986). In addition to the sources cited above, see Naphtali Lewis and Meyer Reinhold, eds., *Roman Civilization: Selected Readings*, 2 vols., 3rd ed. (New York: Columbia University Press, 1990), vol. 1 (*The Republic and the Augustan Age*), selections 25, 26, 37, 104, and 110, and Matthew Dillon and Lynda Garland, *Ancient Rome: From the Early Republic to the Assassination of Julius Caesar* (London: Routledge, 2005), selections 1.14, 2.12–13, 13.42, and 13.54.

Secondary Works
E. Stuart Staveley provides a brief summary of, and largely discredits, various theories about the origin of the dictatorship, adhering closely to the ancient source tradition that makes dictatorship a

Republican magistracy, not a regal one. For an opposing view, see D. Cohen. Arthur Keaveney provides an overview of Sulla's dictatorship, while F. J. Vervaet gives a detailed analysis of its legal basis, demonstrating especially how Sulla's dictatorship differed from its earlier counterparts. An analysis of Caesar's dictatorship in the context of his larger political accomplishments and ambitions can be found in Elizabeth Rawson's article in the *Cambridge Ancient History*, vol. 9 (1994), pp. 438–467, especially pp. 458–467.

Cohen, D. "The Origin of Roman Dictatorship." *Mnemosyne* 10 (1957): 300–318.

Crook, J. A., Andrew Lintott, and Elizabeth Rawson, eds. *Cambridge Ancient History*. Vol. 9: *The Last Age of the Roman Republic, 146–43 B.C.* Cambridge, U.K.: Cambridge University Press, 1994.

Keaveney, Arthur. *Sulla: The Last Republican*. 2nd ed. London: Routledge, 2005.

Staveley, E. Stuart. "The Constitution of the Roman Republic, 1940–1954." *Historia* 5 (1956): 74–122. See especially pp. 101–107.

Vervaet, F. J. "The *Lex Valeria* and Sulla's Empowerment as Dictator (82–79 BCE)." *Cahiers du Centre Gustave-Glotz* 15 (2004): 37–84.

Geoffrey S. Sumi

DIDACTIC, GREEK

See Poetry, Greek, *subentries* Post-Classical Greek Epic *and* Didactic Poetry.

DIDO

See Aeneas; Virgil.

DILETTANTI, SOCIETY OF

The Society of Dilettanti was founded in London in 1734 as a dining club for gentlemen who were alumni of the Grand Tour. Its initial raison d'être was sociable conversation, but cultivating the public's appreciation for classical antiquity soon commanded the group's time and resources.

The Dilettanti launched groundbreaking archaeological expeditions to Greece, Asia Minor, and the Levant. Taking inspiration from Robert Wood's *The Ruins of Palmyra* (1753), its members underwrote James Stuart and Nicholas Revett's *Antiquities of Athens* (1762–1794) and Richard Chandler's *Ionian Antiquities* (1769). These pivotal folios circulated the first empirical illustrations of eastern Mediterranean ruins. In addition to fostering the reception of the neoclassical style in Europe, the society sponsored pioneering topographical surveys that heralded archaeology as a rigorous scholarly discipline.

The society was a close-knit circle of artists, architects, and their aristocratic patrons, and its leading lights were notorious revelers and cultural catalysts. In the spirit of their chief toasts, *seria ludo* (serious matters in a playful vein) and "Grecian Taste and Roman Spirit," they found innovative ways to blend Bacchic conviviality and antiquarian research. The discovery that wax phalluses were being offered as Christian cult dedications in the southern Italian town of Isernia prompted Richard Payne Knight to author *A Discourse on the Worship of Priapus* (1786). Though his penchant for erotic curiosities was the butt of satire in the popular press, Knight's book represented a serious inquiry into comparative religion and the ancient symbolism of procreation. Printed together with accounts of the Isernia votives by William Hamilton and Joseph Banks, the controversial treatise was reissued in 1865 with an essay on the worship of the generative powers in the Middle Ages.

Many of England's most distinguished collections of antiquities decorated Dilettanti members' estates, among them Shugborough, Woburn Abbey, Castle Howard, Wentworth Woodhouse, and the Deepdene. In their capacity as arbiters of "fashionable *virtù*," connoisseurs such as Knight and Charles Townley championed classical art as a model of refined taste. To promote the importance of Greco-Roman antiquity for improving the national arts, they embarked on a third publishing enterprise, *Specimens of Antient Sculpture* (1809–1835). John Samuel Agar was one of several artists who prepared the illustrations, which are considered the finest ever made of ancient sculpture. *Specimens* rivaled the standards of meticulous accuracy established by the Dilettanti's architectural publications. Disputes in 1816 over the British Museum's acquisition of the Elgin Marbles—in part a referendum on the superiority of Greek over Roman art—divided the members and damaged the society's prestige.

With the professionalization of field archaeology, a development in which the Dilettanti were instrumental, the role of enlightened amateurs gradually diminished. During the course of the nineteenth century the group nevertheless fulfilled its mission by subsidizing excavations at Teos, Priene, Didyma, and Naucratis, as well as publications such as William Gell's *The Topography of Rome and Its Vicinity* (1834), F. C. Penrose's *An Investigation of the Principles of Athenian Architecture* (1851)—landmark research on the optical refinements of the Parthenon—and Charles Cockerell's *The Temples of Jupiter Panhellenius at Ægina and of Apollo Epicurius at Bassae near Phigaleia in Arcadia* (1860). The society transformed classical art from a matter of private delight—in the original sense of the term "dilettante"—into one of public consequence. Since its founding in 1734 the Society of Dilettanti has continued to meet regularly, and through its charitable trust it maintains the long tradition of support for the arts and archaeology.

[*See also* Antiquarianism; Archaeology, *subentry* Historical Overview; Classical Tradition, *subentry* Classical Influences on Western Art; Elgin Marbles; Priene; *and* Travel and Tourism in Classical Lands, Modern.]

BIBLIOGRAPHY

Kelly, Jason. *Archaeology and Identity in the British Enlightenment: The Society of Dilettanti, 1732–1816.* New Haven, Conn., and London: Paul Mellon Centre for Studies in British Art and Yale University Press, 2009.

Redford, Bruce. *Dilettanti: The Antic and the Antique in Eighteenth-Century England.* Los Angeles: J. Paul Getty Museum and the Getty Research Institute, 2008.

Claire L. Lyons

DINNERS

See Banquets, Roman; Food and Drink; Wine.

DIO CASSIUS

See Historiography, Latin.

DIO CHRYSOSTOM

(c. 45–118 CE), Greek sophist and philosopher, also known as Dio Cocceianus and Dio of Prusa. Born in Prusa in Bithynia, Dio was a brilliant orator—the epithet "Chrysostom" means "golden-mouthed"—whose career provides our clearest vision of the early Second Sophistic. His surviving corpus, which includes more than seventy orations, demonstrates a huge range of interests. Some are purely sophistic, as with his "In Praise of Hair" and the lost "Encomium of a Parrot." Others supposedly offer direct advice about kingship to Trajan (Orations 1–4). These texts claim a direct engagement with politics at the highest possible level, and that same spirit underpins Dio's many "civic" orations composed for Eastern cities (e.g., Orations 31–34) and for his native Bithynia (Orations 42–50), speeches that provide important windows into the workings of provincial centers. Other works deal with philosophic matters, as with his discussions of Diogenes (Orations 6, 8–10) and his treatises on specific virtues and vices (Orations 16–26). Throughout, Dio shows a deep interest in the Greek literary tradition, whether in his comparison of the myth of Philoctetes as adapted by Aeschylus, Sophocles, and Euripides (Oration 52), his reevaluation of the Trojan War (Oration 11), or his extended narratives that defy easy generic classification (e.g., Oration 7, the "Euboean Discourse," which shares many traits with the Greek novels). This variety of topics fits well with Philostratus' classification of Dio as one of those who combine traits and habits of a sophist and a philosopher.

Three turning points in Dio's career give contour to his era and literary output: his conversion at Rome away from sophistic oratory and toward philosophy under the influence of the Stoic Gaius Musonius Rufus, his relegation from Rome under the emperor Domitian, and his rehabilitation under Nerva. These key shifts encourage us—at times, perhaps, too hastily—to see neat episodes in his career. Yet even if such historicizing goes too far, it is undeniable that Dio at times revels in epideictic braggadocio and at other times pushes a serious philosophical agenda; at times he languishes as the exiled vagabond and at other times relishes being a political insider. And as with the historical writings of Tacitus and Juvenal's satires, we see in Dio a public figure who was forced to adapt to the radical reversals in political climate that accompanied the move from one emperor to another.

Given his influence on later generations and the insights he provides into daily life in the Eastern Empire, Dio enjoys a prominent but still understudied place in the classical tradition. His student Favorinus is another colorful example of a superstar sophist (though his writings are poorly preserved), Dio himself is mentioned by Pliny the Younger (Epistulae 10.81) as a notable provincial figure in his later years, and his orations were studied and imitated throughout the Byzantine Empire. Like his contemporary Plutarch, Dio brings this world to life, but both men also actively create our image of the Eastern Roman Empire through their constant references to the events and literature of earlier eras. Yet whereas Plutarch keeps himself in the background, Dio stations his public face, a cross between a nouveau Socrates and a philosophical Odysseus, squarely between his chosen topic and his audience. In his elegant but conversational style he thus becomes for us a personal guide and apologist for his age.

[*See also* Second Sophistic.]

BIBLIOGRAPHY
Works of Dio Chrysostom
Dionis Chrysostomi Orationes. 2 vols. Edited by Guy de Budé. Leipzig, Germany: Teubner, 1916–1919. Authoritative Greek text.
Dio Chrysostom. 5 vols. Translated by J. W. Cohoon and H. Lamar Crosby. Loeb Classical Library. Cambridge, Mass.: Harvard University Press, 1932–1951. Greek text

with facing English translation. The most easily available complete English text.

Orations VII, XII, and XXXVI. Edited by D. A. Russell. Cambridge, U.K., and New York: Cambridge University Press, 1992. Greek text and English commentary make for the most convenient and thorough introduction to Dio for any audience that reads ancient Greek.

Secondary Works

Bekker-Nielsen, Tønnes. *Urban Life and Local Politics in Roman Bithynia: The Small World of Dion Chrysostomos.* Aarhus, Denmark: Aarhus University Press, 2008. Focuses on the local scene evoked through Dio's writings and argues that politics was not so much "political," in the modern sense, as it was a game of self-promotion.

Jones, Christopher Prestige. *The Roman World of Dio Chrysostom.* Cambridge, Mass.: Harvard University Press, 1978. A biography that situates Dio within his sociopolitical context.

Swain, Simon, ed. *Dio Chrysostom: Politics, Letters, and Philosophy.* Oxford and New York: Oxford University Press, 2000. An excellent collection of essays that explore Dio's career and writings from diverse and productive perspectives.

Tom Hawkins

DIOCLETIAN

(Gaius Aurelius Valerius Diocletianus, c. 244–c. 312 CE), Roman emperor (r. 284–305) who founded the tetrarchy and established new and enduring administrative structures. Born on 22 December near Salona in Dalmatia, he is reported to have been either the freedman of a senator or the son of a scribe who may have been a freedman. He served as a soldier under Claudius Gothicus, Aurelian, and Probus, and may have held a military command in the Balkan province of Moesia prior to becoming commander of the elite imperial corps of *protectores domestici.* His original name was Gaius Valerius Diocles. Upon the death of Carus in Persia and the subsequent murder of Carus' son Numerianus in Bithynia, Diocles was proclaimed emperor by the soldiery near Nicomedia on 20 November 284. Within months he altered his cognomen to Diocletianus. He confronted Carus' other son, the emperor Carinus, in battle in May 285 at the river Margus (Morava R.), where Carinus was slain by his own troops.

Formation of the Tetrarchy and Campaigns. In order to better control the empire, Diocletian appointed as a subordinate Caesar one Aurelius Valerius Maximianus, a fellow Illyrian and soldier, in mid-285 at Milan. Diocletian immediately sent Maximian to suppress the uprising of the Bagaudae, a group of rural peasants under a leader named Amandus, who claimed imperial power. In April 286, Diocletian elevated Maximian to full Augustus and went east to settle relations with Persia and Armenia. By 287 he and Maximian assumed the honorary titles Iovius and Herculius, respectively, thus advertising a personal connection with the gods Jupiter and Hercules and a notional father-son relationship. Diocletian campaigned on the Raetian frontier in 288 and against the Sarmatians on the middle Danube in 289, making his base at Sirmium. In summer 290 he moved to Syria to fight the Saracens, then back to Sirmium and thence to Milan, where he met Maximian in winter 290–291. In the west, the naval commander Carausius had been accused of embezzling loot captured from Saxon and Frankish pirates and had broken into revolt in Gaul in 286. After moving to Britain, Carausius hindered Maximian's attempts to overthrow him. Whether as a result of forward planning at Milan in 291 or simply as a response to the need for additional commanders, Diocletian and Maximian appointed two Caesars to serve as their subordinates. On 1 March 293 Maximian installed Julius Constantius (Constantius I) in this office, and a short time later Diocletian promoted Galerius Armentarius (Galerius) to the same position. The Caesars, both also Illyrian soldiers, were adopted by (and married to the daughters of) their respective Augusti, thus establishing quasi-familial and dynastic links. This system of four-man rule, referred to by moderns as the tetrarchy, had major effects on imperial government for the next century.

Constantius was able to wrest control of northern Gaul from Carausius in 293, and, after Carausius was assassinated by his officer Allectus, to retake Britain in 296. In the same period, Diocletian campaigned on the Danube against the Carpi, many of whom he resettled in Pannonia. Maximian campaigned in Spain and Mauretania against the Moorish Quinquegentiani from 296 to 298. Meanwhile, in 296 and early 297 Galerius advanced against the Sassanid Persian king, Narses, who routed him in a battle near Callinicum in Syria and forced his withdrawal to Antioch. After Diocletian resupplied his army with troops from the Danube, Galerius attacked Persia a second time in late 297 beginning from Satala on the Euphrates border with Armenia. He defeated Narses, captured his treasury and harem, and marched into central Mesopotamia to capture Ctesiphon. By early 299 Diocletian concluded a treaty with the Persians at Antioch which ceded back to Rome control of northern Mesopotamia, including the strategic trading center of Nisibis, and control over the Armenian and Iberian thrones and the northern Mesopotamian satrapies. In 297 Diocletian had faced the revolt of Lucius Domitius Domitianus in Alexandria, which he took after an eight-month siege and narrowly spared from destruction. After traveling as far south on the Nile as Elephantine and renegotiating the Egyptian frontier with the Nobatae, Diocletian moved his residence to Antioch (299–302), and then to Nicomedia, where he was based until 305. This city, in Bithynia, became the de facto capital of the eastern empire until 330, when Constantine declared for Byzantium/Constantinople.

Abdication and Influence. On 23 February 303, perhaps under the influence of Galerius, Diocletian initiated a great persecution against the Christians. Four edicts were issued. These were enforced with leniency in Constantius' northwestern domains, but with severity in Africa, Italy, and particularly in the east. For his *vicennalia* (twentieth regnal anniversary) in late 303, Diocletian traveled to Rome and met Maximian, whom he forced to swear an oath at the temple of Jupiter Optimus Maximus, apparently regarding plans for mutual abdication. Unrest in Rome drove Diocletian out of the city quickly, and on his winter's journey to the Danube and thence to Nicomedia, he grew extremely ill. He went into hiding in the palace but reappeared at an assembly outside Nicomedia on 1 March 305 to announce that he was abdicating, Rome's first emperor to do so voluntarily. He promoted Galerius to Augustus and elevated Maximin Daia, Galerius' nephew, to be his Caesar. With reluctance, Maximian did the same at Milan on 1 May, with Constantius assuming his role as Augustus and the latter's deputy Severus that of the western Caesar. This meant passing over two possible dynastic choices of successor, Maximian's son Maxentius and Constantius' son Constantine, both of whom would later usurp power.

Diocletian returned to his homeland in Dalmatia, where he had constructed a massive retirement villa at Spalatum (Split). There he cultivated vegetables and avoided involvement in government affairs, except that in November 308 he journeyed to Carnuntum on the Danube to consult with Galerius about the chaotic state into which the tetrarchy had fallen. He died on 3 December, most likely in 312. His wife, Prisca, and daughter, Galeria Valeria, remained at the court of Galerius until his death in early May 311. They then sought refuge with Maximin Daia, who later exiled them, and were eventually captured and executed in late 314 by Maximin's rival for eastern power, Licinius. This was the end of Diocletian's line.

Diocletian is notorious for having increased the level of imperial ceremonial and the lavishness of the imperial trappings and court, setting the tone for centuries to come. He was above all a successful general and tremendous administrator who reformed the coinage, the army, the taxation system, provincial administration, and the bureaucracy.

[*See also* Balkans; Bithynia; Christianity; Emperor; Illyria; Imperial Cult, Roman; Rome, *subentry* The Empire; *and* Tetrarchs.]

BIBLIOGRAPHY

Barnes, Timothy D. *The New Empire of Diocletian and Constantine.* Cambridge, Mass.: Harvard University Press, 1982. Indispensable compendium of factual information, especially when supplemented with updates at *Journal of Roman Archaeology* 9 (1996): 532–552.

Kolb, Frank. *Diocletian und die Erste Tetrarchie.* Berlin and New York: Walter de Gruyter, 1987. Standard study arguing for the systematic construction of the tetrarchy.

Nixon, C. E. V., and Barbara Saylor Rodgers, eds. *In Praise of Later Roman Emperors: The "Panegyrici Latini."* Berkeley: University of California Press, 1994. Translation and commentary on the best contemporary source for Diocletian.

Rees, Roger. *Diocletian and the Tetrarchy.* Edinburgh: Edinburgh University Press, 2004. Useful introductory survey.

Noel Lenski

DIODORUS SICULUS

(c. 90–c. 30 BCE), Sicilian Greek universal historian. A native of Agyrium in the northeast part of Sicily, Diodorus—clearly a man of private means—claims (1.4.1) to have devoted thirty years to researching and writing the vast *Bibliotheca historica* (*Bibliothēkē*; *Library of History*) for which he is remembered. After perhaps five years of travel in Europe and Asia Minor, in 60 BCE he took up residence in Alexandria, an ideal site to research books 1–6 of his work. At some point before 45 he moved to Rome, where, he says, he spent "considerable time" because of easy access to the sources he needed. When, or if, he returned to Sicily is unknown. One of the few inscriptions from Agyrium is a grave marker for "Diodorus son of Apollonius." The name, unfortunately, is extremely common, but the coincidence remains notable.

From his own work we get a few hints as to his personality. Diodorus is, like so many ancient writers, a social and political conservative. Conventionally religious, he treats history primarily as an instrument for moral guidance and a witness to heaven's inexorable pursuit of evildoers (a habit that ensured his popularity among Christian apologists); but he also, like Herodotus, has a passion for collecting marvels and exotica. The latest event that he mentions (16.7.1) is Octavian's eviction in 36 BCE of the population of Tauromenium (Taormina) to make room for a Roman *colonia*; of the devastation and widespread confiscation of estates that followed, in an area that included Agyrium, he says nothing. Diodorus may well have lost his own property; it is not impossible that he was proscribed.

Internal evidence strongly suggests that by 30 he was dead, with the final editing of the *Library of History* still incomplete.

The *Library* was conceived on a large scale. It has been convincingly argued that Diodorus originally planned to write forty-two books, in seven hexads, ranging from mythical antiquity to 46/5 and culminating in Julius Caesar's appointment as dictator (see Rubincam, "How Many Books Did Diodorus Siculus Originally Intend to Write?"). But though that last date survives in Diodorus' calculations (1.4.6–7, 1.5.1), in fact his final version consisted of forty books terminating in 60/59, the beginning of the Gallic Wars: the civil convulsions of the late Republic made Caesar's later career too risky to handle. Books 1–6 cover descriptions of the Mediterranean world, both east (1–3: a whole book is devoted to Egypt) and west (4–6), together with pre–Trojan War mythical traditions; in contrast to the rest of the *Library*, Diodorus made no attempt here to impose a chronological framework, reasonably citing lack of reliable evidence (1.5.1). Books 6–10, like books 21–40, exist today only as fragments preserved in digests, excerpts, and citations, mostly Byzantine; books 11–20 have survived intact, however, and give us an all but unbroken narrative sequence from Xerxes I's invasion of 480, through the Peloponnesian War and Alexander's conquest of the Achaemenid Empire, to the eve of the Battle of Ipsus (301). For much of this material, including all Western history, the reign of Philip II of Macedon, and the early wars of the Successors, Diodorus is virtually our only source.

What Diodorus set out to write was "universal history" (*historiai koinai* or *katholikai*), necessarily based on earlier written sources rather than on direct observation (hence also the bookish aspect of his title, *Bibliothēkē*), that presented a general survey of the Mediterranean world and those nations immediately adjacent to it, plus a more or less synoptic history of the major players. The idea was not new. Herodotus had opened up horizons with his panoramic survey of Achaemenid provinces. Panhellenism, as promoted by Isocrates and others, similarly looked to the wider world. Ephorus

(c. 405–330 BCE; much used by Diodorus) seems to have been the first soi-disant universal historian: Diodorus criticizes him (1.3.2–3) for avoiding myth and the doings of "barbarian nations." Timaeus of Tauromenium made Sicily and Magna Graecia a recognized part of the Greek historian's world. Alexander's conquests and the literature that they inspired opened up the East as never before. Polybius (1.3.1) fastened on the meteoric rise of Rome to promote the idea of history as an "organic whole" in which "the affairs of Italy and Africa are interwoven with those of Asia and Greece" toward a new universality. Diodorus' slightly earlier contemporary, the great Stoic scientist, philosopher, and historian Posidonius of Apamea, promoted a fixed cosmic order, under the auspices of Fate, governing all mankind. All his historical explanations were moral; he was also a class-conscious antiradical who believed in being kind to slaves.

These were the predecessors on whom Diodorus drew, and their influence can be detected throughout his surviving text. From Herodotus he borrows the notion of wide-ranging ethnic digressions, with an emphasis on Egypt. Ephorus gave him the idea of dividing a large work into planned groups of books, each with its own preface (*prooimion*), and encouraged his local patriotism. Diodorus' chronological framework, correlating Olympiads and the Athenian archon-year—not always successfully—with the Roman *fasti*, drew on the work of both Timaeus and Polybius. His notion of history as a succession of moral exempla goes back a long way in Hellenistic historiography, but the immediate inspiration for it, as for his treatment of the Roman slave revolts, was undoubtedly Posidonius. Where he goes beyond them all, and knows it—frequently faulting his predecessors for their shortcomings—is in the sheer size and scope of his undertaking.

Until the time of Reinhold Niebuhr and the nineteenth-century analysts, Diodorus' plain narrative style and moral high-mindedness ensured his popularity. After that his reputation plummeted: the new historicist critics dismissed him as an imbecilic scribbler who picked one source for each period (e.g., Ephorus for the fifth century, Timaeus for the West,

Hieronymus of Cardia for the Successors) and transcribed it mindlessly. Hence the regular aphorism that Diodorus is "only as good as his source." Though this dismissive view still commands wide support, a recent new movement argues that Diodorus was in fact a perfectly rational, second-class historian who used multiple sources, died before his text was fully revised, and should be evaluated on that basis.

[*See also* Historiography, Greek.]

BIBLIOGRAPHY

Works of Diodorus Siculus

Diodori Bibliotheca Historica. 5 vols. Edited by Immanuel Bekker, Ludwig Dindorf, and Friedrich Vogel. Leipzig, Germany: B. G. Teubner, 1888–1906. Includes a Greek text and Latin notes.

Diodorus of Sicily. 12 vols. Translated by C. H. Oldfather, Charles Lawton Sherman, C. Bradford Welles, Russel Mortimer Geer, and Francis R. Walton. Cambridge, Mass.: Harvard University Press; London: W. Heinemann, 1933–1967. Includes a Greek text and an English translation.

Bibliothèque historique. Various editors. General introduction by François Chamoux and Pierre Bertrac. Paris: Belles Lettres, 1972–2003. Includes a Greek text, a French translation, and commentary in French.

Diodorus Siculus, Books 11–12.37.1: Greek History 480–431 B.C., the Alternative Version. Translated by Peter Green. Austin: University of Texas Press, 2006.

Secondary Works

Rubincam, C. I. R. "How Many Books Did Diodorus Siculus Originally Intend to Write?" *Classical Quarterly* 48 (1998): 229–233.

Rubincam, C. I. R. "The Organization and Composition of Diodorus' *Bibliotheke*." *Echos du Monde Classique* 31 (1987): 313–328.

Sacks, Kenneth. "Diodorus and His Sources: Conformity and Creativity." In *Greek Historiography*, edited by Simon Hornblower, pp. 213–232. Oxford: Clarendon Press; New York: Oxford University Press, 1994.

Sacks, Kenneth. *Diodorus Siculus and the First Century.* Princeton, N.J.: Princeton University Press, 1990.

Stylianou, P. J. "Introduction." In his *A Historical Commentary on Diodorus Siculus, Book 15*, pp. 1–139. Oxford: Clarendon Press; New York: Oxford University Press, 1998. An up-to-date exposition of the traditional view.

Peter Green

DIOGENES LAERTIUS

(c. 200 CE), author of the most comprehensive and detailed survey of ancient Greek philosophy to survive antiquity. This work, commonly called *Lives of the Philosophers* (the transmitted title, *Lives and Doctrines of Those Who Became Famous in Philosophy, and the Tenets of Each School*, is more accurate but probably spurious), presents summary accounts of the lives, teachings, and writings of more than eighty Greek thinkers from the origins of Greek philosophy in the sixth century to the second century BCE and occasionally beyond. Nothing is known about Diogenes apart from this work. Its contents indicate that he was probably active in the late second or early third century CE: the latest figure cited is Sextus Empiricus (active c. 150–200 CE). It shows no awareness of later developments like Neoplatonism, and its general tenor, including abundant citation of Hellenistic and imperial scholars, suits the classicizing tastes of Second Sophistic authors like Lucian and Athenaeus. Where Diogenes lived, what circles he frequented, and what else he did are insoluble mysteries. Even his name is uncertain: Laertius, most likely a cognomen or toponym, could be his personal name, and Diogenes only a sobriquet adopted from a Homeric epithet for Odysseus, *diogenēs Laertiadēs*, or "Zeus-born son of Laertes."

Philosophical Lives. Diogenes, as seen in his work, was a well-read scholar and industrious compiler but an amateur in philosophy. The *Lives* displays deep respect for the Greek philosophical tradition and wide knowledge of its leading figures and schools, but little engagement with philosophical issues or debates, and no philosophical depth or originality. Yet his work is unique, and uniquely valuable. Written to celebrate a central part of the Greek cultural heritage, it pays special attention to how philosophers interacted with the world around them. The evident aim is to exhibit philosophy less as a theoretical discipline than as a moral and intellectual lifestyle or "way of life" (*bios*), and in all its immense variety and detail. Biography therefore looms largest, though rarely as continuous narrative; rather, a rich stock of anecdotes, ranging from sage admonition and heroic valor to witty jibes and scandalous iconoclasm, breathes life into figures otherwise known mostly through skeletal outlines of their thought. Diogenes shows philosophers in action, at work and at play, among associates and strangers, both friendly and hostile, in public and in private. The result is a fascinating gallery of miniature portraits that vividly illustrate the foibles and follies, as well as the insight and intellect, of its iconic cast.

Organized in a sequence of ten "books" (about fifty pages each), the *Lives* opens by canvassing rival accounts of the origins of philosophy—Diogenes champions Greek over foreign traditions—then outlines a quasi-genealogical scheme of "successions," or chains of teacher-student influence, that structures the rest of the work. The scheme has two main trunks, each of which splits into multiple branches. One trunk, labeled "Ionic" after its Ionian roots, occupies books 1–7. Book 1 highlights Thales and appends a lengthy excursus on ten of his contemporaries known collectively as "wise men" (the Seven Sages). Book 2 runs through a series of Presocratics leading to Socrates and his companions, first Xenophon and then the "minor Socratics." Book 3 is devoted to Plato, and book 4 to his followers in the Hellenistic Academy, including Academic skeptics. Book 5 covers Aristotle and his followers in the Hellenistic Lyceum. Book 6 covers the Cynics, starting with the Socratic Antisthenes as their alleged founder, and book 7 covers the Stoics, as inspired by the Cynics. Diogenes then starts anew with the other trunk, labeled "Italic" after its Pythagorean roots in southern Italy. Book 8 covers Pythagoras and his successors. Book 9 treats another series of Presocratics, leading to Pyrrho and Pyrrhonian skepticism. The final book is devoted to Epicurus and his followers. Within this scheme Diogenes interweaves biographical lore—ranging from precisely dated facts to dubious or impossible anecdotes—with bibliographical data and more or less detailed accounts of the philosophers' doctrines, ideas, and intellectual innovations and achievements. The result is an exceptionally thorough and balanced survey of Greek philosophy from its sixth-century origins down to about 100 BCE, dense with citations of a host of ancient authors, philosophers, poets, historians, and scholars alike.

The work, which is complete except for the end of book 7 (the transmitted text ends abruptly midway through a long catalog of works by the Stoic Chrysippus), is highly derivative in structure and content. Diogenes' main contributions lie in selection and emphasis, and, mainly at the level of detail, in sequencing and citation. For biographical lore he is heavily indebted to Hellenistic scholarship: biographies by Antigonus of Carystus and Hermippus of Smyrna, chronological data from Apollodorus of Athens, teacher-student "successions" from Sotion of Alexandria and others. For philosophical theory he relies on summary doxographies (descriptions of doctrines) from various authorities: digests derived from Aristotle and Theophrastus for Presocratics, Hellenistic and Roman handbooks for Plato and later figures. In many areas his account is also filtered through later writers, including Philodemus, Plutarch, and Favorinus (c. 85–155 CE). Diogenes himself probably read only a small fraction of the numerous works he cites. Yet he remains a neutral reporter throughout, showing no clear sectarian allegiance, even when he twice addresses his reader: a female admirer of Plato (3.47) who apparently disdained Epicurus (10.29).

The ratio of biography to doxography varies from figure to figure, but the most influential figures as a rule receive fuller treatment on both counts. Diogenes typically begins by recording (where known) the philosopher's parents, hometown, and teachers. There follows a medley of information about his (and in one case her) looks, habits, studies, travels, family, civic achievements, and encounters with other famous figures, all seasoned with anecdotes and apothegms to indicate his wit, wisdom, and character. Many lives also outline the philosopher's distinctive theories and ideas, especially on questions of cosmology, ethics, and knowledge. After describing how the philosopher died, the lives typically conclude by citing dates for either his "acme" or his death, or both, and listing his writings, students, and "homonyms" (notable men of the same

name). Diogenes often highlights the death by reciting one or more short epigrams, often of his own composition, that serve as poetic epitaphs proclaiming the figure's lasting fame. His own efforts, which he assembled in a separate collection entitled *Pammetros* ("all meters": 1.63), rarely rise above frigid bathos and cliché, though a few achieve striking point or poignancy.

Influence. The *Lives* is a major source for philosophy before and after Plato and Aristotle. Very little original work survives from either period, and Diogenes preserves much of the information—and misinformation—we have about earlier thinkers from Thales to Socrates, and his accounts of the major Hellenistic schools (Epicureanism, Stoicism, and both Academic and Pyrrhonian skepticism) are among the most informative available. Even his accounts of Plato and Aristotle contain much that we would not otherwise know about their lives and ancient reception.

The most precious gems in Diogenes' treasury are four works by Epicurus; though modest in length, they are the only complete works to survive by any major Hellenistic philosopher: a letter *To Herodotus* summarizing his atomic theory, another *To Pythocles* on celestial and related phenomena, one *To Menoeceus* outlining his ethical principles (10.35–135), and a collection entitled *Key Doctrines* that Diogenes transcribed as the crowning "colophon" to the entire work (10.139–154). Other notable riches include a systematic summary of all three areas of Stoic theory, replete with citations of leading Stoics (7.38–160); rare documents, including wills for Plato, for Aristotle and his three successors in the Lyceum, and for Epicurus, an honorary decree for the Stoic Zeno, and a sheaf of letters to and from his subjects (all or most of them spurious); abundant verse, including more than sixty lines from the lost *Lampoons* of Timon of Phlius, eleven epigrams ascribed to Plato (most likely apocryphal), and even some verses ascribed to Socrates (2.42; cf. *Phaedo* 61b); and numerous booklists, most notably a systematic catalog for Democritus, an intriguing survey of Plato's corpus that records rival classifications of the dialogues and several editorial conventions, and long lists for Plato's first two successors in the Academy, for Aristotle and four of his associates, for the Stoic Zeno and six of his followers down to Chrysippus, and for Epicurus and three of his followers. Excepting Epicurus, however, quotations from philosophical texts are rare and mainly come from early figures, such as the opening lines of two notorious works by Protagoras.

Traces of the *Lives* appear in Byzantine works, but Diogenes remained little known in the Latin West until the Renaissance. Interest exploded after Ambrogio Traversari completed a Latin translation in 1432 (for the Medici family), which inspired so much demand that it joined the first generation of printed texts in 1472, a decade ahead of Marsilio Ficino's Plato; the Greek text did not appear in print until 1533. In the absence of comparable ancient authorities, Diogenes decisively shaped modern views of ancient philosophy. A favorite of humanists like Montaigne (who decorated his rafters with some of the many maxims he cites from it), the *Lives* provided the framework and much of the content for histories of ancient philosophy well into the twentieth century. Critical scholarship, starting in nineteenth-century Germany, has dramatically lowered Diogenes' standing by detailing the errors, distortions, and holes in his text, which is widely disparaged by scholars today. Yet the flaws of a compilation reflect the defects of its sources and authorities. Friedrich Nietzsche, whose first publications include meticulous studies of the *Lives*, offers a fairer assessment when he likens its author to a menial night-porter: no pretender to the throne, Diogenes still holds the keys to the palace of Greek philosophy.

[*See also* Biography; Epicurus; *and* Philosophy, *subentry* Greek Philosophy in the Middle Ages and the Renaissance.]

BIBLIOGRAPHY
Works of Diogenes Laertius
Lives of Eminent Philosophers. Translated by R. D. Hicks. 2 vols. Loeb Classical Library. Cambridge, Mass.: Harvard University Press, 1925. Greek text and English translation on facing pages.

Vies et doctrines des philosophes illustres. Translated by Marie-Odile Goulet-Cazé et al. Paris: Livre de Poche, 1999. French translation with richly instructive notes.
Vitae philosophorum. Edited by Miroslav Marcovich. 3 vols. Stuttgart, Germany: Teubner, 1999–2002. Greek text in vol. 1, with parallel Greek texts in vol. 2 and indices in vol. 3.
Vitae philosophorum. Edited by Tiziano Dorandi. Cambridge, U.K.: Cambridge University Press, in preparation. Greek text based on an improved understanding of the manuscript tradition.
Lives of the Ancient Philosophers. Translated by Stephen White. Cambridge, U.K.: Cambridge University Press, in preparation. English translation.

Secondary Works
Aufstieg und Niedergang der römischen Welt (ANRW) 2.36.5–6 (1992). Studies of key issues and sections.
Barnes, Jonathan. "Nietzsche and Diogenes Laertius." *Nietzsche-Studien* 15 (1986): 16–40.
Giannantoni, Gabriele, ed. *Diogene Laerzio, Storico del pensiero antico*. Elenchos 7. Naples, Italy: Bibliopolis, 1986. Studies of selected sections.
Gottschalk, Hans. "Notes on the Wills of the Peripatetic Scholarchs." *Hermes* 100 (1972): 314–42. An illuminating study of these rare documents.
Mejer, Jørgen. *Diogenes Laertius and His Hellenistic Background*. Wiesbaden, Germany: Steiner, 1978. A critical analysis of Diogenes' methods and sources.
Warren, James. "Diogenes Laertius, Biographer of Philosophy." In *Ordering Knowledge in the Roman Empire*, edited by Jason König and Tim Whitmarsh, pp. 133–149. Cambridge, U.K.: Cambridge University Press, 2007. A probing and sympathetic assessment.

Stephen White

DIOGENES THE CYNIC

(c. 412/403–c. 324/321 BCE), Cynic philosopher. Diogenes of Sinope was the emblematic Cynic philosopher among Greeks and Romans from his own time to late antiquity, and then again in the Renaissance. Our ancient sources for his life, beliefs, and way of teaching are almost entirely anecdotes, notoriously difficult to authenticate and sometimes open-ended in their meaning. According to his biography in Diogenes Laertius (6.20–81), Diogenes wrote dialogues, letters, and tragedies; although none of his writings survives, they could have been among the sources for the many anecdotes told of him throughout antiquity. Diogenes' trademark goal was to "re-value the currency" (*paracharattein to nomisma*), by which he meant to disrupt the customs circulating in society, sometimes because they were distracting people from better alternatives, and sometimes just to demonstrate that they were arbitrary. Ancient biographers attributed his exile from his native Sinope on the Black Sea to an episode involving literal defacing of the coinage, but it is possible that this was a fiction invented from an episode in one of his writings (*Pordalus*, Diogenes Laertius 6.20).

Whatever the reason for his exile, Diogenes came to Athens probably between the 360s and 345, and there he adopted a public mission similar to that of Socrates, confronting people who claimed to know something with the revelation that they did not: according to the anecdotes, this was often achieved with a biting sarcasm, and Plato allegedly called him "Socrates gone mad." Ancient tradition holds that Diogenes learned about Socraticism from Antisthenes, a discerning teacher who accepted the new pupil only after testing his character (Diogenes Laertius 6.21); this relationship has been doubted in modern scholarship on chronological grounds. Diogenes' revelation that a simple lifestyle was sufficient allegedly came from observing a mouse.

In Athens, Diogenes supposedly lived in the open during warm weather and took shelter in a barrel (or wine cask: the Greek is *pithos*) for the winter. He once owned a drinking cup, but after seeing a boy drink water from his hands, he discarded his cup in disgust. He wore no shoes, and he folded his tunic double rather than wearing a woolen cloak over the top: this also enabled him to sleep in it. Once he got old, he carried a walking stick when he went away from town: this symbolizes the itinerant life, but also connotes the authority of a public speaker. In this lifestyle Diogenes practiced radical self-sufficiency (*autarkeia*), courage (*tharsos*) through passivity to fortune, and indifference (*eupatheia*) through reason over suffering. This was in an economic realm, but also social: he found sexual satisfaction through masturbating, and he was unashamed at spitting or urinating on people when the situation called for it.

Diogenes supported himself by begging, which he considered to be repayment for his services. The Athenians allegedly loved him, and replaced his barrel when a youth broke it. Some anecdotes place him in Corinth, where it is said that he died peacefully at age ninety under his blanket, although some followers claimed that he suffocated himself because even in death he should be self-determining. According to the story of the "Sale of Diogenes," possibly a fiction started by the later Cynic writer Menippus, he moved to Corinth because he was sold as a slave to one Xeniades, whose household he then ran as a "good genius" (*agathos daimōn*) and whose sons he educated.

Diogenes' primary message concerned the ends that humans should pursue. Our evidence usually puts this in the negative terms of what should not be pursued: wealth and luxury, the conventions of marriage, and the practice of arts such as philosophy, mathematics, music, or gymnastics when they are done for their own sake rather than for making one better. But many anecdotes also isolate a special quality in being a human or a man. At the Olympics when the herald announced that a contestant had become "victor over the men," Diogenes responded that the athlete had beaten slaves: he, Diogenes, beats men. When asked what he was doing with his torch, Diogenes said that he was looking for a human being. A real human was free from all convention and self-deceit: once released from these trappings, presumably the human nature had a goodness of its own. The ancient evidence does not make this explicit, but this was the understanding in the Renaissance, when Peter Paul Rubens and others illustrated this episode in paintings. Ancient portraiture of Diogenes was also widespread: he is portrayed in his Cynic style with long hair and staff, sometimes in a barrel, and in ambiguous relationship to others, isolated in some respects but often engaged with his eyes.

Diogenes was known as author of a political text called *Republic*, which reportedly went further than Plato in abolishing marriage and the family and allowing incest and cannibalism. Diogenes might have intended to provoke dissent from the status quo rather than advocate such behaviors—he said that he liked to set the pitch too high so that others could hit the right note—but his text was received, seriously, as anathema by later philosophers. He is attributed with coining the term *kosmopolitēs*, "citizen of the universe," by which he seems to have meant that he was citizen of an ideal city, such as existed only "in the universe." That is, his allegiance as a citizen was elsewhere than in Athens or any real city, and in his era there was no way to identify that "elsewhere" in anything but fantastic terms.

[*See also* Cynics *and* Cynicism.]

BIBLIOGRAPHY

Branham, R. Bracht, and Marie-Odile Goulet-Cazé, eds. *The Cynics: The Cynic Movement in Antiquity and Its Legacy.* Berkeley: University of California Press, 1996.

Diogenes Laertius. *Lives of Eminent Philosophers.* Translated by R. D. Hicks. Loeb Classical Library. Cambridge, Mass.: Harvard University Press; London: Heinemann, 1925. See 6.20–81.

Dudley, Donald R. *A History of Cynicism from Diogenes to the Sixth Century A.D.* London: Methuen, 1937.

Susan H. Prince

DIOMEDES

The legendary Greek warrior Diomedes of Argos, son of Tydeus (one of the Seven against Thebes), is most important for his role in the *Iliad*. After Achilles withdraws from battle, Diomedes leads the Greek attack against the Trojans, which culminates in his wounding Aphrodite and Ares at Athena's direction (*Iliad* 5). When Diomedes meets Glaucus, an ally of the Trojans', and an exchange of genealogies reveals their grandfathers' friendship, they form a truce; Glaucus exchanges his gold armor for Diomedes' bronze. This exchange provokes an unusual editorial comment from the narrator on Glaucus' poor judgment (*Iliad* 6.119–236) and creates a byword for inequity (gold for bronze). Diomedes is otherwise a ruthless killer and an effective speaker, associated with the other prudent counselors Odysseus—whom Diomedes accompanies on a nighttime sortie (*Iliad* 10)—and the elderly Nestor. The poem encourages comparison with Achilles by creating parallels between the two young warriors;

overshadowed by a father he cannot remember, Diomedes lacks the complex humanity that makes Achilles the *Iliad*'s central hero.

Elsewhere in the epic tradition Diomedes assists Odysseus in several exploits surrounding Troy's fall. Before going to Troy, Diomedes participates in a successful attack on Thebes by the sons of the original Seven (*Iliad* 4.405–410) and restores his family's rule in Calydon (Apollodorus *Library* 1.8.6). On his return he finds his wife unfaithful (Aphrodite's revenge!) and goes to Italy to found Argyrippa (Arpi); his men are transformed into birds, and he slays the Colchian dragon (Lycophron *Alexandra* 592–632). Diomedes receives a blessed afterlife in the Elysian fields (*Poetae Melici Graeci* 294, 894) and worship in hero cult.

[*See also* Achilles; Homer; *and* Trojan War.]

BIBLIOGRAPHY

Andersen, Øivind. *Die Diomedesgestalt in der "Ilias."* Symbolae Osloenses, supplement 25. Oslo, Bergen, and Tromsö, Norway: Universitetsforlaget, 1978. The best literary study of Diomedes in the *Iliad* and the only book-length one. Diomedes has not received a great deal of attention from English-speaking scholars, apart from numerous article-length discussions of the significance of the exchange of armor.

Fineberg, Stephen. "Blind Rage and Eccentric Vision in *Iliad* 6." *Transactions of the American Philological Association* 129 (1999): 13–41. Though the change that Fineberg posits in Diomedes' character is not convincing, this stimulating article contains a useful bibliography that includes many of the most important interpretations of the significance of the change of armor.

Pratt, Louise. "Diomedes, the Fatherless Hero of the *Iliad*." In *Growing Up Fatherless in Antiquity*, edited by Sabine R. Hübner and David M. Ratzan, pp. 141–161. Cambridge, U.K.: Cambridge University Press, 2009. Focuses on the significance of Diomedes' fatherless state in the poem.

Whitman, Cedric H. *Homer and the Heroic Tradition.* Cambridge, Mass.: Harvard University Press, 1958. Whitman's brief characterization on pages 165–169 remains one of the most vivid and perceptive sketches in English of Diomedes' character and significance in the *Iliad*.

Louise Pratt

DIONYSIA

"Dionysia" is a generic term used to refer to three annual Attic festivals celebrated during the winter months from December to March. The oldest were the rural Dionysia, celebrated in the demes (local residential units in the countryside) in December. The others were the Anthesteria in February and the City Dionysia (also called the Great Dionysia) in March. A fourth festival, the Lenaea celebrated in January, also belongs to this Dionysiac cycle. Wine rituals played a large role in the Anthesteria and Lenaea; dramatic presentations were part of the regular schedule for the rural Dionysia, the Lenaea, and the City Dionysia.

The sources for reconstructing the activities of these festivals are scattered and fragmentary, making it impossible to describe with confidence the sequence of events for any festival in a given century, but there are some highlights that we can attempt to verify by evidence from the Classical period. The Anthesteria and Lenaea celebrated the vintage. At the three-day Athenian Anthesteria events included opening the *pithoi*, storage vessels filled with new wine, to taste it. There was a drinking contest, probably on the second day. This was probably the same day that fathers introduced their very young sons to their first taste of wine, served in tiny pitchers sometimes decorated with pictures of small children. During the Anthesteria the dead were said to roam free. The second day of the festival was considered a polluted time. Temples were closed, and people chewed buckthorn and painted their door with pitch to ward off the pollution of the dead. Events concluded on the third day with a pot of cooked grains (*panspermia*) and sacrifice to Hermes Chthonius, the god who leads the dead to the underworld.

During the Anthesteria fourteen women from families of high standing served as venerable priestesses of Dionysus at the temple of Dionysus in the Marshes, open only one day in the year. Called *gerarai*, these women took their oath of office with the wife of the *basileus* (the Athenian official in charge of the festival) presiding. Each performed a special sacrifice for Dionysus as part of their service. They had to be sexually pure, and their rituals were neither discussed nor reported. Celebrations are said to have included an enactment of a visit by night of the god himself to the wife of the *basileus*. At both the Anthesteria and Lenaea women seem to have had special responsibilities associated with the distribution of wine, but the evidence, mostly vase painting, is disputed. Vases show women dancing around temporary images of the god made by hanging a robe on a stick topped by a mask.

Greek dramas were presented at festivals of Dionysus in the context of traditional rituals. Dramatic performances for the Athenian audience were part of the Lenaea. In March before the City Dionysia could take place, an ancient wooden image of Dionysus had to be brought from the god's sanctuary at Eleutherai on the Boeotian border to the temple next to the theater in Athens. Recalling the myth of the original arrival of Dionysus from the north, this preliminary procession welcomed the god and invited him to be present at his own rituals. Athenian ephebes (young men in training for adult responsibilities) participated in the procession and brought the statue to the theater.

The major procession took place the next day. Ritual objects were carried in the parade that wound its way through the agora to the theater, where, in the sanctuary of Dionysus, at least one hundred steers would be sacrificed to provide meat for a banquet open to the entire citizen body. During the course of the procession, men wearing masks and dressed as satyrs accompanied a wagon (*phallogogeion*) that carried a large wooden phallus to the theater. The processional route and the *orchestra* (central dancing area) of the theater had to be purified before the procession itself could take place. On the processional route, under the protection of their masks, men in costume shouted obscene terms of abuse at each other and at targeted spectators. This ritual abuse was called *tothasmos*, a transitional ritual performed to prepare the audience for the most important stage of the celebrations, the spectacle of drama itself. The phallus was carried into the theater and men, unmasked and dressed like *Silēnoi*, continued to direct insults and jokes at their audience.

The context of Athenian drama was competition. There were separate contests for tragedy and comedy at the Dionysia in the city. The contest for tragedy required three tragedies and a satyr play by each of three dramatists; the contest for comedy required one comedy. The staging of plays lasted four days with, by the end of the Peloponnesian War, five comedies on the first day and three tragedies and one satyr play on each of the next three days. The late-fifth-century audience therefore saw a total of seventeen plays in four days. Being a spectator was strenuous. Winners made dedications to Dionysus in thanks for their success.

Both the Anthesteria and the Lenaea were widespread in Ionia and elsewhere before they reached Attica. The City Dionysia, however, were definitely an Athenian invention. During the second half of the fifth century BCE representatives from other cities allied to the Athenians had to bring their tribute to Athens at the time of the City Dionysia so that it could be exhibited in the theater. These envoys, who were introduced to Athenian drama by their participation in this procedure, must have been an important source of the export of the Dionysia elsewhere. Widespread construction of theaters throughout the Aegean began in the fourth century BCE. By the end of the fifth century BCE it had also become customary at Athens to announce public honors for esteemed foreigners and generous local benefactors to the assembled thousands of citizens at the Dionysia. This practice also spread with the growth of theaters abroad. By the Hellenistic period the Dionysia were popular throughout the Aegean and beyond. Sacrifices to Dionysus, with his priests presiding, accompanied performances of plays by famous Athenian tragedians and by playwrights in other cities dramatizing popular local myths elsewhere.

[See also Dionysus; Music; Theatrical Production, Greek; and Tragedy, Greek.]

BIBLIOGRAPHY

Csapo, Eric, and William J. Slater. *The Context of Ancient Drama*. Ann Arbor: University of Michigan Press, 1995. A collection of important original sources translated into English with lucid commentaries and explanations. Includes glossary, bibliography, and plates.

Humphreys, S. C. "Metamorphoses of Tradition: The Athenian Anthesteria." In *The Strangeness of Gods: Historical Perspectives on the Interpretation of Athenian Religion*. Oxford: Oxford University Press, 2004. An important critique of the (still used) nineteenth-century approach to analyzing the sparse literary sources for Greek festivals. Includes a detailed and heavily annotated discussion of the Anthesteria.

Parker, Robert. *Polytheism and Society at Athens*. Oxford: Oxford University Press, 2005. A major work that surveys all Athenian ritual practice in the context of a polytheistic system. Gives an up-to-date account of Dionysiac festivals.

Wilson, Peter, ed. *The Greek Theatre and Festivals: Documentary Studies*. Oxford: Oxford University Press, 2007. A collection of essays concentrating on inscriptions, material remains, and sculptured monuments; covers the Greek theater from its earliest appearance through the Roman period.

Susan Guettel Cole

DIONYSIUS OF HALICARNASSUS

(c. 60 BCE–c. 7 BCE), Greek historian and literary critic. Dionysius was of a patrician family in his native Halicarnassus, and his admiration for the Romans stemmed from his confidence in their ability to reassert the traditional political power of the Greek elite. Actium (31 BCE) was the event that dated Dionysius' move to Rome, and possibly precipitated it. By his own account he spent more than twenty-two years there, studying Latin, researching at least some archives, speaking with Roman authorities, and writing his history. He may have taught as a rhetorician.

Dionysius' most significant work was the *Roman Antiquities*, a twenty-volume history of Rome, of which we have nine books complete, two nearly so, and fragments of the rest. He begins with the earliest inhabitants of Italy—the Sicels and Aborigines, he maintained—and continues through to the First Punic War (264–241 BCE), the point at which Polybius' history began. Dionysius shows a highly specific geographical knowledge of Italy (he knows Strabo), offers acute judgments on chronology, discusses religion, laws, the constitution, and social life, and has a compendious knowledge of the Greek and Latin sources. Relying on the evidence of Cato the Elder among others, he concludes that the Romans were descendants of Arcadian Greeks (*Roman Antiquities* 1.31). He pauses throughout his history to point out similarities of rite or custom in support of this view. Extended set speeches and a highly detailed, even novelistic, narrative distinguish his historiography. He regards good prose style and high subject matter as keys to the best history. Though popular at the time, his style is not admired today, and he is now more often consulted than read. This is unfortunate, for his work is important evidence for the Greek elite's intellectual investment in Augustan culture and Roman self-representation.

While at Rome, Dionysius also wrote extensive literary criticism on oratory and historiography. Perhaps the most significant is "On Literary Composition." Like Cicero, Dionysius was a vigorous opponent of "Asianism," which was supposed to be florid, effeminate, emotional, and rhythmic. Its opposite was Atticism, a style modeled on the expression and vocabulary of the fourth-century Attic orators. Dionysius paints Asianism as the vulgar and decadent consequence of the oratory flourishing in the kingdoms of Alexander's Successors (*Ancient Orators* 1). Surviving examples of Asianism are too short and too few to determine the validity of his criticism. He believed in a connection between good literary taste (Atticism) and the moral exercise of power; the epochal turn to Atticism he credited primarily to the Roman conquest of the East.

Dionysius' essays on Lysias, Isocrates, Isaeus, Demosthenes, and Dinarchus are extant; those on Hyperides and Aeschines are not. He ranks Thucydides a better historian than Herodotus, and, startlingly, he offers extensive quotations that change Herodotus' original Ionic Greek into Attic, a sign of the depth of his commitment to Atticism. His analyses of the orators are often perceptive, and we have Sappho's "Hymn to Aphrodite" and Simonides' "Danae" thanks to his taste in examples of poetry.

[*See also* Historiography, Greek; Literary Criticism, Ancient; *and* Second Sophistic.]

BIBLIOGRAPHY

Works of Dionysius

Roman Antiquities. 7 vols. Translated by Earnest Cary. Loeb Classical Library. Cambridge, Mass.: Harvard University Press, 1937–1950.

Critical Essays. 2 vols. Translated by Stephen Usher. Loeb Classical Library. Cambridge, Mass.: Harvard University Press, 1974–1985.

Secondary Works

Bonner, S. F. *The Literary Treatises of Dionysius of Halicarnassus: A Study in the Development of Critical Method*. Cambridge, U.K.: Cambridge University Press, 1939.

Gabba, Emilio. *Dionysius and the History of Archaic Rome*. Berkeley: University of California Press, 1991.

C. M. C. Green

DIONYSUS

Dionysus, the god of wine, was recorded by name on Greek Linear B tablets as early as the Mycenaean period, but in classical myth and ritual he often appears as a traveler from elsewhere. He had few temples but could be encountered anywhere. As a god of arrival, he was constantly on the move and capable of sudden changes. A hymn tells how pirates kidnapped him and failed to recognize his divine status even though their ropes could not hold him. In retaliation the god entwined the mast with ivy, strung grapevines along the sail, and made wine to flow through the ship. When he made a bear appear and transformed himself into a ravening lion, the crew dove into the sea, where he changed them into dolphins (*Homeric Hymn* 7).

This story, in which people are punished for failure to recognize the god of wine as a divine authority, belongs to a type of myth in which the god's arrival is resisted. In some versions three daughters of a king, inflicted with bacchic madness, dismember a child as punishment for local insult to the god. In his *Bacchae*, Euripides presents a version that takes place at Thebes, the birthplace of Dionysus. In the play the god returns to Thebes to punish his

Dionysus. Interior of a black-figure kylix showing Dionysus in a boat with a vine. Exekias, Siren Painter, sixth century BCE. STAATLICHE ANTIKENSAMMLUNG UND GLYPTOTHEK, MUNICH, GERMANY/THE BRIDGEMAN ART LIBRARY

mother's three sisters for plotting the death of his mother, Semele. He claims to have traveled from as far away as the lands of the Bactrians and the Persians to bring his rites (*teletai*) to Thebes. His cousin Pentheus, now king, fails to recognize the god and rejects his rituals. He is determined to rid the city of the dangerous stranger, who punishes the women of Thebes with a madness (*mania*) that drives them into the mountains. The confrontation between Pentheus and the god culminates for Pentheus in a scene that requires him to dress as a female to spy on the women. Mistaking him for a lion, they tear him limb from limb, and his mother,

the deluded Agave, carries her son's head home in triumph.

Challenging Dionysus carries a great penalty. His gifts must be treated with care. Another pattern of resistance is associated with the introduction of wine, considered a dangerous substance that had to be controlled and carefully used. In an Attic version King Icarius receives Dionysus and introduces the local inhabitants to wine. When they become drunk, they believe they have been poisoned and kill Icarius. When his daughter finds her father dead, she hangs herself. Such story patterns reflect ambivalence about the power of wine and reveal anxiety about coming to terms with a divine power whose gift could be both pleasant and also destructive.

Greek customs of communal wine drinking illustrate the need to avoid the god's anger. The density of Dionysiac imagery in Attic vase painting indicates that the popularity of the god increased with the development of the nucleated polis, or city-state. Dionysus appears on more Attic black-figure pottery of the sixth century BCE than any other god does. The male community functioned best when the god was recognized and the drinking of wine controlled by the protocols of the *symposion*, communal wine drinking associated with banqueting, both private and public, where males ate and drank according to a prescribed order. The Greek standard required mixing wine with water. In a poem of Anacreon, with some irony the speaker orders a slave to bring a mixing bowl for mixing water with his wine in a ratio of ten to five "so that I can once again act the role of a proper *bassara*," or a foxy (female) follower of Dionysus (Anacreon 356a). Contrasting the barbarian custom of drinking undiluted wine, another poem enjoins the group to avoid drinking in Scythian style, "but let us practice drinking with control among beautiful hymns" (Anacreon 356b).

Temples for Dionysus are not common. He was worshipped in the countryside, but traces of his cult are also found in the heart of the city, especially in and around the theater. Successful choruses inscribed dedications to him, and his priest officiated at the sacrifices that framed the performances of his plays. The theater, with its emphasis on the delusion and illusion created by the use of costume and masks, was the prime place to celebrate the Dionysiac experience. Dionysus himself is a character in tragedy, most famously in Euripides' *Bacchae*, and also in comedy in Aristophanes' *Frogs*, where he journeys to the land of the dead to mediate a competition between Aeschylus and Euripides.

Dionysus is hard to pin down because his identity is constantly in flux. His critics are unable to tell whether he is lion, bull, man, or god. Some think his gifts are poison. Others welcome him with lively anticipation of a good time. They say that he spent the three winter months at Delphi, but he had no temple there, although his female followers were depicted on the pediment of Apollo's temple. He was a god, but Philochorus of Athens in the fourth century BCE located his tomb at Apollo's Delphic shrine. The Dionysiac boundary between mortal and immortal was very fluid. Dionysus is the only Greek divinity to share his name with his worshippers. He is called *Bakcheus* or *Bakchos*; his worshippers are called *Bakchos* (masculine) or *Bakchē* (feminine). Inscriptions on gold indicate that as early as the fifth century BCE private groups practiced secret bacchic rituals (mysteries) in anticipation of aid from Dionysus after death.

The public face of the god is displayed in the cities of the Hellenistic period where actors called "artists (*technitai*) of Dionysus" performed both classical dramas and new tragedies written to glorify the myths of individual cities. Dionysus enjoyed great popularity especially in the eastern Mediterranean. Many cities prided themselves on legends of wine miracles as gifts from the god in their honor. In imitation of the god's triumphal conquests of foreign lands, Hellenistic kings and Roman emperors claimed the title "New Dionysus." Wealthy families all the way from northern Europe to Cyprus and beyond decorated their homes with Dionysiac scenes on their walls and Dionysiac mosaics on their floors.

With Dionysus, however, it is difficult to tell whether art imitates life or life imitates art. The influence of Euripides' *Bacchae* was very strong. When the Roman general Marcus Licinius Crassus was slaughtered at Carrhae in 53 BCE, his severed head and right hand were sent to his enemy, the Parthian king. The body parts arrived, it is said, during a performance of this very play, just at the moment when a Greek actor was about to perform the part of Pentheus at his death. Handing his costume to someone else, the actor took advantage of the new prop and played the role of Pentheus' mother Agave instead, with the head of the Roman triumvir standing in for that of her son (Plutarch *Crassus* 33.1–4).

[*See also* Bacchus; Delphic Oracle; Dionysia; Gods, Greek, *subentry* The Olympian Gods; Maenads; Orphism; Satyrs; *and* Wine.]

BIBLIOGRAPHY

Carpenter, Thomas H., and Christopher Faraone, eds. *Masks of Dionysus*. Ithaca, N.Y.: Cornell University Press, 1993. A collection of twelve articles by major scholars of Greek religion; covers the various forms of the god and his rituals.

Casadio, Giovanni. *Storia del culto di Dioniso in Argolide*. Rome: Grupo Editoreale Iternazionale, 1994. A detailed study of Dionysus concentrating on a single region.

Isler-Kerényi, Cornelia. *Dionysos in Archaic Greece: An Understanding through Images*. Translated by Wilfred G. E. Watson. Leiden, The Netherlands: Brill, 2007. An English translation of the Italian edition published in 2001. The most recent study of Dionysiac iconography, with excellent plates and an extensive bibliography.

Seaford, Richard. *Dionysos*. London and New York: Routledge, 2006. A general introduction to the nature of Dionysus and the various forms of his cult.

Susan Guettel Cole

DIOSCURI

See Castor and Pollux.

DIPLOMACY

See Interstate Relations.

DISEASE

See Health and Disease.

DIVINATION AND DIVINERS

Divination, attempting to predict the future or to determine if the gods approve of a course of action, was widely practiced by peoples of the ancient Mediterranean, and the Greeks and Romans were no exception. The practice presumes divine omniscience, that is, the ability of the gods to know everything, including the course of future events. It also presupposes a concern on the part of the gods to communicate to mortals through signs, prodigies, and omens. Signs could be conveyed in numerous ways, including through the casting of lots, the seemingly random selection of verses from a book, dreams, or the observation of the behavior of animals. Prodigies are occurrences that appear to violate the natural order of things, such as talking mules or statues sweating blood. An omen is something spoken in regular conversation that is taken to be prophetic although the speaker did not intend it to be so.

Greek Divination. Though less prominent than the consultation of oracles, divination was an essential part of Greek religious practice. One of the oldest and most popular forms was divination by interpreting the behavior and song of birds (ornithomancy). Indeed, Calchas and Helenus, two prophets in Homer's *Iliad*, are both described as excelling in interpreting the flight of birds (1.69, 6.76). Bird omens are common in Greek literature, notably the omen of the snake and the sparrows in Homer's *Iliad* 2.301–332, the twin eagles and the hare in Aeschylus' *Agamemnon* (104–121), and the ominous birds observed by Tiresias in Sophocles' *Antigone* (998–1004). In Aristophanes' comedy entitled *The Birds*, birds boast that people rely on them to foretell the future in every matter of business or love (716–718).

Another common form of divination among the Greeks was the inspection of the entrails of slaughtered animals, mostly goats, lambs, and calves—though dogs and pigs were used on some occasions (Pausanius 6.2.4–5). The practice is called extispicy, from the Latin *exta* (entrails). Of particular interest was the shape of the animal's liver. Though the details are lost to us, the sources are consistent on the most general principle: a healthy liver was a good sign, but if the organ lacked a particular lobe, the gods were displeased and death was imminent (Plutarch *Cimon* 18 and *Alexander* 73). Extispicy was also used to consult the gods about proposed military expeditions (Xenophon *Anabasis* 6.4.9–5.21).

Roman and Etruscan Divination. The most famous practitioners of extispicy in the ancient world were the Etruscans in Italy. Two inscribed mirrors from Etruria bear pictures of the practice being performed by a *haruspex* (plural, *haruspices*), a priest who specialized in extispicy and the reading of weather signs. On both mirrors, the *haruspex* examines the liver he holds in his hand, as he leans forward resting on his left leg, which is propped up by a rock beneath his foot. A bronze model of a liver (presumably made for teaching purposes) was found near the town of Piacenza in 1877. It is marked into quadrants, each containing the name of an Etruscan god—presumably the god responsible for the message conveyed by that portion of the organ. The skill of Etruscan *haruspices* was so well respected that the Roman senate regularly consulted them before responding to prodigies, especially lightning strikes. After Etruscan territory was under Rome's control, the senate passed a law (at some point prior to the mid-first century BCE, but the sources are not specific) to ensure that the study of haruspicy was maintained in Etruria (Cicero *On Divination* 1.92; Valerius Maximus 1.1.1).

The Romans always identified the *haruspices* as Etruscan. A Roman form of official, public divination was practiced by a different group of priests called augurs, who determined the gods' opinions by "taking the auspices," that is, by observing the flight and behavior of birds, including both wild birds and the sacred chickens (Cicero *On Divination* 1.29 and 2.7), or by interpreting thunder and lightning. Signs could either be met with accidentally (oblative, i.e., freely offered/given) or sought out specifically (impetrative, i.e., sent by the gods in response to a request from a priest or magistrate). One procedure for taking impetrative auspices is described in Livy's *History of Rome* (1.18): after seating himself on the top of a hill, the augur marked out quadrants in the sky (*templum*, plural *templa*) using his curved augur's staff (called a *lituus*). The priest then asked Jupiter to send him clear, unambiguous signs within the boundaries of the *templa* he had just marked out. Once the signs he had specifically requested were sent, the augur accepted them and the augury was complete.

The augurs formed one of the four great public groups (colleges) of priests of the Roman state, the others being the *pontifices*, epulones, and priests for overseeing rites (*sacris faciundis*). By the late second century BCE, augurs were publicly elected from among candidates put forward by the college. By the end of the Roman Republic, there were sixteen augurs at any given time. Successful candidates retained their office for life. The senate did not consult the augurs on how to respond to prodigies; rather individual augurs assisted public magistrates, who took the auspices at the beginning of important state occasions (whence "inauguration"), such as public meetings, gatherings of the senate, and elections, as well as before military expeditions. On some occasions an augur took the auspices himself. As a college, the augurs were sometimes asked to issue rulings about the interpretation of the auspices.

Despite some small evidence for private individuals taking the auspices at events such as weddings, there is no indication that this practice was widespread in the historical period. Essentially, augury was performed by public priests and was tied to the political life of Rome. Numerous other forms of divination were available to private individuals, such as sortition (drawing lots), astrology, and oneirology (dream interpretation). Augury was thought to have been linked to politics since the very founding of the city: it was through augury that Romulus and Remus settled their dispute over which brother would found the new city (Livy 1.6–7). Since the gods had to agree before public business could be undertaken, unfavorable auspices were sufficient grounds to cancel elections or public assemblies. Improper interpretation of the auspices or incorrect performance of the ritual invalidated the results of a public vote. Failure to heed the warnings delivered through augury was uniformly thought to result in death and destruction.

Divination was a popular subject for intellectual inquiry and philosophical debate from the earliest times for both Greeks and Romans. Philosophers held opinions ranging from complete acceptance of the validity of divination as a way to understand the thoughts of the gods, to doubt about some forms and acceptance of others, to disregard for the practice altogether. A catalog of Greek philosophical opinions on the topic is found in the introduction to Cicero's treatise *On Divination* (written 45–44 BCE). This work in two books, one presenting the argument for divination and the other against it, is our most important ancient source for evidence of divinatory practices among the Greeks and Romans.

[*See also* Cicero, *subentry* Philosophy of Cicero; Delphic Oracle; Magic; Oracles; Priesthoods, Roman; Priests and Priestesses, Greek; Prophecy; Religion, *subentry* Roman Relgion; *and* Sibyls and the Sibylline Books.]

BIBLIOGRAPHY

Cicero: On Divination Book I. Translated with introduction and commentary by David Wardle. Oxford: Clarendon Press; New York: Oxford University Press, 2006.

Halliday, William R. *Greek Divination.* London: Macmillan; Chicago: University of Chicago Press, 1913. Reprint, Whitefish, Mont.: Kessinger Publishing, 2003. Also accessible via The Ancient Library http://www.ancientlibrary.com/divination.

Haynes, Sybille. *Etruscan Civilization: A Cultural History.* Los Angeles: J. Paul Getty Museum, 2000.

Rawson, Elizabeth. *Intellectual Life in the Late Roman Republic.* Baltimore: Johns Hopkins University Press, 1985.

Scheid, John. *An Introduction to Roman Religion.* Translated by Janet Lloyd. Bloomington: Indiana University Press; Edinburgh: Edinburgh University Press, 2003.

Celia E. Schultz

DIVORCE

See Marriage and Divorce.

DODONA

See Oracles.

DOME

A dome is a convex vault or ceiling in the shape of a hemisphere. Because a dome is in essence an arch rotated around its vertical axis, the dome preserves one of the arch's structural advantages: widely spaced vertical supports that create a broad unbroken interior expanse. Many of the terms used to describe the parts of an arch apply equally to a dome. The "springing" is the point at which the curved segment of the dome begins. The term "intrados" refers to the inner, or lower, surface of the dome, while "extrados" refers to the exterior, or upper, dome surface. In addition are several specialized terms for domes: the "drum" is a cylindrical or polygonal base from which the dome springs. The "oculus" is a round opening at the apex, or crown, of the dome. The term "haunch" describes the portion of the dome just above its springing. Many domes also have "ribs," radial bands of masonry that run from the springing to the crown.

Although most Roman domes are simple hemispheres, many other varieties were known. A saucer dome is a shallow dome with only a slight curvature. A semidome, or half dome, is just that: half of a hemispherical dome; semidomes are often used to roof a semicircular space such as an apse. A segmented dome is composed of curved sections that rise from a polygonal base; some feature ribs that define each section. More complex are melon or umbrella domes, which are segmented domes with an additional, outward curvature in each section of masonry.

A dome, similar to an arch, distributes the downward force of its weight in an outward manner, and thus the haunch of a large dome often requires a buttress to help counterbalance its outward thrust. Step rings are a common buttressing device. These circular bands of masonry were added to the extrados of a dome just above the springing and came into use in the second century CE; the most famous are those on the Pantheon in Rome (c. 116–128 CE). Before the adoption of step rings, simple masonry walls abutting the extrados served as buttresses—for instance, in the so-called temple of Mercury at Baiae, from the late first century BCE. To help regulate a dome's weight and thrust, Roman architects frequently adjusted the composition of its concrete, a compound made from mortar and an aggregate, typically pieces of stone. At the crown, where a lightweight material was advantageous, builders would use a lightweight aggregate such as pumice, but when strength was a priority, such as at the haunch, a heavier stone aggregate was used.

The construction process for a dome resembles that for a vault: a formwork, or wooden mold, for the concrete was built atop timber scaffolding, called centering, which supported the dome for two to three weeks as the concrete cured. Because the extrados of a dome was typically exposed to the elements, precautions had to be taken to ensure its longevity. Typically the exterior of a dome was waterproofed with a layer of hydraulic cement (known by its Italian name, *cocciopesto*). Some rare commissions received a more luxurious treatment and were covered with expensive bronze tiles: for example, the Pantheon was originally sheathed in gilt bronze roof tiles, and when these were removed in 663, a lead covering was installed in their place.

The earliest extant Roman domes belong to early first century BCE bath complexes in Pompeii, Italy. A renovation of Pompeii's Stabian Baths circa 80 BCE added a *laconicum* (sweating chamber) with an unusual conical dome and an oval oculus. Pompeii's Forum Baths, built at about the same time, had a similar domed space. Such domed sweating rooms were ideal, according to Vitruvius, who advocates that a *laconicum* be roofed with a hemispherical concrete dome; he continues to describe in detail a bronze device that could be suspended from the dome's oculus to regulate the room's heat (*De architectura* 5.10.3–5). Given how conservative Vitruvius' architectural taste was, it is not surprising that he champions vaulted bath ceilings out of the belief that their curved surfaces helped optimize the flow of heat in the rooms.

The earliest preserved concrete dome dates from the Augustan period. Built in the late first century BCE as part of a bath complex at Baiae, the so-called temple of Mercury has a hemispherical dome with an interior diameter of 70.7 feet (21.6 meters) and a circular oculus. The decision to add irregularly placed masonry buttresses after the dome was raised betrays the experimental nature of the architect's design. Over the next few decades Roman architects mastered the structural principles of the dome, as seen in the virtuoso design of a domed,

octagonal room in Nero's Domus Aurea (Golden House), built circa 65 CE. There an eight-sided segmented dome with a diameter of about forty-three feet (thirteen meters) is supported by slender piers rather than by a solid drum. The space was lit by an oculus, and the architects—Severus and Celer—designed a system of extrados buttresses that allowed for clerestory lighting in the neighboring rooms; this creative resolution of the competing demands for light and counterthrust attests to their mastery of the structural dynamics of the dome.

The most renowned of all Roman domes is that of the Pantheon in Rome, which since antiquity has been lauded as an architectural marvel. Built circa 116–128 CE under Hadrian and "vaulted over in lofty beauty" (Ammianus Marcellinus 16.10.14, writing c. 390), the Pantheon has a hemispherical concrete dome with square coffers and a round oculus that encloses an immense, unbroken interior space (the interior diameter is about 142 feet, or 43 meters). Hadrian had an especial interest in architecture and is said to have made architectural drawings of melon domes (Cassius Dio 69.4.2, writing c. 230). Unsurprisingly, Hadrian's villa in Tivoli, Italy (c. 125 CE), contains many innovative domed and vaulted forms, including an impressive melon half-dome over the so-called Serapeum, an outdoor dining pavilion.

In the late third century and early fourth century, large domed tombs—many modeled on the appearance of the Pantheon—were the vogue for Rome's elite. The dynastic tomb erected by Maxentius on the Via Appia circa 306–312 exemplifies the new type of grandiose funerary monument. The tomb mimics the Pantheon's characteristic combination of a round, domed cella with a pedimented facade, but on a smaller scale—its diameter is 82 feet (25 meters)—and with the addition of an annular crypt intended for the sarcophagi of Maxentius and his descendants. After the Empire the dome went on to become one of the central architectural expressions of the Christian church, achieving new and unprecedented glory in the Byzantine world.

[*See also* Arch; Architecture, *subentry* Forms and Terms; Pantheon; *and* Vaults and Vaulting.]

BIBLIOGRAPHY

Adam, Jean-Pierre. *Roman Building: Materials and Techniques.* Translated by Anthony Mathews. London: Batsford, 1994. Chapter 6 offers a comprehensive introduction to the topic, though some of Adams's dates have been questioned.

Lancaster, Lynne C. *Concrete Vaulted Construction in Imperial Rome: Innovations in Context.* New York: Cambridge University Press, 2005. A primary resource on the construction, development, and structural dynamics of Roman concrete domes.

MacDonald, William L. *The Pantheon: Design, Meaning, and Progeny.* Cambridge, Mass.: Harvard University Press, 1976. A fundamental source on Rome's most famous dome and its antecedents.

Elisha Ann Dumser

DOMESTIC ARCHITECTURE

Greek and Roman houses shared some superficial resemblances in plans and structure, but their underlying principles of organization differed considerably. Both the Greeks and the Romans built unroofed spaces, whether courtyards or atria with rooftop openings, into their homes in order to illuminate and ventilate the domestic interiors. Greek houses were usually planned with the idea of separating private family life from the gaze of nonfamily members, whereas Roman houses were usually planned so that outsiders could literally see through the whole house. The differences are the result of disparate social practices: the Greeks considered the *oikos* (house and family) as private, while the Romans considered their houses as conveyers of the image of wealth and status.

Greek Houses. In their plans, Greek houses throughout history represent a mediation between the outside world and the inside. In earlier periods the open air of the court contrasted with the enclosed rooms; in the Hellenistic period the public rooms for entertainment contrasted with the private spaces for family life. The houses of early Iron Age Greece had a variety of forms, including rectangular, oblong, and apsidal, depending in large part on the materials of their construction; those with rectilinear plans were covered with flat roofs, and those with curvilinear ends were roofed with thatch. The walls were formed of low stone socles topped with mud brick, a combination of materials that continued in use as the preferred form of wall structure through the Hellenistic period. Early examples of Greek domestic architecture had two other features that persisted in later periods: a southern orientation and an open courtyard. The first is noted by Classical authors, including Xenophon (*Memorabilia* 3.8.8–10) and Aristotle (*Oeconomica* 1345a), as preferable for providing light and warmth in the winter months when the sun is in the Southern Hemisphere and for allowing a cooler environment when the sun is overhead in summer. The courts of these early dwellings were simply open spaces situated to the south of the one- or two-room houses, such as at Megara Hyblaea in eastern Sicily.

The Archaic period (600–480 BCE) saw changes in Greek houses that resulted both from an improvement in construction techniques and more importantly from an evolution in political and social structures. Perhaps the more noticeable and most lasting change was the inclusion of the unroofed courtyard within the built structure of the house, a change that allowed the activities conducted in the court to be hidden from public view. Interior courtyards are not a regional feature; they appear in houses both on the Greek mainland, such as in the Archaic houses in Athens, and in colonial sites, such as Monte San Mauro in Sicily. The enclosed courtyards of Archaic houses do not sport either full peristyles or even colonnades; rare evidence for single posts provides proof of shed roofs built on one side of some domestic courts. Connected to the change in the location of the domestic courtyard is the form of roofing. Baked clay tiles that were first developed in the seventh century for temples came to be used in houses in the later Archaic period. Terra-cotta tiles enabled the residents to collect the water that ran off the pitched roofs during the rainy season.

From a relatively early date the courtyards of Greek houses appear to have had two common, albeit not ubiquitous, forms. In mainland Greece and to the west, many houses from the late Archaic period into the Hellenistic had a broad corridor to

Greek House. Remains of ancient houses in Priene (Samsun Kale, Turkey). VANNI/ART RESOURCE, NY

the north of the courtyard that served as both an entrance and a buffer to the important rooms located on the north side of the house. The corridor was often fashioned as a portico, with columns or pilasters screening it from the open court. The excavators at Olynthus, in northeast Greece, borrowed the term *pastas* from Vitruvius 6.7.1–7 to refer to this corridor. In contrast, some houses, such as those at Priene and Colophon in Asia Minor, have a common architectural unit, labeled the *prostas* by the excavators of Priene. The term—also borrowed from the same passage of Vitruvius—labels a two-room suite with open porch, often distyle in antis to the south, and a larger square room behind. The *prostas* is considered by many to have descended from the megaron unit of Bronze Age architecture. In effect, both the broad corridor of the *pastas* and the porchlike *prostas* have the same effect of shielding the inner rooms to the north from the direct rays of the sun or the bustle of daily life in the courtyard. Many early studies of Greek domestic architecture were concerned with establishing a typology of houses based on whether they possessed a *pastas* or a *prostas*, a fixation that limited the examination of how life was lived in the various buildings.

Although Greek domestic architecture of the Classical period is not significantly different in form from that of the late Archaic, several new rooms appeared in Classical houses. A vestibule was added to serve as a buffer between the public world outside the house and the private world within, and its doorway to the street was usually positioned so that there was no direct line of sight from the entrance into the core of the house. The resulting single-entrance courtyard house enabled the Greeks to limit access to the *oikos* and so maintain control of social behavior in the house. Common to many Classical houses, but not ubiquitous, is the *andrōn*, a square room with a low platform along its walls; on the platform sat couches on which all the male diners reclined, facing toward the center of the room. The *andrōn* was a place for entertaining guests, and there is little evidence that it had much use in daily life. The dining rooms were sometimes entered through their own anterooms, spaces used both to buffer the noise of a raucous symposium and for the preparation of the diners' meal. Houses without purpose-built *andrōnes* could accommodate a dinner party with the proper arrangement of couches in any suitable room.

Roman House. View of the garden with birdbath, Domus Vettiorum (Casa dei Vettii), Pompeii, Italy. PHOTOGRAPH BY ROBERT B. KEBRIC

There is little evidence that Greek houses of the Archaic period possessed upper stories, but literary sources, such as Lysias 1 and Lysias 3.6 (*Against Simon*), note their existence in Classical houses and suggest that they were used as private living space. Given that mud brick was the most common building material for the walls of houses, neither it nor the wooden joists and ceiling beams have survived to reveal much about the appearance of upper floors. More telling are staircases, usually surviving only in the bottom-most stone step, from which a wooden flight of steps once rose. Such step blocks appear in the courtyards of some of the Classical houses at Olynthus and in one at Athens.

It has long been a truism that Greek houses were arranged so that the women within were secluded from outsiders; both the layout that ensured privacy and the written sources appear to confirm this

belief. In his *Oeconomicus* (9.5), Xenophon wrote of the *gynaikōnitis*, the women's quarters, a series of rooms that also figure prominently in the account of Greek houses by Vitruvius; this purported description of Greek houses by the first century BCE Roman architectural historian has long colored interpretation of Greek houses. A close examination of the use of the term *gynaikōnitis* in the fifth and fourth centuries BCE reveals that it most often indicates the quarters for female slaves, who were probably sequestered so that they did not have sexual relations with their male counterparts. Women's quarters in Greek houses were likely determined as much by the time of day and who was in the house as by any other factor. The distribution of assemblages of cookware and household tools shows that women probably had the run of the house—especially the courtyard, which served as the center of daily life—for most of the day, and they retreated to more secluded rooms when unrelated men were present in their homes.

Because of the ephemeral nature of daily worship in Greece, physical evidence for domestic religion is sparse. Prayers, fires in the hearth, hung foliage, and incense marked many household rites. The hearth (*hestia*) was the center of worship in the home, although few fixed hearths have been found in Classical and Hellenistic houses; portable braziers that burned charcoal and were used for heating and cooking were the likely substitutes for a built fireplace. The Athenians in particular celebrated the rites of passage—birth, marriage, and death—at the family hearth, although deities other than Hestia were recognized in household rites. Zeus Herkeios in particular appears in the written sources. Some houses possessed actual altars, but large immovable altars were rare; portable altars made of terra-cotta or stone are more frequently found. Many houses contained terra-cotta figurines, most of which played a role in domestic worship in the Classical period. In Hellenistic houses some figurines may have instead served as domestic decor.

Interior decoration is virtually unknown in Archaic Greek houses and is uncommon in the Classical period (480–323 BCE). The few attempts at embellishing the interior of the Greek house appear in the *andrōn*, where the intended audience was the invited male guest. Mosaic floors were framed by the platforms for the dining couches. Mythological scenes appear in the floors, with Dionysiac scenes preferred, a logical choice given that the *andrōnes* were the location of the symposium. Evidence for wall painting is poorly preserved in Classical houses because it was done on plaster on the now-degraded mud-brick walls. Remains from Olynthus suggest that some paintings mimicked monumental masonry.

Attempts have been made to identify type houses in Classical cities: that is, houses of identical lot size and similar plan that were the physical expression of *isonomia*, equal political status in the democratic city-state. House lots of comparable size built in blocks and framed by the urban grid of streets are attested in both colonial cities, such as Megara Hyblaea, and refounded cities, such as Olynthus

and Piraeus in mainland Greece. But Athens, the democratic polis for which we have the best evidence, reveals no traces of equal-sized house lots. Social equality in the polis was not the same as economic equality, and this difference may account for the absence of equal-sized housing lots in many city-states.

Greek Farmhouses. Considerable attention has been paid to houses in urban areas, but archaeologists have uncovered farmhouses in parts of the Greek world, particularly in eastern Attica and colonial sites around the Black Sea. Although rural settings did not impose the constraints of limited space and proximity of neighbors experienced in urban environments, there are distinct similarities between the houses in the countryside and those of the cities. The southern orientation of rooms, the unroofed courtyards, and some of the purpose-built rooms, such as the *andrōn*, are found in farmhouses. Towers, of either square or round plan, are often built into the rural homes; the towers' upper floors probably served as strong rooms to protect valuables, including grain, as well as vulnerable family members in areas far from the protection of friends, family, and neighbors.

The latter fourth century BCE represents a turning point in the form and size of Greek houses. The modest dwellings of the Classical past were eclipsed by larger, more complexly planned, and more elaborately decorated homes. The trend toward luxury was in large part a response to the rise of Alexander the Great and the Successors. As individual political power in the polis was replaced by that held exclusively by the kings, the agora and public spaces no longer served as the arena for powerful men. Houses became larger and incorporated increasingly more architectural and decorative forms that were previously found in the public areas of the polis. The influence of the Macedonian palaces on domestic architecture and decoration is unmistakable. Double courtyards, multiple dining rooms, numerous floor mosaics, and faux marble painted stucco all began there and ultimately found their way into private homes, first of the wealthy and later of the middle classes.

Hellenistic houses usually had peristyles in their courtyards, often with the Doric order on the ground floor and the Ionic in the upper. The courtyards were invariably paved; the modest terra-cotta tiles or mosaics with pictorial scenes provided an impervious surface to facilitate the runoff of water into cisterns that lay under the courts. In houses with two courtyards, one was usually the focal point for rooms used for entertaining guests. The *andrōn* of the Classical period persisted in the Hellenistic, but the pavement was no longer fashioned with a platform, probably to allow a more flexible use of the space and more variation in the arrangement of the dining couches. Interior decoration of all media abounds in these spaces; along with the expansion of houses, floor mosaics experienced a technical shift, with the pebbles previously used replaced by cubic tesserae. In their appearance the resulting pavements more closely approximated painting and thus produced a more impressive effect. Domestic sculpture seems to have been completely absent in Classical houses, but in the Hellenistic period sculpture was displayed in courtyards and in rooms for entertainment. Though domestic sculpture was first used for household ritual, the numerous images of Aphrodite and Dionysiac images from Hellenistic houses more closely approximate domestic decor.

The second courtyard in some Hellenistic houses contrasted markedly with its more highly decorated neighbor. Second courtyards appear to have had a more purely domestic function, seen in the lesser attention to both the architectural and the decorative programs, as well as in the service nature of many of the surrounding rooms. Here one found the kitchen and bathroom, rooms that were less frequently built in Classical houses as dedicated spaces. Hellenistic houses at Morgantina, Monte Iato, and Eretria prove that the domestic quarters warranted as much space as the public quarters did, even if they were less impressively decorated.

Roman Houses. In some respects Roman houses varied greatly from their Greek cousins. The Roman house (*domus*) of Republican date had an axial arrangement that encouraged the viewer to enter the house. Social norms dictated this arrangement that ran so counter to the Greek tendency toward keeping the interior of the house private. In the ideal Roman house the street door, the vestibule (*fauces*), the atrium, and the *tablinum* (study for the *paterfamilias*) were aligned axially so that passersby in the street or those entering the front door might see into the house. The interior decoration of mosaics and painted stucco were created with the intent of further enhancing the impression of wealth and status. In some houses of modest means, such as the House of the Samnite at Herculaneum, the openings to rooms were positioned so that the effect of grandeur might be enhanced. These features speak to the way in which Roman houses were used as physical expressions of wealth and status, but the axiality might have been inherited from earlier Etruscan homes.

The Roman house was seen by visitors at its best during the morning *salutatio*, when clients would pay their respects to their patron in his home. Positioned in his atrium or *tablinum*, the patron would be surrounded not only by domestic trappings and expensive decor, but also by images of his ancestors, placed in the atrium or in the family shrine (*lararium*). The legitimacy bestowed by his ancestry was a further enhancement of the patron's status. The use of Roman domestic architecture and decor as conveyors of status was manipulated to great effect by the first emperor Augustus, who reinforced his position as *primus inter pares* (first among equals) by living in a Republican-style house of no remarkable size on the Palatine Hill. In the second century CE and after, the axially located atrium was no longer the dominant form in the house; an apsidal hall of often grand scale and monumental decoration replaced the atrium as the location for the *salutatio*.

In the second century BCE when the Romans came into direct and frequent contact with the Greeks, forms from Hellenic architecture began to pervade the Italian peninsula. In houses, that Greek influence can be seen in the addition of colonnaded courtyards, clearly borrowed from Hellenistic domestic architecture. Republican houses have one or even two courtyards, which are most often planted with a garden, rather than paved in the

Greek fashion. The domestic courtyards were rapidly integrated into the plans of Roman houses in order to enhance the display for guests, and they were decorated not only with carefully chosen plants but also with fountains, sculpture, and furniture. The fountains and their plumbing provide ample evidence of the extent of private water supply in Roman towns and cities.

The concepts of public and private appear not to have been so sharply defined in Roman houses as they were in Greek, probably because the Roman home was used to convey messages of wealth and status to outsiders. The *cubicula* or bedrooms were more than private chambers for sleeping; written evidence supports their having been used for meeting business associates as well as for intimate encounters. Though slave quarters have been adduced from both textual sources and graffiti on the walls of undecorated rooms, many slaves slept on the floor outside or even in the rooms of their masters.

Guests were entertained in a wide variety of rooms that the ancient writers call *triclinia* and *oeci*; although the latter word is a Latinized form of *oikos*, there appears to be nothing Greek about the elaborately decorated chambers found in the Roman homes. The Roman practice of dining three to a couch in the triclinium differed from the Greek, and the rooms in which the triclinia were placed differ accordingly. Whereas the Greek *andrōn* was usually closed off from the rest of the house and its inhabitants, the Roman dining room was often open in such a way that the diners had carefully planned views of the decorative glories of the house. Later Roman houses were sometimes provided with a *stibadium*, a semicircular couch on which the diners reclined all together. The *stibadium* might be placed either in an apsidal room or in a garden setting and was positioned to provide an optimal view of the house and its decor.

The tendency seen in Hellenistic houses to create specialized rooms such as kitchens and bathrooms continues and is expanded in Roman houses. Kitchens with built countertops for food preparation and latrines with drains are found in even modest Roman homes. During the high Empire and later, bathing complexes complete with a full sequence of *tepidarium*, *caldarium*, and *frigidarium* were constructed in private houses and villas.

In the imperial cities such as Rome and Ostia there was extensive urban housing in *insulae*, apartment buildings that bear a remarkable resemblance to their modern counterparts. *Insulae* were usually several stories tall and housed many people, with several apartments located on each floor. Common courtyard space in the center of the building, usually equipped with a well and sometimes with a semiprivate latrine, was the only feature reminiscent of the typical *domus*. The apartments might comprise just a few rooms, usually without the axial arrangement found in the homes of the more well-to-do. The construction of the *insulae* was notoriously shoddy; the frequent fires in Rome can be attributed in large part to the poor construction, the inferior materials, and the overcrowding in the many *insulae*.

Roman Villas. In the Roman countryside, one found villas that were luxurious vacation homes or were working farms or, on occasion, were both. The coast of Italy was lined with villas belonging to the wealthy and successful men of Rome; individuals such as the politician and orator Cicero or the emperors might possess several country homes for relaxation. In their overall plan, villas contain most of the same rooms that Roman houses do and follow some of the same general layout. Notably different from Roman townhouses and from Greek houses before them, Roman villas often were situated in the landscape so that the home was seen to best advantage from a distance and so that the villa might have an optimal view over the surrounding country or seaside. Colonnaded loggias and carefully placed windows framed the view and manipulated access to that view. Vacation villas displayed wall paintings and mosaics that rivaled those in the urban houses; the role of the house as a conveyor of the message of wealth was alive and well in the villa, where the patron entertained many guests.

Villas that served as working farms were also impressive in scale and were outfitted to allow for the production of wine, oil, or other agricultural commodities. Seaside villas from the late Republic onward were often provided with *piscinae* (fish farms). In general the living quarters of working villas were not as sumptuously decorated as the buildings dedicated to the relaxation of the owner. Farm managers might occupy the domestic quarters of the farming villas, and one large complex at Settefinestre in Italy has accommodations for the large number of slaves who worked the fields.

[*See also* Baths; Fountains and Nymphaea; Furniture; Gardens; *and* Mosaics.]

BIBLIOGRAPHY

Cahill, Nicholas D. *Household and City Organization at Olynthus.* New Haven, Conn.: Yale University Press, 2002.

Clarke, John R. *The Houses of Roman Italy, 100 B.C.–A.D. 250: Ritual, Space, and Decoration.* Berkeley: University of California Press, 1991.

Ellis, Simon. *Roman Housing.* London: Duckworth, 2000.

Hales, Shelley. *The Roman House and Social Identity.* Cambridge, U.K.: Cambridge University Press, 2003.

Hoepfner, Wolfram, ed. *Geschichte des Wohnens.* Vol. 1: *5000 v. Chr.–500 n. Chr.: Vorgeschichte, Frühgeschichte, Antike.* Stuttgart, Germany: Deutsche Verlags-Anstalt, 1999.

Hoepfner, Wolfram, and Ernst-Ludwig Schwandner. *Haus und Stadt im klassischen Griechenland.* 2nd ed. Wohnen in der klassischen Polis 1. Munich: Deutscher Kunstverlag, 1994.

Jameson, Michael. "Private Space and the Greek City." In *The Greek City from Homer to Alexander*, edited by Oswyn Murray and Simon Price, pp. 171–195. Oxford: Clarendon Press; New York: Oxford University Press, 1990.

Mielsch, Harald. *Die römische Villa: Architektur und Lebensform.* Munich: C. H. Beck, 1987.

Nevett, Lisa. *House and Society in the Ancient Greek World.* Cambridge, U.K.: Cambridge University Press, 1999.

Pomeroy, Sarah B. *Xenophon Oeconomicus: A Social and Historical Commentary.* Oxford: Clarendon Press; New York: Oxford University Press, 1994.

Wallace-Hadrill, Andrew. *Houses and Society in Pompeii and Herculaneum.* Princeton, N.J.: Princeton University Press, 1994.

Walter-Karydi, Elena. "Die Nobilitierung des Wohnhauses: Lebensform und Architektur im spätklassischen Griechenland." *Xenia* 35 (1994): 5–81.

Barbara Tsakirgis

DOMITIAN

(Titus Flavius Domitianus; 51–96 CE), emperor of Rome from 81 to 96, the last ruler of the Flavian dynasty. Domitian was the youngest child of the emperor Vespasian and was born in Rome during his father's consulship. Domitian was raised and educated in the city—although, unlike his elder brother Titus, not in the imperial court—and he showed an interest in literature and poetry that Tacitus and Suetonius derided as "feigned." He was likely in Rome at the time of the death of Nero in 68 and certainly was there during the so-called Year of the Four Emperors, 69, although the details of his life at that time are not known. On 18 December 69, Domitian, only eighteen years old, along with his uncle the prefect of the city and his cousin, both named Titus Flavius Sabinus, came into conflict with Vitellius and his troops. As a result the Flavians took refuge on the Capitoline Hill; Domitian's uncle was killed in the ensuing siege, but Domitian escaped, possibly disguised as a worshiper of Isis. Two days later Vitellius was dead, Vespasian—still absent from the city—had been proclaimed emperor, and Domitian took a public role as his father's representative. Domitian's ambitious attempts to exert authority at this time brought him into conflict with Vespasian's generals and earned him a reputation for greed and arrogance. When Vespasian returned to the city in the fall of 70, he rebuked Domitian for his behavior.

It was at this time that Domitian married Domitia Longina, the daughter of the Neronian general and victim Corbulo; Domitian may have intended this marriage to help him begin his military career. However, although Vespasian gave him many honorific titles in the 70s—including suffect consulships in 71, 73, 75, 76, 77, and 79; the titles Caesar and *princeps iuventutis*, normally given to imperial princes; and numerous priesthoods—he had few real responsibilities. Even after Titus' accession in 79, Domitian's public presence was limited. So at the time of Titus' death in September 81 and Domitian's accession to power the following day, his public reputation was based entirely on his arrogance in

70 and his subsequent retirement and literary indulgence.

Domitian's style of rule was openly autocratic, which made him unpopular with senators. He refused to repeat Titus' vow not to try any senator on capital charges; he monopolized magistracies, holding the consulship ten times as emperor and, in 85, having himself declared *censor perpetuus* (censor for life) without a colleague; and he limited the senate's authority and relied on a closed group of advisers consisting of imperial freedmen, relatives, and some members of the senate. He was the first emperor since Tiberius (r. 14–37) to spend significant amounts of time outside the city, either in his villa at Alba (twenty miles from Rome) or on military campaigns on the Rhine or Danube frontiers. On the basis of these campaigns he celebrated multiple triumphs and adopted triumphal dress even in the senate, although Tacitus contrasts the general Agricola's real successes in Britain with Domitian's trumped-up victories. He imposed his literary and artistic tastes on his courtiers, earning him the nickname "the bald Nero," and he sought to be addressed as "master and god."

In 89 a rebellion broke out on the Rhine under Saturninus, the governor of Germania Superior. This may not have been a serious conspiracy, and Domitian dealt with it swiftly. However, the incident made the already paranoid emperor even more cautious, and the 90s saw numerous attacks on senatorial and aristocratic leaders. In particular Domitian lashed out against the relatives and friends of Publius Clodius Thrasea Paetus and Helvidius Priscus, the Stoic senators who had been executed by Nero and Vespasian, respectively. He expelled philosophers and astrologers from the city on two occasions, in 88/9 and in 95/6, perhaps fearing some kind of intellectual resistance. In 95 he turned against his own family, executing his cousin Titus Flavius Clemens (consul for that year), along with a number of members of his own household; he also banished Clemens' wife, Domitian's own niece Flavia Domitilla, even though he appears to have thought of Clemens' two sons as his potential heirs.

As emperor, Domitian adopted a severe attitude toward public morality that seems at odds with his private excesses. In 83 and in 90 he oversaw the trials and executions of Vestal Virgins on charges of immorality. He promoted a religious platform heavily reminiscent of that of Augustus, including a celebration of the Secular Games (*ludi saeculares*); he also instituted the Capitoline Games. He particularly identified Isis and Minerva as his personal patrons, although he also promoted the worship of his deified father and brother, as well as the *gens Flavia* (the spirit of the Flavian family); Domitian completed and dedicated a temple to Vespasian and Titus at the western end of the Forum in about 87.

Domitian undertook numerous expensive public building projects in Rome and beyond, including the construction of the Via Domitiana that joined Rome to Naples, numerous temples, and the lavish imperial residence on the Palatine. In addition, he was the first emperor to increase the pay of the legionary and auxiliary soldiers, an act that made him popular with the army. It was probably in connection with this action that Domitian devalued the currency, which seems to have allowed him to leave behind a full treasury.

Domitian had a son with Domitia Longina, but the child was dead by 81, and it is possible that his brief divorce from his wife in 83 or 84 may have been motivated by his concerns over the succession. He looked to his extended family for an heir, but he seems to have been unable to trust fully even his family. Suetonius identifies the death of Clemens as the act that led some of Domitian's own palace officials and the Praetorian prefects—and possibly also Domitia Longina—to conspire against him, and Domitian was assassinated on 18 September 96. His death greatly upset the army, which sought to deify him, but the senate was overjoyed and condemned his memory.

[*See also* Flavian Family and Dynasty; Trajan; *and* Vespasian.]

BIBLIOGRAPHY

Boyle, A. J., and W. J. Dominik, eds. *Flavian Rome: Culture, Image, Text*. Leiden, The Netherlands, and Boston: Brill, 2003. A collection of articles on the history, society, culture, art, and literature of the Flavian period.

Darwall-Smith, Robin H. *Emperors and Architecture: A Study of Flavian Rome.* Brussels, Belgium: Latomus, 1996. An overview and discussion of the monumental architectural program of the Flavian emperors, most of which was completed under Domitian.

Jones, Brian W. *The Emperor Domitian.* London and New York: Routledge, 1992. A biography of the emperor Domitian that covers the major events of his reign and explores the political, military, and administrative issues connected with his reign.

Nauta, Ruuard R. *Poetry for Patrons: Literary Communication in the Age of Domitian.* Leiden, The Netherlands, and Boston: Brill, 2002. A study of the literary culture of Domitian's court, particularly on the relationship between the emperor and the poets Statius and Martial.

Karen Acton

DORIANS

Dorians were one of the three principal subdivisions of the ancient Greeks, the other two being Ionians and Aeolians. Pan-Hellenic genealogy derived their name from Dorus son of Hellen: Aegimius son of Dorus adopted Heracles' son Hyllus and made him an heir side-by-side with his two sons; the three became the eponymous heroes of the Dorian tribes—Hylleis, Dymanes, and Pamphili. The Dorians of the historical period occupied large territories in the Peloponnesus (Sparta, Argos, Corinth, Sicyon, Epidaurus) and adjacent lands (Megara, Aegina); their settlements were spread over the eastern Mediterranean (for example, Crete, Melos, Rhodes, Cos, Thera), as well as over Italy (Taras, Rhegium), Sicily (Syracuse, Acragas, Gela, Himera), and North Africa (Cyrene). The Dorian communities were distinguished by their specific dialect, their division into three tribes (the Ionians had four), and by their political, social, and religious institutions. Sparta and Crete, where the pre-Dorian population was not allowed to become part of the community but was subjugated and reduced to serfdom, are often considered as representing the characteristically Dorian system of rule.

According to Greek tradition, the Dorians migrated into the Peloponnesus from their homeland in the northwestern region of Epirus soon after the Trojan War; they were led by kings who traced their descent to Hyllus ("the Heraclids"): this is why the emergence of the Dorians in southern Greece was traditionally referred to as "Return of the Children of Heracles." After having defeated and displaced the inhabitants of the land, the Achaeans, the Dorian leaders divided the territory of the Peloponnesus by throwing lots: this is how the historical regions of Argos, Sparta, and Messenia (later conquered by Sparta) were created. At the same time, it is important to keep in mind that the widespread term "Dorian invasion" or, which seems more preferable, "the coming of the Dorians," relates to miscellaneous population movements from the periphery to the center of the Mycenaean world that took place at the end of the Bronze Age, by no means all of them associated with the Dorians proper (thus the southward movements of the Boeotians and northwestern Greeks should also be taken into account).

The "Return of the Children of Heracles" is represented in ancient sources as having taken place in two stages: after the first attempt to conquer the Peloponnesus, the Dorians turned back to their base on the plain of Marathon, only to return and to complete the attack after three generations. The Dorians' first attempt to enter the Peloponnesus is envisaged as an advance of the full-scale army led by Hyllus; yet, joint forces of the Peloponnesians succeeded in stopping the invaders at the Isthmus of Corinth, where Hyllus was killed by the Arcadian Echemus in a single combat. It was only three generations later that the Dorians actually conquered the Peloponnesus. They did not come now through the Isthmus but crossed the Corinthian Gulf from Naupactus in the northwest, being guided on their way by the one-eyed Aetolian Oxylus; the latter brought with him many Aetolians (a northwestern Greek tribe), who occupied what was to become Elis. Finally, the population of the Peloponnesus fled before the invaders and concentrated in new areas, first and foremost

---

The Dorians in Verse

But Heracles unvanquished sowed your stock:
  take heart! Zeus bows not yet beneath the yoke.
Fear not the throng of men, turn not to flight,
  but straight toward the front line bear your
    shield,
despising life and welcoming the dark
  contingencies of death like shafts of sun.
    (Tyrtaeus, Sparta, seventh century BCE; translated
      by M. L. West)

They sleep, the mountain peaks,
  the clefts, ridges, and gullies,
  and all the creatures that the dark earth feeds,
  the animals of the glen, the tribe of bees,
  the monsters of the salt purple deeps.
They sleep, the tribes
of winging birds...
    (Alcman, Sparta, seventh to sixth century BCE;
      translated by M. L. West)

In spring the Cydonian quince-trees
watered from freshets of rivers
where Nymphs have their virginal gardens
blossom, and vine-shoots are growing
under the shade of the branches;

but Love in me at no season is laid to rest.
Like the North Wind of Thrace that comes blazing
with lighting, he rushes upon me,
sent by the Cyprian goddess
with withering frenzies, dark-lowering,
undaunted, and from the foundations
he overwhelms and devastates my heart.
    (Ibycus from Rhegium, Italy, sixth century BCE;
      translated by M. L. West)

Join me, Muse, in rejecting stories of battle,
  and celebrate weddings of gods and banquets
    of men
and feasts of the blessed
when the swallow in springtime rings out.
Such are the lovely-haired Graces' gift to the public
That we must sing, devising an elegant Phrygian
    melody,
at the arrival of spring.
    (Stesichorus from Himera, Sicily, sixth century
      BCE; translated by M. L. West.)

— *Greek Lyric Poetry*. Oxford World's Classics.
Oxford: Oxford University Press, 1994.

---

in Achaea and Attica. The Dorian kings who entered the Peloponnesus were the Heraclids Temenus, who became king of Argos; his brother Cresphontes, who became king of Messenia; and their nephews Eurystheus and Procles, who became kings of Sparta.

The late emergence of the Dorians in southern Greece is strongly suggested by the dialect map of the region. The Doric dialect, which, together with northwestern Greek, belongs to the west Greek group, is a typical peripheral dialect, which has retained many archaic features that were lost in the dialects of the central group. But in the historical period Doric is found wedged in between such more advanced dialects as Arcadian on the one hand and Attic on the other, thus indicating its intrusive character. This and other evidence supplied by the dialects is clear-cut to such a degree that it urges us to assume the "coming of the Dorians," whether or not a tradition of the Dorian invasion is available. However, many archaeologists dispute this tradition, arguing that, although the break in continuity at the end of the second millennium BCE is incontestable, "the coming of the Dorians" as such has not been sufficiently corroborated by the archaeological record.

While especially acclaimed by ancient authors on account of their superior warfare, the Dorians also contributed to Greek culture in music ("Doric mode"), poetry, drama, art, and architecture ("Doric order").

[*See also* Greek, *subentry* The Greek Language; Heraclidae; Language, Theories of; *and* Peloponnesus.]

BIBLIOGRAPHY

Primary Works

Apollodorus. *The Library.* Translated by J. G. Frazer. Cambridge, Mass.: Harvard University Press, 1921. Loeb Classical Library. Book 2, Chapter 8.2–5.

Diodorus Siculus. *Library of History.* Translated by C. H. Oldfather. Cambridge, Mass.: Harvard University Press, 1935. Loeb Classical Library. Vol. II, Book 4, Chapter 58.1–5.

Herodotus. *The Histories.* Translated by Aubrey de Selincourt. Revised by John M. Marincola. New York: Penguin, 2003. Penguin Classic. Book 9, Chapter 26.

Pausanias. *Guide to Greece.* Translated by Peter Levi. Harmondsworth, U.K.: Penguin Books, 1971. Penguin Classics. Book 1, Chapter 44.10; Book 2, Chapter 18.6–7; Book 4, Chapter 3.3–5; Book 5, Chapters 3.5–4.2; Book 8, Chapters 5.1 and 6, and 45.3.

Plato. Laws. Translated by A. E. Taylor. In *The Collected Dialogues of Plato.* Princeton, N.J.: Princeton University Press, 1961. Book 3, 683–685.

Secondary Works

Cartledge, Paul. *Sparta and Lakonia: A Regional History 1300–362 B.C.* London: Routledge & Kegan Paul, 1979. pp. 65–87.

Finkelberg, Margalit. *Greeks and Pre-Greeks. Aegean Prehistory and Greek Heroic Tradition.* Cambridge, U.K.: Cambridge University Press, 2005. pp. 140–149.

Malkin, Irad. *Myth and Territory in the Spartan Mediterranean.* Cambridge, U.K.: Cambridge University Press, 1994. pp. 33–45.

Margalit Finkelberg

DRACO

(or Dracon, fl. 621/0 BCE), Athenian lawgiver. In response to civil strife, the Athenians empowered Draco to compose Athens' first written laws in the archonship of Aristaechmus (621/0 BCE); what (if any) position Draco held in the Athenian government is unknown. (The constitutional reforms attributed to Draco in [Aristotle] *Constitution of the Athenians* 4 are generally regarded as inauthentic; cf. Aristotle *Politics* 1274b15–16: "There are laws of Draco, but he made his laws for an existing constitution.") In 594/3 BCE, Solon repealed all Draco's laws except those dealing with homicide, which remained in force down through the Classical period (479–323 BCE). While some modern scholars believe that the legislative activity of Draco was limited to the field of homicide and that later Athenians incorrectly extrapolated a wider code of laws, references to obsolete Draconian laws on topics other than homicide by Classical and later authors (e.g., Xenophon *Oeconomicus* 14.4–5, on theft; Lysias fragment 40b Carey, on idleness; Aeschines 1.6, on education; Plutarch *Solon* 17.2, on idleness, petty theft, and temple robbery) support the traditional account.

Draco's laws were originally inscribed probably on wood or other perishable material; no contemporary copy has survived. But in 409/8 BCE the Athenian state ordered that Draco's homicide law be republished on stone. This inscription survives (*Inscriptiones Graecae* I, 3rd ed., no. 104; translation and commentary in Gagarin [1981]); substantial parts of the beginning of the inscribed law are legible and/or can be supplemented by quotations of the law in fourth-century BCE sources (in particular Demosthenes 23 and [Demosthenes] 43).

In the surviving clauses, Draco asserts a distinction between intentional and unintentional homicide; most scholars believe that he punished the former with death and the latter with exile (though Gagarin argues for a penalty of exile for intentional killing). Under his law, killing with one's own hand and conspiracy to kill incur equal liability. The inscription mentions two groups of magistrates: the "kings" (on whose identity see Gagarin, 46–47), who "shall judge [the defendant] guilty of homicide whether he killed with his own hand or conspired [to kill]" (lines 11–13), and a court of fifty-one *ephetai* (probably a subcommittee of the Council of the Areopagus), who are to determine whether a killing was intentional or unintentional (lines 17–18) and who have the right to render a verdict in at least some cases (line 13). The prosecution of a homicide is to be conducted by the victim's male relatives down to and including first cousins once removed, with further relatives and members of the victim's phratry empowered to assist in the prosecution (lines 20–23; cf. [Demosthenes] 47.71–72). Draco also makes provision for the pardon of a killer by his victim's kin, but only if the group entitled to pardon does so unanimously (lines 13–19).

By the Classical period (479–323 BCE) Draco had gained a reputation for severity, and it was believed that Solon had abrogated most of Draco's laws because their penalties were excessively harsh (Plutarch *Solon* 17, citing the fourth-century BCE Athenian statesman Demades); we have insufficient evidence of the nature of Draco's code as a whole to judge this assertion.

[*See also* Law, Greek.]

BIBLIOGRAPHY
Primary Works
Lewis, David, ed. *Inscriptiones Graecae* I, 3rd ed., fasc. 1, no. 104. Berlin and New York: de Gruyter, 1981. The definitive text of Draco's reinscribed homicide law, with editorial annotations and supplements.

Secondary Works
Carawan, Edwin. *Rhetoric and the Law of Draco.* Oxford: Clarendon Press, 1998. A study of Draco's law and subsequent developments in the Athenian law of homicide, with commentaries on surviving speeches from Classical Athenian homicide lawsuits.
Gagarin, Michael. *Drakon and Early Athenian Homicide Law.* New Haven, Conn., and London: Yale University Press, 1981. A detailed analysis of Draco's homicide law, with attention paid to the pre- and post-Draconian treatment of homicide and comparison with other ancient Greek laws.
MacDowell, Douglas M. *Athenian Homicide Law in the Age of the Orators.* Reprint. Manchester, U.K.: Manchester University Press, 1999. Originally published in 1963. The seminal modern study of Athenian homicide law.

David D. Phillips

DRAMA

See Comedy, Greek; Comic Theater, Roman; Satyr Play; Theater Buildings; Theatrical Production, Greek; Theatrical Production, Roman; Tragedy, Greek; *and* Tragedy, Roman

DREAMS AND DREAM INTERPRETATION

In ancient Greece and Rome, dreams were a continuous subject of interest. In Homer's understanding the dream is a discrete divine entity that Zeus sends as he wills. It sits at the sleeper's head and delivers a message that arouses a person from sleep. Homer uses dreams to great literary effect, and he highlights their social role. He subtly undercuts Agamemnon's public standing in the *Iliad* (book 2) by having him get a false dream: it was widely thought that greater people were more likely to have truer dreams. In the *Odyssey* (book 19), Penelope reports a dream to Odysseus, who is concealing his identity, that subtly invites him to reveal himself and highlights dreams as a form of indirect and intimate communication. Penelope further points out that dreams are unreliable, claiming that there are two gates for them, the true and the false, a notion that Virgil carries through in the *Aeneid*, having Aeneas (book 6) exit the underworld by means of the gate of false dreams.

Throughout antiquity, dreams were considered among the most common means by which people get signs of the future through divination. Plato thought that dreams arrived by means of the liver (*Timaeus* 71a–d), while Aristotle thought that they were the result of subtle movements in the still night air that a sleeping soul, because it is unencumbered with the day-to-day management of the organism, could detect and unconsciously correlate into a predictive image of what was over the horizon (*On Divination by Dreams*). The Stoics saw dreams as resulting from the nature of the soul, which in their view was a hunk of god itself. During sleep our sentience becomes coextensive with divine sentience, again when we are liberated from the concerns of waking life.

Perhaps the most powerful description of dreams as a predictive system, though, comes not from a philosopher but from a practitioner. Artemidorus of Daldis (second century CE) leaves behind the only extant example of what was a rich genre of dream books in antiquity. He gives some schematic thoughts on how dreams work, drawing from ancient allegorical theory, as well as from the philosophers, but he says that his real method is empirical. He claims to have collected examples from marketplace diviners all around the Mediterranean and gathered many hundreds of examples. He has a noteworthy interest in context and usually claims multiple meanings for a given dream image, depending on the social identity of the dreamer. Cormorants predict extreme danger for sailors, for example, but for all others they symbolize courtesans, difficult wives, or swindlers. Dreams have a prominent place in magical divination as well. In the so-called Greek magical papyri, we find a genre of "spells to the lamp" that center on inducing a predictive dream in the performer. The spells often involve Apollo and are to be performed toward one's bedside lamp.

Dreams were also prominent in ancient medicine. Large temple complexes dedicated to Asclepius, the most famous of which is at Epidaurus, offered healing dreams to the sick. Patients began with an interview with the local priests, went to sleep inside the temple, and then received an incubation dream from the god. Stone stelae near the site advertise past successes and attest that all manner of ailments might be cured—headaches, worms, traumatic injuries, and extended pregnancies. The inscriptions depict the god curing not by fairy dust but by performing medical procedures, including invasive surgeries. Aelius Aristides' diary, the *Sacred Tales* (second century CE), details his personal relationship with Asclepius by means of his dreams, which involved visitations from the god both inside temples and out, with elaborate and harrowing cures prescribed—from the drinking of quantities of hellebore, to fasting and vomiting, to emersion in freezing rivers in winter. Hippocratic doctors find dreams useful as well. The *On Regimen* turns to dreams as a diagnostic mechanism. The author sees sickness as arising from imbalance in the body. These imbalances set in stealthily, and dreams serve as an early warning mechanism. When the body is asleep the soul becomes sensitive to more subtle internal bodily states; the soul reflects these conditions in dreams, which for this author speak in a fascinating language. The soul dreams of features of the cosmos that bear an allegorical relation to parts of the body that are imbalanced—for example, swollen rivers indicate too much blood, or the dry crust of the earth predicts an onset of skin rashes.

[*See also* Asclepius; Magic; and Medicine.]

BIBLIOGRAPHY
Primary Works
Aristotle. *On Sleep and Dreams.* Edited and translated by David Gallop. Warminster, U.K.: Aris & Phillips, 1996. Parallel Greek and English text, along with notes.
Artemidorus. *The Interpretation of Dreams.* Translated by Robert J. White. Park Ridge, N.J.: Noyes Press, 1975. A translation with commentary.
Cicero. *De divinatione, liber primus.* Edited by Arthur Stanley Pease. 2 vols. Urbana: University of Illinois, 1920–1923. An edition with commentary.
Hippocrates. *Vol. 4 of On Regimen.* Edited and translated by W. H. S. Jones. Loeb Classical Library. London: Heinemann, 1923.

Secondary Works
Behr, C. A. *Aelius Aristides and the "Sacred Tales."* Amsterdam: A. M. Hakkert, 1968.
Hanson, John S. "Dreams and Visions in the Graeco-Roman World and Early Christianity." In *Aufstieg und Niedergang der römischen Welt* 2.23.2 (1980): 1395–1427.
LiDonnici, Lynn R. *The Epidaurian Miracle Inscriptions.* Atlanta: Scholars Press, 1995.
Lieshout, R. G. A. van. *Greeks on Dreams.* Utrecht, The Netherlands: HES Publishers, 1980.
Oberhelman, Steven M. "Dreams in Graeco-Roman Medicine." In *Aufstieg und Niedergang der römischen Welt* 2.37.1 (1993): 121–156.

Peter T. Struck

DRESS

See Clothing.

DROYSEN, J. G.

(1808–1884), German historian. Johann Gustav Droysen was a historian of the highest importance whose writings virtually created a new historical epoch, the age of Alexander the Great and his successors. Down to Droysen's time Greek history was seen as ending in the time of Demosthenes (d. 322 BCE), and the following period as one of decay and collapse. Droysen followed the hint of some earlier thinkers and called it the age of Hellenism (*Hellenismus*). This term hardly seems linguistically or historically accurate, for Hellenism can also mean the whole story of Greek civilization. Even more dubious is the term "Hellenistic" for his new period, which Droysen saw as the era in which Greece and the Near East fused in a new culture. The word *Hellenistai* originally referred to Jews who spoke Greek, not to Greeks who were part of a mixture of Greek and eastern cultures. But Droysen's terminology, even if inaccurate, has conquered and is now universally used.

He was born in the Pomeranian town of Treptow, the son of an army chaplain, from whom Droysen inherited a deep Christian faith. His father died when Droysen was but eight, and only with the support of friends could he attend a gymnasium and then the University of Berlin. Here he was influenced above all by August Böckh in classical philology and Georg Wilhelm Friedrich Hegel in the philosophy of history; the latter taught that history is a continuous path toward spiritual progress and Droysen saw Alexander as, even unknowingly, contributing to this movement.

Droysen's earliest publications included a translation into German of the tragic dramas of Aeschylus (2 vols., 1832). He followed this path with a translation of the comedies of Aristophanes (3 vols., 1835–1838). Meanwhile he wrote his first important contribution to historical scholarship, his biography of Alexander. In its revised edition it formed the first of three volumes narrating the history of Hellenism. The second volume was on the successors of Alexander and their continual wars down to about 280 BCE; the third, on the Hellenistic world and its passage to the control of Rome by about 220 BCE. Alexander, in Droysen's portrait, was the supreme hero, the man who ended one epoch and began another. In such admiration of Alexander, W. W. Tarn, the British historian, is Droysen's disciple. Droysen's biography shared, and indeed largely established, the fascination with conquest and military success often characteristic of German historiography.

Droysen was also a Prussian patriot in the highest degree. As a boy he lived during the wars of liberation (*Freiheitskriege*) by which Prussia was freed of French domination. In 1840 he was appointed professor of history at Kiel and took an active part in Prussian politics. Appointed professor at Berlin in 1859, he devoted himself to what he considered his masterpiece, his gigantic history of Prussian politics and the Prussian monarchy down to 1756.

He often lectured on the theory and methods of history. In 1937 his papers and notes on these topics were assembled and published. Some theorists of history consider these writings even more important than his historical narratives. It is regrettable that very little of Droysen's vast legacy has appeared in English translation.

[*See also* Classical Scholarship, *subentry* Modern Classical Scholarship.]

BIBLIOGRAPHY
Primary Works
Droysen, Johann Gustav. *Geschichte des Hellenismus.* Edited by Erich Bayer. 3 vols. Basel: B. Schwabe 1952–1953. Includes *Geschichte Alexanders des Grossen* (originally published 1833); *Geschichte der Diadochen* (originally published as *Geschichte der Nachfolger Alexanders*, 1836); and *Geschichte der Epigonen* (originally published as *Geschichte der Bildung des hellenistischen Staatensystems*, 1843).

Secondary Work
Momigliano, A. D. "J. G. Droysen between Greeks and Jews." *History and Theory* 9, no. 2 (1970): 139–153.

Mortimer Chambers

DRUGS

See Pharmacology.

DRUIDS

The druids were a priestly class of the ancient Celts of Gaul (roughly modern France), Britain, and Ireland. They may have also existed in other Celtic areas such as northern Italy, Spain, and Galatia in

Asia Minor, but written evidence is lacking. Druidic duties focused on sacrifice and divination but also included teaching and rendering judgments. The earliest information about the druids derives from the first-century BCE Greek philosopher Posidonius of Apamea who traveled in Gaul before Caesar's conquest. As preserved in the writings of Strabo, Diodorus Siculus, and later historians, Posidonius records that the druids alone were allowed to perform sacrifices and consult the gods. Although the stories of human sacrifice by the druids were highlighted by Posidonius and other classical authors, such events were probably rare. Recent archaeological finds from Gaul and Asia Minor, however, confirm that such gruesome sacrifices did take place among the Celts.

In his *Bellum Gallicum* (Gallic War) written in the mid-first century BCE, Julius Caesar notes that the druids held a privileged place in Gaulish society along with the warrior class. Druids judged cases involving murder, inheritance, and boundary disputes. If anyone ignored their decisions, the offenders were subject to shunning by the tribe and excommunication from all sacrifices. In wars between tribes, druids were considered sacrosanct and could halt a battle by stepping between opposing lines.

Gaulish parents were anxious to have their children trained as druids even though the process could take as long as twenty years. The ancient Celts used writing, but all druidic knowledge was considered sacred and was passed to students orally in verse alone. Caesar records that the druids of Gaul elected a chief during an annual convocation in the land of the Carnutes tribe (near modern Chartres). We know little of genuine druidic doctrines aside from their belief in reincarnation. The few druidic rituals preserved by the first-century CE writer Pliny the Elder involve divination using mistletoe cut from oak trees and the brewing of medicinal herbs.

The Roman invasion of Britain in the first century CE unleashed a flurry of propaganda against the druids as a bloodthirsty and barbaric cult worthy only of destruction. Authors such as Tacitus, Suetonius, Pomponius Mela, and Lucan stress the horrors of druidic human sacrifice to justify the ongoing conquest of Britain. By the third century CE, the druids were portrayed more benignly as a largely vanished priesthood reduced to brewing potions and fortune-telling. As a young soldier in Gaul, the future emperor Diocletian is reported to have met a female druid working as a tavern keeper who foretold that he would one day rule the empire.

Druids are recorded in early Irish laws and stories composed after Saint Patrick's missionary work in the fifth century CE. Tales of Patrick's celebrated battles with the druids for influence over Irish kings are a later creation drawing heavily from the Bible and hagiography, but enough reliable evidence remains from Irish sources to show that druids continued to exist in Ireland through the early medieval period.

[*See also* Celts; Gaul; *and* Posidonius of Apamea.]

BIBLIOGRAPHY

Aldhouse-Green, Miranda. *The World of the Druids*. London: Thames and Hudson, 1997.

Piggott, Stuart. *The Druids*. London: Thames and Hudson, 1975.

Philip Freeman

DURA-EUROPOS

Europos, a city on the Middle Euphrates in modern Syria that was also known in antiquity as Dura and is known today by the compound Dura-Europos, was an important settlement and military post on the Hellenistic-Parthian-Roman frontier for more than five hundred years. Its significance today is primarily archaeological, especially with regard to military and religious history, and it is notable for the large number of papyri and artifacts of daily life, Roman arms and armor, and religious art and architecture found there.

Founded as Europos circa 300 BCE, likely by Nikanor, a general of Seleucus I, the city was settled—according to a papyrus found at the site— by Macedonian Greek cleruchs. Domestic and public buildings, including temples to Artemis and Zeus Megistos, clustered at the intersection of the river and desert roads, and two large residences—the fortified citadel palace and the *stratēgion*—stood on the highest points of the city. Adjacent farm plots supported the Macedonian and local Semitic population. Language, government, legal systems, coinage, and religion were officially Greek.

The city, corresponding to the "Dura" mentioned by Isidore of Charax in *Parthikoi Stathmoi* (first century CE), was occupied by Parthia circa 113 BCE and remained under Parthian control until 165 CE. Prosperity from the caravan trade along the Euphrates and westward across the desert to Palmyra generated population growth and civic expansion. The city's excellent natural defenses were supplemented by a stout fortification wall; within this wall an orthogonal street grid was centered on an agora. The Macedonian temples to Zeus Megistos and Artemis were expanded, and new temples in increasingly Mesopotamian style were dedicated to Semitic gods such as Bel. Votive reliefs honored synchretic Greco-Parthian/Aramaic gods such as Zeus Kyrios-Baalshamin. Palmyrenes resided at Dura, and strong ties to their native city are evident in the dedication by Palmyrenes of the temple of the Gaddé (Tychai) of Dura and Palmyra and of the Mithraeum, as well as in the importation of Palmyrene limestone and sculpture. Aramaic and Palmyrene inscriptions appear in temple dedications and Parthian coins circulated in Dura, but language and laws remained officially Greek.

The Romans briefly captured the city and dedicated an arch to Trajan in 116 CE, but Parthia regained control in 121. An earthquake damaged the city in 160. In 165, Dura fell to the Romans under Lucius Aurelius Verus, and it served as a Roman garrison on the eastern *limes* for nearly a century. Status as a Roman colony was granted around 211. Roman Dura was a crowded city of many languages, religions, and cultures, with significant intermixture of Romans and locals in both military and civilian life. The northern part of the city became the Roman camp. The civilians concentrated in the southern part, in homes that were often divided and shared with businesses, and continued to farm along the Euphrates. An amphitheater and several Roman baths were built, as were temples to Adonis and Jupiter Dolichenus. Small communities of Christians and Jews each converted a private house into a place of worship, both decorated with extensive figural wall paintings. Wall paintings and relief sculpture adorned the Mithraeum, and several pagan temples featured votive wall paintings and votive and cult reliefs. Written documents on parchment and papyrus found throughout the city reveal details of both military and civilian life.

The first attack and possible occupation of the city by the Sassanians under Shapur I in 253 resulted in the construction of a huge embankment to reinforce the defensive wall on the vulnerable desert side of the city. Buried and thus preserved in the embankment were the synagogue, Christian baptistery, Mithraeum, and temples of Adonis, Aphlad, Zeus Kyrios, and Bel, as well as numerous houses and objects of daily life, including such rarely preserved objects as textiles, leather, bone dolls, and baskets. Under the defensive wall and towers, siege tunnels and mines filled with bodies and weapons were discovered, providing vivid evidence of the attack and counterattack that resulted in the city's fall. Following the Sassanian victory, Dura was evacuated and destroyed.

Explored by Bruno Schulz, Friedrich Sarre, and Ernst Herzfeld in 1898 and 1912 and identified from a painted inscription as "Dura" by James Henry Breasted in 1920, the site is known through excavations in 1922–1923 by the French Academy under Franz Cumont (who discovered the name "Europos" for the city); through joint excavations from 1928 to 1937 by Yale University and the French Academy of Inscriptions and Letters, led by Michael I. Rostovtzeff and directed by Maurice Pillet (1928–1931), Clark Hopkins (1931–1935), and Frank Brown (1935–1937); and through the current ongoing Franco-Syrian excavations directed by Pierre Leriche under the aegis of the Centre National de la Recherche Scientifique (CNRS) in Paris, begun in 1986. Finds from the site are in the National

Archaeological Museum, Damascus, and the Yale University Art Gallery, which also houses the archive from the Yale University–French Academy excavations.

[*See also* Archaeology, *subentry* Sites Elsewhere in the Middle East; Christian Art; *and* Syria.]

BIBLIOGRAPHY

Baur, P. V. C., and M. I. Rostovtzeff, eds. *The Excavations at Dura-Europos: Preliminary Reports of the First–Ninth Seasons.* New Haven, Conn.: Yale University Press, 1929–1952. See also, by various authors, the volumes of *The Excavations at Dura-Europos Conducted by Yale University and the French Academy of Inscriptions and Letters, Final Report* (New Haven, Conn.: Yale University Press, 1943–2004).

Cumont, Franz. *Fouilles de Doura-Europos.* Paris: P. Geuthner, 1926.

Leriche, Pierre. "Europos-Doura Hellénistique." *Topoi Supplement* 4 (2003): 171–191.

Leriche, Pierre, ed. *Doura-Europos: Études.* Occasional supplement to the journal *Syria*, (1986–).

Susan B. Matheson

DYES

See Textiles.